1964 Ferrari 158

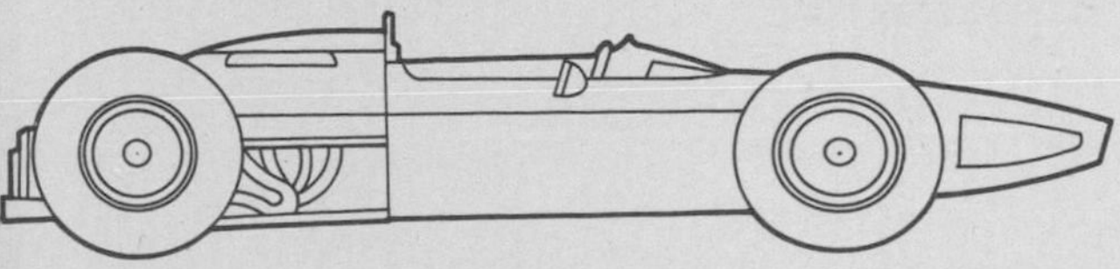

1965 Lotus-Climax 33

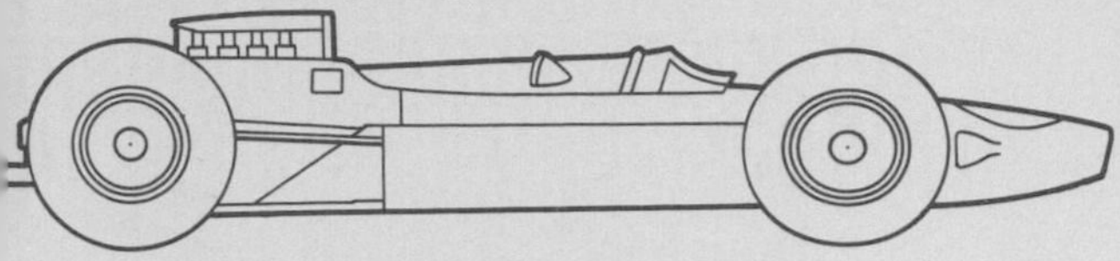

1966 Brabham-Repco

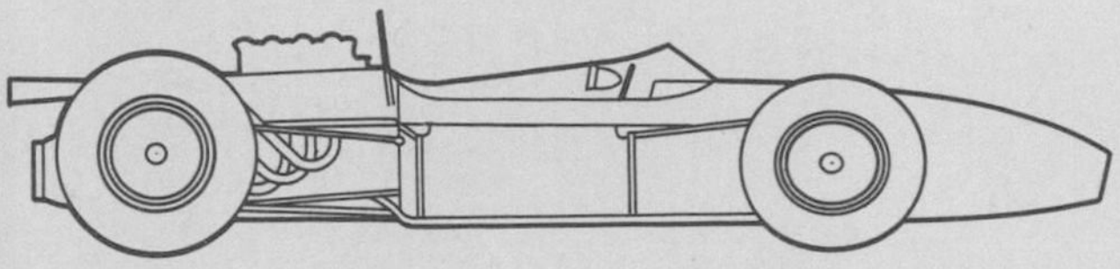

1967 Lotus-Ford 49

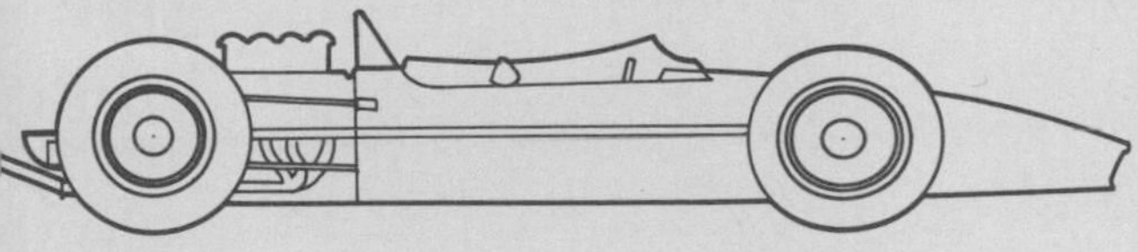

1968 Lotus-Ford 49b

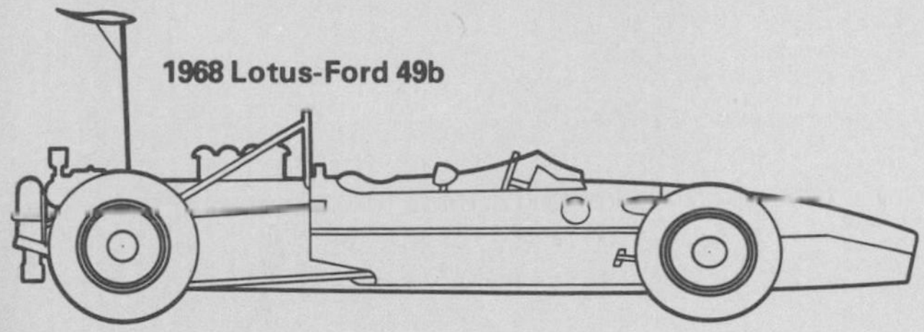

1969 Matra MS 80

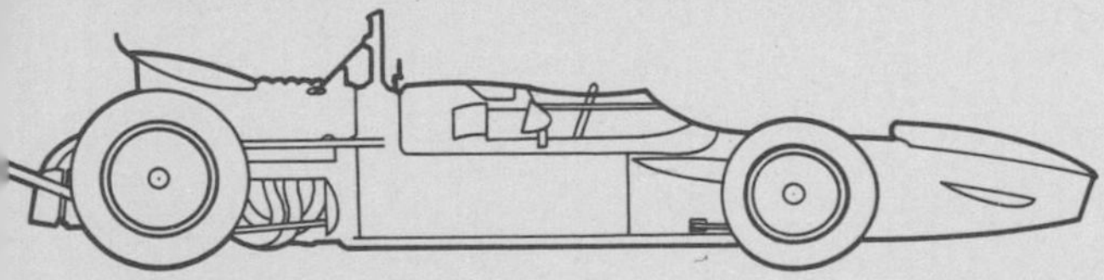

1970 Lotus 72

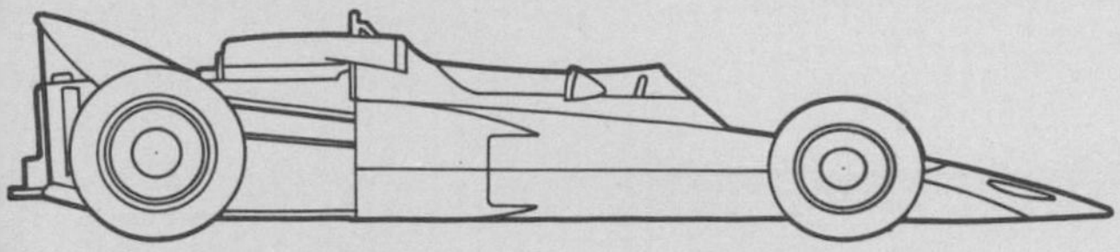

1971 Tyrell-Ford 003

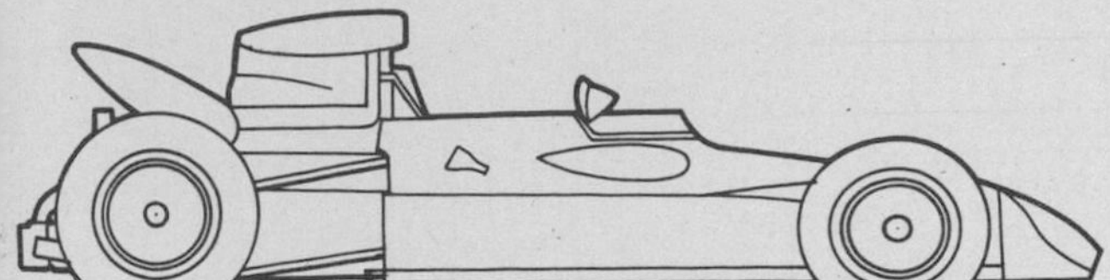

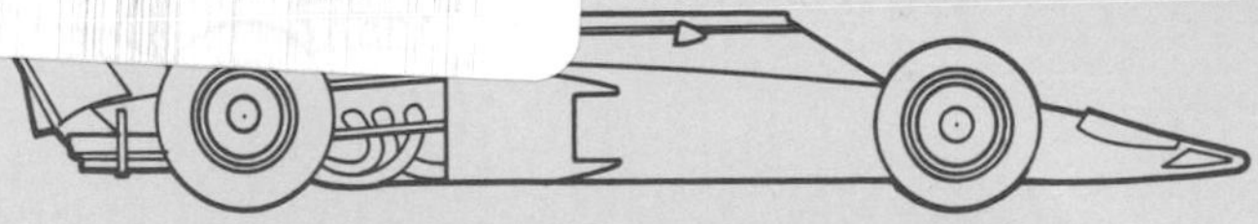

1973 Tyrell-Ford 006

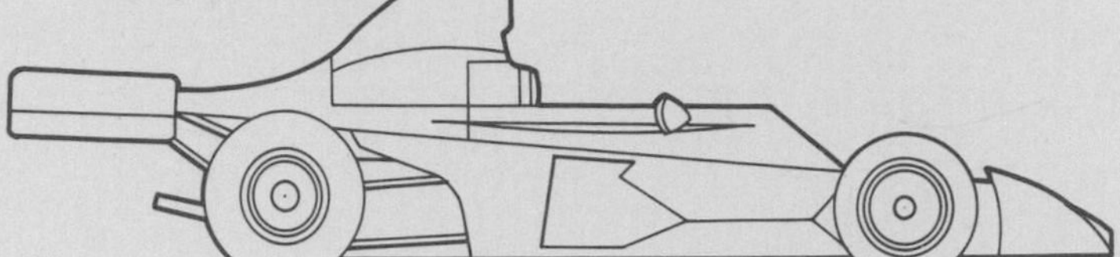

1974 McLaren-Ford M23

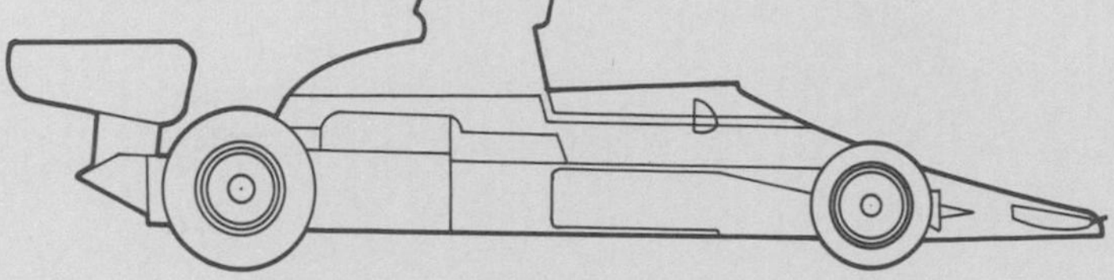

1975 Ferrari 312F

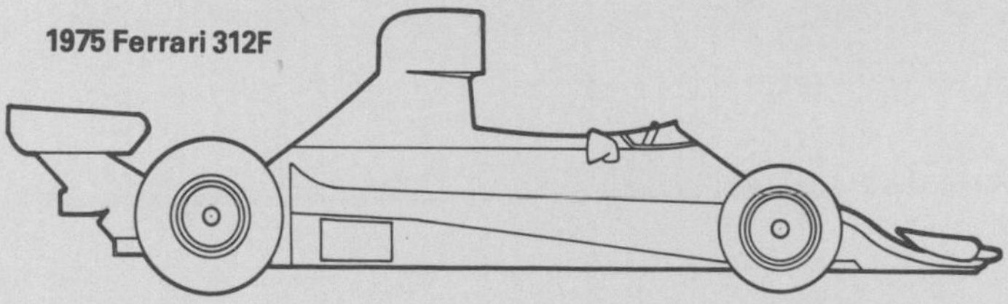

1976 Tyrell-Ford Project 34
Six wheeler

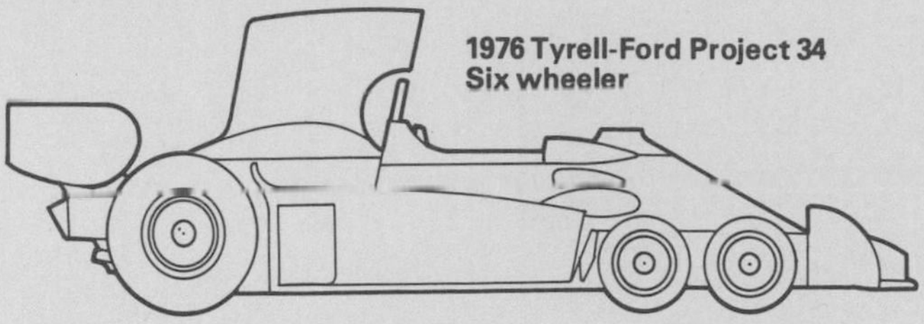

1977 Wolf

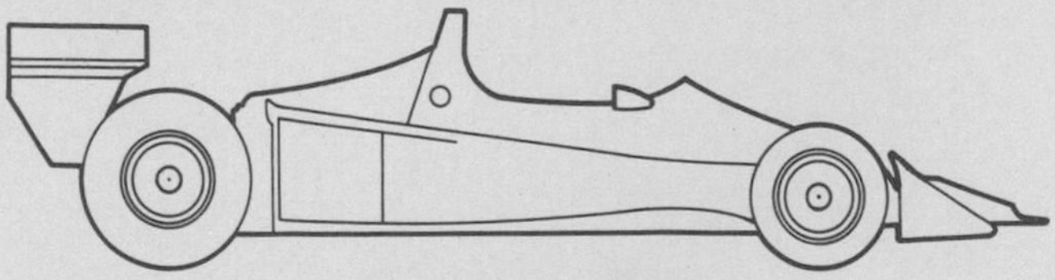

1978 Lotus 78

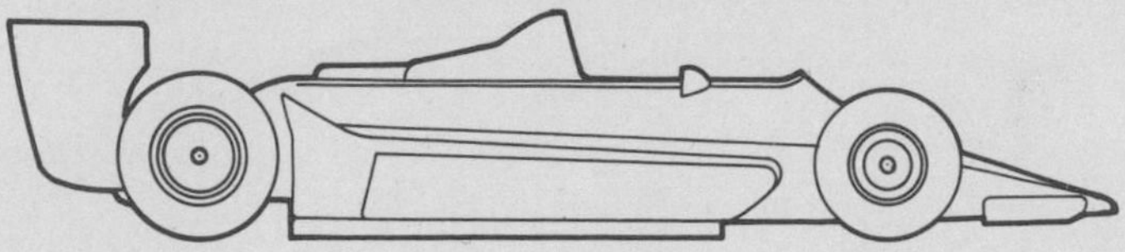

1979 Ferrari 312

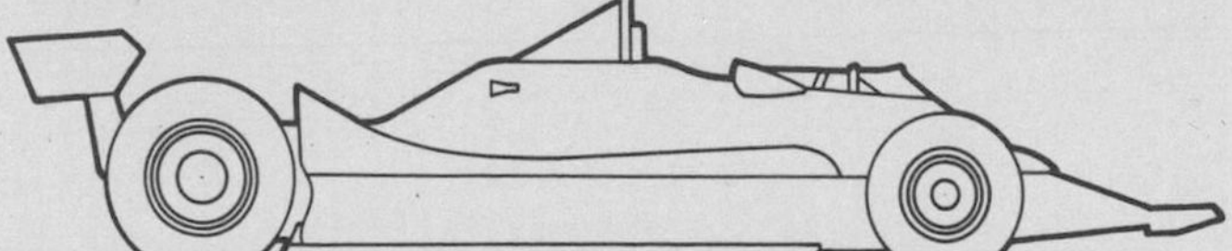

THE GUINNESS GUIDE TO GRAND PRIX MOTOR RACING

Eric Dymock

GUINNESS SUPERLATIVES LIMITED
2 CECIL COURT, LONDON ROAD, ENFIELD, MIDDLESEX

Captions to chapter pages

1950: The first world champion, Dr Guiseppe Farina, masters his sliding Alfa Romeo 158 on the way to winning the inaugural world championship race—the British Grand Prix at Silverstone.

1951: Fangio sets off towards his first world championship, at the age of 40. His Alfa Romeo adopts a rear-end squat as he accelerates away at the start of the French Grand Prix. He won the race at the wheel of Fagioli's car (which started from the third row) after his own (No 4) was delayed with a misfire.

1952: Too late. The complexities of the V16 BRM engine defeated its creators. By 1952 it had been by-passed, and Formula 2 rules were adopted for Grand Prix racing.

1953: Fangio (Maserati No 23) takes a sidelong glance at the opposition at the start of the British Grand Prix. Hawthorn (Ferrari) just visible past Fangio's car is lagging behind, but Ascari in another Ferrari won, with Fangio second.

1954: Silver Arrow. The Mercedes-Benz streamliner which proved such a handful for Fangio in the British Grand Prix at Silverstone. But the dents caused by the trackside markers may have been due to aerodynamic effects unsuspected even by Mercedes' formidable team of technicians.

1955: By now Britain was an established force in Grand Prix motor racing. Stirling Moss wears a union jack on the tail of his victorious Mercedes-Benz in the British Grand Prix.

1956: Mike Hawthorn grapples with the 2½-litre P25 BRM.

1957: Tony Brooks (left) and Stirling Moss share the glory of winning the British Grand Prix for Vanwall. Between them, aristocratic drivers of an earlier era, Earl Howe and Lord Selsdon.

1958: Vanwalls lead the field at the start of the Belgian Grand Prix at Spa-Francorchamps.

1959: The arrival of the rear-engined cars. The start of the French Grand Prix at Rheims, with Tony Brooks (Ferrari No 24) racing ahead beside Jack Brabham (Cooper-Climax No 8), and Phil Hill (Ferrari No 26) just ahead of Maurice Trintignant (Cooper-Climax No 10) and Stirling Moss (BRM No 2).

1960: Youngest Grand Prix winner, Bruce McLaren in the new, lower Cooper-Climax.

1961: Phil Hill waits in the Ferrari by the pit counter at Monaco.

1962: Conference at BRM. Graham Hill (in car) discusses the work to be done overnight before a race with the BRM mechanics.

1963: Victory lap at Monza for Jim Clark and Colin Chapman (with cup) after clinching the world championship for drivers and constructors. Mike Spence hangs on precariously to the tail of Clark's Lotus 25.

1964: World champion John Surtees drives his Ferrari through the famous Karussel on the punishing Nürburgring during the German Grand Prix. The concrete ditch on the inside of the corner is employed as a bumpy make-shift banking which stresses the suspension to its limits

1965: The first of Jackie Stewart's record-breaking series of 27 Grand Prix victories was the 1964 Italian Grand Prix at Monza. Leading into the Parabolica, he heads Graham Hill (BRM), Jim Clark (Lotus) and Dan Gurney (Brabham).

1966: In the first year of the 3-litre Formula, several teams still had 2-litre engines. Jim Clark drives No 6 Lotus in the Dutch Grand Prix with a 2-litre Coventry-Climax, and would probably have won but for a tiny hole in the water pump casing.

1967: Jim Clark's fifth and final victory in the British Grand Prix was achieved with the engine conceived with him in mind—the Ford-Cosworth DFV—which was to dominate Grand Prix racing henceforth.

1968: John Surtees (Honda No 14) Bruce McLaren (McLaren No 2) and Chris Amon (Ferrari No 9) make up the front row of the grid at the start of the Italian Grand Prix. Behind them are Jacky Ickx (Ferrari No 8) and Graham Hill (Lotus-Ford No 16). But the winner of the race was reigning world champion Denny Hulme in the wingless McLaren No 1, whose superior speed along Monza's long straights gave him the advantage.

1969: Cutting the corner before the pits put Jochen Rindt (Lotus 49) on to the second row of the grid for the French Grand Prix, but the Clermont-Ferrand track's switchback curves made him feel sick. He discarded the full face helmet he wore during practice, borrowed an open one from Piers Courage for the race, but retired after 23 laps.

1970: The race leaders have already gone, but Jackie Stewart and Jochen Rindt were to retire from the Belgian Grand Prix on the Spa-Francorchamps track, and Pedro Rodriguez (Yardley BRM No 1) scored a popular win, breaking the grip of the Cosworth-Ford cars. Chris Amon (March-Ford) who led on the opening lap was second. Behind Rodriguez is Jacky Ickx (Ferrari), Jack Brabham (Brabham-Ford), and Jean-Pierre Beltoise (Matra-Simca).

1971: Montjuich's barrier-lined track through Barcelona's controversial park. Jacky Ickx (Ferrari) negotiates the twisty lower section in the 1971 Spanish Grand Prix. Ickx finished second, one of his best results in a frustrating season.

1972: With Lotus back on its feet, the cars became officially known as John Player Specials to match the sponsor's cigarettes. Emerson Fittipaldi won the world title by one of the most comfortable margins ever.

1973: Jackie Stewart turned the tables on Emerson Fittipaldi by winning five of 1973's Grands Prix, and his last world title.

1974: Every year at the Italian Grand Prix, the track-side advertising hoardings are painstakingly erected, and every year the spectators, like caterpillars on a gigantic cabbage make holes for their unofficial grandstands. The extra weight has led to collapse of the supports, and at least one fatality, but every year the process is repeated.

1975: The field sweeps into the first corner at the Nürburgring with Niki Lauda (Ferrari No 12) in the lead after making the first-ever lap of the track in under seven minutes. Behind him, Carlos Pace (Brabham-Ford No 8), Patrick Depailler (Tyrrell-Ford No 4), and on the outside of the Sudkehre, the eventual winner, Carlos Reutemann (Brabham-Ford No 7).

1976: Six-wheeled sensation. Designed by Derek Gardner in an effort to reduce the frontal area of the modern Formula 1 car, the Tyrrell six-wheeler (driven here by Jody Scheckter) showed promise, but development proved problematical.

1977: All-enveloping helmets and fire proof face masks hide all but the eyes of the modern racing driver. Carlos Reutemann comes between the advertising.

1978: The return of the supercharger. Renault became one of the few major car manufacturers to play an active role in Grand Prix racing, taking the technically demanding option presented by a high-efficiency 1½-litre turbocharged engine.

1979: First South African world champion driver, Jody Scheckter in his familiar yellow and white helmet.

To Janet

Editor: Beatrice Frei

Design/Layout/Artwork: Don Roberts Associates

Illustrations: These are all from Geoffrey Goddard's collection, except for pictures appearing on page 177 (Nigel Snowdon), 178/9 (All Sports/Steve Powell), 182/3 (Automobiles Ligier), 184/5 (Nigel Snowdon), 187 (Chris Rogers)

Acknowledgements are also given to Motor Racing Publications Limited, for permission to publish a quote from Laurence Pomeroy's *The Grand Prix Car* (Vol 2)

End Paper Artwork: Pat Gibbon

Published in Great Britain by
Guinness Superlatives Limited, 2 Cecil Court, London Road, Enfield, Middlesex

Colour Separation by Newsele Litho Limited, London and Milan

Set in 10/11 pt Times Roman

Printed in Great Britain by Ebenezer Baylis and Son Limited,
The Trinity Press, Worcester, and London

Bound by Leighton Straker Bookbinding Company Limited, London

British Library Cataloguing in Publication Data
Dymock, Eric
The Guinness guide to Grand Prix motor racing
1. Grand Prix racing - History
I. Title
796.7'2 GV1029.15
ISBN 0-85112-206-X

Contents

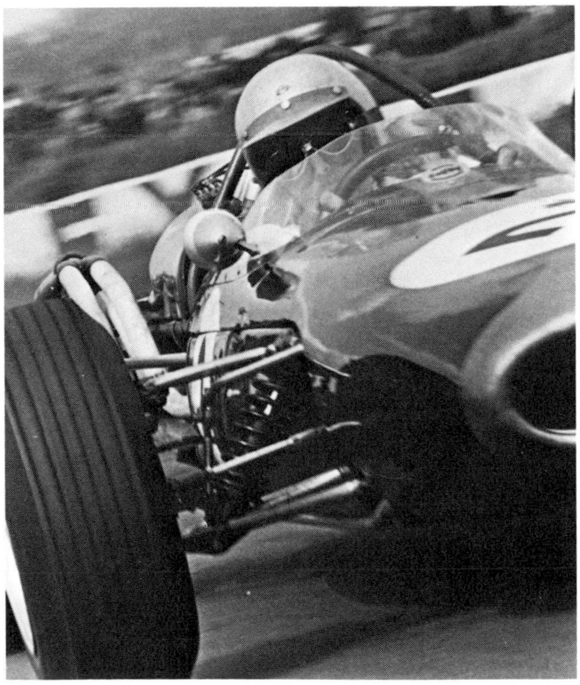

Foreword

I was delighted to be asked to write a foreword to the *Guinness Guide to Grand Prix Motor Racing* for two main reasons. First of all, motor racing has always been my favourite sport; indeed, for a long time, it was virtually my whole life. But perhaps even more important is my conviction that of all the different facets of the fascinating world of motor racing, it must be Grand Prix competition which is the fastest, toughest, most specialised, most challenging and most worthwhile of all.

Yet it's necessary to qualify that statement. Whenever you talk about Grand Prix racing, you have to remember that not every Grand Prix race is a real Grand Prix. At the very beginning of motor racing, everything was very simple and very clear: there was only one Grand Prix, *the* Grand Prix, and that was the one organised and run each year by the Automobile Club of France, which attracted the best cars and the best drivers from all over Europe. Over the years, such was the prestige of this event, more and more races were named after it. Usually the Grand Prix label was applied first to the very biggest international events for thoroughbred racing cars: the Belgian GP, the German GP, the Grand Prix of Europe.

The trouble is that there has been a tendency to devalue the currency. In more recent times, the Grand Prix tag has been used for every kind of event for just about every kind of car, most of which would never qualify as true Grand Prix machines. So if you agree with me that a real Grand Prix race must always be an international event for single-seat Formula One cars driven by world-class drivers, then this is the book which will tell you what you want to know. Perhaps they should have called it the *Guinness Guide to* Real *Grand Prix Motor Racing*—then there could be no possible confusion!

Stirling Moss

Introduction

It is no accident that the *Guinness Guide to Grand Prix Motor Racing* turns out to be something of a history of Grand Prix racing since 1950. Any guide to the condition of the sport—or the activity, which releases one from being too precise about what Grand Prix racing actually is—requires explanation.

In the case of the premier league of international motor racing, the explanation lies in its evolution. The 1973–4 oil crisis, for example, had its effect on Grand Prix racing along with many other aspects of Western, civilised life. Authors, even those writing for a relatively specialised and probably knowledgeable audience, ignore such signposts of their times at their peril.

Certainly, Grand Prix racing does have its origins in the classic contests that began in 1906. It did scale the heights of romanticism in the Twenties. And it did achieve greatness in the Thirties.

Keith Duckworth has pointed out some of the shortcomings of the world championship. With his customary gift for reaching at the very basis of any subject to which he turns his mind, he said, 'If a drivers' world championship is to have any meaning, all the cars must be the same. Equally, a manufacturers' world championship presupposes that all drivers should be the same, and since neither of these conditions have the faintest chance of being met, the whole thing would appear to be a waste of time.'

Yet despite Duckworth's unquenchable logic, Grand Prix racing is inextricably bound up with the world championships.

Modern Grand Prix racing may not have truly started with the dropping of the flag at the British Grand Prix on 13 May 1950, but that was the moment when, for a great many people, it began to matter. Henceforward, the Twenties and Thirties would appear no more than an elaborate rehearsal for the epic theatricals to come. Revolutionary changes were to follow; technical developments came with bewildering speed. But the shift in emphasis away from the team, or the country of origin of the team, towards the driver, altered the entire nature of the business.

That is why the best guide to Grand Prix racing as it is now lies in a study of its evolution since 1950, and in particular the years after 1966 when the 3 litre Formula began.

The features on technical developments, personalities, or occasions of special significance emphasise the diverse nature of Grand Prix racing. Its wide range will be seen in the detailed results tables at the end, to which must be applied the customary *caveat* that whilst every effort has been made to make them the most accurate of any compilation, they necessarily rely heavily on the word of other people. Even present day race reports are not invariably accurate, in particular regarding reasons given for cars retiring, and even on matters of detail such as the order of the starting grid, which can change greatly from that published by the race organisers. The reasons may be breakdowns, accidents on the warming-up lap, or plain subterfuge by specially competitive drivers. In a very few cases, it has even been necessary to apply a little inspired conjecture.

Inevitably, a book such as this must draw upon the work of others, as well as be the result of first-hand experience. In particular, thanks are due to other authors, such as Laurence Pomeroy, Leonard Setright, William Court, Doug Nye, William Boddy, S C H Davis, Denis Jenkinson, Cyril Posthumus and many more. My gratitude is also due to the book's editor, Beatrice Frei, without whom it might never have taken shape. Finally, also to my wife, to whom it is affectionately dedicated. Her help and support throughout have been unstinting.

Sutton Veny,
Wiltshire.

The Formative Years

Motor racing was more than ten years old before the French coined 'Grand Prix' for a new sort of competition in which the cars raced round a course starting and finishing in the same place. It was not entirely new (even the title had been used before) but the greatest races hitherto had been from Paris to Bordeaux, or Paris to Madrid.

Although roads were the obvious places on which to race, it was some time before they were closed to ordinary traffic in the interests of safety. Some of the town to town races had been murderous affairs, so one of the first considerations that shaped the destiny of early Grand Prix races was how to run them without endangering the public.

Finding a satisfactory reason for running them turned out to be more problematical. There was plenty of enthusiasm for proving one design better than another. Besides it was an exciting pastime for the wealthy, but that was not quite enough. The cause, instead was that of '... the encouragement of industry'. That seemed important enough to commend itself to the man in the street, and Governments.

The Automobile Club de France, conceiving France as the natural home of the automobile (conveniently overlooking the vital role played in its invention by Daimler and Benz) decided it must also run the most important motor race in Europe.

The French had been frustrated over the only major international races, the Gordon Bennett series, to which they were allotted, by the international committee, one three-car team the same as everybody else. This did not square with their aspirations at all, so they determined to put the matter right with a motor race which would be grander in every way than the Gordon Bennett. Thus was born a competition for a race with a 'Great Prize'.

It was a simple enough plan. The weight of the competing cars was fixed at 1000 kg/2205 lb, and they were to start at 90 sec intervals from 06.00 to cover a 103.18 km/64.12 mile circuit of roads near Le Mans on Thursday 25 June, 1906. The following day they would cover the course a further six times, making twelve laps in all, and the winner would be the car which managed the task in the shortest time.

Of the 32 starters, eleven completed the set distance which everyone agreed was rather long at 1238 km/769.3 miles. The winner was the Hungarian driver Ferenc Szisz in his red Renault in a total of 12 h 14 min 07.0 sec (an average speed of 101.195 kph/62.879 mph). Felice Nazzaro of Italy was second in a FIAT and Albert Clément was third in one of his father's Clément-Bayards.

Despite rolling and tar sealing, the roads were a worry, and to deal with the puncture problem, the first Grand Prix did produce a notable innovation.

For the fortunate Renault, FIAT, and Clément-Bayard teams, detachable rims with tyres already mounted, reduced the time for changes from a quarter of an hour to under five minutes. It was the only major technical development in the 34-car field, made up mainly of cars with four-cylinder engines between 12 and 18 litres.

The motive was not quite sport. the philosophy of the Grand Prix was described by *L'Auto*: *'Ah, oui, la Grande Epreuve est la passionnante épreuve que ce Grand Prix l'Automobile Club de France, grande bataille industrielle de l'automobile.'* Yet the response from rival motor industries was poor. Ten French manufacturers entered 25 cars, three teams of three cars each came from Italy and Germany, but none from Britain or the United States.

The significance of the Grand Prix was making a motor race a contest between individual cars, instead of, as in the Gordon Bennett, between teams of cars representing countries. The cash prize was also big

Triumph for Mercedes: the 1914 French Grand Prix. The German team earned a telegram from the Kaiser for their 1-2-3 victory. The third placed car of Otto Salzer races through the Virage de la Mort.

enough to be significant. At modern values it represented something around a quarter of a million pounds.

It was this as much as anything else which distinguished the Grand Prix series, certainly for as long as the French kept the title for themselves. Other forms of racing went their own way, for instance sports cars, or racing on special tracks such as Brooklands, even then being constructed near Weybridge in Surrey. But the Grand Prix, or Grosser Preis, or Gran Premio became established as the richest, the biggest, and the best for the cars that were fastest and the most advanced. It did not always live up to its ideals, but it remained the racing which caught the imagination most firmly.

The regulations were a problem from the beginning. Another of the international committees, which it was fashionable to form, thought it would encourage designers to draw up more realistic cars if they had to work to a fuel consumption limit. It would discourage freaks, and help develop the motor industries which these well-meaning committees and Automobile Clubs were trying to promote. Furthering industry was considered public-spirited—a commendable activity for the nobility and gentry.

The first 'formula' allowed cars 231 litres/50.8 gallons of fuel for the next Grand Prix in 1907, equivalent to 9.4 miles per gallon. A minimum weight was tried later, together with a limitation on the diameter of the cylinders. A maximum body width was suggested and in 1913 another fuel consumption limit of 20 litres per 100 kilometres/14.12 mpg. Almost in desperation to discover a simple, easily verifiable standard for competing cars, the solution was adopted the following year of all cars having the same cylinder capacity.

In the French Grand Prix of 1914, the engine swept volume was fixed at 4½ litres, and the weight at 1100 kg/2425 lb. The race was run at Lyon and became one of the most famous Grands Prix ever.

The Automobile Club de France decided it was to be their greatest 'Grand Prize'. Having chosen the site, they spared no expense to make it the best. They built unmatched facilities for spectators, of which the crowning glory was a 4000-seat grandstand reputedly costing £12000. This provided a view of the competing cars for about 2½ miles/4km as they roared up La Montagne Russe, and through the Jaws of Death on the finishing straight. The naming of sections of the track was nothing if not picturesque.

But only six days before, the opening shot of the Great War was fired in Sarajevo. With the assassination of Archduke Ferdinand, the war clouds were gathering, and the Grand Prix, in which the chief protagonists were France and Germany, acquired a new significance.

It was a triumph for Mercedes. Their technical superiority vanquished the French hero Georges Boillot, who had won for Peugeot in 1912 and 1913, in an emotional finish to an intense contest. Despite having an engine which reached an astonishing 3000 rpm, and new four-wheel brakes, Boillot lost the 20 lap 752.6 km/467.64 mile race in the final stages. The winners were the well-prepared cars of Christian Lautenschlager, Louis Wagner, and Otto Salzer.

Twenty years later, SCH Davis, the famous sports editor of *The Autocar*, who witnessed what came to be called The Greatest Grand Prix wrote:

'There was something more than motor racing in the atmosphere as the crowds made their way dustily from the course. Never before has there been that curious indefinable feeling and everyone was extraordinarily quiet. Had the gift of foresight been ours, what, I wonder, would one have thought; as it was there was quite distinctly the feeling that a menacing though invisible presence had been manifest. The thing disappeared in an hour or two, normality returned; but though we knew nothing of it, there had come faintly on the wind the echoing thud of guns. The brooding shadow was death, the end had come to a generation. Never again would the Grand Prix seem the same. Castles in the air had vanished beyond return. The roads we had known were to see not racing cars but millions upon millions of men, to bear armoured fighting machines and countless numbers of guns. When next we saw the Mercedes Grand Prix engine it was in a fighting aeroplane—it had in fact been the beginning of one before the race. Team headquarters, which were so pleasant a memory vanished in a hell of shellfire, their shattered debris to hide the still more deadly machine gun. Men had reached their journey's end. Perhaps it was as well we did not know.'

It was the first 1-2-3 finish in a Grand Prix, but the end of an era. Within a month Europe was at war. The Kaiser sent a telegram congratulating the Mercedes team and drivers, but the fruits of their victory were not the expected sales of cars so much as the machines with which the war was fought.

Racing resumed in a different world. In 1922 the international committee of motor clubs formed a special sub-committee to supervise the sport, known as the Commission Sportive International (CSI), with a particular brief to ensure that Grand Prix racing should conform to some common pattern. Complete uniformity was not achieved until after the Second World War, because many organisers preferred their own rules. Cars conforming to the international rules were not always available; local drivers wanted to race amongst themselves.

Generally, however, races recognised as the most important, so-called grandes épreuves, came to be run under the combination of engine capacity limits and weight restrictions, as decided by the CSI from time to time ever since. These formulae, as they came to be known, were dictated by a number of considerations, including plain economic practicality. It made sense in the hard times after the Great War to enable sports cars to double up as Grand Prix cars. The splendid cause of encouraging industry would not be helped by firms overspending

Tazio Nuvolari acknowledges the cheers after winning the 1938 Donington Grand Prix for Auto Union. The legendary Italian was one of the few drivers who mastered the German rear-engined monsters.

in their anxiety to do well in racing in the hope of selling cars.

As the lean years of the Twenties drew to a close, those manufacturers who did take part in racing (they included Sunbeam, Fiat, Delage, Alfa Romeo, Aston Martin, and the Americans Miller and Duesenberg) mostly withdrew. This left room for the wealthy amateurs with their sports cars such as the classic, pointed-tailed Type 35 Bugatti, the artistically engineered eight-cylinder car that was the epitome of the sports-racer from its introduction in 1924. Its elegant proportions, the product of a family noted as much for its sculpture as its engineering, influenced the dreams of speed of an entire generation.

Technical improvements became a matter of evolution. Together with the 1½-litre Delage, the Bugatti was amongst the last of the great two-seat racing cars. Sports car racing, led by the example of Le Mans, was going its own way; Grand Prix racing continued to be the category where cars tended to be built if not exactly regardless of expense, at least with out and out racing as their primary purpose. With improved reliability, riding mechanics became an anachronism, and drivers either had to fend for themselves if they broke down, or else they could stop at the replenishment pits. The mechanic was not required to ride in the cars after 1924, but it was ten years before his departure was acknowledged and his seat dispensed with.

The first Grand Prix cars were descendants of the city to city racers of the early years of the century. They had tall engines and almost no bodywork, and relied on sheer size for power. By 1912 the search for efficiency led a Swiss engineer, Ernest Henri, to employ a cylinder head layout for the 1912 Peugeot which remained the classic for high performance engines ever after. This had two overhead camshafts working inclined valves in hemispherical combustion chambers. Henri also employed four valves per cylinder.

The Mercedes which ran Henri's Peugeots to a standstill in 1914 were rather lower built, and were brought out again after the war, equipped with four-wheel brakes, to win the 1922 Targa Florio in Sicily. Duesenberg won the 1921 French Grand Prix with hydraulic brakes, and an important stage in the development of the supercharger was marked by another Henri design, the 1924 Sunbeam 2 litre. The car which dominated the later years of the 2 litre Formula which ran from 1922 to 1925 was, however, the P.2 Alfa Romeo. It was designed by the great engineer Vittorio Jano, with a supercharged eight-cylinder engine, and it carried on winning, even when the race organisers chose to ignore the 1½-litre Formula which followed in 1928–30.

The first car to exploit the change in the rules allowing the passenger seat to be done away with, was the P.3 Alfa Romeo, known as the 'monoposto', or single-seater. Once again the brainchild of Jano, it could do 150 mph, and with its eight-cylinder engine and twin superchargers, won its first race. Its only real opposition came from another Italian car, the 2.9-litre Maserati, for which hydraulic brakes were re-invented a decade after the Duesenberg. Its drivers were the great Campari, and later the incomparable Nuvolari after he had fallen out with the manager of the Alfa Romeo team, destined to have the longest association of anyone with Grand Prix racing, Enzo Ferrari.

Mussolini had already decided to employ motor racing as a means of enhancing national prestige, when the 750 kg Formula was introduced in 1934. This laid down that racing cars had to weigh not more than 750 kg/1654 lb. Alas, the CSI had reckoned without the redoubtable Hitler, who saw Grand Prix racing as a fine advertisement for his regime. He established a state fund, from which Mercedes-Benz and Auto Union drew, to field cars with powerful engines and lightweight construction which easily defeated the badly-framed regulations. Auto Union took over from Dott Ing Ferdinand Porsche the design for a revolutionary 16-cylinder, rear-engined car with independent suspension. Mercedes-Benz produced a more orthodox car which failed to score an immediate success. In 1934 it won only four races, two major and two minor. It suffered, along with Auto Union, particularly humiliating defeats in the French Grand Prix at Montlhéry and the Swiss Grand Prix at Berne.

The French, however, were soon eclipsed, the British provided no opposition, and soon only the Italians looked like any match for the all-conquering Germans. In 1935 they were beaten only four times, and even when the formula changed in 1938, to a maximum engine capacity of 3 litres supercharged and 4½ litres unsupercharged, they carried on, invincible. Even as the German armies rolled across Europe in the opening phase of the Second World War, the final races of the Thirties were still being run. The Franco-British ultimatum on Poland expired at 11 am on 3 September 1939, yet at 5 o'clock the same afternoon, the flag went down on the start of the Yugoslav Grand Prix. Two-car teams from Mercedes-Benz and Auto Union blandly faced one another—Manfred von Brauchitsch, nephew of the German Field Marshal, and Hermann Lang in the W163 cars with which Mercedes-Benz had won every race but one during the season, and Tazio Nuvolari and Hermann Müller in D-Type Auto Unions.

A leaden sky reflected the mood of Europe on that sombre day, as von Brauchitsch and Lang took their customary lead. In his eagerness Brauchitsch spun and lost time, whilst Lang suffered a disappointing end to the season of which he was the uncrowned champion, retiring after being struck by a flying stone.

Müller lost the lead through a stop to change his Auto Union's tyres, finishing third behind the wily master, Nuvolari, with Brauchitsch second. So, even as the torpedoed *Athenia* began to settle in the icy waters of the North Atlantic, and the first tragic casualties of war were sustained, the chequered flag fell on six years that had taken Grand Prix racing beyond the realms of mere sport into an Olympian arena of international propaganda, where the principal consideration had been prestige and a technological ideology. It had been a struggle between nations the like of which would not be seen again until the space race of the Sixties, and whose echoes would reverberate for ever down the motor racing halls of fame.

While Auto Union, as William Court says in *Power and Glory*, '. . . went to share the long, eternal sleep of Fiat, Delage, Sunbeam, Peugeot and the other departed champions,' and the Mercedes-Benz technicians turned their attention to more pressing matters elsewhere, the Italians, not yet at war, were able to carry on.

The significant race of 1939 turned out to be not that last tense Grand Prix by the shores of the Adriatic, but a minor, though unaccustomedly rich event on the other side of the Mediterranean. Promoted to enhance Italian prestige in Libya, across Mussolini's *Mare Nostrum* in a new outpost of the Italian Empire, the Tripoli Grand Prix was mounted on a lavish scale at the 13.09 km/8.14 mile New Melleha circuit. From 1935–8, the Germans had triumphed, winning the first three places in every race, but for 1939 the Italians had an answer.

Overwhelmed by the Germans in every major race for the best part of a decade, the Italian state automobile factory, Alfa Romeo, had turned instead to motor racing's second division, the so-called voiturette formula. This had a pedigree as long as that of the premier league with its demand for engines of 3 litres supercharged, and 4½ litres unsupercharged, in cars weighing not less than 850 kg/1874 lb.

Voiturettes had run before the First World War with an engine capacity limit of 3 litres, which had become in turn the benchmark for Grand Prix cars in the impoverished world which followed. The largely amateur category was drawn up for cars of 1100 cc or 1½ litres, the races tended to be shorter, less demanding, and qualifying for titles such as Trophy, or Coupe, rather than the magic of Grand Prix.

By the mid-Thirties, voiturettes had a calendar of their own, with Bugattis and Maseratis competing against the successful British ERAs until the storybook intervention in 1936 of the daring Richard Seaman in his immaculate black, ten-year-old Delage. It was into this class that Enzo Ferrari, the Alfa Romeo racing manager, threw the designer Gioacchino Colombo. His challenge was to produce a car with a 1½-litre supercharged engine, complying with the smaller formula which was expected to become the basis of the 1941 Grand Prix rules.

The outcome was one of the greatest racing cars of all time, the Alfa Romeo Type No 158 (15 for 1.5 litres, 8 for eight cylinders) a masterpiece of precision with a tubular frame, a pointed tail, and a Latin elegance that at least made it look a match for any Teutonic adversary. The Alfettas, as they became known, finished first and second in their first race, the 1938 Coppa Ciano Junior at Leghorn.

Together with the promise of the contemporary Maserati, the 4CL, the successful début of the Alfetta persuaded the Italian Automobile Federation to decree that for 1939, principal races on Italian territory would be for voiturettes. Tired of the scourge of the swastika on the Grand Prix tracks of the world, the Italians simply changed the rules, and changed them in particular for their prestige event coming up in May in North Africa.

But the designers at Auto Union and Mercedes-Benz were as capable as Enzo Ferrari at reading the signs for the future. Eight and twelve-cylinder engines to the smaller limits were already on their drawing boards, and while the Italians seemed to have the initiative during 1938, a rude awakening was in store.

When Marshal Balbo dropped the starter's flag for the Tripoli Grand Prix of 1939, the masses crowding in from the desert saw not the keenly awaited demonstration of Fascist Italy's prowess, but the annihilation of the Maseratis, and the humiliation of the Alfa Romeos, by two W 165 Mercedes-Benz cars. These were scaled-down miniatures of their 3-litre stablemates, developed in secret and, as always, faultlessly prepared. Hermann Lang and Rudolph Caracciola outclassed the opposition, finishing first and second. The works Maseratis never completed the first lap of the race, and only one of the 158 Alfa Romeos survived, a distant third.

The driver was Emilio Villoresi, and a development programme was immediately taken in hand to put things right. Within two months however, Villoresi had died testing the revised design at Monza, and in any case the effort had come too late. By the time the return match could be staged at Tripoli in 1940, the Germans were preoccupied elsewhere and it mattered little that the beautiful little red cars won at a higher average speed than the Mercedes of the year before. If the Mercedes had returned they might have been faster still. When the flag came down this time, the Alfas were shipped back quickly to Italy and put away, only emerging seven years later, into a very different world.

It was to be ten years before Grand Prix racing finally shook itself completely clear of the Thirties. Immediately after the war it was unthinkable that the Mercedes-Benz and Auto Union teams should be revived. Germany was not allowed to take part in racing and in any case the resources were no longer available. The Auto Union factory at Chemnitz was in the Eastern Zone, behind that iron curtain which, in Winston Churchill's words, was coming down, '... from Stettin on the Baltic to Trieste on the Adriatic'. The Stuttgart factory of Mercedes-Benz was in ruins from Allied bombing, and would soon be far too busy producing vehicles for the reconstruction of West Germany to have anything to do with motor racing.

The reconstituted Alliance Internationale des Automobile Clubs Reconnus (AIACR) now called itself the Fédération Internationale de l'Automobile (FIA), but still delegated sporting affairs to a sub-committee—the Commission Sportive Internationale (CSI). This quickly adopted the proposed 1941 Formula A for such Grand Prix races as anyone cared to run, on the grounds that plenty of cars were available with 1½ litre supercharged or 4½ litres unsupercharged engines without anybody going to the trouble of building new ones. Materials and money were in short supply, petrol was scarce, and there was no question of reviving Grand Prix racing on the extravagant pattern of the Thirties. But motor races of a sort there would surely be.

Nice managed a Grand Prix in 1946, and so did Marseille, with Maseratis winning both. The sights and sounds of racing cars returned at Albi, in South-West France, with another Maserati victory, and a pre-war ace at the wheel, the great Nuvolari. Many races were run under Formule Libre rules with sports cars competing against single seaters, but the principal race of that first post-war season was to be the Grand Prix des Nations at Geneva.

It was a muted affair by the standards of the Thirties, held on a 2.94 km/1.83 mile circuit made up of streets and boulevards near the Palace of the League of Nations by the lake side, with the novel hazard of tramlines at two places. The significance of the occasion was the return of a works-supported team, the Alfa Romeos, the Type 158s having spent the greater part of the ten years since their conception by Ing Colombo reputedly hidden in a cheese factory. Behind the wheel, their pre-war drivers Giuseppe Farina, the handsome Doctor of Law and nephew of the famous Pinin Farina, Count Trossi the adventurous Italian aristocrat, and Jean-Pierre Wimille, former works Bugatti driver and the fastest man in France. The beautiful Alfettas carried all before them, and did so again in the Circuit of Turin, longest of the generally brief revived races at 280 km/174 miles, won by Achille Varzi, once Nuvolari's greatest rival. It was Trossi's turn in the 83 km/52 miles Circuit of Milan at the end of the season.

Motor racing had come back with more than a touch of *déjà vu*. Italy was more than a match for anyone, although the French had cars too, such as the ponderous 4½-litre Talbot, hardly nimble but economical enough to catch out the thirstier cars in longer races by spending less time in the pits refuelling. The flamboyant and popular Monegasque Louis Chiron used one to win the 1948 French Grand Prix at Rheims but only because the Alfas stayed away. The British campaigned their few elderly ERAs but they were no match for the Italians despite some spirited efforts by private owners such as Bob Gerard. Alongside the all-conquering Alfa Romeos, Maserati steadily developed the 4 CL into the 4 CLT, and ultimately the lowered 4 CLT 48, known as the San Remo model after a victorious début. One of the few cars developed in Britain was the disappointing E-Type ERA, but for the most part challengers from Britain and France were privately financed and ill-conceived with little influence on the course of events. The most significant long-term development for Grand Prix racing in Britain was the growth of club racing amongst energetic enthusiasts returned from the war, with well developed skills, and a talent for improvisation nurtured on the battlefields of the world.

Home-built specials, or Hot-Rods as another nation and another generation came to call them, were made at an astonishing rate. The slopes of trial hills, and the English eccentricity of 'mudplugging' by the amateur builders of spidery sports cars was a far cry from the sophistication of the elegant red racing cars from Modena or Milan. But at Shelsley Walsh and Prescott, at club meetings on the former Battle of Britain satellite aerodrome of Goodwood, or on the recently-surfaced little track at Brands Hatch in Kent, a new generation of engineers and drivers were feeling their way. If the playing fields of Eton decided Napoleon's fate at Waterloo, the destiny of Italian motor racing was forged in the back-yard garages of suburban London.

Meanwhile, the nationalistic triumphs of Nazi Germany in Grand Prix racing were belatedly noted in France and Britain. The French Government commissioned a Grand Prix car from the Centre d'Etudes Techniques de l'Automobile et du Cycle. Veteran designer Albert Lory produced a neat looking V-8 with torsion bar suspension, but when Raymond Sommer let in the clutch on the start line of the 1947 French Grand Prix, it broke a half-shaft.

That project never recovered. An ambitious British scheme for a co-operative racing car, funded by a motor industry hoping to benefit from the prestige of international domination the way the Germans had in the Thirties, fared little better. Its V-16 engine and complicated chassis engineering proved too much for the resources available. Materials shortages delayed matters, despite official blessings. Quarrels broke out amongst the Trust set up by Raymond Mays, who had been largely responsible for the pre-war ERA (English Racing Automobiles); and the BRM (British Racing Motors) car suffered humiliating delays, and proved disappointing when it did appear.

The Italians continued to be the pace-makers. Alfa Romeo took a year off in 1949 to concentrate on the development of a new road car. Maserati continued with the development of their 4 CLT, and Ferrari reappeared as a constructor in his own right. The former Alfa Romeo team manager had founded a dynasty of sports and racing cars which, in the classic manner, were working their way through the lower strata of motor racing, but doing so in a manner which pointed ultimately to Grand Prix racing. The Maserati brothers, Ernesto and Bindo, had sold out the firm bearing their name and established their break-away OSCA (Officine Specializate Costruzione Automobili) although they had yet to fit a projected V-12 engine into their first Grand Prix car.

The dark days of the Forties drew to a close with the scene set for a return to normal. The tracks had been re-establishing themselves with the French Grand Prix, back at the Rheims-Gueux circuit under the auspices of the Automobile Club de Champagne. Monaco had been revived, and there was racing again on the wooded Bremgarten, on the outskirts of Berne, traditional home of the Swiss Grand Prix. Spa-Francorchamps was back on the calendar for a long-distance sports car race, then for the Belgian Grand Prix. Holland was in the picture, with Zandvoort, in the sand-dunes on the North Sea coast, a track built amongst the breastworks of Hitler's *Festung Europa* (Fortress Europe). In Britain, while Donington Park remained optimistically and determinedly on the calendar, a proper Grand Prix had been established by the RAC on the former Bomber Command airfield at Silverstone.

The final ingredient, giving Grand Prix racing the impetus to enter the Fifties with no more than a formal acknowledgement that the Forties had existed at all, came from the CSI's decision that henceforward there would be an annual competition for the world championship of drivers.

The cars in existence after the war comprised 1½-litre supercharged former voiturettes, and 4½-litre unsupercharged cars of the pre-war Formula A. The 4½-litre cars had fared badly racing against 3-litre supercharged adversaries, opinion leant towards a 1941 formula calling for the supercharged: unsupercharged ratio to be changed. The roll-call of available cars for the projected 1946 Formula was as follows:

France

Talbot—There were several six-cylinder 4½-litre models with offset single-seater bodies such as had run at Rheims in the 1938 French Grand Prix, and one basically similar car with a single-seater body which ran in the 1939 French Grand Prix.

Delahaye—One single-seater, twelve-cylinder unsupercharged 4½-litre model.

Britain

Alta—This was a 1½-litre four-cylinder car with independent suspension and a tubular frame of pre-war design.

ERA—Six-cylinder, 1½-litre cars built between 1934 and 1937 for the voiturette formula, with Roots superchargers in three types, the A- and B-Types having rigid front axles, and the later C-Type independent front suspension. The 1939 E-Type had a redesigned engine with a shorter stroke, a tubular chassis, independent front suspension, and a de Dion rear axle.

Italy

Alfa Romeo—Eight-cylinder in-line engines, with single Roots-type supercharger, trailing-arm front suspension, tubular frames and swing-axle rear suspension, Type 158. The engine was one bank of Colombo's V-16 design prepared for the pre-war 3 litre s/c–4½ litre u/s Formula. The twin overhead camshafts were driven, together with the supercharger, by gears at the front of the engine. Four cars survived the war.

Maserati—A number of four- and six-cylinder, 1½-litre cars were available in 1946, some dating back to 1934; but for the most part they were 1939 4 CL types which had a four-cylinder engine with a single Roots supercharger, independent front suspension by torsion bars and wishbones, and a live rear axle on quarter-elliptic springs.

1950

1950

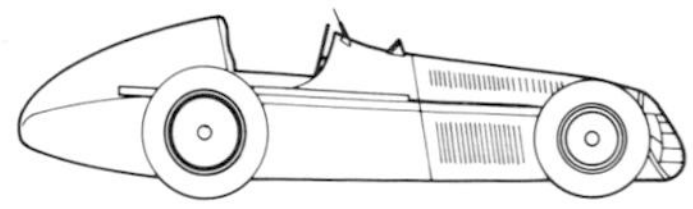

The Fifties had dawned before motor racing finally put the Thirties behind it. The watershed was 1950, the first year of the drivers' championship. The new decade saw Europe recovering from the chaos and tragedy of the Forties, with the Allied military Government of Germany dismantled, and the opening shots of the new war in Korea too far off to be heard by the public at large. All across Western Europe car manufacturers were replacing models carried over from 1939, with designs conceived in a brave new world. In Britain petrol came off the ration, and Germany re-entered international motor racing, with the revival of the dramatic Nürburgring, staging a race for Formula B cars.

The $1\frac{1}{2}$s/c–$4\frac{1}{2}$u/s Formula A proposed for 1941 and re-adopted after the war, remained in force, together with many of the cars such as the 158 Alfa Romeos, but the ranks of the pre-war drivers were beginning to thin. The break with the Thirties lay more in the changes wrought during the active second half of the Forties than the first. This period witnessed the loss of Jean-Pierre Wimille, killed practising for the 1949 Buenos Aires Grand Prix in a Gordini. Achille Varzi, a great ace of the Auto Union team, skidded on a wet road at Berne, overturning his 158 Alfa and died in the wreckage. Yet another blow was the death in 1948 from cancer of a former President of Alfa's Scuderia Ferrari racing team, Count Carlo Felice Trossi.

The disappearance of these pillars of the motor-racing establishment together with the work on their new production car gave Alfa an opportunity to drop out of racing in 1949—the continued absence of real opposition was almost embarrassing. Of the other, now older drivers, Chiron and Etancelin still raced but were nearing the end of their careers, and Nuvolari was a sick man. New names were appearing, such as the Argentinian Juan Manuel Fangio. Although he had been thought too old at 38, his success with a Maserati in 1949, his experience in the rough and tumble of South American racing, and above all his masterly driving, ensured his place alongside Farina in the Alfa Romeo team of 1950.

The races counting towards the new world title began with the British Grand Prix in May, followed by the Grands Prix of Monaco, then Switzerland and Belgium in June, the French Grand Prix at Rheims in July, and the Italian Grand Prix at Monza at the beginning of September. A driver's best four performances out of the six races would count, with points for finishing places; eight for winning, with second, third, fourth, and fifth receiving six, four, three, and two points respectively. A single point was awarded for fastest lap, and in view of the widespread practice of drivers taking over a colleague's car during a race, points thus gained were divided.

The rationale behind the scoring system remains obscure, but the best-of-four rule was clearly intended to prevent a walkover by one of the Alfa Romeo drivers. Grand Prix racing was not yet closely competitive, nor the cars well-matched. With the Alfas so much faster than anything else, some interest, it was hoped, would be lent to the competition by a system that discounted some results. The shared points for shared drives would be an obvious source of trouble, and the fractions have been matters of contention ever since. The scoring was to be changed a number of times over the years, but no entirely satisfactory, or even logical, arrangement ever emerged.

Problems during the early years included the wide disparity between the performance of different makes of car, with drivers' skills of little avail unless exercised at the wheel of an Alfa Romeo or, a little later, a Ferrari. Races were still often won by wide margins of a lap or two, and drivers, in any case, frequently had to drive to the orders of a team manager.

Changes in philosophy were to follow in the wake of the world championship, but meantime, teamwork remained a principal feature, with the main effort still directed towards a victory for the marque rather than glory for an individual driver. In the case of Alfa Romeo, the rationale for racing was still the sale of production cars, an idea carried forward from those precursors of Grands Prix, the Gordon Bennett races, and sustained throughout the years when it was mainly car manufacturers seeking prestige who took part. The same influence was visible in the Thirties with Mercedes-Benz and Auto Union. Here the reputation of the State was the main consideration, and although, human nature being what it is, drivers could not be reduced to ciphers, it was still mostly the team that mattered.

Individual effort in motor racing was left to the amateurs until the drivers' championship came along to change things. Contemporary reports of Grand

Prix races continued to pay little attention to the institution of the title or its progress.

The Americans, on the other hand, thought Grand Prix racing a quaint sort of institution and ignored it, making the **world** championship for many years no more than the FIA's earnest expression of internationalism. Indianapolis was eventually dropped from the scoring, and so far as its influence on Grand Prix racing is concerned, can be largely disregarded. The FIA's efforts to bring European and American racing together went for the most part unrewarded, although traffic of one sort and another did occur, for different reasons, in the fullness of time.

For 1950, racing form remained largely a matter of who was likely to come second after the Alfa Romeos. Only Ferrari seemed able to take advantage of the Alfas' year off in 1949, by virtue of being the only manufacturer who had made a well-organised, and apparently well-financed, effort. In France the CTA-Arsenal had been stillborn, and the 4½-litre Talbots were no longer likely winners. In Britain the BRM was not ready, and the ERAs, dating back to 1934–6, had been no match for the Alfa Romeos even when they were new. The under-financed Alta was never a serious contender, and the E-Type ERA lurched from crisis to crisis—a pattern that the BRM was to follow unerringly in its turn. Although now officially back within the comity of nations, Germany had not had time to re-enter Grand Prix racing, but Italy's early defection from the Axis had allowed her to revive not only the omnipotent Alfa Romeos, but also develop the promising Ferraris and a generation of Maseratis which was only just beginning to be outmoded.

The success of the Alfa team was never in doubt. In the first championship Grand Prix ever, at Silverstone on 10 May 1950, they fielded a team of four cars for Farina, Fangio, Fagioli, and Parnell. Mindful of the potential market in Britain for their road cars, Reg Parnell was invited to make a guest appearance, a gesture appreciated by the huge crowd estimated at well over 100 000 which turned up, many gaining entry in the crush without the formality of paying. Ferrari did not come to Silverstone for the race, courtesy-titled Grand Prix d'Europe and attended by Their Majesties King George VI and Queen Elizabeth; so the Alfas' opposition consisted of a team of Talbots, together with an assortment of privately entered Maseratis, ERAs, and an Alta.

The Alfas were never hard pressed, although Fangio retired with a broken oil pipe, leaving Farina an easy winner from Fagioli and Parnell, gaining an extra championship point for setting fastest lap.

The new championship had a good start. Following the return of the Alfa Romeos at Silverstone, the Monaco Grand Prix the same month turned out to be a dramatic race. Revived only with difficulty in 1948, and not run at all in 1949, the 1950 race in the tiny principality, on its traditional course round the still-picturesque harbour, saw Farina skidding on spray blown over the sea wall at Tabac corner, and causing a multiple accident on the first lap. It was one of the most remarkable incidents ever in Grand Prix racing. Within a few seconds of the start, the field was reduced from 19 cars to ten, which almost at once became nine when Froilan Gonzalez's Ferrari caught fire. The burly Argentinian driver escaped with light burns, the only casualty of the day. His fellow-countryman Fangio became the hero of the afternoon when he picked his way through the wreckage and saved face for Alfa Romeo.

The Alfas remained supreme, but in second place that day was Alberto Ascari, son of the great Antonio Ascari, in a new long-chassis, two-stage supercharged Ferrari, the Type 125 which had been the spearhead of the new make's challenge since it became established in its own right.

Nobody knew better than Ferrari the magnitude of his task in challenging Alfa Romeo. To tackle it he employed a young designer, Aurelio Lampredi, to develop Colombo's engine to the point where it would constitute a threat. After all, it had been beaten by Fangio at Monte Carlo by no more than the length of a refuelling stop.

Eliminate this delay, as the slower Talbots did, and Ferrari knew he had the beating of the Alfas. He

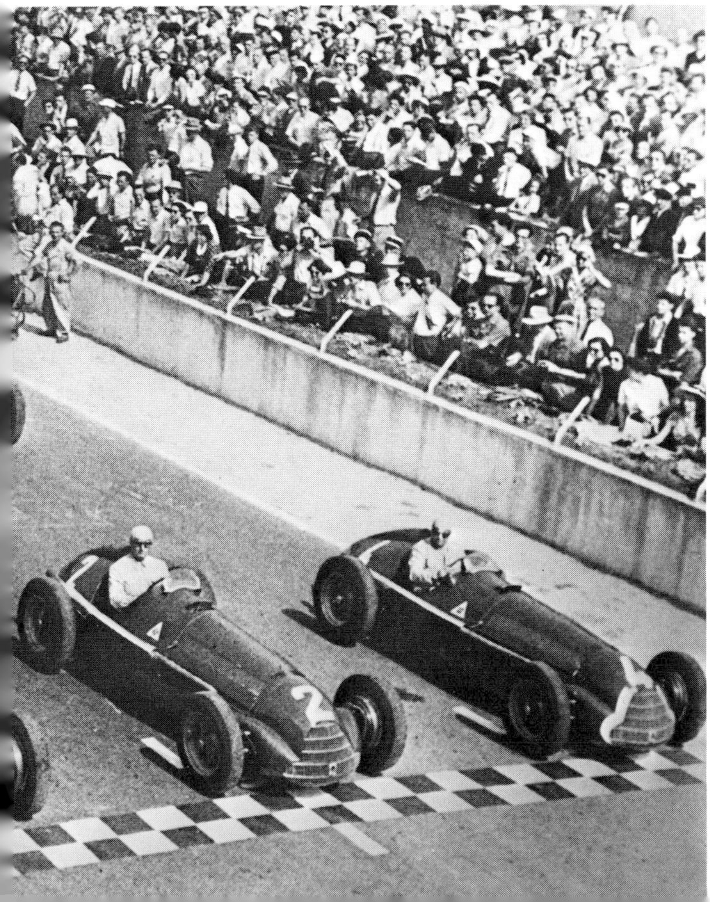

Rheims, the starting grid of the French Grand Prix. On the front row, the supreme Alfa Romeos, Fangio (No 6), Farina (No 2), and Fagioli (No 4). On row two are the Lago Talbots of Etancelin (No 16, with his cap turned back to front), and Giraud-Cabantous (No 18). No 20 on the row behind is Raymond Sommer's Talbot, alongside him are the Maseratis of Franco Rol and Froilan Gonzalez, while behind in No 22 is the ill-fated Pierre Levegh (Talbot). Fangio won, with Fagioli second, and significantly, although he started from the very back of the grid, Peter Whitehead was third in a Ferrari.

Enzo Ferrari (b 1898)

Enzo Ferrari was born near Modena, and got a job as test driver with a small car firm, where his experience made him the obvious choice in 1919 to drive their first racing car. He joined Alfa Romeo in 1920, abandoning ambitions to be a journalist or an opera singer, and beginning instead a long association with motor racing.

Ferrari was never a great driver, but he finished second in the Targa Floria, the Sicilian road race. In 1923, after winning the Circuit of Ravenna, he was presented, according to his own rather egocentric account of the incident, with his prancing horse emblem by the parents of Count Francesco Baracca, an Italian air ace, killed near the end of World War 1, and whose squadron insignia it had been. Ferrari added the yellow heraldic colour of Modena, and the symbol appeared on all the cars with which Ferrari was associated thereafter.

These included cars of the Alfa Romeo racing stable—or Scuderia—which Ferrari ran, establishing himself in Modena as a commercial racing car agent. He prepared his own and private entrants' cars for racing, but it remains doubtful whether the Scuderia was any more than a front organisation for Alfa Romeo's own direct participation in racing. An arrangement like this is often popular with car manufacturers as a means of gaining approbation for victories without suffering the odium of defeats. An official racing team cannot shelve responsibility when things go wrong, yet a win reflects credit—whoever is the driving force. Ferrari says he remained on the Alfa payroll, and that the Scuderia while independent was still '. . . umbilically tied' to the factory, an ironical choice of words in view of the matricidal analogy which followed his final defeat of Alfa Romeo.

The classic racing Alfas which represented such significant stages in the evolution of the Grand Prix car, the P2, and the Type B known as the P3 'Monoposto', which exemplified the single-seater racing car for over 20 years, all raced under the Scuderia Ferrari banner. In 1938, however, dissatisfied with the failure to compete effectively with the all-powerful Germans, Ferrari was dropped. The umbilical cord was severed, with an injunction from Alfa Romeo preventing re-formation of the Scuderia Ferrari for four years.

The autocratic, huffy, former driver defied it. In the truncated 1940 Mille Miglia there was a car built to the design of Ing Alberto Massimino, by Ferrari's Auto Avio Costruzione, of Viale Trento Trieste in Modena. It was made largely from Fiat parts and put together in the space of four months for Alberto Ascari, whose father had driven for, and been a close friend of, Ferrari. In deference to the legal ban, it was known only as the 815 (8 for eight cylinders, 15 for 1.5 litres) and the bodies for the two cars were made by Touring of Milan. Despite their anonymity, the 815s were the first Ferraris; and although neither finished the course, they were the founders of a dynasty of cars that was to dominate Grand Prix racing, and many other sorts of racing besides, for 40 years.

Ferrari's small factory machined aircraft parts, then moved just outside Modena to a patch of land Ferrari owned in Maranello, and was bombed twice towards the end of the war. Here in 1945 Ferrari at last put his name to a car that would embody all the most exciting, extravagant and advanced automotive ideas that would have been daring at any time, but in war-torn Italy seemed outrageous.

Taking former Alfa Romeo personnel such as the faithful Luigi Bazzi, and Ing Colombo with him, Ferrari conceived a V-12 engine, and installed it in a chassis which bore more than a passing resemblance to Alfa Romeos of the past, down to the oval tubular frame borrowed from the Type 158 which Ferrari had commissioned Colombo to design in 1938.

The 125, as it was called under Ferrari's system of numbering, derived from the capacity of an individual cylinder, was Ferrari's staple car in sports and racing forms, stripped for racing, or endowed with sketchy bodywork for the road. The engine was enlarged to 2 litres, and in 1949 Ferrari took advantage of Alfa Romeo's sabbatical year to gain 32 outright victories including the Formula A Grands Prix of Holland (Villoresi), Italy (Ascari), and Switzerland (Ascari). The Silverstone International Trophy (Ascari), and the Grand Prix of Rosario (Farina) were other Formula A wins, while the name dominated Formula B, with Ascari and Villoresi winning the Grands Prix of Brussels, Luxembourg, Rome, Bari, Naples, Monza, and Rheims. In sports car racing Ferraris won the Targa Florio and the Mille Miglia (Clemente Biondetti), and the 24 Hours' of both Spa and Le Mans (Luigi Chinetti), while private owner Peter Whitehead completed a triumphant season for Ferrari by winning the Grand Prix of Czechoslovakia.

There was only one challenge left, and that was to settle the old score with Alfa Romeo. In September 1949, Ferrari set his new designer Lampredi working on a car to do just that.

knew the 15-year-old design was fully stretched, with higher and higher supercharge pressures, which in time would affect reliability. Lampredi was reluctant to follow anything other than the classic supercharged path himself, but with the benefit of experience, and the feel for motor racing that made him such a formidable figure, Ferrari overruled him. What he had in mind was a technical development of the sort that would punctuate the history of Grand Prix racing many times in the years to come.

Meanwhile, the Swiss Grand Prix on the Bremgarten proved another victory for Alfa Romeo, despite Luigi Villoresi's efforts with the latest twin overhead camshaft, de Dion axled, supercharged Ferrari. It lasted only nine laps, and Ascari also retired in a second car. Farina and Fagioli won for Alfa Romeo, with Louis Rosier third in one of the ponderous Talbots which were proving such an object-lesson to Ferrari. Fangio's Alfa dropped out, another hint that the pressures within the now highly-developed straight-eight engine were taking their toll.

It was at the next race, the Belgian Grand Prix on the fast, Spa-Francorchamps circuit in the Ardennes, that Ferrari showed his hand. Rumours of a new unsupercharged Ferrari were confirmed when a 3.3-litre car was wheeled out, an interim model on the way to a full 4½-litre, taking advantage of the upper capacity limit allowed by the formula. The cylinder dimensions of 72 mm bore by 68 mm stroke, giving a capacity of 3322 cc, clearly gave room for expansion, Lampredi having at last agreed with his patron that the supercharged engine would eventually be defeated by its own complexity and heavy demand for fuel, so long as the relationship to unsupercharged engines remained in the ratio of three to one. This ratio had been proposed as long ago as 1938; ten years' intensive engine development had outdated it.

The Alfas were developing between 220 and 235 horse power per litre. To match them Lampredi needed to achieve 70 to 80 horse power per litre, not a difficult task even with a normally aspirated engine with carburettors. This figure would give his cars comparable performance with the Alfas, and the penalty of the extra weight, inevitable with the larger engine, could be more than compensated for by not having to stop so often for fuel. Yet over and above this, Lampredi was already thinking of 100 horse power per litre.

Spa was not a success for Ferrari. Villoresi drove a supercharged car and Ascari the 3.3 litre, but the Alfas lapped at 4 min 37 sec (Farina's best practice lap) while Villoresi could only manage fourth fastest at 4 min 47 sec, and Ascari was behind the Talbots with 4 min 49 sec. Both cars suffered delays in the race, leaving Alfa victorious and Ascari fifth, a lap behind.

A milestone in the post-war development of the Grand Prix car was the 1950 French Grand Prix, with Fangio's practice lap in the Type 158 Alfa of 2 min 30.6 sec—1.6 sec faster than the 1939 record set by Hermann Lang's W 163 Mercedes-Benz. Fangio had 340 bhp at 8500 rpm, Lang 483 bhp at 7800 rpm. Fangio had 1½ litres supercharged and eight cylinders, against Lang's 3 litres supercharged and twelve cylinders. The Alfa's top speed along the main straight of the Rheims–Gueux circuit was nearly 180 mph; the Mercedes flat-out in fifth probably nearer 190 mph, yet the smaller car, nimbler on the corners, benefiting from developments in tyres and brakes, was every bit as fast round the 7.81 km/4.85 miles of smooth, *Route Nationale* amidst the woods and fields of Champagne. The lesson that lap speeds were more than a function of engine power was not a new one, but its implications were not yet fully grasped. The engine test-bed was to remain the principal tool of the technologists of motor racing. The science of

Ferrari's relationship with his drivers was at best variable. Together with Scuderia Ferrari officials showing the 1956 Lancia-Ferrari, are a group of the most famous; Peter Collins (second from left) Olivier Gendebien, Marquis de Portago (with arms folded), Juan Fangio, and Eugenio Castellotti.

the chassis engineer and the aerodynamicist had not yet affected the fundamental shape of the car laid down nearly 20 years earlier.

Another landmark at this race was the demoralisation of Maserati. There were works cars from this famous factory here for Chiron and Franco Rol, Scuderia Ambrosiana cars for Parnell and David Hampshire, a Scuderia Achille Varzi car for Gonzalez, and a Maserati-Milan (a development of the handsome 4 CLT model with bigger superchargers) for Bonetto. They were outclassed even by the Talbots, and all were out of the race before 15 of the 65 laps had gone on this hot July afternoon.

Ferrari again entered the 3.3 litre car, but it was no match for the Alfa Romeos in practice, and was withdrawn. Ferrari won the Coupe des Petites Cylindrées for Formula B cars that accompanied the Grand Prix, with a promising new driver, Stirling Moss, in third place driving an HWM, but Fangio and Fagioli comfortably won the Grand Prix from Peter Whitehead's privately entered Ferrari.

For the non-championship Grand Prix des Nations at Geneva, one of the now rather crowded calendar of Formula A races promoted sometimes as holiday attractions all over Europe, Ferrari had one car with enlarged cylinder bores, 80 mm instead of 72 mm, giving a capacity of 4.1 litres, ever nearer the full 4½. The drivers in Geneva, encouraged perhaps by their new-found status with a world title of their own, staged a protest over the course, which had a section of straight with opposing streams of traffic separated by no more than a line of straw bales. The section was shortened, but the race took place.

Both Ferraris, driven as usual by Ascari and Villoresi, now had de Dion rear suspension, improving traction for the ever increasing power. Fangio was fastest in practice with a time of 1 min 46.7 sec, but the Ferraris were both snapping at his heels, both with 1 min 48.7 sec, in second and third places on the starting grid. In the race, only Fangio was able to stay ahead of Ascari, Villoresi unfortunately crashing while lying fifth, with seven laps to go, Ascari retiring shortly afterwards with water coming out of the exhaust pipes. The Alfas were left in command, but the writing was on the wall, and the next race, at the beginning of September, the sixth and final round of the world championship, was the most important of all. On the doorstep of both protagonists was the Grand Prix of Italy, at Monza.

Fangio held the championship lead when the cars assembled for the 80-lap race round the 6.27 km/3.89 mile track in the Royal Park on the outskirts of Milan. Alfa Romeo entered five cars for Farina, Fagioli, Fangio, Consalvo Sanesi, and Piero Taruffi, while Ferrari had Ascari in one car, Dorino Serafini replacing the injured Villoresi in the other. The Alfa engineers had wrung every ounce of power from their engines, making modifications to them throughout the season, super-tuning some cars in an effort to draw out the opposition, running others with higher axle ratios in the hope that lower engine speeds would ensure survival.

For a country as dedicated to motor racing as Italy in the Fifties, when it was the centre of the Grand Prix world, Monza was the focus of attention. During practice, Ascari was beaten only by a fraction of a second for pole position on the grid, after breaking the old lap record. The engine stroke had been increased from 68 mm to 74.5 mm, bringing the capacity to the full 4494 cc, and for the first time since that Tripoli débâcle in 1938 the Alfas started a classic Grand Prix with no guarantee of winning.

Ascari led Farina for two experimental laps, the acceleration of the V-12 providing him with an advantage coming out of the corners, but to the great relief of the Alfa Romeo top management lining the track, retired six laps later. The Ferrari pit handed over Serafini's car to Ascari during a pit stop for tyres, but he was too far behind to make any impression, although later in the race, despite the loss of third gear, he overtook Fagioli and finished second. Fangio retired twice—one Alfa suffered gearbox trouble, so he took over Taruffi's, but it broke as well.

The pace had been exhausting. Only seven cars out of 20 completed the 502 km/312 mile race; but by and large the Alfa ranks held, and Farina won, pacing himself with great care as the threat from Ascari receded, from 182.83 kph/113.60 mph on lap 20 when he was fighting the Ferrari off, to 176.54 kph/109.69 mph on the closing lap.

The failure of Ascari's first car had been due to a porous cylinder block, but although the Alfa Romeo drivers Farina and Fangio were victorious in the world championship, winning all six races between them, and setting every fastest lap and fastest practice time, it was clear that in 1951 a more serious challenge was coming.

For the engineers a winter of development lay

Although Dr Farina gained a reputation for appearing relaxed at the wheel, he is working hard to keep control of his Alfa Romeo in this fine action shot at Silverstone. Note the linen wind helmet; crash helmets were not yet compulsory, and many drivers raced with bare arms.

ahead for their basically 13-year-old design, the first four examples of which had been largely assembled by the Scuderia Ferrari at Modena, and so held few secrets. They were plainly being stretched to their mechanical limits, while Ferrari were going confidently ahead with a design still in the first flush of youth. While Alfa felt obliged to miss the final, non-championship race of the season, the Grand Prix of Penya Rhin on 29 October, on the Pedralbes circuit outside Barcelona, Ferrari fielded three cars, two 4.5-litre models for Ascari and Serafini, and a 4.1 litre for erstwhile Alfa driver Piero Taruffi.

They won without difficulty on the 6.27 km/3.89 mile circuit after a 50-lap race distinguished by the first appearance in a Grand Prix (at any rate a race with the title Grand Prix, even though not a title round) of the BRM. It was only the second time the BRM had raced. The immensely powerful, but over-complicated and under-developed cars had failed to appear in time for the British Grand Prix in May, and had disgraced themselves when a drive-shaft broke on the start line of the International Trophy at Silverstone in August. Reg Parnell won two minor races at Goodwood at the end of September, which encouraged the British Motor Racing Research Trust to enter for Barcelona with a view to a full season's racing in 1951.

Alas, it only served to emphasise the car's shortcomings. While it proved faster than even the Ferraris over a timed kilometre on the long Pedralbes straight (299.27 kph/185.95 mph against 286.4 kph/177.9 mph) it was slower through the corners. The BRM's acceleration was also inferior, so its lap times were slower. Parnell managed to hold fourth place behind the Ferraris on the first lap, but retired on the next with failure of the drive to the supercharger. Peter Walker worked his way up to fourth by half distance, but his car retired too.

For Ferrari, the triumph only increased their confidence. The BRM had remained a threat only so long as it never actually put in an appearance; now it stood revealed as over-ambitious and under-financed, so could be effectively dismissed from the Italians' calculations. The home of motor racing, it seemed, was still firmly located on the Plain of Lombardy and likely to remain there.

Giuseppe Farina (1906–66)

Becoming the first world champion driver turned out to be the summit of Farina's career. His 16 years in motor racing were punctuated with crashes, beginning with his first event, when he was studying law at Turin University. It was the Aosta–Grand St Bernard hill-climb in which he entered a second-hand Alfa Romeo 1500 against his father who finished fourth. Farina finished in hospital.

He graduated as a Doctor of Law, and undaunted, drove privately entered Maseratis and Alfas in 1933–4, attracting the attention of Nuvolari, under whose guidance he developed a polished, relaxed style at the wheel, sitting well back with arms at full stretch. He is often given credit for setting the example to the new generation of drivers in his stylish posture, but they were beginning to find this stance more practical in any case, as steering became lighter, requiring much less muscle than before.

When Alfa Romeo officially re-entered racing in 1938, Farina was one of their drivers, and he became Italian champion twice at the wheel of the 158s, to which he returned after the war, winning the Grand Prix des Nations, one of the first races, in 1946. He drove Maseratis in 1948 and Ferraris in 1949, but returned to Alfa until they finally withdrew in 1952.

Farina then joined Ferrari, but, ever a temperamental driver, was unhappy with his position in the team, and he was overshadowed by Ascari. He was injured in 1954 while leading the Mille Miglia in a Ferrari, recovering only to be badly burned while practising for the next race when a ruptured fuel tank flooded the cockpit with blazing petrol.

Farina carried on racing determinedly in 1955, and as late as 1957, at the age of 51, made two ill-judged attempts on the Indianapolis 500. Accidents continued to dog this brilliant, but often excitable driver, and he died in a road crash, when his Lotus-Cortina skidded on an icy road near Chambéry, while on his way to watch the 1966 French Grand Prix.

1951

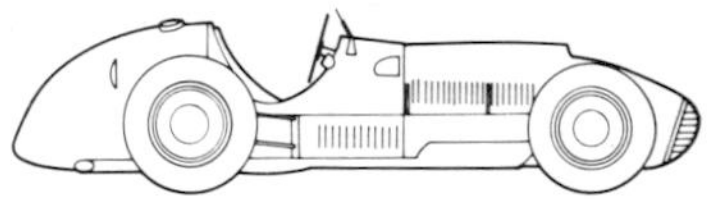

Winter in Modena and Milan saw intensive development programmes by Ferrari and Alfa Romeo, mostly concerned with increasing power. The output of the Alfas in 1946 was 254 bhp at 7500 rpm, then two-stage superchargers were fitted, producing 310 bhp at 7500 rpm. Overhauling the exhaust system, and other changes, produced 350 bhp at 8500 rpm on the 1950 test bench.

By the spring of 1951, supercharger boost had been increased and the water circulation system altered to pump coolant directly towards the exhaust ports in the cylinder head, now almost incandescent despite valves packed with sodium. Triple downdraught Weber carburettors gulped in air from a forward-facing trunk, and the magneto was moved to save it from the effects of the heat thrown off the exhausts. The high temperatures and pressures within the engine were an increasing source of worry, and in the end yet another ploy had to be tried.

The choice of fuel in 1951 was still free, the obligatory 'pump' fuel still several years off. Indeed the 75 octane 'pump' fuel of the post-war period was indifferent stuff for road cars, let alone highly tuned racing engines. Alcohol burns relatively coolly, so the Alfa's fuel was liberally laced with it to keep down the temperature on the critical exhaust side of the engine. Together with very large angles of valve overlap, this reduced the fuel consumption of the now redesignated Type 159 to less than 1.8 litres per 100 km/$1\frac{1}{2}$ mpg, so a number of cars were rebuilt with side fuel tanks, and all 159s had additional tanks in what turned out to be the only space left within the car's 250.2 cm/8ft $2\frac{1}{2}$in wheelbase, the driver's cockpit. Even so, a maximum capacity of 65 gallons/295 litres still provided less than 100 miles/160 km of racing.

The modifications increased the car's power to 404 bhp at 9500 rpm, well over twice its original 190 bhp of 1937, but at the penalty of a fuel load weighing over 250 kg/5 cwt, or around 20 per cent of the total weight of the car. Even with different spring rates to allow for it, the handling was seriously affected, and it was impossible to use full power until some of the fuel had been used up.

Ferrari on the other hand were a long way from getting the most out of their engine. Power had been increased from 330 bhp at 6500 rpm, to 380 bhp at 7500 rpm with two sparking plugs per cylinder. Ascari and Villoresi were once again engaged as drivers, winning two races at the beginning of the season at Syracuse and Pau, without the Alfa Romeos putting in an appearance.

The newest Ferrari was held in reserve until the first clash was expected at the Grand Prix of San Remo, but at the last minute Alfa declined to join battle, and Ascari won. A confrontation was eagerly awaited at Silverstone for the non-championship International Trophy in May, but this proved an inconclusive occasion washed out by a thunderstorm, and in any case the Alfa once again declined to appear.

There were seven world championship events in 1951, the Grands Prix of Switzerland (Berne), Belgium (Spa), France (Rheims), Britain (Silverstone), Germany (Nürburgring), Italy (Monza), and Spain (Pedralbes). Monaco had decided on a sports car race, but Spain was uprated, and Germany included for the first time.

From Silverstone the rain followed the contestants to the Bremgarten circuit for the Swiss Grand Prix, won by Alfa from Ferrari by less than a minute, but the pattern for the season was set in practice. Both makes broke the 1950 record speed, lapping at 168.07 kph/104.43 mph in the case of the Alfa, and 164.47 kph/102.19 mph for the Ferrari. But the result was again inconclusive. Ferrari's number one driver, Ascari, had been burned in the Formula 2 race, and the veteran Taruffi to whom he handed over his car was not in the same class, while Villoresi, in the other new Ferrari, crashed after only 13 laps. Taruffi drove

Alfa's Waterloo. The 4.5-litre Ferrari proved too much for the Type 158/9 Alfa Romeo. Ascari shared second place in the French Grand Prix, and by the end of the season, the $4\frac{1}{2}$-litre unsupercharged car was in the ascendant.

the race of his life, overtaking the reigning world champion Farina, and finishing second, but had it been Ascari . . . ?

By the Belgian Grand Prix the Ferraris were at full strength, with three new cars for Ascari, Villoresi, and Taruffi, against the Alfas of Fangio, Farina, and Sanesi, all tuned to concert pitch for this fast circuit, with its murderous Masta straight. One Alfa was now equipped with de Dion rear suspension featuring heavily dished rear wheels to accommodate wide brake drums, an innovation that was to prove the undoing of their fastest driver.

But both teams were approaching 200 mph on Masta, Fangio and Farina exceeding 9000 rpm, and calling for bigger 7.00 × 19 in. rear wheels for race day. Five drivers broke the previous year's lap record in practice, Fangio (4 min 25 sec); Farina (4 min 28 sec); Villoresi (4 min 29 sec); Ascari (4 min 30 sec); and Taruffi (4 min 32 sec).

The Alfas' tank capacity had been raised to over 70 gallons/318 litres, some of which they now had to work off in the opening laps, which Villoresi led, before Farina engaged him in a furious passing and re-passing duel lasting for three long circuits of the Spa track. Farina gradually took the initiative, lapping at 186.64 kph/115.97 mph, then 190.02 kph/118.07 mph on laps four, and five, and reaching 192.11 kph/119.37 mph on lap six, whereupon Fangio went faster still, setting a new record and the race's fastest lap in 4 min 22.1 sec, a speed of 193.90 kph/120.48 mph.

Fangio took the lead, but his new wheel jammed on its splines during a tyre stop, and Farina was able to get in front again and remain there, even after a second stop for fuel and tyres on lap 25, occupying only 39 sec—pit crews drilled against the stopwatch for moments like this. Ascari and Villoresi finished second and third, fully 3 min in arrears after 2 hr 45 min of racing, but in 1951 this was considered a close-run thing.

Alfa's experiments with the de Dion axle had been as a result of problems cropping up during the search for more speed. The increases in power had resulted in more wheelspin, as the narrow-section tyres of the day fought for grip. Tyres wore out quickly on the Ferraris as well, and they had already adopted de Dion, with its arrangement for keeping the tyre at right angles to the road, instead of altering camber and toe-in with which the Alfas had previously been content. Likewise, brakes had to be expanded until they practically filled the wheel, blanking off a useful route for the cooling air, necessary to dissipate the heat generated in stopping 1-ton racing cars from almost 200 mph.

The existence of the 4½-litre Lago Talbot (left) and the Type 158 Alfa Romeo (right) pointed the way for the first post-war Grand Prix Formula. Farina (No 2) overtakes Pierre Levegh (No 44) in the French Grand Prix.

The Alfas no longer enjoyed the luxury of racing in line ahead, never again finishing with a team intact, and although they fought off the opposition at the French Grand Prix at the beginning of July—extended to 77 laps, 603.37 km/374.91 miles just to make sure even the Ferraris would stop for fuel—their subjugation was at hand.

Round four of the 1951 championship was at Silverstone on 14 July, and four Type 159 Alfa Romeos faced three Type 375 Ferraris driven by Ascari, and Villoresi, together with an older 12-plug version. This was driven by Froilan Gonzalez, a plump, energetic Argentinian who had come to Europe in 1950 to drive the blue and yellow Scuderia Argentina Maserati. He had attracted attention in the spring of 1951 by defeating an admittedly badly prepared team of 1939 Mercedes-Benz 3-litre cars in Argentina, with a 2-litre Ferrari. He was given a works drive by Alfa Romeo, but his big opportunity had come in the recent French Grand Prix at Rheims, when Taruffi took ill. Gonzalez deputised, and shared the second-place car with Ascari.

Now he was driving on the flat airfield track in a spectacular manner, elbows flailing, his bulk overflowing the sides of the cockpit, and to such effect that he was not only the fastest Ferrari driver, but beat the Alfa Romeos as well. Silverstone was

Juan Manuel Fangio (b 1911)

Grand Prix racing generally throws up one driver who is regarded by his contemporaries as the exemplar, and throughout the Fifties this was Juan Manuel Fangio. He was the driver the others strove to match—there was little hope of ever beating him in a straight conflict. He was the driver who could be relied upon to get the best possible performance from his car, whatever the conditions, consistently and safely.

Fangio was 40 when he won his first world title, and four more were to follow before this greatest of all drivers quit motor racing and retired to his native Argentina. An extraordinary man with bow legs, almost indolent movements, but searching, penetrating eyes, he was born on 24 June 1911 in Balcarce, a small town 200 miles from Buenos Aires, the fourth of six children in an Italian immigrant family. While still a teenager he got a job as a garage mechanic, survived a severe bout of pneumonia and did his military service as an officer's chauffeur. Cars were an absorbing interest, and a garage customer took him on as a racing mechanic.

In 1934 Fangio opened a garage in Balcarce, beginning his career as a driver in long, hot and dusty road races across the Andes that lasted for days. His successes created a certain amount of civic pride in Balcarce and in the absence of a wealthy sponsor, a whip-round was organised amongst peasants who, in his own words, '... would slice a loaf thin to save a penny'. Yet they subscribed with enthusiasm to buy Juan a proper racing car. Their judgement was astute , but it was 1939, and by 1942 motor racing even in neutral South America was in abeyance. Frustrated, Fangio kept his hand in by driving furiously in his old Ford over the routes of the pre-war races in the mountains.

Fears that he would be too old for motor racing when it resumed persisted, and he was already 36 when he finished third in the Buenos Aires Grand Prix of 1947, at the wheel of his faithful Chevrolet. He continued campaigning with the old car until the Automobile Club of Argentina bought Maseratis for Fangio and another local driver Oscar Galvez. Fangio's first year in Europe, 1948, did not seem a success, yet his talent was so remarkable that it had been recognised by drivers such as Villoresi, Varzi, and Wimille, and his fame spread.

The following year proved more rewarding, with a series of victories at San Remo, Pau, Perpignan, Marseille, Monza, and Albi, and the Fangio legend was launched. The enigmatic driver from the other side of the world began to be regarded with a sense of awe which was never lost.

His career suffered a setback in 1952, with his only serious injury in a racing car. Exhausted with travelling from race to race, he drove a Maserati at Monza, crashing on the Seraglio, and breaking his neck. It was 1953 before he came back, but he quickly rediscovered form, and led the Mercedes-Benz team during 1954 and 1955, setting a record total of Grand Prix victories that stood until 1968.

Racing in the rain. Juan Fangio splashes through the downpour at the Silverstone International Trophy. After winning his heat, the final was stopped after six laps, and Reg Parnell (Thinwall Ferrari) declared the winner.

Alfa Romeo withdrawn

For Alfa Romeo, 1951 was the end of the road. To continue racing in the face of Ferrari opposition invited disaster, and there was insufficient time to develop a new $1\frac{1}{2}$-litre car. The Government department responsible for financing the motor industry refused to grant the cash, and there was no Scuderia Ferrari able to act as a politically acceptable decoy.

Silverstone had been their first defeat since a minor race in 1946, ending an unbroken run of 25 victories in five and a half years, a record that would stand throughout the history of modern motor racing.

The cars were consigned to the Alfa Romeo museum, and the racing department wound up. Perhaps Alfa would never have gone into Grand Prix racing in the Forties had they not had Colombo's design, and the laid-up racing cars lying in that famous cheese factory. Yet their two championships laid the foundation of their sporting reputation after the war, from which their production cars continued to benefit ever after. The specialised engineering of the supercharged 159A as it became, may have had little to do with road cars of any generation, but the glamour, and the association with success was carried through with an expertise and dash that put the name of Alfa Romeo amongst the motor racing immortals.

still a relatively slow Grand Prix circuit. The lap speeds at Spa and Rheims had been around 120 mph/193 kph, while Silverstone had only just reached 100 mph/161 kph. Here the high top speed of the Alfa was of no avail against the punch of the V-12 out of the fast bends. Gonzalez started the race from pole position, and just over two hours later, the long reign of the Alfa Romeos was at an end.

It was a gripping spectacle, with Fangio and Farina treading carefully during the opening laps, their cars heavy with fuel, and catching Gonzalez after ten laps. But even Fangio with all his magic was unable to draw away. On lap 49 he had to refuel and change his rear tyres, losing 1 min 13 sec to the flying Ferrari which lost less time when its turn came, so despite all the greatest driver of his time could do, Gonzalez was able to ease up towards the end, and win by 50 sec.

For Enzo Ferrari it was an emotional affair. Honour had at last been satisfied in his 13-year quarrel with Alfa Romeo, and he wrote later, 'I wept with joy; but my tears of happiness were blended with tears of sadness, for I thought that day: "I have killed my mother".' He wrote to Alfa's Managing Director, 'I still feel for our Alfa the adolescent tenderness of first love, the immaculate affection for the mamma.'

His wistfulness made no difference at all on the Nürburgring a fortnight later at the revived German Grand Prix, when only Fangio's Alfa Romeo survived—and that in poor shape. Ascari won, and Ferraris filled five of the first six places. Ascari even broke Caracciola's 1937 race record with the 5.6-litre Mercedes-Benz, on a circuit that placed a premium on roadholding, in particular the ability of the rear wheels to gain traction through the 172 corners of this tortuous track in the Eifel Mountains.

At Monza, Fangio was fastest in practice, but Ascari won yet again with Gonzalez second; after a long hard race, Ascari lost the lead only briefly to Fangio whose car threw a tyre tread. After six races, three to Alfa, three to Ferrari, the twelve-cylinder cars were in the ascendancy, and the final round of the championship at Barcelona seemed a foregone conclusion.

Both teams had been making further changes during the season to try and extract the last ounce of speed. The Ferraris had longer tails and larger fuel tanks; Alfa Romeo had another shot at getting the exhaust system right, and turned the air trunk to breathe in the cooler environment of the cockpit instead of the torrid zone under the bonnet. Detail changes like these, however, were to be the downfall of Ferrari and the salvation of their rivals.

After the Italian Grand Prix, the title lay between Fangio and Ascari, the former leading by a few points. The Pedralbes circuit at Barcelona included a section of the wide Avenida Generalissimo Franco which cuts right across the city before heading off in the direction of Madrid. Speeds on this long straight with the now much modified cars were clearly going to be high, and tyres critical. Ferraris chose 16 in. rear wheels with wide-section tyres, while Alfa

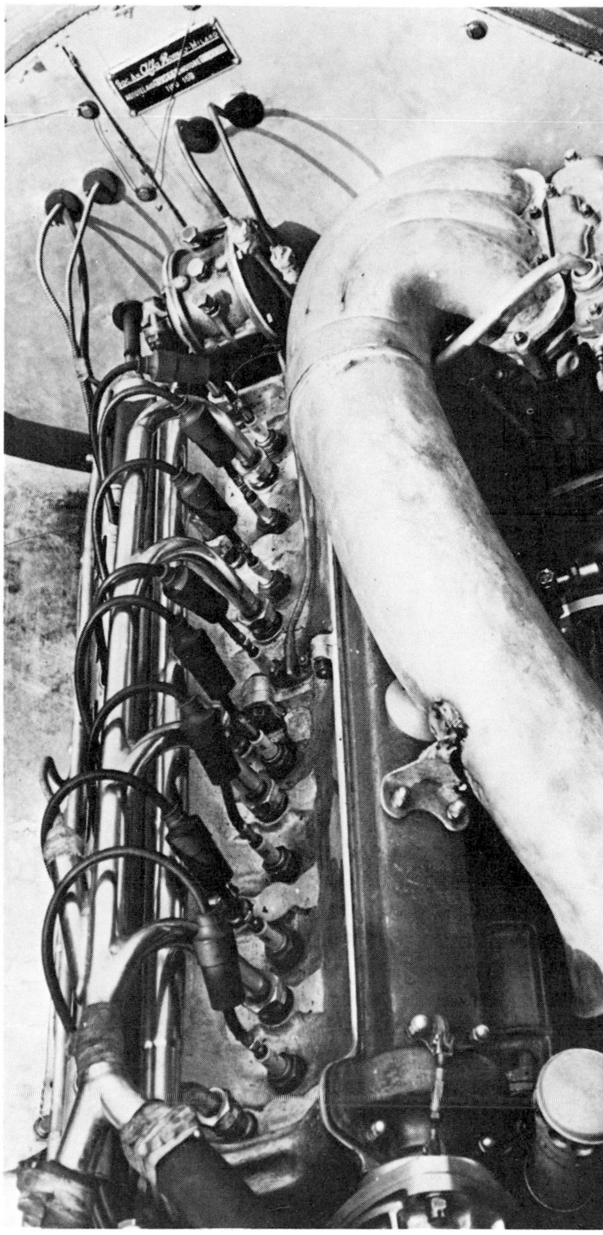

The last great racing straight-eight. The Alfa Romeo 159 1½-litre supercharged. The trumpet on this model is collecting warm air from under the bonnet for the Roots blower. The final version drew it from the scuttle instead.

Romeo preferred 18 in. wheels with narrow section tyres. Although Ascari put up the fastest time in practice, at 173.9 kph/108.1 mph, which was 15.9 kph/9.9 mph faster than his Ferrari over the same course a year earlier, in the race he threw tyre treads on the punishing 2.8 km/1¾ mile straight, leaving Alfa Romeo to win, and Fangio to clinch his first of five world championships.

The technical achievements of Ferrari and Alfa Romeo during 1951 were summed up by Laurence Pomeroy FRSA, MSAE in Vol 2 of *The Grand Prix Car* shortly afterwards. 'The difference in speed . . . may perhaps best be realised by imagining that they (the Alfa Romeo and the Ferrari) had been asked to

cover a single lap 43.1 miles/69.3 km long made up of the circuits at Berne, Spa, Rheims, Silverstone, Nürburgring, Monza, and Barcelona put, as it were, end to end. The fastest Alfa Romeo would have covered this lap (about equal in length to the Dieppe circuit of 1912) in 26 min 25.2 sec at an average speed of 97.8 mph/157.4 kph and the fastest Ferrari would have come past 12.6 sec later at an average speed of 97.1 mph/156.2 kph. The total eclipse of all rivals of these two Italian cars can perhaps be best appreciated by a safe estimate that none of them would have reached an average of even 90 mph/144.84 kph on such a hypothetical circuit.'

Of these rivals, the decline of the Talbots was hastened by financial trouble which prevented a works team taking the field, while the Maseratis were overwhelmed by the technical superiority of the two leading protagonists. Two BRMs made a last-minute appearance in the British Grand Prix where they finished fifth and seventh, but although they had a trouble-free run on this occasion the cars were still far from right. The cockpits overheated, badly burning the drivers, and at the Italian Grand Prix a desultory performance threw the team further into gloom, dispirited the sponsors, and cast doubt on prospects for the car in 1952.

In October the FIA decided to extend the life of the Formula, now generally referred to as Formula 1, up to the end of 1953 providing time to get ready for a change to new limits of 2½ litres for unsupercharged, and 750 cc for supercharged engines in 1954.

The climate of opinion had run against supercharged cars on the grounds that they were expensive to build, complicated, generally unreliable, and in a phrase that would be repeated often in the years to come, too far removed from the average car in the street. A problem endemic in the structure of the FIA and the CSI, throughout the history of Grand Prix racing was their tendency to reflect the views of the race promoters rather than the competitors, which would lead to conflict in the years ahead. One of the earliest manifestations of this was nervousness over what was felt to be the rarefied atmosphere of Grand Prix racing, and the need to relate it to the cars ordinary people drove. Another abiding fear was a shortage of competitive cars, and

Above right: Mainstay of the private entrant in the opening seasons of world championship racing, the 4CLT 'San Remo' Maserati. The 1950 world champion Dr Farina tries one at Goodwood.

Above left: The venerable Talbot was in the tradition of a Grand Prix car which could double as a sports car when necessary. Louis Rosier, seen here in the 1951 British Grand Prix used a similar car equipped with mudguards and lights to win the 1950 Le Mans 24 Hours.

effectively banning superchargers seemed to the legislators a neat way of keeping costs down, and making cars 'realistic', so that the big car manufacturers might be tempted to take part.

Even the nationalised Alfa Romeo factory found the cost of developing their supercharged car crippling. It was becoming obvious they were about to call it a day, and the FIA's new rule changed the ratio between unsupercharged to supercharged engines from 3:1 to 3.3:1. Had the proportions been left as they were and the u/s engine reduced to 2½ litres, the blown limit would have been set at 833 cc. Instead, what seemed to be wanted was a simple, straightforward unsupercharged Formula 1, and in the event that is what they got. With 500 cc racing now well established, and drivers such as Stirling Moss lapping the Nürburgring at 118.6 kph/73.7 mph, perilously close to the speed of a number of Grand Prix cars, a 750 cc supercharged car may have seemed at least an outside possibility. None emerged, and the theorists who prophesied that the effect of the new rules would be unopposed 2½-litre cars, were right.

Mercedes-Benz had designed a 1½-litre supercharged car for the old formula, their ill-starred foray to South America at the beginning of 1951 being part of a plan to reorganise their racing department. Gonzalez had shown their reappearance to be premature, and with only two years of the formula to run, they put their plans away and decided to wait.

Meanwhile the race organisers worried, lest in 1952 the absence of Alfa Romeo would leave Ferrari with a succession of walkovers that no one might care to come and watch.

1952

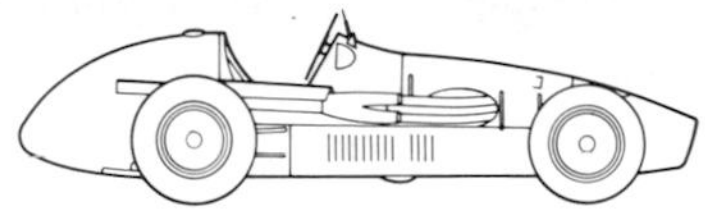

The BRM team soldiered on at Monza, testing and re-testing their recalcitrant V-16. Its performance was crucial to the development of Formula 1 in 1952, as race organisers began making up their minds whether to run their Grands Prix for Formula 1, or the 2-litre unsupercharged/500-cc supercharged Formula 2. The BRM was by far the most powerful car in the history of the $1\frac{1}{2}$-litre formula. As early as 1949, with its two-stage centrifugal supercharger, it had shown over 400 horse power on the test bed—already a match in theory for the still developing 159 Alfa Romeo. By 1952, 500 bhp was in prospect, but the car was behind schedule, underdeveloped, and unreliable. With Alfa out, the Ferraris would have no opposition, and Grand Prix fields would be down to a handful of cars.

When the BRM failed to appear for a non-championship Formula 1 race at Turin in April, national automobile clubs all over Europe decided on Formula 2 events, and once again organised seven championship races during the season. Spain was dropped from the series, but the Dutch Grand Prix on the new coastal circuit at Zandvoort, near Haarlem, was included for the first time. Even the British, anxious as they were to see their over-publicised Grand Prix contender take part in some real racing, had to comply with the adoption of Formula 2 for the Silverstone round. Although they kept inventing excuses for Formula 1 or even Formule Libre races for the sake of encouraging the now much disparaged project, time for the BRM had finally run out. The car that had made the most dramatic noise ever heard on the race track—a banshee-like shriek—was to be remembered for little else—apart from its complexity and its failures.

The adoption of Formula 2 for the next two seasons suited Enzo Ferrari, whose cars had dominated it since 1949; but for a number of reasons he had embarked on a diversity of new designs in 1950-1. On short, twisty circuits his cars were being given an uncomfortable time from rivals such as the French Simca-Gordini and the British HWM, both relatively unsophisticated, using components borrowed from production cars. Also, Ferrari had an eye to the future, and wanted to influence the FIA's thinking about future formulae. A new 2-litre engine seemed called for to deal with Gordini and HWM, and if it could be easily enlarged to $2\frac{1}{2}$ litres for the talked-about 1954 formula, so much the better. Ferrari was never above a little manipulation of the FIA, and from experience knew that the well-publicised existence of an engine that caught the mood of the legislators, might inspire them to make the appropriate decision.

In what appeared at first to be a complete reversal of his policy, hitherto permutations of V-12s, Ferrari commissioned Lampredi to design a 2 litre four cylinder. With this he recommenced racing in Formula 2, which he had all but abandoned to concentrate on crushing Alfa Romeo. Formula 2, he reasoned, would provide him with a development programme and place him in a competitive position for 1954. Events would frustrate him, but for the moment he took the view that a four-cylinder engine was the way to go, encouraged by the pre-eminent motor cycle racing engine of the day, the Norton 500 cc, producing 100 bhp per litre. If Norton could manage it, so could Ferrari.

The wholesale switch to Formula 2 in 1952 had more immediate advantages. Now Ferrari had both a potent V-12 for fast circuits, and his newly completed Type 500 four cylinder (which raced first as a $2\frac{1}{2}$ litre,

Tracks

Of the Grand Prix venues established so far, the Swiss had a traditional home, the Bremgarten road circuit near Berne in publicly owned forest, where the Grand Prix had been inaugurated in 1934. The roughly diamond-shaped 7.28 km/4.52 mile circuit of public roads was to host every one of the 14 Swiss Grands Prix run until the authorities banned motor racing in 1955.

Spa-Francorchamps in Belgium was composed of public roads, and had seen its first Grand Prix in 1925, won by Antonio Ascari in an Alfa Romeo. It enjoyed a grim reputation partly because of its speed, and partly because, like other circuits, when cars crashed there was invariably something hard by the trackside to crash into. Richard Seaman died here in a Mercedes-Benz in the 1939 Belgian Grand Prix.

The British Grand Prix was largely a post-war invention but it was by now well established, having been held at Silverstone every year since 1948, even though the course had been changed from year to year. Monza on the other hand went back to 1922, since when the Italian Grand Prix had been held elsewhere only in 1937 (Leghorn) and the post-war crisis years of 1947–8. Its distinguishing feature was that besides the road circuit laid out within the confines of a Royal Park, simulating a normal road, there was also a slightly banked oval, and link roads which could be used in conjunction with one another. The banked track had been incorporated in the races between 1922–8 and 1931–3, and was about to be rebuilt.

Zandvoort, in the Netherlands, was brand new, but the Nürburgring had been built by German unemployed in 1926–7, and had hosted every German Grand Prix since, on the most dramatic track in the world.

The odd race out was the most ancient, the French Grand Prix. It had been run at Le Mans on two different Circuits de la Sarthe, and also at Dieppe, Amiens, Lyon and Lyon-Parilly, Strasbourg, Tours, Montlhéry, Miramas, Comminges, Pau, and Rheims, and Rheims-Gueux. Except for Montlhéry and Miramas, all were public road circuits, but together they established the principle that no single track enjoyed: an inalienable right to run a national Grand Prix.

Above: Alberto Ascari in the Formula 2 Ferrari with which he won six of the seven world championship races.

Below: Stirling Moss made his mark in the HWM, one of a handful of British entrants who found themselves 'promoted' to Grand Prix racing following the adoption of Formula 2 rules.

because development was so far advanced at the end of 1951). The V-12 was never needed. Ferraris won every round of the championship, Ascari won every race except one, and even though Colombo had forsaken Ferrari and joined Maserati to work on the six-cylinder A6GCM, opposition was weak.

Taruffi won the odd race, the Swiss Grand Prix for example, while Ascari was engaged in an unsuccessful attempt on the Indianapolis 500 with a modified $4\frac{1}{2}$-litre Ferrari. Giuseppe Farina finished second four times, to take second place in the championship behind Ascari. Taruffi, the third Ferrari driver was third in the points table, and sharing fourth place was Rudi Fischer, a Swiss driver with a privately entered car, whom Ferrari exploited to try out prototypes for the factory at Fischer's expense.

The driver with whom Fischer shared fourth in the championship was Mike Hawthorn, who had shot to fame in a single afternoon at Goodwood, with one of the new Cooper-Bristols. Hawthorn exemplified the newcomers arriving in Grand Prix racing behind the jubilant Ferraris, not merely drivers like himself or Moss, Peter Collins, and Lance Macklin, but also new cars such as the HWM and Connaught, and the Cooper-Bristol. From being talented amateurs, or semi-professionals in the Second Division, the wholesale shift to Formula 2 suddenly catapulted these fresh-faced youngsters into the premier league of motor racing, and while Ferrari was being congratulated as his cars took one chequered flag after another, the movement that would eventually take the initiative in Grand Prix racing away from Italy, gathered speed.

Ascari was a worthy enough world champion. It was hardly a vintage season, but it was won handsomely by the best car, and a driver at the height of his powers, probably a match even for Fangio. It had also been a crowded season. Although there were still only seven rounds of the world championship, all still in Europe except the anomalous Indianapolis event, there were plenty of other races as well. No fewer than seven counted as Grands Prix de France; at Pau, Marseille, Montlhéry, Rheims, Sables d'Olonne, Comminges, and La Baule. Ferraris won all but one, the fast Rheims circuit favouring the Gordini of the new French hero, Jean Behra. The championship French Grand Prix took place on the new Rouen Les Essarts circuit, laid out in a wooded valley near Rouen, and formed out of the RN 138 and the RN 840 with a link road between. There had been a short circuit here between the wars, and its creation by the Automobile Club de Normand demonstrated another phenomenon with which Grand Prix racing was gradually to become more familiar, the rivalry of circuits over which should stage the national Grand Prix.

Traditional venues were faced with challengers,

some of them with formidable advantages which would be magnified later on, as demands were made for more safety and better facilities. The national automobile clubs, or ACNs as they were known (such as the RAC in Britain, or the Automobile Club de France) had no tracks of their own, and were only responsible for sanctioning the race. It was run by a promoter, which could be a track owner, or a motor club, or a combination of both.

Now the choice of venue was becoming a matter of importance, with the cachet of world championship in the title, and the prospect of world-wide publicity. It became competitive as promoters' prospects of profit increased. With district or city prestige at stake, in some cases it became a local political issue as well, which meant that Government funds soon became available, even if only for encouraging tourism. The progress by which Grand Prix racing became an extremely wealthy, international, professional sporting entertainment was beginning. Doors opened on every side to new means of making money, Ferrari leading the way as a team, with Stirling Moss soon to show drivers how best to exploit their commercial opportunities.

The finances of motor racing

When Alfa Romeo withdrew at the end of 1951, they were the last Grand Prix team of the classic era to run on a subsidy from the State. The Mercedes-Benz and Auto Unions of the Thirties, Alfa themselves under IRI, the *Istituto per la Ricostruzione Industriale* (the Italian government's nationalisation corporation) and even the ill-starred CTA-Arsenal, had all been run under subsidies from the taxpayer. These days were now at an end.

Ferrari derived a little income from the manufacture of road cars, having phased out his war-time machine tool business. However, the racing team was run as a commercial proposition to sell, and even run cars belonging to wealthy private owners, such as the Swiss Ecurie Espadon of Fischer and Staechlin, or the Formula 1 car of Englishman Peter Whitehead. Running cars for other people was, after all, a traditional activity of the Scuderia Ferrari, amongst whose customers had been Alfa Romeo with its IRI subsidy dating back to its nationalisation in 1933.

Ferrari had also enjoyed retainers from tyre and oil companies, and his reputation ensured his team the highest starting money whenever it appeared. This was a system of payments by race organisers to defray expenses, since prize money was mostly derisory—a mere £1750 for the opening Grand Prix d'Europe in 1950, while starting money came to £4600 of which £600 was allocated to British entries. Starting money was an important source of income, particularly to teams like Ferrari who had developed a keen sense of their value as crowd-pullers. Advertising, beyond a discreet badge on drivers' or mechanics' overalls, or in terms of acknowledging 'technical assistance' from a supplier of spark plugs or carburettors, was unknown. Commercial sponsorship in the formal sense existed only in America, although there were wealthy patrons of racing teams in Europe. Fiat began to play a part in funding Ferrari, to ensure it remained amongst the better-off teams, which was the next-best thing to a subsidy from the government. Fiat relied upon a certain enhancement accruing to Italy in general, and the Italian motor industry in particular, of which they comprised the major portion.

Much later, when professionalism was firmly established in motor racing, what came to be known as 'rent-a-drive' was much disparaged. Yet it was already a feature of Formula 1 racing in 1952, with wealthy enthusiasts willing to pay for the privilege of driving for a famous team, in a competitive car. Some rent-a-drivers went on to gain great distinction. Yet the best years for drivers still lay in the future. Motor racing was still a team business, cash still the problem of the team management. Patronage, sponsorship, or retainers were still a matter for discretion. To most teams, motor racing was a sporting pursuit like yacht racing, or skiing, or big game hunting, for which they expected to pay—there seemed little choice. Breaking even was the best they could hope for, making a profit was hardly ever thought of, except perhaps by Ferrari.

Simca Gordini, as their name implied, obtained help, mostly in kind, from Simca, the French branch of Fiat as it was at the time, and on whose engines they relied. Connaught had connections with the British firm of Lea-Francis, while HWM was a private venture relying on a small garage in south-west London, called Heath Walton Motors. John Heath was a partner and it had premises at Walton-on-Thames, hence the name. Stirling Moss recalls how he and Heath, who was to die taking part in the 1956 Mille Miglia, used to beg and borrow components or services from a normally well-disposed British motor industry to keep the shoe-string operation going.

Professional drivers were in the ascendancy, but their status as an attraction at races and thus candidates for starting money, only began to blossom as the world championship took root. They now had a role enjoyed by only a few in the Thirties, men such as Nuvolari, or Caracciola. Now, like the teams, drivers were looking for retainers from fuel and tyre companies, and getting them. Advertising endorsements became a well-established practice, and drivers no longer had to rely on a private income or another job to provide their livelihood. A star like Ascari in a Ferrari was still worth more starting money than an unknown Stirling Moss in an HWM, even at Silverstone, at least until the underdog looked like winning. Gradually amateurism was fading.

Starting-money wrangles continued to be a feature of racing for many years, with Ferrari in particular wielding his bargaining power by theatening not to appear, even threatening to withdraw his team from racing altogether, his pronouncements gaining prominence all over the world, adding handsomely to his value. Negotiations over money were carried on in deadly secret, lest team A discover what team B was getting. Horse power figures were methodically leaked to improve prospects, and failures glossed over. There were no cartels, no alliances, no closed shops—motor racing was still inhabited by the fiercely independent.

But in 1952, safety was at last acknowledged. Drivers' crash helmets were made compulsory.

1953

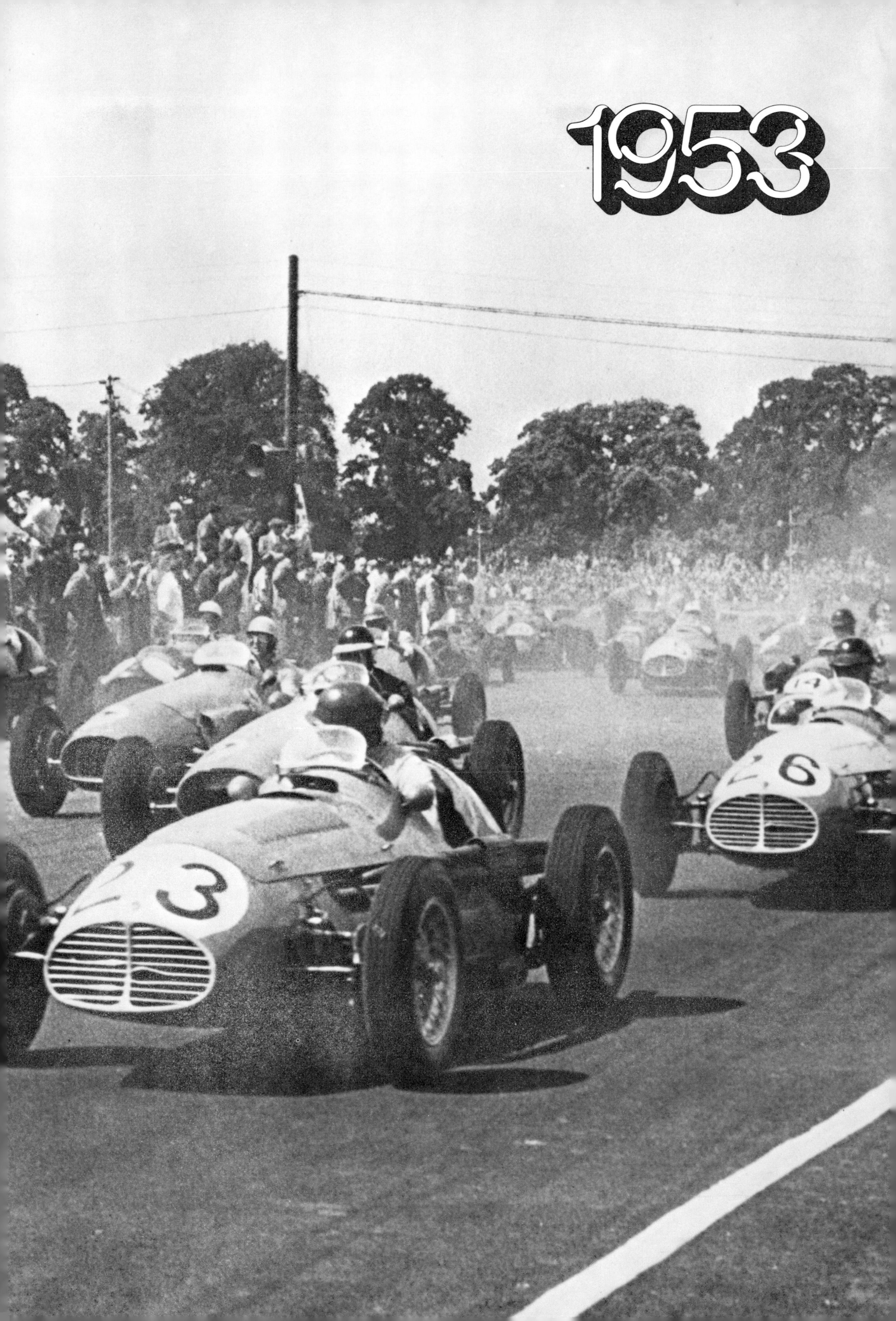

1953

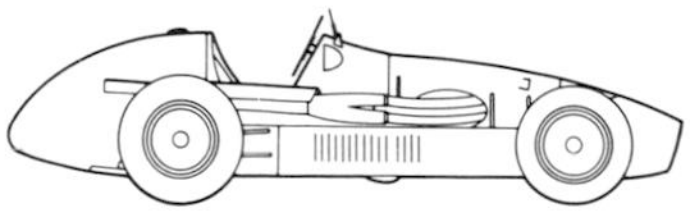

The second year of Formula 2 racing appeared to be much the same as the first. Ferraris won every race except one, and Alberto Ascari the world championship, but it was by no means a repeat of the easy conquest of 1952. Maserati offered such a strong challenge that Fangio, recovered from his injuries, was runner-up, winning the final round, after a series distinguished by the closest racing seen in Grands Prix for the best part of 20 years, even though the cars themselves were relatively unspectacular.

The season also saw the first world championship round outside Europe, the first of Ferrari's 'withdrawals' from motor racing, and Ascari's almost monotonous succession of victories come to an end, after a record nine in a row. The spell lasting from the Belgian Grand Prix in 1952 to the same race in 1953 was broken by the first British driver to join a major team *and* win a grande épreuve since Richard Seaman. He was Mike Hawthorn, whose arrival also brought a new youthfulness to Grand Prix racing. Farina had won the 1950 title at the age of 44, Fangio was already 42, and although Ascari was regarded as young, even he was 35. Hawthorn was barely 24, and by the middle of the season had proved that skill and daring were just as important ingredients in the make-up of a racing driver as experience.

Hawthorn and his challenge to the older drivers caught the imagination, particularly in Britain. The popular press turned its attention to motor racing, hitherto regarded as of interest only to a minority of enthusiasts, taking it a step further towards recognising individual accomplishment, instead of being primarily a team sport.

The Maserati which was to offer the challenge to Ferrari, was developed during the winter of 1952–3 by the redoubtable Gioacchino Colombo, and was essentially a modern, six-cylinder engine within a modified version of the familiar 4CL's tubular chassis.

An output of 208 bhp was claimed for the basically 1947 A6 sports car engine with a 15:1 compression ratio; but a more realistic figure would be the 198 or so, on the 13.75:1 ratio normally used for racing, as opposed to bench testing. Enhancement of horse power figures was popular, not merely to intimidate the opposition, but because a new, exciting version of what was really the same old car could be good 'Box-Office'. Engineers' vision was sometimes clouded by the starting money bargaining going on from the office next door. Nevertheless, this was close to the magic figure of 100 bhp per litre, regarded by contemporary engineers as just about the best obtainable by a conventional engine, with carburettors and alcohol-based fuel. Maserati's higher power output compared with the Ferrari was unfortunately offset by the narrower range of rpm in which it was available. Furthermore, Colombo's concentration on the engine disregarded the unpalatable fact that his car, and the already obsolescent Simca, were the only ones still running with a live rear axle.

A new face in Grand Prix racing. Mike Hawthorn's broad smile lit up the world championship when he became the first English driver to be signed by a major European team for a generation.

After a period of relative safety, the season opened with a tragic accident in the Argentine Grand Prix in January, involving Giuseppe Farina. A youth ran on to the track, and was killed by Farina's Ferrari. The driver lost control, and the car swerved into the crowd, killing and injuring several more spectators.

Accidents of this sort were by no means new, and the attitude of authorities had been established as long ago as 1903, when the French government stopped the Paris–Madrid at Boulogne, and effectively ended the days of town-to-town races. Farina's tragedy served to emphasise the importance of keeping spectators well out of reach of racing cars, a serious problem particularly in places where administration was lax, and nothing more substantial than a rope or a slender fence was thought necessary. However, Argentina 1953 was a warning that went unheeded. Sadly, the accident was regarded in Europe as an aberration in a country unaccustomed to motor racing, at a track where safety precautions were inadequate, and not worth action elsewhere.

Ascari won in Argentina; Fangio's Maserati only lasted one-third of the distance although it was lying second when it went out. Ascari won again at Zandvoort; Farina in a second Ferrari in his shadow, and again Fangio dropped out, this time with axle trouble. Gonzalez took up the cudgels for Maserati and finished third. In Belgium, Fangio was still out of luck and crashed, and it was left to the third Argentinian in the Maserati team, young Onofre Marimon, to take third place.

It was clear by the time the French Grand Prix came round that Maserati and Ferrari were evenly matched, with Ferrari winning on reliability. What then happened was not only ample proof that there was nothing to choose between them in speed, but a

Grand Prix took place that went down in the annals of motor sport as The Race of a Lifetime.

Britain's place in the field was still probationary. The fiasco of the BRM had not been forgotten, nor how it had hastened the demise of a popular and successful formula. No worthy British car had appeared for the best part of 30 years. Jaguar had just beaten Ferrari and Alfa Romeo at Le Mans, and snatched victory in the 12 Hours sports car race preceding the Grand Prix. But the British had done well at Le Mans before, similarly, in a pattern that would become repetitive, at a time when Grand Prix racing was somewhat in the doldrums. In Formula 2 the HWMs had become outclassed, Cooper, another make of promise, had lost Hawthorn, and nobody else had driven them as capably. Stirling Moss had wasted 1952 with his ERA, and his 1953 car was no better.

Despite a record of good finishes, Hawthorn was still regarded as something of a novice. The Grand Prix world at large had not had the benefit of the *Daily Express* to point out how good the 'Farnham Flyer' really was. Within the Ferrari team which comprised two world champions, Farina and Ascari, and the veteran Villoresi, Hawthorn was definitely the number four driver. Besides, recognition of anything British was difficult following the Rheims sports car race, which Jaguar had won when the leading Ferrari was disqualified in the early hours with a flat battery.

Gonzalez (Maserati) started the Grand Prix with half-full tanks, to secure an early lead and try to draw the Ferraris into a pursuit which might overstrain their engines. The Ferraris drove as a team, slipstreaming one another on the long straights. They passed and re-passed each other, and when Gonzalez stopped to refuel, Hawthorn was in front as they caught up with Fangio in the other Maserati.

Fangio was slightly faster down the straights, but Hawthorn could out-brake him into the corners. Together they drew away, wheel to wheel, while to the rear Ascari and Farina in Ferraris, and Gonzalez, his tanks replenished, and Marimon in Maseratis elbowed one another round the hairpins. They tucked in behind on the straights, all as intent seemingly, on racing one another as they were on avoiding the accident to the leaders which now looked inevitable.

For 150 miles, from around half distance to the end of the 60-lap race, Fangio and Hawthorn were neck and neck, first one leading, then the other. Once, at the new Garenne hairpin, Hawthorn rammed the back of Fangio's car, denting it. The Maserati was handicapped on the slow corners following the loss of second gear, and it was on one of these corners, Thillois on the last lap, that the race was decided. With the crowd gasping with excitement, all round the circuit, Fangio made one of his rare mistakes. He slid the tail of his car wide, and Hawthorn held him off, to win by 40 metres after $2\frac{3}{4}$ hours of the closest motor racing ever seen. The day had perhaps gone when races were decided by laps; minutes were more usual, but here, it was down to seconds, and fractions of seconds.

Hawthorn's victory broke Ascari's run of success, although he came back to win the British Grand Prix a fortnight later. What was important, however, was that a new name had become established. Hitherto, only Gonzalez had been able to break the Farina-Fangio-Ascari deadlock—they had won every world championship race but one, since the title began.

For the third race in a row, Fangio finished second at the Nürburgring, which was won by Farina after Ascari was delayed when a wheel came off and he had to complete a lap of the track on a brake drum. But Ascari clinched his second title, winning the Swiss Grand Prix after dropping to fourth with a pit stop. The final race of the season was a repetition of the excitement earlier in the season.

Like Rheims, Monza favoured out-and-out speed, with the Maserati's indifferent behaviour on corners becoming less important, so the two great rivals were once again evenly matched. In the course of the race, the lead changed no fewer than 22 times. The straw bales marking the edge of the track grew frayed with cars brushing them as drivers sought every inch of the road for racing. Farina's patience with Ascari finally gave out in the excitement, and he joined in, racing his colleague every bit as determinedly as he raced the opposition.

What happened at the South Curve as the cars swept round in close formation towards the finish has been a matter for debate ever since. Certainly, the duelling Ferraris and Maseratis tangled, and only Fangio managed to pick a way through unscathed, to win his first Grand Prix since Spain in 1951.

Ferrari's threat to withdraw from racing before Monza (like all his others over the years, soon withdrawn) resulted in the cancellation of the Spanish Grand Prix, leaving Ascari with the world championship for the second time, Fangio runner-up, and Farina third. But it was the arrival of Hawthorn, fourth for the second time, that was the vital new element. He achieved a 100 per cent record of finishes, and had won his first Grand Prix in style. Ahead of names such as Villoresi, and Gonzalez, he demonstrated conclusively that the Grand Prix Establishment was by no means invulnerable.

This was the state of design at the end of 1953. Drivers still preferred cars with a natural tendency to understeer, that is to say run wide on corners. They preferred plenty of power to spin the rear wheels, and induce oversteer, or slide the tail wide. Throttle control was a delicate business, and the smooth curve of the torque graph against engine speed critical. Sudden bursts of power, such as the V-16 BRM suffered from, could produce an uncontrollable skid, in which the driver was helpless.

The technique of balancing power against centrifugal force on corners had a number of flattering descriptions, such as 'power slide', and 'four wheel drift'. In fact the execution of the manoeuvre was nothing like so refined as the terms surgest, and except as practised by a very few top drivers could be a very messy procedure indeed. The grip the cars had on the road was still little better than that of a good contemporary sports car, or even a well-developed touring car. Braking was better, but pedal pressures were high, and tyres still not much wider than those of a road car. Aerodynamics remained no more than a vague notion that frontal area ought to be kept down, and the drivers could be seen crouching behind the wheel on the straights, searching for those elusive last few mph. Racing car design remained in the realms of the sculpting tradition of the great Bugatti, while science still had much to teach a largely empirical branch of engineering.

The new formula—straws in the wind

With the 1954 formula imminent, racing car constructors had to decide how they were going to cope with the change. Ferrari appeared for practice at Monza with what was effectively a prototype 2½ litre. Its tubular space frame suggested that the engineering of the successful 300 SL Mercedes-Benz and the small British sports cars, such as the Lotus, had not gone unnoticed. The 'Squalo', or Shark, had bulbous tanks on the sides, but it did not handle well, and was consigned to second-rank drivers for the race.

BRM indicated they might be willing to make a 750 cc supercharged car by effectively chopping their V-16 in half, but the entire project was now in such dire straits that it never came to anything. Fangio, Gonzalez, and Ken Wharton had driven BRM V-16s in the Albi Grand Prix, but beyond proving the car was now immensely fast, it had achieved little owing to thrown tyre treads.

Yet the BRM was to bear fruit in an unexpected way. One result of the quarrels which had broken up the original Trust was an entry for this race of a 4½-litre Ferrari by Tony Vandervell. As the manufacturer of Vandervell bearings, he called it the Thinwall Special, not a title that commended itself to the Grand Prix Establishment, smacking as it did of commercial sponsorship, which was generally thought rather vulgar. The redoubtable Mr Vandervell, however, insisted, and it was discovered with a general sense of chagrin that nobody could stop him. The Thinwall Special was the forerunner of a new make, the Vanwall, a racing car destined to have a pronounced influence.

Technical developments

The development of engines as a process of modification and refinement, rather than radical change proceeded apace, but the overall shape and general arrangement of the racing car had moved forward little since the Thirties. The true single seater had emerged with the 'Monoposto' Alfa Romeo P3 of 1932, when the reality of having no riding mechanic (they had not been written into the regulations since 1924) was at last accepted. The next car to set an important trend was the Mercedes-Benz W125 of 1937, with a number of technical novelties including a chassis frame made from two parallel, oval-section tubes of 1.5 mm thick nickel-chrome molybdenum—expense was not important to Mercedes-Benz.

The engine was an eight-cylinder, twin overhead camshaft in-line of 5.6 litres, and supercharged. With it, Daimler-Benz designers under Director Wagner conformed with the more usual practice of mounting the supercharger between the carburettors and the engine, but in most other respects, the rest of the racing world followed where they led. Independent suspension at the front was by coil springs and wishbones, while at the rear a de Dion axle was employed—not a new idea in itself, but a complete breakaway for Grand Prix cars.

It was an important departure. Rear axles had hitherto been rigid, or 'live', that is to say they comprised a beam with the final drive in the middle, supported on semi-elliptic leaf springs on the chassis.

Independent rear suspension had been tried as a method of improving cornering and grip, usually by means of swinging half-axles pivoting on the centre line of the car, but these suffered from the inherent fault that while the middle remained fixed, the wheels described an arc on bump and rebound.

It was in an effort to keep the rear wheels parallel to one another (which meant they would remain more or less parallel to the road) that the de Dion system was employed. It had been invented in principle before the turn of the century, and in the case of the Mercedes-Benz had a tube running behind the line of the drive shafts connecting the wheel hubs, and located by a hardened steel ball running in a slot at the back of the final drive. The springing was by torsion bars, and the wheel hubs were trailed on arms connected to the chassis.

The W125 was streamlined, with the fuel in a shapely tank within the pointed tail. It was the most powerful car ever seen in Grand Prix racing, with 646 bhp at 5800 rpm, and remained so. Its pattern was followed in cars such as the Type 158 Alfa Romeo designed contemporaneously, initially with swing axle rear suspension, but changed as the engine became more powerful, to de Dion. The pattern was followed in Ferraris right up to the 1953 Formula 2 cars, although their engines varied from twelve cylinders to four. Maseratis likewise conformed, except in their refusal to adopt the de Dion, or an independent system for the rear, and suffering as a result. Fangio's victory in the 1953 Italian Grand Prix was the last ever for a car thus equipped.

The layout of the W125 was followed by almost everyone, with the notable exception of Dr Porsche with his pre-war Auto Unions and his far-sighted but abortive post-war mid-engined Cisitalia, but these only tended to emphasise the absence of radical innovations in the general arrangement of racing cars for the best part of two decades.

1954

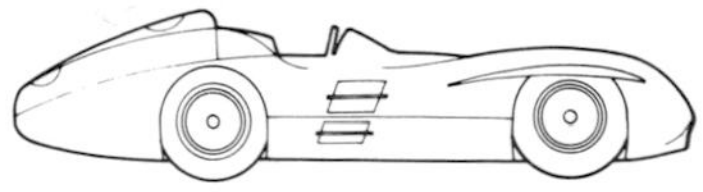

The changes implicit in the new formula were not obvious at first. The step from 2 litres to 2½ litres was not, after all, very great, and designs could be, and were, carried over from one formula to the next without much change. But there were other forces at work which would have a profound influence on Grand Prix racing. One of the most important of these was the declaration by Mercedes-Benz that they intended returning to the track in 1954. Lancia, too, said they would join in for the first time in their long and distinguished history, a further threat to the pattern of events established since 1950.

Yet at the beginning of the season, things did remain much as they were, with the habit-forming practice of the annual change-round of drivers in time for the Grand Prix of Argentina in January. Ascari and Villoresi were no longer with Ferrari, having signed for Lancia—who would not be ready until late in the season. Instead, Ferrari took on Gonzalez from Maserati, and retained the services of Hawthorn and Farina. Fangio remained at the wheel of a Maserati until his Mercedes-Benz became available.

Once again there were eight races, with Spain restored and Zandvoort cancelled, but the first, in Argentina, turned out to be an inconclusive affair. It was interrupted by rain, and when the track was wet, Fangio's Maserati had the advantage, but when it was dry the Ferraris of Farina and Gonzalez took the lead. It may have said more for Fangio's driving than it did about the way the Ferraris handled, but Fangio won nonetheless. Ferrari protested vigorously that extra mechanics had worked on his car, their fury erupting after Hawthorn had been disqualified for a push start. It appeared to the Italians that local officials were discriminating in favour of their home-grown hero, not the last time such a charge would be levelled.

Hawthorn almost won the non-championship Buenos Aires Grand Prix, his car blowing up on the last lap. This left Maurice Trintignant to inherit victory in a privately entered Ferrari, earning himself a place in the works team to the anger of Louis Rosier, who had counted on Trintignant to continue driving for him. Squabbles over who should drive for whom were not new, but the world championship began to give them an extra bitterness. Places in works teams were coveted because they carried the opportunity of acquiring more handsome points totals which, in turn affected a driver's signing-on fee for the following year. The professional element was gaining ground.

By April the picture became clearer, showing that just as during the final year of Formula 2, the Maseratis and Ferraris were evenly matched; indeed in the non-championship Syracuse Grand Prix, Marimon's Maserati and Gonzalez's Ferrari tied for fastest practice lap. Non-title races continued to proliferate; there were no fewer than 28 in 1954, but for the most part they failed to offer enough starting money or prestige to attract the major teams. They were contested instead by private owners who bought 'production' versions of cars such as the Maserati 250F or even built their own. Britain had the BRDC International Trophy in May, as well as the Grand Prix in June. New circuits at Aintree, Oulton Park, and Snetterton also ran Formula 1 events, giving small teams an opportunity to obtain race mileage, and even a little income from such starting and prize money as was available. These were useful training grounds for drivers to match themselves against established names, or in some cases, such as the Syracuse race, for the works teams to try out new ideas without the pressures associated with a round of the world championship.

Fangio made certain of the championship race at Spa in Belgium, despite problems with his rain visor (a thunderstorm was expected) which caused him to lose the lead to Farina; but he recovered and drove a typical Fangio race, mastering every other driver in the 14-car field.

Rheims, on 4 July, on a hot summer afternoon, saw the French Grand Prix and the dramatic return of the Mercedes-Benz team. At the time it seemed to signal the dawn of a new era, and certainly some things would never be the same again, but as events turned out, it was but a brief flash of light. No manufacturer would ever again field such a radical technical *tour de force*, because racing cars henceforward would advance, within the strictures of their regulations, in such a way that even small gains in performance would become progressively more difficult to obtain. Few great leaps forward remained that would not be outlawed in the interests of safety, or else the general welfare of the racing community. It was also the last time for over 20 years that a major car manufacturer would commit the necessary resources, in an activity where the *pace* of technological change, as opposed to its magnitude, became so rapid that only small, flexible teams would be able to make the instant response necessary to keep up.

The 'Silver Arrows' as the Mercedes-Benz were quickly dubbed, not only looked different, with their full-width streamlined bodywork, they *were* different. Fangio and Kling won the race in style, after setting off from the grid in a specially low first gear engaged for acceleration and ignored thereafter. It was one example of the attention to detail in which the Germans indulged, but this did not save the team's third car, driven by Hans Herrmann, which retired laying an undignified smoke screen across the fields of Champagne, which was nothing however, compared with the havoc wrought amongst its rivals.

The pace had been devastating. Ascari (Maserati) was out after one lap, Hawthorn (Ferrari) out after two, his engine disintegrating spectacularly on the long straight, past the main public enclosure. He finally spun on his own trail of oil, and disappeared backwards up an escape road. Gonzalez (Ferrari) retired by lap 13, and of the 21 cars which started, only five survived the long, sunny afternoon. Meanwhile the winners, for much of the race, were 10 miles ahead of anybody else and able to stage a

One Italian answer to Mercedes domination was the long-awaited Lancia D50, seen here in Ascari's hands during practice for the Spanish Grand Prix where it showed such promise.

The shape of names to come. Peter Collins at Snetterton in Tony Vandervell's 1954 Thinwall Special, really a 4½-litre Ferrari, and the forerunner of the Vanwall.

Vanquisher of the Mercedes team at Silverstone, José Froilan Gonzalez, winning his second British Grand Prix. His car—a Ferrari 625.

The first Vanwall Special. After the series of Thinwall Specials, Vandervell began racing his own car. Peter Collins at practice for the Spanish Grand Prix.

formation finish a few yards apart.

Rodney Walkerley, Sports Editor of *The Motor*, summed up the general frustration in his report of the race, with his famous, 'Well, there you are, they're back.' Yet surprisingly, the Mercedes' début at Rheims did not set the pattern for the rest of the season.

Fangio had trouble at the British Grand Prix with the oil drums marking the edge of the track. It was an unsatisfactory system made necessary by the wide open spaces of the former airfield circuit, and the wide bodywork was blamed, apparently making it difficult for the driver to place the car accurately because he could not see the front wheels. Yet Fangio, although he did not enjoy sports cars, could still drive the entire course of the Mille Miglia, with its walls and fences close by the roadside, unscathed. The dents in the elegant curves of the Mercedes were the result of the rather unexpected effect on the handling of the large, flat areas of body on Silverstone's relatively fast bends. The aerodynamic properties of bodywork of this sort were not fully understood, but they did entail the car's suspension being set up in such a way that the transition from understeer to oversteer took place too abruptly, catching out even the great Fangio from time to time.

Yet it was his talent that saved the season for Mercedes-Benz. The extravagantly engineered cars were beaten at Silverstone, and Fangio's was the only Mercedes on the front row of the starting grid at the next race, the German Grand Prix at the Nürburgring. The streamliner was replaced by a more conventionally bodied car and Fangio finished first, ahead of two Ferraris, with Kling fourth. In the Swiss Grand Prix Fangio won again, with a Ferrari second, Herrmann's Mercedes third, and a Ferrari fourth. Fangio narrowly avoided defeat from a Maserati 250F in Italy after a notable drive by Stirling Moss, and in the Spanish Grand Prix at Barcelona the tables were again turned. All three Mercedes gave trouble, and Fangio was lucky to finish in third place driving a car smothered in oil, while Hawthorn won his second Grand Prix in his Type 750 'Squalo' Ferrari four cylinder. The Mercedes had never been within striking distance of the lead, and instead, the long-awaited Lancias proved the fastest cars, although neither finished.

So, although Rheims had been a triumph, Mercedes achieving their psychological advantage from the beginning, there was little doubt by the end of the year that the team had no room for complacency, despite Fangio's taking the world championship. This was nothing like the clean sweep to which German teams had been accustomed in the Thirties. Indeed the Lancias, by their speed in Spain, looked a real threat for 1955.

Alas, in one of those cataclysmic shifts of fortune that would change the entire world of motor racing almost beyond recognition, the New Year turned out to be very different from its bright prospect. The 1954 casualty list was short, with the death in practice for the German Grand Prix of the promising young Argentinian Onofre Marimon, protégé of Fangio and friend of Gonzalez, whose career never recovered. No one in their worst imaginings could guess the horror that awaited in 1955.

Cars for the new Formula

One car which appeared at the start of the new formula turned out to be one of the longest-lived and most popular racing cars of all time. The Maserati 250F was the spearhead of the works challenge from the beginning, and remained the mainstay of private entrants throughout. Well-proportioned, elegant, and every Fifties schoolboy's vision of a racing car, it harassed the Mercedes throughout 1954–5 and the Lancia-Ferrari in 1956. In its developed form it provided Fangio with his third world championship in 1957.

Its ancestry lay amongst the previous generation of Maserati single-seaters. Racing car design outside the extravagant world of Mercedes-Benz was still generally a process of evolution rather than clean sheets on the drawing board. From the Formula 2 car of the year before, the 250F inherited a 2½-litre version of the 2 ohc six-cylinder engine, with three twin-choke Weber carburettors, but the tubular chassis with its de Dion rear axle was new. The chassis was not a space frame in the strictest sense and few features of design put the car on the technical level of the Mercedes-Benz, yet its inferiority in performance was negligible.

Ferrari, who had seemed so well prepared for 1954 turned out to be nothing of the sort. He produced bewildering permutations, based on a four-cylinder engine in a number of tubular chassis designs, mostly stemming from the 1953 car, but with variations for example in the short chassis 'Squalo', which for all its dramatic appearance was heartily disliked by its drivers. Lampredi had to replace the leaf spring IFS by coil springs, and improve the handling before Hawthorn had the means with which to win the final Grand Prix of the season.

The Mercedes was producing 260 bhp plus, the Ferrari about 250, and the Maserati and the new Lancia D 50, 260; yet the Lancia proved to be the fastest car of the season at that important race in Barcelona. Designed by Vittorio Jano, the D 50 had a number of novel features, but in contrast to the Mercedes-Benz, much of its philosophy was based on the 'feel' or instinctive engineering of the great artist-engineer, rather than the efficient, highly mathematical conclusions of a design team, and an office full of draughtsmen and stress engineers.

Yet Jano was as capable of innovation as anyone. The engine of the D 50 pioneered a notable idea which was not repeated for ten years, with the stressing of the crankcase and cylinder block to play a part as the structure of the car. It had always been considered that the strains imposed would prove unacceptable, but Jano went ahead, and it worked.

The Lancia was the first V-8 in modern Grand Prix racing. Also, the gearbox *and* the clutch were in unit with the final drive, following the example of the firm's famous Aurelia sports car. Yet the most obvious novelty of the D 50 was the outrigger fuel tanks within the large fairings on each side. Lying between the wheels, they served the double purpose of streamlining in a notably turbulent area, and maintaining the weight distribution as the fuel was used up, so the car did not start a race tail heavy, nor finish quite the reverse. The light, tubular chassis featured independent suspension at the front, and de Dion at the rear.

Gianni Lancia had inherited his family's enthusiasm for racing cars. His successes with the Aurelia sports cars and the V-6 D 24 had been encouraging, but the Formula 1 venture was expensive. Ascari and Villoresi had been engaged at great cost long before the cars were ready, and although the results on test and at Barcelona were good, much work lay ahead during the winter to develop the 1955 model.

In view of the technical might of Mercedes, and the apparently well funded and adventurous engineering of the three leading Italian makes, the French and British efforts appeared unimpressive. Gordini enlarged the 1953 Formula 2 car, but it was still not powerful enough, and not reliable. HWM was now out of contention, but another make appeared at Silverstone for the British Grand Prix, and also later in the season in Italy and Spain. This was the Vanwall, driven by Peter Collins, and in time, it, not the BRM, would take the initiative in Grand Prix racing away from Italy, to its short-term benefit, securing it, to its long-term detriment, in Britain.

The first Grand Prix car to employ the engine as a stressed part of the chassis, the side-tanked Lancia D50 with veteran Luigi Villoresi at the wheel.

Tony Vandervell was a Ferrari-come-lately. A motor racing enthusiast all his life, he had built up his bearings empire assiduously and successfully. Joining the BRM project with enthusiasm, he was disillusioned by what he saw as wasteful, if well meaning, incompetence. To Vandervell there was only one way to travel and that was first class; so, much as he disliked the Ferrari and its winning ways, he bought one, and set about learning how to run a racing team himself.

By 1954 he was ready with a new car of his own. Following his association with the Norton motor cycle racing team, the engine was designed round four of these highly developed and amazingly successful single-cylinder units working on a common crankcase. Vandervell's aim was to put a British car on to the starting grid of Grand Prix races with the express intention of beating the Italians at what was then regarded as their game.

Meanwhile Connaught, a rather smaller project from Send, in Surrey, was reaching an important stage in its development. Rather like HWM, Connaught Engineering was a small private company, privately financed by Kenneth McAlpine, which had built a series of Lea-Francis-based sports cars, then tackled Formula 2 with success. It found itself making Grand Prix cars when the formula changed, and was now pioneering such advanced techniques as fuel injection (by Hilborn-Travers) and disc brakes (by Dunlop). Connaught still tended to fill the role of gallant losers, rather than representing a real threat to the combined might of Modena, Maranello, and Stuttgart. But together with Cooper, now Vanwall, and the growing number of British drivers who followed Hawthorn and Moss, they made the British presence in international racing felt. British cars and drivers had now won the most publicised motoring competitions of their time, Le Mans and the Monte Carlo Rally. It seemed only a matter of time before together they won a Grand Prix as well.

Winning a world championship was still not an idea that could be seriously entertained.

Mercedes-Benz W196

The car with which Mercedes-Benz made their comeback was one of the most complex and advanced ever seen. Some of its features set the pattern for years to come, others were not seen again for a decade, and at least one was so costly, and so demanding in engineering effort, that it was never seriously used again.

The tubular chassis was unlike any car before, a true space frame within the strictest definition of the term, with the stresses spread evenly throughout the structure, which was composed of triangles of straight tubes. The engine was an in-line eight cylinder, the last great straight eight ever in Grand Prix racing, although only its broad scheme was traditional. It lay over at 70° to reduce the height of the car, it had fuel injection, and the valve gear was desmodromic, that is to say the valves were closed mechanically, and not simply by springs.

The two blocks of cylinders were welded fabrications, a form of construction Mercedes-Benz had preferred over casting for racing engines since 1914. The crankshaft was built up on the Hirth system, and ran in roller bearings. With a capacity of 2496 cc, it produced 260 bhp at 8500 rpm, slightly over the magic 100 bhp per litre. Later versions would reach 290 bhp, but the engine was still in the early stages of its development when work on it ceased prematurely, after only two of its planned five years' span.

In the independent suspension of all four wheels, a notable feature was the return to swinging half-axles at the rear, but of a novel design which did not suffer from the unwanted change in camber. It was pivoted about a point a mere 6 in/15 cm above track level, keeping camber change to a minimum, in conjunction with a Watts linkage. The gearbox location above the rear axle improved weight distribution, and helped drivers find traction from the most powerful racing engine of its time, although in its first season the persistent understeer made it a tricky car to handle.

Mercedes did not consider disc brakes sufficiently developed for their car, although they had been used by Connaught, and most effectively by Jaguar to win Le Mans as long ago as 1953. Drum brakes of sufficient size and power for Formula 1 were too big and heavy to fit within the wheels, where they represented an unacceptable unsprung weight. Instead, they were fitted inboard, on the end of short shafts from the front wheels, giving rise to speculation that the car could be converted to four-wheel drive should the need arise. Ducts directed cooling air to the rear brakes and the transmission, and the workmanship of the car was exemplary. The team was run by Alfred Neubauer, who had commanded them in pre-war days in the same authoritarian manner, and its efficiency and thoroughness presented a formidable challenge in an era when an amateur approach was not only the rule, but was still held to be desirable.

1955

1955

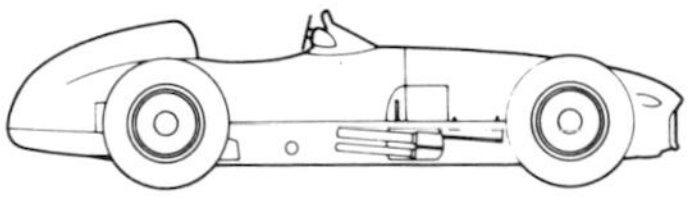

With the world championship in its fifth year, Grand Prix racing seemed to be poised for great development. Throughout the world, interest had never been greater. With Stirling Moss recruited to their team it appeared likely that Mercedes-Benz would carry all before them, yet this was, if anything, an enhancement. Motor racing spectators will invariably turn out to see winners; foregone conclusions do not seem to matter.

The challenge from Lancia added spice, and there was the promise of large, competitive fields with the proliferation of new models such as the Maserati 250F. The Vanwall looked a more likely proposition than before when Mike Hawthorn contracted to drive it, and even BRM was now on a firmer footing. It had been taken over by the Owen Organisation, who were playing in a new team by running one of the graceful 250F Maseratis.

Alas, it was not to be. The Le Mans disaster hung like a pall over the 1955 motor racing season which began in confusion, and ended with a melancholy toll of dead and injured. Along with other forms of motor sports, Grand Prix racing would never be quite the same again.

Under a fierce summer sun, the season began in Buenos Aires, where the Grand Prix of Argentina was won by Fangio in the Mercedes-Benz. Only he and another Argentinian, Roberto Mieres (Maserati) who finished fifth, were able to complete the distance without assistance. Heat exhaustion compelled everyone else to hand over their car for a spell, which showed up one of the shortcomings of the championship scoring system. The Ferrari which finished second was shared by Gonzalez, Farina, and Trintignant, and the one which came third by Trintignant, Farina, and Maglioli. Moss, Herrmann, and Kling took turns in the Mercedes which came fourth, so a complicated calculation was necessary to work out the points table afterwards.

The basis was still 8:6:4:3:2 for the first five finishers, with an extra point for fastest lap. The drivers of the second, third, and fourth place cars effectively shared the points in this case, earned by the *car*. Thus, Fangio gained 9 points, Farina and Trintignant $3\frac{1}{3}$ (2 for sharing the second-placed car, $1\frac{1}{3}$ for sharing third), Gonzalez and Mieres 2 (for sharing second place and for sixth place respectively), Maglioli $1\frac{1}{3}$ (for a share of third), and Moss, Kling, and Herrmann 1 each (for sharing fourth). The total equals the race's full allocation of 24 points.

The Lancias were in the picture briefly, Ascari gaining the lead for the opening laps, but retiring after 20. The team gained some encouragement from a clean sweep in the non-championship Turin race, following a winter of frenzied modification and change to Jano's design.

Ferrari were similarly active, completely re-working their Type 555 Squalo which had been so successful at Barcelona the year before. It was given a new, lower frame and fatter tanks at each side, earning it the sobriquet 'Super Squalo'. The older Type 625 was changed as well, but with neither car handling well, the team was in a turmoil of indecision. Maserati on the other hand only had to tidy up their 250F to sell it in ever-increasing numbers. Moss's car was equipped with disc brakes, and Maserati were happy with the development of a car which, they felt with some justification, was next best only to the Mercedes-Benz.

The second championship round was the Monaco Grand Prix, the great race at last re-established on its classic course, after a somewhat chequered post-war career. Mercedes-Benz arrived in style, with several permutations of car—some short-chassis, some long, some with inboard brakes, some outboard—so that Fangio and Moss had plenty to choose from in order to discover which was best round the tight hairpins, and along the short straights of the demanding street circuit. A later generation would build racing cars in which the suspension, brake balance, and so on would be adjustable instead, achieving much the same effect rather more conveniently.

Herrmann crashed his Mercedes in practice and put himself in hospital, but Fangio and Moss led off, sandwiching Ascari on the front row of the starting grid—racing cars were still narrow enough for three abreast not to be a crowd even at Monaco.

It was just as Moss coasted to a halt with engine trouble that 1955's tragic chain of events began. Ascari inherited the lead, his Lancia as ever handling sensitively, and in an astonishing accident which remains puzzling to this day, ran wide at the chicane, rode over the straw bales, and plunged into the harbour in a cloud of smoke and steam.

Ascari surfaced at once, and swam to the rescue boat with nothing worse than a shaking, while Maurice Trintignant scored an unexpected win for Ferrari. But less than a week later, Ascari, at Monza during unofficial testing in preparation for the week-end's Supercortemaggiore sports car race, borrowed a Ferrari to shake off the effects of the accident.

He crashed after only three laps, the car rolling over, and Ascari, the champion driver of the world, was dead. By an uncanny coincidence, he had been killed, like his father, on the 26th of the month, at the age of 36, leaving a widow and two small children.

Ascari's death was also the last straw for Lancia, and they did not enter the next race, the Belgian Grand Prix, although their driver Eugenio Castellotti borrowed one car as a private entry. It turned out to be the only real opposition the Mercedes-Benz team had on the fast track at Spa. Fangio and Moss got into their stride at once with cars from which the damaging understeer had now been more or less eradicated, the team efficient and resourceful, and the opposition getting a look in only briefly by displays of bravura such as that of Castellotti.

Before the next race, the Dutch Grand Prix, Le Mans had cast its shadow over an increasingly cheerless season which also saw three fatal accidents in the Tourist Trophy, at Dundrod and the death of the Italian veteran Clemente Biondetti in Florence at the age of 56.

John Arthur Brabham (b 1926)

The small British specialist sports car makers would try almost anything. Cooper, who had graduated from 500 cc single seaters to sports and racing cars such as the successful Cooper-Bristol, had developed a small, streamlined 1100 cc car, nominally a sports car, but with a central driving position, and the 'passenger seat' covered over as was the fashion. With a Coventry-Climax engine behind the driver but ahead of the rear wheels, making it what may be termed *mid*-engined as opposed to *rear*-engined, it had proved outstandingly successful in the short, sprint-type races which were such a popular feature of domestic club meetings. Its tail was cut short, and concave in accordance with Kamm's theories that lopping it off was logical because only an impractically long tail would achieve any measurable reduction in drag.

A stretched version of the Manx-tailed Cooper, as it came to be known, was developed. Having regard to the earlier success of Cooper in Formula 1, a Bristol six-cylinder engine enlarged to 2.2 litres was installed, driving the rear wheels through a gearbox adapted from a front-drive Citroën and turned, as it were, back to front.

This unlikely car was driven in the 1955 Grand Prix at Aintree by the son of a Sydney greengrocer, Jack Brabham, born 1926 and a former Australian dirt-track champion. Brabham had bought 500 cc Coopers, and later a Cooper-Bristol, so when he came to England, the Coopers' tiny works at Surbiton was his obvious starting-off point. This historic entry of the first car with the engine behind the driver to contest a grande épreuve since the days of Auto Union was the result.

With a time of 2 min 21.2 sec round Aintree, compared with the winning car's 2 min 0.4 sec, Brabham risked being overtaken by the leaders every six laps. He was slower than most of the field in the 500 cc race, and belonged more properly in the sports car race, although he would not have made much impression there either.

The taciturn Australian was, however, made of sterner stuff than many of the huge crowd packed round the Liverpool track would have given him credit for. He had to abandon the little car after 41 laps when the engine failed, but he had not only made a bit of motor racing history. Within a very few years, driving his funny racing cars with the engine at the wrong end, he would re-write it.

The Le Mans disaster

The catastrophe of 11 June 1955 came at 6.29 pm, just short of two and a half hours into a race which had begun with a lively duel between Fangio (Mercedes-Benz 300 SLR) and Mike Hawthorn (D-Type Jaguar), which broke the Le Mans lap record ten times, leaving it to Hawthorn at 193.963 kph/120.52 mph. Castellotti's Ferrari joined in for a time, but it was outpaced.

The first pit stops were due, and Hawthorn, pulling in briefly baulked Lance Macklin's much slower Austin-Healey, which in turn swerved into the path of the Mercedes-Benz driven by veteran French driver Pierre Levegh. The Healey's sloping tail acted as a launching ramp, and the Mercedes hurtled on to the safety embankment at high speed, and with such force that the engine and front suspension broke free, crashing into a crowded enclosure.

Levegh and 82 spectators died, many more were badly injured, and the tragedy stunned the world. The AC de l'Ouest did not stop the race, on the grounds that confusion was likely to result, and hamper the rescue services—probably the right thing to do. The world's press, along with anxious relatives jammed the telephone lines, and it was not until the small hours of the morning, following an emergency meeting of the Directors, that Daimler-Benz finally got word to Neubauer to withdraw the cars, by now well in the lead.

Hawthorn won for Jaguar, but the investigations and the recriminations had barely begun. Some facts were beyond dispute. Levegh, for example, at the age of 50 had been an unwise choice by the German team. Probably a little self-conscious in the post-war world, they wanted a driver who had become a folk-hero to the French in a gallant, but ill-advised, drive in the 1952 race. At the wheel of a Talbot, he had single-handedly taken on the 300 SL gull-wing coupé with which Mercedes-Benz played-in their racing department, but threw the race away in the closing hour through sheer exhaustion.

In 1955, Levegh's 300 SLR was equipped with a controversial air brake, a hydraulic flap raised in the tail to assist braking from high speeds. It was never implicated in the accident, even in view of later researches into the unexpected effect of aerodynamic appendages. It was not even in use at the critical moment. Nevertheless, by association, aerodynamic devices were suspect, and designers left them strictly alone for a long time to come.

The width of the road was inadequate at Le Mans, in view of the speeds of the cars and the activity that was to be expected around the pits. Also, Hawthorn and Macklin seem to have misunderstood one another, Macklin was taken by surprise, and his swerve was wide. But like so many accidents, no single blameworthy feature ever emerged. Yet the chain of events leading up to the tragedy set off a reaction, from which motor racing was to emerge greatly altered.

The immediate effect was the wholesale cancellation of races, including the German and Swiss Grands Prix. The Swiss banned racing for ever afterwards. The French, rather more understandably, stopped it until safety arrangements were investigated, while a similar enquiry in Britain, conducted by a commission appointed under the RAC, concluded that stringent spectator safety measures would continue to be applied. In some countries a few minor events were held in an atmosphere of hostility, and in America the ruling body of the sport, the Automobile Association of America announced it would no longer have anything to do with racing, even at Indianapolis.

The Dutch carried on with their race without Lancia or Vanwall, Ferrari still in fruitless pursuit of the Mercedes team despite the return of Hawthorn. Maserati managed to put on something of a show but once again, it was the dash of a driver, in this case Luigi Musso, rather than the speed of his car that saved complete dishonour. Fangio and Moss had total command, Moss even diverting himself by discovering, in the later stages of the race, how much he could drive using top gear alone, such was the lead the pair enjoyed, and such the astonishing flexibility conferred by the Bosch fuel injection.

At Aintree (at which the British Grand Prix was due to alternate year by year with Silverstone) on the last corner of the final lap round the track, laid alongside the famous Grand National course, Moss thrilled his home crowd by passing his team leader to win. It was his first Grand Prix victory, run strictly to the team plan, with the silver cars filling the first four places.

Inevitably the season ended on a downbeat. The Italian Grand Prix was run at Monza on the new banked track combined with most of the old road circuit which gave a lap 10 km/6 miles long. The combination gave trouble, however, because different tyres and suspension characteristics were demanded by the banked section, where centrifugal force pressed the cars down on their springs, and the flat and level points of the course. Working out the compromise taxed even Mercedes-Benz, but they won just the same, and Fangio clinched his third world title.

Yet it was Moss, still only 26 years old, who emerged as the hero of 1955. His performances in the 300 SLR sports car in the Mille Miglia, the Eifelrennen, the RAC Tourist Trophy which he won with John Fitch, and the epic Targa Florio which he won with Peter Collins despite two dramatic accidents, marked him out as one of the greatest drivers not only of his day, but of all time.

The bitter memory of Le Mans lingered on at the press conference on 22 October, when 'after deliberation' the directors of Daimler-Benz decided to 'absent (Mercedes-Benz sports and Formula 1 cars) irrevocably from motor racing for several years'.

The cars were only at the beginning of their development, the four-wheel-drive versions were never built, and the plan to take part in racing for five years was abandoned. The firm said they wanted to concentrate on their production cars again and had achieved what they set out to do. In terms of publicity which was the reason for racing, they probably had, because the reputation for excellence which they had established in competition is remembered to this day. Fangio and Moss were paid off, the racing department disbanded, and the cars disposed of to motor racing museums where they bear silent testimony to remind the world of one of the greatest racing cars ever. Those in Mercedes' own museum are dusted down, fired up from time to time, and driven, their curiously flat, blaring exhaust note still capable of bringing a glazed look to some senior members of Daimler-Benz management, as they approach middle age . . .

Lancia—the end . . . Lancia-Ferrari—the beginning

Following the death of Ascari came the revelation that the Lancia firm was in deep financial trouble. The cost of the Grand Prix team was held partly responsible for the collapse of the family concern which had been building distinctive sports and touring cars since 1906. The Lancia family was forced to sell out, and the group which took over promptly called a halt to the racing programme.

The problem over what to do with the team and the racing cars remained. They were offered to Maserati, but with some justification they felt that their own 250F was a better car than the D 50 which had required such extensive and perhaps over-frequent modification. Ferrari on the other hand was in difficulties with his Lampredi-designed Squalo and Super Squalo four-cylinder cars. He had already said, as part of his annual fund-raising campaign, that the Scuderia Ferrari was in need of more support if it was to carry on. So, with a customary display of magnanimity, Enzo undertook to 'rescue' Lancia from their predicament.

On 7 July 1955, Ferrari learned that his bid was successful, and through Fiat, the AC d'Italia, and the ANFIAA, Italy's motor industry trade association, he took over the team, complete with designer Jano, and an annuity from Fiat of 50 million lire (over £30 000) for at least the following five years. Ferrari was handed the six racing cars, transporters, and spares, together with wealth beyond the dreams of any other manufacturer except perhaps Mercedes-Benz. But Mercedes were soon to take their leave, and Ferrari seized the opportunity to add a further asset to his team—Fangio.

Top: The sun shone for Fangio, on the way to his third world championship in the British Grand Prix at Aintree. Middle: the four Mercedes in the familiar line-ahead fashion, with Fangio in the lead from Moss, Karl Kling, and Piero Taruffi, with Roberto Mieres' 250F Maserati bringing up the rear. Bottom: In his battered crash helmet, Juan Manuel Fangio, by any standards the greatest Grand Prix driver of all time.

The thin end of the wedge, Syracuse

The final event of the European season was a non-championship Grand Prix at Syracuse in Sicily. Maserati entered a team of four cars, and in the absence of Ferrari, working and worrying over the Lancia design and the problems of transforming it into the Lancia-Ferrari, it looked like being an easy victory. First day's practice seemed to confirm the prospect, with four fastest times.

On the second day however, a new Connaught arrived at the circuit, driven by a little known student dentist, Tony Brooks who, up till then, had never so much as sat in the car. By his third lap, Brooks had beaten the Maseratis' time, sending them into a frenzy of activity. When the race began Brooks split the team on the front row of the grid, and went on to win by the handsome margin of 50 sec. Brooks had gained the first Grand Prix win for a car equipped with disc brakes, and the last for a car with an epicyclic, preselector gearbox.

The race was not a grande épreuve, nor did it count for the world championship, but he had beaten leading cars and leading drivers such as Villoresi and Musso, and the race *did* have the title Grand Prix.

It was the first such victory for a British driver at the wheel of a British car since the 1924 San Sebastian Grand Prix, won by Sir Henry Segrave's Sunbeam. A turning point in the history of Grand Prix racing had been reached.

An early attempt to produce a slippery, wind-cheating shape for a Grand Prix car was the British Connaught. Later, the rules were amended to prohibit enclosure of the wheels. Following the Connaught at Aintree is Stirling Moss (250F Maserati).

Mercedes, Moss, and the Mille Miglia

The Germans' racing policy for 1954–5 encompassed both Formula 1 and sports car racing under one technical plan. This was for the W 196 Grand Prix car to be adaptable, with a 3-litre instead of a 2½-litre engine, to be a sports car with two seats.The result was the W 196 S, or the 300 SLR as it was called to establish a relationship (a rather distant one as it turned out) to the firm's production 300 SL sports model.

Announced in prototype form in 1954, the 300 SLR was not ready for racing until the Mille Miglia in 1955. This great Italian road race which dated back to 1927, and started in Brescia, ran down the Adriatic coast, across the Appennines to Rome, then back by way of Florence and Bologna to the finish at Brescia some 1000 miles and ten hours later. An anachronistic and spectacular survivor of the great town to town races at the turn of the century, the Mille Miglia demanded an intimate knowledge of the traditional course. Clemente Biondetti, who won it four times, lived on the route and practised it assiduously. The Marzotto brothers likewise knew it in detail, and except for 1931 (Caracciola, Mercedes-Benz), only Italians driving Italian cars had won.

It was an event enshrined in tradition, such as the legend that the leader in Rome never won the race, but in 1955 Stirling Moss and Denis Jenkinson not only refuted that particular piece of folklore, but won at an average speed of 157.55 kph/97.89 mph which remained the record for the race, stopped for ever by an accident involving spectators in 1957. With Jenkinson reading what rally drivers would come to call pace notes, it was one of the greatest drives of Moss's distinguished career.

1956

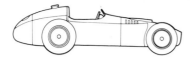

Ferrari were far from happy with their new car, and Fangio was probably fortunate to win his fourth world championship with it. Maserati's 250F handled better, but grew less reliable as the season wore on, and both cars underwent a prolonged and untidy period of development in the face of pressure from Vanwall, and, rather surprisingly, BRM.

Fangio had been joined by Peter Collins, Luigi Musso, and Eugenio Castellotti, but the engineers at Maranello were having a struggle with the Jano-designed Lancia-Ferraris, having scrapped the Squalo and Super Squalo four-cylinder cars. The sensitive Lancias were proving difficult to put right, yet they could not be discarded. Fiat had considered them full of promise, and were paying handsomely to have them raced. In any case, Ferrari had no assurance, in view of the Squalo fiasco, that a new design of his own would be any better. Lampredi departed, discouraged, joining Fiat to work on gas turbines, and Ferrari was left with the task of making the Lancias as Ferrari-like as he could.

For the first race in Argentina, at the end of January, the side tanks were emptied, and the fuel redistributed mostly to a big tank in the tail. Lancias appeared with Ferrari suspension, and Ferraris with Lancia engines. The exhausts of the V-8 were routed through the side pods, which were streamlined into the body sides, then gradually dispensed with altogether. Even Jano's clever idea of stressing the engine as part of the chassis was forsaken, and it was braced with a tubular frame instead.

Maserati, now with Moss, Jean Behra, and Cesare Perdisa fared little better. Half-way through the season, they had to revamp their six-cylinder 250F in an effort to keep up, and they avoided the non-championship Syracuse Grand Prix in April, where they had been so humiliated by Connaught the previous October.

Further evidence of how serious a challenge the Italians faced came at the Silverstone International Trophy in May. During the opening stages of the race, Fangio and Collins in Lancia-Ferraris were outpaced by Mike Hawthorn's BRM, and then beaten over the full 60 laps by Stirling Moss, released in the absence of Maserati to drive the new Vanwall. His 100.47 mph/161.69 kph for the 180 mile/289 km race was faster than the old lap record (1 min 45.2 sec, Farina 4.5 litre Thinwall special 100.16 mph/161.19 kph), and he shared a new record (1 min 43.0 sec, 102.3 mph/164.6 kph) with Hawthorn.

Colin Chapman of Lotus had been called in to redesign the Vanwall's suspension, and de Havilland aerodynamicist Frank Costin had equipped it with an efficient body shape. The British cars were using four-cylinder engines in which Ferrari firmly believed, but had reluctantly been forced to abandon. They had disc brakes which neither Ferrari nor Maserati had, and Vanwall was well ahead in fuel injection technology such as only Mercedes-Benz had hitherto been able to use successfully.

Fangio took over Musso's Ferrari to win the first world championship round in Argentina, despite a protest by Maserati about a pushed start. Moss replied with a convincing victory at Monaco after Fangio, having damaged his own car in fruitless pursuit, took over Collins's. This needle match between the two greatest drivers of their time was renewed at Spa, for the Belgian Grand Prix three weeks later, at the beginning of June. There Moss did a practice lap in 4 min 14.7 sec, to which Fangio replied, after a great deal of effort, with one in 4 min 9.8 sec.

The race in Belgium belonged, however, to the new British hero, Peter Collins, who won after both the leading protagonists had dropped out. In the next race, a month later, the French Grand Prix at Rheims, a new Bugatti provided an interesting, if short-lived diversion. Designed by the versatile Colombo, with an eight-cylinder engine mounted transversely behind the driver, it anticipated the Lamborghini Miura, and a number of notable design features by some ten years. The novel suspension kept up the Bugatti tradition for racing cars with beam axles, although the idiosyncratic engineering that embraced them, gave the impression of a principle sustained with scant regard to practicality. Alas, the final gasp of the classic *pur sang* lasted only 18 laps before it retired, and was never raced again. The other French eight cylinder, the Gordini, was likewise out of its depth.

Of more lasting significance was the speed of the new Vanwall, with Hawthorn joining Harry Schell, the enthusiastic Franco-American at the wheel. A third car was driven during practice by Colin Chapman who, besides being a gifted designer, was also a formidable driver; but on this occasion he followed Hawthorn (a frequent adversary in club races) into Thillois while bedding-in brakes, and they collided. Chapman's car was too badly damaged to take part in the race, although Hawthorn's was quickly put right. It might have seemed an inauspicious introduction to Grand Prix racing, but Chapman was already well established both as a driver and an engineer. He never drove in a Grand Prix again, but in the long term he was to exert a more profound influence not only than any of his contemporaries, but greater than almost anyone else in the whole history of Grand Prix racing.

Fangio remained the driver to beat. But after leading in the opening stages, his car gave up, and Peter Collins became not only the third British driver to win a Grand Prix, and the first to win two in a row, but also the first to head the world championship.

The British Grand Prix, back to its traditional Silverstone venue, was a further warning to the Italians, who still tended to use well-tried solutions to the problems of racing car design, against the new science-based projects such as the Vanwall. Even though the British teams' recipe of a four-cylinder engine within a tubular frame was still essentially low-technology (and low-budget) they were employing engineers who tended to work within the disciplines of formal engineering without feeling

Peter Collins (Ferrari) suffers from a certain amount of understeer in the D50 car still with its outrigger tanks inherited from the Lancia design. Ferrari engineers spent the greater part of the season redeveloping the cars.

Peter Collins (b 1931)

Amongst the drivers produced by the proliferation of club racing in Britain, in particular 500 cc racing during the early Fifties, Peter Collins was outstanding. Following the deaths of R. M. Dryden and Alf Bottoms, with whom he had teamed up, he went for bigger cars, joining John Heath's HWM team along with Stirling Moss and Lance Macklin.

Collins drove sports cars with Aston Martin, and Tony Vandervell engaged him for the Thinwall Special, forerunner of the Vanwall. In 1955 he joined BRM, to drive first the Owen Maserati 250F and then the early $2\frac{1}{2}$-litre BRMs, but it was as Stirling Moss's co-driver in the 300 SLR Mercedes-Benz that Collins scored one of his best-known successes, in the Targa Florio.

He joined Ferrari in 1956, acquiring valuable experience from Fangio, just as Moss had done at Mercedes-Benz the year before, and gaining his two notable victories in the Belgian and French Grands Prix. Unlike Fangio he attracted the warm friendship of Enzo Ferrari, which was to turn out an unusual accomplishment for any Scuderia Ferrari driver through the years. He only incurred displeasure when he married Louise King—a distraction, Ferrari considered—in 1958 at the age of 26, before he was killed driving a Ferrari at Nürburgring.

The son of Patrick Collins who ran a large motor business in Kidderminster, Peter Collins enjoyed a boisterous friendship with Mike Hawthorn and a reputation for sportsmanship; this was enhanced by his gesture to Fangio at Monza, which made him, during his tragically short career one of Britain's best sporting ambassadors.

inhibited by them. The approach to motor racing of the three nations reflected in some ways their national traditions, with Mercedes-Benz methodical and thorough, using large resources, highly qualified staff, and achieving something of a technological overkill. The Italians on the other hand tended to be artist-engineers, relying more on their feel for metalwork, and instinct for machines to win through, and to their credit and excitement they usually did. The new British engineers compromised with resources, and made cars that could gain from improvisation in the field. They had no tradition about how racing cars ought to look or even behave, so radical design perhaps came more easily to them.

Chapman was a gifted, formally trained technician, while the Coopers were talented craftsmen. Both were quick to seize new developments such as disc brakes and were not afraid to be first to proscribe the outworn, such as centre-lock wire wheels, considered as natural to racing car design as having the driver sit bolt upright behind the engine. More important, the Italians stuck to firmly sprung racing cars when the Germans and the British moved to softer springing combined with a stiff frame, aimed at improving road holding, to make up for any deficiencies the British, at least, may have suffered in engine power.

Tony Vandervell tries out one of his new Vanwalls; its unpainted body shape was developed by aerodynamicist Frank Costin in pursuit of Vandervell's ambition to '. . . beat the b----y Italians.'

Above all, these newcomers were competitive, and their ideas began to bear fruit with the arrival of Tony Vandervell, who set the standards of investment necessary to win races. No British team had ever been funded so generously, nor organised so efficiently. Vandervell bought the best advice, and shared his consultants' enthusiasm for radical solutions, such as Costin's dramatic new body shape, in which the air intakes were in high pressure and the outlets were in low pressure areas, the driver was cowled, and the tail high.

To complete the picture, British engines were now producing power that matched any others, and at Silverstone the speeds of the cars through a timed 176 yd/160.9 m stretch of straight was as follows:

Hawthorn (BRM) 137.4 mph/221.1 kph
Schell (Vanwall) 136.88 mph/220.28 kph
Brooks (BRM) 136.36 mph/219.45 kph
Fangio (Ferrari) 134.83 mph/216.98 kph
Collins (Ferrari) 134.33 mph/216.18 kph
Moss (Maserati) 133.83 mph/215.37 kph

Discovering even the hitherto much despised BRM was faster, galvanised Maserati and Ferrari to even greater efforts before the season's end.

By Silverstone, in July, Collins led the world championship with 19 points against Behra's 14, and Fangio's 13. During the opening laps the BRMs of Hawthorn and Brooks led, helped on by the splendid low-speed torque of their four-cylinder engines; but first Hawthorn dropped out with axle trouble, and then Brooks had his throttle jam open, and he had a 120 mph end-over-end crash, from which he was lucky to escape. The car caught fire and was burned out. Moss took the lead, but he too retired, with axle failure on the Maserati, and Fangio scooped up his second victory of the season.

The Vanwalls did not go well at Silverstone, and the BRMs were still new, so they both missed the German Grand Prix the following month and were taken to task by Denis Jenkinson, the irrepressible Continental Correspondent of *Motor Sport* for not putting up a fight. It gave the Italian teams some respite, and left Fangio without a great deal of opposition.

By the time they lined up at Monza in September, the Maseratis had acquired a Vanwall-type snout, the driver was similarly cowled-in, and they had an experimental chassis with the frame lowered by 2 in/5 cm, and the engine inclined at 6° across the car so that the driver could sit beside the drive line instead of on top of it. During practice the bumpy Monza banking gave trouble, with cars breaking up as a result of the 180 mph/289 kph, heavy g pounding, a problem which put Fangio out of the race after only 20 laps.

The pace was crippling, with the Vanwall of Harry Schell trading blow for blow with the Ferrari, and the Maserati of Moss, in a hectic race which left the lap record in tatters, and Moss the holder at a speed of 218 kph/135.5 mph.

In the race for the world championship, Collins and Behra both had 22 points, which meant they had to win at Monza *and* set fastest lap to have any chance of beating Fangio to the title. Behra was already out of the race, and so was Fangio, while his Ferrari team mates Castellotti and Musso were too absorbed with their own problems of stripping treads and the destiny of the Italian championship, to spare him any thought. Not so Collins. Sportsmanship is not unknown in motor racing—but more often by its breach than its observance. Collins came into the pits, and volunteered his car, so that Fangio might secure second place, and with it clinch the world championship.

Enzo Ferrari himself joined in the Italians' applause over Collins's action. Ferrari recalls in his memoirs a meeting he had had with Collins, whom he admired greatly. He had been asking Collins his opinion . . . 'I'm not asking you to step down for Fangio; I wouldn't ask anybody that. All the same, I'd like to know what you think about the position now that it's touch and go.'

According to Ferrari, Collins never hesitated. 'I never imagined that anyone who was only twenty-five could get to be world champion. I've still plenty of time. Fangio must remain world champion because he deserves it, and I'll let him have my car every time it might help him.'

Ferrari says that, had Collins not given up his car at Monza and earlier in the season at Monaco, Fangio would, '. . . with mathematical certainty', not have been world champion. Indeed, in view of Ferrari's quarrel with Fangio already simmering, and due to erupt bitterly in the years to come, the old man would probably have preferred Collins to have taken the crown.

1957

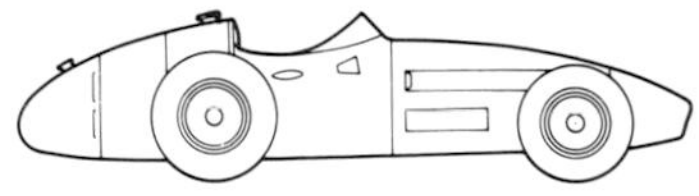

Fangio left Ferrari—both of them embittered—and went back after a three-year absence to Officine Maserati, his racing car a new version of the venerable 250F. For Enzo Ferrari, he had not a good word, accusing him of treachery, the sabotage of his cars, and even female enticements to sap his energy before a vital race. Ferrari in turn denounced the world champion for his 'persecution mania', and in a resounding philippic refuted the, '. . . concoction of betrayals, sabotage . . . and deceit'.

It was an undignified interlude in Fangio's career, but it serves to emphasise the delicate nature of the relationships Ferrari was to have with drivers throughout his life. The moment anyone seemed to divert attention from his beloved cars, Ferrari lost interest in him, and he was either dismissed, or his position somehow made so intolerable that he left.

Yet Mike Hawthorn returned. His cars were made 4 in/10 cm longer to accommodate his six-foot plus frame, and as the best driver in the world after Fangio and Moss, ever a match for the occasion, he was made welcome. Ferrari would later describe his manner as, '. . . rather absent', and found his unpredictableness, '. . . disconcerting'. He was joined in the team by his great friend Peter Collins, whose marriage still lay far enough in the future for him to remain a favourite, together with Castellotti and Musso. Moss, Brooks, and the new, likeable Welsh driver Stuart Lewis-Evans were to drive the improved Vanwalls. BRM began the season with Ron Flockhart and Roy Salvadori, neither amongst the front rank of Grand Prix drivers, although during the season Flockhart would gain his second Le Mans victory in a row. Jean Behra, Harry Schell, and a new Argentinian, Carlos Menditeguy, joined Fangio at Maserati.

In 1956, Switzerland, Holland, and Spain had failed to run their Grands Prix, and in 1957 in the wake of the Suez crisis, they were joined by Belgium. Demands for increased starting money on top of financial difficulties for the Belgian organising club were to blame, in particular the sums asked by Ferrari and Maserati. In order to keep the number of championship races up to seven, the CSI took the unusual step of promoting the Pescara Grand Prix to championship status, thus giving Italy two rounds counting towards the title, to the indignation of the French, who had a perfectly good race at Rheims which they felt merited the distinction rather better.

Pescara was a descendant of the pre-war Acerbo Cup race which dated back to 1924, when it had been won by Enzo Ferrari, driving an Alfa Romeo. It was one of Ferrari's few personal victories, but it made no difference to his strictures on works cars taking part in modern races over Italian road circuits. He forbade it, and only one car was reluctantly loaned out for this occasion.

Fangio made short work of the first three races on the championship calendar. Ferrari were still hampered by difficulties with the Lancias, of which almost the only recognisable feature left was the V-8 engine. They appeared during the season with side tanks and without them, then with the fuel drained from the tail and put in turgescent swellings on each side of the body. Swing-axle rear suspension was tried and rejected, the exhaust system was changed again, then the front suspension, and the tubular frame—the list seemed endless.

It was to no avail. Three cars retired from the first round in Argentina, held during the European winter in January; and the fourth, that of Castellotti, lost a wheel. Sadly, it was Castellotti's last race. Not long afterwards he was killed in what Ferrari called a '... banal' accident, testing a new car at Modena. Ferrari blamed involvement with a girl for Castellotti's '. . . confused emotional state', and, '. . . a momentary slowness in his reactions.'

Castellotti's death followed that of the British driver Ken Wharton. After sharing the fifth-placed car in the Argentine Grand Prix with the Marquis de Portago, Wharton was killed in a racing accident in New Zealand. The colourful Spanish aristocrat died in the spring of 1957, along with Ed Nelson his American co-driver, and ten bystanders in the Mille Miglia, which led the Italian Government to proscribe the race henceforth.

At Monaco, on the tricky, narrow track, Fangio once again demonstrated his extraordinary talent for keeping out of trouble where he had made one of his unaccustomed mistakes the year before. Moss took the lead soon after the start in the Vanwall, suitably snub-nosed to make it more manageable in the traffic. Collins was in hot pursuit, but on the third lap, Moss took the chicane too fast, and crashed. He dislodged the long poles marking the edge of the track, and in avoiding them, Collins crashed as well.

Means of identification

Early Brooklands meetings inherited the traditions of the turf for no better reasons than they were the only ones available. Thus racing cars gather together in a paddock, and the chief official is called the clerk of the course. The entire affair is still known as a race meeting, so it is hardly surprising to find the first drivers wearing jockey's silks for identification.

Although the practice died out in later years, the tradition of painting the cars in national colours went back even further, to the Gordon Bennett races at the turn of the century. Some of the colours allotted to national teams then became permanent, such as blue for France, yellow for Belgium, and white for Germany. Italy adopted red later on, and the United States blue and white. Green was given to the English driver Charles Jarrott for the 1900 Gordon Bennett because, as a supposedly lucky colour in France, it was expected to compensate for his starting number, which was 13.

British racing green was never a strictly defined colour, and varied from the olive adopted for the Vanwalls, the very dark green used by BRM, and the very light shade used by Stirling Moss for his Maserati and, later, the British Racing Partnership cars.

Germany came round to a metallic silver instead of white, and Prince Bira personally registered a particular light blue, rather gallantly taken from the colour of a girl's dress, together with yellow as the colours for Siam. Cars with Scottish connections tended to adopt the metallic dark blue used by the famous team of Ecurie Ecosse, while drivers often added national flags, such as the Union Jack Moss had painted on the tail of his Mercedes.

A long list of international racing colours was drawn up, often making a racing car's chassis or bonnet a different colour. By 1957, however, the chassis was no longer revealed, and the system fell into disuse.

The colours were officially distributed as follows:

Argentina: blue, black, chassis and wheels, yellow bonnet. *Numbers:* red on white.
Austria: blue, white chassis and wheels. *Numbers:* white.
Belgium: yellow. *Numbers:* white.
Bulgaria: green, white bonnet. *Numbers:* red.
Brazil: yellow, green chassis and wheels. *Numbers:* white.
Chile: red, white chassis and wheels. *Numbers:* red on white.
Czechoslovakia: white, blue bonnet, red chassis and wheels. *Numbers:* blue on white.
Egypt: mauve. *Numbers:* red on white.
Estonia: upper part white, lower part blue, black chassis and wheels. *Numbers:* black.
Finland: black. *Numbers:* blue on white.
France: blue. *Numbers:* white.
Germany: white. *Numbers:* red.
Great Britain: green. *Numbers:* white.
Hungary: white, red bonnet, green tail. *Numbers:* white.
Irish Republic: green with yellow line along side. *Numbers:* white.
Italy: red. *Numbers:* white.
Latvia: black, white bonnet. *Numbers:* black.
Lithuania: chequered blue and yellow, blue wheels. *Numbers:* white.
Luxembourg: grey, red bonnet. *Numbers:* white.
Monaco: white with red stripe along side. *Numbers:* black.
Netherlands: orange. *Numbers:* white.
Poland: white, red chassis and wheels. *Numbers:* red.
Portugal: red, white chassis and wheels. *Numbers:* white.
Romania: blue, red chassis and wheels. *Numbers:* white.
Siam: blue, yellow wheels and yellow stripe along side. *Numbers:* white
South Africa: buff, green bonnet, white wheels. *Numbers:* black on white.
Spain: red, yellow bonnet. *Numbers:* white.
Sweden: upper part yellow, lower part blue, transverse blue stripes on bonnet. *Numbers:* white.
Switzerland: red, white bonnet. *Numbers:* black.
United States: white, blue chassis and wheels. *Numbers:* blue.

The dying days of the classic 250F Maserati. This elegant racing car was soon to be eclipsed by the newer designs from Vanwall, yet was still able to take Fangio, at the age of 46, to his fifth world title.

Having taken over the Vanwall from Tony Brooks, convalescing from his Le Mans injuries, Stirling Moss speeds towards his historic victory at Aintree.

Fangio picked his way through as he had on that other famous occasion in 1950. Hawthorn, following, was less fortunate. He and Brooks in the second Vanwall collided, sending the Ferrari into the wreckage of Collins's car. Brooks recovered, and went on to finish a brilliant second to Fangio, less than half a minute behind, but the three leading British drivers were out.

The Formula under which the Grands Prix of 1957 were run had been intended to last from the beginning of the 1954 season to the end of 1957, and when the CSI decided to extend it to 1960, they reintroduced Formula 2. This was in response to tracks which could no longer afford the world championship teams, and revived the pre-war voiturette racing, together with the well-remembered precedents of those occasions when it turned out to be the next Formula 1.

The new class came into effect in 1957, for cars with unsupercharged $1\frac{1}{2}$-litre engines, running on 'pump' petrol, which meant that alcohol and other chemical mixtures were forbidden. Cars were already being made which complied with the new regulations; amongst them were the Cooper-Climax, and one of these was entered, somewhat venturesomely, in the Monaco Grand Prix, by Jack Brabham. With only 1.9 litres the Monaco entry appeared uncompetitive, but with the customary mechanical and accidental toll on the 16-car field, it was third of the six survivors at the end of 103 laps. The astonishing performance came to an end when the fuel pump drive failed two laps from the finish. Brabham pushed the car over the line to take sixth place, yet the success made no outward impression on the Grand Prix Establishment.

Cars with the engine behind the driver continued to suffer from the deeply ingrained reputation gained by the Auto Union 20 years before, of being a difficult car to drive. Only a few alert engineers would concede a case for putting the engine's weight over the driving wheels as a means of getting the wheels to grip. The time for the change was not yet ripe, however. Circumstances needed to alter a few more essential elements in the equation to even things out; but in time they would, and when that took place, a revolution was inevitable .

In July, Fangio won the French Grand Prix, held

at Rouen les Essarts, with Vanwall deprived of Moss through illness, and Brooks recovering from an accident at Le Mans. By the time of the British Grand Prix at Aintree, later the same month, Fangio had a handsome lead towards his fifth world championship.

During the run-up to the Grand Prix, British enthusiasts received the bad news that the British Automobile Racing Club's difficulties over starting money were proving the last straw for Connaught, coming on top of cancellation of the Dutch and Belgian races. Income from racing was insufficient, and Kenneth McAlpine, who had financed the team, withdrew support. The cars, spares, engines, and even an experimental model were all put up for auction, and the little team that had done so much to put Britain on the motor racing map of the world was suddenly gone.

However, restitution of British fortunes came on race day, 20 July, a turning point for Grand Prix racing in general, and British participation in particular.

Brooks was still feeling stiff from his accident, but Moss and he did sufficiently well in practice to sandwich Behra's Maserati on the front row of the grid. Moss took the lead when the race began, but by lap 21 his Vanwall was misfiring, and he was forced into the pits. Brooks lay sixth. To bring his car in and send Moss out in it cost time, which dropped it to ninth. Meanwhile, Behra (Maserati) driving at the peak of his form was firmly in the lead.

It was a race brimming with excitement, as Moss fought back with the Vanwall, repeatedly breaking the lap record, and although still well down the field, overtook car after car in one of the best drives of his career. Behra, alerted by signals, responded. By two thirds of the race distance of 90 laps, he was matching Moss's speed, leading from Hawthorn (Ferrari), with Lewis-Evans (Vanwall) third, Collins fourth, and Moss fifth. Spurred on by a crowd hungry for a home win, Moss broke the lap record once more with 1 min 59.2 sec (90.6 mph/145.77 kph), passed Collins, and together with Lewis-Evans tackled Hawthorn. Then, on lap 69 everything seemed to happen at once.

Behra's clutch and flywheel assembly split asunder, and as Hawthorn came alongside the crippled Maserati, a piece of debris from the disintegrating transmission punctured Hawthorn's

Lying second in the British Grand Prix—Mike Hawthorn (Ferrari). But while fighting off Moss and Lewis-Evans (Vanwalls) Hawthorn punctured a tyre on debris from the disintegrating clutch of the leading Maserati, and fell back.

rear tyre. Fate had delivered the two leaders to the flying Vanwall, at one fell swoop.

Delighted cheers from a capacity crowd greeted the first occasion when a British driver had won the British Grand Prix in a British car. Moss and Brooks were the heroes of the day, along with Tony Vandervell, whose ambition to, '. . . beat the red cars', had at last been fulfilled.

Two weeks later, the tough, abrasive Nürburgring was cruel to the Vanwalls, and Fangio won the German Grand Prix after a memorable race, increasing his lead in the world championship, showing he had lost none of his skill even at the ripe age, for a racing driver, of 46.

At Pescara, later in August, Moss won from Fangio, followed by yet another remarkable race at Monza as the season drew to a close in September, the trees round the historic park tinged with autumn colour. Three Vanwalls on the front row of the grid drove home the message that green cars would henceforward be in the same competitive league as the red cars of Italy. Vanwall, Maserati, and Ferrari fought out the race on equal terms, running one another into the ground, with Moss the victor from Fangio and the German Count Berghe von Trips in a Ferrari.

By the end of the season, the teams were making ready for the changeover to petrol for 1958. Ferrari with some relief announced that the ill-starred Lancia would be replaced with a new V-6, which had been developed initially for Formula 2, and in customary Ferrari fashion, scaled-up to 2½ litres. Vanwall were more worried about effects of the change on engines like theirs, relying heavily on alcohol for internal cooling. Yet, except amongst the more thoughtful students of motor racing, the trend to mid-engined cars, already apparent in the Formula 2 designs that were making their appearance, still seemed to strike no chord in Formula 1. Brabham's efforts with the Coopers remained a matter for surprise, a gallant effort, a movement towards simplicity and lightness suitable for less powerful cars, but with no real application in the world of front-rank Grand Prix teams. His Monaco performance was explicable by the freakish nature of the track, and the mechanical mortality with which it was associated. Dr Porsche's 1947 Cisitalia, and Ing Colombo's Bugatti were likewise regarded sceptically, as theoretical eccentricities which, being short of achievement on the track, could therefore be ignored.

Yet they had not been overlooked altogether. Behind the smoked glass of elegant, cool design offices in Maranello, or scribbled on the backs of envelopes behind closed doors in Surbiton, Bourne, and Hornsey, England, a new generation of racing cars was being conceived.

Fangio at the Nürburgring

The 1957 Grosser Preis von Deutschland was run in hot August sunshine over the Nürburgring, the 22.8 km/14.17 mile circuit in the Eifel Mountains, where 200 000 people often camped in the woods over the long weekend of the race. The Ferrari team of Hawthorn, Collins, and Musso decided to run non-stop throughout the 22 laps, not expecting to change tyres or refuel.

Maserati, on the other hand, had a wear problem, indicating a pit stop would be necessary; so Fangio decided to start with a half load of fuel, taking on more at the inevitable tyre stop. Starting with a 170 lb (77 kg) advantage would, he reasoned, enable him to gain enough of a lead to remain in front afterwards.

Of the 51 world championship races in which Fangio took part, he started from pole position 28 times. This was one of those occasions, yet it was Hawthorn who led for the first two laps from Peter Collins. Fangio took stock, then as the fuel load became lighter, took command of the race. By lap three he was past both of his adversaries, and then proceeded to invoke all his reserves of skill to build up the advantage necessary to provide time for his tyre change and refuel. It was a display of virtuosity that left the crowds gathered round the fences, and lining the road that wound amongst the pine-clad slopes, gasping in admiration.

Time and again he broke his own circuit record, gaining from the Ferraris at a rate of seven seconds every lap. By the twelfth, just after half distance, he came into the pits for his tyre change. It was not one of the best-arranged stops. Before he got under way again, 53 sec had elapsed, and the two young Englishmen were three quarters of a minute ahead of the 46-year-old veteran Argentinian.

It seemed all over; but this shy, retiring man in the battered brown crash helmet was the greatest driver of his day, and raised the driving of a racing car to new heights of achievement. As the fuel load in the Maserati again lightened, and the new tyres were scrubbed in, he went faster and faster, breaking the record on every one of those momentous laps, and leaving it at 9 min 17.4 sec, an average speed of 147.27 kph/91.51 mph.

By the time the Ferrari pit was aware of the danger, it was already too late. Laps at the Nürburgring lasting almost ten minutes meant opponents could make up a good deal before a pit crew became aware of it, and 20 minutes before their driver got the message. So almost as Hawthorn and Collins were being alerted, Fangio was in their mirrors, and by lap 20 he was upon them.

Collins, whose clutch was giving trouble, was picked off without difficulty, and in another half-lap, Fangio took Hawthorn. His old adversary of that famous French Grand Prix of 1953 gave chase, and even managed by dint of inspired driving to keep up. But this time the legendary Fangio made no mistakes. The young lions were no match, and he took the chequered flag for one of his greatest races, and one of the most dramatic Grands Prix of modern times. It was Fangio's 24th Championship Grand Prix victory and, as it turned out, his last, setting the seal on the career of the greatest racing driver in the world.

1958

1958

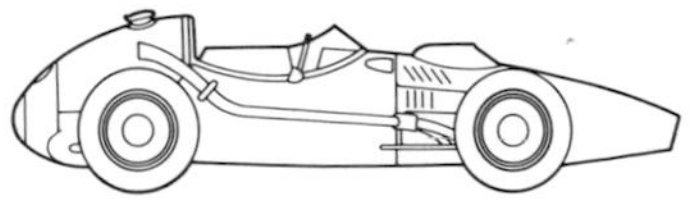

The profound nature of the changes in the rules for 1958 were not at first apparent. An effort to trim the scoring system, and attempts to attract cash into Grand Prix racing, seemed relatively unimportant at the time, yet their effects were to be incalculable. The 1957 decree that drivers must cover one-third of the race distance to be eligible for championship points, went some way towards removing fractions from the title table. The 1958 amendment that only one driver may score points in one car brought about more fundamental changes. Race tactics would never be quite the same again.

An anodyne agreement with the oil companies for a change to what was euphemistically known as 'pump' petrol had been intended to increase the money flowing into motor racing. It was the CSI's job to make sure organisers and competitors were able to work in a favourable economic climate. Advertising endorsements of the oil companies' products had been employed for years, but they were perceived as rather empty and worthless treaties by motorists who knew that racing car fuels were witches' brews of greater volatility than anything *they* were ever likely to encounter.

The change was to influence racing car design, and also, tragically, make a business that was already dangerous, even more so. Together with the shorter races demanded by promoters who thought them a better draw for the crowds, the consequences would be far-reaching.

The motives were practicality and profit; their influence for good or ill remains a matter of debate. For the purist, to whom a motor race was the better the longer it went on, the changes were a disaster. In the long term they would banish the tactical pit stop, such as Moss had at Aintree, or Fangio at the Nürburgring. The sense of anticipation that came when a leading car was running short of fuel, or wearing out its tyres, was lost. After changing to petrol, cars would need less fuel capacity, with their consumption almost halved, and following the trend to shorter races, even less still. A pit stop of any sort would signal virtual retirement from the contest, because ground thus lost could never be made up. Non-stop racing became essential, and drivers were no longer called upon to conduct a disciplined race, saving tyres, or conserving brakes to last the distance. All that mattered was driving to the absolute limit, on every lap, with no quarter asked, given, or expected.

For those spectators looking for outright thrills, however, it was a new era. No longer was it essential to follow the event with a lap chart. The car at the front was the car in the lead, and it became easier to keep track. Yet the new circumstances gave motor racing at Grand Prix level the characteristics of the pressure cooker: the higher the heat, the greater the pressure, and the greater the pressure, the higher the heat, compressing the cooking into a shorter time.

The taste, alas, was not the same. The practice of changing drivers during a race was a relic of the days when the object of a motor race was to race motors, and not drivers. The world championship had been encouraging *driver* racing, and the newly introduced restrictions on their swapping cars would, it was hoped, prevent the games of 'musical cockpits' with drivers leaping from car to car in their efforts to reach the finish. It tended to appear slightly comic, yet the change meant there was no longer the same incentive to make those spectacular dashes from the back of the field which had been such a characteristic of 1957.

The scoring retained its essential flaws, as 1958 would amply demonstrate. Mike Hawthorn returned to Ferrari and rediscovered his old form, winning the championship with one victory, five second places, a third, and a fifth, against Stirling Moss's four outright victories. Was a world champion the driver who won most races, or the one with the most consistent car? The question was never satisfactorily answered, but the scoring system was altered largely as a result of Hawthorn's narrow triumph.

It was the closest Moss ever came to the world championship. It was his fourth year as runner-up. Yet because he never won, it was the title that lost the status, rather than Moss. There was obviously something wrong with it, if it failed to elect the best driver in the world after the retirement of Fangio.

The immediate result of the new fuel regulations was the withdrawal of Maserati. Sports car racing had sapped the little firm's resources; the noisy V-12 engine which appeared intermittently in 1957 had proved temperamental and unsuccessful, so the last 250F was made over to Fangio, and after 30 years amongst the leading names in motor racing, Maserati, so far as Grand Prix racing was concerned, disappeared. It was a sad demise for the company responsible for the immortal 8C, and the 4CL series that was the backbone of Formula A in the Forties. The ill-starred V-12 would rise again from the ashes, but as a Grand Prix contender, Maserati itself was finished.

The new V-6 Ferrari, called the Dino after Ferrari's son, who had died of leukaemia in 1956, was well suited to the 130 octane Avgas specified for Formula 1 (it would not be real 'pump' petrol for several years to come) for which it was, in any case, designed. The Vanwall, however, was less in harmony with the new fuel. The four cylinders whose head design was based on the 500 cc Norton motor cycle, and the crankcase from a Rolls-Royce military engine had withstood 310 bhp on the already forbidden nitro methane, and 290 bhp on alcohol, but was reduced to 262 bhp on petrol.

The loss of cool-burning alcohol also threatened trouble with high cylinder head and valve temperatures, making the institution of the first Manufacturers' Cup seem inauspicious for Vanwall. The scoring was to be the same as for the drivers' title, except that should one make of car finish a race first and second, only the points for first would be allowed, and so on down to fifth, the highest placed car alone counting. Runaway scoring was thus prevented should there be a preponderance of cars

John Michael Hawthorn (b 1929)

The deaths of Collins, Musso, and Lewis-Evans during that painful 1958 season confirmed Mike Hawthorn's resolve to retire. He had had three distressing years, and at 29 took the opportunity of being the first British world champion to bow out. Racing, he always said was for enjoyment, and he had ceased enjoying it. He wanted to put the tragedies behind him, go back to the garage at Farnham, Surrey, and settle down.

Mike Hawthorn was born in Yorkshire in 1929, and in 1931 his father, Leslie Hawthorn, bought the TT Garage in order to be closer to his beloved Brooklands, where he raced motor cycles. It was 1950 before the family began racing cars, two Rileys, an Imp and a Sprite, with which they were successful at the Brighton Speed Trials. Mike went on to distinguish himself in the cars, especially in club racing on the nearby Goodwood circuit in Sussex.

In 1952 a family friend bought the Cooper-Bristol with which Hawthorn established himself internationally. After a sensational first outing in the Goodwood Easter Meeting, where the dashing young man (he was still only 23) in the bow tie showed himself a match for some of the best-known names in motor racing, he received offers from BRM and drives in the Thinwall Special. He even drove a Sunbeam, and won a Coupe des Alpes in the Alpine Rally.

Ferrari's offer came for the 1953 season, resulting in the memorable duel with Fangio in the French Grand Prix. Hawthorn became the first British driver to win a grande épreuve since the Twenties and, almost overnight, was a national hero. His flamboyant character, and his obvious enjoyment of mechanical things such as cars and motor cycles, earned him a devoted following. His boisterousness struck a chord in the imagination of a generation which preferred its heroes to drink beer and smoke a pipe, loving life in the cherished tradition of the Spitfire pilots of recent memory.

In 1954 Hawthorn's career started to go wrong. He burned his legs in an accident, then became the victim of a newspaper campaign concerning his failure to do National Service. The Korean War, quiescent now, but still fresh in the public mind, brought questions in the House of Commons about how this apparently strapping young man was able to, 'avoid his obligations to his country'. The accusations were ill-deserved. Hawthorn suffered from a serious kidney complaint which made him medically unfitted for military service. Not surprisingly he did not want to publicise the fact, already knowing it was likely to prevent him surviving much beyond middle age. To make things worse, his father died in a road accident, and in 1955 the unhappy young man signed for Vanwall in order to remain in Britain, and run the family business.

Before the season was finished, however, he had become disillusioned with the car, and returned to Ferrari, but not before being involved in the Le Mans disaster and the obloquy that came after it. In 1956 he tried BRM, but again suffered accidents and failures, so he rejoined Ferrari once more in 1957.

Enzo Ferrari described Hawthorn's driving as '. . . unpredictable' and, as he saw it, '. . . disconcerting'. Certainly it never had the artistry of Moss, nor the native cunning of Fangio. Ferrari said he was, 'capable of facing up to any situation and getting out of a tight corner with a cold and calculated courage and an exceptional speed of reflexes [but] he was nevertheless liable suddenly to go to pieces'. The explanation for Ferrari's view of course, was Hawthorn's essential humanity, which did affect him, for example when he withdrew from the race after Collins's crash. As Ferrari was to demonstrate many years later over Niki Lauda, he was never able to understand, forgive, or in the event, tolerate drivers who did not share his rustic views on courage and behaviour.

Mikc Hawthorn died one grey morning, in January 1959, within weeks of announcing he would not drive a racing car again. He skidded his Jaguar saloon on a wet Guildford by-pass in Surrey, and driving at speed as he always did, crashed disastrously and was killed. He was mourned by the youth of a nation which he had taken to the forefront of motor racing

belonging to one make.

Vanwall and BRM were absent from the first round of the 1958 championship, the Grand Prix of Argentina in January, so the small field was made up of six Maseratis, three Ferraris, and Stirling Moss's solitary Cooper-Climax. Behra (Maserati), Hawthorn (Ferrari), and Fangio (Maserati) led in turn, but all met trouble and Moss took the initiative, carefully conserving his tyres to win by 2.7 sec from Luigi Musso (Ferrari). The curious looking, diminutive, four-cylinder Cooper, its engine seemingly at the wrong end, giving away nearly half a litre to its rivals, had won its first world championship Grand Prix—the first for such a car since the days of Auto Union before the war.

Yet an air of unreality persisted over Moss's victory. The pundits were not convinced. They thought it was due to other teams being unready for the start of the new season, the small field, Moss's virtuosity, the brilliant way he had looked after his tyres. Even when Maurice Trintignant won the very next race at Monaco with Rob Walker's Cooper-Climax, it was only after the faster cars (including Moss's Vanwall) had once again failed. Perhaps the little cars *were* only winning through reliability. It was probably the now more familiar name of Jack Brabham in fourth place at Monaco that finally persuaded the traditionalists to concede, that for some circuits at least, the new rear-engined cars might have a place in the scheme of things.

The Cooper, furthermore, was not the only novelty at Monaco. Colin Chapman's Lotus cars were already well established in British racing, and also at Le Mans, with radical, lightweight, and well thought out tubular frames which contributed to their remarkable road holding. Lotuses were made with a variety of engines in Marks 9, 10, and 11: the Mark 12 was a Formula 2 single seater with a Coventry-Climax engine. The firm's first road car, the Elite, with its load-bearing reinforced glass-fibre body, and destined to become a classic, had just been announced. This was a further demonstration of Chapman's versatile mind which had already influenced the design of racing car suspension. He

Fangio's last race. In an uncompetitive Maserati, five times world champion Juan Manuel Fangio takes part in the French Grand Prix. Afterwards, the greatest Grand Prix driver slipped away to an unannounced, and honourable retirement.

had shown his mastery of the subject by the part he had played in the Vanwall. Now, the Lotus 16 appeared, a Vanwall in silhouette, and a racing car in miniature.

Chapman had trimmed it down to the essentials, and produced an ingenious, spidery car that was driven at Monaco by Cliff Allison, where it finished sixth. It clearly had a long way to go before being a winner; but Chapman, only just turned 30, already had a reputation for success, for innovation, and for tackling fundamental problems in novel ways.

The British filled the first two rows of the grid at Zandvoort in May, and Moss (Vanwall) won from the BRMs of Schell and Behra, with Roy Salvadori fourth in a Cooper-Climax, Hawthorn (Ferrari) fifth, and Allison's Lotus again sixth in a further demonstration of Anglo-Saxon prowess. Musso's Ferrari could finish no better than seventh, followed by two more Coopers, and a solitary Maserati was tenth.

Tony Brooks joined the ranks of Grand Prix winners in his own right in the Belgian race at Spa in June. There was no longer anything remarkable about a Vanwall victory, but what was astonishing was the performance of Allison's tiny Lotus on the immensely fast road circuit amongst the wooded Ardennes. Although four minutes behind the leaders after 24 laps, it might have won had the race been 25. As he crossed the finishing line the gearbox of Brooks's Vanwall jammed; Hawthorn in second place broke a piston, and as he passed the flag, the suspension of Lewis-Evans's Vanwall collapsed. For the Lotus to come so close to winning a Grand Prix this early in its first season, was a notable achievement. This race also saw the first girl driver taking part in a world championship Grand Prix. The glamorous Italian Maria Teresa de Fillipis finished tenth in her Maserati, two laps in arrears.

At the beginning of July, after a close race, Hawthorn won the French Grand Prix, but in sad circumstances. The talented, and patriotic Italian, Luigi Musso died while in pursuit of the English driver, in a 150-mph crash on the long Gueux bend. Musso was, according to Enzo Ferrari, '. . . the last Italian driver of International class . . . the last example of that school of aces, beginning with Nazzaro that was distinguished by perfection in style'.

It was also the last race of the charismatic Fangio. Out of contention, on the third row of the grid with his now forlorn Maserati, he finished fourth; then quietly, without making any formal announcement, retired from racing. Already a legend, he hung up his helmet at the age of 47, and went back to Argentina. His appearances at tracks thereafter were in the role of spectator, or official where invariably (in contrast

One of Britain's best drivers of the Fifties, Tony Brooks takes his Vanwall to victory in the Belgian Grand Prix.

Peter Collins' last victory was the British Grand Prix at Silverstone. A fortnight later this outstanding driver died on the Nürburgring.

With its rear suspension redesigned by Colin Chapman, the P25 BRM was at last competitive. French driver Jean Behra in the British Grand Prix at Silverstone.

Second place at Silverstone for Mike Hawthorn, who preferred the four-spoke steering wheel, and small aero screen with which his Ferrari is equipped in the British Grand Prix.

to other retired drivers), he was treated deferentially, instead of being mobbed. To his admirers, and even to Enzo Ferrari, his stature as a driver was the highest ever.

In the championship, Hawthorn and Moss were level pegging, with 23 points apiece, Hawthorn edging ahead at Silverstone by finishing second to Peter Collins, while Moss retired the Vanwall. Roy Salvadori (Cooper) finished third, a matter of yards ahead of Lewis-Evans (Vanwall) showing once again that in the new, shorter races the small light cars were competitive on any track.

Moss had little better luck in the German Grand Prix, due to magneto failure after only four laps, leaving Tony Brooks once again upholding the honour of the team, scoring his second victory of the season. Alas, once again it was in distressing circumstances. Just after Brooks overtook the Ferraris of Hawthorn and Collins on the downhill bends towards Adenau on the eleventh lap, Collins lost control and crashed, receiving fatal injuries. It was a tragic conclusion to a career that was in full flourish, and broke up the carefree, happy trio of English drivers who were leading an assault that was changing the face, and incidentally also the principal language, of Grand Prix racing.

Moreover, in the nature of things, new drivers were already waiting in the wings. In the same race, the Formula 2 section was won by a brilliant, and very youthful New Zealander who was also to exert a strong influence on motor racing. His name was Bruce McLaren.

For the first time, Portugal was included in the world championship series, at the 7.407 km/4.602 mile circuit on the outskirts of Oporto, with cobbles, plenty of camber changes, and even tramlines. It had all the customary features of a true road circuit, including kerbs, walls, and even lamp posts by the track side, protected rather hopefully by straw bales. Unusually, the races on it were run anti-clockwise.

By August the championship was still very close, and Moss needed to score the maximum points to keep up with Hawthorn. He won, but failed owing to misinterpreting a pit signal to set fastest lap. Instead, it went to Hawthorn and with it the vital single point that would make all the difference at the season's end.

Misfortune struck Moss again at Monza the following month, when his gearbox failed, and even though Hawthorn, too, had trouble, he scored yet another second place, and it was left to the final round in Morocco to decide the outcome.

At Ain Diab, Casablanca, Moss had to win *and* set fastest lap, with Hawthorn, no higher than third. Hawthorn, on the other hand, only had to keep Moss in sight to clinch the title. Backed up by his new American team mate, Phil Hill, Hawthorn fought his way through, and finished second.

Once again the Grand Prix world was plunged into gloom by a fatal accident. A shadow was cast across the track by the smoke pall from the Vanwall of Stuart Lewis-Evans who was terribly burned when his tanks caught fire after a crash. He was flown back to England, but died within a few days.

Fires in racing cars were by no means unknown in the days of chemical fuels, but despite their reputation as 'explosive' mixtures, they were relatively less dangerous than petrol in the ruptured tanks of a racing car. Lewis-Evans was the first victim of the changeover to petrol that may have been commercially satisfactory, but would remain treacherously perilous in the years to come.

1959

1959

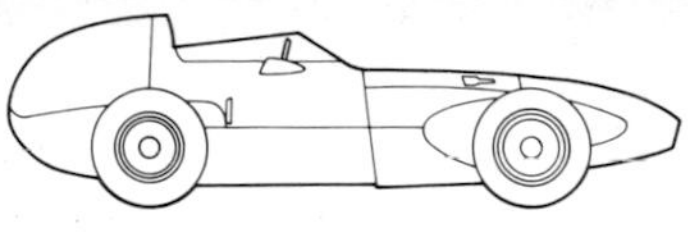

By the beginning of the 1959 season, it was clear that Fangio really had retired. There was no longer even an Argentinian Grand Prix for him to win. Hawthorn, the world champion, was dead; so motor racing had lost two of its best drivers, whose skill and daring, and capacity for racing to the finish against the odds, had enlivened so many Grands Prix. Peter Collins and Luigi Musso were gone; and Tony Vandervell, still deeply affected by the loss of Stuart Lewis-Evans, decided to withdraw the Vanwall team. His own health had failed and, although there were some half-hearted attempts at revival, with a small staff kept on after the formal disbandment, the vigour of the project left with Vandervell, and the first team to win the Manufacturers' Cup was no more.

Tony Brooks went to Ferrari, busily modifying their V-6 Dino, and even having a change of heart over disc brakes. Vanwall had made their own, holding their American Goodyear patents close to their chest, while most of the rest used Girling or Lockheed. Ferrari was amongst those who relied on a Dunlop design after Hawthorn had insisted on disc brakes at Monza the year before. He had prevailed upon Ferrari engineers to take a set off the late Peter Collins's road car to race with, leaving the rest of the team to manage as best they could with bi-metallic drums. As drum brakes they were exemplary, but they were no match for their British rivals' discs.

Already, it was becoming evident that 1959 was to be a turning point. The shorter races were now established, giving designers as fundamental a new set of ground-rules as if the Formula *had* been changed. Instead of three hours or 500 km/311 miles, races were now two hours or 300 km/186 miles, and together with cars' lower fuel consumption (from around 5–6 mpg on alcohol to 10–11 mpg on petrol) it was possible for competitors to go through without a refuelling stop. This meant in turn that cars could be altogether smaller and lighter, which would mean less wear on the tyres, and less fatigue on the drivers who could now sustain their concentration, and deliver a peak performance for the entire race distance.

Taken together, these factors brought about the greatest revolution in the history of racing car design. With lighter cars needing smaller, slimmer fuel tanks, the ratio of engine weight to all-up weight altered in favour of the mid, or rear-engined layout. The wholesale changeover which ensued was not so much due to the inspiration of John Cooper, or subsequently Colin Chapman, as to the logical result of changed circumstances to which, as it turned out, Cooper and Chapman had a ready-made reply.

Hawthorn's year was the last for front-engined cars. No world champion would ever drive such a car again. The 1959 season saw the last* victory in a world championship event for a front-engined** car taking part in a championship Grand Prix. The change was swift. Of the 16 cars on the grid of the first race of 1959 at Monaco in May, seven were rear-engined. The way to winning had suddenly become so clear that the trend towards a stereotype that would be such a prominent feature of the years ahead, was already distinguishable. Later the same month in the Dutch Grand Prix, 13 of the 15 starters were on Dunlop tyres, whose nylon carcass was proving superior to anything hitherto. Disc brakes were universal, and so were Weber carburettors. For the first time since 1950–1, design was approaching uniformity, and so, as a result, was performance. The lap time spectrum was becoming narrower, with little more than a second separating the first two rows of the grid, instead of several seconds. Two years after winning the world championship, a 250F Maserati, for all its classic lines, was a motor racing dinosaur, skulking at the back of the field, dropping into an automotive limbo from which it would only emerge with the popularity, years later, of historic car racing.

Newcomers, like Aston Martin, encouraged into Formula 1 by their success in sports car racing (and who would win the 1959 World Sports Car Championship) were out of date before they started. They appeared with the elegant DBR4/250, a car in the classic mould, showed some speed at Silverstone, but quickly withdrew, being no match for the nimble rear-engined cars that were gaining the upper hand.

The championship series lost Argentina, but gained a North American Grand Prix for the first time. Sebring, the Florida airfield circuit, had already held a round of the sports car championship, so avoiding the obligation to hold a non-championship Formula 1 race before their round would be sanctioned.

Monaco saw the Coventry-Climax cars attain their full 2½ litres, and the appearance of two teams of Coopers. One was composed of the works cars of Brabham and Bruce McLaren with four-speed gearboxes based on the venerable Citroën; and the other was Rob Walker's Stirling Moss car with a five-speed gearbox by Colotti. Moss, Behra (Ferrari), and Brabham fought it out, the two former retiring, with Jack Brabham scoring his first world championship victory, and setting fastest lap.

BRM at last broke their vexing spell of misfortune at Zandvoort. After more than ten years they scored their first Grand Prix victory when the wealthy Swede, Joakim Bonnier, took the chequered flag in the Dutch Grand Prix in May, with a car that had been completely redesigned over the winter to meet the changed conditions. The major alterations of the year before, when the car had been made more compact, had been rounded off with another Colin Chapman consultancy job, employing what had come to be known as Chapman struts in the rear suspension. The changeover to petrol had cost the engine only a matter of 18 bhp, the low-speed torque of the four cylinders was virtually unimpaired, and

*Ferrari won the 1960 Italian Grand Prix with front-engined cars, but owing to the special circumstances of this race, it is not usually taken into account. See pages 69, 70.
**A Ferguson four-wheel-drive car took part later, but it is not regarded as a 'normal' ie rear wheel drive car. See page 73.

Top: Superstitious as ever, Stirling Moss had his P25 BRM painted the lightest green he could find to satisfy the requirements of international rules for racing colours, but in the French Grand Prix failed to obtain his favourite racing number seven. It was all to no avail. Although he set fastest lap, he retired following a spin. Bottom: Jack Brabham takes up a characteristic crouch in the mid-engined Cooper-Climax at Aintree, on the way to victory in the British Grand Prix and the world championship.

the car was almost as wieldy as the Cooper, and although heavier, it had more power.

Furthermore, BRM could discern which way the wind was blowing, and by Monza late in the year had about-faced their new design to try out an experimental rear-engined BRM during practice.

The Ferrari V-6 remained the most powerful, with 290 bhp against the Coventry-Climax engine's 239. Consequently, on the high-speed straights of Rheims, where power remained vital, Tony Brooks and Phil Hill in their Ferraris reigned supreme. Brabham won the British Grand Prix at Aintree, leading all the way, but the Ferraris were still fastest on the extraordinary Avus circuit in West Berlin.

The German Grand Prix had been moved from the traditional Nürburgring, where it suffered from two years of disappointing receipts, to the Avus, a track dating back to the First World War, with its famous banking put up for the 1937 Avusrennen. A highlight of Berlin life during the Third Reich, when crowds of between 300 000 and 400 000 were commonplace, Avus in 1959 saw barely 100 000 in a divided city, making the Berlin Senate's subsidies imperative.

Composed of two parallel straights with a hairpin at one end, and the wall-of-death banking at an angle of 43° at the other, the modern Avus had been abbreviated owing to much of it lying in the Grünewald, within the Russian Zone of the city. When it had been 20 km/12.43 miles long, Bernd Rosemeyer (Auto Union) set the lap record at a speed of 276.38 kph/171.73 mph in 1937. On the shorter 8.3 km/5.2 mile Avus, the W 196 Mercedes-Benz Stromlinienwagen had achieved 224 kph/139.19 mph in a non-title race, using the rather bumpy, brick-faced speed bowl. Several teams had experimented with full-width, wind-cheating bodies with varying success, and Avus in 1959 seemed just the place to exploit them.

For the Grand Prix, however, the authorities forbade streamliners. Aerodynamics was still an inexact science, and when Jack Brabham had tried an aerodynamic Cooper, the hitherto little-known phenomenon of aerodynamic lift nearly took control of the little car. It was hardly surprising of course, with the car doing two or three times the speed at which light aircraft will take off, weighing considerably less, and with a body that was getting perilously close to an aerofoil in section.

It is surprising that it took almost 20 years before anyone stood the idea on its head and 'inverted' the aerofoil so that, instead of producing lift, it resulted in downforce to help cornering grip. So-called ground effect cars still lay a long way in the future, but the Avus ban on full-width bodies was later enshrined in the international regulations for Formula 1, which came to insist on what were known as open-wheelers.

The Grand Prix was divided into heats, both won by Tony Brooks (Ferrari), but the meeting was marred by the death, in the sports car race preceding the Grand Prix, of Jean Behra. An audacious, vigorous driver, and the best in France, Behra had fallen out with Tavoni, the Ferrari team manager, and he died when his Porsche RSK spun on the banking during rain. In another accident, Hans Herrmann had a miraculous escape when his BRM toppled end over end, throwing him out at high speed, leaving him dazed but little more than bruised in the road, while the car spectacularly destroyed itself.

Brooks's victory was the last for a front-engined car in a fully-contested world championship race. The changeover to rear engines was now proceeding so quickly that older cars speedily became uncompetitive, and Stirling Moss had no difficulty winning with the Cooper first at Oporto, then at Monza, where all he had to do was keep up with the front-engined Ferraris in his much lighter car, wait until their inevitable tyre changes, and carry on to victory.

Monza proved to be the *coup de grâce*. If the little Cooper could vanquish the Ferraris here, it could beat them anywhere. It was now winning demonstrably on merit, and not by default, or because the circuit was a twisty one, and sooner or later it was evident that every racing car constructor had to conform.

The final race of the season was the new United States Grand Prix at Sebring, on the 5.2 mile/8.34 km airfield circuit, where the leading Ferrari, driven by Brooks, finished three minutes, or nearly a full lap behind Coopers driven by Bruce McLaren and Maurice Trintignant. It was McLaren's first Grand Prix victory, and in only his eighth race he became at 22 years 104 days the youngest driver ever to win a world championship Grand Prix.

Brabham's world championship emphasised that the rear-engined car had come to stay, and with it a new style of racing team, a new approach to Grand Prix racing, and even a new style of driving. The time-honoured methods were now outworn. The Ferrari way, with all its riches but somewhat hide-bound conventionality, was unable to meet the challenge swiftly enough. BRM with their rear-engined experiment showed willing, but they were still not completely convinced they ought to make the change. John and Charles Cooper had hit upon the solution almost by accident. It is not being unkind to them to say they probably did not know how to build a Grand Prix car any other way, but they were a small, flexible organisation, with no internal dissensions, pragmatic, practical, and willing to work all night if necessary to produce quick solutions to the problems of the race track.

The fuel regulation and the short races favoured their approach, and the cars were two years ahead of everyone else's as a result. All the ingredients had been there at the crucial moment, brought together opportunely by Jack Brabham. Furthermore, Brabham had a flair for innovation in his quiet Australian way. As one of the first drivers to translate his experience at the wheel into practical engineering, he pioneered a number of important developments.

Drivers as a rule never had much direct bearing on designs or specifications of the cars they drove: Brabham's influence was functional in the sense that he would often carry out work on it himself. Drivers did not descend from the cockpit and take up a welding torch, at any rate not in the exclusive world of Grand Prix racing. The gulf between the theorist and the man at the wheel had been a wide one. Brabham narrowed it.

A refinement which was to prove almost as important to motor racing as the advent of the rear engine was hit upon by the Cooper team along with Brabham. This was the incorporation of threaded joints in the front suspension, allowing the length of the upper front wishbone to be altered, thus changing the camber angle of the front wheels. As a consequence, the amount of over or understeer could be varied as a driver felt appropriate for any track upon which he was called to race.

The new Formula 2 had provided the Coopers with an opportunity for the mid/rear-engined configuration to be developed, and they won eight of the ten Formula 2 races of 1957, and all 19 in 1959. Coventry-Climax developed their four-cylinder engine with twin overhead camshafts specifically for motor racing, enlarging it from 1.7 litres, to 1.9, 2.2, and for 1959, the full 2½ litres, and sold them to Cooper and Lotus.

The mid-engined layout had a number of advantages. It saved the weight of a long transmission line, and a frame supporting a compact engine and transmission could be made correspondingly lighter. But the principal benefit concerned the car's polar moment of inertia—the so-called 'dumb-bell' effect. A car with its weight concentrated at each end (as in a dumb-bell), will acquire a large moment of inertia, or behave like a flywheel with a heavy rim. It will be reluctant to spin, but difficult to stop once it has started. But with the weight concentrated in the middle, it will be more like a flywheel with a heavy hub and a light rim, namely easy to spin, but quick to stop.

The advent of the Cooper illustrated the search for road holding, as opposed to good handling. Designers had endowed their cars with a high polar moment of inertia, which conferred good directional stability—in other words they tended to sit on the road well at speed. On corners the driver would exercise control partly through spinning the rear wheels, using the large resources of power, and partly through the steering.

Understeer, the 'running wide' tendency on a corner went more naturally with cars of great power. But understeer consumes power as a result of the front wheels tending to scrub off speed as they are turned. If the understeer is reduced, however, the high polar moment makes the handling sluggish and unresponsive. But if, instead, a low polar moment is introduced by concentrating the car's weight towards the centre, as in the mid-engined configuration, the driver has a car which has more consistent handling, is less likely to take him by surprise, and becomes less dependent on sheer power for control.

This was the car which developed in the dawn light of the Sixties.

1960

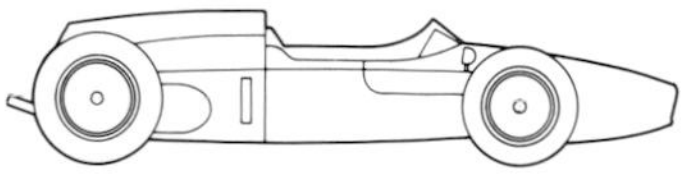

The final year of the $2\frac{1}{2}$-litre Formula was at best inconclusive. After the excitement of the changeover to rear engines, and despite the startling pace of development which saw the slowest cars on 1960 grids faster than the fastest ones of 1959, there was a sense of anticlimax. It was heightened as the year drew to a close, by rancour over the Italian Grand Prix, and the running dispute which the British teams had with the CSI over the new Formula due to come into force in 1961. The British had been opposing the $1\frac{1}{2}$-litre proposals ever since they were mooted in 1957, and it now looked as though Grand Prix racing would be split asunder by the quarrel.

The taciturn Brabham scored his second world championship; once again he and the Coopers showed great skill and flair, yet had Stirling Moss not been temporarily excluded after an accident in the disastrous Belgian Grand Prix, the story might have been very different.

At the end of 1959, Colin Chapman had decided that the arguments in favour of rear-engined cars were too strong to ignore, and set to work producing his Mark 18. BRM had already tested their rear-engined car and had a full team of them ready to race early in the season, with Bonnier, American, Dan Gurney, and Graham Hill. Ferrari followed the BRM example by simply taking a Dino 246 engine and installing it in a back-to-front version of their existing car.

The difference between them and the Lotus, and even the difference between the Lotus and the Cooper, was that Chapman had taken the first of his great strides in design that were to become such a characteristic of his progress in the years ahead. The Mark 18 Lotus—not the pioneering Cooper, was the car which was to set the standards of performance and engineering, not only for 1960, but for the opening years of the new formula to come. One of Chapman's objectives was to create a car in which Formula 1 or Formula 2 engines could be installed, because he wanted Team Lotus to be ready whichever way the controversy over the new Formula developed. This implied the use of a chassis structure capable of dealing with any engine between $1\frac{1}{2}$ and $2\frac{1}{2}$ litres.

His 1959 front-engined car had not been a success. He had aimed at making it light (which it was). He had aimed at keeping down wind resistance (which he had; the tubular frame was enclosed in a most slim-fitting envelope) and he had succeeded in building an extremely low car. The engine was canted in the frame, and angled so that the driver did not sit on top of the drive line—but it proved an unsatisfactory car to handle, owing to too much understeer.

The new rear-engined car weighed about the same as its predecessor, and even the weight distribution was little changed. It was still very low-built, Chapman realising that the most inhibiting feature in the frontal aspect of a racing car was the height of the driver sitting at the wheel. If the driver could be prevailed upon to lean back, however, he could take up longitudinal space, of which there was plenty, and reduce the overall height. The new Lotus, with its driver reclining, was under 30 in/76 cm tall.

The components of the new Mark 18 were carefully distributed inside the slimmest practicable silhouette, minimising drag, in a tubular frame which was light and stiff. The most significant result was a new class of road holding, achieved by a novel arrangement at the rear, and suspension geometry which reduced the roll axis to within an inch or so of the road surface. The result of the new hub carriers at the back, combined with the employment of the drive shafts as upper suspension arms, kept the outside

Top left: Jack Brabham was ready to take the Cooper team to victory when conditions favoured the lightweight, mid-engined layout the Coopers had used since manufacturing motor cycle engined 500 cc cars.

Above: John Cooper points anxiously the direction Jack Brabham should take in the British Grand Prix at Silverstone. Together with mechanics 'Noddy' Grohman, Mike Barney, and 'Ginger' Devlin, he is encouraging Brabham to catch up on the leading BRM. The signal means placed second, 2 seconds behind, with seven laps to go. The entreaty was successful. Brabham won the race, and a second world championship.

rear wheel, to which the weight of the car was transferred on corners, vertical. The full area of its tyre contact patch gripped the road surface on corners, transmitting braking or accelerating torque more efficiently than any previous arrangement.

The Lotus was, in short, a revelation. It did not appear at the first race of the season, the Grand Prix of Argentina in February, where Bruce McLaren followed up his Sebring success of the previous year by winning his second Grand Prix in a row. Instead, it won at Monaco in May, in the wet, on its first appearance—a feat which Chapman would repeat more than once during the course of a distinguished Grand Prix career.

At Zandvoort, Moss (Lotus) came fourth after dropping to the back of the field following a puncture, and Jack Brabham scored the first of five victories that would give him the world title. Moss, alas, broke both legs during practice for the next race, the tragic Belgian Grand Prix in June, when a stub axle failed. He came back at the end of the season, and beat the Coopers in the United States Grand Prix at Riverside, California; but Brabham had the title securely in his pocket, and the season became yet another sorry chapter in the history of Moss, the greatest driver never to win the world championship.

By then the mood of the season had deteriorated with one row over the new formula, and another concerning Monza. The Italian Grand Prix organisers reinstated the 1955 banked track, and planned to run the 1960 Grand Prix on the combined road and track course. Unfortunately, the Grands Prix of 1955 and 1956 had shown that the two sorts of track were incompatible, the tyre and suspension characteristics necessary for racing on one proving unsatisfactory, and even dangerous, on the other.

Still, the Monza authorities insisted. The Grand Prix must run on both. There was widespread suspicion that the high-speed circuit was perceived as perhaps the last opportunity for a victory by the front-engined Ferraris. The new, rear-engined versions were still not ready. The Anglo-Saxon invasion by the Vanwalls and their like had been a bitter enough pill to swallow, but now the hordes of little, rear-engined cars seemed to be spoiling Italians' traditional appreciation of a sport which they still tended to regard as their own. It did not seem like sharp practice, to try and gain a little advantage for the home team. The organisers' concern was probably not so much the result of pure chauvinism, as an anxiety to provide hope for a home win to large numbers of potential spectators.

The British boycotted Monza. It was not only inconvenient for them, but with the newer, less robust cars on the bumpy banking, the heavy g loadings would have been unacceptably dangerous. Phil Hill led home a procession of Ferraris to a hollow victory.

Hill and Richie Ginther, both Americans, were amongst the new drivers making their name at Ferrari, together with the German, von Trips, and the former Lotus driver, Cliff Allison. Dan Gurney was driving for BRM together with Bonnier and Graham Hill. He had graduated from sports cars after starting off as a mechanic, and later became a driver with Lotus. Innes Ireland, the Scottish sports car driver, led for Team Lotus, losing his colleague Alan Stacey in the catastrophic Belgian race after being struck in the face by a bird at 140 mph. Another young British driver, Chris Bristow (Cooper-Climax), died when he went off the road racing Willy Mairesse (Ferrari). It was the only Grand Prix of modern times to suffer two fatal accidents, which followed Moss's mishap during practice, and injuries to Mike Taylor (Lotus-Climax) in his first Grand Prix when the steering column broke. It was a distressing dêbut for another young driver, who had already developed a dislike of Spa with the death there the previous year of the immensely brave and popular Scottish driver Archie Scott-Brown. The newcomer was a compatriot, 25-year-old Jim Clark.

There was also a new make of car in 1960, which, alas, only made the history books as the last conventional front-engined racing car to take part in a world championship Grand Prix. This was the Scarab, built and financed by the wealthy American Lance Reventlow, and driven by him and Chuck Daigh. It had all the ingredients expected of a modern Grand Prix car, a tubular frame, and a sloper four-cylinder engine, with expensively-developed desmodromic valves like those of the W 196 Mercedes-Benz. But it had taken too long to put on the road, and needed a Chevrolet gearbox when it made its appearance at Monaco, two years too late to have any hope of success.

Despite the wrangles of 1960, the 2½-litre Formula was, generally speaking, a success. Design and engineering were in a lively condition, world-wide interest had been sustained, and the racing was closer than it had ever been. The traditionalists continued to mourn the passing of the pit stop, and maintained that the rear-engined cars had not the visual appeal of their predecessors. The new cars' road holding tended to make them less spectacular, but the Formula, all in all, was so successful that many people wanted to keep it.

As late as the closing months of 1960, nobody knew for certain how the new year, and the new Formula were going to develop.

The racing Coopers

The British 500 cc movement not only nurtured many of the new British drivers—it also witnessed the birth of the unlikeliest world champion team of all.

Charles Cooper had been racing mechanic to Kaye Don, racing and record-breaking motorist of the period between the wars. When the class for motor-cycle engined, single-cylinder cars began after the war, Charles cobbled one up for his son, John, its chassis built from the halves of scrap Fiat 500 'Topolinos', welded together, back to back. That is to say all four wheels were independently suspended, using a high-mounted transverse leaf spring, and a lower wishbone to each wheel, with a telescopic shock absorber. The engine was a JAP Speedway.

Nearly all subsequent Coopers were built to much the same recipe, namely independent suspension all round, rear engine, and from 1952, a chassis of welded steel tubes. The 500 cc car was such a success that orders for replicas flowed in, including one from Stirling Moss. Over the years, the little single-seaters with the alloy wheels were refined, slimmed, lightened, and success followed success. Indeed, it was largely due to the overwhelming mastery of the Cooper marque that the class lost popularity and died.

The Coopers' engineering was largely instinctive, and surprisingly often dead right. They made their cars by taking the previous design, and adding a bit here, or taking off a bit there as seemed appropriate. Proper engineering drawings only came much later, the byword for production was expediency, and changes of a radical nature such as the abandonment in 1958 of the transverse leaf spring were only carried out when they became absolutely unavoidable.

Coopers were not noted for their sophistication. Most of the sports-racing cars followed the same established pattern, including the bob-tailed car which Brabham adapted for Formula 1. Its distinctive rear was later rumoured to owe less to the theories of the distinguished Professor Kamm, than to John Cooper's anxiety that it should fit the transporter.

It was 1960 before the Coopers caught up with features which their rivals considered imperative, such as chassis frames made entirely from straight tubes, triangulated in the classic manner. Previous Coopers had used curved tubes to the horror of more formally trained engineers, but with no apparent ill effects. The rear suspension of the Formula 1 cars was altered to double wishbones and coil springs, an anti-roll bar was fitted, and also disc brakes.

Amongst the Coopers' better commercial deals was one with BMC (British Motor Corporation) to put their name on a special version of the Mini, which was raced in the Coopers' livery of dark green, with two longitudinal white stripes up the bonnet. The little saloons' amazing road holding and almost indecent speed somehow epitomised the effect of the Cooper in Formula 1. They had the same unnerving impertinence in their cheerful challenge to the Establishment, and their effortless, winning ways.

1961

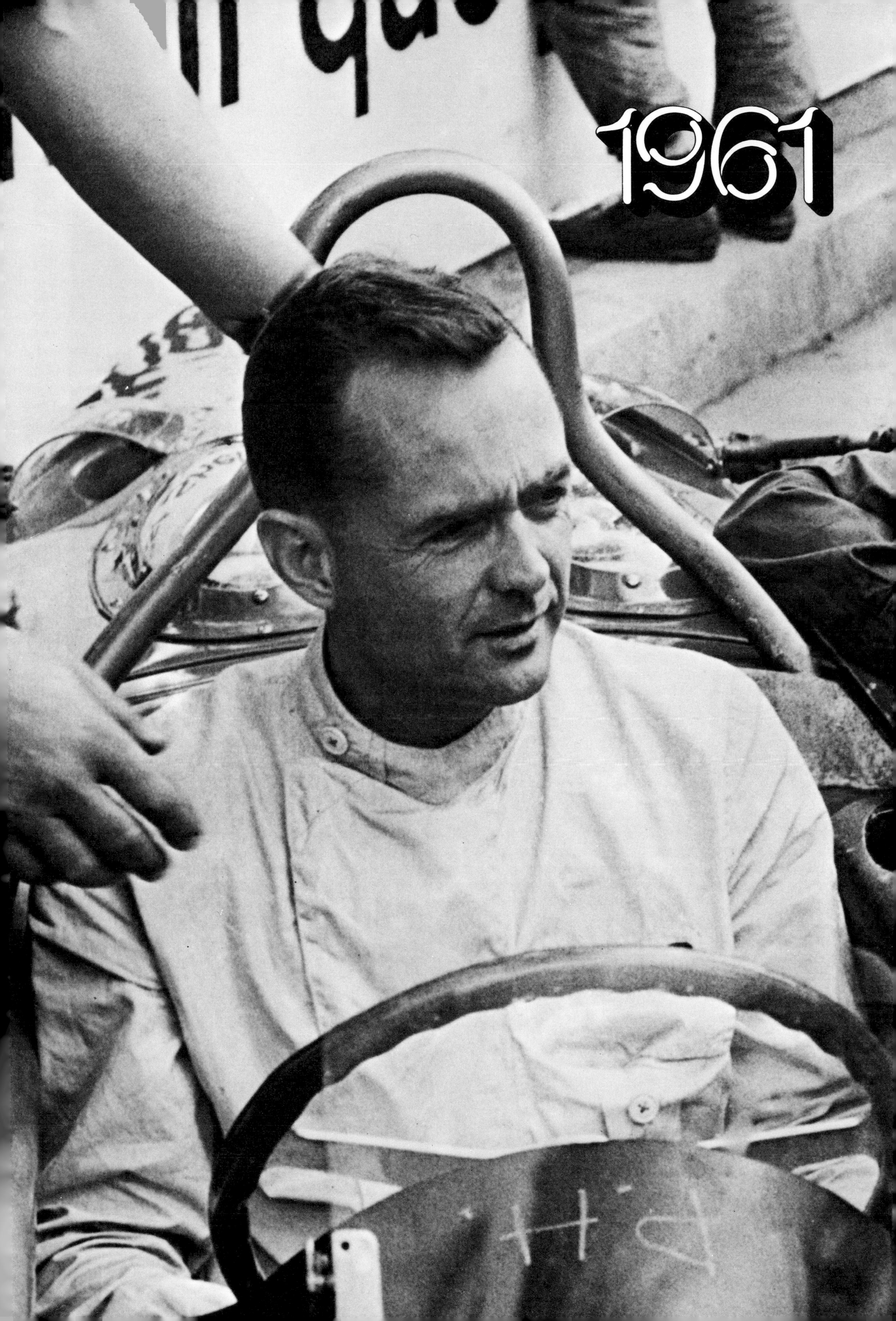

1961

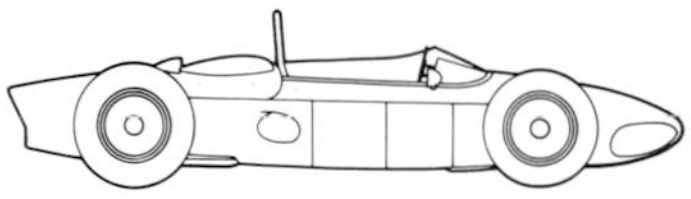

The closing years of the 2½-litre Formula had seen the rise of the proprietary engine, and in the final season Coventry-Climax won every race with the exception of the unrepresentative Italian Grand Prix. The British constructors' almost complete dependence on Coventry-Climax became the basis of their opposition to change. There was no equivalent source of 1½-litre engines in prospect, and they saw their new-found success in danger of slipping away.

So, when the FIA, in one of their perennial exercises aimed at putting European and American racing on the same footing, suggested an alternative 3-litre Formula in which both could take part, the British greeted the idea with enthusiasm. Jack Brabham already had an entry for Indianapolis, and with any luck, a world-wide shift to the Inter-Continental Formula as it came to be known, seemed likely to follow.

A few of the Continental race organisers hinted that they might be prepared to run their Grands Prix for 3-litre cars should sufficient support be forthcoming. Ferrari suggested he might build a 3-litre single-seater using one of his sports car engines. And following the precedent of 1952–3, when Formula 2 had been co-opted despite not being the officially prevailing Formula 1, Inter-Continental might conceivably have followed suit. Some race promoters shared the British view that the 1½-litre cars might be dull to watch, and preferred to keep their options open, so for different reasons, all parties kept the idea of Inter-Continental alive.

A number of things brought matters to a head. The first was a refusal by Coventry-Climax to make a larger version of their four-cylinder engine. They built a 2750 cc edition for Brabham's Indianapolis attempt, but considered it unsuitable for enlargement to the full 3 litres. They did, however, hold out hope for a continuation of the Cooper and Lotus series of successes by undertaking the design of a new 1½-litre V-8. They had tried a V-8 once before, principally for Connaught in 1954–5 but their participation in Formula 1 had not been on the same level then. They were worried lest the new 1½-litre would prove unsuccessful, so although it would not be raceworthy until nearly the end of 1961, it held out the promise that British constructors would not be left high and dry.

The matter was decided for Ferrari at a non-championship race in April, the Syracuse Grand Prix, the same race which had set such a trend with Tony Brooks's victory for Connaught in 1955. Ferrari had had a drubbing in recent years, and it was probably lack of confidence that worried him about a 1½-litre Formula, until he tried out a new version of the V-6 Dino engine at Syracuse. The full Cooper, Lotus, and BRM teams had hurried there from the Aintree 200, and were expected to walk all over the solitary Ferrari, a works car lent out to an unknown Italian, Giancarlo Baghetti. He had been sponsored for the drive by some public-spirited Italians in their search for someone to replace their lost generation of Ascari, Musso, and Castellotti.

An astonished 27-year-old Baghetti beat not only the British, but also a hard-driving Dan Gurney's Porsche, and at once it was clear that if an inexperienced newcomer could win so convincingly, then Ferrari had nothing to worry about for the rest of the season.

The secret lay in the disposition of the cylinders of the V-6 at 120° instead of 60°, which not only made the engine lower, but also provided inherently better balance for higher rpm and more power. With his customary optimism Ferrari suggested it was already developing 190 bhp, but the true figure for the start of the season was probably nearer 180–5 bhp. Yet it was still substantially better than the existing four-cylinder Climax, and almost as good as the so far unraced V-8.

Ferrari quickly made up his mind. A formidable team of cars was put in hand for Phil Hill, Count von Trips, Richie Ginther, and Willy Mairesse. No new 3-litre cars suitable for Inter-Continental were making their appearance, so the race organisers began to come out in favour of the 1½-litre Formula 1, and the dithering British found themselves racing last year's Formula 2 cars (they had nothing else ready) whether they liked it or not.

The opening championship round in the middle of May allayed any fears that the new smaller cars might fail to provide exciting motor racing. At the Monaco Grand Prix beside the warm waters of the Mediterranean, in spring sunshine, Stirling Moss put on one of the best drives of his career in a memorable race. He showed that despite the apparent uniformity of the new 1½-litre cars, an outstanding driver was still capable of influencing the result.

His entrant was Rob Walker, a wealthy member of the Johnnie Walker whisky family who had himself raced at Brooklands, and continued taking part in speed events and hill climbs right up to 1957. Besides a notable collection of cars, he owned the RRC Walker Racing Team based at Dorking in Surrey, employing a number of distinguished drivers including Peter Collins and Tony Brooks, who drove a variety of highly competitive cars in their distinctive Scottish blue.

At Monaco, Walker had both a Cooper and a Lotus 18 for Moss to choose from. He was unable to provide him with the latest Lotus 21 because Colin Chapman's team was retained by Esso, and Walker's by BP, and Esso refused to allow their rival the best equipment. It was the thin edge of a commercial wedge that would steadily be driven home as racing became ever more dependent on sponsorship, and less on sportsmanship.

With his year-old car Moss was at an obvious disadvantage. Against the new Ferraris with their flared 'nostril' air intakes, the blue Lotus seemed to have no chance. Ginther set a blistering pace during the opening stages with the 120° car, and five laps passed before Moss appeared composed enough to reply. By lap eight he was only 1½ sec behind, with Bonnier in pursuit driving one of the silver Porsches with fuel injection (but drum brakes), and it took the pair a further five laps to break the tough little Californian's concentration and get past.

Ginther was small and determined; he had been a passenger to Phil Hill in a 4.1-litre Ferrari in the Carrera Panamericana, the famous Mexican road race, and Hill took him to Ferrari as a test driver. Bonnier was unable to keep up as the other two works Ferraris came through to back Ginther. The best practice lap stood to Moss at 1 min 39.1 sec with the car unencumbered with fuel, the track clear, and conditions at their best. The pace was now 1 min 37.0 sec, and on lap 84 Ginther did 1 min 36.3 sec, to which Moss replied on lap 85, with—1 min 36.3. Together they were a tenth of a second off the best time round Monaco recorded by a racing 2½ litre.

Moss won, an achievement only the best driver in the world could pull off on a circuit where a masterly performance could still make a difference. He was in the prime of his career: he could lap the entire field on a wet Silverstone during the Inter-Continental BRDC International Trophy race, and he even won the German Grand Prix on the Nürburgring later in the season with a further display of virtuosity. The rest of the year, however, belonged to Ferrari, and they won more or less as they pleased. Among their victories was von Trips and Hill at Zandvoort in a remarkable race unique in the annals of the world championship because all the 15 starters completed the distance non-stop, nobody retired, no car came into the pits, eight were on the same lap as the winner, and the margin between first and second was less than 1 sec. Uniformity, it seemed, had arrived.

At Spa, in high summer, the Ferraris finished in the first four places. Baghetti, showing all the signs of being a skilled and gifted driver in the face of great provocation from the established aces, won the French Grand Prix. It was a rather more knife-edged affair with the works cars retiring, and the tyro narrowly saving the day by a tenth of a second from Dan Gurney's Porsche on the final straight. Unfortunately, it was to no avail: at the end of the next season Ferrari failed to exercise his option on him, and Baghetti's meteoric career was virtually over. Teams who might have signed him were inclined to give the credit to the car, and the sad, talented Italian was forgotten in the hurly-burly, unforgiving high-speed world of Formula 1.

Count Berghe von Trips, the first German to win a Grand Prix for 22 years (his victory at Zandvoort 16 years after the end of the war was greeted with little enthusiasm by the Dutch spectators) won again at Aintree in the rain. The race saw the first four-wheel-drive Grand Prix car built for ten years, the Ferguson P 99, make an inconclusive appearance in the hands of Jack Fairman and Moss. The decade would nearly be out before the experiment was repeated.

The first example of the new Coventry-Climax V-8 engine was secured by Jack Brabham for the German Grand Prix at the Nürburgring, and he made the front row of the grid with it. Eagerly awaited by all the other English constructors, they eyed it enviously but only briefly, for Brabham went off the road on the first lap. Moss had another at Monza, where the British overcame their reservations concerning the banked track, and BRM gave theirs its first outing, as well, but neither were ready for real racing. In any case everything was overshadowed by the death there of von Trips, together with 14 spectators in a horrifying accident, which proved worrisome for years to come. Season after season, whenever Clark and the equally hapless Colin Chapman were in Italy, they were subjected to endless questioning in an effort to discover some scapegoat for the tragedy. As it was, it bereft Grand Prix racing of its potential world champion, and Phil Hill took the title in a way which did less than justice to his thoughtful, dedicated driving over the season, probably a more accomplished performance, given his highly strung

The nose of Phil Hill's Ferrari dips under, braking for the Station Hairpin at Monte Carlo. In the background the Hotel Mirabeau, later demolished, which gave its name to the preceding Mirabeau Corner. But the corners of the tight little circuit round the Principality gave Stirling Moss a chance to show his mastery, and the Ferraris finished second and third to his Lotus.

Carlo Chiti (left) with Phil Hill. The Ferrari engineer later led the breakaway ATS team, and subsequently was in charge of Alfa Romeo engine development.

Phil Hill (b 1927)

Victory at Monza in 1960 made Phil Hill the first American to win a classic Grand Prix since 1921, when Jimmy Murphy won the French Grand Prix in a Duesenberg. In 1961 Hill also became the first American world champion.

Born in 1927 in Miami, Florida, and brought up in Santa Monica, California, Hill began racing with an MG TC, and although he gained the world title, probably had an even more outstanding career as a sports car driver. He won Le Mans (with Olivier Gendebien) three times, 1958–61–2, in Ferraris, on the last occasion breaking Hawthorn's five-year-old lap record.

Amongst his other great victories in sports cars were the 1958 Sebring 12 Hours and the Buenos Aires 1000 Kms (with Peter Collins); the 1959 and 61 Sebring 12 Hours (with Gendebien); the 1960 Buenos Aires 1000 Kms (with Allison); and the Nürburgring 1000 Kms (1962 with Gendebien, 1966 with Bonnier). In 1967 he won the BOAC 6 Hours at Brands Hatch with Mike Spence in the winged Chaparral 2E.

The championship was nonetheless one of the pinnacles of Hill's career. The inevitable quarrel with Ferrari followed, and Hill left at the end of the next season, along with Ing Chiti and team manager Tavoni in favour of the ill-fated ATS project.

Hill was taken on by Ferrari in 1955 to drive sports cars and found Formula 1 always promised him but taking years to come about. When it did, Hill discovered the political difficulties in the team resulting largely from the tortuous lines of communication between the race track and the cool, dark, bare office in Marenello where Enzo Ferrari brooded with the photograph of his dead son, never seeing a race. An autocrat to his fingertips, Ferrari would furiously demand an explanation from the engineers when the cars went wrong. It was years before Hill discovered they usually blamed the driver.

Yet the most difficult feature of his Formula 1 seasons with Ferrari was probably the manner in which drivers were drawn into conflict with one another, and sometimes also with the engineers. The Commendatore clearly believed that in order to get the best out of the individuals in the team, their combative nature had to be exploited. Thus, he refused to designate a number one driver—one with the right to the best car, to lead the team and to gain the best chance of the championship.

The pressure was intensely wearing; more so following the accident in which von Trips met his death, throwing Hill into a turmoil of indecision and despair. He agreed to remain with Ferrari for 1962, but after finding he could not get on with the new team manager Dragoni and the engineer Forghieri, who replaced the ATS defectors, and discovering the 1962 car even more difficult to handle than the 1961 had been, Hill left.

The ATS foundered, and although Hill remained at the wheel until 1967, still driving from time to time in Formula 1, his Grand Prix virtually finished the last time he stepped out of a Ferrari. Articulate, sensitive, cultured, if sometimes irascible, Hill's essential talent was probably not so obvious in 1961 as it appears by hindsight. Ferrari ought to have given him a Grand Prix car many years before he did, but instead surrounded Formula 1 with so much mystique that the Californian wasted time before coming to grips with it. Given that time, he might have been amongst the great Grand Prix drivers.

nature, even than that of the late von Trips, the mature, polished professional.

Inter-Continental was quietly forgotten. The little $1\frac{1}{2}$-litre cars provided closer racing than before, so the race organisers were happy. The British had not entirely lost the initiative, and the new V-8 promised well for the new season. The FIA recognised that the time was still not ripe for a unification of European and American racing, and Ferrari's decision to stick with the official Formula was vindicated. Jack Brabham's foray to Indianapolis seemed only moderately successful at the time; he was ninth with his little rear-engined car in a field of fierce-looking Indy roadsters, and the expedition probably did little to improve his poor season with the Cooper in Formula 1. Yet it did show that some cross-referencing on each side of the Atlantic in the manner cherished by the FIA *was* possible although not in the formal way envisaged by Inter-Continental. In the long term, some cross-pollination was inevitable, but the lessons Brabham learnt were not wasted. Quietly, they were absorbed by the rising genius of the motor racing world, Colin Chapman.

The surprise of the 1961 season lay at the end. The United States Grand Prix on its new, permanent course in the hills above the picturesque small town in upstate New York, Watkins Glen, saw the first victory in a world championship race for Team Lotus. Moss had already won at Monaco and on the Nürburgring in a Lotus car, but this was the first time the works team had prevailed—a team which henceforward would virtually write the history of Grand Prix racing. It was also the first, and as it turned out the only victory for Innes Ireland, the colourful, skilled, but sometimes brittle Scottish driver who had unfortunately little opportunity to enjoy his laurels. He recovered from his early-season Monaco accident and gave Lotus a brilliant victory in the non-title Solitude Grand Prix, but after Watkins Glen he was sacked by Chapman, who believed he had found someone better. Chapman never kept a component on his cars, or a member in his team on whom he thought he could improve, and it was Ireland's misfortune that he happened to be in the same team as another brilliant natural driver in the mould of Nuvolari, Fangio, and Moss—Jim Clark.

Formula 1—the 1961 regulations

Taking effect at the beginning of 1961, and intended to last until the end of 1963 but later extended for a further two years, the new Grand Prix Formula specified engines between 1300 cc and 1500 cc, and for the first time superchargers were specifically forbidden. The new code called for 'pump' fuel as defined by the CSI's Technical Committee, which meant in practice that the new commercially available premium fuels of around 100 octane replaced Avgas. A minimum weight of 450 kg/approx 990 lb or 8.9 cwt was specified not only to discourage designers from employing expensive alloys so that costs might be contained but also, hopefully, so that they would desist from the flimsy cars about which the legislators were becoming increasingly worried. Lotus in particular were suspect following breakages, such as occurred in the Belgian Grand Prix the previous year.

The CSI were still essentially distrustful of the new wave in Grand Prix racing. They still spoke French, and the French texts of the regulations were still the ones which were invoked in the event of a dispute. There remained a residue of suspicion over the new and very lightweight engineering with which Colin Chapman was so closely identified together with, by implication, the other English radicals. Chapman had also shown great talent at building cars to the letter of any regulations which the CSI cared to write, not something found commendable in the cloistered councils of the august.

Many of the changes which came in with the new regulations were aimed at making racing safer. The Le Mans disaster, and the fatal accidents which had punctuated every season since, had brought the matter to everyone's attention. The CSI saw their duty clearly. This was not only out of a regard for safety for its own sake, but they had to bear in mind the energetic anti motor racing lobby which, for example in Italy, was capable of uniting the Roman Catholic Church and the Communist Party in seeking its wholesale and immediate prohibition.

Circuits had been forced to spend money on improvements, in particular to the pits areas. Corners had been eased, and spectators moved back, and now it was felt it was the turn of the cars. Unhappily, not every innovation had its intended effect. Some indeed turned out to be downright dangerous.

Stationary cars had always been a hazard both on the starting grid, or stalled following a spin, so self-starters seemed a good idea. They had been a feature of sports car racing for years, but required single seaters to have a battery for the first time, a small 12-volt dry cell unit usually tucked under the driver's knees. But this created the new danger of electrical fires despite the mandatory master switches.

Seat belt attachments were demanded although there was as yet no obligation on drivers to wear them. Some, notably Stirling Moss, would have refused, still clinging to the belief that it was better to be thrown out in an accident. The first roll-over safety bar was specified, but not its dimensions, and the frail little hoops which appeared would have been quite useless in the event of a car overturning. Bodywork likely to impede the driver leaving in case of emergency was forbidden, and so was bodywork between the wheels. Dual braking systems were demanded, and in a well-merited recognition of the dangers inherent in the fuel now in use, fillers and breathers were made to conform with certain minimum standards. Oil replenishment was no longer allowed during races, preventing leaky cars being topped up, only to spill more for others to skid on.

Minimum race length remained at 300 km, or two hours, with the maximum at 500 km. Nine races were scheduled, the championship points scoring was amended to 9, 6, 4, 3, 2, and 1 for the first six finishers, the point for fastest lap was scrapped, and only a driver's five best performances were counted. Indianapolis, always an anomaly, was at last dropped from the table.

Monaco, the contenders

The opening race of the new season, the Monaco Grand Prix, demonstrated the enthusiasm for the new formula amongst entrants. Over-subscribed entry lists were to be a regular source of trouble. This was particularly true in the restricted conditions of the principality with its newly installed, glamorous Princess Grace.

The Monaco starters were limited to 16, and for 1961 each works team was guaranteed two cars. Most were coming round in any case to the notion of two-car teams which was as much as they could cope with during an ever busier season. At Monaco these were as follows:

Cooper: Jack Brabham and Bruce McLaren
Lotus: Innes Ireland and Jim Clark
BRM: Tony Brooks and Graham Hill
Ferrari: Phil Hill and Count von Trips
Porsche: Jo Bonnier and Dan Gurney

Stirling Moss (RRC Walker Racing Team Lotus) qualified for one of the guaranteed places as a past winner of the race, and so did Maurice Trintignant with his privately entered Cooper-Maserati. This made twelve, leaving four places on the starting grid to be fought for on the basis of practice times amongst:

Richie Ginther (third works Ferrari)
Hans Herrmann (third works Porsche)
Olivier Gendebien and Lucien Bianchi (Ecurie National Belge Emerysons)
Masten Gregory (Cooper)

Michael May (Lotus), and the cars of the two new British hire purchase teams. These comprised UDT-Laystall running Lotuses for Cliff Allison, making a painful recovery from his injuries of the previous year and Henry Taylor, and Yeoman Credit managed by Reg Parnell and running Coopers of which one was driven by John Surtees. In all, 21 cars practised, the non-qualifiers turning out to be the Emerysons, Masten Gregory in his old Cooper, Innes Ireland who crashed heavily the day before the race, and Henry Taylor whose car gave trouble.

Count 'Taffy' von Trips who would probably have been world champion in 1961 but for his tragic accident at Monza.

C A S Brooks (b 1932)

During the winter of 1961–2 Tony Brooks announced he was retiring from Grand Prix racing. Overshadowed by Moss and Hawthorn, Brooks was nevertheless instrumental in the development of the British presence in Formula 1 racing. A dental student when he began racing in 1952 with a Healey Silverstone, Brooks fell into that rare category of 'natural' drivers who seem to have been born with exactly the right deftness, acuity of vision, or speed of reaction that fitted them for driving a racing car.

Without ever having raced abroad, or driven a Formula 1 car before, Brooks won his famous victory for Connaught in 1955 against a full team of Maseratis, thrice breaking Marimon's 1954 lap record. It was an amazing feat and swept him into the BRM and subsequently the successful Vanwall team. Out of his 38 Grands Prix, Brooks shared one win with Moss and won five on his own, gained three pole positions, and three fastest laps. His best place in the world championship came in 1959 at the age of 27 when he was with Ferrari, and had just married an Italian girl.

Equally skilled in sports cars, Brooks drove for Aston Martin, winning the Nürburgring 1000 Kms in 1957 and sharing a TT with Moss. But in Formula 1 he began to miss the power of the big 2½-litre cars, and with his garage business in the shadow of the old Brooklands track to look after, he gave up. Quietly spoken and gentle in manner, Brooks could nevertheless be a determined driver on the track in a stylish, undramatic, precise way that put him amongst the best drivers of his time.

1962

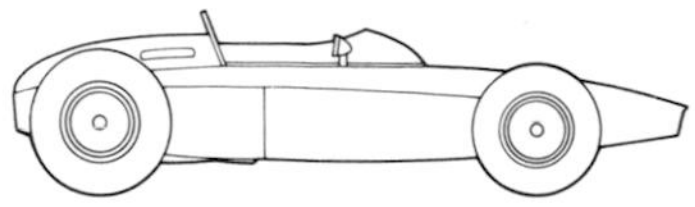

After the season of Ferrari glory in 1961, there followed their almost total eclipse. The Commendatore staged one of his dramatic withdrawals from racing in September, a month later than usual, then suffered the loss of his key staff at the turn of the new season. Even though the team was announced with the customary *brio*, with new cars and improved 120° V-6 engines (and a four-valve version to come) it was destined not to be another Ferrari year.

The Coventry-Climax V-8 was coming on stream, and BRM had their V-8 almost operational, although of the three engines the Ferrari was still certainly the best developed. Porsche's horizontally opposed eight cylinder remained in the offing, giving the season a new openness. No longer every January could the pundits reach agreement on form. No longer was there one make, or perhaps two, on which to lay a safe bet. Up to half a dozen teams could now start a season with much the same chance of success.

It still seemed inconceivable that Ferrari could go through the year without a win, for the first time (except for 1957) since the year after the Championship began. There was consolation in the sports car field and the newly established if somewhat nebulous GT category of racing, but in Formula 1 they faced a bleak prospect.

The British now had no fewer than four leading teams, Lotus, Cooper, BRM, and Lola and by the start of the season proper, the first named of these had introduced a new model that once again would lay down the criteria for racing car design for years to come. For the second time in as many seasons (and not for the last time) Colin Chapman produced a car which every other constructor would sooner or later imitate. Within a few months almost every other team would, somewhat sheepishly, produce a car which copied the principal features of the Lotus, in this case the so-called monocoque of the Mark 25, probably the most elegant, and best-proportioned single-seat racing car ever made.

Cooper found themselves without Jack Brabham in 1962 when he decided to break away and form his own Brabham racing organisation, Motor Racing Developments, along with his fellow Australian Ron Tauranac as designer. Brabham appeared first with a Lotus until his own car was ready. As back-up driver for Bruce McLaren, Cooper took on Tony Maggs, a young South African who had been driving for Ken Tyrrell's apprentice school team of Formula Junior Coopers. The new Formula 1 Cooper was lower, but rather bulkier than its rivals, and did not promise to be as light as the Lotus—indeed nothing was.

Most teams intended to run two cars, but contrary to the trend Ferrari announced three drivers, Phil Hill, Giancarlo Baghetti, and 20-year-old Ricardo Rodriguez, the elder of wealthy Mexican brothers who had been racing Ferraris since they were sixteen. Ferrari also announced six-speed gearboxes and an adjustable link in the rear suspension so that the rear wheel toe-in could be quickly adjusted, following Brabham's example in the new art of 'chassis tuning', although at the time it looked more like indecisiveness over design than anything else.

BRM chief engineer, and architect of Graham Hill's world championship victory, Tony Rudd (left) with Richie Ginther.

There was an important change at BRM. Not only was Tony Rudd now chief engineer, but Alfred Owen, who had been responsible for financing the team since the collapse of the BRM Trust, had issued an ultimatum. BRM, he said, must win two Grand Prix races, *and* remain within their budget, or face closure within six months.

BRM was almost as beset as Ferrari with internal disputes and rivalries, but Rudd was given a free hand to deal with the administrative problems and get on with the job of winning. Richie Ginther joined them from Ferrari to replace Tony Brooks, Graham Hill was kept on, and the new car opened the season at the BRDC 'May Silverstone' with a dramatic victory on the very last corner of the International Trophy race. Hill overtook Jim Clark a matter of yards from the chequered flag, lifting the morale of the team to heights it had not reached since its creation 14 years before.

It set the pattern for the season. Hill and Clark fought out the championship round by round, but alas without intervention from Stirling Moss. At the Goodwood Easter Monday meeting Moss received injuries which not only kept him out of racing for the remainder of the season, but ended his distinguished career.

Graham Hill scored his first championship Grand Prix victory on a track that had been kind to BRM already, Zandvoort. With the BRM's distinctive, tall stackpipe exhausts (later replaced to improve the V-8's torque curve) he beat Clark's new Lotus 25 which had led for the first eleven laps, but had been delayed with trouble in the ZF gearbox.

At round two in June, Clark gained pole position on the grid and set fastest lap, but the Monaco Grand Prix was a race the great Scottish driver was destined never to win. On this occasion he suffered gearbox trouble once again while Hill, who was to make Monaco his special stamping ground, led until eight laps from the end when his engine blew up and laid an oily trail down to the station hairpin.

The Belgian Grand Prix at Spa was close, with Clark scoring his first Grand Prix victory and setting fastest lap, but Hill's second place gave him the lead in the world championship. At Rouen for the French Grand Prix there were no Ferraris, Clark went out with suspension trouble, Hill with a broken fuel injection pump, leaving Gurney to prove just how open the season was by scoring both his *and* Porsche's first Grand Prix victory. Three races had provided three first-time winners.

At Aintree, amidst the industrial environment of Liverpool, Clark made no mistakes, and his car ran faultlessly. He gained pole position in practice, set fastest lap, and led all the way; Chapman could ask no more of his brilliant young driver than that. Hill was fourth, but he still led the championship with 19 points to Clark's 18. The BRM held the edge on reliability, but if the Lotus kept going it invariably won.

Jack Brabham gave up his temporary Lotus 24 at the German Grand Prix on the Nürburgring, and became the first constructor-driver of modern times with his new Brabham Coventry-Climax, retiring after nine laps. He was still a giant in the Grand Prix world after his twin world titles, and always had the choice of the best engines Coventry-Climax could provide, so a great deal was expected of his new car—too much perhaps because running-in a new team takes time.

White paint on Jim Clark's wheels show how close he took his new Lotus 25 to the walls bordering the Monte Carlo track. Yet Monaco was a race the great Scottish driver was destined never to win.

As an indication of the growing number of cars available for world championship Formula 1 racing, no fewer than 29 were entered for the German Grand Prix, of which 26 started. Ferrari was able to field a fourth car driven by Lorenzo Bandini, Baghetti's rival for the 'scholarship' drive of the year before. Porsche had a third eight-cylinder car and there were private owners aplenty, emulating Formula Junior drivers from all over Europe who were coming to Britain to buy competitive cars rather than follow the chancier path of developing their own. The United Kingdom's prowess in Grand Prix racing was leading to the establishment of an entirely new industry. Firms were growing up all round the country to build, service, and repair racing cars, engines, and components for the amateur and semi-professional categories being established as a major leisure activity in Europe, South Africa, Australia, and North America.

Jim Clark accidentally knocked off the switch on his Bendix fuel pumps at the start of the German Grand Prix, the only time in the season when the car was let down by the driver, and it cost Clark dearly. He was left behind on the opening lap, but it was a characteristic of his driving that under such circumstances he felt it important to make amends, whether he had been to blame or not. On a wet track he worked his way back to fourth, before a lurid spin made him decide that enough was enough. Hill won his second victory of the season, and led the championship by 18 points to Clark's 21.

At Monza, Clark was again fastest in practice but he retired in the race, while BRM's already brimming cup of success overflowed with first *and* second places, and Hill had 37 points. As the season drew to a close, on the penultimate round of the championship, however, Clark replied in a closely fought race in which he and Hill lapped the entire field by three-quarters distance. The destination of the title now lay in the final round, the new South African Grand Prix at East London, on the shores of the Indian Ocean.

It had been a crowded season. Four Grands Prix, two of them full-length world championship races had been held on consecutive week-ends in July, another had been due on 9 September at Albi in South West France, but was cancelled when the Italian Grand Prix was moved to 16 September: nobody wanted to risk championship cars so close to a championship race, and the overcrowded nature of the calendar was called into question.

The European Grand Prix season was stretching, and this time the cliff-hanging championship went right to the end of December. Ferrari and Porsche did not go to South Africa. Porsche were getting jittery about Formula 1 and had released their drivers to go elsewhere in 1963. They had always been class winners in sports car racing, building up an impeccable reputation by doing well with smallish cars. Their days of outright wins at races such as Le Mans were still to come. They had won one Grand Prix with a little help from dropped-out leaders, but

BRM

The foundation of the BRM took place as early as March 1945 with the publication of a manifesto setting out the principles of running a co-operative racing car which would not have to depend on the patronage of wealthy individuals. Instead, the motor industry contributed collectively towards its support, expecting to gain prestige in proportion to the car's success.

With the BRM the opposite occurred, and the industry was amongst those berated for its failures. The original project foundered, and its assets were bought by Mr (later Sir) Alfred Owen on behalf of the industrial empire known as the Owen Organisation. This was outright ownership, not sponsorship which means payment by means of a fee, loan or grant towards a team's upkeep in return for advertising.

Contrary to the late Raymond Mays' original intention, however, it put BRM back into the lap of a wealthy individual, which had been the downfall of his ERA cars before the war. The BRM management turned out to be cumbersome and inefficient. Following the débâcle of the original V-16, the 2½ litre held out promise but little else during the years of the 2½-litre Formula. Turning out a real winner seemed beyond the capabilities of the team based at Bourne, Lincolnshire, in the grounds of the Mays family home. The cars were well engineered, well prepared, and well driven, but even lucky wins eluded them until the reorganisation and the famous ultimatum of 1962.

The principal architect of the recovery was Tony Rudd who, as a young engineer, had been loaned to BRM by Rolls-Royce to work on the V-16's supercharger, and stayed on. He was appointed team manager and chief engineer and told to get on with it, and win two championship Grand Prix races or face closure.

One of the most elegant BRMs was the Tresilian designed P25, driven here by Mike Hawthorn in the 2½-litre Formula.

After a series of good performances in the middle of 1962, Rudd felt confident enough to write to the ascetic Mr Owen concerning his plans for 1963, receiving a curt reply reminding him it was *two* Grands Prix. While the letter was in the post, however, the team won the German Grand Prix, their future was assured, and they were on their way to the world championship.

It proved to be the summit of the BRM's achievement. The V-8 was their greatest engine ever, winning the Monaco Grand Prix four times in a row—the final occasion in 1966 when it ran as a 2 litre in the first year of the 3-litre Formula. It was second in the 1962 United States Grand Prix, and won it each of the following three years. As a 2 litre it also won in the 1965 Tasman Series by winning seven of the eight races (it came second in the eighth) and BRM were runners-up in the world championship for every one of the three years that followed Hill's 1962 triumph.

The project had at last achieved what its founder Mays had intended albeit after a hard struggle and four years behind Tony Vandervell. It was too good to last. When the formula changed in 1966, BRM went into a decline from which it never recovered. Its moment of glory had passed and all the lessons painfully learnt about being small, wieldy and responsive were forgotten. Only Ferrari enjoyed a longer participation in Grand Prix racing than BRM—and had rather more to show for it.

Stirling Moss in the dark blue Rob Walker Lotus. The greatest driver never to win the world championship, Moss was driving a Lotus at the time of his near fatal accident in 1962.

Stirling Moss (b 1929)

A minor race in the Easter Monday Goodwood meeting of 1962 brought to an end the remarkable career of the best driver in England, and one of the greatest ever, Stirling Moss. His frustration at being runner-up in the world championship for four years in a row (1955–8) and third for a further three (1959–61) only showed in greater determination and energy. At the wheel of a Lotus equipped with a V-8 engine, with the Rob Walker team well-organised and competitive, Moss had never been in a better position than he was at the start of 1962.

But at Goodwood, where he had begun his great career at the age of 18, driving the Walker Lotus in the light green of the UDT team, he crashed. Moss was competing in the 42-lap Glover Trophy Race, and started from pole position, but the car was not running well, and he stopped with gear selector trouble, rejoining after three laps.

Moss believed in giving spectators their money's worth (and incidentally making some for himself) and set about breaking the lap record with the car, of which he expected so much in the season to come. But as he came up to overtake Graham Hill's BRM, by now firmly in the lead on the 35th lap, and with the record already equalled, Moss changed down into fourth, drew almost alongside, and on the entry to St Mary's corner, a 120 mph/approx 190 kph right hander, went charging across the grass before plunging at almost undiminished speed into the bank.

Why the greatest driver in the world was unable to mitigate the effects of leaving the track during the 60 yards or so before he hit the unyielding earth wall, remains inexplicable. Perhaps the engine failed, or the throttle stuck, but there was no firm evidence of either. The Lotus folded in two and Moss received serious head injuries, and damaged his shoulders, legs, and ribs. For several days his life hung in the balance, and his recovery took many painful months.

It was a year before he sat in a racing car again, a Lotus 19 in which he tested himself, to help make up his mind if the combination of eye and hand that had made him the greatest driver of his day were impaired. He decided they were, and at the age of 32 he had driven in his last professional motor race.

It was a decision later regretted, taken probably in the belief that had he carried on racing he might have been amongst the also-rans, something he would have been unable to bear. Reflecting on other drivers who recovered from accidents and lost none of their cunning, Moss could most likely have done the same. He chose not to, and although he remained close to racing he was never active in running his own team. He preferred instead the life of the freelance, which came to encompass many business enterprises, design projects, and journalism that kept his name very much alive in the years to come.

raced for commercial prestige on behalf of their road cars and they were not achieving it—a measure of how competitive it was becoming—so they quietly withdrew.

The difficulties of the championship scoring system came up again in South Africa. Hill had 43 points gross, 39 net, and Clark 30 either way. Hill had to forfeit two of his scores on the 'best five' principle, part of the championship small print designed to prevent one driver out-stripping everyone else. For the final race, therefore, Hill could increase his score only by winning. Clark too had no option but to win because he was nine points behind, and a win here would give him the title on the basis of four wins to Hill's three—the tie-decider. Hill had the consoling advantage that should Clark fail to finish the title was his no matter what happened.

Clark was on pole and led handsomely for 61 of the 82 laps before a puff of smoke from the twin tail pipes of the Climax V-8 portended trouble. The little green car rolled into the pits and Clark was out of the race. A tiny bolt had worked loose in the distributor housing, resulting in oil loss and disaster for the engine. The title belonged to 33-year-old Hill, with the colours of the London Rowing Club on his helmet, and BRM.

It had been a thrilling season for everyone except perhaps Ferrari who had not been seen since Monza, and whose collapse was completed by the departure of Phil Hill to join the breakaway faction at ATS. A Grand Prix without an Italian team or driver would have been unthinkable a few short years before, yet it happened twice in 1962. Almost the entire Grand Prix 'circus' had become British, and the drivers came mostly from England, South Africa, the United States, Scotland, Australia, and New Zealand. The revolution in racing, the change round in design, and the centre of pressure (but not the rock-like core of the CSI) had shifted to the very edge of the Continental shelf.

Jim Clark's first Grand Prix victory was the Belgian Grand Prix of 1962. He took the lead about one-third of the way through the race, and won Team Lotus their second victory—the first for the revolutionary Lotus 25.

Lotus 25

Chapman had, it seemed, only introduced the space frame Lotus 24 to try out a number of features for his real masterpiece, the Mark 25. In fact the 25 evolved from a flash of inspiration when Chapman was working on the backbone frame of the Lotus Elan sports car which itself originated as a jury-rig. He hit upon the idea of splitting the backbone frame in two and sitting the driver between the halves which could also act as fuel tanks. Locating rigid tanks in a tubular frame, which was continuously twisting and buckling, had always been a headache, but incorporating rubber bag tanks in his 'catamaran' hull on aluminium sheet riveted together in a style reminiscent of aircraft technology, seemed to be the answer. Furthermore the new V-8 with its strong crankcase had come along just at the right time for the monocoque development, and so had Team Lotus's rather short, slim drivers who fitted the narrow cockpit snugly, behind one of the smallest steering wheels, 12 in/30 cm across, ever seen on a modern racing car.

The term 'monocoque' is used to describe a car built with a stressed skin, box-like hull, literally shell-like, and the 25 was of such startling simplicity it was surprising that nobody had thought of it before. Chapman's tubular frames were already crammed with novelties, such as using the tubes to pipe cooling water and oil between the rear engine and the radiators at the front, to save the weight of the plumbing. But the tubular 24 was destined to be no more than a back-up, the car that was sold to customers in line with a works team's standard practice of keeping something with a little extra to themselves.

The 24 became no more than the prototype for the suspension, engine, transmission and wheels for the 25—the lowest, smallest, slipperiest Grand Prix car ever built. Glass reinforced plastic, already widely accepted as bodywork material, provided the neat cover on top of the bathtub-like hull, really two longitudinal fuel tanks, and the complete car scaled exactly the minimum weight which the sages of the FIA had considered the all-but-impossible irreducible minimum.

Chapman hung the front suspension coil spring and damper units inboard to take them out of the airstream and reduce drag. The success of the complete design can be demonstrated by comparison with the contemporary Brabham. With the engine in place, the Lotus monocoque would twist through one degree with the application of a force of 2400 lb ft; the comparable figure for the Brabham was only 1000 lb ft, allowing the Lotus vitally softer springs to help it most on slow corners.

Brabham retained the tubular space frame longer than anyone because in some senses it was more practical and easier to repair, but it was certainly not as safe. After Stirling Moss's accident in which the tubes trapped the driver for a life-risking half an hour, Jim Clark refused ever to race such a car again.

Most of the Lotus imitators did not have the confidence to build a complete monocoque right away. They preferred hybrids in which the engine remained within its own tubular frame, or the aluminium panels were used merely for stiffening. But while the others were making up their minds, the Lotus was already a generation ahead, and set for a record-breaking series of victories that left the Grand Prix world gasping.

1963

Jim Clark and the Lotus 25 proved almost invincible in 1963. He scored the maximum possible points in the world championship—a unique achievement—and by winning seven Grands Prix, established the record for the greatest number of victories in a season. Richie Ginther and Graham Hill (BRMs) shared second place, while the seeds of the following year's title were sown with the recruitment, by Ferrari, of John Surtees who finished in fourth place.

Amongst the losers of 1963 was the ATS team, accompanying the declining fortunes of the 1961 world champion Phil Hill, and Giancarlo Baghetti. Porsche confirmed their withdrawal, leaving Dan Gurney to join the consistently-improving Brabham team, and Jo Bonnier went to Rob Walker. Chris Amon came from New Zealand to join the Reg Parnell team and begin a 14-year Grand Prix career destined to be filled with distinguished second places. The British Racing Partnership's Lotus BRMs were driven by a waning Innes Ireland, and a waxing Swiss graduate of Formula Junior, Jo Siffert. They were joined by the Texan Jim Hall, who was to achieve fame later on, as the father of the Chaparral sports car.

The addition of the Mexican Grand Prix in November made the championship more worthy of its world title, and brought the number of qualifying races to ten.

Jim Clark's domination of the season did not begin straight away. Graham Hill won the opening race, the Monaco Grand Prix in May, in which he was becoming accustomed to doing well. His team, BRM, were delighted when Clark lost the lead and failed to finish after his gearbox broke. But on 9 June, Clark scored his second successive win in the Belgian Grand Prix at Spa-Francorchamps, despite appalling conditions. Several cars went off the road, in an uncomfortable reminder of the dangers of racing in the rain on that narrow ribbon of public highway in the Ardennes. The unpredictable nature of the weather, and the unguarded margins of Spa, still the fastest of the championship courses with a lap speed of well over 130 mph/approx 210 kph was already making it a target for safety critics. Chris Amon gained the distinction in this race of being the youngest driver ever to compete in a world championship Grand Prix, at the age of 19 years 324 days.

Later the same month, Clark won again, at Zandvoort in the Dutch Grand Prix, a lap ahead of the entire field. Dan Gurney brought Brabham an encouraging second place in a race that saw the début of a new Italian driver, Lodovico Scarfiotti. He was brought into the Ferrari team to replace Willy Mairesse who had been injured at Le Mans.

Despite a misfire, Clark was untouchable in the French Grand Prix at Rheims on 30 June. Graham Hill stalled on the start line and should have been disqualified for a push start, but his sentence was commuted to a minute's penalty, which allowed him to keep his third place, but forfeit his championship points.

Excitement in the British Grand Prix at Silverstone on 20 July was provided by the battle which developed for second place, behind the imper-

Left: Jim Clark (Lotus 25) on his way to winning the French Grand Prix at Rheims, his third in a row towards the 1963 world championship, and his fourth meeting on the same set of Dunlop tyres.

Right: Monaco, the opening stages of the Grand Prix, with Dan Gurney (Brabham-Climax) pursuing Jo Bonnier (Cooper-Climax) through the hairpin in front of the old Mirabeau Hotel. Gurney went out with transmission trouble, and Bonnier finished seventh.

turbable Clark. This was between John Surtees, getting into his stride with Ferrari, and Graham Hill. It was resolved only on the last lap, when Hill's BRM ran out of fuel and he coasted across the line to take third place.

Moving over to race cars has been a tempting step for racing motor cyclists ever since the days of Nuvolari, and the British Grand Prix witnessed the début of Mike Hailwood (Lotus) and Bob Anderson (Lola), who finished eighth and twelfth respectively. Hailwood subsequently went back to motor cycles, but it was yet another former motor cyclist—John Surtees—who interrupted Clark's series of victories the following month.

At the Nürburgring on 4 August, Surtees scored his first victory in a car Grand Prix, becoming the first driver in modern times to win Grand Prix races on two and four wheels. It was also the first victory for Ferrari for two years, their longest period of failure since the Formula 1 championship was established in 1950. Clark had trouble with his Coventry-Climax engine misfiring, and had to be content with second.

A worrying feature of the German race was an unexpected spate of accidents. Both Sciroccos (formerly Emerysons) crashed without injury to their drivers Tony Settember or Ian Burgess, and Count Carel de Beaufort was lucky to escape after rushing off from the pits, where his mechanics had just spotted that one of his wheels was in a dangerous condition. The wheel came off, and the impetuous Dutch driver was only just able to bring the car to a safe stop.

The luckless Mairesse, back in the Ferrari team, went off the road on the humpback following the Flugplatz, receiving further injuries to add to his Le Mans burns, this time bringing his career at the wheel to an end. Chris Amon landed up in hospital beside his fellow New Zealander Bruce McLaren as a result of accidents, although their injuries were not serious. And Lorenzo Bandini, steadily establishing himself as the most competitive driver in Italy, collided with Innes Ireland, eliminating his Italian entered BRM and also Ireland's Lotus.

It was concern over accidents like these that had led to the formal setting-up of the Grand Prix Drivers' Association (GPDA) at Monaco in 1961. With Stirling Moss as a founder member it was the successor to the earlier Union des Pilotes Professionels Internationaux (UPPI), and was concerned chiefly with safety and conditions for drivers. The GPDA organised a petition affecting the following race, the Italian Grand Prix at Monza on 8 September. The organisers intended to use the controversial banked track once again, but the drivers were against it. The matter was only resolved when the Italian police, still concerned about spectator safety in the aftermath of the 1961 von Trips tragedy, said arrangements on the banked sections of the track were inadequate, forcing the Automobile Club di Milano to revert to the 5.74 km/3.57 mile road circuit.

Graham Hill walks disconsolately back to the pits after completing 17 laps of the Belgian Grand Prix in second place, then retiring when his BRM's gearbox failed. Grinning mechanic on the left has reason to be pleased. He is Dick Scammell, in charge of Jim Clark's car which is heading for victory.

It made no difference to Clark, who won again after an exciting race, another real Monza slipstreamer, in which he shared the lead with Hill, Surtees, and Gurney. But Clark's luck was out at Watkins Glen for the United States Grand Prix on 6 October, when it was his turn to stall on the line. It was a testimony to his skill, and the handling and road-holding of the Lotus 25 that he was able to fight back, and in the course of 2 hr 20 min of racing, recover from 20th and last place to finish third. He started a lap and a half in arrears and might even have finished second, had not his engine given trouble towards the end.

Mexico on 3 November also belonged to Clark, with Brabham gaining another second place for his own make of racing car, a further indication that his new team was on the threshold of success. And in East London just after Christmas, Clark crowned a copybook season by gaining pole position on the grid of the South African Grand Prix, and leading it from start to finish.

He gained 73 points gross, and on the basis of his best six scores kept the maximum net possible, 54. Hill and Ginther tied with 29, and although Ginther actually scored 34, under the 'best six' rule, he was awarded third place owing to the tie-breaking clause, Hill's two outright wins giving him the advantage.

Arguments for change: the case for 1966

Technical progress during 1963 included the development by Coventry-Climax of a fuel injection system. This enabled the British constructors to compete effectively in engine power with the Ferraris, which had benefited from their close association with the carburettor firm founded by Ferrari's old friend, Eduardo Weber. BRM had six-speed gearboxes, and hulls built on a semi-monocoque basis, following the trend set by the Lotus 25. Yet the BRMs were not as light, low, or as narrow in cross-section as the Lotus, and proved less reliable.

On the legislative front, January 1963 saw proposals put forward for the change of Grand Prix formula due in 1966. Formula 2 in 1964–5 was to be for four-cylinder engines of 1000 cc in cars weighing 420 kg/926 lb and Formula Junior was due to be replaced by Formula 3. This was also for cars of 1000 cc, but with engines based on production units from homologated touring cars.

The application of production engines to Formula racing was significant. It inferred that Grand Prix racing could also use production engines, as a means of halting the rising spiral of costs. A Coventry-Climax V-8 was already £5000, and the investment and upkeep of a team met the income from starting money, only for those who were successful and won prize money as well. Bonuses from tyre and accessory manufacturers were a help, but they too only went to teams which won. It looked as though Grand Prix racing might price itself so highly that spectators would no longer be prepared to foot the bill.

So, it was felt that engines based on a production car, a large American V-8 for example, might lead to a reduction in costs. The major components would be standardised and cheap, and the large investment for the design and development of a pure racing engine would be unnecessary. In America, Can-Am racing was getting under way with production-based engines in big, exciting cars which, it was suggested, might have the additional advantage of tempting the major car manufacturers to endorse racing for publicity purposes.

As Can-Am was to show, however, turning production engines into racing engines was not always a cheap alternative. Stressing production components with racing power outputs tended to make them unreliable, and one of the most expensive parts of maintaining a racing team—the between-race overhaul—was by no means eliminated. So the traditionalists, calling for 'pure' racing engines, won the day. When the 1966 Formula arrived, it was for engines designed from the outset for maximum power, and two to three hours' duration, the very limits of engineering endurance at the lightest weight practicable. As yet, there were no thoughts about how they were going to be paid for.

What was clear, however, was that the doubts expressed about the $1\frac{1}{2}$-litre cars were in some respects justified. They presented no great spectacle, even though the racing was closer than ever. The cars were small, and since the change to rear engines and wide tyres, they appeared to corner as though on rails. The skill and precision with which they were driven was scarcely evident to the spectators, on whom the sport depended so heavily.

In an effort to give onlookers their money's worth, it was proposed to reverse the trend of post-war formulae, and increase engine size from $1\frac{1}{2}$ litres to 3 litres unsupercharged. Improvements in braking and road holding, it was felt, could now cope with the increase in power. After all, 3-litre sports cars were racing in large numbers apparently without running undue risks. Their existence was also a compromise offered to advocates of the production engine philosophy. With plenty of sports car engines around, there would be no need to design and develop expensive, new Formula 1 power units. The new Formula emerged with the principle that world championship Grand Prix racing *ought* to be for the most progressively engineered racing cars of all, more or less intact.

Dan Gurney on the far side (Brabham-Climax) gets off the line a fraction ahead of Jim Clark (Lotus-Climax No 18) and Graham Hill (BRM) as the front row moves off, tyres wreathed in smoke, at the start of the French Grand Prix. Clark proved the winner.

Starting procedures

While Le Mans continued the tradition of beginning races with the drivers sprinting across the road, starting their engines and driving off, modern Grands Prix always had the well-established grid pattern. In this, the starting order was decided on the basis of practice times during the days before the race, the fastest cars on the front row of the grid, slowest to the rear.

The object was not to handicap slower cars further, but to achieve a massed start without too much confusion, or danger, as fast cars and slow ones all made for the first corner in a bunch. With the fast cars already a few yards in front, they were more likely to get cleanly away, spreading the field out safely. Races were seldom decided by the few yards distance of a starting grid.

The fastest car occupied what came to be known as 'pole' position—'on the pole', from the practice of starting alongside the starter's pole, on the more favourable side of the track with regard to the first corner.

With the increasingly competitive nature of racing, however, the 20 to 25 cars on the grid tended to be evenly matched, and they sometimes did arrive at the first corner in a bunch. This had not been a very serious situation hitherto, but it was causing more concern as increasingly wide tyres led to increasingly wide cars. In the early Sixties, tracks could generally still accommodate several cars abreast, and grids arranged in 4-3-4 ranks were not uncommon.

Much more serious were the problems of stalled cars. To show that their self-starters worked, it was the practice to stop engines on the grid, start after the warm-up lap, and run them for a few moments before the starter's flag went down. Once started, racing engines could not be allowed to run long before moving off, as with no cooling fans, they quickly overheated.

Accordingly, no time was allowed any laggards to churn their way into life, and when the flag fell, the field would sweep off, those at the back forced to swerve their way past anyone stationary with a dead engine.

With the added complications of taut nerves, and smoke from exhausts and spinning tyres, a stationary front runner could be approached from the back of the grid at as much as 80–90 mph/approx 135 kph and collisions occasionally did occur.

In an effort to deal with the problem, the cars were lined up for the 1963 United States Grand Prix at Watkins Glen, a few yards short of the line on a dummy grid. There, engines were started and preliminaries completed, then the cars rolled slowly forward, paused for ten seconds, for the national flag to signal the start of the race. Cars which failed to start were thus left on the dummy grid where they could be dealt with at leisure.

The experiment proved a success, and from 1964 on the dummy grid system was generally adopted for most forms of racing. Exceptions were in America where the rolling start was preferred, in which a pace car accompanied the grid for a controlled lap of the track, say at 50 mph/80 kph, before they were released for racing. Le Mans clung to the echelon formation until safety harness came into general use, making the run-and-jump start impractical, and a rolling start was gradually introduced there too.

As Grand Prix cars became wider still, grids were narrowed to 3-2-3, and finally to staggered 2-2-2, giving more space between the cars laterally, but extending grids longitudinally so that those which still faltered could be passed by back-markers at as much as 100-125 mph/approx 185 kph. The dummy grid system was progressively modified, but it never completely eliminated start line accidents, and neither did the traffic lights which gradually replaced officials, whose curious ways of starting races may have added to the spectacle, but sometimes did little for the cause of safety.

The brothers Rodriguez and the Mexican Grand Prix

The Mexican Grand Prix came and went within eight years, its rise and fall identified with the fortunes of the Rodriguez brothers, Pedro and Ricardo. At the age of 14, Ricardo, the younger and faster, had been motor cycle champion of Mexico, and by the time he was 20, his brilliant driving, together with the backing of a wealthy and influential family, had put him in the seat of a Formula 1 Ferrari. During the 1962 season, he picked up four world championship points.

Enthusiasm for the brothers' exploits abroad including Le Mans, and their two consecutive wins in the Paris 1000 Kms sports car race, encouraged the inauguration of the Mexican Grand Prix. The new track in Mexico City was the highest at 2225 m/7300 ft ever used for a world championship Grand Prix, but at the inaugural race in 1962, Ricardo, one of the first drivers to go out for practice, crashed Rob Walker's Lotus-Climax, and was killed.

Pedro went on to a distinguished career in long distance racing (winning Le Mans in 1968, and Daytona, Monza, Spa, and the Österreichring Manufacturers' Championship races in 1971) and in Formula 1 where he won two Grands Prix before he died in 1971 during a minor sports car race. The following year the Mexican Grand Prix died too. Interest in it subsided after the organisers failed to control the crowds at the 1970 race. It was threatened with the loss of championship status, and the 1971 race was cancelled.

The story of Mexico exemplified how drivers from nations hitherto unrepresented in Grand Prix racing often helped to sustain certain rounds of the world championship. Sweden's desire to see Ronnie Peterson in action in his own country helped establish the track and the Grand Prix at Anderstorp. The year after his and Gunnar Nilsson's deaths, it was cancelled. Jochen Rindt's success was instrumental in the making of the Österreichring at Zeltweg; and South Africa's anxiety to retain a foothold in any international sport, and in particular motor racing with Jody Scheckter, helped find money for the South African Grand Prix. The Canadian Grand Prix found a new lease of life when Gilles Villeneuve won the revived race in 1978, and the upsurge of interest in Brazil that followed Emerson Fittipaldi (and the subsequent sale of TV rights to several seasons of Grands Prix to that country alone) brought millions of pounds into the sport.

International interest in local drivers was not lost on those concerned with making Grand Prix racing a commercial proposition. Mexico was long remembered as an object-lesson in gaining—and keeping—new rounds of the world championship.

1964

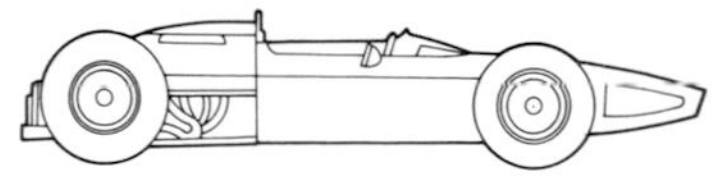

For the second time in two years, and the fourth time in all, the world championship was decided in the final round. What made this occasion unique was the dramatic final lap of the last race, when the issue still lay with John Surtees, Jim Clark, and Graham Hill.

In May Jim Clark began the season in customary style by leading the opening stages of the Monaco Grand Prix until a loose roll bar threatened to delay him. Once again he adapted his driving style to take account of the problem, but then the Lotus lost oil pressure about which even Clark could do nothing.

Towards the end of May, at Zandvoort, Clark achieved a flag to flag victory with another faultless performance in the Dutch Grand Prix, driving the same car with which he had won the year before. Run in more clement weather than the previous season, the Belgian Grand Prix at Spa, in June, produced an astonishing finish.

With fuel accounting for a high proportion of the start line weight of the small $1\frac{1}{2}$-litre cars, drivers tried to begin races with the minimum in the tanks. From tests during practice, each car's consumption was measured—it varied from car to car and track to track, depending on mixture settings, and the gear ratio and tyre sizes, between 7 and 10 mpg.

The idea was to start with just the right amount of fuel, so that there was no excess weight to affect acceleration. For Spa, Dan Gurney loaded his Brabham with what seemed like sufficient for 32 laps round the Francorchamps track, 450 km/279.6 miles, and longer than most races owing to the high speeds. The distance was dictated by the requirement for world championship races to last two hours.

Gurney was fastest in practice, and took a comfortable lead, while Clark and Graham Hill fought out second place with Bruce McLaren (Cooper). Hill had the edge on speed, and took the lead when the unfortunate Gurney dashed into his pit with three laps to go, calling for more fuel. His pit crew believed his misfiring must be due to something else. Their calculations indicated he ought to have plenty, and in any case they had no fuel available and promptly sent him back into the race.

In the meantime, Clark had also called at his pits for water to cool his engine, overheating in his desperate slipstreaming battle with Hill. Then Hill, too, spluttered to a stop. The BRM's fuel pump had failed on his final lap, leaving an overjoyed McLaren in the lead. But *his* glee was short-lived, for rounding the hairpin at La Source within sight of the finish his engine, too, fell silent.

Almost unbelievably he had run short of fuel as a result of the blistering pace in the hot weather. At a painful 15 mph/about 25 kph he coasted downhill towards the chequered flag, listening to the approaching roar of Clark's Coventry-Climax V-8 echoing off the wooded hillsides as he approached, braked for the hairpin, and accelerated past with a matter of yards to go.

The bemused officials forgot to give Clark the chequered flag, and he carried on quite unaware he had won. He, too, in turn stopped, out of petrol, to commiserate with Gurney on the far side of the circuit, while the reception committee stood around in the sunshine, waiting for him to reach the winner's podium for the third year in a row.

A pensive John Surtees, the 1964 world champion sits at the wheel of his Ferrari. Of all the drivers who drove for the Scuderia Surtees found genuine warmth in his relationship with the autocratic founder.

Gurney won the French Grand Prix a fortnight later at Rouen, giving Brabham *their* first Grand Prix, where he had scored for Porsche two years before. Clark led until half distance, pulling away from Gurney by a comfortable half second a lap, but went out with piston failure as a result of a stone being drawn into the engine.

Brands Hatch ran the British Grand Prix for the first time in 1964. The future of Aintree was uncertain, and five years previously Brands had invested in an extension of the original kidney-shaped circuit, to 2.65 miles/4.26 km, to ensure it was capable of playing host to a round of the world

John Surtees (b 1934)

The 1964 world championship not only marked the peak of John Surtees's unusually long (13 years) career as a racing driver, but it was also the achievement on which his subsequent reputation as a constructor largely rested.

Enzo Ferrari had shown an unaccustomed warmth towards Surtees, 'Il Grande John' 'Great John' as the enthusiastic Italian press called him after he had won seven world championships (four in the 500 cc and three in the 350 cc class) riding Italian MV-Agusta motor cycles. During his time with the Italian factory, Surtees had learned to eat, think, and even talk like an Italian, and his stock stood high.

But there was more behind Ferrari's almost avuncular regard for Surtees. During the Thirties, besides the Scuderia Ferrari racing cars, he also ran a motor cycle team with Rudge and Nortons, and acquired a high regard for the faculties of the men who rode them. Motor cyclists' lives are vulnerable to the most trifling errors, which may pass unnoticed at the wheel of a car. And when English riders distinguished themselves during the post-war era on Gileras and Moto-Guzzis, Ferrari determined to put his theories on their merits to the test.

Although not an academically trained engineer, Surtees had completed a practical apprenticeship with Vincent motor cycles, so his knowledge of engineering was by no means superficial. Well-qualified engineers (with all their inhibitions) tend to be rare in motor racing which often requires the empirical solutions of an artistic, or in the case of Colin Chapman, inspired engineer.

So when Surtees met up with Eric Broadley, the Lola designer who, like Chapman, combined brilliantly the inspirational with the institutional, the effect was profound. Surtees absorbed Broadley's strictures on chassis design as he became deeply involved, not merely with the track testing of the racing cars, but with every aspect of their design and construction. To anyone with an engineering bent, it was an exciting prospect, and to Surtees it was the key to progress.

The first time Ferrari asked him to drive, Surtees refused, but he agreed when the offer was repeated for 1963. His reception by the technicians at Maranello was muted at first. They were accustomed to drivers who simply got into the car and drove; one who wanted to take a hand in the design was a novel experience, but Surtees's reputation, carried over from his motor cycling days, won through and the arrangement seemed to be working. It must have worked, for it won Ferrari and Surtees the 1964 world titles.

Things began to go wrong when Eugenio Dragoni, a middle-aged friend of Enzo Ferrari's, replaced the long-established Tavoni as Team Manager. A retired pharmacist with a faintly feudal view of Italy in its former pattern of separate city-states, he saw the job as a means of promoting the interests of his fellow *Milanese*, the young Lorenzo Bandini.

The first crisis came in 1965 in a race at Mosport, after Surtees crashed when the suspension of his Can-Am Lola broke. He very nearly died from his injuries, but there was scant sympathy at Ferrari, where it was felt that had he only stuck to Ferrari cars, the accident would never have happened. So far as they were concerned, Surtees's wounds were self-inflicted.

He made a good recovery, but Dragoni never missed an opportunity to drop hints about Surtees's fitness. Bandini should be the number one driver; he was young, bronzed, and obviously in better physical shape than Surtees, who was always naturally pale, and rather thin. Surtees had to put matters right with Mr Ferrari and he won two important races at the beginning of 1966; but by June, at the Le Mans 24 Hours race, Dragoni's campaign was affecting the whole conduct of the team, and Surtees could stand it no longer. He stalked out, probably the only driver to leave Ferrari to the old man's genuine regret.

He completed the season at the wheel of a Cooper, but the worthy cars from Surbiton were being overtaken by the high technology of their rivals. Compensation lay in winning the Can-Am series in his Lola, then Surtees spent two years developing the Honda Formula 1 car before going to BRM and subsequently forming a team of his own.

After taking part in 111 Grand Prix races, of which he won six, gained eight pole positions, and set eleven fastest laps, Surtees retired in 1973 when his cars had won both the European Formula 2 and Formula 5000 Championships, but never a Grand Prix.

World motor cycle champion in the 500 cc class in 1956, and 1958-60, and 350 cc champion in 1958-60, John Surtees was the only two- and four-wheeled title holder.

championship when the occasion arose. It had already run major international sports car races, and although it never sought the 'classier' style, or the Garden Party atmosphere of the British Racing Drivers' Club at Silverstone, it had the advantage of being probably the best spectator course in the Grand Prix world, with the cars remaining visible for the best part of half a lap.

Only 2.8 sec separated Clark's winning Lotus from Graham Hill's BRM at the end of the British Grand Prix. The two had rarely been more than a few lengths apart throughout. It was a race of stalemate, with neither driver able to score the advantage—Hill unable to overtake with his BRM, difficult to drive and needing a constant 10 000 rpm in the higher gears; Clark unable to pull away, each waiting for the other to make a mistake.

Races with cars passing and repassing were becoming the exception, as engine power, speed, and handling became more closely matched than ever; and although spectators by and large enjoyed the close wheel to wheel racing, many longed for the daring manoeuvres and the refuelling stops of the past. There was nostalgia for day-long pursuits, rather than sprints amongst the singularly look-alike little cars with their now almost out-of-sight drivers recumbent behind perspex screens.

The German Grand Prix at the beginning of August saw the first appearance of the Japanese Honda, and sadly, the last of the popular Dutch driver Count Carel de Beaufort, who died of injuries received during practice when he crashed his four-year-old Porsche into a tree.

Honda appeared with a formidable team of mechanics and technicians, and were greeted warmly in the fond hope that their arrival might signal the intention of their rivals in the passenger car sales battle to follow. Car manufacturers were still being urged to take a stake in Grand Prix racing; there were even hopes that Mercedes-Benz might be encouraged to return, but they never did. Honda's driver, a little-known American, Ronnie Bucknum, performed creditably, however, finishing 13th *in his first race in a single seater*, after starting last. He gained seven places on the first lap, and although he went off the road in the closing stages, the Honda had done rather better than anyone expected.

John Surtees won at the Nürburgring with Graham Hill second, which took Hill to the top of the world championship table, after having been second to Jim Clark. Unlike 1963, however, no clear leader was emerging, and the next race, Austria, only served to confuse matters more .

On 23 August, Lorenzo Bandini won his first, and, as it turned out, his only world championship Grand Prix. It was a victory largely by default, for the retirements included Hill's BRM, Surtees's Ferrari, both Lotuses, both Brabhams, and both Coopers.

Phil Hill's Cooper burns at the Austrian Grand Prix, a victim of the changeover from alcohol-based fuel to petrol, although the driver escaped without injury.

Above: Honda arrive at the Nürburgring. A German policeman finds the Oriental team worth more than a passing glance.

Below: The first Honda Grand Prix car set the engine transversely in the chassis. A 60° V-12 with needle roller crankshaft main and big end bearings, and fuel injection, it won the last 1½-litre Grand Prix of all.

McLaren's Cooper went out with engine trouble, and Phil Hill's was destroyed in a fire after crashing. Of more significance than Bandini's victory perhaps, was the performance of a young local driver in his first Grand Prix. Jochen Rindt coaxed his Rob Walker Brabham BRM up to third place before the steering broke.

If Austria was inconclusive, Monza at the beginning of September, and Watkins Glen in October held the key to what was to follow. Surtees won the Italian Grand Prix, and Graham Hill scored his second successive American victory at Watkins Glen, to which the entire circus of cars, spares, and tools and equipment were now air-lifted.

The growth and efficiency of this form of transport was instrumental in the world-wide expansion of Grand Prix racing. It made the extension of the season practical, and also had the effect of conferring a new-found unity amongst the Grand Prix Constructors. Arrangements for the massive air freight operation for the North American and Mexican races brought the teams together, and it was perfectly logical for them to co-operate in flying everything in one aircraft, or perhaps two. It kept the cost within bounds, and from there it was but a step towards co-operative negotiations with the appropriate race organisers to pay for it. Thus, the principle of competitors striking joint agreements with race organisers came into being. The implications for the future were far-reaching, although at the time it seemed no more than a useful and apparently straightforward expedient.

The leading contenders arrived in Mexico, Hill with 39 points, Surtees 34, and Clark 30. Once again the vagaries of the scoring system complicated matters. Clark's chance of victory lay in the tie-break of race wins, of which he already had three; but Hill and Surtees needed to finish lower than fourth, so the odds were against Clark.

It was closer between Surtees and Hill, and even if Surtees won, with Hill in second place, the title would belong to Surtees.

Hill's chances of fending Surtees off seemed to vanish when he retired early in the race, and Clark looked all set to win both race *and* title until the last lap but one.

The order was Clark, Gurney, Bandini, and Surtees. But Clark had noticed an oil streak on the track at the hairpin. He altered his line to avoid it, but realised next time round that the streak changed line as well, showing that it was coming from his own car. He slowed slightly, but it made no difference. An oil pipe leaked away his chances of a second world championship, and as he creaked round his 64th lap, his engine gradually seizing up, Gurney took the lead.

This made Hill, waiting anxiously in the pits, the potential champion, but it only took a signal from the Ferrari pit to change things. Bandini let Surtees by into third place, which quickly became second as Clark's engine stopped on the final lap. John Surtees, at the age of 30, was champion driver of the world after the closest finish ever.

For Clark, it was a bitter moment. It was not sufficient, it seemed, to be the world's fastest driver with the world's fastest Grand Prix car to win the world championship, and he watched one close rival win the race, and another snatch the driver's title for himself, and the constructor's cup for Ferrari. Clark had won three of the ten races, Surtees, Gurney, and Hill only two apiece. He had led four others before dropping out with mechanical trouble. But for two relatively trifling problems with his cars in the final races of 1962 and 1964, Clark would have been world champion three years in a row, and with his 1965 title still to come, would almost have matched the mighty Fangio.

Jim Clark with his roll bar coming loose in the Monaco Grand Prix. The greatest driver of his day, Clark adjusted his driving to suit, but was thwarted from winning nonetheless.

1965

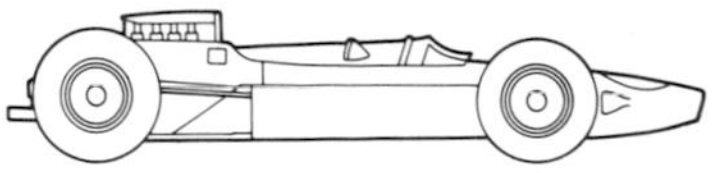

Following Stirling Moss's accident in 1962, a replacement as the leading driver in Grand Prix racing was not long energing. The principal contenders were Jim Clark, Graham Hill, John Surtees, and Dan Gurney. Hill and Gurney 'peaked out' early on, the former finding it difficult to sustain performances based on determination and courage rather than natural aptitude. As time passed, Gurney's motivation seemed to diminish, and he dissipated his efforts through tinkering with his cars, rather like Surtees. For his part, Surtees suffered from the unseemly quarrel with Dragoni, which might have been settled by someone more diplomatic.

Yet Jim Clark did not inherit the crown by default. He had native skill of a sort that few individuals possess, a genius for getting the best from his car, unmatched by anyone since Fangio. Had Moss carried on racing, there might have been little to choose between them, but from 1963 on, Clark was the master.

The final year of the $1\frac{1}{2}$-litre Formula went more or less according to form, with Jim Clark winning six races out of ten, BRM still runners-up, Dan Gurney still a vigorous contender, and Surtees in disarray along with Ferrari. But there was one new element.

From time to time, drivers arrive in motor racing for whom a brilliant career is fondly forecast. Sometimes they do well, a few even make it to the top, but most champions are the product of years of struggle; most Grand Prix fortunes are attained painfully, and for every individual who makes the grade, scores drop out on the way.

In the very first race of 1965, the Grand Prix of South Africa at East London on New Year's Day, one driver took part in his first championship race, and went on to be not only the greatest driver of his generation, but also to influence the entire future of Grand Prix racing. At the age of 25, Jackie Stewart drove the number two BRM and gained a championship point in his first race. He was third in his second and second in his third, and before the season was over he had won one, and lay third in the world championship. It was an astonishing feat, a meteoric ascent, and he was to remain at the top for a long time to come.

Clark won that opening race, but when the circus came to Europe, he and Team Lotus were preoccupied elsewhere. Colin Chapman had long had his eye on the riches of Indianapolis, the 500-mile Memorial Day classic in Indiana, which had been dominated for a generation by the big, front-engined roadsters with their Offenhauser engines, and they had become so specialised they competed nowhere else.

Chapman knew he had the technology to start a revolution in the curiously staid (from a design standpoint) world of oval circuit racing. Nothing radical had been successful at the Brickyard, as it was called in recollection of its former brick surface, for the best part of 30 years. The car Chapman prepared was rear-engined, low built, and small, rather like the Lotus Grand Prix cars, but with a 500 horse power, 4200 cc American Ford V-8 engine.

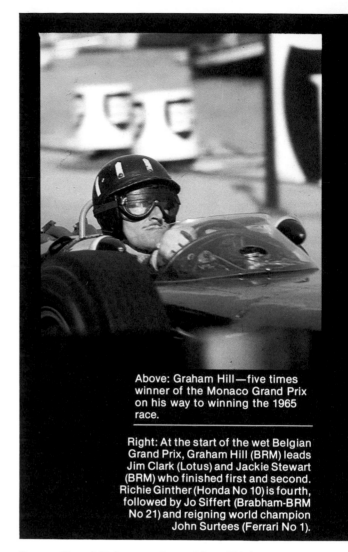

Above: Graham Hill—five times winner of the Monaco Grand Prix on his way to winning the 1965 race.

Right: At the start of the wet Belgian Grand Prix, Graham Hill (BRM) leads Jim Clark (Lotus) and Jackie Stewart (BRM) who finished first and second. Richie Ginther (Honda No 10) is fourth, followed by Jo Siffert (Brabham-BRM No 21) and reigning world champion John Surtees (Ferrari No 1).

The 1965 race was Jim Clark's third attempt. On his first, in 1963 he had finished second to Parnelli Jones, on his second he retired while leading, surprising the Americans into taking his challenge seriously enough to copy the hitherto risible Lotus wholesale.

The team spent the whole of May getting ready, and were rewarded with the first non-American victory at Indianapolis since Dario Resta won for Peugeot in 1916. It was the first time the race average speed exceeded 150 mph/241.40 kph, the first victory for a rear-engined car, the first for a V-8 (breaking the Offenhauser monopoly) and a notable achievement for Ford, now deeply committed to a competition programme embracing rallies, Le Mans, Formula 2, and in time, Grand Prix racing as well.

While Lotus were away scoring their historic victory, Graham Hill won his third Monaco Grand Prix in a row. It was a memorable race which Hill led for 24 of the 100 laps, before arriving at the chicane to find Bob Anderson's Brabham-Climax almost stopped in the middle of the track. Hill was forced to take the escape road, then stop, get out and push the

car back (uphill), restart, and pursue the leading four who had gone past, on a circuit where overtaking is notoriously difficult.

He set a new track record on lap 82 with a time of 1 min 31.7 sec 123.89 kph/76.98 mph. He made up the 38 sec he had lost, and by lap 65 was in front again after one of the best drives of his career. Paul Hawkins of Australia became the second driver to retire from Monaco by plunging into the harbour, swimming free of his sinking Lotus-Climax and reaching the quayside uninjured.

Once again the Belgian Grand Prix at Spa-Francorchamps in June was beset by thunderstorms, but Jim Clark won it nonetheless, and for the fourth time in a row. BRMs pursued him throughout the season, and on this occasion it was the car of his fellow Scot Jackie Stewart which was second. The French Grand Prix found a new home at the Charade circuit, Clermont-Ferrand, a spectacular 8.055 km/ 5.005 miles of public roads in the mountains of the Auvergne. Clark and Stewart once again dominated the race; at the British Grand Prix at Silverstone the following month it was Hill's turn to pursue Clark, then Stewart's again at Zandvoort a fortnight later. The Dutch race was the scene of a famous incident in which Colin Chapman was arrested and charged with assaulting a policeman.

Clark was able to clinch the title rather earlier than usual, with his fifth win in a row, at the German Grand Prix on 31 July, once again with Hill's BRM at his back. But his run of success was over. Although he took pole position at the Italian Grand Prix in September, Jackie Stewart forced his way through to score his first ever grande épreuve victory. Hill won the penultimate round of the championship series at Watkins Glen in October, to complete his second hat-trick of the season.

The final race of the $1\frac{1}{2}$-litre Formula was a curiosity. Richie Ginther had campaigned the interesting Honda throughout the year with only moderate success—he finished sixth twice, his best results in a season punctuated by retirements. But the altitude of the Mexico City circuit seemed to suit the carburation of the Honda, Ginther gained the second row of the starting grid, and led the race from start to finish. It was the first victory for a Japanese car in a Grand Prix, Ginther's first (and only) one, and the first for a car with Goodyear tyres, breaking the Dunlop monopoly which had existed almost throughout the $1\frac{1}{2}$-litre Formula.

COVENTRY-CLIMAX

Leonard Lee, the managing director of Coventry-Climax Engines had announced withdrawals from racing before, but like those of Enzo Ferrari, they had turned out to be premature. In October 1962, for example, they decided 'to withdraw from Grand Prix racing at the end of the year, as it is no longer economic. Commitments . . . with owners of our engines will be fulfilled, and [we will] supply spare parts . . . It is, of course, our sincere regret . . .'

Lee's concern was over the increasing cost of the engine produced by his little firm, whose business was not racing engines at all, but fork lift trucks and industrial units for small power plants, such as portable fire pumps. The original engines seized upon by the Fifties' sports racing car industry had indeed been developed from those designed for pumping water through firemen's hoses, light in relation to their power.

At the time they cost £1000. A four cylinder for the 2½-litre Formula had been £2250. The new FWMV, as it was called, the V-8 which dominated the 1½-litre Formula was £3000 in 1962. But in the way of these things the price had almost doubled, with the increasing complexity of developments such as the 32-valve cylinder heads. Lee's conception of Grand Prix racing as something people did largely for fun was already a little old-fashioned; it was now thoroughly commercial. Nevertheless, he was worried that such a precarious business as racing might suddenly fold up, leaving his firm with some very expensive investments on its hands in the shape of unsold engines. The cost of the proposed 3-litre Formula appalled him.

His conservative little firm was accustomed to clients with a more conventional business background than motor racing teams, and it was causing the directors acute discomfort, particularly when at least one racing team got the idea that Coventry-Climax ought to be paying *them* rather than the other way round. Other suppliers paid bonuses for the publicity value of wins, but Coventry-Climax would rather have gone back to fire pumps. Accordingly, the racing teams went to their fuel, tyre, and accessory sponsors, more cash was found to pay for the engines, and Lee was persuaded to remain in the business a little longer.

He had two talented engineers, Walter Hassan, who had been involved with racing engines since the Twenties, and Harry Mundy, later a distinguished technical editor of the magazine *Autocar*. As technical director and chief designer respectively, they produced and developed a range of engines, culminating in 1964 in a very advanced 1½-litre, horizontally opposed 16 cylinder. It was introduced in the final year of the formula, but never raced. The 32-valve V-8 was fast enough for Jim Clark to win the championship without difficulty, even though it did give trouble in the final races. Also, the last stages of developing the complex 16 cylinder took longer than expected.

Astonishingly, a four-valve version of the 16 cylinder was also planned, which would have required engineering of watch-making precision, but it was never built. Coventry-Climax decided against an engine for the 3-litre Formula, and with the announcement that the 16 cylinder was under test came the news that British constructors would need to look elsewhere in the future.

There was talk of supercharging either the V-8 or the flat-16 to compete under the 3-litre rules, but it was never done. Unlike the days of the 1½-litre Alfa Romeo, alchohol was no longer permitted in the fuel where it could act as an internal coolant, and supercharging with petrol, in the prevailing state of the art, would have led to disastrous temperatures and pressures. Besides, a suitable small supercharger was not available, and small turbo-chargers had not yet appeared.

As a stop-gap, Coventry-Climax agreed to build 2-litre versions of the 1½-litre V-8 for Lotus to run during the opening year of the 3-litre Formula, largely in recognition of the victories Jim Clark had gained them. But the break was otherwise final and complete. Hassan and Mundy went on to design and develop the Jaguar V-12, and Coventry-Climax was subsequently absorbed by British Leyland.

Coventry-Climax ushered in the principle of the proprietary engine, doing away with the idea that cars and engines were naturally the product of the same manufacturer. They won 96 major Formula 1 races, of which 40 were world championship Grands Prix.

The pressure groups

The control and marshalling of individuals connected with a Grand Prix became more vexatious with the passing years, as the incident between the Dutch police and Chapman emphasised. Grand Prix racing had come to represent their livelihood, to a body of drivers, mechanics, journalists, administrators and others, who were quite unlike the wealthy amateurs or state-subsidised technicians of years gone by.

Racing was supporting a small, but significant industry with a substantial investment in cash and careers, which demanded a firmer commitment to security and continuity than the FIA had hitherto provided. The Grand Prix community never expected long-term guarantees, but as a body of self-styled professionals, it began to question the amateur stance taken by the FIA and the race organisers, whom they often felt were over-represented on the CSI.

The direct result was the setting-up of protectionist groups and committees, such as the Formula One Constructors Association (FOCA), the GPDA, and significantly at Zandvoort in 1968, of the International Racing Press Association (IRPA) by the distinguished French motor racing journalist, Bernard Cahier.

Campaigning for recognition, better press facilities, passes, and access to the track, IRPA found its voice in Cahier. The GPDA, advocating improvements in safety facilities and related matters, found a vigorous new spokesman in Jackie Stewart. In the meantime FOCA maintained a discreet solidarity, content to gain influence over financial affairs slowly but surely, and for the time being, without a major-domo.

COVENTRY-CLIMAX VICTORIES 1958-65

1958:	Argentina	Cooper	Stirling Moss
	Monaco	Cooper	Maurice Trintignant
1959:	Monaco	Cooper	Jack Brabham
	Britain	Cooper	Jack Brabham
	Portugal	Cooper	Stirling Moss
	Italy	Cooper	Stirling Moss
	United States	Cooper	Bruce McLaren
1960:	Argentina	Cooper	Bruce McLaren
	Monaco	Lotus	Stirling Moss
	Holland	Cooper	Jack Brabham
	Belgium	Cooper	Jack Brabham
	France	Cooper	Jack Brabham
	Britain	Cooper	Jack Brabham
	Portugal	Cooper	Jack Brabham
	United States	Lotus	Stirling Moss

Total $2\frac{1}{2}$-litre Formula, 15

1961:	Monaco	Lotus	Stirling Moss
	Germany	Lotus	Stirling Moss
	United States	Lotus	Innes Ireland
1962:	Monaco	Cooper	Bruce McLaren
	Belgium	Lotus	Jim Clark
	Britain	Lotus	Jim Clark
	United States	Lotus	Jim Clark
1963:	Belgium	Lotus	Jim Clark
	Holland	Lotus	Jim Clark
	France	Lotus	Jim Clark
	Britain	Lotus	Jim Clark
	Italy	Lotus	Jim Clark
	Mexico	Lotus	Jim Clark
	South Africa	Lotus	Jim Clark
1964:	Holland	Lotus	Jim Clark
	Belgium	Lotus	Jim Clark
	France	Brabham	Dan Gurney
	Britain	Lotus	Jim Clark
	Mexico	Brabham	Dan Gurney
1965:	South Africa	Lotus	Jim Clark
	Belgium	Lotus	Jim Clark
	France	Lotus	Jim Clark
	Britain	Lotus	Jim Clark
	Holland	Lotus	Jim Clark
	German	Lottus	Jim Clark

Total $1\frac{1}{2}$-litre Formula, 25

Analysis: $1\frac{1}{2}$-litre Formula 1961–5

The winners

Drivers:	Jim Clark	19
	Graham Hill	10
	Dan Gurney	3
	John Surtees	3
	Phil Hill	2
	Stirling Moss	2
	Count Berghe von Trips	2
	Giancarlo Baghetti	1
	Lorenzo Bandini	1
	Richie Ginther	1
	Innes Ireland	1
	Bruce McLaren	1
	Jackie Stewart	1
Cars:	Lotus Coventry-Climax	22
	BRM	11
	Ferrari	9
	Brabham Coventry-Climax	2
	Cooper Coventry-Climax	1
	Honda	1
	Porsche	1
Engines:	Coventry-Climax V-8	22
	Coventry-Climax 4 cyl	3
	BRM V-8	11
	Ferrari V-6	7
	Ferrari V-8	2
	Honda V-12	1
	Porsche 8 cyl	1

Fastest practice laps

1961		**1962**	
P. Hill	5	J. Clark	6
S. Moss	1	G. Hill	1
von Trips	1	J. Surtees	1
Brabham	1	D. Gurney	1
1963		**1964**	
J. Clark	7	J. Clark	5
G. Hill	2	D. Gurney	2
J. Surtees	1	J. Surtees	2
		G. Hill	1
1965			
J. Clark	6		
G. Hill	4		

Total:

J. Clark	24
G. Hill	8
P. Hill	5
J. Surtees	4
D. Gurney	3
J. Brabham	1
von Trips	1
S. Moss	1

TYRE DEVELOPMENT

Richie Ginther's unexpected victory in Mexico brought to an end the formula which had led to the smallest cars ever in modern Grand Prix racing. To some extent the criticisms of 1960 had proved justified. The cars were sometimes not very exciting to watch, and with the technical advances they had made did tend to resemble slot-racers. Against that, there had been tangible progress in design, stemming largely from their closely matched power output which had forced engineers to seek other means of bettering performance. This was achieved by improving handling and road holding with constant development of suspensions, and also, equally significant, the creation of new tyres.

Tyre widths had been increasing, a development encouraged in Grand Prix racing by the Indianapolis experiences of Lotus. The transatlantic traffic in racing technology had not all been one way. Carcass construction improved, tread widths increased, and instead of accepting the tradition of one tyre suitable for all conditions, new softer compounds appeared, giving dramatic improvements in grip. But these were accompanied by restrictions preventing their use in wet weather which, in turn, led to different compounds and tread patterns for tyres which *were* to be used in the rain.

Once again, a technological advance had been made which would fundamentally affect the development of Grand Prix racing. It seemed at the time no more than a logical development, given the increased competitiveness, and it had the added virtue of apparently making things safer, particularly in wet weather. The notion that greater grip, leading to higher cornering speeds, might only mean that the speed of the accident went up, had not yet dawned.

Prohibitions or restrictions on tyre development seemed unnecessary, even though their influence was acknowledged, particularly by suspension designers. In any case, restrictions on tyre compounds or materials would have been almost unenforceable, and an inch here or there on widths seemed hardly significant. The magnitude of the increases were probably not envisaged by the CSI, but they quickly outpaced the rule requiring notice of major changes. The constructors' anxiety for stability had demanded a year's grace before they could be compelled to make any important design changes, and by the time the implications of the wide tyres were realised, cars had changed, and a reversion to the old order would have been iniquitous.

Above all, it was feared that if tyre development were to become hidebound by rules, there was danger of discouraging the American tyre companies, Firestone and Goodyear, both of whom were interested in equipping the cars of the impending 3-litre Formula. Pirelli, Engelbert, and Continental had all dropped out of racing, Pirelli as long ago as 1958 when Maserati had been their last customer, leaving Dunlop with a monopoly.

Competition from Firestone and Goodyear would bring new cash, with three tyre companies competing to retain teams, and there was still worry over how the new formula was to be paid for. The CSI of course was not only looking after the financial well-being of the teams. As a sub-committee of the FIA it was heavily representative of the Grand Prix organisers, which made it see its duty plainly. It was obliged to create a commercial environment in which the teams could prosper, or there might be no teams to run in the Grands Prix they represented. The CSI could not afford to stand in the way of competitors' enrichment, so the new, potentially troublesome wide tyres were passed on the nod. The financial boat was not to be rocked so close to the imposition of a new formula with all its investment risks, and the changeover from wheel-shaped wheels to drum-shaped wheels got under way.

The 1½-litre Formula had turned out to be relatively safe, despite concern about the small and apparently fragile cars. The worst accident was at Monza in 1961 involving von Trips and the spectators, but this had little to do with the cars. It was put down to the Ferrari team's efforts to keep Clark out of their slipstream. Gary Hocking, Carel de Beaufort, and Ricardo Rodriguez died in practice accidents, Rodriguez not even at a title race. Apart from von Trips, no driver died in the course of the 47 championship races during the formula's five-year span. Other racing during the period produced its customary toll, but despite the usual lurid accidents and a number of injuries, at least some of the most serious hazards seemed to have been removed from world championship racing.

The most significant advance in engine design was the advent of the V-8s, first by Coventry-Climax, then BRM, and belatedly by Ferrari who consigned the V-6 Dino to a sports car, and eventually a production car. It remains a Ferrari classic, and even became the basis for the famous Lancia Stratos engine many years later.

By 1963 Lucas fuel injection was standard equipment on the British cars, Bosch on the Ferrari, and although it made little difference to power outputs, unmanageable torque curves were smoothed out, making the cars rather easier to drive. For the final season, Ferrari had also developed a horizontally opposed twelve cylinder which failed to come up to expectations on this occasion. Porsche had tried an air-cooled flat-eight, but they retired before it had an opportunity to fulfil its potential.

BRM took the Lotus 25's monocoque structure a stage farther by enclosing the driver in what was effectively a tube with a hole scooped out of the top—a strong riveted aluminium fuselage structure. Like Lotus, BRM mounted the front springs inboard, on rocker arms in an effort to reduce frontal area, which was steadily increasing owing to the ever-wider wheels and tyres.

Three of Jim Clark's six victories in 1965 were scored with a development of the Coventry-Climax V-8 to 32-valve configuration; three were with the standard 16-valve version. Had the 32-valve not let him down at Monza, Watkins Glen, and Mexico City, where it blew up in practice, his run of success in the Lotus, now designated Type 33 following changes to the wheels and suspension, might have been on a par with 1963.

The Honda which won the final race was a novel design with its engine mounted transversely in the rear which reduced the wheelbase, but increased the frontal area. It was the only V-12 to race throughout the formula.

1966

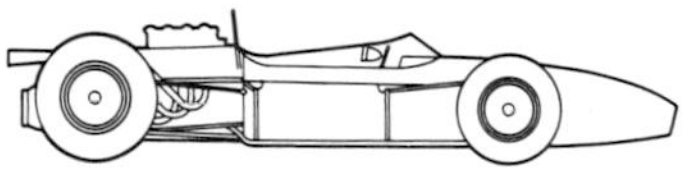

In its sixtieth year, Grand Prix racing reached what has come to be regarded as its modern age. Nineteen sixty-six began the longest-lived formula ever, with a period of reform in which commercial sponsorship became well established, and the competitors gradually gained control. Judged by its world-wide popularity, there was no doubt about the success of the 3-litre Formula, but some aspects of the changes it brought provoked strong disagreements, and encouraged further fragmentation of interests within racing. Technical development followed an unexpected course, with results that were unforeseen, sometimes dangerous, and which often presented difficulties, political and practical, for the ruling body.

During these 60 years, lap speeds had doubled. Disregarding the periods of the two wars, they went up by roughly two per cent per annum, although the rate of increase varied. The greatest took place in the four years 1934–7, when the German Auto Union and Mercedes-Benz intervention put it up by 16 per cent.

After 1945, the annual rise slowed to under one per cent; but it is surprising that it went up at all, in view of the reductions in power output of Grand Prix engines under the various formulae. From 600 bhp or more in 1937, it fell to under 400 bhp between 1947 and 1951, then to less than 300 bhp from 1954 to 60, and 200 bhp or so during the period of the $1\frac{1}{2}$-litre Formula just ended.

The gains had come from other sources, including a reduction in the weight of cars by around one-third, a reduction in frontal area of about the same, together with improvements in braking, suspension, and tyres. It followed also, from predictions on the 3-litre Formula by the late Laurence Pomeroy, that with engines of 450–500 bhp ' . . . if the well-proved dogma advanced in *The Grand Prix Car* were maintained to the effect that lap speeds, *all other things being equal*, varied as the sixth root of power per square foot of frontal area, circuit speeds would rise by 18 per cent or from say, 110 mph to very nearly 130 mph'.

Writing in *Automobile Year*, 'Pom' went on to say precisely why this increase could not go on. Unless four-wheel drive were employed, he hypothesised, a power to weight ratio of more than 400 bhp per ton would result in excessive wheelspin, and cars were already cornering at, '. . . what is likely to be a limiting speed, as side forces are equalling, or even slightly exceeding gravity'.

'Pom's' perpetual caveat, of course, lay in the phrase, 'other things being equal,' which as he knew perfectly well, they hardly ever were. Yet he was not the only one who believed that the new formula would result in much larger, heavier cars, which would need four-wheel drive to transmit their power to the road.

The light $1\frac{1}{2}$-litre cars were already finding difficulty, so it remained to be seen how much heavier cars would need to be, if the extra power of 3-litre engines was not to disappear in tyre smoke.

Distributing the drive to all four wheels was the obvious solution, so the first cars of 1966 tended to be regarded as interim models, with one notable exception. This was the BRM, seen as the prototype of how cars of the new formula would turn out. It was large, heavy, and complicated, rather like those of the previous large-engine formula in the Thirties, but of course lower, mid-engined, and with wide tyres. BRM made the expected provision for four-wheel drive, and following their world championship

The teams

Nearly 20 makes of car had appeared during the course of the $1\frac{1}{2}$-litre Formula, and although many more would come and go in the years ahead, the 1966 grids were composed principally of the familiar makes such as BRM, Ferrari, Cooper, Brabham, Lotus, and Honda, together with two new ones. These were McLaren, and one variously referred to as a Gurney-Weslake, AAR (for All-American Racers, which strictly speaking they were not, or Anglo-American Racers, which they certainly were) or later on Eagle, AAR Eagle, Gurney-Eagle, or American Eagle.

BRM: An ambitious programme was conceived by BRM's chief engineer, Tony Rudd, in the logical expectation that 3-litre cars would be altogether larger and heavier than $1\frac{1}{2}$-litre cars. The V-8 had been outstandingly successful, and Rudd's plan was based on the premise that having evolved a highly satisfactory cylinder head, there was a compelling argument for keeping it.

Accordingly, he in effect 'flattened out' the 60° V-8 to 180°, and produced a horizontally opposed eight cylinder; doubling up two such engines one on top of the other produced a 16 cylinder, composed of four banks of four cylinders. Twice $1\frac{1}{2}$ litres equals 3 litres, and when the two crankshafts were geared together the engine rêsembled the letter H laid on its side, and became known as the H-16. The layout was known in aviation with the Napier Sabre and Rolls-Royce Eagle engines, but was unique in Grand Prix racing.

It had a number of commendable features. It was short—very little longer than the $1\frac{1}{2}$-litre V-8. It was light in relation to its anticipated 600 horse power. Like the notable Lancia D 50 of 1954 it was also a stressed part of the car's structure, and it was adaptable to four-wheel drive. BRM had already undertaken experiments with a four-wheel drive car, and ran one in practice for the 1964 British Grand Prix, so they were well ahead, against the day when the enormous power of the H-16 was expected to make it necessary.

Unfortunately, the H-16 coincided with the return of a bureaucratic regime at BRM. Up to 1961, Sir Alfred Owen had spent a million pounds on it, and now, well into a second million and flushed with success, he began in 1962, and subsequent successes, gave every appearance of a team that knew what it was doing.

Ferrari were much fancied at the beginning of 1966 as well, with their V-12 car logically enough developed from the 3.3-litre Le Mans prototypes. There were new teams to take into account, such as McLaren and Eagle. Cooper struck up an alliance with Maserati to use a 1957 V-12 engine. The outlook for Lotus and Brabham was less encouraging. Lotus were making do with Coventry-Climax engines enlarged to 2 litres, but giving away 100 horse power or more, and Brabham was due to try an Australian engine developed from an American Buick . . .

The unexpected happened. The big, heavy cars did not win—small light ones did instead. The results were so unexpected that even commentators as redoubtable as Pomeroy were caught out. He need not have worried about the accuracy of his own, '. . . well-proved dogma'. It was right after all. Lap speeds duly went up by just about the magnitude his famous formula forecast. Developments took place which would challenge his assertion that four-wheel drive was the only solution to the problem of wheelspin, and cars would shortly be capable of cornering with side forces not merely equalling the pull of gravity, but substantially exceeding it. Before the formula was many years old, means were found of cornering at well over 2g, accelerating at almost 1g, and braking at 1.8g.

Most such developments, however, lay in the future. Engines were still expected in 1966 to be the primary source of improved performance. The new formula somewhat optimistically laid down a series of specifications for gas turbines taking account of the air-flow area at a fixed point between two stages of the power turbine, together with the pressure ratio of the compressor turbine. Wankel engines were admitted on the basis of an equivalency formula, taking twice the volume of the difference between the maximum and minimum capacity of the working chamber.

The Wankel's equivalency was always a dubious one, but no case was ever made for change. There were plenty of objections to it as a racing engine already, not least the cost of development and its high fuel consumption. Fuel load was also a critical factor against the gas turbine, but at least it would be tried, whereas the Wankel was not.

Supercharged two-strokes seemed an outside possibility for the formula, but none was ever produced. Considering the fashion at the time for making racing motor cycles go faster by multiplying the number of cylinders, 'Pom' envisaged a 32 piston, unsupercharged 3-litre two-stroke built around an eight-throw crank pin (ie a V-16 with parallel pistons in each block) giving 550 bhp at 12000 rpm. Not surprisingly, nothing like this was ever produced either, and to make sure it never was, a limit of twelve cylinders was imposed in 1971.

Economic facts still discouraged flights of fancy in 1966. Grand Prix racing was becoming richer, but not sufficiently so to undertake, unaided, the design and development of many new engines. The same doubters who had worried over the $1\frac{1}{2}$-litre Formula, worried over the 3-litre for much the same reason—they did not know where their next engines were coming from. Still, there remained the prospect of a full season of nine races, with such teams as there were, using what engines they could.

---

giving BRM other jobs to do. A business man, he and his industrial empire wanted to see some return on their investment.

BRM was given projects, such as the Le Mans Rover-BRM gas turbine car, in order to impress the motor industry to which Rubery Owen was such a substantial supplier. BRM made a 1000 cc engine for the Formula 2 market, and its design office was burdened with projects for which it was ill-prepared. The Owen Organisation saw it as a source of bright ideas for a wide range of engineering work, not all connected with racing, and some of it not even connected with cars. But amongst the various engines they were called upon to draw up, was a number of V-12s . . .

This division of effort merely exacerbated the problems which arose with the H-16. The planned power output was nowhere near realised, indeed the BRM engineers were lucky to see 400 bhp on the test bed. Moreover, vibrations set up by the two crankshafts threatened literally to shake the engine to pieces, crankshaft counterweights detaching themselves even after the H-16 had been passed fit for racing.

So, development took time; the team started in 1966 with the faithful V-8s, and the 16 did not race until September. It appeared in practice at Monaco, Spa, and Rheims. However, not only the engine, but also the massive transmission proved troublesome. It was autumn at Monza, before two cars started in a Grand Prix—Hill's retiring with engine failure, and Stewart's going out with a fuel leak.

The works H-16 BRMs' most encouraging performances of the season were in the non-championship Oulton Park Gold Cup race, which both Stewart and Hill led before they broke down, and at Watkins Glen. There, Hill's transmission broke, and Stewart stopped in a cloud of steam and smoke. In the final race of the season, the Mexican Grand Prix, Stewart got up to third place before a crankshaft counterweight went.

Perversely, the opening races with the V-8 proved not unsuccessful. With 1916 cc versions producing 270 bhp, Jackie Stewart won the Monaco Grand Prix and Graham Hill was third, but by mid-season, 3-litre rivals were getting into their stride, and making the success of the H-16 a matter of urgency.

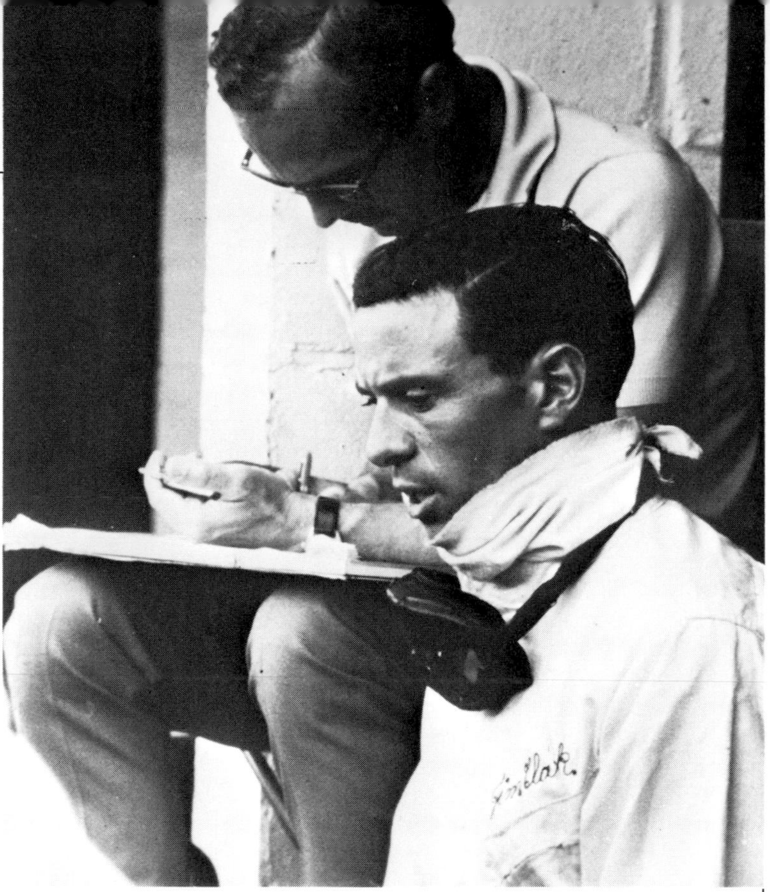

Great minds. The ingenuity of Colin Chapman's designs, and the brilliance of Jim Clark's driving dominated the middle years of the 1960s.

Lotus: Faced with the prospect of using 245 bhp, 2-litre Coventry-Climax V-8s, the future for Lotus looked bleak, at least for the time being. Ford of Britain had already stepped into the breach left by Coventry-Climax with a commission for a new Formula 1 engine; but it would not be ready until 1967, so Colin Chapman was forced to look elsewhere. There was talk of a 3-litre version of the 4.2-litre V-8, which Ford of America had produced for Lotus's assault on Indianapolis, but there seemed little likelihood of that being ready before the still-secret Ford of Britain project. In any case, there was no certainty of success, so the idea was abandoned.

In the meantime, Chapman was forced to become a customer for the BRM H-16. With their new-found commercialism, BRM were only too pleased to sell an engine, even to a rival, relying on the well-established motor racing tradition that a works team keeps first choice of all the best equipment, with the latest modifications, in order to retain a competitive edge. Lotus could expect no concessions.

Clark's defence of his world championship turned out to be a series of disasters. At Monaco, for the first round of the new season, he set fastest time in practice, despite having less power than his principal rivals. Even though his gearbox stuck in first at the start, he fought his way back up the field on a difficult overtaking circuit. He reached second place before a rear upright broke, forcing him out.

At Spa an assembly fault put him out within a mile or so, and he did not start in the French Grand Prix at Rheims after being struck in the face by a bird during practice. He finished fourth in the British Grand Prix despite a pit stop and led the Dutch, until the crankshaft damper broke and two stops dropped him to third.

Clark crashed at the Nürburgring, once again after setting fastest practice time through his brilliant driving. But it was clear that 1966 was going to follow the pattern of one year up—one year down, which Lotus were already establishing.

The slow pace of development of the H-16 engine was no help. It was not seen in a Lotus until Monza, where Clark struggled up to second place before retiring, but the engine, although not faultless, had shown an encouraging turn of speed.

At Watkins Glen, Lotus entered Clark in a Coventry-Climax car. After setting fastest time in practice with the H-16, he decided to race it. A camshaft breakage on the final lap of practice, decreed a change to another engine that had put two rods through the side at Oulton Park a fortnight earlier; but Clark was not discouraged.

It turned out to be his only lucky break of the season. Lorenzo Bandini dropped out of the lead when, according to Ferrari, a spark plug electrode knocked a hole in a piston (an unlikely sort of failure, the plug manufacturer observed sourly) and Jack Brabham's engine broke a tappet at half distance. John Surtees might have pressed Clark, had he not lost time colliding with Peter Arundell's Lotus, so Clark was able to bring the H-16 through not only to its first race finish, but also its first (and only) victory.

The resulting boost to BRM morale inspired them to press on with development for a further year. The engine was already taxing their patience, however, and failures of the crankshaft coupling gears persisted. Lotus seemed to have solved the problems of installing the 700 lb/317 kg engine and transmission rather better than BRM, on account of their experience with the Indianapolis car. The Lotus H-16 handled better, and had a more efficient cooling system, which made it appear that BRM's problems *were* capable of solution whereas they were, in most respects, beyond it.

Ferrari: After BRM, Ferrari seemed to be best prepared for the new formula. In 1961 they had had the V-6 which was developed from Formula 2. This time they had a formidable array of 3-litre engines, and an impressive record of racing them in sports cars. There was even the same good omen of an easy victory in the non-championship season opener, the Syracuse Grand Prix. John Surtees still led the team following his 1964 world championship, and was making a good recovery from his Can-Am accident. Lorenzo Bandini looked more capable than ever as a back-up

The quarrel with Dragoni was reaching a critical point, however, and the new car suffered from a handling difficulty that was proving difficult to eradicate. Like most other designers, those at Ferrari agreed that 3-litre cars were likely to be big and heavy, but the new model was merely cumbersome. Surtees had trouble keeping ahead of Stewart's 2-litre BRM at Monaco, before retiring with differential failure; afterwards he won the Belgian Grand Prix, his last race for Ferrari.

Lorenzo Bandini led the French Grand Prix at Rheims, while Surtees's replacement (with whom he never got on) Mike Parkes, finished second. No matter how they tried to conceal it, the departure of their best driver left Ferrari in disarray. They failed to come to the British Grand Prix, blaming a metal workers' strike, and were late turning up for the Dutch, where both cars crashed. The German Grand Prix at the Nürburgring was unsatisfactory, and it was not until the Italian Grand Prix in September that things began to look up.

The V-12 engine had new, three-valve-per-cylinder heads, and although Dragoni's proposed Bandini victory was thwarted by a fuel leak, Lodovico Scarfiotti won Ferrari's home race—his fourth Grand Prix drive ever, and his only win.

The momentum was not sustained. Bandini suffered an undignified exit from the United States Grand Prix after leading, and the team missed Mexico to concentrate on the following year's sports prototypes—a measure of the diminished priority Formula 1 now took, following the defection of John Surtees.

Cooper: After Jack Brabham left to form his own team in 1961, some of the steam went out of the modest little partnership that he had taken into Grand Prix racing. It was not really equipped for the high technology pervading Formula 1, and had been sustained largely by the ingenuity of Brabham, together with the Coopers' own practicality. But practicality is plentiful, and ingenuity is not. They never displayed the same faith in the judgement of young Bruce McLaren, and looked quite baffled over what to do next. They turned up at race after race with the same cars, undeveloped, unmodified, capable of picking up occasional wins, but well out of the progressive league exemplified by Lotus, BRM, and Ferrari. Moreover, with Brabham's departure, their relationship with Coventry-Climax altered. Unlike Lotus, they no longer had any claim on 'development' engines, and were treated like any other customer.

Jonathan Sieff of the Marks and Spencer family, a motor sport enthusiast and former driver himself, bought the Cooper team, and through his ownership of Chipstead Motors eventually brought about a change in fortune. Chipstead held the British concession for Maserati road cars, and Sieff brought Maserati and Cooper together to provide an engine to replace the Coventry-Climax.

Maserati had never lost interest in racing, and even built and tested a 1½-litre V-12, but Formula 1 was beyond their means. They had developed a 3-litre V-12 from the 2½ litre of 1957, and used it for sports car racing. It was effectively ten years old, and the process of developing it for Formula 1 had to take into account fundamental changes, such as the introduction of petrol. Carburettors were abandoned in favour of fuel injection, and the ignition coils replaced with a transistorised system. By the end of the season, the engine was giving 340 bhp, together with a useful spread of torque, but it was big, heavy and extremely long.

It not only needed a large, bulky car, but it also suffered from an unusually high piston speed, leading to unreliability. However, like the BRM, it *was* ready in time for the first race. If it could race competitively in the opening years of the 3-litre Formula, Cooper and Maserati would have time to develop something more up-to-date. Cooper were experienced in modern chassis design, if not exactly innovators, but they did run a current Grand Prix team, so Giulio Alfieri of Maserati was already thinking about alternative 3-litre engines, or even a supercharged 1½. Multiple cylindered two-strokes might be dismissed as flights of fancy, but conventional supercharged engines were not—yet.

So far advanced were Cooper with their Maserati-engined car, which was under test by the autumn of 1965, that they were able to construct some for sale to private owners. Two appeared in races before the works car.

Although Bruce McLaren had gone, Cooper still had the services of the aggressive Jochen Rindt and Richie Ginther, who agreed to drive for them until his Honda was ready. John Surtees joined after he fell out with Ferrari half-way through the season, so there was no shortage of talent for testing, development, and racing.

For all that, Cooper obtained no more than moderate success. The high spots were at Spa, where Rindt led most of the way (although only after many of the likely winners had plunged off the road in a sudden shower) and the Nürburgring, where Surtees and Rindt finished second and third. Surtees might have won in America had he not suffered a collision; he would probably have been able to deal with Clark's Lotus-BRM. As it was Rindt finished second, with Surtees third. Surtees made amends with a convincing victory in the final round in Mexico, and Cooper-Maserati finished third in the Constructors' Championship, one point behind Ferrari, by now acknowledged the fastest car of the season.

Brabham: Motor racing has been defined as the art of the practical. Anything which works is automatically right, and Jack Brabham was thus, by definition, a pragmatist. It was partly fortuitous, partly opportunist, but mostly a gift for making the best of the available materials that created a racing car which did not follow the established tenets of design.

Faced with the familiar problem which confronted all the former Coventry-Climax clients, Brabham had to look elsewhere for an engine. He found it in his native Australia. The firm of Repco was the largest manufacturers of automotive parts and service equipment in the Southern Hemisphere. With a motor industry obliged to incorporate a substantial proportion of domestically produced ingredients, Repco had acquired substantial engineering expertise. It had also acquired Phil Irving, an engineer who, like Harry Mundy of Coventry-Climax, had connections with the technical press.

Developed from an aluminium Buick, the Australian Repco V-8 won the world championship for Brabham cars for the opening two years of the 3-litre Formula. In 1966 form it produced less power than any of its rivals, but was reliable, light, and consistent.

Repco had supported Brabham throughout his racing career, and it was to them that he turned in his search for a new engine. They had been busy adapting a design suitable for the 2½-litre Tasman Series of races, which often provided Grand Prix teams and drivers with a useful source of income during the close season.

Lacking the resources to design and develop a racing engine from scratch, Irving took an existing production cylinder block, and grafted on new heads. The engine on which his choice fell was an aluminium V-8, which General Motors had put into production for Buick and Oldsmobile 'compact' cars, but which they discarded, once techniques for thin walled castings in iron rendered the expense of aluminium unnecessary. It was the same pushrod overhead valve engine, together with certain production facilities, which was bought by Rover for their coming series of 3500 saloons.

Repco Engineering of Melbourne's modifications were more radical than the Rover Company of Solihull's. Irving's new cylinder heads had single overhead camshafts, and with Daimler con rods and a Laystall crankshaft, he soon had a 3-litre racing engine out of the 3½ litre, linerless 90° V-8. The original cylinder bore was maintained, the central camshaft disposed of, and the two new camshafts driven by chain. The result was a sturdy, thoroughly straightforward engine which, although lacking a number of classic racing engine features (it retained parallel in-line valves) did have good torque at low and medium speeds. Compared with the 400 bhp minus of the H-16 BRM, and the 380 of the Ferrari, or even the 340 of the Cooper-Maserati, the Repco's 300-315 bhp was modest indeed; but unlike several of its rivals, it *was* available when the flag fell for the start of the first race, the non-championship South African Grand Prix on 1 January 1966.

The car into which Brabham put the new engine was essentially a stop-gap. Using a tubular space frame because it was cheaper and easier to repair than a monocoque, Brabham had built the front half of the BT 19, as it was called, to accommodate the proposed flat-16 Coventry-Climax 1½ litre. It was in every respect a 1½-litre car, with the customary low weight of 1142 lb/518 kg, including engine. This was its most significant feature, because none of the other contestants in 1966 were anywhere near as light. The 500 kg/1102.3 lb minimum weight limit specified in the Formula 1 regulations was so that constructors would not skimp on materials to save weight. Strength and safety were still equated with weight, and the new, light cars from Britain were still strongly suspect, more so whenever accidents took place following a suspension breakage, or a sheared drive shaft. It seemed most unlikely that anyone would build a car down to the limit, at least for a year or two.

There were signs that Brabham had hit upon the right recipe in the very first race. He led the South African Grand Prix and set fastest lap, before retiring with injection pump trouble. He retired again at Syracuse, but by the

Silverstone International Trophy in May he was able to defeat John Surtees's Ferrari. The car suffered gearbox trouble in the first championship round at Monaco, finished fourth at Spa, then during the month of July, Brabham virtually swept the board on the way to his third world championship, at the age of 40.

He won the French Grand Prix at Rheims, the British at Brands Hatch, the Dutch at Zandvoort, then on 7 August, the German at the Nürburgring. By coming second in the Mexican Grand Prix at the end of the season, Brabham had 42 points against John Surtees's 28. He became the first driver to win the world championship in a car of his own manufacture, and with those four straight victories, re-wrote the handbook for the single seat racing car designer.

Brabham's fellow Australian, Ron Tauranac, drafted the chassis (the BT type nomenclature came from their surnames) but the conception was undoubtedly Brabham's. He proved that 3-litre Grand Prix cars need not be massive and unwieldy. A small, nimble car that was reliable and easily mended when it went wrong could still win races, even though it was inferior in power. He was on the first row of the grid four times, three of which were on the pole. His successes were not achieved merely by reliability, or even, as sometimes happens at the beginning of a season, by the rest of the field simply not being ready.

In the course of the year an improved version of the car, known as the BT 20 was produced. This had 1½ in/3.8 cm extra on the wheelbase and 1 in/2.5 cm on the track, a modified space frame and slightly wider body, and 15 in/38 cm wheels instead of 13. New Zealander Denny Hulme, who had joined from the Formula 2 team, drove a second car, sharing the front row of two starting grids with Brabham, finishing second in the British, and third in the French, Italian, and Mexican Grands Prix. Hulme took fourth place in the world championship.

McLaren: Bruce McLaren's side-line was Can-Am. He had set up his own team in 1963, to run two 2½-litre Coopers in the Tasman Series, but after winning the New Zealand Grand Prix, his antipodean season ended in tragedy with the death of his team mate, 25-year-old American Tim Mayer, in a practice accident before the final race at Longford, Tasmania.

Later the same year, Mayer's brother Teddy, a tax lawyer, became a partner in the McLaren team, and their first project was a car for the series of races that was to become famous as Can-Am. This was the Canadian-American Challenge Cup, which McLaren's cars would, in time, dominate.

They started with the ex-Roger Penske Zerex Special, a Cooper Monaco sports car in which Penske had replaced the Coventry-Climax four-cylinder engine with an aluminium Oldsmobile V-8, the same engine which was destined to form the basis of the 1966 Repco. McLaren's new car won first time, so he set out to build others.

His next step was to leave Cooper and form his own Formula 1 team. Once the principle of the proprietary engine had been established, Formula 1 teams proliferated. The investment necessary to design and build a chassis was trifling compared with what it cost for an engine, but until there was a more regular source of supply to replace Coventry-Climax, McLaren, like the rest, was faced with the problem of where to find them.

Colin Chapman had turned down the idea of adapting the 4.2-litre four-cam Indianapolis US Ford V-8, but McLaren was already into the engine modifying business for his Can-Am project, and undertook a development programme for the American V-8 until such time as he could become a customer for a BRM V-12.

McLaren's chassis design was undertaken by Robin Herd, a young Oxford graduate with a double first in physics and engineering, straight from the drawing boards of Concorde. With characteristic thoroughness, Herd started from first principles, and introduced a novel form of construction for the monocoque. He used Mallite, a sandwich of balsa wood between sheets of aluminium, but it proved a difficult material with which to work. Shaping it to the necessary curved form turned out to be an unnecessarily complicated, lengthy, and expensive process considering such benefits as it offered, and it was dropped the following year.

The engine was a more obvious failure, with frequent bearing trouble, and for the Belgian Grand Prix at Spa, McLaren fell back on an Italian V-8 of 265 bhp in order to put in some race mileage. The car only ran in practice, and after blowing up at Zandvoort, it was not entered for any further races until a revised Ford engine was ready for the US Grand Prix in the autumn. All in all, it was an inauspicious first season, yet McLaren was a team with a businesslike look about it, a strong technical and financial base from which to work, and it was expected to do well.

Eagle: Like McLaren, Dan Gurney took advantage of the proprietary engine philosophy to set up his own team, with himself as the leading driver. Like McLaren it was operated with a strong American connection (making Indy cars—one, Lloyd Ruby's, led the 1966 race for 68 laps) but like McLaren, establishing an engine supplier proved difficult.

Amongst the V-12s which began life in the BRM drawing office under Aubrey Woods, Gurney's was to be developed by an engineer famous for his studies of gas flow in cylinder heads. Harry Weslake had a small works near Rye in Sussex, and this was where Anglo American Racers also set up shop. Chassis design was in the hands of Len Terry, who had done some work on the Indianapolis Lotus as a freelance consultant, and he adapted a prototype on which he had been working for BRM, as a basis for the Eagle.

The Weslake four-valve heads took time to get ready, so Gurney had to make do with a 2.7-litre, four-cylinder Coventry-Climax, dating from the 2½-litre Formula of 1954–60. Unlike McLaren's stop-gap engine, Gurney's proved surprisingly competitive. Following the principle which Brabham had discovered of light weight and practicality, and despite being well down on power, Gurney managed fifth place in the French Grand Prix on the very fast Rheims circuit.

The Eagle really drew attention to itself in the British Grand Prix, however, when Gurney made some significant improvements to the suspension. It set third fastest practice time and finished fifth, to record the new make's first world championship points. At Zandvoort Gurney was fourth fastest in practice, and lay fourth in the race when he had to make a pit stop as a result of a leaking cylinder head gasket. Similar trouble delayed him in the German Grand Prix, but the new car held out the promise of success once the Weslake V-12, which was already giving 350 bhp on the bench, was installed.

But yet again, the development of a new engine proved a troublesome, laborious, and time-consuming business. Overheating, crankcase pressurisation, and throttle linkage problems plagued the Eagle until the end of the season. Gurney was not the first to discover that engines often behave differently in the car from the laboratory conditions of the test bed.

Honda: Winning the final race of the 1½-litre Formula encouraged Honda to build a 3-litre car. In view of their successes with motor cycle racing engines using large numbers of small cylinders working at astronomically high revolutions (not to mention the fond imaginings of 32 cylinders) their choice of a V-12 seemed almost prosaic. The car did not appear until the Italian Grand Prix in September, and it immediately became apparent that the Japanese engineers had not had the prescience of Jack Brabham, to design something small, light, and practical.

The Honda weighed nearly half as much again as the 500 kg minimum weight allowed. In fact it was 243 kg *above* the limit on the Monza weighbridge. Nonetheless, Richie Ginther worked his way up to second place before a tyre tread disintegrated, and he crashed, breaking his collar bone.

Honda's return was thus inconclusive, but before the end of the year they reached an agreement that John Surtees was to drive for them in 1967.

At the approach to Tabac on the Monte Carlo circuit Graham Hill's 2-litre BRM (left) duels with Jochen Rindt's Cooper Maserati, one of the new 3-litre cars for the new formula.

The H-16 BRM was a technical accomplishment of the highest order, overtaken by less sophisticated but more practical cars such as the Repco Brabham. Graham Hill practises the H-16 at Rheims for the French Grand Prix, but elected to use a 2-litre for the race. The H-16 did not race until Monza.

The formula changed, but the pattern of the world championship races remained much the same as in 1965, with the exception of the South African Grand Prix on 1 January. This was run as a non-championship event, because the FIA thought it too early for a full-blown qualifying round. As it was, Monaco in May still saw plenty of teams without 3-litre cars, including Lotus and BRM. Brabham had only one Repco, Denny Hulme starting with a four-cylinder, 2.7-litre Climax instead. One of the Ferraris was a 2.4 litre, and Parnell Racing had a Lotus 25 with a 2-litre engine for Mike Spence.

It was indicative both of the testing nature of the Monte Carlo course, and the dubious reliability of the new cars, that the race was won by Jackie Stewart's 2-litre BRM. Lorenzo Bandini was second in the 2.4-litre Ferrari, Graham Hill third in the second 2-litre BRM, and the only other classified finisher was American Bob Bondurant in yet another 2-litre BRM. Only two of the 3-litre cars were running when the chequered flag came down, and one of these was 25 laps behind. Only John Surtees's Ferrari had offered any opposition to the 2-litre cars.

Yet Monaco, as usual, could be considered a special case. The nature of the track, the good record here of BRM (this was their fourth win in a row) could have affected the result, and it was still unrealistic to imagine that any team without 3-litre power could expect to do well over the season.

The Belgian Grand Prix at Spa the following month was inconclusive as well. It was won by John Surtees in a 3-litre Ferrari, with Jochen Rindt second in a Cooper-Maserati. But the field was reduced by half on the first lap, after one of the most significant series of accidents ever in Grand Prix racing. It was almost as much of a turning point as the Le Mans disaster of 1955. Fortunately it was nothing like as serious, yet it did emphasise that the difference between fatal and non-fatal accidents was often a matter of luck.

The race began on a dull afternoon. As the 16-car field streamed down the hill from the start line to Eau Rouge, and up the opposite slope, heading off into the thickly wooded countryside, rain was already falling on the far side of the 14.1 km/8.77 mile course. Phil Hill set off from the back of the grid with a McLaren-Ford festooned with cameras for the making of sequences for John Frankenheimer's film *Grand Prix*. What he saw from the cockpit was more dramatic and frightening than anything imagined by a scriptwriter.

Jim Clark was out within a mile or so of the start, perhaps as events turned out, counting himself fortunate that Coventry-Climax had left a camshaft drive sprocket loose, expecting Lotus to re-time the engine when it was put in the car. They did not, and Clark's hopes of a fifth consecutive victory here vanished in a wrecked engine.

As the remainder of the field came to the difficult series of downhill sweeps at Malmedy, at speeds of around 150 mph/approx 240 kph they found the road awash. It had been raining for several minutes, and Jo Bonnier (Cooper-Maserati), Mike Spence (Lotus BRM), Denny Hulme (Brabham-Climax), and Jo Siffert (Cooper-Maserati) all went off the road. Although there were no injuries, Bonnier's Cooper finished up poised with the front wheels overhanging an unguarded ravine.

A mile or so away, on the famous Masta straight, the water lay in an enormous puddle which caused the wide tyres, despite their rain grooves, to skid across the surface. Grand Prix drivers were encountering almost for the first time a phenomenon little-known in the days of narrow tyres—aquaplaning.

The BRMs of Bob Bondurant, Graham Hill, and Jackie Stewart went out of control at once, Stewart's crash being by far the most serious of the afternoon. His BRM was severely damaged, trapping the driver, with petrol from the split tanks drenching his clothing and the surrounding grass. Ignoring the danger of explosion, Hill and Bondurant laboured to undo the steering wheel and release Stewart, who was in great pain from a broken shoulder and a cracked rib, and burning from the effects of the fuel on his skin.

It was the worst accident of Stewart's career, and he never forgot it. There was a delay in getting him to the circuit medical centre, which he found dirty and inefficient. There was a delay in getting him to hospital from which, largely as a result of the efforts of Louis Stanley, Sir Alfred Owen's brother-in-law, he was flown back to St Thomas's Hospital in London. He had been appalled by the whole experience, and vowed to lead a crusade on driver safety, which would exercise the minds and actions of people in Grand Prix racing for a long time to come.

The Belgian Grand Prix had been shortened over the years from 36 laps to 32 laps, and for 1966 it was 28 laps. The Ferraris of Surtees and Bandini shared the lead as news of the accidents filtered back. Then Jochen Rindt forced his way through the spray, and it looked as though he might win his first Grand Prix. But he was having trouble with the limited slip differential, and when Surtees overtook in the closing stages, there was nothing he could do to retaliate. Theirs were the only cars to complete the distance. Others, even amongst the cars still running, were less fortunate. Despite a brave drive in the appalling conditions, one non-qualifier was a French driver with a future in motor racing. His name—Guy Ligier.

Jack Brabham won the fastest Grand Prix race ever staged in France, at Rheims, repeated the triumph with a 1-2 for his team at Brands Hatch, won at Zandvoort when Clark's car overheated, and rounded off one of the most remarkable months in motor racing by winning a wet German Grand Prix. Within a few weeks, every designer in the business was looking at ways of making a 3-litre car that would be light, reliable, and much more like the 1½-litre cars they had just discarded than they had ever thought possible. Brabham had won the constructors' and drivers' titles convincingly with 320 bhp and a tubular chassis, where 400 bhp and a monocoque had been regarded as essential. Theories were of no avail if they failed to win races. Four-wheel drive was disregarded, for the moment at least. Brabham had demonstrated that there *was* an alternative, and if he was not to run away with 1967, others had little choice but to copy.

Drivers—a new deal

By 1966, professional drivers had acquired a world-wide role, bringing them into touch with other sorts of racing, leading in turn to a cross traffic that would have important consequences for Grand Prix racing. Indianapolis, for example, not only taught Lotus how to use wide tyres and build a big car for the BRM H-16 engine. It showed drivers that there were races where they could earn more in an afternoon than they took home from the entire Grand Prix season. The 1966 prize fund for Indy was $691 808, which included $30000 in lap prizes, and $545 239 in Speedway prizes. By 1970 it would rise to over $1 000 000, and one of the principal beneficiaries was invariably the winning driver.

Drivers became jet-setting travellers from country to country during the week, taking part in widely different sorts of racing at the weekends. Jim Clark drove Lotus sports cars, and also Ford Lotus-Cortinas, his spectacular three-wheeled cornering technique enlivening many touring car races, particularly in Britain. Clark often drove in three events in one afternoon, which obviously delighted the newly competition-conscious Ford Motor Company. Their links with Lotus were close, and having the world champion identified with their products became an integral part of their appeal to young buyers. Clark even drove a Lotus-Cortina in the 1966 RAC Rally with conspicuous success.

Jackie Stewart was amongst those who took part in Formula 2 racing, although he was careful not to over-commit himself. He already believed in extensive test sessions aimed at tuning his cars—and even his team—to concert pitch, and except for a few appearances in Lotus-Cortinas or sports cars, confined his activities to F.1, F.2, Tasman, and for 1966 only, Indianapolis.

Phil Hill, Jo Bonnier, Lorenzo Bandini, and Pedro Rodriguez had regular drives in world championship sports cars. These races occupied alternate weekends during the European summer, with events such as the historic Targa Florio, the Nürburgring 1000 Kms, and Le Mans. Lodovico Scarfiotti also distinguished himself in the European Mountain Championship, which included the long hill-climbs at Rossfeld, Mont Ventoux, and Cesana-Sestriere.

Jackie Stewart, Graham Hill, and Jim Clark took part in the Tasman Series during the Australian and New Zealand summer, Stewart winning the series, and BRMs seven out of the eight races. These three drivers nearly finished in the same order at Indianapolis in May. Stewart led the Memorial Day classic from lap 147 to 192, dropping back eight laps from the end with falling oil pressure, leaving Hill with an unexpected victory.

Bruce McLaren and Chris Amon won the 1966 Le Mans 24 Hours race for Ford, and also took part in the six-race Can-Am series for sports cars conforming to International Group 7 rules, meaning in effect two-seat racing cars. Their rivals in the $360000 championship included Dan Gurney, and John Surtees who won it in a Lola-Chevrolet, after winning rounds at St Jovite, Riverside, and Las Vegas.

The second round of the Can-Am at Bridgehampton, at Long Island's Hampton Bay on 18 September 1966, was notable for the first appearance of a new shape in motor racing. This was a new model Chaparral, driven by Phil Hill, with a device called, for want of a better term, a 'flipper'. This was a wide wing, on tall columns near the tail of the car, which, under control of the driver, tilted on corners to act like an aircraft wing in reverse, producing downthrust instead of lift. The effect was to press the rear tyres on to the track surface and provide extra grip. It was not an air-brake such as Mercedes-Benz had used on their 1955 300 SLR sports car. Instead, it was the first effective aerofoil to take part in a modern motor race, running in 'clean' air out of the turbulence caused by the car's passage through the air.

It looked bizarre, and nobody was very sure whether it worked or not. Chaparral were rather secretive about it for a time. It seemed just another of those 'spoilers' which were already familiar on cars with full-width bodies, now going so fast that special aerodynamic arrangements were required to 'spoil' their tendency to take off. One thing was sure, however, there were no regulations covering it.

So, the globe-trotting drivers went hurrying back to their Grand Prix teams, to report on the riches to be found elsewhere—and the curious devices to be discovered on cars on the other side of the world . . .

1967

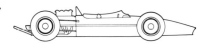

The world calendar grew longer with the South African Grand Prix restored to championship status, taking place at Kyalami for the first time, and the first Canadian Grand Prix at Mosport. The indecisive nature of the opening races in 1966 had largely gone, with Cooper-Maserati doing well in the closing rounds of the season, as though to convince the doubters that perhaps theirs *was* the way to go after all. And as though to confirm it, Pedro Rodriguez scored his first Grand Prix victory on 2 January 1967.

The move to Kyalami, which had already been used for a number of secondary South African races, was not unexpected. The Grand Prix was by now a major international sporting occasion. It needed to take place closer to the main centres of population, so it went from the resort town of East London to Kyalami, about half way between Johannesburg and Pretoria.

As the season wore on, three V-12 engines were to gain one victory apiece—Cooper-Maserati at Kyalami, Eagle in its solitary splendour at Spa, and the curious occasion of Honda at Monza. The rest of the year belonged to the V-8s. And it was not just the Repco this time, but a new V-8 destined to become the most famous and successful engine in the entire history of Grand Prix racing. The Ford-Cosworth DFV won its first race, and carried on winning throughout the modern Grand Prix era.

After Rodriguez scored his unexpected victory in South Africa, the first European race took place at Monaco on 7 May. It was an unhappy affair in which Denny Hulme, in his second season with Brabham, scored his first Grand Prix victory, but for the first time since the von Trips disaster in 1961, a driver crashed fatally during a world championship Grand Prix race. Lorenzo Bandini, at the age of 31, was trapped when his Ferrari overturned at the chicane on his 82nd lap, while placed second. The car caught fire, and Bandini died from his injuries the following day.

Monaco's safety record had been a good one, but perhaps because of that, the fire fighting and rescue services were unprepared, adding emphasis to Jackie Stewart's calls for greater safety at all circuits. Yet Monaco, strangely, had *been* safe, and while Stewart's recommendations for wide run-off areas and crash barriers seemed justified in most places, the proximity of walls and kerbs and buildings to the trackside here, had not taken a serious toll. Indeed only three drivers had ever been seriously injured at Monaco since racing began in 1929 (in each case during practice) and three had died. The 54-year-old veteran driver Luigi Fagioli died three weeks after being injured when he crashed in the Tunnel, practising for the 1952 sports car Prix de Monte

John Surtees's victory in the Italian Grand Prix demonstrated to the Japanese that his advice on chassis design was worth listening to. Based on Lola practice, his winning car was lighter, faster, and handled better than the earlier Honda.

Carlo. Dennis Taylor of Britain was killed when his Lola hit a tree on the incline leading to the chicane, during a heat of the 1962 Monaco Junior Grand Prix, and Norman Linnecar, also of Britain, died at Ste Devote during the only motor cycle Grand Prix at Monaco, in 1948. An official died after being struck by a wheel which broke off Richie Ginther's BRM during the opening lap accident in 1962.

Hulme won with the previous year's Repco Brabham. The engine which Brabham himself blew up during practice was a redesign intended to provide more power for 1967. The pattern of season-by-season development was being continued after a fashion during the new formula, and Repco completely changed the head and block, leaving very little of the original Buick. It failed to produce a great deal more power, however, and it was certainly not enough at the next race, the Dutch Grand Prix at Zandvoort, in the first week of June.

Graham Hill had left BRM at the end of 1966. He was disillusioned with the H-16, and clearly felt threatened by Jackie Stewart, so he returned to the team with whom he had first driven in Formula 1, Lotus. He intended overcoming the traditional underdog role of the second driver in Team Lotus that had proved so troublesome in the past, by being publicly appointed Equal Number One with Jim Clark. As a former world champion with a reputation for determined driving, he could demand such a title.

No form of words, however, could disguise the fact that the two drivers were poles apart in ability. Yet Chapman, as usual, was being shrewd. With Clark and Hill, he had the strongest team of drivers in the world. They were essentially complementary, and to match them, he produced a car that would go down the years as a Grand Prix classic, the Lotus 49.

The Lotus-Ford, as it was called in deference to the firm who were not merely the paymasters of the Ford-Cosworth engine, but also its progenitor in some practical senses as well, looked correct from the very beginning. It was brand new, but its presentation and preparation were exemplary. There was no hint of hurried assembly, or the crudeness that so often betrayed teams that found themselves short of time. The car gleamed with polished steel and chrome; it was resplendent in green and yellow, and looked right in every detail.

In fact its development had been carried out at breakneck speed. Clark, by now a tax exile, had not so much as sat in the car before Zandvoort, and even Hill had done precious few miles in it. Hill was fastest in practice, but Clark, unaccustomed to the new car, was on the third row of the grid. There, he had the unnerving experience of seeing a marshal stroll past during the tense seconds before the flag

The most successful Grand Prix engine of all time. The Ford-Cosworth DFV dominated world championship racing for more than ten years, and in a turbocharged version became the Indianapolis DFX. As installed in the Lotus 49, the crankcase acted as a stressed part of the chassis.

went down. With surely a reckless excess of zeal, the hapless official tried pushing Denny Hulme's Brabham back, amongst the revving, smoking welter of noise, when the start was given. The field took off, leaving him frozen to the spot and, miraculously, unscathed. No pedestrian was ever in such traffic and survived.

Hill led for the first ten laps, before rolling in to the pits with a dead engine. Faulty gear hardening had broken teeth off the timing gear, and he was out. Harley Copp and Walter Hayes, watching from the corner behind the pits, were nonetheless satisfied. Their new V-8 had proved competitive. It had led the race, and Jim Clark was working his way through from sixth place as he grew more familiar with the car.

Six laps later he took the lead, and almost unbelievably, kept it for the remainder of the 90 laps. Motor racing history had been made, and 4 June 1967 went down as the first victory of the Cosworth, and the start of a new chapter.

Gurney's Eagle won at Spa later the same month with Jackie Stewart second, his best place ever in an H-16 BRM. But he, too, was becoming disenchanted with the car, despite the promise of more power from improved versions of the engine, and the expectation of the V-12 to come. Jim Clark had told him what the Cosworth was like, and Stewart knew Lotus had an exclusive right to it for one year only. After that, it would be on sale to any team which might likewise reflect credit on Ford. Stewart was already a candidate.

The French Grand Prix on 2 July took place on the new Bugatti circuit at Le Mans. The Automobile Club de l'Ouest had run their 24 Hours race as usual in June, but they felt that Le Mans was more than the home of just one major race a year. It was also the time-honoured home of all motor racing; indeed all mechanised sport. Had not the first Grand Prix been run here 61 years before, and did not some of the first flights in Europe take off from its hallowed soil?

Well, of course, they had. But the two hundred thousand who regularly gathered to see the 24 Hours race every year, were not all necessarily motor racing enthusiasts. *Les Vingt-Quatre Heures du Mans* was an occasion: the Grand Prix was not. It was a two-hour sprint on a curious new track despised even by the drivers, who referred to it contemptuously as 'Mickey Mouse'.

In fact the Bugatti circuit was no more 'Mickey Mouse' than many on which they were to race in the years ahead. It was laid out largely within the *Circuit Permanent's* car parks, and used the same pits straight, but it was flat, and looked thoroughly artificial. Sparse crowds filled the yawning grandstands, and the experiment was never repeated.

Yet the track was a safe one. It was built with all the precautions the GPDA wanted; run-off areas were provided where a spinning car would lose speed before hitting anything. There was a safe, slow approach to the pits; there were escape roads and crash barriers. At places where cars might go off, there were even layers of light wire netting on poles, designed to catch cars and progressively slow them down, cushioning the impact layer by layer.

With these 'catch fences' as they became known, the Bugatti Circuit was a foretaste of things to come, an arid, featureless place, and to make matters worse, it was a dull race. Brabham and Hulme were the only two to complete the 80 laps; Jackie Stewart was a lap behind, Jo Siffert two, and eight cars retired before lap 50, including both Lotus 49s. If tracks like that produced racing like this, were they really wanted? Safety crusaders were called unkind names.

At Silverstone, a fortnight later, Jim Clark won the British Grand Prix for the fifth time in six years. It was another triumph for the new Lotus, but Hill's car had to come into the pits with a loose suspension bolt, following a rebuild after an accident during practice. Out of four races, Clark won two, but Hill had not finished any. All he had to show was fastest lap in the French Grand Prix. Equal Number One was not a rank recognised by Dame Fortune.

Denny Hulme won the German Grand Prix at the Nürburgring in August, after Clark and Gurney dropped out, then the circus was whisked across the Atlantic for the new Canadian Grand Prix at Mosport, in the hills above Lake Ontario. Throughout its history, Mosport had problems with the weather, and the inaugural Grand Prix pointed the watery way ahead. Jim Clark's Lotus had a lead of a minute and a quarter when the rain got into the ignition. Denny Hulme dropped back when he had to make two stops for clean goggles, leaving Jack Brabham to score his second victory of the season. Hulme was second, Dan Gurney third, and Graham Hill, managing to finish for the first time in the season, fourth two laps behind.

Monza was memorable for a different reason. By 10 September, the cars were back from Canada, and a surprise was the new Honda, built in six weeks in England, on advice from Surtees, who had begun to feel he was getting nowhere with the overweight, lugubrious V-12. Its more than passing resemblance to a Lola resulted in the new car being dubbed the 'Hondola', but it was smaller, 200 lb/about 91 kg lighter, and demonstrably worked. Honda was belatedly recognising the Brabham principle, which Cooper and BRM had also apparently overlooked with such unhappy results.

In the race, it looked as though Graham Hill's luck was about to change, and he seemed headed for a comfortable win. After two of the scheduled 68 laps, Clark displaced Gurney's Eagle for the lead, but had some difficulty dealing with Hulme, who darted out of the slipstream on the long Monza straights and actually passed on lap ten. Three laps later, Clark was in the pits. A puncture cost him over a lap, and by the time he returned to the race, the two Brabhams had got the better of Hill.

Slipstreaming, of course, could be used for more purposes than overtaking. A faster driver can also 'tow' a team mate to a higher speed than he may be

able to achieve on his own, and as Clark, an entire lap behind, caught up, Hill hung on to him. With the close understanding between the Lotus drivers, their cars almost touching at close on 180 mph/290 kph, Hill was 'sucked' along in Clark's wake to get clear of Brabham and Hulme, and back into the lead. Hulme's engine found the strain too much and overheated, while Clark, his job of helping his colleague done, gradually pulled ahead again. He began an astonishing progression from 15th place and a whole lap, over 5 km/approx 3½ miles in arrears.

It was one of the most brilliant performances in the career of the greatest driver of his day. Clark pulled away from Hill at the rate of two seconds per lap. On lap 26 he set a new record for Monza in 1 min 28.5 sec (233.898 kph/145.337 mph) gaining as many as three places on one lap. By half distance he was seventh, by lap 48 fifth, and lap 54, fourth.

On lap 58, ten laps from the end, a broken-hearted Hill coasted into the pits with that recurring Cosworth problem, broken timing gears. Brabham took the lead, and almost at once Clark passed Surtees and lay second. There was now no stopping the Flying Scot, and on lap 61, almost incredibly, Clark was back in the lead after one of the most convincing demonstrations of driving skill since Fangio's famous German Grand Prix almost exactly ten years before.

Alas, on his final lap the Lotus faltered, and Clark's painfully built-up lead was halved. The pace was consuming fuel faster than Chapman had bargained for, and although there was still about a gallon and a half left in the tanks, it was being picked up only intermittently. Surtees shot by, and then Brabham. The Australian, head down in characteristic hard-charging fashion, even managed to pass the Honda on the final corner—but Surtees pulled ahead again in the sprint to the finish with Brabham a matter of feet behind. The timekeepers gave the interval as 0.2 sec.

Watkins Glen, the penultimate round of the 1967 season, was almost, by contrast, an anticlimax. It was nearly as dramatic for Clark, however, who won despite a rear wheel hanging at a crazy angle, owing to a broken suspension arm for the final 2½ laps. Graham Hill was second, only the second race he had completed all season.

By the last round in Mexico, the championship lay between Hulme and Brabham. Jim Clark won the race, his 24th victory, matching Fangio's ten-year-old record of Grand Prix wins, but Hulme took the title with a safe third place.

Quiet, tough New Zealander Denny Hulme gives a touch of opposite lock to his Repco Brabham on his way to winning the 1967 world championship.

Cosworth

Colin Chapman's search for an engine to replace the Coventry-Climax had led him back to one of his earliest collaborators. Keith Duckworth had worked for Lotus at Hornsey as a development engineer. He later formed Cosworth Engineering together with another ex-Lotus colleague, Mike Costin, brother of Frank, the aerodynamicist who had designed the bodywork for the Vanwall. COStin and DuckWORTH put more than their names together. Along with a third director, Bill Brown, they put their combined practical and theoretical skills towards an engine design and tuning business, which was already supplying racing engines and so-called 'conversion' equipment in substantial quantities, when Chapman asked Duckworth if he could design a Formula 1 engine.

Duckworth thought he could, so Chapman went off to find the money. The Ford Motor Company had already backed Cosworth in the production of the 1000 cc SCA engine for Formula 2 racing, loosely based on a Cortina. Duckworth put the cost of the Formula 1 project at £100000—much less than Ford of America had spent on their Indianapolis engine, and a mere trifle compared to what it had cost Ford to win Le Mans.

Chapman already had strong connections with Ford through the Lotus Cortina. Harley Copp, Ford of Britain's Vice-President of Engineering, and Walter Hayes, a former journalist, then Ford's Director of Public Affairs, agreed that Ford ought to take a chance on the brilliant young engineer. Duckworth was still only 33.

A little incredulous, aware of the daunting nature of the task, Ford advanced £25000 for an engine based on another of their production units, the 116E four-cylinder Escort, for the 1967 Formula 2. This permitted engines up to 1600 cc, and a four valves per cylinder layout was envisaged, so Duckworth with breathtaking originality dubbed the engine FVA, for Four Valve Type A.

When he doubled-up the FVA to make a 3-litre V-8, he called it, logically enough, the DFV, or Double Four Valve. The nomenclature was consistent with his great capacity, similar to Chapman's, for utter fundamentalism, combined with a deep flair for thinking out engineering problems. He tackled them head-on, and astonishingly got most of his answers right first time. For a new engine to achieve sufficient reliability to finish its first race was unusual. To win its first race was, in modern Grand Prix racing, unique.

Denny Hulme (b 1936)

Although not one of the best-remembered world champions in the mould of Clark, Fangio, or Ascari, Denny Hulme was nevertheless a worthy one. Taciturn like Brabham, he had appeared, it seemed, from nowhere, and not many people knew him. He cared little for self-advertisement, concentrating on getting on with the job, and turning in some extremely polished performances during his two years in the 3-litre Formula with Brabham.

The title set the seal on Hulme's reputation as a driver, yet while Phil Hill, John Surtees, and Giuseppe Farina all seemed to have won it at, or just after, they had reached the peak of their careers, Hulme's best days were still to come. He never won the title again, but his grit and courage in the years ahead, particularly after the painful burns to his hands following an alcohol fuel fire at Indianapolis in 1970, earned him great respect.

Born in New Zealand in 1936, the son of Clive Hulme who won a VC in Crete during the Second World War, Dennis Clive Hulme graduated from an MG TF to a single-seater Cooper-Climax. This earned the New Zealand International Grand Prix Association's 1960 'Driver to Europe' scholarship, which had sent Bruce McLaren to England two years earlier.

It was 1964 before Hulme's big break came, when he joined Jack Brabham's team for the Tasman Series. Formula 1 drives followed intermittently, and it was the first year of the 3-litre Formula before Hulme had established his place on a regular basis. He finished second with Ken Miles in a Ford at Le Mans, but after winning the world championship, stuck to single seaters and Can-Am racing with his friend Bruce McLaren.

It was in Can-Am that Hulme's toughness showed best. With the big orange McLarens, his favourite racing cars, he won the series in 1968, and again in 1970, when he carried on despite the tragic death of Bruce McLaren in a testing accident at the beginning of the season.

Hulme retired in 1974, a veteran of 112 Grand Prix races, of which he won eight. Rather surprisingly he gained pole position only once, the South African Grand Prix of 1973, but he set fastest lap seven times. Happy with his nickname of 'The Bear', earned through his reputation for irascibility—probably more of a protective shell than he would ever admit—he returned to New Zealand with his family after a notable ten years in Grand Prix racing.

1968

DUNLOP
PNEUMATICI
Mobil
Gulf
Gulf
Gulf
Gulf
TROL
Gulf
MICHELIN
Campagnolo
PIRELLI
SU MISURA
SU MISURA
SU MISURA
ARAL
ARAL
ARAL
ARAL
FINA
75

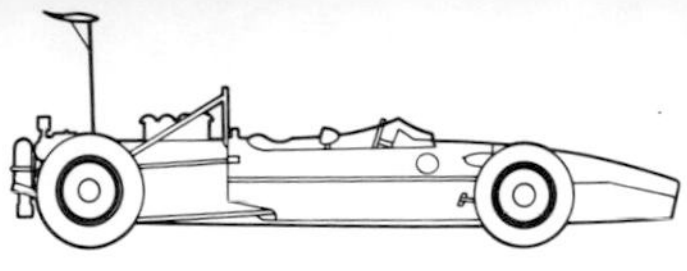

Development of Grand Prix cars did not stop with the introduction of the Cosworth engine, but it followed a different course. A horse-power stalemate was reached as it established ascendancy, winning every Grand Prix but one in the long 1968 season, in which Spain brought the qualifying races to twelve. The last time a proprietary engine had achieved such dominance was with Coventry-Climax in 1962, when Chapman's solution had been the Lotus 25, an immense step forward in handling and road holding. A similar solution would need to be found now, but suspension and chassis design seemed to have reached the point where such gains were small.

With the end of the Lotus monopoly, there was a proliferation of Cosworths. McLaren and Matra International obtained theirs. BRM gave up the H-16 and tried the V-12, Matra Sport joined in with *their* V-12, Cooper gave up the Maserati and bought V-12s from BRM. Dan Gurney's Eagles had a miserable season, closing down in Europe at the end of it.

Sadly, there were other partings of the ways in 1968. Between April and June, four drivers died in one of Grand Prix racing's saddest summers. Jim Clark, Mike Spence, Lodovico Scarfiotti, and Jo Schlesser were lost to a stunned Formula 1 world that seemed to grow older with each bereavement. Somehow, it seemed, motor racing would never be the same again.

In many ways, it never was. Although only Schlesser died during a Grand Prix, safety became more urgent. Improvements to tracks and cars, and changes in regulations became more pressing than ever; the question was not so much whether to make changes, as how, and how fast. There was still no clear agreement over what was required. The GPDA said the tracks needed changing. More safety barriers should be put up; trees, walls, bankings, and buildings were to be moved back. The penalty for error was to be made less severe.

The tracks disagreed. They were deep in the process of changing the system of payment for races. Starting money was being gradually abolished. Instead, the constructors were pressing for (and obtaining) an arrangement for paying every finisher according to his position at the end of the race. Instead of each team haggling beforehand, the entire race purse was split up according to merit. It was fair and equitable, but it did imply bigger purses, and the tracks argued that it left less cash for safety improvements.

Clark died in a Formula 2 race at Hockenheim. The explosive decompression of a tyre—a blow-out—was later blamed: there was still much to learn about wide, hand-made, fragile racing tyres. He was not even in the lead. He had no hope of winning; it was inexplicable. It was like Stirling Moss's crash all over again, except that Clark hit a tree, and died at once.

Mike Spence was practising at Indianapolis. As a driver he was reaching a stylish maturity, and his loss was a serious one for BRM. He hit the retaining wall at speed, and was crushed in his disintegrating car. Scarfiotti was killed practising for one of his beloved hill-climbs. Schlesser was a Formula 2 driver, pressed upon John Surtees in an ill-judged attempt to boost Honda's sales in France. He lost control of the experimental, air-cooled Honda V-8, considered by Surtees as unready to race, on the downhill curves at Rouen in the wet. It overturned and caught fire. Armco barrier put up to prevent a repetition of the tragedy only caused another, when Gerry Birrell, the promising Scottish driver crashed into it five years later. There seemed no answer to the chain of disasters.

The last Grand Prix Clark won was the first for Gold Leaf Team Lotus, although when he drove to victory at Kyalami, his car was not yet in the unfamiliar red, white, and gold. The CSI had at last relaxed the restrictions on advertising on racing cars, and Lotus were the first to take advantage.

Formula 1 had always had a slightly patronising attitude to Americans, with their Red Ball Specials (Graham Hill's 1966 Indianapolis winner) or Zink-Urschel-Slick Trackburners. Yet now it was emulating them, with racing cars painted up like cigarette packets. Traditionalists were appalled, although the effects of sponsorship did not seem serious at first. It had no great influence on how teams were run, and only in the long term affected some aspects, such as the choice of drivers.

Those engaged for 1968 included Clark and Hill for Lotus, but after Clark died, Jackie Oliver came in from Formula 2. After Spence was killed, Richard Attwood joined Pedro Rodriguez at BRM. Hulme joined McLaren, a surprise after his 1967 championship, but a well-judged move, while Jochen Rindt took his place at Brabham. Rindt had still not won a Grand Prix. His talent was plain to see ever since his sensational defeat of Graham Hill on 18 May 1964, at the Whitsun Crystal Palace Formula 2 meeting, yet he never managed to be in the right team at the right time. The Cosworth was overpowering the Repco-Brabhams, now stretched up to (and beyond) their limits.

Unlike Rindt, Jackie Stewart knew exactly when to move. He left BRM, unconvinced about the new V-12, and together with his mentor Ken Tyrrell, started the Matra International team, using Ford-Cosworth engines. Stewart had never stopped driving for Tyrrell. When his Cooper BMC days were over, and he was with BRM in Formula 1, Tyrrell engaged him in a Formula 2 Matra. Following the Brabham principle of using the smallest practicable car, this needed only a minor redesign with the British V-8 on the back, to enable it to race in Formula 1 and give France a contender (at least by proxy) in Grands Prix. Tyrrell's sponsorship from Elf, the French national oil company, had a French driver in the small print, in this case the unlikely, though skilled, Johnny Servoz-Gavin.

A missile and aerospace firm, Matra appeared on their own account with a V-12, driven by Jean-Pierre Beltoise and Henri Pescarolo, but it was never as successful as the Anglo-French team of Tyrrell's.

Jim Clark (b 1936)

Excepting the Le Mans disaster, no tragedy in a sport that had seen many, was felt so keenly as the death of Jim Clark. The reasons lay deeper than simply the high personal regard in which Clark was held. They were deeper than his well-moulded Scottish character, or his natural modesty, visible not only to motor racing enthusiasts, but radiating to a world audience.

Jim Clark's accident was a convincing demonstration of the vulnerability of the racing driver. His genius at the wheel had been such that a generation grew up believing that a driver could be adroit enough to outwit death. Clark always seemed to be in *some* control of his car, even to the extent of minimising the consequences of an accident after it had started. Commentators would gasp, and say, 'Look at Jim Clark controlling that spin.'

If anyone could keep control, it was he. Yet on the grim April day at Hockenheim, even Clark became a passenger in a racing car. The entire motor sporting world went into a state of shock. If motor racing could kill Jim Clark, it could kill anybody. A host of illusions that had built up around the sport were shattered. It was like war games suddenly being conducted with live ammunition. An activity where 'dicing with death' had been taken lightly was no longer fun. The death of Clark meant that, after all, survival in a racing car could be just a matter of chance—an incalculable risk. Retired drivers may boast of never having drawn blood throughout their career, but the credit obviously did not entirely belong to them.

It was a coincidence, of course, yet the loss of Clark and the total commercialisation of motor racing took place almost simultaneously. Sponsorship and advertising was a gradual process compared to the sudden, paralysing blow of his death. However, once advertising took root, the idealism of motor racing as a modern, gladiatorial struggle, or even as a sport in the strictest sense of amusement, or game, simply disappeared. With Clark, the heroic element still seemed to be present. Without him, Grand Prix racing began to change. Its motivation became less and less a contest amongst cars and drivers and engineers. It became a promotion, a spectacle, a means of making money—a circus.

In a sense it was a replay of the Thirties, where the motives had been nationalist propaganda. Now individuals and groups began to infiltrate, recognising the commercial possibilities of the interest in racing rather, perhaps, as Dr Goebbels had seen it 30 or so years before. It became a means to an end.

In both cases of course, it produced memorable motor racing. But it was *different* motor racing.

Jim Clark's boyhood gave little clue to the role he was to play in the development of Grand Prix racing. He was born at Kilmany in Fife, Scotland, on 14 March 1936, the only son of a wealthy farming family. In 1942 they moved to Edington Mains, a farm near Duns in Berwickshire.

Amongst Clark's earliest connections with motor sport was in 1948, when his eldest sister married a local farmer who raced a Brooklands Riley Nine, and owned a 3-litre Bentley. Clark watched Guiseppe Farina race the Thinwall Special on Charterhall, a nearby airfield track, where he later drove in some of his early races.

He took part in rallies and sprints in a Sunbeam and then a Triumph TR3, racing for the first time in June 1956 with his friend Ian Scott-Watson's DKW Sonderklasse on Crimond, another Scottish airfield circuit, in Aberdeenshire. Recognising Clark's astonishing skill, Scott-Watson traded in the DKW for the ex-Billy Cotton Porsche 1600S, and by 1958 Clark was racing regularly in club events in Scotland and the North of England.

His exploits with the Porsche led to the reformation of the Border Reivers team with an already famous D-Type Jaguar, TKF 9, which had been raced by Archie Scott-Brown and Henry Taylor. Of 20 races in which the D-Type was entered Clark won 12, taking part in his first Continental event at Spa, the race in which Scott-Brown lost his life.

With the Reivers' Lister-Jaguar and Scott-Watson's Lotus Elite, Clark made an impression on Colin Chapman, almost beating him in a race at Brands Hatch. This led to a Lotus works car for Formula Junior and Formula 2, and in time, Formula 1.

His rapport with Chapman was complete. Although untutored as an engineer, Clark mastered the new art of 'setting-up' the suspension and trim of a racing car. As his career progressed, he overcame some of his natural reserve, although not to the extent that he ever enjoyed self-advertisement or making speeches. He was never a public performer like his team mate Graham Hill, nor had he the business acumen of his fellow Scot Jackie Stewart. But he had a skill that outstripped them all, and a sense of responsibility to the *aficionado* seldom seen in a racing driver. Jim Clark happily earned a substantial income from motor racing, but riches were not his inspiration—taking part was.

Jim Clark was world champion in 1963 and 1965. But for some ill-disposed fate he would have been champion in 1962, 1964, and 1967 as well. He was amongst the very last of the great sporting racing drivers.

Ferrari meanwhile promoted another of Tyrrell's discoveries, Jacky Ickx from Belgium, to their team, together with Chris Amon. Cooper lost Scarfiotti before the season was properly under way, followed closely by Brian Redman, injured when his front suspension broke at Spa. It was the beginning of the end for the team which had won the world championship in 1959–60, but had now run out of ideas. At the end of the year it also ran out of sponsorship, when BP withdrew partly as an economy, partly in protest at the rising costs foreseen for the 3-litre Formula.

Clark and Hill dominated the South African Grand Prix on 1 January, Jackie Stewart leading somewhat impertinently for the first lap, in his essentially Formula 2 Matra. But by May, when the field lined up for the Spanish Grand Prix on the new track at Jarama near Madrid, Clark and Spence were dead, and the GPDA were already sensitive to matters effecting safety.

Jarama had been built with the catch fences and guard rails they wanted—a new artificial circuit with the permanent installations for which they had so long campaigned. Yet they were still apparently not satisfied. The race was very nearly cancelled because the GPDA said its members would not take part until the safety barriers were properly installed. They were too high, and Jackie Stewart had collided with one at the inaugural meeting, his car sliding underneath, coming to rest with the steel so close that it knocked the peak off his helmet. A foot or so more and he would have been beheaded.

Loose gravel and marker cones which threatened to fly into drivers' faces were other points of contention. Stewart was a non-starter owing to a wrist injury, Hill won for a distraught Team Lotus, and Rodriguez crashed his BRM. The new Grand Prix on the new track was a portent of more trouble to come.

At Monaco, Hill repeated his triumph with a fourth, record-setting victory round the historic track. He was driving the curiously shaped new edition of the Lotus 49, with wings on the nose-cone and an upswept tail. They called it 'The Wedge', and it proved to be the thin end of a change that would engulf racing in one of its most acrimonious quarrels for years.

Aerodynamics was an area where designers hoped to gain an advantage, but not in the familiar sense of reducing drag to gain speed on the straights. That had already been tried in 1963 with the reclining driver, inboard suspension, and the enclosure of everything encloseable in a tight-fitting envelope. There were limits to how slim cars could be. Drivers could not lie down any further or they would not be able to see. In any case, the massive tyres were now the limiting factor in frontal area; it was a field of diminishing returns.

That left aerodynamic aids to cornering. On 24 June 1956 a Swiss engineer, Michael May, was due to drive a Porsche Spyder in the Supercortemaggiore sports car race with an aerofoil above the open cockpit, tilting through angles of —3° to +17°, acting through the centre of gravity of the car. The object was to apply increased loading on the tyres when cornering, but the Italian scrutineers turned it down, and it never raced. That left the Chaparral to show the way in 1967, with its 'flipper' flicking up and down on command from the driver. Its success encouraged a closer look at means of using the science of aerodynamics in an altogether new way.

Above: Graham Hill at Monaco, a race which he won five times. In 1968 he drove the Lotus 49 'wedge' with nose fins and the embryonic tail wing disguised as an air scoop for the rear oil cooler. Earlier in the season (below) he won the Spanish Grand Prix at Jarama, the team's first Grand Prix in the full John Player livery, and their first since the loss of Jim Clark.

Chapman's 'wedge' Lotus was a tentative step. The technology needed exploring, and so did the regulations. As he had found with his Indianapolis turbines, any radical idea that turned out too fast too soon, ran the risk of wholesale bans by authorities anxious to preserve the status quo. But having piloted his own aircraft for some time, and knowing that his cars often achieved take-off speeds, the Chaparral solution appealed to him. Essentially, this involved taking an aircraft wing and inverting it, so that instead of lift, it generated downforce.

The principal difficulty lay in where to apply the aerodynamic stress. The Chaparral fed its downforce straight into the rear wheel hubs, with the advantage

BP
9
LOTUS
FORD

STP

Jackie Stewart's greatest race

For three days, the cloud base lay below the 620 m/2034 ft highest point of the Nürburgring. For three days, the Grand Prix world kept its raincoats on, and spectators at the German Grand Prix huddled under umbrellas and tarpaulins. All round the circuit, which threaded its way amongst the pine trees and the hills of the Eifel, they waited. In their dripping encampments hidden in the swirling mist, they expected the race to be cancelled.

Practice had been a fragmentary affair, with sessions postponed or called off, and on the Sunday, the race itself was delayed to give the fog a chance to lift. Visibility was around 100 m/330 ft, and during the morning warm-up, Stewart tried his car first with a wing, then without, while Jackie Oliver crashed, knocking two wheels off his Lotus 49.

Jacky Ickx had been fastest in official practice, with 9 min 4.0 sec at a time when a good Nürburgring lap should have been nearer eight minutes. On race morning, the conditions were so bad, with rivers of water running across the track, that Stewart was hard pressed to get under ten minutes. He was still easily the fastest, however, channels pumping the water away from the tread of his Dunlops, giving him more grip than anyone else in the 20-car field.

Grip or not, a driver's main problem was how far he could see. This was a difficulty at the Nürburgring in any case, as the road dived down behind blind crests, and dipped amongst the trees into dark valleys that concealed sharp bends. Yet here were the world's best drivers about to lap the track at nearly 90 mph/approx 145 kph. The lap record in the dry stood to Dan Gurney at 165.96 kph/103.12 mph and the cars reached 170 mph on the rather undulating 'straight'. And the racers included the most vigorous campaigner for motor racing safety of all.

The combination of Jackie Stewart, Matra Ford MS 10 and Dunlop tyres proved almost invincible in the wet races of 1968. Here he splashes through the rain in the French Grand Prix at Rouen.

Stewart's views were not always popular. He had been pilloried by a vociferous minority who still believed that danger was somehow ennobling. There were still those who thought that motor racing achieved greatness by its constant conflict with death.

He would have none of this. And at the German Grand Prix, he was about to silence his critics. Starting from the third row of the grid, he took the lead half-way round the first long, rain-soaked, drizzly lap. By the time the field came past the pits trailing long plumes of spray, he was 9 sec in the lead. By the end of the second lap, he was an astonishing 34 sec ahead. By the third it was 47 sec. By lap four, 58 sec, while a mere 9 sec covered the next four cars, Hill (Lotus), Amon (Ferrari), Rindt (Brabham), and Ickx (Ferrari).

Vic Elford, the rally driver attempting Grand Prix racing with Cooper, went off the road at Pflanzgarten. Jean-Pierre Beltoise (Matra V-12) went off at Hohe Acht. Chris Amon (Ferrari) spun into the ditch at the Nordkehre, while Stewart went faster than ever. He set the race's fastest lap with a time of 9 min 36.0 sec (142.67 kph/88.67 mph). By the end, he was over 4 min ahead of Hill, half a lap in 14, and Hill was fighting off Rindt, only 4 sec behind.

Stewart splashed his blue Matra, almost invisible in the mist, across the finishing line, and drove round the long South Curve, and back up behind the pits. He stopped, got out of the car, and stood chatting to officials before the second car could be heard.

Ascari; Fangio; Moss; Clark; there had always been a driver who was better than all the rest. Now, there was a new one—Jackie Stewart.

of imposing the load on the tyres alone. A body-mounted wing merely tended to force the car down on its springs, as though with an increase of weight. Chapman was already developing a full wedge shape for his Type 56 gas turbine Indianapolis cars, and as a first stage applied a similar, though less extreme, solution to the 49, now known as the 49B.

At the Belgian Grand Prix in June, the prospect of the fast Spa circuit brought out further aerodynamic experiments. There was still some doubt about how effective they really were, or how much they merely contributed to drivers' psychological well-being. Some, such as the 18 in/45 cm wide moulding on the engine cover of the McLaren, had a negligible effect through being too small and situated in a turbulent part of the airstream. Honda applied a sheet of aluminium almost out of sight behind the engine. The more elaborate structure on the Ferrari was on such frail struts that its downforce must have been of small account.

Lotus discovered that the tail wedge had to be counterbalanced by vanes on the nose, and when Brabham joined the wing cars at Spa, he too employed nose tabs to prevent the car adopting a tail-down attitude. A month afterwards, at the French Grand Prix, any doubts about the efficiency of wings was resolved in an accident which threw a frightening new light on the whole issue.

The Lotuses appeared with wings on tall struts, and Jackie Oliver quickly discovered one of their more dramatic side effects. Coming up close behind Richard Attwood's BRM, Oliver's Lotus suddenly went out of control, writing itself off, with the gearbox and rear wheels 30 m/98 ft from the rest of the car. It was a 140 mph/225 kph accident, and the driver was lucky to escape without injury, but it served the purpose of showing how much was still to be learned about wings.

McLaren now carried them, followed by Honda, Matra, and BRM. Brabham was the first to use two, mounting an extra one over the front wheels, and before the end of the season Matra, Lotus, and Ferrari had movable wings, like the Chaparral and the May cousins' Porsche, though smaller. Matra's was worked by means of an electric motor, and actuated by the brakes, while Ferrari's was hydraulic, from gearbox oil pressure and feathered when the driver flicked a stalk on the steering column. The Lotus arrangement was a simpler one, in which the wing was tilted on corners by means of a pedal working a system of cords. Already, however, the dangers of wings were becoming apparent; Amon spun during the Italian Grand Prix after a hydraulic line failed.

Mounting remained an inexact science. Wings sometimes fell off, and there was still disagreement about whether they should be mounted securely on the chassis, or on the suspension, where they were subject to vibration. Either way, no regulations took them into account beyond perhaps those stipulating that bodywork (always rather quaintly called 'coach-work' in English translations of FIA rules) must not project beyond the wheels. Some wings did, but it could be (and was) argued that wings were not 'bodywork' within the meaning of the rules. Furthermore, and by way of confirmation that wings *did* work, there was a serious outbreak of drive shaft failures.

Graham Hill won Monaco despite a spirited pursuit by Richard Attwood, hurriedly drafted into the BRM team following the death of Mike Spence, and the serious accident which ended the Grand Prix career of Chris Irwin. It was hardly a classic Monaco, however, with only five cars running after 17 laps, Jackie Stewart still a spectator following his wrist injury, and Ferrari absent.

Back at the wheel, however, Stewart very nearly won the Belgian Grand Prix. Amon's Ferrari led the first lap, followed by John Surtees (Honda) for nine laps, until the suspension broke. Stewart then ran short of fuel, handing Bruce McLaren the first victory for his new make of car.

Stewart made up for it a fortnight later, scoring the first win for Matra-Ford in a wet Dutch Grand Prix. Jacky Ickx scored his first victory in the tragic French Grand Prix at Rouen, another circuit where the choice of tyres for the wet road proved vital. Jo Siffert won a hard-fought British Grand Prix at Brands Hatch, *his* first ever, and the first for Rob Walker since the days of Stirling Moss.

Grand Prix racing also found itself locked into yet another modern phenomenon, a 'tyre war'. Lotus, Ferrari, Cooper, and Honda were on Firestone; both sorts of Matra (and BRM part of the time) were on Dunlop, and Eagle, Brabham, McLaren (and BRM the rest of the time) were on Goodyear. The tyre firms were major sources of revenue for the teams through retainers and bonus payments. Firestone, however, like Coventry-Climax and Ferrari before them, were going through one of their 'withdrawal' periods. Yet they managed to score best in 1968 with six victories, leaving Dunlop and Goodyear three apiece.

But it was the spectacular victories of Dunlop that stole the show, in particular their wet weather triumphs in Holland and Germany, boosting an advertising campaign for road tyres with extra grip in the rain. The Matra's low camber change suspension, designed to keep the tyre at 90° to the road, allowed Dunlop to design a very flat, low-profile tyre with a height to width ratio which was reduced in the space of a season from 50 per cent to 40 per cent. Other cars with different suspension characteristics demanded more round-shouldered tyres, illustrating the 'fine tuning' now being done at the initial stages of design to match up components.

The result was that when Firestone withdrew, or changes in the rules sought to outlaw features of design such as wings, the unscrambling process could affect some cars more than others.

The Italian Grand Prix at Monza should have marked the début of two American drivers with distinguished Indianapolis careers. Mario Andretti and Bobby Unser were entered by Lotus and BRM

Winner of the British Grand Prix at Brands Hatch, Jo Siffert (Rob Walker Lotus 49).

respectively, then flew to the United States after practice to take part in the Hoosier 100. The organisers were expected to waive the CSI's rule, preventing drivers from racing during the 24 hours before a Grand Prix. But despite the prospect that the popular Italo-American Andretti would add substantially to the crowd, the AC di Milano stuck to the letter of the law, and forbade it. Andretti did take part in the United States Grand Prix a month later, earning the profound respect of the Grand Prix 'regulars' by taking pole position on the grid, and holding second place for 13 laps. But he was only to flirt with Formula 1 for almost a decade, before his talent gained the recognition it deserved.

Hulme's hopes for defending his title were raised when he won the Canadian Grand Prix, only to be dashed by transmission trouble in the United States Grand Prix, and an accident in Mexico when the McLaren's suspension failed. Stewart won in the US, and for the second time in four years, three drivers came to the final in Mexico, each with a chance to finish champion. But after Hulme's accident, Stewart's fuel pump failed, leaving Hill with a secure lead, and his second world title.

Plumber's nightmare. The exhaust system of the Ferrari was changed several times to try and gain more power from the V-12 engine.

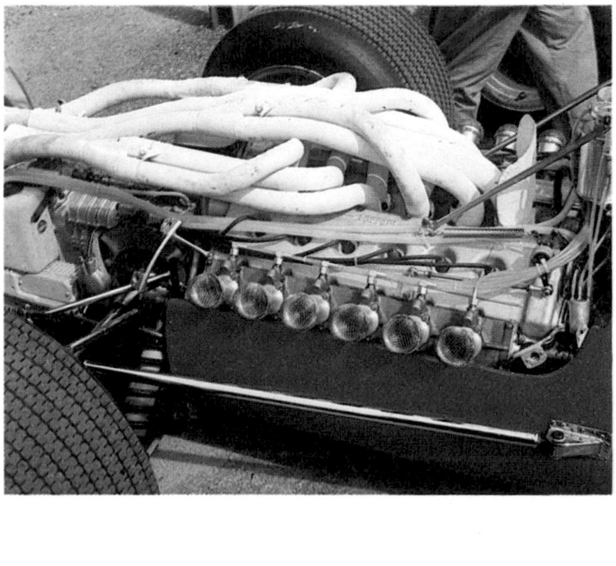

1969

1969

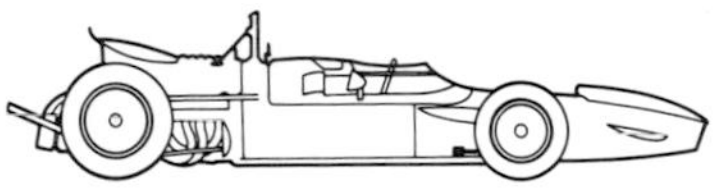

By winning all eleven Grands Prix in 1969, Cosworth brought their three years' total to 26. While they sought an answer to Duckworth's DFV, Ferrari slipped into a temporary decline; BRM fell into disarray, while Matra V-12, Honda, Cooper, and Eagle disappeared altogether. Brabham at last gave up the Repco and went over to Cosworths, and by the end of the season, the British Standard Racing Car also included the Hewland gearbox, with its easily changed ratios. Lotus gave up their ZF gears, as part of the general consensus of design, and even wings became part and parcel of the modern Grand Prix scene.

Yet Formula 1 engineers were about to drive into the race track's biggest cul-de-sac. Four-wheel drive had long been accepted as the most efficient means of transmitting the 400-odd horse power of the 3-litre engines. Astutely, Pomeroy had already observed how engineers could be expected to proceed.

The Lotus 49 had been intended only as a mount for the Cosworth engine; Chapman believed that with a brand-new power unit he would have his hands full in any case. What he wanted was a simple, robust, reliable chassis, in which it could get over its teething troubles. Indeed the only completely new two-wheel drive car to appear during the season was from Matra, the bulbous MS 80.

Regulations drawn up in the aftermath of Bandini's accident came into effect, requiring on-board fire extinguishers, and a stout roll-over bar aimed at preventing a driver being trapped underneath his car. Seat belts became mandatory, although most drivers already followed the example of Jackie Stewart who had first used them in his BRM in the German Grand Prix of 1967.

The tyre war continued, with Dunlop winning six races, Goodyear three after their improvement near the end of the season, and Firestone two. Following Honda's departure, John Surtees began his acrimonious relationship with BRM; Jacky Ickx took Rindt's place at Brabham; Rindt went to Lotus, and Beltoise joined Ken Tyrrell.

From the start, the season belonged to Jackie Stewart. At Kyalami, where the South African Grand Prix was now a firm 1 March fixture, opening the new season instead of being a postscript to the old one, he led from start to finish. He drove a bi-plane 1968 Matra MS 10, having tried out the MS 80 only in practice. All the cars had wings, mostly tall and on stalks, which grew taller still, like jungle plants seeking the sun, as they stretched towards 'cleaner' less turbulent air.

By 4 May they were at their height, ready for the first Spanish Grand Prix on the Montjuich Park circuit with which the city fathers of Barcelona had met the challenge of Jarama-Madrid. Representations by the GPDA resulted in Armco barriers as much as three tiers high to protect the spectators, as well as safeguard the drivers. Le Mans, 1955, still cast its shadow.

The Lotus cars wore the tallest and biggest wings, with Chapman adding a lip on the trailing edge to increase downforce to around 600 lb/approx 270 kg. There was no longer any doubt that wings worked. The question was only how to get the best out of them.

Rindt was fastest in practice, and he and Hill started from the front row of the grid. Hill was lying third on lap nine, when his wing 'topped out' at the crest of the rise just after the pits, instantly buckling. Deprived of its down-thrust, which had prevented the cars from taking off on the 160 mph/257 kph crest, the Lotus went out of control and crashed headlong into the barriers. Hill was fortunate to climb uninjured from the wreck.

Rindt, who had been outspoken on wings, was in the lead. His views had been greeted with enthusiasm by a press which generally felt that wings were a defacement of Grand Prix racing. His remarks gained emphasis however, when like Hill's his wing failed, sending his car end-over-end, coming to rest within yards of the still smoking remains of Hill's. The Lotus was bent almost double, trapping Rindt inside, and the further course of wing development was at once settled. It was as well neither driver was killed, or the CSI's inaction on the matter may well have been more culpable.

Later in the race, Jacky Ickx's wing crumpled, depriving him of second place; Chris Amon seemed certain to win until his Ferrari failed him, so Jackie Stewart inherited victory in the still-new Matra MS 80.

It was nearly a month to the Monaco Grand Prix, but the CSI was still unable to meet and decide what to do about wings until after first practice. The AC de Monaco, with rather more sense of urgency, wanted to ban them on its own, until reminded by the Formula One Constructors that the rules could not be changed without risk to the race's world championship status. So the Club backed down, and awaited the result of the CSI's rather laboured deliberations.

It was not that the Constructors necessarily wanted to preserve wings with all their obvious hazards, but by now some cars were designed round them, and their performance depended on wings. Taking them off willy nilly would penalise some cars more than others. Removing them permanently meant redesign and expense, and also that the research on them up till now had been largely a waste of Constructors' money, even though they had been acting within the rules. They did not want the matter resolved race by race, but they did want it cleared up quickly.

The CSI's belated decision was, however, characteristically equivocal, largely because no agreement was reached on a basic definition of wings. It was all very well banning aerodynamic devices, but was a radiator duct not an aerodynamic device? The little tray which Lotus now fixed round the rear of the car was blandly described as a means for deflecting air into the oil cooler. Nobody could argue with that, no matter whether they privately believed it was an aerodynamic aid by another name. Chapman, as usual, was sticking to the letter of the

Racing to the closest finish of his career, Jackie Stewart (Matra-Ford MS80) beat Jochen Rindt's Lotus to the line by 8/100ths of a second in the Italian Grand Prix.

law. The CSI's quandary was one with which they were to become familiar, namely how to control a technical development without stifling ingenuity.

Part of the rationale for racing was supposed to be innovation—it always had been—but it seemed unwise to allow wings to get out of hand and risk a repetition of Barcelona. The ever-wider tyres were worrisome as well, especially at circuits such as Monte Carlo, where in many places, there was no longer room for two cars side by side, and no possibility of widening the track.

Another legacy of Barcelona was Graham Hill's new full-face helmet, designed to prevent facial injuries such as Jochen Rindt had suffered. Drivers' features had long since disappeared behind a mask of fire-resistant Nomex fibre, to prevent the inhalation of smoke and flame. After Bandini's accident, Jackie Stewart had made available, through the GPDA, the knowledge that a driver could die in seconds through breathing hot toxic fumes. Now, Hill began wearing the new type of helmet which Dan Gurney had pioneered in 1968, and which soon became universal.

Hill won his fifth Monaco Grand Prix in seven years from the dashing young English driver, Piers Courage in his Frank Williams Brabham. Jackie Stewart dropped out with a broken drive shaft. Rindt was still not fit after Barcelona, and on the strength of his spirited pursuit of Hill the previous year, was replaced by Richard Attwood, who finished fourth.

Rindt was back at the wheel by Zandvoort on 21 June, where there were several interpretations of the Monaco ruling that wings which were not part of the car's bodywork, were henceforth forbidden. Or at least they would be until the CSI could think of another way of putting it.

The French Grand Prix returned to the Charade circuit 760 m/approx 2500 ft up in the mountains near Clermont-Ferrand, for the first time since 1965. Some sort of order was brought to wings, and as an admission of their existence, their height was limited to 80 cm/31.49 in above the lowest point on the chassis, and their width to 110 cm/43.3 in. But there was no restriction on where they were to be mounted on the car. Once again, different interpretations of the badly drafted regulations appeared, with several teams getting the better of them by mounting the wing well behind the back wheels, where it would achieve the greatest effect.

The CSI's vacillation and ineptitude betrayed the weakness of their control over Grand Prix racing, which had been apparent for many years, but rarely challenged. The Constructors were by now more or less agreed that despite their imperfections, wings ought to stay, and they got their way without much of a struggle.

It still looked as though four-wheel drive might offer a better alternative in the long run, which is probably what the CSI hoped. In any event, wings (of sorts) remained, and Jackie Stewart scored his fourth victory in five races with Jean-Pierre Beltoise overtaking Jacky Ickx (Brabham) on the final lap, to give Matra a 1-2 in their home Grand Prix, and French motor racing an important shot in the arm.

Ickx was a thorn in Stewart's flesh for the rest of the year, for while Stewart won the British Grand Prix at Silverstone on 19 July, Ickx managed to coast across the line to finish second. Jochen Rindt mounted a strong challenge until the side panel of his wing fouled a tyre, and all three Lotus-Fords (Rindt, Hill, and the Rob Walker car of Jo Siffert) ran out of petrol.

Ickx was on form again in the German Grand Prix

at the Nürburgring, where he used the improving grip of his Goodyears to good effect, and beat Stewart. But at the beginning of September, the tenacious little Scot clinched his title by winning the Italian Grand Prix. Monza's reputation for thrilling races was sustained by a tight group of cars, up to eight at a time, wheel to wheel, slip-streaming a matter of inches from one another. Rindt, Hulme, and Courage shared the lead, but Stewart had rehearsed the finish by installing a gear ratio which got him from the Parabolica to the line, ahead of the rest.

Ickx won the Canadian Grand Prix after knocking Stewart off the road, and Rindt the American at Watkins Glen. This was the race which virtually ended Graham Hill's Grand Prix career. After spinning, Hill got out of his car to give it a push start. Unable to do up his seat belts again, he made for the pits at racing speeds, but suffered a blow-out, and broke both legs when he crashed.

In Mexico Denny Hulme rounded off the Goodyear recovery by winning from Ickx and Brabham, while Stewart battled for fourth with Rindt. With the leading teams using virtually identical engines, not only races, but also world championships were now decided by the smallest advantages. Winners were those with tyres that had a fraction more grip; wings exerting a shade more downforce; cars honed a degree or two closer to perfection, an art of which Stewart proved a painstaking master.

Formula for failure: four-wheel drive

When he designed the Cisitalia in 1948, Dr Porsche asserted that four-wheel drive was essential. Mercedes-Benz said it was right as long ago as 1937, and were still making plans for it 20 years later. Alfa Romeo studied it for a projected 1954 Grand Prix car. Keith Duckworth, whose success with the Cosworth lent great weight to his opinions, had just built his first racing car—with four-wheel drive. And Formula 1 had not forgotten the astonishing performance of the Ferguson P 99 in the wet 1961 Oulton Park Gold Cup, when Stirling Moss ran rings round the two-wheel drive cars. BRM tested the P 67 in 1964, and four-wheel drive turbine cars were running away with Indianapolis. In the dry, it would get the power to the road; in the wet, it would be essential to success. Even Colin Chapman was about to replace the Lotus 49 with the Lotus 63, and with a track record like his, there was no longer room for doubt. Other teams prepared to follow suit.

Duckworth's rational engineering mind was appalled by the wheelspin he had seen on the Lotus 49, placing huge demands on the skill of drivers such as Jim Clark. There was even a special DFV developed for the Cosworth car, cast totally in magnesium. Robin Herd left McLaren to work on it, and he and Duckworth produced one of the most dramatic looking Grand Prix cars ever.

It never raced. But the very existence of the Cosworth gave four-wheel drive fresh impetus, and by the Dutch Grand Prix in 1969, Lotus and Matra were both trying out four-wheel drive cars. The Lotus was the more mature, having as an ancestor the Pratt & Whitney turbine cars built for Indianapolis. The Matra appeared almost makeshift, with a tubular space frame, and the ready-made Ferguson Formula four-wheel drive system. Like the rest of the 1969 crop of 4-w-d cars, it had inboard brakes to reduce unsprung weight.

Mechanical complication was a penalty of all the systems. Another was weight, and a third expense. But the most disabling turned out to be the drivers. Torque split was crucial to four-wheel drive, in other words the proportion of the tractive effort applied to the front or rear wheels. It could be adjusted to 40–60, or 50–50, but drivers found the choice almost impossible. They clung to the familiar feel of two-wheel drive, and endeavoured to choose the torque split which made the car behave most like those they were driving already.

Their conservatism devalued the whole exercise. They refused to accustom themselves to the characteristics in the middle of a racing season with its pressure for results, and championship points. There was no time to deal with the massive understeer problems from which all the cars suffered.

The Matra had a further shortcoming. Its space frame (made necessary by room needed for the gearboxes, drive shafts, and differentials) was not as stiff as the outwardly similar MS 80. It was difficult to tell how much it felt different because of four-wheel drive, and how much because of the flexible nature of the frame.

In the Lotus, Chapman had made so much effort to concentrate the weight in the middle, that the driver's feet stuck out ahead of the front cross-shaft. This influenced Hill's and Rindt's views from the start, because it was almost impossible to get out of the car in a hurry, and threatened severe leg injuries in an accident.

Stewart tried out the MS 84 during practice for several Grands Prix, recording satisfactory middle-of-the-grid times, but he never raced the car. The four-wheel drive Lotus was generally left to John Miles, because neither Hill nor Rindt wanted anything to do with it until it was competitive. Chapman tried Mario Andretti in an effort to benefit from the experience of a driver familiar with four-wheel drive at Indianapolis, but Andretti crashed it at the Nürburgring. McLaren tried Derek Bell in their car at the British Grand Prix, but they too enjoyed little success.

Johnny Servoz-Gavin gained four-wheel drive's solitary championship point of the season by finishing sixth in the Canadian Grand Prix. Jochen Rindt came second in the Lotus 63 in the non-championship Oulton Park Gold Cup, but the real test of four-wheel drive came with the Grand Prix of the United States at Watkins Glen. Even Andretti, acknowledged amongst the world's best drivers, and thoroughly experienced with 4-w-d was unable *on a wet track* to get within striking distance of Rindt's practice times.

By the end of the season, interest had evaporated to the point where Servoz-Gavin drove the Matra MS 84 in the Mexican Grand Prix, with the drive to the front wheels disconnected. The great experiment was over. By the time the field assembled for the first races of 1970, a new generation of cars was on the way; and with the legislative difficulty largely solved, designers found they could achieve all that four-wheel drive promised more simply, more effectively, and above all for next to nothing—with wings.

1970

1970

Grand Prix racing was influenced by disasters more than once: Le Mans in 1955, Bandini in 1967 and Jim Clark in 1968. In 1970, it suffered a new series of blows that closed up its ranks yet again.

While 100000 people would turn up at tracks for the Austrian or United States Grands Prix, millions more were dismayed by the deaths of Bruce McLaren, Piers Courage, and Jochen Rindt. Three of the sport's leading drivers dead within four months, one of them 1970's posthumous world champion, was hardly the hallmark of a modern, civilised activity.

There was, further, a terrifying accident in Spain, and another at the start of Indianapolis. Race tactics in Formula 3 were worrying the authorities. Costs spiralled upwards, racing became more dependent on sponsorship, and sponsorship more dependent on goodwill, a clean 'image', a sportsmanlike appearance. The deaths not only made racing appear gloomy. A cereal manufacturer would not want endorsements by stars who might be dead by the time the corn flakes reached the breakfast table.

Yet a major new non-automotive sponsor did appear. It took two years for anyone to follow the Lotus initiative, and link the sponsor firmly to the team by name. BRM did so with Yardley in a way that became common. But by the end of the year, Dunlop were amongst those of Formula 1's traditional paymasters who, like Esso, Shell, and BP the year before, found the going rate too high, and withdrew. Teams shed obligatory crocodile tears, but their dismay was only public. They had sources of wealth as yet untapped.

The great supply of competitive engines at the now moderate cost of £7500 each, encouraged new teams. Monocoques and suspensions were easy to copy. Talent was not required, and with sponsors willing to pay for the new-found advertising medium, cash was freely available. Teams were founded, such as March, its name an acronym of Max Mosely, Alan Rees, Graham Coaker, and Robin Herd, its first directors.

From their new headquarters in Bicester, they set out in grandiose style, hiring public relations consultants, obtaining sponsorship from STP, and nominating Chris Amon as their leading driver. Yet their biggest *coup* was to have their cars running in the blue of Ken Tyrrell's team.

In fact, it was not so much of an achievement under the circumstances. Tyrrell had been caught out by developments at Matra, whose new partnership with Simca and Chrysler made involvement with Ford Cosworth engines unacceptable. He was left to find a constructor for a car for the world champion to drive, not something a rival would undertake with equanimity. March, on the other hand, had nothing to lose. Their gain lay in tempting sponsors through the reflected glory of Stewart having 'chosen' their car.

For a moment, it even looked as though Herd's version of the British Standard Racing Car might be successful. Stewart won the Spanish Grand Prix at

Huge crowds attended the Austrian Grand Prix on the new Österreichring, hoping for a victory for their hero, Jochen Rindt. The 1964 race, held on a nearby airfield was Rindt's first Grand Prix and, alas, the 1970 event on the brand new track was to prove his last.

Jochen Rindt (b 1942)

To the customary characteristics for a racing driver, of competitiveness, opportunism, and physical acuity, Jochen Rindt added a dash of rebelliousness. He had a keen memory for detail; he was an astute businessman, and, rare for a racing driver, he had a lively imagination.

Although born in Germany of a German father, Rindt was brought up by his maternal grandmother in Austria. His parents were killed in a bombing raid on Hamburg in 1943 when Jochen was a year old, and he grew up in Graz, not far from the site of the future Österreichring. His family was sufficiently wealthy to send him not only to the best schools, but also, after some difficulty with his teachers, to England. He sailed near Chichester, and watched his first motor race at Goodwood.

There was a conflict between his education, first at Innsbruck then at Aachen, towards a degree in economics, and cars. Economics lost. By the time he was 21, he had sold his inheritance, and gone from a Formula Junior Cooper to the Formula 2 Brabham with which, at the 1964 Whitsun meeting at Crystal Palace, he burst upon an astonished motor racing world.

It was not until he joined Lotus, however, that Rindt attained the ranks of serious championship contenders. Unlike Jackie Stewart, his friend, rival, and neighbour in the village of Begnins, overlooking Lake Geneva, success proved elusive. He seemed to have the knack of joining teams in their years of decline, and although he won Formula 2 races more or less as he pleased, and even Le Mans 1965 with Masten Gregory in a Ferrari, Grand Prix laurels eluded him.

By the time he joined Lotus in 1969, he knew exactly what he wanted, but his relationship with Colin Chapman was to be a stormy one. More accustomed perhaps to drivers playing the role of confederate, Chapman was taken aback by one who worked on his own account. Rindt demanded a car that would win, and complained bitterly when he failed to get it. There were meetings, quarrels, and threats on both sides. Yet each realised the brilliance of the other, and they remained together, arguing to the end . . .

Following the Monza crash, Chapman's cars once again came under suspicion. The cause of Jim Clark's accident had not yet been satisfactorily explained, and now the wisdom of inboard front brakes on drive shafts was called in question. Once again, nine years after the von Trips accident, Chapman was pursued by the Italian authorities, who claimed this time that a design fault was to blame for a fatal accident. They held the drive shaft responsible for the loss of control, and the barrier the cause of Rindt's death, but their drive shaft conclusion remains dubious.

Lotus had had their share of mechanical failures, and during the innovative period of wings these included a disproportionate number of rear drive shafts. It was also true that Lotus cars were less 'over-engineered' than their contemporaries. Weight *was* reduced to a minimum. Yet it was reduced much more scientifically than on any other racing car. Chapman and his designers relied far more than his apparently less adventurous colleagues on well-proved engineering principles. The reasons for the seemingly high rate of failures was more likely their prominence (Lotus was consistently the car most often in the lead of Grands Prix from 1962 onwards) and their exposure (Lotus cars competed, mile for mile, more than any other make over the same period).

Clark's accident was later shown not to have been the result of a Lotus failure, nor was Rindt's. Yet the loss of these two great drivers within two years marked the end of an era. Ironically, they took place during a period when interest became focused on drivers as never before. Partly, perhaps, due to their greater standardisation, cars played a lesser role.

Drivers on the other hand, attained a new-found stardom in the gossip columns and on the TV screens. Celebrity status became part of their stock-in-trade as the world of advertising endorsements, and women's magazine rights to their family life opened up.

The familiarity of their faces added poignancy to tragedies such as Rindt's which, despite their denials, inevitably added tangible value to the take-home pay of the survivors.

Jarama in April. But it was a fleeting moment of glory that March were never to recapture.

Tyrrell, in any case, had other plans. Before the season was over, he replaced the March with a new car of his own make, determined never again to be caught without a car worthy of Jackie Stewart's generous talents. Tyrrell engaged Derek Gardner from Harry Ferguson Research, and set him to work in deadly secret. He designed a car that was essentially a copy of the MS 80 that had brought Stewart the title. It formed the basis of a new dynasty of racing cars that would earn it for him twice more.

Jochen Rindt's tragic, unique feat of being the posthumous world champion was brought about partly through the absence of a suitable car for Stewart, and partly from his own competitive, robust style of driving. But it also owed much to the car which Colin Chapman rescued from the ashes of the four-wheel drive débâcle, the Lotus 72.

It had ingredients from other Lotuses as well, such as the thin wedge shape, designed to funnel air on to the huge rear wing which Chapman was now convinced was a vital component of the modern racing car. Radiators were banished to each side, housed in outrigger pods where they would not disturb the precious flow of air. The brake discs were inboard, those at the front on short shafts, where they could be individually cooled, and became part of the sprung mass of the car. Chapman's final refinement of rising rate suspension to get the best out of the new tyres that were becoming available, set another milestone in the development of the single-seater racing car.

Jochen Rindt on his way to winning the Dutch Grand Prix in which his friend Piers Courage died.

Rindt's season began inauspiciously, with him retiring in the South African Grand Prix at Kyalami, at the beginning of March. The career of the Lotus 49 was extended yet again, as the creation of the new 72 fell behind schedule, a legacy of the time wasted on the abortive four-wheel drive project. It was not until the Spanish Grand Prix in April that the car was ready to race.

This turned out to be a troubled event from the very beginning. There were arguments amongst the officials, and then the accident in which inefficient fire services failed to prevent two cars from being completely burnt out. It was just the sort of race which infuriated the GPDA and the Constructors alike. The confusion and ineptitude lent substance to their claim, now voiced more often, that running such a highly professional sport as motor racing was not something that could be left to amateurs. By definition, *they* were the professionals, while the unpaid, volunteer officials of the organising clubs *who also nominated the delegates of the CSI*, were the amateurs.

The only crumb of comfort from the accident was that despite the instant conflagration, after Jacky Ickx (Ferrari) and Jackie Oliver (Yardley BRM) collided (the BRM broke a stub axle) both cars' tanks brimming with a full load of fuel, the drivers escaped. It was a testimony to the seat belts, which meant they were not knocked unconscious by the impact, and the Nomex clothing which gave them time to leap to safety. Ickx sustained only minor burns, and Oliver was unhurt, even though the cars' own extinguishers turned out to be hopelessly inadequate.

Amongst proposals canvassed later was one to reduce the fuel load from the 50 gallons/227 l which reduced both cars to ashes and scrap metal within minutes, to around 30 gallons/140 l. Refuelling stops, it was supposed, would brighten up races, although fires could happen just as easily during replenishment, and since it would only mean exchanging one hazard for another, the idea was dropped.

Carrying fuel in tanks which would not leak so easily proved of more practical value, and the problem was tackled with a new sense of urgency. There was still a reluctance to give up petrol, however, and employ something with a lower flash-point. Many of the fuel companies who had been behind the changeover in the first place had now withdrawn, but there were others taking their place, prepared to enrich motor racing and, indirectly, influence the regulations.

Rindt retired from the Spanish Grand Prix after only nine laps, Stewart winning the March's sole Grand Prix for many a year. Graham Hill finished

French Grand Prix, Clermont-Ferrand. Henri Pescarolo (Matra-Simca MS120) is about to be overtaken by Jack Brabham (Brabham-Ford) into fifth place on the 13th lap. Behind them are Denny Hulme (McLaren-Ford M14D) and Ronnie Peterson (March Ford 701).

fourth, still in great pain from his American accident, and now driving the Rob Walker Lotus 49.

Monaco in May saw Jack Brabham fight off, until the final lap, a determined Jochen Rindt. On the final corner, anxiously looking in the mirror for Rindt, who had worked his way up from seventh, Brabham made an uncharacteristic blunder. He braked for the hairpin, and for once the calm detachment that had seen the Australian through so many Grands Prix was not enough. The car brushed a barrier, and momentarily stopped.

Rindt seized his chance, and in an instant was past, while Brabham recovered to finish second. It was also the first Grand Prix for a new driver, who had made his reputation in Formula 3 and Formula 2—Ronnie Peterson.

The Belgian Grand Prix at Spa at the beginning of June was an occasion becoming more rare as the spirit of the new professionalism took root; a victory greeted with warm applause even by rivals. BRM, in their Yardley livery, had produced a new car at the beginning of the season, the P 153 designed by Tony Southgate. They had not won a Grand Prix since the start of the 3-litre Formula, but on the long, fast straights of Francorchamps, Pedro Rodriguez, accustomed to fast sports cars on the perilous circuit, fought off Chris Amon's March to win by 1.1 sec, breaking a Ford-Cosworth monopoly that had lasted for 20 races. It was the first BRM victory for four years and it was popular. BRM were still held in respect; they just seemed down on their luck, while Rodriguez was admired as a fighter. More important, it showed the Cosworth *could* be beaten, an effective reply to critics, who saw Cosworth domination as stagnation, and dubbed Formula 1 (perhaps a little unfairly) 'Formula Ford'.

Rindt won the Dutch Grand Prix on 21 June, leading most of the way, but it was an occasion that brought him little cheer. Piers Courage overturned his de Tomaso, a new design which Frank Williams had commissioned from Ing Giampaulo Dall'Ara. The car caught fire, but this time there was no leap to safety. Courage was trapped underneath just as Bandini had been, and perished in the flames. The Dutch fire fighters drew back for the few, vital moments as the flames took hold, and the Grand Prix world, dazed by the death of Bruce McLaren at Goodwood on 2 June was shocked again by the loss of Courage three weeks later. The roll-over bars, the on-board extinguishers, the fire-resistant clothing, the course marshalling—all the safety improvements of the past few years were unable to save the popular, brave young driver.

Rindt and the Lotus scored their second victory in a row at the French Grand Prix at Clermont Ferrand in July, though they were outdistanced early in the race by the Ferrari of Jacky Ickx, and the V-12 Matra of Jean-Pierre Beltoise. Ferrari was making something of a comeback with the flat-twelve 312B engine hung from a cantilevered extension of the chassis. Matra had completely altered their V-12 since it appeared in 1968, but it continued to be an unfulfilled promise.

Rindt won the British Grand Prix, once again at the expense of Jack Brabham, who ran short of fuel on the last lap, his engine guttering to a stop within sight of the chequered flag. Yet another of the year's newcomers appeared for the first time in this race. Now that Lotus had Type 49s to spare, they gave one to a bright young Brazilian, who had risen from Formula Ford to Formula 1 within the astonishingly brief space of 18 months. Emerson Fittipaldi could hardly have guessed that he was about to emulate Jackie Stewart, and before the season was over, score his first Grand Prix victory.

Lobbying over safety was now achieving more tangible results, and the German Grand Prix was moved from the Nürburgring to Hockenheim. The GPDA felt that the classic Nürburgring had not kept pace with the increasing speeds of Grand Prix cars. Faster cornering and lighter weight caused them to take off at several points, and scrape the track at

One of the most successful partnerships in motor racing—Jackie Stewart and Ken Tyrrell. The 1970 season was their last with Dunlop. For 1971 they changed to Goodyear—and won their second world championship.

others. Setting spring and suspension rates was proving impossible.

Hockenheim's two long straights, linked by a fast curve, and the series of tight turns through its unique stadium typified the modern flat, billiard-table track. There were plenty of run-off areas now that the trees had been cleared following Jim Clark's accident. The track was criticised for its arid nature, but there was no doubt about the atmosphere in the crowded stadium when Rindt led the way. The cheers could be heard even above the engines, as he claimed his fourth victory in a row, his fifth out of eight races, making him almost unassailable for the world championship.

Jacky Ickx led a Ferrari clean sweep in Austria; then, as the cars assembled at Monza, the autumn leaves starting to turn in the famous royal park, it seemed too late for anyone to offer a realistic challenge to the brilliant Rindt. He was at the peak of his form, and the Lotus 72 was the best car of the season.

Disaster came during practice. Rindt's car went out of control on the approach to the Parabolica. It veered off, caught a wheel on a guard-rail upright, and as the tail of the car swung round, the hull was rent asunder. Rindt suffered severe injuries, and despite efforts to save him, died soon afterwards.

For the third time within months, racing was stunned. Clay Regazzoni currently winning the European Formula 2 Championship won the Grand Prix from a saddened Jackie Stewart. But it was not until the United States Grand Prix in October, with a victory by the young Emerson Fittipaldi, that Rindt's points total was put beyond anyone's reach. The FIA pronounced him the sport's first posthumous world champion. They could do little else, short of making a rule that the champion had to be alive.

It had been a season of change. At the end of it Jack Brabham announced his retirement, but new drivers soon closed up the gaps in the ranks. Besides Fittipaldi, Peterson, and Regazzoni, there was François Cevert, the handsome Frenchman who joined Tyrrell. There was Rolf Stommelen from Germany, and the Italian, Andrea de Adamich, who brought Alfa Romeo back into Formula 1 with their V-8 sports car engine mounted in a McLaren. It was less powerful than the Cosworth and less reliable. De Adamich was also one of the handful of Formula 1 drivers who regularly wore glasses. The McLaren team used Dan Gurney after their leader's death, then he too, announced he would retire from active driving, and Peter Gethin, a veteran of Formula 5000, took his place. Gethin scored a solitary point when the Canadian Grand Prix moved to its alternate circuit at Ste Jovite. A new team was set up by John Surtees, who drove a McLaren before appearing at Brands Hatch with his own TS 7—yet another name with which to prefix the Ford Cosworth engine.

1971
Shell
Firestone
4
4

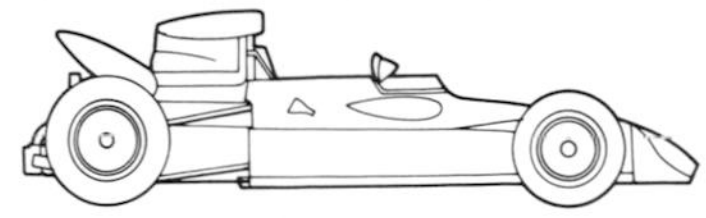

In some senses Grand Prix racing settled down in the Seventies. Technical progress was slower at first, and there was no substantial improvement in performance until the ground effect cars arrived much later. Speeds increased through increments in cornering power, which more than doubled to $2\frac{1}{2}$g, amply fulfilling Pomeroy's prophecies, although in a way of which he never dreamt.

The improvement came about firstly through detail changes in tyres, and aerodynamics. The widespread use of glass reinforced plastics for bodywork enabled frequent alterations in the shape of cars, with air boxes for example, growing taller and more bizarre. These were designed to gulp air into the engine under pressure at speed, but they were unsightly, and their size was eventually restricted. Nobody minded. Cars were no slower and the boxes had become a nuisance through swallowing road debris. The teams had been afraid to take them off just in case they lost the advantage.

Nose cones sweeping the road were an attempt to improve aerodynamics underneath the car. Designers would try almost anything to gain a precious second or two. Their closeness to the ground was never taken account of by the regulations, largely because it seemed to be something that would be self-limiting in any case. Yet it turned out an important precedent for the ground effect cars that were to follow.

Fundamental changes took place in the politics of Grand Prix racing, as the competitors filled the vacuum created by the slackness of the International Sporting Commission. CSI members' conservatism, or even *laissez-faire* came about through a general inability to agree. They were unwilling to impose sanctions on anyone who broke rules, but what upset the GPDA and the Formula One Constructors most was their continued commitment to the Grand Prix organisers. It was something that remained implicit in the CSI's constitution; in their remit as appointees of the national automobile clubs (ACNs) who sanctioned the races.

The Constructors now formally convened at regular meetings. In the finishing order of the 1971 Constructors' World Championship, they now comprised Tyrrell, BRM, March, Ferrari, Lotus, McLaren, Matra-Simca, Surtees, and Brabham, and called themseves the Formula 1 Association. As they became more articulate, more demanding, and more challenging, the CSI perhaps made this annual award to them with less and less enthusiasm.

The races were a triumph for Tyrrell and for Jackie Stewart, who won Spain, Monaco, France, Great Britain, Germany, and Canada. François Cevert in the number two Tyrrell was second to Stewart in France and Germany, and became France's leading driver when he won the United States Grand Prix at Watkins Glen.

Tyrrell's cars remained essentially copies of the Matra MS 80, refined in detail, always faultlessly prepared, and invariably brilliantly driven. Stewart's consistency as a test and race driver would have won him the title even without the verve and speed to elbow his way to the front of race after race. His Monaco Grand Prix was a copybook example.

He set fastest time in practice, 0.8 sec better than his own pole position the year before. He led the race at a record speed 2.65 kph/1.65 mph faster than Jochen Rindt did in 1970. Under pressure from Ronnie Peterson, Stewart set fastest race lap as well, in 1 min 22.2 sec, 137.69 kph/85.55 mph, a new record, once again a full second faster than Rindt.

It was much the same in the French Grand Prix at the new Paul Ricard track, near Bandol in sunny Provence, which quickly gained ground on Monaco as the favourite of the Grand Prix socialites. Ricard was the epitome of the modern, purpose-built track, although it still had its critics on account of the remoteness of the cars. They were so far away that much of the spectacle was lost, but the GPDA welcomed the well-planned layout and the track facilities, the built-in safety, with low kerbs and a wide margin for errors.

While the construction was financed by M. Ricard, the aperitif magnate, Marlboro, forced by the growing restrictions on conventional cigarette advertising to look for new methods, paid for installations, such as the novel signalling bridge. This was intended to replace the customary flag signals by flashing lights. Technical difficulties persisted, however, and the first Grand Prix on the fine new track, with its pits complex looking like an airport terminal and its air-conditioned press room, began like all the others, with a man waving a flag.

By winning the Austrian Grand Prix (Jo Siffert) and the Italian Grand Prix, which made Peter Gethin winner of the fastest Grand Prix ever at 242.55 kph/150.71 mph, BRM secured second place in the

Above: Winner of the fastest-ever Grand Prix, Peter Gethin who won the Italian Grand Prix at Monza in a Yardley BRM P160 at an average speed of 242.57 kph (150.73 mph) by 0.01s from Ronnie Peterson (March-Ford 701).

Right: The finishing 'straight' at the Nürburgring. Jacky Ickx (Ferrari) leads Chris Amon (Matra-Simca MS120B). Both cars retired from the German Grand Prix.

championship, even though Ronnie Peterson was the drivers' runner-up with his March. But BRM's euphoria was short-lived. After scoring a brilliant second place in the Dutch Grand Prix on 20 June, and driving in the French Grand Prix in July, Pedro Rodriguez died taking part in a minor sports car race at the Norisring.

He could never resist a race; he had just won the Daytona 24 hours, the Monza 1000 Kms, and the Spa 1000 Kms, in a brilliant season with the immensely fast Porsche 917s, and had been given the opportunity to drive an old love, a Ferrari. It was the year's second fatality in championship sports car racing. Ignazio Giunti, after a promising start in Grand Prix racing for Ferrari, was killed in a scandalous accident during the Buenos Aires 1000 Kms, when Jean-Pierre Beltoise, who should have known better, pushed a broken-down Matra into his path.

BRM were to grieve once again before the end of the year, when Jo Siffert crashed at Brands Hatch during a meeting celebrating Jackie Stewart's world championship. Siffert only broke his leg, but died when flames engulfed his car, the third occasion during the season when fire played a part in a fatal accident. He gained the dubious distinction of being the only driver to die racing a BRM in the make's 25-year history.

In a year of such holocausts, Ronnie Peterson represented the other side of the coin, surviving crash after crash almost unscathed. In both Formula 1 and Formula 2, he showed astonishing courage and outstanding talent. Many of the accidents were not his fault, and time and again he would step out, unharmed from wrecked cars. His driving was reminiscent of his fellow Scandinavians in rallies, when they either won or went off the road in the attempt. Peterson would brake a little later, slide a little more sideways, and try a little harder than anyone else after the style of Jochen Rindt. He was less smooth than Stewart, less polished than Ickx, and perhaps not quite so aggressive as Regazzoni, but on his day he had the beating of them all.

In Formula 2, he followed Jacky Ickx (1967), Jean-Pierre Beltoise (1968), Johnny Servoz-Gavin (1969), and Clay Regazzoni (1970) as the last driver to win the European Formula 2 Trophy before it became recognised as an FIA Championship in its own right. He had a Formula 2 March under an arrangement whereby he drove the works car, but obtained income from sponsors, such as Vicks, by selling them space on the car, or on his overalls.

The system was known by the rather deprecatory term of rent-a-drive, implying that such appointments went only to those who could afford them, rather than those selected on merit. This was not new in itself, wealthy amateurs having been doing much the same since the dawn of motor racing. It enabled a number of drivers to set themselves up as professionals in Formula 1 amongst whom some began, like Peterson in 1971, with a March. By raising a personal loan from an Austrian bank, these included a slim, 22-year-old called Niki Lauda.

Peterson had still to win a Grand Prix, but driving a March that was little better than the model Stewart had scrapped, he gained an impressive list of second places. Monaco, Silverstone, Monza, Canada, and the non-championship race at Hockenheim were notable performances.

The season had more than its share of non-title Formula 1 races. Argentina staged one on 24 January, as a 'dry run' for a world championship round in 1972. Chris Amon lived up to his growing reputation for ill-luck by winning in his Matra-Simca—he was still without a victory in a 'proper'

Grand Prix. There were three British non-title Formula 1 races at the beginning of the season, the Race of Champions at Brands Hatch on 21 March, won by Clay Regazzoni's Ferrari, the Rothmans International Trophy on 9 April won by Pedro Rodriguez (BRM), and the traditional 'May' Silverstone run by the British Racing Drivers' Club on 8 May. This turned out to be the last Formula 1 victory for Graham Hill, driving the otherwise unsuccessful Brabham, nicknamed 'lobster claw' on account of its radiators mounted each side of the nose.

Fourth place in the Spanish Grand Prix at Barcelona was the best Pedro Rodriguez could do for the Yardley-BRM team in April, but two months later he finished second to Jacky Ickx's Ferrari at Zandvoort. But the gallant Mexican did not see the season out. Like his talented brother Ricardo, he died at the wheel in a racing accident.

On 28 March, a new track, the Ontario Motor Speedway airlifted the entire Formula 1 circus to California for the Questor Grand Prix, billed as the War of the Worlds (Formula 1 v. Formula A, with American 5-litre production-based engines). This was also intended to be a dry run for a future championship Grand Prix, and was won by Mario Andretti in a Ferrari. Unfortunately, the multi-million dollar circuit proved a flop despite heavy promotion, and although it established the principle that the United States *could* have a West Coast Grand Prix as well as the East Coast one, it was not going to be run here. What it also did was confirm the 'package deal' Grand Prix. It proved that, given enough money, the Formula 1 circus was for sale.

Non-championship Formula 1 races proliferated, with Jacky Ickx winning the Jochen Rindt Memorial Trophy at Hockenheim on 13 June, and John Surtees the Oulton Park Gold Cup on 21 August. Spectators always turned out to see the stars in action, something of which race promoters were becoming increasingly aware. But on 24 October, the smoke from Jo Siffert's funeral pyre rose above Brands Hatch, and the trail of debris made further racing impractical. Peter Gethin was named the winner of a race everyone wanted to forget. It was virtually the end of the road for non-championship Formula 1.

It cost the teams almost as much to turn out as it did for a Grand Prix, with neither commercial return nor the prospect of championship points. There was little to be gained and now, as with Siffert, so much to be lost. Henceforward, teams would only appear when the stakes were high, and if that meant uprating a race to Grand Prix status in order to secure appropriate value, ways and means would be found to do it.

Lotus did not recover from the death of Jochen Rindt quite as they had from that of Jim Clark. There was no gritty Graham Hill to pull them through, only a still inexperienced Emerson Fittipaldi, and the rather weaker Dave Walker and Reine Wisell. Walker distinguished himself by crashing twice at Zandvoort, once in the 72 during practice, and once in the turbine 56b during the race. It was not an easy car to drive, with 4-w-d, and a bothersome throttle lag, which meant the driver had to put his foot down several seconds before he wanted the power to come in. Besides, the car was too heavy to be a success. After winning the Championship in 1970, Lotus failed to win a race in 1971. The turbine was an interesting technical exercise, but it proved an unnecessary distraction while Fittipaldi built up race experience, and prepared himself for a more fruitful season to come.

Air boxes were not the only fad of 1971; so was rising rate suspension, the feature that had given the Lotus 72 such an advantage. McLaren tried it, but failed to master it, and joined the losers while they did so. Matra never won either, except in Argentina, which did not count. But the real disappointment of the season was Brabham. Jack Brabham himsef had gone, and the team he left was short of cash. His partner, Ron Tauranac remained, but the stage was set for its ownership to change, which it did, to a man who once described himself as 'a business athlete'. In his way, he would influence the course of Grand Prix racing in the years to come as much as any driver, or any engineer. Brabham was bought by Bernard Ecclestone.

Grand Prix racing's new order

Brabham was by no means Bernie Ecclestone's first motor racing venture. When Connaught Engineering was auctioned off in 1957 he purchased it, and ran in the Tasman Series with Stuart Lewis-Evans and Roy Salvadori. He continued in Europe during the following year with Archie Scott Brown and Ivor Bueb. Ecclestone had driven the motor cycle engined 500 cc cars himself, but a bad accident forced him to retire, and he decided to devote himself to the motor trade and the business side of motor racing.

Following the deaths of both Lewis-Evans and Scott-Brown, Ecclestone withdrew from motor sport; but he returned as a result of his friendship with Jochen Rindt. He managed Rindt commercially, and on joining Lotus in 1969, Colin Chapman appointed Ecclestone to manage the Lotus Formula 2 team.

A financial and executive interest in Motor Racing Developments (as the Brabham firm was known) was a first step to buying it outright in October, 1971. The intention was for Tauranac to continue designing the cars, but it proved impossible for him to work with Ecclestone, so he left. 'The most important thing for anyone in business is to be able to make decisions quickly . . . This means that the top job is a one man job. If there are two top men a lot of time is wasted just trying to agree', said Ecclestone.

He carried this philosophy through to the Formula 1 Association, or the Constructors' Association, as it was more generally known. Although their meetings were almost always conducted in secret, he soon emerged as spokesman, and decisions more and more bore the stamp of the diminutive, but increasingly powerful, owner of the Brabham team.

'If I were a runner or a driver you would expect me to go for that last hundredth of a second. I'm a business athlete and it is that last penny which makes all the difference, not in hard cash—but in the satisfaction of knowing that a deal has been pulled off in the best possible way . . . Away from business I never bother to check bills, but every invoice which goes through my office goes under the microscope . . . In my work I am acting as a competitor against other competitors . . .'

1972

GOODYEAR
elf
elf
elf
4

Marlboro - BRM
Marlboro - BRM
Marlboro - BRM
BP
17
HEUER
Firestone
Marlboro
BRM
17

Until ground effect cars became established, the principal influence on Grand Prix racing moved away from the drivers, the engineers, or even the governing body. Racing was entering the realms of professional sport as exemplified by golf, tennis, or ice-hockey. Races began to influence the course of events less. But the commercial ambitions of individuals inside, and world events outside began to matter more.

Motor racing had survived the Suez crisis of 1956 with no more than a few cancellations and the renewed criticism of those who had been against it already. It was still recovering from the Le Mans disaster, and the calendar had been thinned out.

The 1973 Middle East War was yet to come, but the looming energy crisis was providing food for thought. The 3 Litre Formula had been extended on account of its popularity, and also on account of the opposition proposals for change provoked. Previous alterations, the CSI recalled, had met with vigorous protest. In 1960–1 the British had supported the breakaway Intercontinental group, and in 1965–6 Coventry-Climax had withdrawn leaving a good deal of uncertainty and confusion until the Ford-Cosworth supplied the power to keep the teams in business.

By 1972 these same teams had become so influential that the CSI dared not even suggest change. They had little reason to. A thoughtful few felt an element of fuel conservation desirable, but formulae with fuel consumption limits had been tried as long ago as 1907 and found wanting. They suffered from administrative problems; spectators preferred races won by the fastest, not worked out by mathematics afterwards. Tampering with awards was never satisfactory, especially over technicalities.

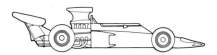

Left to themselves, the CSI might have listened to the fuel consumption formula proposed by eminent engineers such as Keith Duckworth. Creating an engine efficient in energy consumption he considered a far greater challenge than one merely producing maximum power within a set of arbitrary dimensions.

Instead, however, things were left as they were. Further attention was paid to safety, circuit inspections were made more rigorous, and the standards of the CSI's circuit safety committee were enforced, if necessary with demands for installations to be built or modified before racing took place. The crusade for safety suffered a cruel jolt, however, with the death, in June, of Jo Bonnier, long a campaigner, and President of the GPDA. At the age of 42, Bonnier had retired from Grand Prix racing, hanging up not only his helmet, but also his Cooper-Maserati on the wall of his home in Switzerland. Yet he still drove sports cars, and it was in one of his Lola T280s that he unaccountably collided with a Ferrari at Indianapolis Corner on the Le Mans circuit.

Bonnier's efforts on behalf of the GPDA had resulted in the CSI's circuit safety committee, of which he was a member. They largely brought about the decision to drop the Spa-Francorchamps circuit from the 1972 calendar, and take the Belgian Grand Prix to the new Nivelles-Baulers track in June. Laid out along the now-customary safety lines, Nivelles was never a popular circuit and suffered chronic financial trouble. It also had another important drawback. Like Spa, it lay in the French-speaking part of Belgium, and the Flemish-speaking Limbourg province wanted the Grand Prix, if it was to be transferred anywhere, moved to the new, rather primitive little track at Zolder.

A world championship Grand Prix, with its prestige and, equally important, the economic benefits it could bring, was still a winning issue for local politicians, or, as in this case, sectarian interests. The German Grand Prix remained at the now much-modified Nürburgring, but the CSI safety committee decided they had had enough of 150 mph slipstreamers at Monza. Two chicanes were ordered, because being a royal park, Monza was unable to cut down trees, or make the sort of modifications that had been no more than a matter of money in Germany.

Furthermore, Ing Bacciagaluppi, the Monza circuit director, was worried about the mounting pressure from the authorities. Fearing more trouble like that which followed Rindt's fatal accident in 1970, he fell in with the plans to make the circuit slower. Accordingly, two chicanes, one at the Curva Grande and one at the Curva del Vialone, were built to break up the slipstreaming bunches which had been such a feature of Monza for years.

Above right: The Nürburgring winds its way through the Eifel Mountains, probably the world's most dramatic racing circuit. On the opening lap of the German Grand Prix, the leading Ferrari lays down the racing line.

Above left: Jackie Stewart's Tyrrell bears some resemblance to the rotund shape of the Matra MS80 which it replaced. Compare this shot of Stewart on the last corner at Clermont-Ferrand with the similar one of his friend Jochen Rindt on page 125.

Left: In the rain-soaked Monaco Grand Prix of 1972, Jean-Pierre Beltoise secured the last victory for a BRM. On the treacherous track, he led from start to finish, with only the Ferrari of Clay Regazzoni finishing on the same lap.

The competitive side

The races of 1972 proved a triumph for Lotus. They were now John Player Specials, painted black and gold and were in effect modified versions of the Type 72, known as the 72D. Emerson Fittipaldi, at 26, became the youngest world champion, by winning the Grands Prix of Spain, Belgium, United Kingdom, Austria and Italy.

His principal adversary was Jackie Stewart, and for the first four years of the Seventies, they shared the title.

Champions were continually unable to mount a successful defence of their titles, and none was able to repeat Jack Brabham's success of 1959–60. Stewart blamed the strain of the closing races, when a team and driver with the championship in sight are under great pressure.

Stewart's second championship in 1971 proved such a strain that he succumbed to a stomach ulcer in 1972, keeping him out of the Belgian Grand Prix, and probably slowing him at Spain and Monaco. He also had the handicap of a car with neither the potential nor the development programme of Fittipaldi's Lotus. He managed to win the opening race in Argentina from Denny Hulme, and led for a long way in South Africa, but he was out-driven on 1 May by Fittipaldi in Spain.

As happened so often, Monaco turned out to be something of a curiosity. Jean-Pierre Beltoise splashed his way to victory for BRM, the last ever for a make now in sharp decline. There was mounting criticism over the dangers of racing in the rain, particularly from drivers accustomed to racing in America. There, as in sports where danger is not even an important element, such as lawn tennis or cricket, competition stops when the rain starts.

With Stewart ill, Fittipaldi won at Nivelles, but Stewart bounced back at Clermont-Ferrand. Fittipaldi reversed the positions at Brands Hatch, and then Jacky Ickx upset the pattern at the Nürburgring. It was the first victory for a Ferrari for 14 months—since Ickx won the wet Dutch Grand Prix in 1971. The result might have been different but for a collision between Stewart and Ronnie Peterson (March) on the first lap. It was a superficial brush, but it landed Stewart behind the second Ferrari of Clay Regazzoni, of whose tactics Stewart had a good deal to say afterwards. Regazzoni blocked him at every turn, until Stewart crashed on the final lap.

It did not affect the championship position, because Fittipaldi was also out, with a cracked gearbox casing. Stewart had his Tyrrell 005 back in action at the Austrian Grand Prix in August, the race where he had clinched the championship the year before. At an average speed of 214.51 kph/133.29 mph it was the fastest race of the year, Fittipaldi running him close until the Tyrrell's handling deteriorated, and Stewart slipped out of the points.

At Monza, it was Fittipaldi's turn to win and decide the championship.

The season ran out with Stewart winning both the Canadian and American Grands Prix, a season when new makes proliferated as the Cosworths spread and multiplied. A winning team, it seemed, took only £10000 and a monocoque frame. Brabham began experiments with the Weslake-Ford V-12, another descendant of the old Gurney-BRM engine; and Tecno plunged into Formula 1 with a Ferrari-like flat-12 of their own. But their career was short-lived. The Brabham V-12 never raced, and the Italian Tecno proved troublesome, despite the efforts of former Vanwall team manager David Yorke and drivers Derek Bell and Nanni Galli.

McLaren acquired sponsorship from Yardley, and were successful with their modified M 19 model; Surtees remained long on promise but short on fulfilment, while March discovered yet another of motor racing's design dead-ends with the 721X. Robin Herd's theory was that by placing the gearbox behind the engine, but ahead of the rear axle centre line (instead of behind) the mass would be brought closer to the centre of the car. The resultant low polar moment of inertia (or dumb-bell effect) was intended to make the car handle better.

It did not, and before the season was half over, Ronnie Peterson announced he would drive for Lotus in 1973.

One race Fittipaldi did not win was the Monaco Grand Prix, run in drenching rain, making the cars difficult to control with their ever-wider tyres.

1973
elf
5
Ford

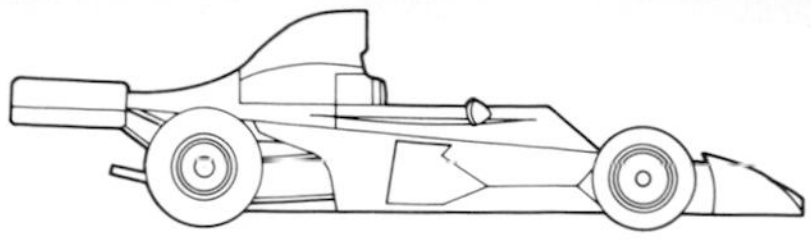

If world championship racing began in 1950 as a series of ripples on a small pond, by 1973 it was making real waves. It was becoming contentious and the disagreements between the Formula One Constructors and the International Sporting Commission (CSI) were bitter. Furthermore, the backwash was visible from the outside, as the protagonists enlisted the support of the press. Yet, by the year's end, the Yom Kippur War and the Arab oil embargo had changed everything—Grand Prix racing, together with every other familiar aspect of life in the modern, western world.

The industrial crisis and the world recession that followed the Arab/Israeli conflict plunged racing into the common pool of gloom. The full implications were not grasped until 1974, which was probably just as well because the confrontation between the competitors and the authorities which many people were expecting had become imminent. As it was, the schism was at least postponed, and perhaps avoided altogether.

The militant aspect of the dispute went back to 1972, when practice for some races was interrupted by wrangles over cash. At the Monaco Grand Prix, the Formula 1 Association (the Constructors) had locked their cars in the big garage on the Avenue Princesse Grace, until the Automobile Club de Monaco agreed to 25 starters as negotiated in what

Argentina was experiencing a spate of kidnappings when the Grand Prix circus turned up in January, which meant a lot of armed guards at the Sheraton Hotel. Defending champion Emerson Fittipaldi won the opening round, taking the lead from François Cevert's Tyrrell with ten laps to go. He also won the second race, on his home circuit of Interlagos, at São Paulo, with Stewart second after a fruitless pursuit of the John Player Lotus.

Kyalami in March turned out to be an eventful race for Jackie Stewart. He crashed heavily during practice, and so started in François Cevert's Tyrrell from 16th place. In the unfamiliar car, equipped with an untried rear suspension arrangement which he had never driven, he managed to avoid Regazzoni's accident, and climbed through the field to finish first. Peter Revson (McLaren) of the Revlon cosmetic family, having decided at last to take motor racing seriously, came in second.

Fittipaldi won the Spanish Grand Prix on its return to Montjuich, the 50th Grand Prix victory for Lotus, putting them coincidentally one ahead of the total won by Ferrari since 1950. Ronnie Peterson, who had joined Fittipaldi in the team, led for much of the way, but dropped out when the tricky course, with its hairpin bends and frequent torque reversals, proved too much for the gearbox. Graham Hill took part in the first race with his new team of Embassy Shadow.

The Belgian Grand Prix at troublesome Zolder in May was run on a track which became more treacherous with every lap. Only a perilously narrow groove on the racing line remained fit for driving on. Jackie Stewart had been the track's severest critic, but when it came to racing on it, he showed that he was master. It was like driving on a tightrope, from which eight cars slipped off, but Stewart won just the same.

He won again at Monaco, with Fittipaldi second, but this ding-dong had gone on long enough. Nobody else had won a race since Jacky Ickx in Germany the previous August. Denny Hulme broke the spell, celebrating his appointment as president of the GPDA by winning in Sweden convincingly for McLaren. Ronnie Peterson won the French Grand Prix at Ricard, followed by the astonishing British Grand Prix at Silverstone.

Accidents involving a large number of cars were still rare, and any which stopped a race almost unknown. Even the Monaco Grand Prix in 1950 had carried on despite the litter on the quayside by the Tabac. Multiple pile-ups and red flags were an American phenomenon—or so everyone thought before the British Grand Prix on 14 July which turned out to be the first in an extraordinary series of British Grands Prix.

Amongst the 28 starters were some newish drivers. David Purley failed to reach the grid in his March following a practice accident, but amongst those who did were Jackie Oliver and George Follmer, driving for Shadow, new to Formula 1 after their success in Can-Am. They were at the back of the grid along with Graham Hill in his Embassy-sponsored Shadow, and Graham McRae in yet another new make, the Iso, which was once again a creation of Frank Williams's fertile sponsorship efforts. Mike Beuttler was a newcomer in a private March, and Rikky von Opel took part in an extravagantly-styled Ensign. Von Opel, of the German family that gave their name to the car, was alongside Roger Williamson (March) in his first Grand Prix, sponsored by the enthusiastic Tom Wheatcroft of Donington fame.

John Watson had his private Brabham, and Howden Ganley from New Zealand was in the second Iso, while nearer the front was James Hunt, with a March belonging to the new Hesketh team. Niki Lauda was on the fourth row with his BRM, immediately behind a keen young South African whom McLaren had picked up almost straight out of Formula 3, Jody Scheckter.

Like any new driver, Scheckter was out to make his mark, and he put the McLaren on the third row of the grid. The pace car dutifully sped round, with the grid in tow, then they paused on the long, fast, right-hand sweep past the grandstands, and set off.

Ronnie Peterson took the lead, with Jackie Stewart tucking in behind. Lauda snapped a drive shaft in a manner strangely reminiscent of the BRM's first appearance at Silverstone over 20 years before. The car trickled forward a few feet and stopped, the rest of the grid swerving past on each side. All, that is, except Jackie Oliver's Shadow. Coming from the back of the grid, Oliver had reached second gear, and approaching 70 mph collided with the stationary BRM knocking off the left rear wheel.

Both drivers were thus out of their cars, and witnesses to one of the most comprehensive accidents in the history of Grand Prix racing.

was known as the Geneva Agreement. This was a scale of payments for teams against a contract which guaranteed race organisers a full field of Grand Prix cars.

Monaco had already been persuaded to raise the number of starters to 18; now the Constructors were demanding 25. What they feared, however, was that the CSI might take the part of the AC de Monaco in the quarrel.

They were also concerned about the announcement by Prince Metternich, the President of the CSI, of proposals for new safety legislation. For 1973, it was decreed, cars must have a deformable structure, surrounding the fuel tanks with impact-resistant material to reduce the risk of fire. In addition, the cars were to have less capacity for fuel, and pit stops were to be compulsory.

The Constructors were in agreement about the deformable structures, but disagreed profoundly about the pit stops. The immediate quarrel at Monaco was solved, but the row over pit stops dragged on. By October 1972, after press conferences and public pronouncements, the real cause of the disagreement became evident. The circuits decided to resist the Constructors' demands for ever increasing race purses, and formed themselves into a new organisation called Grand Prix International (GPI). Their object was to negotiate common financial

Stewart outbraked Peterson at Becketts, so by the time the field came streaming round Woodcote at upwards of 150 mph/240 kph at the end of the first lap, he was well in the lead from Peterson (John Player Lotus) and Carlos Reutemann (Brabham). Behind them came two McLarens, the one on the outside driven by Scheckter, who seemed determined to overtake not only his team mate, but Reutemann and Peterson as well.

Scheckter wanted to make an impression, but not like this . . . The McLaren kicked up the dust on the outside of the corner and it soon became clear that the driver had made a colossal error of judgement. In his anxiety to make up on the leaders he ran wide. Jody fought off the inevitable accident all the way round a corner which had been described as one of the most difficult in all motor racing. The bump in the middle, the oil droppings and water left from the cars which just over a minute ago were boiling themselves dry on the grid, the rubber dust left from their departure, all conspired against him.

The white McLaren went off the edge of the track, Scheckter caught it again, but by the time it was opposite the pits, all was lost. It slammed into the wall, and bounced back into the road broadside-on to the approaching cars.

Several cars still found their way past. But for many, there was no hope. The McLaren blocked much of the track, the remainder quickly filled with swerving, braking and spinning cars, and in collision after collision the entire area soon looked as though struck by a freak typhoon. Fire extinguishers popped off, there was debris everywhere, but by some miracle, only one injury. Andrea de Adamich lay trapped in his car near the pedestrian bridge with a broken leg. The rest were able to vault out and follow Scheckter to the pit wall, waiting to see what would happen when the survivors who had got through, came round at 150 mph for their second lap . . .

The starter hung out the red flag, the seldom-used signal to stop the race. Stewart came streaming through Woodcote, but before he reached the wreckage and the rescuers in the middle of the track, held up his hand to warn those behind, and managed to stop safely.

The race was re-started after the track was cleared, and Peter Revson scored a popular victory for McLaren. But the accident was not forgotten. It had been costly for several teams, including Surtees, which lost Mike Hailwood's Jochen Mass's, and Carlos Pace's cars along with the chance to win any cash after the re-start.

Yet while people were still congratulating one another on the effectiveness of the safety measures which had seen almost everyone safely through such a massive shunt, came the Dutch Grand Prix and the grim accident to Roger Williamson.

Tyre failure was blamed, and the guard-rail was badly installed, but it proved that motor racing remained a dangerous business. Stewart won the race, with François Cevert second in the Tyrrell. Fittipaldi's hopes of defending his title received a setback when he crashed, and injured his ankles. The Tyrrell twins repeated their victory at the German Grand Prix a fortnight later, at the beginning of August.

Some cars always suited some circuits better than others, and the Österreichring, with its long, extremely fast sweeping curves, never matched well with the handling characteristics of the Tyrrell. Stewart arrived in Austria with an 18-point advantage over Fittipaldi, who led until seven laps from the end of the 54-lap race. A loose fuel pipe put him out, letting Peterson by to win, and Stewart swept through to second place, increasing his advantage in the world championship to 24.

Peterson won again in the Italian Grand Prix at Monza, ironically ending Fittipaldi's chances of the title, which Jackie Stewart clinched with fourth place. Peter Revson won the confused Canadian Grand Prix where the organisers' lap charts were unequal to keeping track of a race where the cars were continually in and out of the pits changing their rain tyres.

Cevert's death, and Stewart's decision not to drive in what would have been his hundredth Grand Prix, cast a pall over the United States Grand Prix. The race itself was another triumph for Ronnie Peterson, with James Hunt a surprise second, boosting the morale of the new Hesketh team, and giving them the necessary encouragement to carry on building their own car for the following year.

But would there be a following year? The October War was about to cast the long shadow of the energy crisis, and before the following season, the future of not only motor racing, but much of what the western world regarded as its customary way of life, hung in the balance.

terms with the Constructors, making them in effect a sort of commercial equivalent of the CSI. The relationship was emphasised by the appointment of an energetic Dutchman, Henri Treu, as organiser soon after he had been dismissed as Secretary General of the CSI.

By December, GPI announced an ultimatum in response to the Constructors' demand for a minimum of £103000 for each of the 15 qualifying rounds of the 1973 world championship. GPI's final offer was £53000, and they gave the Constructors until 14 December to accept, or they would approach the CSI to change the rules for the world championship.

The CSI, hand-in-glove with Grand Prix International since their membership overlapped, obligingly approved the opening up of the world championship to Formula 1, Formula 5000, USAC*, and Formula 2 cars. They hoped to reassure the race organisers that come what may, races could take place even without the leading members of the Constructors' Association. What they were also hoping for was pressure from drivers, anxious to secure world championship points.

GPI members comprised the race organisers of Austria, Britain, Belgium, Brazil, Canada, France, Germany, Italy, Monaco, Holland, South Africa, Spain, Sweden, and the United States. Argentina did not join in (but this seemed unimportant at the time) owing to the political trouble caused by the return of General Perón. Their race seemed in doubt anyway, and the likelihood of its cancellation endangered the next one (the new Grand Prix of Brazil at Interlagos) because the expenses for the airlift of cars and teams would have to be borne by one organiser instead of two.

The deadlock seemed total, with the Constructors threatening to run the entire world championship series on their own. They had the cars and the drivers—circuits could be found. They could probably, in the climate of 1972–3, also have found the money. Marlboro's budget would have stretched to it.

The members of GPI each placed a bond of £12000 as proof of their solidarity, but instead of having several months in which to sort out the problem (the first European race was not due until the end of April) the world championship races began to happen in January whether they liked it or not.

Argentina stubbornly refused to be cancelled, and with half the air-freight charges down to them, Brazil could hardly cancel on their own; besides, the Fittipaldi fans in Brazil would have revolted if they had.

Alex Blignaut of Kyalami pleaded to be treated as a special case. The South African Grand Prix prize fund traditionally included the air-freight charges, so it could not be held at the £53000 minimum. Europe would need to look after itself. Political considerations weighed heavily on South Africa as well, since the Republic was losing representation in so many sports, and pressure was strong on Blignaut to keep the country's foothold in motor racing.

With three races already run, by the time the circus arrived in Europe, the idea of running the world championship for any category except Formula 1, with any drivers except those already scoring points, was unacceptable. The Constructors' Finance Committee of Max Mosley of March, Phil Kerr of McLaren, and Bernie Ecclestone of Brabham had won the day by observing the principle of 'divide and rule', refusing to have anything to do with GPI or Henri Treu whom they heartily disliked, and negotiating directly, circuit by circuit.

The least edifying episode of the whole undignified business was the Formula 1 Association's press conference at the London Racing Car Show in January, 1973, when they tried to make a case by pleading poverty. It was already obvious that running a Grand Prix team had become a highly profitable operation, to which the equipment and resources of the teams themselves bore witness. Spare cars, spare engines, large transporters, their growing number of motor homes and private aircraft were testimony to the principle whereby a modern Formula 1 team secured its overheads by means of sponsorship, and relied on winnings to provide most of the profit.

The Belgian Grand Prix was the occasion of the next squabble. It was scheduled for Zolder on 20 May which must have taken the little circuit by surprise because, although it had run races for categories up to Group 7 Interserie, it was far from ready to play host to a Grand Prix.

During the winter, listening to the wrangling between GPI and the Constructors and fearing their race might never be run, Zolder felt disinclined to invest in re-laying the track surface. Accordingly, the work was carried out much too late, when the weather had deteriorated.

Emerson Fittipaldi had already reported that the surface was breaking up, and with three weeks to go, Formula Vee drivers refused to race on the new track. Fragments were breaking off, showering their cars with small stones. The surface had not had time to settle, and the wrong 'mix' had been used. There was no choice but to bring the road rollers back and do the job over again.

The GPDA was adamant. Zolder was unsafe. Practice was stopped on the first day, and the contractors worked overnight to try and put things right. But the new top dressing would not adhere to the one underneath, and the drivers still condemned it. The CSI, they pointed out, had broken their own rule that a world championship Grand Prix would not be sanctioned until a track had run a non-championship race. Also tracks were to be approved two months before the race, to prevent such troubles. The CSI had approved the circuit on the basis of promises concerning the track surface, which the organisers had no hope of fulfilling.

Jackie Stewart gave journalists a conducted tour of

*Cars conforming to the United States Auto Club formula.

Jackie Stewart (b 1939)

Jackie Stewart's final season at the wheel took him to the top of the league table of Grand Prix winners, his total of 27 victories topping both Jim Clark's and Fangio's, although he did not score as many pole positions or set as many fastest laps as either.

Yet he was probably the most *complete* driver in the history of Grand Prix racing. Stewart's talent extended to getting the best out of his team, his tyre fitters, his engineers and designers; even perhaps to getting the best out of Ken Tyrrell, although Tyrrell probably believed it was the other way round. Stewart even got the best out of (some would say, exploited) the media, and he became a polished television performer.

From his early days in the family business, a prosperous Jaguar dealership at Dumbuck, overlooking the Firth of Clyde near Dumbarton, John Young Stewart's capacity for self-confidence was boundless. It was different from cockiness because it was so well-merited. His confidence in himself was justified by events. He was an Olympic class shot, and from the moment he followed his elder brother into motor racing, success followed success.

From the very beginning, Stewart paid close attention to detail. True, he was gifted with a natural sense of balance, and an uncommon instinct for gaining a quick grasp of situations, which he described in his articulate way, as like slowing down the action of a film. But while 'natural' drivers are unusual, his gifts were not unique. What set him apart was his devotion to success, and a painstaking, careful, diligent application of energy to putting every fragment of his operation together. He would get involved in each stage of planning, design, and production; and he spent time building up a relationship with the sponsors—in the Tyrrell's case, Elf and Goodyear. He was a relentless tester of different tyre compounds and constructions, relying on his graphic descriptions of how his cars behaved, to inspire his engineers and tyre designers.

A later generation of racing car technologists tried to replace Jackie Stewart's singular interpretative skills with all manner of electronic wizardry. Their failure only emphasised the genius for car control he was able to display. Together with his strong will, and a dash of cool aggression, Jackie Stewart was a formidable adversary.

He was also able to make the most of his success; not simply in cash terms, although he was the richest racing driver of his day. He laid good lines of communication with the press, although many thought him brash and arrogant. He could usually silence his critics with an amazing performance such as his German Grand Prix of 1968, or the Italian Grand Prix of 1973, when, rather like Jim Clark at *his* last race there, he re-passed almost the entire field after being delayed by a pit stop. He even achieved the near-impossible of a fastest lap 0.8 sec faster than his own best practice time.

No driver before or since aspired to Jackie Stewart's status as a socialite, an ambassador, or simply a celebrity. His self-confidence never departed him; it never needed to. Everything he touched seemed to turn to gold. It has even been suggested that his failures were carefully planned to appear someone else's fault.

His very survival was a factor in his success; world champions generally turned out to have a high mortality rate. Stewart's accumulation of wealth continued long after he stepped out of a racing car for the last time, while his field of activities widened to include business and television all over the world.

His influence on motor racing at all levels was incalculable.

the potholed surface, and the arguments between drivers and teams became heated. The Constructors' problem lay in their contract, which assured Zolder a full field of cars. The team managers lined the cars up in front of the pits to indicate that if practice did not go ahead, it would be the *drivers'* fault, not theirs. It would then be the drivers who were in breach of contract.

The deadlock was broken by Jacky Ickx who, conscious of his obligations to his fellow countrymen, left the GPDA debate, got into his Ferrari, and began practising. His colleagues were left with little option but to join him. They raced only under protest, and with the catch fence at one corner alone claiming six victims, the drivers' contention that the circuit was indeed dangerous was amply borne out. Fortunately, on this occasion, there were no injuries . . .

There was a quarrel over money at Silverstone, where the Formula 5000 option was very nearly invoked. Colin Chapman had more legal trouble in Italy, where he was still hounded by the police over the 1970 accident. The GPDA's efforts to turn itself into a sort of trade union for *all* racing drivers, and

The also-rans in the Austrian Grand Prix. Twice world champion Graham Hill, driving his own Embassy Racing Shadow Ford, leads the similar UOP works car of Jackie Oliver, Rolf Stommelen's Ceramica Pagnossin Brabham-Ford BT42, and Rikki von Opel's Ensign-Ford. All retired from the race.

not only those in Formula 1, foundered. It failed to attract the hundreds of members necessary to support a secretariat, and Nick Syrett, who had left the British Racing and Sports Car Club to run it, resigned. It reverted to its former role as the representative body of Grand Prix drivers alone, and Robert Langford became its secretary.

The drivers and the press fell out over who should be allowed in the pit road, and the International Racing Press Association (IRPA) staged a demonstration in Austria in their defence. Some refused to report the race by way of retaliation, which brought the matter home to the sponsors. Yardley and McLaren had writs flying back and forth at the end of the season over who should sponsor the team for 1974, and the lap charting of the Canadian Grand Prix was a shambles . . .

It was the sort of season that irritated the traditional motor racing fan, and even disappointed those who had come to regard Grand Prix racing as a well-organised, modern, professional sport.

Yet the darkest shadow over Grand Prix racing still lay in its danger. Early in the season, Mike Hailwood distinguished himself by stepping into the fire surrounding Clay Regazzoni's Ferrari and pulling the dazed and helpless driver clear in an act of outstanding bravery for which he was later awarded the George Medal.

But at the Dutch Grand Prix in July, similar heroism by David Purley failed to save the life of Roger Williamson. The baleful eye of television caught the fatal moments after Williamson's March overturned, close to where Piers Courage lost his life in 1970. It caught Purley's frenzied attempts to pull his friend to safety. It caught his impotent fury with the fire marshals who recoiled from the first flicker of flames. It caught him beseeching them to try and save the so far uninjured driver, trapped underneath the car. It caught Purley's grief as the fire took hold, and 25-year-old Williamson perished before his eyes.

Whilst many sports, such as climbing, are demonstrably dangerous, death on a mountainside is a private affair. Roger Williamson's, in only his second Grand Prix, seen by millions, had a pagan horror about it, as the cameras dwelt on Purley's gallantry, and his dumb-show mime as the firemen drew back. A second George Medal went to the brave ex-paratrooper, while Zandvoort was denounced for allowing the duplicate tragedy to happen.

The death of François Cevert during practice for the Grand Prix of the United States at Watkins Glen cast further gloom on the season. It cast gloom also on the climax of Jackie Stewart's career, and what would have been his hundredth Grand Prix. Distressed by the death of his handsome young friend, Stewart withdrew from the race, and announced that he had been, in any case, about to retire from racing. Cevert was one of two drivers to die in 1973 on the steel guard rails which the safety lobby had so enthusiastically endorsed. There seemed no answer to an annual toll—despite the improvements there had been to cars, to tyres, to tracks, and to equipment. Yet probably without the safety crusade, the dangers inherent in the increased speed and cornering power of the cars, would have made racing unacceptable in a modern, civilised society.

1974

1974

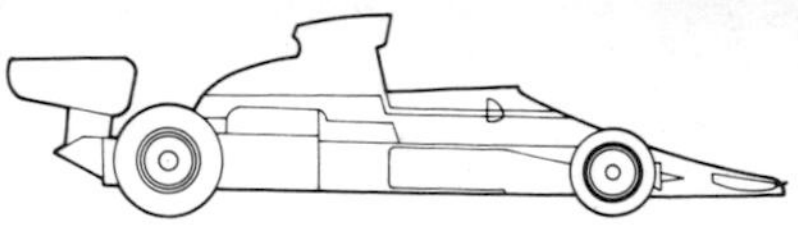

The fuel crisis that caused long queues for petrol throughout Europe also brought the protagonists of Formula 1 racing into line. Rallies were curtailed or cancelled. Races were shortened. Sponsors withdrew from every other form of racing and some, such as Interserie and Can-Am, virtually ceased to exist. Manufacturers like Ford and BMW withdrew from touring car racing.

Britain, where nearly all the Formula 1 teams had their homes, was in the grip of the three-day week. Industrial trouble affected the racing car industry along with every other. It would have been absurd to carry on a quarrel in the face of a crisis such as this, so the looming confrontation between the authorities, the FIA and its sub-committee, the International Sporting Commission (CSI) on the one hand, and the Formula 1 Constructors (the Formula 1 Association) on the other, had to be postponed. The battle lines were still drawn, but conflict was put off for the time being.

Astonishingly, all 15 scheduled Grands Prix did take place, the only one materially affected being South Africa, which was put back from the beginning of March till the end owing to a temporary ban on motor sport by the South African Government. The petrol queues and the weekend closures by filling stations in some parts of Europe had their effect on attendance at races, but the sponsors still mostly paid up. Amongst those contributing regularly to Formula 1 were Marlboro, John Player, Embassy, Yardley (who had their own McLaren team after the row over who should be principal sponsor), Texaco, Elf, UOP, Duckhams, and Fina. The ranks were swelled by the addition of Bang & Olufsen, Hitachi, Matchbox, and First National City Bank. Some of the new sponsors, such as Bang & Olufsen, and even established ones like Texaco and John Player, were not content just to buy a connection with a team. They bought a Grand Prix as well: B & O the Belgian, Texaco the Swedish, and John Player the British.

Most surprising of all amongst the problems affecting Grand Prix racing was not lack of support, but too many entries for each race. The continuing availability of the competitive Ford-Cosworth engine, the wide choice of cars, and even the second-hand engines, cars, and material which could be picked up relatively cheaply, created a seemingly endless supply of new teams. The Formula 1 Constructors postponed their plans for a sort of Grand Prix closed shop, and it was agreed that for the moment, anybody with a suitable car could enter for a race. The fastest 25 would start, subject to being able to achieve 90 per cent of the lap time of the fastest car; a necessary provision to keep the very slowest off the course.

Some of the new teams came from America, with Penske and Parnelli making what turned out to be short-lived attempts to join Shadow in Formula 1. Maki from Japan made an even shorter-lived effort, while the driver changes included the significant one of Emerson Fittipaldi moving from Lotus to McLaren.

With the departure of Jackie Stewart, there was a real vacancy for a driver who would follow in the Fangio-Moss-Clark-Stewart tradition of being *the* one to beat. Ronnie Peterson was the obvious candidate, yet he suffered from the Jochen Rindt trouble of driving for a team that was either past its peak, or leaving one just before reaching it. Jacky Ickx had huge reserves of talent which he seldom felt inclined to call upon, or so it seemed. He was unhappy at Ferrari. Fittipaldi for a time appeared to be the most likely driver; he had all the qualifications—a meteoric rise to fame, a world championship, a record of success against the formidable opposition of Jackie Stewart himself. Yet nobody came forward to fill the breach for fully a season.

Carlos Reutemann, Jody Scheckter, Niki Lauda, Carlos Pace, all were fast drivers close to the front rank, but somehow not quite ready to follow such distinguished wheel tracks.

As for the cars, at the end of 1973 there seemed no doubt that the 1974 world champion would be powered by a Ford-Cosworth engine, But no sooner had the races started than a competitor appeared. The 1974 season saw a return of Ferrari from the wilderness to which it had been consigned almost since the start of the 3-litre Formula. From the day John Surtees walked out following his row with Dragoni, Ferrari had lurched from crisis to crisis, winning some races by default, but never with a team which looked a serious contender for the world championship.

In 1973, Jacky Ickx had been so disillusioned he had left, his capacity to win untapped. Arturo Merzario had taken over, but he was essentially a lightweight, in the figurative as well as the literal sense. For most of the races Ferrari had fielded only one car, and twice they failed to turn up at all.

Angered by the decrepitude into which his name had fallen, and recovering from an illness, Enzo Ferrari in his mid-seventies, stubborn as ever, decided not to join BRM in decline, in the face of the Ford-Cosworth onslaught. He had fought Ford off on the commercial front ten years before, when the Detroit giant had sought to buy him out. Now, Ferrari gave up racing sports cars, and carried out a thorough reorganisation of his racing department. To a man brought up in the racing traditions of small workshops and wizard tuners, his programme was nothing short of revolutionary.

The 1973 car had not lived up to expectations. The new chassis had not given the improvement in road holding for which it had been designed and the engine was not delivering the power which had been expected. For 1974 two drivers had been taken on after a dismal time with BRM; neither seemed front runners. Regazzoni was back after falling out with Ferrari the year before, and Niki Lauda was, after all, no more than an Austrian who had obtained his drives through coming up with the sponsorship cash to buy them.

Ferrari's priceless asset was Fiorano, the test track

The beautiful people at Monte Carlo. The celebrities walk from the Hotel de Paris to the pits, a Monaco ritual which included (leading) Walter Hayes, a Vice President of Ford Motor Company, and perhaps the man chiefly responsible for the Ford-Cosworth DFV engine. Jackie Stewart (in sunglasses) now retired from racing, walks with his wife, Helen, while following them, their week-end guest film star Elizabeth Taylor.

which had been equipped with Fiat money, and was unique in Formula 1. Lotus had a test track on the runways of Hethel, others had the use of tracks round the world, racing circuits where security was negligible and facilities no more than could be brought in the back of a lorry.

Ferrari had a track behind a high wall, close to the factory where a corner in next week's race could be simulated; a track which could be flooded for wet weather tyre testing. Ten television cameras with video tape recording equipment could show the technicians how a car behaved; and at four places twelve photocells in the track, in addition to Heuer timing, could gauge the improvements of minute modifications without having to rely on driver opinion. The timing equipment could be instantly linked to the Univac computer in Zürich to assess the implications of changes which might work in one place and not in another. A skid pan could relay steady-speed cornering data, and Goodyear joined enthusiastically in a programme to tailor a tyre for the new, changed car which resulted.

The Ferrari's problems included poor acceleration off the line. It had always used more fuel than the V-8s, thus its start-line weight was heavier. It was only late in the race that it competed on level terms. Fuel consumption was reduced by five per cent. Pick-up out of corners never had the punch of the V-8s, so now it was improved with a change in the torque curve to give better acceleration without sacrificing the power it already had at the top of the range, some 30 bhp. The low engine (a horizontally opposed twelve cylinder) gave better air flow to the rear wing, and a lower centre of gravity to the car.

Niki Lauda was able to exploit the improvements. As events turned out, however, he was not yet ready to be world champion. He took the opposition aback by winning in Spain in April, and Holland in June. He was second in Argentina, Belgium, and France, backed up ably by Regazzoni; then he made a blunder in the British Grand Prix which probably cost him the race, brought a sour note to the whole season, and he never finished a race again for the rest of the year.

Towards the end of the British Grand Prix, Lauda dropped back with a puncture. He had led for 69 of the 75 laps, but his slowly deflating tyre allowed Scheckter into the lead in the Tyrrell. By lap 74 he realised he would not reach the finish without changing the wheel, so he sped into the pits. But after a lightning stop, he found his exit barred by the crush of photographers and officials round the finishing line where Scheckter was taking the flag.

Ferrari's new team manager, the efficient young lawyer Count Luca Montezemolo, immediately protested that Lauda had been unreasonably prevented from completing the course. The result seemed important at the time, because Lauda was leading the world championship. The case dragged on for months, becoming a *cause célèbre* as the first world championship Grand Prix to be decided in the court room rather than on the track.

In the end, it was all academic. Lauda was awarded fifth place on appeal to an FIA tribunal in September, gaining him two points, and losing Reutemann and Hulme one each. It made no difference to Lauda, because he failed to finish another race for the rest of the season.

His mistake had been in ignoring his team's instructions to come in as soon as the puncture occurred.

He had further lessons to learn as the season wore on, but there was no doubt about the revival in Ferrari fortunes. The Ford-Cosworth remained supreme by weight of numbers if nothing else, but it was no longer unchallenged. The task facing designers was now two-fold. Not only had they to find means of improving road holding; they had to find sufficient improvement to make up for their power deficit *vis-à-vis* the Ferraris.

Clay Regazzoni (Ferrari) scored his first victory for

four years in the German Grand Prix at the Nürburgring, the race in which Mike Hailwood crashed, virtually ending his motor racing career. Hailwood had first raced cars as long ago as 1963, but then returned to motor cycles. Coming back to cars in 1968, after winning 75 two-wheeled Grands Prix, a dozen Isle of Man TTs, and ten world championships, he drove in Formula 1 first for Surtees.

It was not a success, but he was making more headway with McLaren when he broke both legs in a collision with one of the Nürburgring's crash barriers. Hailwood's greatest success in cars was winning the 1972 Formula 2 championship, and coming second in Formula 5000 in 1973, but his heart was always in motor cycling where he proved his greatness by coming back in 1978 and 1979, and winning two more TTs.

The revival in Brabham fortunes was confirmed by two victories for Carlos Reutemann, Austria in August, and the United States in October, while the open nature of the entire season was emphasised at Monza in September, when Ronnie Peterson (John Player Lotus) became the only driver up till then to win more than two races.

The championship was still close. After Monza, with two races to go, Clay Regazzoni led with 46 points, Jody Scheckter was second with 45, and Emerson Fittipaldi third with 43. Then Fittipaldi won the Canadian Grand Prix with Regazzoni second, making them joint leaders with 52 points, and the final race of the season became the decider.

Scheckter in the Elf Tyrrell was the outside chance, but he lasted only 44 of the race's 59 laps. After that, all Fittipaldi had to do was remain in front of Regazzoni, in which he was helped by the Ferrari suffering suspension trouble and calling at its pit. Fittipaldi was able to secure his second world title with a safe fourth place.

Thus, the season that had been in danger from the oil crisis and its aftermath, came to an end. If anything, Grand Prix racing emerged stronger than before. If a world-wide shortage of petrol was unable to stop it, and an international recession affected its prosperity hardly at all, it seemed that there was a great future for it.

The tragedies, unfortunately, continued. Peter Revson died at the beginning of the season, when his Shadow had a suspension failure during a private test session at Kyalami. Aged 35, Revson started racing along with Mike Hailwood in 1963, and returned to a career that was becoming brighter with every race. His death in the blazing car added poignancy to Hailwood's rescue of Regazzoni a few weeks later. Silvio Moser, 33, died on 25 April in a sports car during the Monza 1000 Kms race. The diminutive Swiss driver had taken part in Grand Prix races with an ATS-Cooper, Brabham, and the unsuccessful Bellasi cars. At the season's end, Helmuth Koinigg, the 25-year-old Austrian, became another victim of the unforgiving guard rails at Watkins Glen. It was only his second Grand Prix.

Emerson Fittipaldi (b 1946)

In Brazil, Emerson Fittipaldi was to motor racing what Pelé was to soccer. He demonstrated the truth of the dictum that if a young racing driver is going to reach the top, he nearly always shows it at once. When he won his first world title, it was only a little over two years after he took part in his first Formula 1 race. When he won his second, he was still only 28, but as with several champions, his titles proved the summit of his career. After being runner-up in 1975 he never won another Grand Prix.

Jackie Stewart drove his first single-seater in 1964, won his first Grand Prix in 1965, but had to wait until 1969 to win the championship. It took Jochen Rindt two more years. Even Jim Clark was in single-seaters for three years before his first championship. It took Fangio four years; Mike Hawthorn six. Stirling Moss tried for ten, and never won it.

Fittipaldi was 15 when he won his first motor cycle race, and at 20 was winning five races out of seven in the Brazilian Formula Vee series. He and his elder brother Wilson were inseparable, until Emerson left their native São Paulo, alone, and went to England to drive in Formula Ford, and take lessons at the Jim Russell school. He won his second race, went on to win three out of eight in his first season, and never finished lower than fourth.

Despite a late start in Formula 3, he won the British Lombank Championship with eight victories in twelve races, so by the age of 23 he was in demand for Formula 2. In the event, he leap-frogged that class and went straight into Formula 1, being catapulted to the leadership of Team Lotus following Jochen Rindt's accident at Monza in 1970.

He remained a winner in Formula 2, but not surprisingly his first season in Grand Prix racing proved difficult. It was not helped by a road accident which cracked his ribs and injured his wife, and he missed the Dutch Grand Prix.

But was his success founded upon the sudden maturity of the Lotus 72 in time for his first title, and the McLaren M23 in time for his second? His failure to follow up with the ill-starred Copersucar prompts the question. Fittipaldi played his part ably enough in the devolopment of both cars, however; his test driving was invariably more effective than that of Ronnie Peterson, who joined him in the uneasy 'equal number one' driver role. There was a healthy rivalry between the perhaps inappropriately cool Latin, and the instinctive Swede.

On the commercial front, Fittipaldi ruffled feelings. When he left Lotus he took Texaco sponsorship with him, which created difficulties at McLaren with Yardley. When he left McLaren to form Copersucar, he did so abruptly, incensing Teddy Mayer. His stand against the Constructors in Spain in 1975 was probably not easily forgiven, although it showed him as one of the more highly principled drivers of modern times. Mayer accused him of going off, '. . . in an unwavering pursuit of riches'. Spain 1975 showed that Fittipaldi was a driver not easily bought off, or bullied.

1975

Conti TS
Conti TS
Conti TS
TEXACO
Beta
UTEN SILI
elf
elf
8
4
11
12

Grand Prix racing became increasingly a story of broken rules and rows. Niki Lauda's 1974 British Grand Prix was the first to hit the headlines with a courtroom battle. Now, protests flew thick and fast; lawyers joined the mechanics, team managers, sponsors, and public relations men in the Grand Prix circus. The quarrel between the Constructors and the CSI, postponed from 1973, began afresh. Racing itself seemed to matter progressively less.

Yet a more bizarre element was still to come. With the virtual disappearance of the drivers from the Grand Prix political equation, the years since the UPPI, and the GPDA (formed in 1961) came to nothing. At the Spanish Grand Prix, the Constructors put the drivers firmly in their place with a stern warning that a long queue of replacements awaited their seats, their racing overalls, and their earning power. Drivers' options were further reduced by the continued decline in alternative forms of racing.

There were 15 races scheduled, but Canada was peremptorily cancelled, not by the CSI which nominally had the only option to do so, but by the Constructors, flexing their political muscle. Four races were cut short by rain, demonstrating once again that tyre development made racing in wet weather at best problematical, at worst dangerous and a waste of time. Rain upset several more races, so that although Niki Lauda won his first world championship by a convincing five victories in a season where only Emerson Fittipaldi won more than one, a statistician would look askance at the sample.

In the technical field, a number of teams undid some of the 'advances' they had made. Stage by stage, McLaren removed the theoretically superior rising rate suspension on the M 23, and reverted to an older style of airbox. Tyrrell reverted to outboard front disc brakes on their 007 model, and changed the torsion bar rear suspension back to coil springs. Lotus turned their Type 72 back almost to the pattern in which it had raced during 1973.

Designers seemed to be chasing their tails in their desperation to find the small improvements that would give them an advantage. The days were long past where the leading teams could win races by a lap, or achieve walk-overs in line-ahead formation. Tenths of seconds separated the cars on the grid, a few lengths after two hours' racing. Inevitably some circuits, such as Zandvoort, became known as most suitable for Ferraris, while others seemed better matched to particular Cosworth-engined cars.

Tyres produced as many questions as answers, with tyre technicians and car designers alike puzzled by identical tyres producing different results on different circuits. Drivers could be so perplexed by choice that even those in the same team could choose different tyres for the same race.

With Lauda now a mature, practised winner, the Ferrari recovery was complete. The 312T (the 'T' for *transversale*, describing the disposition of the gearbox) was fully developed with their principal driver steadily acquiring a reputation for cool, computer-like driving on the test track, and skilled, tactical behaviour in races.

All that remained to destroy the harmony of a successful season's competition was the weather, and the hard-headed rush of the Constructors into the vacuum left by the flight of the CSI.

Above left: With the traditional champagne shower Niki Lauda celebrates his victory in the French Grand Prix for Ferrari. James Hunt was second in the Hesketh, and Jochen Mass (right) third for McLaren.

Above: Trouble in Spain, and four angry world champions tell the press what they think (left to right) Graham Hill, Emerson Fittipaldi, Niki Lauda, and Jody Scheckter.

Once again, the problem stemmed from the widely differing outlooks of the two organisations. The CSI, aware of the need to reduce cornering speeds in the cause of safety, wanted to limit the effect of tyres and wings by reducing their dimensions. The Constructors would have none of this, agreed to freeze the dimensions of wings and cars, but insisted that if the tracks wanted to cut cornering speeds, they must do so by introducing chicanes. The Constructors were still unable to agree amongst themselves on any measure which would restrain the cars' cornering power without penalising one design more than another. Instead they chose to pass the problem on.

It was never solved. The chicanes proved only a palliative, and the ever-higher speeds invariably rendered the previous year's circuit changes inadequate in any case. The drivers were worried about the improved traction reducing braking areas, thus further reducing overtaking opportunities, which were already diminished by the width of the cars. Zolder, Silverstone, and Watkins Glen all acquired chicanes, but only after the safety issue had come to a head right at the beginning of the European season, in Spain.

When the GPDA safety committee went out to inspect the track in Montjuich Park, Barcelona, they discovered much of the Armco barrier had only been loosely bolted together. Several of the stanchions were not firmly installed, and racing was refused until they were.

The CSI were ineffectual. They said the circuit conformed to their regulations, and did not seem much interested in the GPDA point of view. The Constructors kept out of the argument as long as they could, until the organisers, the RAC de Cataluña y Baleares reminded them about their contract. This promised a Grand Prix, and if they could not provide one, they would be in breach of contract and the police would impound the cars pending litigation. As the Constructors well knew, this could take months.

The prospect of the season ahead, with all the other contracts for all the other Grands Prix concentrated the minds of the Constructors wonderfully. The Barcelona paddock was a derelict sports stadium with only one exit which the police could cover quickly and easily. Within minutes, the entire Grand Prix circus with its cars, equipment, transporters, and spare engines could be literally at gunpoint. A drawback of the package deal Grand Prix stood instantly revealed.

To the drivers, it was a matter of life or death. Peter Revson had died when a bottom guard rail came off its post, and the car careered over it. François Cevert had received terrible injuries when the Watkins Glen guard rail came apart. There were again reservations about the Watkins Glen rail in 1974 but the GPDA had agreed to race. The result

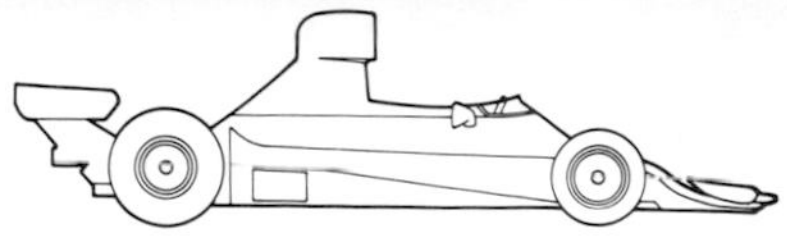

The races

Emerson Fittipaldi started the 1975 season much as he had finished 1974—by winning. He took first place for McLaren in the Grand Prix of Argentina, and his fellow countryman, Carlos Pace, followed up by winning the Grand Prix of Brazil for Brabham. Fittipaldi came second, thus retaining his lead in the world championship. The South African Grand Prix saw the first lady competitor since Maria Teresa de Filippis in 1958–9. An Italian girl, Lella Lombardi (March) started from the back of the grid, and retired after 23 laps with engine trouble. The race was won by Jody Scheckter, who emulated the exploit of his predecessor in the Tyrrell team, Jackie Stewart, by crashing in practice and winning with the spare car.

The Spanish Grand Prix ended before half distance, so Jochen Mass only earned half points for winning, 4$\frac{1}{2}$ instead of 9, and Fittipaldi kept his lead. Monaco was also curtailed, but only by three laps so Niki Lauda gained the full score for winning a race in which a shower of rain resulted in accidents to one third of the 18 starters.

Fittipaldi lost his lead at round six, the Belgian Grand Prix at Zolder which Lauda won, and the Ferrari took the chequered flag again at Anderstorp for the Grand Prix of Sweden. This race confirmed Lauda's new mastery of race-craft, when he climbed through the field from sixth, to take the lead eleven laps from the end.

It was a maturity which James Hunt also unexpectedly showed in round eight at Zandvoort. Once again rain dictated the course of events, and the field started on wet weather tyres. Hunt was the first driver to gamble on a change to dry tyres as the road dried out, and Lauda was never able to make good the time Hunt gained during his few laps' advantage. Illustrative also of the narrowing margin between winning and losing, Hunt had set his suspension to suit dry weather, while Lauda had tuned his Ferrari for the wet, Hunt's slightly superior handling giving him the edge on his opponent. It was the first victory for Hunt and the short-lived Hesketh team which had boasted they would bring fun back to the Grand Prix scene. It was a brave effort, but the smiles must have faded at the cost to Lord Alexander Hesketh, not only of subsidising a Formula 1 team, but also paying for the style in which the operation was carried out. This extended to helicopters, a large yacht in Monte Carlo harbour, and the most extravagant parties seen in Formula 1 since the Thirties.

Lauda won round nine, the French Grand Prix, increasing his lead in the championship, then, at Silverstone, rain brought confusion once again. This was the third British Grand Prix in a row to end in controversy. Sixteen cars crashed, and 19 made stops of one sort or another in a race which began on a dry track, but was almost rained off after 20 laps. Most of the field came in to change tyres, then it dried out after a while, only to rain again after a further 30 laps. A cloudburst hit Silverstone with many cars back on 'slicks'—dry weather tyres with smooth treads which made a wet track as slippery as ice. The race was stopped eleven laps early with the official lap chart in some doubt about the finishing order, due to the passing and repassing during the showers, and the large number of pit stops. Emerson Fittipaldi, one of the few drivers who had neither stopped nor had an accident, was named the winner; so he kept second place in the championship, while the British Grand Prix furthered its reputation for eccentricity.

Punctures spoiled the German Grand Prix at the Nürburgring. They had given trouble before due to the thin casings of the soft-compound tyres into which flints or road debris would quickly work. Nine cars out of 24 were affected, of which six retired, two suffering accidents as a result of tyre failures. The winner, Carlos Reutemann, was one of the handful of drivers fortunate enough to avoid punctures.

Neither of the American teams who had come to Europe in 1974 enjoyed much success. Andretti persevered with the Vel's Parnelli, but in the Austrian Grand Prix the Penske team suffered the loss of their driver, Mark Donohue, due to a curiously unlucky accident. Following a blow-out, Donohue's car went off the track during the warm-up session on race morning. It was a high-speed accident, by no means the first of the weekend, but Donohue mowed down a catch fence and a safety barrier before coming to rest on top of a marshal's post. One of the marshals later died from his injuries while another was also injured. Donohue, however, seemed unhurt at first as he was cut out of the wreckage of his car. But in hospital he lost consciousness, and despite an operation, died from an internal brain haemorrhage two and a half days later.

Until his death at the age of 38, Donohue had been one of motor racing's great all-rounders. He had won the Indianapolis 500 in 1972, and only a week before the accident in Austria, set a new world speed record for a closed circuit. He drove a lap of the Alabama International Motor Speedway, Talladega with his Can-Am-winning Porsche 917-30K at a speed of 221.160 mph/355.92 kph. He was thrice Trans-Am Champion, but also drove in long-distance sports cars, USAC, and NASCAR racing before tackling Formula 1.

Austria turned out to be yet another wet race, stopped after 29 laps, with Vittorio Brambilla scoring his only Grand Prix victory. He was so overcome when he took the chequered flag in his March that he spun and damaged the nose of the car.

For the second time in the season, only half championship points were awarded because the race had not reached half distance. Lauda was still in front, and clinched his title in round 13 at Monza, when Regazzoni led a Ferrari triumph, with Fittipaldi second. Fittipaldi never gave up, even in the final race at Watkins Glen, despite being baulked in his pursuit of Lauda by Regazzoni.

was that Helmuth Koinigg had been beheaded when his car went under a badly secured barrier.

The Constructors never flinched. They made a play of tightening up a few nuts on the rails themselves, but it needed several weeks' work to make Montjuich safe. Then they warmed up the cars in the pits, and told the drivers in strong terms to get in and drive.

Only Emerson Fittipaldi stood his ground. He did the minimum three practice laps in second gear, then withstood the derision of the crowd, and stalked off. The remainder felt insecure enough to do exactly as they were told.

Within a year, the GPDA as a separate entity was no more. It was absorbed into the Formula One Constructors' Association, or FOCA, as it was coming to be known. The drivers had been failed by the CSI, and hamstrung by their employers. They still had a safety committee, but if they wanted things done in future, it would not be by militant action.

The immediate result of carrying on racing at Montjuich was a repetition of the accident in 1969, but with rather more tragic consequences. When Rindt and Hill crashed after their wing failures, the guard rails had saved uncounted spectators. But when Rolf Stommelen went over the same crest, and the carbon fibre mounts of the wing on his Graham Hill racing car failed, the rails were not high enough for the job. While Stommelen was injured, a fireman and a photographer were amongst four people killed.

The race was stopped, and the winner, Jochen Mass, his face dark with fury, almost assaulted the organising committee. It had been a sordid affair from which no one, except perhaps Fittipaldi, emerged with much credit. The major share of the culpability belonged to the organisers and the CSI, but FOCA also emerged in a poor light.

A result of the accident, as in 1969, was a demand for new rules concerning wings. The CSI secretary, Claude le Geuzec, gave the Constructors notice that a change was on the way, but once again the statutory period of grace was demanded before the implementation of a fundamental change in the rules. The CSI capitulated in view of FOCA's ability to make its own rules. As a compromise, the CSI Formula 1 Group was created, essentially as a committee to consider Formula 1 separately from other motor racing. It was to be composed of representatives of the CSI and FOCA, but in practice, it would merely rubber-stamp FOCA decisions concerning the rules, the calendar, and anything else. Having subdued the drivers, FOCA now proceeded to subdue the CSI.

As a further demonstration of power, FOCA refused to turn up for the Canadian Grand Prix because the organisers failed to meet a deadline for a decision on the race purse. The Canadians flew to Europe to try and achieve a change of heart, and even took the matter to court. It was to no avail. A press statement had been issued saying there would be no race at Mosport, and indeed there was not.

What the two sides had been working out was a basis for paying for a 26-car grid as a package. The race organisers paid FOCA and FOCA decided the distribution of £92400 for each European Grand Prix. Under the proposed three-year agreements with the tracks, this would rise to £165000 in 1977, and £190000 in 1978, plus an allowance for inflation, and a bit extra depending on the previous year's attendance. FOCA were not above chartering a helicopter to photograph the crowd as one means of monitoring attendance.

The two North American races were priced at $440000 plus transportation for personnel, together with air freight for the cars, rising to $500000, and later $565000. The payout system was never revealed, but it was based on proportions for the top scorers in the championship, the finishing order in the race, and the fastest 20 cars in practice. Thus it was possible for a car which qualified lower than 20th and finished below 20th place to earn nothing at all. It gave new teams who had not scored in the FOCA championship little opportunity to share. They also had to pay their own transportation for races outside Europe. In short, FOCA had negotiated a self-perpetuating arrangement for a Grand Prix closed shop. And it had managed it with the active participation, if not the actual connivance, of the body that was supposed to be governing it.

Carlos Pace (Brabham-Ford BT44B) finished third in the Monaco Grand Prix.

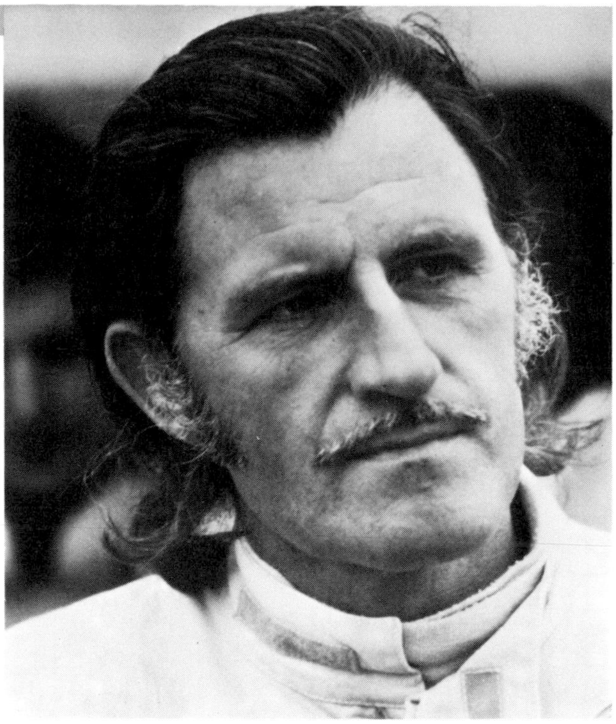

Graham Hill (b 1929)

The longest Grand Prix career of all belonged to Norman Graham Hill, OBE, who took part in 178 races over a period of 18 years. He won 14 of them, and was world champion twice; with BRM in 1962, and Lotus in 1968. He was also the only driver to win the triple crown of the Formula 1 world championship, the Le Mans 24 Hours (1972, with Henri Pescarolo driving a Matra Simca 670) and Indianapolis (1966, driving a Lola).

There was no family wealth to help Hill to the top of the motor racing tree; his arrival pre-dated sponsorship, so he was forced into the time-honoured stratagem of working as a mechanic and talking his way in. He was in his twenties, a former engine room artificer in the Royal Navy, when he saw an advertisement inviting young hopefuls to drive a racing car at Brands Hatch for five shillings per lap. It was a 500 cc motor cycle engined Cooper, and Hill recalled, 'I decided to have a whole pound's worth'.

He threw up his job and went to look after the racing school's cars, but this ended when the school went bust, and Hill joined the dole queue. He registered as an out of work racing driver, and collected 32s 6d (£1.62½) a week until things got better.

In due course they did. Hill bartered his services as a mechanic for the chance to drive racing cars, until he obtained a job with Colin Chapman's Lotus team, becoming one of their regular drivers at the end of 1957. The following year, Lotus entered Grand Prix racing, and Hill went with them.

Success came with Hill's move to BRM with the gutsy, tough driving for which he became famous. Never a gifted, natural driver in the effortless mould of Jim Clark or Jackie Stewart, Graham Hill had to work to shave every tenth of a second off his lap time. He had to make up in teeth-gritting, breath-holding determination what he lacked in talent, and his supporters came to love him for it. They could more easily identify with him, with his humanity, than with the deft genius of his two Scottish rivals. They sensed Hill was an artisan amongst artists, which made his victories all the sweeter when they came.

His recovery from his 1969 accident at Watkins Glen made Hill's a household name. Despite his leg injuries, his spirit was indomitable. He appeared on television from his hospital bed, wrote a book, gave interviews, and always the message was the same, 'I'll be racing again in March'.

Doctors shook their heads but, sure enough, limping and in pain, his left leg permanently bowed, little strength in his ankles and with restricted movement in his foot, he was back at the wheel by the South Africa Grand Prix of 1970. Although he never won another Grand Prix, he did win the 1971 International Trophy to scenes of enthusiasm not often seen at a motor race. He still had two more Formula 2 wins to come, and the astonishing victory at Le Mans, with legs that might have confined less determined men to a wheelchair.

Hill's breezy public persona concealed a tough commercial edge. His affability could vanish the moment business was discussed, and his associates could discover that the only thing he drove as hard as a racing car was a bargain.

He announced he would retire at Silverstone in 1975. He campaigned for disabled drivers and for traffic wardens. In 1971 he was voted best after-dinner speaker by the Guild of Professional Toastmasters, and his dry humour made him a natural for television.

He was flying his beloved Piper Aztec back to Elstree from Marseille on 28 November after a test session at Ricard with his young protégé Tony Brise. One of the most promising newcomers to appear in Britain for some time, Brise (23) was to be the principal driver for the Embassy Hill team, but the testing of the new car had not gone well.

Hill trusted in his familiarity with the approach to Elstree to put down in a light fog. Three miles from the runway threshold, the little aircraft plunged into trees on Arkley golf course. Hill's team died with him. Besides himself and Brise, Ray Brimble (34) his team manager, the designer of the car, Andy Smallman (24), and mechanics Terry Richards (26) and Tony Alcock (35) were killed. The cars never raced, and the team was quietly disbanded.

GRAHAM HILL'S GRAND PRIX RESULTS 1958 – 1975

The Longest Track Record

Graham Hill competed in more world championship Grand Prix races (178) than anyone else. He won the world championship in 1962 and 1968.

Grand Prix	Car	Result
1958		
Monaco	Lotus 12	lost wheel
Holland	Lotus 12	engine
Belgium	Lotus 12	engine
France	Lotus 16	engine
Britain	Lotus 16	overheating
Germany	F 2 Lotus 16	oil pipe
Portugal	Lotus 16	accident
Italy	Lotus 16	sixth
Morocco	Lotus 16	16th
1959		
Monaco	Lotus 16	fire
Holland	Lotus 16	seventh
France	Lotus 16	radiator
Britain	Lotus 16	ninth
Germany	Lotus 16	oil radiator
Portugal	Lotus 16	accident
Italy	Lotus 16	engine
1960		
Argentina	BRM P25	oil pressure
Monaco	BRM P48	seventh
Holland	BRM P48	third
Belgium	BRM P48	engine
France	BRM P48	accident
Britain	BRM P48	accident (*)
Portugal	BRM P48	gearbox
United States	BRM P48	gearbox
1961		
Monaco	BRM P57	fuel pump
Holland	BRM P57	eighth
Belgium	BRM P57	ignition
France	BRM P57	sixth
Britain	BRM P57	engine
Germany	BRM P57	accident
Italy	BRM P57	engine
United States	BRM P57	fifth
1962		
Holland	BRM P57	fifth
Monaco	BRM P57	sixth
Belgium	BRM P57	second (**)
France	BRM P57	ninth (*)
Britain	BRM P57	fourth
Germany	BRM P57	first (*)
Italy	BRM P57	first (*)
United States	BRM P57	second
South Africa	BRM P57	first

Grand Prix	Car	Result
1963		
Monaco	BRM P57	first
Belgium	BRM P57	gearbox (**)
Holland	BRM P57	overheating
France	BRM P61	third
Britain	BRM P57	third
Germany	BRM P57	gearbox
Italy	BRM P61	16th
United States	BRM P57	first (**)
Mexico	BRM P57	fourth
South Africa	BRM P57	third
1964		
Monaco	BRM P261	first (*)
Holland	BRM P261	fourth
Belgium	BRM P261	fifth
France	BRM P261	second
Britain	BRM P261	second
Germany	BRM P261	second
Austria	BRM P261	ignition (**)
Italy	BRM P261	clutch
United States	BRM P261	first
Mexico	BRM P261	eleventh
1965		
South Africa	BRM P261	third
Monaco	BRM P261	first (*)(**)
Belgium	BRM P261	fifth (**)
France	BRM P261	fifth
Britain	BRM P261	second (*)
Holland	BRM P261	fourth (**)
Germany	BRM P261	second
Italy	BRM P261	second
United States	BRM P261	first (*)(**)
Mexico	BRM P261	engine
1966		
Monaco	BRM P261	third
Belgium	BRM P261	accident
France	BRM P261	engine
Britain	BRM P261	third
Holland	BRM P261	second
Germany	BRM P261	fourth
Italy	BRM P83	engine
United States	BRM P83	gearbox
Mexico	BRM P83	engine
1967		
South Africa	Lotus 43	ignition
Monaco	Lotus 33	second
Holland	Lotus 49	camshaft drive (**)
Belgium	Lotus 49	clutch
France	Lotus 49	gearbox (**)(*)
Britain	Lotus 49	engine
Germany	Lotus 49	suspension
Canada	Lotus 49	fourth
Italy	Lotus 49	engine
United States	Lotus 49	second (**)(*)
Mexico	Lotus 49	transmission

GRAHAM HILL'S GRAND PRIX RESULTS 1958 – 1975

Grand Prix	Car	Result
1968		
South Africa	Lotus 49	second
Spain	Lotus 49	first
Monaco	Lotus 49b	first (**)
Belgium	Lotus 49b	transmission
Holland	Lotus 49b	ninth
France	Lotus 49b	drive shaft
Britain	Lotus 49b	transmission (**)
Germany	Lotus 49b	second
Italy	Lotus 49b	lost wheel
Canada	Lotus 49b	fourth
United States	Lotus 49b	second
Mexico	Lotus 49b	first
1969		
South Africa	Lotus 49b	second
Spain	Lotus 49b	accident
Monaco	Lotus 49b	first
Holland	Lotus 49b	seventh
France	Lotus 49b	sixth
Britain	Lotus 49b	seventh
Germany	Lotus 49b	fourth
Italy	Lotus 49b	ninth
Canada	Lotus 49b	camshaft
United States	Lotus 49b	accident
1970		
South Africa	Lotus 49c	sixth
Spain	Lotus 49c	fourth
Monaco	Lotus 49c	fifth
Belgium	Lotus 49c	engine
Holland	Lotus 49c	n/c
France	Lotus 49c	tenth
Britain	Lotus 49c	sixth
Germany	Lotus 49c	engine
Italy	Lotus 72	withdrawn
Canada	Lotus 72	n/c
United States	Lotus 72	clutch
1971		
South Africa	Brabham BT33	ninth
Spain	Brabham BT34	steering
Monaco	Brabham BT34	accident
Holland	Brabham BT34	tenth
France	Brabham BT34	engine
Britain	Brabham BT34	accident
Germany	Brabham BT34	ninth
Austria	Brabham BT34	fifth
Italy	Brabham BT34	gearbox
Canada	Brabham BT34	accident
United States	Brabham BT34	seventh

Grand Prix	Car	Result
1972		
Argentina	Brabham BT33	puncture
South Africa	Brabham BT33	sixth
Spain	Brabham BT37	tenth
Monaco	Brabham BT37	twelfth
Belgium	Brabham BT37	suspension
France	Brabham BT37	tenth
Britain	Brabham BT37	accident
Germany	Brabham BT37	sixth
Austria	Brabham BT37	fuel injection
Italy	Brabham BT37	fifth
Canada	Brabham BT37	eighth
United States	Brabham BT37	eleventh
1973		
Spain	Shadow DN1	brakes
Belgium	Shadow DN1	ninth
Monaco	Shadow DN1	suspension
Sweden	Shadow DN1	ignition
France	Shadow DN1	tenth
Britain	Shadow DN1	chassis
Holland	Shadow DN1	n/c
Germany	Shadow DN1	13th
Austria	Shadow DN1	suspension
Italy	Shadow DN1	14th
Canada	Shadow DN1	16th
United States	Shadow DN1	13th
1974		
Argentina	Lola T370	engine
Brazil	Lola T370	eleventh
South Africa	Lola T370	twelfth
Spain	Lola T370	engine
Belgium	Lola T370	eighth
Monaco	Lola T370	seventh
Sweden	Lola T370	sixth
Holland	Lola T370	transmission
France	Lola T370	13th
Britain	Lola T370	13th
Germany	Lola T370	ninth
Austria	Lola T370	twelfth
Italy	Lola T370	eighth
Canada	Lola T370	14th
United States	Lola T370	eighth
1975		
Argentina	Lola T370	tenth
Brazil	Lola T370	twelfth
South Africa	Lola T370	withdrawn
Monaco	Hill GH1	failed to qualify

(*) fastest lap
(**) fastest practice lap
n/c not classified as a finisher

The withdrawals were both due to practice accidents. In the Italian Grand Prix of 1970 Hill's Rob Walker car was withdrawn until the cause of Jochen Rindt's fatal crash was established. In 1975 Hill badly damaged his Lola during practice for the South African Grand Prix, and the car could not be repaired in time.

1976

elf
3
SCHECKTER
elf
Tyrrell
3
GOODYEAR
GOODYEAR
elf
GOOD YEAR

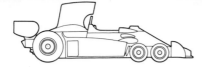

Only Fangio won the world championship three times in a row. In 1976 Niki Lauda failed to repeat the feat by one point. But for a near-tragic accident at the Nürburgring in August, he might have succeeded. Instead, James Hunt, like Mike Hawthorn, Phil Hill, and John Surtees before him, won by the narrowest of margins—perhaps without the merit of any of them. Yet it was the most dramatic, closest-fought title of all. Once again, the role of the drivers was played up, and the popular press made the most of the bitter, rain-swept finale at Mount Fuji. In the heat of the chase, even the motive of Grand Prix racing—money—tended to take second place. What did not alter, however, were the disputes and the off-track wrangles, which took place in the unedifying glare of world-wide publicity.

From Round One in Brazil on 25 January, to Round Sixteen in Japan on 24 October, the title chase was a personal struggle between two men—James Hunt and Niki Lauda. From Interlagos, where Lauda arrived glowing with the successes of 1975, to Fuji, where the strain of the most testing months of his life showed in Hunt's face when he knew he had won. From Interlagos, where Hunt snatched pole position from Lauda by a bare 0.02 sec, to Fuji, where that one precious point decided the destiny of what was already a very rich title.

It was Grand Prix racing at its most international, a return to the Gordon Bennett era for one fleeting year, with the blond, blue-eyed Anglo-Saxon hero against the Teutonic technocrat of the track. Alas, neither really deserved the adulation. They both turned out to be huffy and acquisitive, though Lauda demonstrated astonishing bravery, the virtue Hunt's countrymen treasured so much. Hunt betrayed an aggressiveness which must have seemed more properly a failing of the 'other side'. To Hunt, the game was winning, not merely taking part, and while he certainly earned his title, Lauda earned something more—respect.

The CSI had already lost some significant aspects of its power: deciding who should run Grands Prix for example, and when. In 1976 its rule book was shown to be faulty, its judicial process ponderous and out of tune with the demands of a modern, professional sporting activity. It lost an opportunity to regain control of Grand Prix racing when FOCA proved unable to agree on much else beyond money.

The new President of the CSI, Pierre Ugeux, and the Secretary, Claude le Geuzec, went to Kyalami to discuss a new approach to rule enforcement with FOCA, which resulted in a scrutiny of the cars taking part in the Spanish Grand Prix. The results were contentious. A new appeals procedure introduced half-way through the season overturned another decision, affecting the British Grand Prix. The world championship was bedevilled throughout by delay and uncertainty, which may have added to the excitement, but complicated matters, and puzzled all but the most diligent followers of racing.

The early part of the 16-race series was dominated by Niki Lauda. The Ferraris were on form, and Hunt's pole position in Brazil seemed no more than a momentary aberration. Lauda won after taking over the lead from his team mate Clay Regazzoni in the opening laps. Hunt crashed after his throttle stuck open, but his new McLaren team was not the only one in trouble. The race was a low point in Lotus fortunes. The new Type 77 John Player Lotus was uncompetitive, team mates Andretti and Peterson collided in the race, and Peterson decided to leave following a row with Colin Chapman. It was also the season's only appearance of the BRM. Now under the control of the late Sir Alfred Owen's brother-in-law, and known as the Stanley-BRM, it lasted just two painfully slow laps.

Lauda scored his tenth Grand Prix victory in South Africa in March. Towards the end of the race, however, one of his tyres went down, and Hunt very nearly caught up. The British driver finished second, only 4 sec behind, taking joint second place in the

One of the most controversial drives of James Hunt's controversial career was the British Grand Prix at Brands Hatch. He was later stripped of his well-deserved victory after protests by the Ferrari team following the accident which halted the race on the first lap.

championship with six points against Lauda's 18.

The Ferraris were still unbeatable in the next race, the new United States Grand Prix (West) at Long Beach, California. Clay Regazzoni won on the novel street circuit, an attempt to give a little Monegasque *cachet* to the otherwise rather dreary West Coast town. The tight turns between the high barriers produced an unusual crop of drive shaft failures owing to the rapid torque reversals. The brief straights and heavy braking also produced a number of accidents, as the drivers bumped and bored one another on the narrow streets. One such incident eliminated James Hunt following a minor collision with Patrick Depailler which led to a well publicised and heated exchange afterwards. It was the first public quarrel in a season that was to witness several more.

Lauda's second place at Long Beach seemed to put him well on the way to a second world championship with 24 points to Patrick Depailler's ten. Hunt was only fifth with six. For a few hours Spain on 2 May looked as though it might change things. Hunt won after overtaking Lauda, who was in great pain as a result of having damaged his ribs in a tractor accident at his new Salzburg home. He still led the championship with 30 points, but Hunt lay second with 15 as King Juan Carlos presented him with the winner's garland.

The upset came within hours. Adopting a firmer scrutineering policy in accordance with the new relationship with the Constructors, the CSI officials decreed that the wing on Hunt's McLaren was illegal according to the regulation dimensions *to which the Constructors had instructed them to adhere.* Hunt was accordingly disqualified, and Lauda named the winner, giving him 33 points, while Hunt reverted to six. McLaren protested vigorously that disqualification for a wing 1.8 cm/0.7 in too wide was a severe penalty, and gave notice of appeal—a process noted for tedium and delay.

The new regulations fixing wing dimensions and lowering airboxes did not specify the number of wheels a car had to have, an oversight of which Ken Tyrrell and his designer Derek Gardner took advantage with the introduction in Spain of their six-wheeled car. They thought they had hit upon an important new development, and for a time it looked as though they had. Neither Tyrrell nor Gardner were the sort to indulge in flights of fancy, or publicity gimmicks, consequently the car had to be taken seriously.

It turned out rather like the experiments in four-wheel drive—at best inconclusive. Gardner's theory was that the small front wheels would diminish the frontal area of the car at a critical point in the airflow. The object was principally reduced drag to confer a high top speed on the straights; the extra grip expected for steering and braking was regarded merely as a bonus. Depailler gained the second row of the grid with the car, but crashed following a

James Hunt (b 1947)

The fourth English-born world champion, like Mike Hawthorn, Graham Hill, and John Surtees, won the title narrowly. In public, he would invariably say how he would have liked to be able to share the championship with Lauda, but in private he had no doubt he had earned it. He displayed little animosity towards his rival, indeed they later became close friends; Hunt's breezy charm won him many friends. His good looks also won him the hearts of pretty girls the world over, and surprisingly often he won over their mothers as well, who saw a certain arrogant, slightly rebellious quality they liked to find in their own sons.

Hunt's sponsors enjoyed the articulate way with which he could handle the press or the public, and he was a tireless worker. He became, like so many drivers, a hero for schoolboys who could detect a sense of his never having quite grown up. The break-up of his marriage to Suzy, made him a gift to the gossip writers who represented tangible income to modern Grand Prix drivers. Publicity could be turned into money because it attracted bigger fees from sponsors. It had become as important as race wins—perhaps more so.

Although his parents were relatively wealthy, the way to the top was not always easy for James Hunt. His father was a stockbroker, but the only contribution he made to the career that made his son a millionaire, was to put up with him at home for a time, free, after Hunt had left Wellington College.

Hunt's mother had taken a job to educate her family of four boys and two girls. 'James was extraordinarily difficult as a boy,' she said. 'He was always against authority; the only one who ever screamed at night as a baby. He used to fly into tantrums, but they were over quickly, and he never bore a grudge.'

Unlike Lauda, he had no generous loan with which to buy his first Formula 1 drive. He spent several years saving his earnings as a telephone rental salesman towards building a racing Mini. When that did not work, he took out a rather shaky hire-purchase agreement for a Formula Ford car. The deposit was the proceeds from the sale of the Mini, and the monthly payments represented the bulk of his earnings, so it was as well he was able to live at home for nothing.

The slice of luck in Hunt's climb to the top came in the shape of Lord Alexander Hesketh, who helped him through a period of his career in Formula 3 when his succession of accidents earned him the nickname 'Hunt the Shunt'. Hesketh subsequently went into Formula 1, and when he withdrew, Hunt picked up the spare McLaren drive following the defection of Emerson Fittipaldi to form his Fittipaldi Copersucar team.

Hunt's erratic driving had made him an unlikely choice for any of the regular team managers in Formula 1, until he had shown what he could do with the Hesketh. With McLaren he was mature, careful, diligent, and extremely competitive.

With the title won, however, he shot his bolt. He remained with McLaren for two more years, but found the going hard, and complained that the new generation of ground-effect cars deprived drivers of the initiative. In many ways this was true, but it was nothing new in motor racing. In the days of the 158 Alfa Romeo, or the W 196 Mercedes-Benz, no amount of skill could take a driver to the front without a car of the very highest calibre.

On his own admission, Hunt simply lost interest. He became aware of the dangers of motor racing, and in 1979 he joined the Wolf team, but retired before the season was half finished.

brake failure. As a maiden outing, however, Spain was regarded as a success, and Project 34, as it was called, was adopted for the Tyrrell team as the car of the future.

On 16 May, Lauda seemed to set the seal on the defence of his title by leading the Ferraris home to a 1-2 victory. At Monte Carlo later in the month he led from start to finish, the only surprise being the performance of the six-wheeled Tyrrell. The demands of the tight, round-the-houses track seemed to suit the car exactly, and Jody Scheckter was second. But Lauda had a towering 51 points in the championship against the joint second place of Regazzoni and Hunt, still stuck on 15.

The six wheelers scored their first victory on 13 June, in the Swedish Grand Prix at Anderstorp, and while both first and second places seemed to support Gardner's and Tyrrell's confidence, the track favoured handling characteristics which did not do well on others. Lauda finished third, Hunt fifth.

Round eight took place at the Paul Ricard track, where the French Grand Prix was run on 4 July. Hunt took over the lead when both Ferraris failed within a few laps of one another with broken crankshafts. It was Lauda's first mechanical trouble in 17 races—a testimony to the Ferrari's outstanding reliability. It hardly seemed a turning of the tables, but as Lauda had dominated the first half of the season, so Hunt was about to dominate the second.

The improvement in Hunt's fortunes began the day after the French Grand Prix. Before it, the score had been Lauda 55, Hunt (in fourth place) eight. On the Monday following the race, however, the FIA's International Court of Appeal reinstated Hunt's Spanish Grand Prix win, so within the space of 24 hours, his eight points became 26 and he was once again joint second with the consistent Depailler. Lauda was back on 52 points through being reclassified second in Spain, and although the margin was still wide, from Hunt's point of view it was an improvement.

The British Grand Prix, on 18 July, proved yet another in a controversial series. On the first corner, the unusually difficult Paddock Bend at Brands Hatch, the Ferraris of Lauda and Regazzoni collided—the result of an injudicious attempt to take the lead by the impetuous Swiss driver. The multiple pile-up which followed involved a number of cars, including Hunt's McLaren, which limped on, badly damaged.

Debris on the road caused the clerk of the course to stop the race on safety grounds, ordering a restart after the prescribed 20 min. The CSI rules allowed any 'runner' at the time of stopping to take part in the restart, but what constituted a runner? Was it a car that was racing, or one, like Hunt's which was merely running? It covered half a lap under its own steam before coming into the pits by a back entrance, where it was hurriedly repaired in time for the restart. This was delayed while team managers argued with officials, barracked by the crowd who left no doubt what *they* thought of the idea that Hunt might not be allowed to restart.

Hunt did restart and won a convincing victory when Lauda suffered gearbox trouble, but as with Spain, the row dragged on through protest and appeal for months. As matters stood, however, Lauda's lead was cut—58 points to 35. Hunt's challenge was now viable.

At the beginning of August, events took a new turn. Lauda was outspoken on the dangers of the Nürburgring. His complaint was no longer about the hazards of racing on a track with perhaps more than its share of difficulties; the Germans had not long since spent millions of D-Marks on improvements to satisfy the drivers. The basis of his criticism was that recognising the impossibility of having marshals' posts short distances apart on a 23 km (approx 14 mile) circuit, it could be a long time before help reached an injured driver.

His view was shared, but the drivers agreed to race there one year more—under protest. It was as though Lauda had a presentiment of disaster.

The uncertain weather made the choice of tyres problematical. On the second lap, Lauda hit a kerb and his Ferrari's suspension broke, sending the car plunging off the road at high speed. It caught fire, but the driver was pulled clear by prompt action on the part of fellow drivers Brett Lunger, Guy Edwards, Harald Ertl, and Arturo Merzario, who had stopped, or collided nearby. Lauda's burns were grave. His helmet had been wrenched off in the early stages of the accident, depriving him of the piped air from his life-support system, and he had breathed the searing, poison-laden flames for those vital moments that could make the difference between life and death.

Help arrived in due course, and the injured driver was flown off by helicopter, but the news that night from Mannheim University Clinic was bad. His burns were serious, his condition critical. On the following Tuesday a priest was called to give the last rites. His arrival prompted Lauda to begin his fight back to life.

Hunt won the restarted race, and a fortnight later finished fourth in Austria, to come within eleven points of his rival, slowly convalescing from his terrible injuries. The Austrian race was won by John Watson, his first, and the first for the Penske team, appropriately at the track where they had lost Mark Donohue the year before.

At the end of the month Hunt won the Dutch Grand Prix, to come within two points of Lauda. It might not be the best way to win a world championship, but in the circumstances he could do little else. Lauda's recovery would be slow; he had been near death, and there seemed little prospect of his racing again during the season.

But at Monza, a mere six weeks after his accident, Lauda was back. Scarred, gaunt, and ill, his lung tissue growing painfully slowly. Yet he not only drove a racing car again, but he drove it resolutely and well. All he lacked was the time to carry out his customary test programme, otherwise it was much the same Lauda under the red helmet.

He arrived to find another row breaking out. This time the CSI's scrutineers had discovered a discrepancy in the fuel being used by the McLarens of Hunt and Jochen Mass, and John Watson's Penske. Their Saturday practice times were accordingly disallowed, and since Friday's practice was washed out by torrential rain, all three were obliged to start from the back of the grid.

The McLaren management, in the person of Managing Director Teddy Mayer, were furious. They claimed it was a reprisal by the Italians to even the score for the British Grand Prix. The issue was much more complicated than that of course, and there was a great deal of behind-the-scenes bargaining to get the cars to start at all. They had in effect been disqualified until some private entrants conveniently withdrew, leaving vacant spaces on the grid. Faced with the possibility of seeing their cars non-starters, some of the sponsors bought their way out of trouble.

The real culprit in the dispute was once again the rule book. The octane of the fuel allowed in Formula 1 was defined as the highest commercially available in France, Germany, Great Britain, and Italy. There was doubt about exactly what that was, and further doubt on the test methods used to measure the strength of the samples. The margin of possible error was wide. But there was no time for a legal argument this time; the sentence was the back of the grid, effectively ruining Hunt's chances of adding substantially to his score.

Lauda was fourth and Hunt failed to finish, so Ronnie Peterson was able to gain the sole victory in a full-length classic Grand Prix in the entire eight-year history of the works March Formula 1 team.

During the three weeks before the Grand Prix of Canada at the beginning of October, the FIA announced that Hunt had been stripped of his victory in the British Grand Prix. So, instead of the score being Lauda 61, Hunt 56; it was suddenly Lauda 64, Hunt 47. From five points, the gap widened to 17. It was an astonishing decision, and drew attention once again to the ineptitude of the governing body, and the inadequacy of their appeals procedure. Settling the results of races months after the event was plainly absurd.

The decision galvanised the McLaren team and Hunt in Canada. They won after setting fastest time in practice, and went on to the United States with at least a fighting chance of still taking the championship. At Watkins Glen, Hunt ran yet another superb race with Lauda, back in fine form, third. With one race to go, there was a bare three points in it.

Lauda was still a bruised and dazed man. To have survived such an ordeal at all was commendable, to race a miracle, but to race competitively was heroic. Ironically, the only critic of his decision to withdraw from the Japanese Grand Prix because of the appalling conditions was Enzo Ferrari—to whom he had brought so much credit throughout three seasons at the wheel of his cars. It was a more forthright action than ploughing on at reduced speed and blaming the car or the tyres, or inventing some other weak excuse. Instead, Lauda quit. Hunt finished third in a sensational race, and won the title.

It was a story-book achievement. Hunt made a fortune out of it, and Lauda got everything in the world except the title and a new face. He carried the scars for ever after. And as so often at the end of a season, in the excitement and clamour surrounding a new champion, an important straw waving in the wind was overlooked. Mario Andretti had just given Team Lotus their first victory since 1974.

The inflation of the Grand Prix bubble

For the 1976 British Grand Prix, Brands Hatch gave up the annual struggle with FOCA over the purse. They simply doubled admission prices to the race, improved the promotion, and, as FOCA had been telling them for years—it worked.

With more grandstand seats available than ever before, they were sold out by 27 February. Over 30000 people paid to watch the two practice days, 77000 on race day. As a comparison, attendances at the other Grands Prix were as follows:

Brazil (weather hot, dry)	70000	Brands Hatch (weather hot, dry)	77000
South Africa (weather hot, dry)	70000	Nürburgring (weather wet, cloudy)	200000 (est)
Long Beach (weather warm, dry)	77000 (paid)	Austria (weather hot, humid)	40000
Spain (weather warm, dry)	85000	Holland (weather hot, dry)	65000
Belgium (weather warm, dry)	55000	Italy (weather warm, light rain)	100000 (est)
Monaco (weather warm, dry)	53000 (paid)	Canada (weather warm)	85000
Sweden (weather cool, dry)	33000	Watkins Glen (weather warm, dry)	90000
France (weather hot, dry)	95000	Japan (weather cool, very wet)	72000

Attendance figures for Grands Prix should be treated with caution. Some promoters try and inflate them, others, for a variety of reasons which vary from country to country, tend to play them down. For races such as Long Beach and Monaco, the paid attendance takes no account of those who watch free of charge from balconies, rooftops, and other vantage points. Figures for the Nürburgring necessarily include a certain amount of guesswork owing to the large numbers of spectators who camp all weekend, in the woods and hills surrounding the circuit. Austria in 1976 was not representative owing to Lauda's accident, and the non-appearance of the Ferraris; nevertheless, these figures suggest that well over 1¼ million people attend Grands Prix each year.

The British Grand Prix meeting, including the three supporting races, cost £258000 to stage, of which the Formula 1 share was £150000—nearly twice as much as it had cost only four years before, when John Player agreed to sponsor it at £25000 a year. In 1972 this covered a third of the costs, but by 1976 it represented only 15 per cent.

1977
MARTI
Valvoline

1977

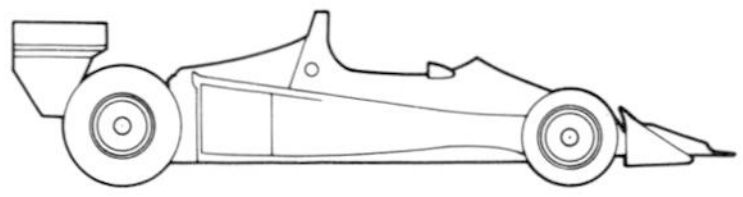

In contrast to the histrionics of 1976, the following season came almost as an anticlimax. Ferrari remained supreme. Perhaps the cars were less spectacularly fast than they had been in Lauda's first championship year, or the opening races of 1976, but their reliability was restored, and the post-accident Lauda was more cautious, more content to race for a place than before. With so many races in the championship the title was more likely to go to the driver of a *reliable* car than the driver of one that was merely fast.

Mario Andretti won more races than Lauda; the victory in Japan had been the culmination of a season's keen effort. The new Lotus proved to be a thoroughly effective car which was not only fast, but, as so often in the past, represented a technical achievement by Colin Chapman of the very highest order.

Behind the closed doors of Ketteringham Hall, with a team which included Tony Rudd, formerly of BRM, designer Ralph Bellamy, and aerodynamicist Peter Wright, Chapman introduced a new concept into racing car design. It became known as the 'wing car', or 'ground effect car' and within twelve months revolutionised not only racing car design, but also became one of the few developments of modern single-seater design to have a practical lesson for road cars as well.

The wing car demonstrated the influence aerodynamics could have on cornering performance. It also showed an increasingly energy-conscious world how important aerodynamics could be in the realms of fuel conservation. The proper management of a car's (or a lorry's) airflow was shown to provide advantages not only for improved cornering power, but also for fuel economy.

More so than ever before, the season was one of rapidly changing fortunes. The most trifling modification, or the most fundamental seemed to produce no more than marginal improvements. Differences between teams and drivers, between cars or engines, were down to the slimmest they had ever been. The effect was to increase the importance of the Ferrari's reliability, or the Lotus's faster cornering to a greater degree than a few years earlier.

It also produced some bizarre results, such as the success of the new Wolf team, which won their first race ever, the opening Grand Prix of the season in Argentina. Jody Scheckter, who had left Ken Tyrrell to his six-wheeler, started in eighth place, and took the lead six laps from the end of a race which proved the first of his three victories during the season. He won from Carlos Pace, the promising Brazilian driver in a Brabham, using for the second season a horizontally-opposed twelve-cylinder Alfa Romeo engine. It was the best result so far for the combination of Brabham and Alfa Romeo which had begun with an adaptation of the V-8 with which Alfa had had some success in sports car racing. A great deal was expected of the flat-12 with each new season, and although it was very powerful—around 510 bhp, about the same as the Ferrari—it was never as

reliable, and never really overcame the heavier fuel consumption, and consequently heavier start-line weight.

The second of the South American races proved a triumph for Carlos Reutemann. In his second drive for his new team, Ferrari, Reutemann took advantage of Lauda's disastrous practice session, and enjoyed a short-lived lead in the world championship. By South Africa Lauda was in the winner's circle once again, and Scheckter also ahead on points.

Alas, it was a sad Grand Prix. The most successful Welsh driver since Stuart Lewis-Evans, 27-year-old Tom Pryce, was killed when he struck a marshal running across Kyalami's main straight. Nineteen-year-old Jansen van Vuuren had been taking a fire extinguisher (needlessly as it turned out) to Renzo Zorzi's Shadow just over the blind crest of the hill, and was caught at full speed by Pryce's car. Both men died instantly. Within days Carlos Pace also died in a flying accident in South America.

The second Long Beach Grand Prix witnessed an increasingly worrisome phenomenon of modern Grand Prix racing, an opening-lap accident. Wide cars, narrow tracks, and the closely matched performance of individual machines made overtaking more problematical than ever, particularly at tracks such as Monte Carlo and Long Beach. Here, a good grid position was essential. Drivers were prepared to take extra risks in the opening lap, and this, together with the nervous tension to be expected

Mario Andretti (John Player Lotus No 5) and John Watson (Brabham Alfa Romeo No 7) go off the road in a shower of sparks on the first lap of the Belgian Grand Prix at Zolder. The closely matched cars and the stress of the opening moments of a Grand Prix made incidents like this increasingly common.

at the beginning of any competitive event, produced a rising incidence of first-lap crashes.

The first corner at Long Beach was typical. It was rather like Paddock Bend at Brands Hatch the year before. The start of the race was on Ocean Boulevard (it was later changed to Shoreline Drive, which created problems of its own) with a sharp right-hander downhill into Linden Avenue, followed immediately by a 90° left and right, then the sweeping left-hander on to one side of the dual carriageway on Shoreline Drive.

Jody Scheckter made a good start, and led the field into the first right, from the second row of the grid. Andretti held to the outside of the corner, while Reutemann and Lauda took his inside. Once again, however, as at Brands, rivalry within the Ferrari team precipitated a crisis. Reutemann left his braking too late in his anxiety to outmanoeuvre Lauda, locked his front wheels, and ploughed straight on. Lauda and Andretti managed to duck behind him, and get through the turn safely; but the cars behind, faced with an almost stationary Ferrari in the middle of the corner, were less fortunate. John Watson (Brabham Alfa Romeo) tried to follow Lauda and Andretti, but was hit by Hunt's McLaren which was lifted high in the air as the cars' wheels touched.

Landing back on the track, it stopped, so there were now two cars blocking the corner. In avoiding them, Clay Regazzoni (Ensign) and Vittorio Brambilla (Surtees) also collided. As seemed to happen often to Brambilla, his accident acquired a comic element. His car came to rest at roughly the same place as he had finished his race the year before; and when marshals tried moving it to a safer place, it ran away from them, down the hill, and crashed, driverless, into the barrier on the other side of the track.

Andretti won the race in the new Lotus 78, then went on to dominate the Spanish Grand Prix at Jarama, setting fastest time in practice, and leading from start to finish. Niki Lauda withdrew on race morning after changing gear with such vigour that he cracked a rib, a legacy of one of his previous year's injuries.

At Monaco, Scheckter scored the Ford Cosworth engine's 100th Grand Prix victory, and at round seven in Belgium on 5 June, Gunnar Nilsson, the popular, young Swedish driver, scored his only Grand Prix victory. Nilsson joined Team Lotus after a meteoric career in Formula Atlantic, quickly establishing himself as talented, likeable, and a very capable back-up driver to Andretti. In this case, Andretti needed a back-up, having rather carelessly collided with Watson's Brabham on the first lap of a very wet race indeed.

At Nilsson's home race in Sweden, in another upset to form on the singular Anderstorp circuit, Jacques Laffite scored his, and the V-12 Ligier Matra's first Grand Prix victory. It was the first time an all-French team, car, driver, and engine had ever won a world championship Formula 1 race, and a sign that the French challenge, after many years, was at last likely to bear fruit. The new school of French cars and drivers, assiduously backed by Elf and Renault in Formula 2, was bringing results. Renault's new, turbocharged Grand Prix contender had been an open secret for most of the season, and took part in its first race soon after Laffite's triumph.

It was not ready for the French Grand Prix at Paul Ricard, which Andretti won. Renault were making a cautious approach; they wanted to win Le Mans with their well-established sports cars before taking Formula 1 too seriously.

Hunt won at Silverstone on 16 July, but he was already out of the running for a repeat of 1976; the jinx on anyone winning two years in a row once again proved too much. Lauda's careful driving, and the consistent reliability of the Ferrari gave him a lead by round ten, of 39 points against Scheckter and Andretti, who were level pegging in second place with 32.

The German Grand Prix was moved to Hockenheim partly because of Lauda's outspokenness over Nürburgring and his accident. The drivers' petition of 1976 alone might not have been sufficient—the accident plus the influence of Bernie Ecclestone (the GPDA was coming under the wing, formally as well as practically, of FOCA) was. Lauda must have gained a certain satisfaction out of winning the race, and setting a milestone for Goodyear—their 100th Grand Prix victory.

The season ran out with Alan Jones scoring his first victory in Austria, and also Shadow's only Grand Prix win. Hunt and Andretti had an undignified row at Zandvoort after colliding, while Andretti scored his fourth victory of the season in the Italian Grand Prix at Monza—one more than Niki Lauda, but Lauda had already clinched his second world championship.

He was so sure of it that he did not take trouble to compete in the last two races of the season, the Canadian and Japanese Grands Prix. He had finally fallen out with Ferrari, and the customary recriminations flew back and forth. Hunt added to the Grand Prix follower's growing disillusionment with champion drivers by refusing to attend the organisers' celebrations after winning the race in Japan. He had no police escort to help him catch his flight home. Hunt was already in trouble for punching a marshal in Canada following a collision with his team mate Jochen Mass. Drivers' reputations were definitely on the down-turn at the end of 1977.

Flying inversion

Colin Chapman had already admitted defeat with the Lotus 77 while work on the epoch-making 78 was well under way. The 77 might have been another breakthrough, such as the 25 or the 49 or the 72 had been. Its conception resulted from the superior performance of short wheelbase cars on circuits with tight turns, such as Monaco or Long Beach, while long wheelbase cars behaved better on the faster tracks, with wide, high-speed bends. Furthermore, narrow cars were faster in a straight line than broad ones on account of their lower frontal area, while wide tracked ones were better on circuits which placed a premium on road holding.

Barring a different car for each circuit (which would be impractical) it seemed logical to design a car which would be fully adjustable in every direction. It could be made short wheelbase for short circuits, long, narrow, or wide as the drivers and engineers decided.

Unfortunately, as with the four-wheel drive episode, drivers proved unequal to the task of telling the engineers what they preferred. For their part, the engineers were unable to educate the drivers in the technicalities, and confusion reigned in Team Lotus throughout most of 1977. By the end, they had scrapped much of the adjustability of the 77 and were making a competitive car out of it, but as Chapman himself observed, '. . . if the big things aren't right, you can mess about with the small things 'til the cows come home and you are never going to make it'.

Andretti won the final Grand Prix of 1976 after a season spent 'sorting' the design together with the inexperienced Nilsson. Bit by bit, design features destined for the still-secret Type 78 were tried out; the importance of aerodynamics underneath the car had long been known, and the 77 was run with rows of brush bristles sweeping the track surface to channel the air flow the way the aerodynamicists wanted. The brushes were used, and nobody objected—so yet another feature that was to become controversial was introduced quietly, and a precedent established simply because there was no rule covering it, and no case for objecting.

The Lotus 78 took the concept a stage further. With the former Eagle, BRM, and Shadow designer Tony Southgate now a member of the team, it was introduced after a gestation period probably as long as any Lotus. It was no sudden flash of inspiration this time. The document outlining the idea of a 'wing', or 'ground effect' car was presented by Chapman to Tony Rudd in August 1975, a month before the formal announcement of the 77. Rudd told the story of the 27-page concept document to Doug Nye for his book *Theme Lotus* (Motor Racing Publications, 1978) 'He realised that in racing we were down and out, and that we'd got it all wrong by the latest standards. And he made the right long-range strategic decisions while still involved in racing day-to-day. He not only suggested the way to go, but he also listed all the things he didn't know, and then he left it to me and a bunch of new boys to tell him all the answers.'

The principle was to employ the car itself to produce the downforce necessary to help cornering. Wings above the car had reached more or less their limit of development given the regulations governing them, and the only way forward in view of the closely matched performance of every available engine was to improve a car's speed through corners.

Influenced by the World War 2 de Havilland Mosquito aircraft's inner wing section with its cooling radiators cowled in the leading edge, side pods were developed for the Lotus 78 after extensive wind tunnel tests. The entire car was then in effect an upside-down wing, forcing itself downwards as the air was speeded up and rushed past the curved surfaces underneath. A vital component of the design was the skirt, which now became rather more substantial than the row of bristles, and was passed on the nod by the authorities who once again had to concede that it broke no rules.

Similarly, the side pods were essentially radiator ducts, not wings within the meaning of the regulations, and Lotus took great care that the secret of the car, the underside, was hidden from view. Not until it had raced, and the necessary precedent been set, was the real purpose of the mysterious pods revealed. Chapman's triumph lay not merely in the invention of a new concept in racing car design, but in doing so within the rules, stage by stage, without provoking any reaction from either the CSI or his fellow competitors.

The car, according to Andretti, felt '. . . like it's painted to the road'. The American proved a successful test driver, establishing a relationship with Chapman not unlike that achieved by Jim Clark. Their rapport was complete, and success was assured. But for agonisingly unreliable engines, and a number of trifling mechanical failures, Andretti would have been world champion in 1977. By the beginning of 1978, he was invincible.

1978

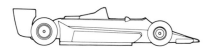

The arrival of the ground effect car gave a new lease of life to the Cosworth engine as it entered its second decade. Andretti and Peterson were so much faster than anyone else that they won races more or less as they pleased, except when Andretti made a characteristic mistake—as at Austria—or the John Player Lotuses suffered breakdowns—as at Brands Hatch. They proved as uncatchable to their Cosworth colleagues as to the twelve-cylinder Ferraris or Brabhams, and Andretti's title was taken with the most sweeping series of victories since 1963.

Yet his moment of triumph turned to ashes in the accident at Monza which claimed the life of Ronnie Peterson. And a season that started in the searing summer sunshine of South America blew itself out in the sleety rain of a Canadian winter. It ended with a shiver of grief over not only one of the ablest and most popular drivers racing had ever known, but also, it seemed, over a whole era of Grand Prix racing. At the October Congress of the Fédération Internationale de l'Automobile (FIA), the CSI was finally given the autonomy for which it had pleaded so long, and a new president, Jean-Marie Balestre, formerly of France's powerful Fédération Française du Sport Automobile, was elected. His objective quickly became clear. He was pledged to halt the erosion of the CSI's influence which had marked the strongly conservative regime of Prince Amaury de Merode of Belgium, as president of the FIA.

Under him, the non-sporting elements had turned down the CSI's proposals for a bigger budget, blocking the efforts of the Secretariat, and dismissing Henri Treu. The resulting paralysis of the CSI continued through the secretaryship of Claude Le Geuzec, replaced with the arrival of Balestre by Yvon Léon. One of Balestre's reforms, once autonomy was achieved, was to rename the CSI the Fédération Internationale du Sports Automobile (FISA).

It remained to be seen how effective Balestre's efforts in challenging the grip of Bernie Ecclestone and FOCA on Grand Prix racing would be. Some of his attemps bordered on the fatuous, and he failed to halt a manoeuvre which enabled FOCA to control the only drivers who could take part in Grand Prix races. Even non-FOCA teams were forced to consider only drivers who had gained FOCA approval, effectively removing yet another sanction which a more influential CSI/FISA might have employed to regain control.

Andretti won the Grands Prix of Argentina, Belgium, Spain, France, Germany, and Holland. He finished second in Long Beach, and was moral victor of the tragic Italian Grand Prix at Monza. The hapless AC di Milano achieved their second fluffed start of the day and penalised Andretti for jumping it, naming Niki Lauda (Brabham Alfa Romeo) the winner instead. Andretti was thus unable to match Jim Clark's record of seven Grands Prix in a season following Monza's sordid and unworthy decision. In a sad epitaph to the season, Andretti failed to score in the final two races, while Jean-Pierre Jarier, never a particularly distinguished driver, was able to demonstrate the overwhelming superiority of the Lotus 79 by setting fastest lap at Watkins Glen, and taking pole, and almost winning the Canadian Grand Prix at the new circuit on the grounds of Montreal's Expo 67 site.

This race was won by the new Ferrari driver, the controversial Gilles Villeneuve, in one of those convenient home wins which guaranteed the race's continuation, pleased the partisan crowd, and offered the sponsors (and FOCA) the prospect of continued reward in the future.

Yet FOCA proved by no means a united band of brothers when the Brabham team tried to introduce their new car in the Grand Prix of Sweden at Anderstorp. This was the famous 'fan' car with which Bernie Ecclestone and his talented South African designer Gordon Murray very nearly took the 'ground effect' concept a stage further by means of a huge fan driven off the engine. In conjunction with more substantial and firmer skirts than anything seen so far, the fan drew air from underneath the car, effectively 'sucking' it to the ground as a means of generating great downforce. The car's adhesion was greater than any Grand Prix car yet seen, and Watson and Lauda posted second and third fastest laps in practice.

Right: The controversial Brabham BT 46B, the famous 'fan' car with which Niki Lauda won the Grand Prix of Sweden at Anderstorp. Despite protests, the car was declared legal, but banned from further racing thereafter.

Below: Carlos Reutemann took advantage of a momentary hesitation by Niki Lauda at Clearways to put his Ferrari into the lead, and win the British Grand Prix.

parmalat
parmalat
parmalat
parmalat
parmalat
parmalat
BRABHAM
ALFAROMEO
GOODYEAR
GOODYEAR

The employment of fans to create a suction effect was not completely new. The Chaparral 2J of 1970 had tried a similar ploy. Driven in Can-Am by Jackie Stewart, it used a 45 hp Snowmobile twin-cylinder two-stroke engine to drive fans which sucked air from underneath the car, the area sealed by skirts made of Lexan, a thermoplastic material. It was consistently faster than the opposition, but was promptly banned on the grounds that the fans constituted a movable aerodynamic device, forbidden since the earliest days of wings.

Ecclestone had hoped to take a leaf out of Colin Chapman's book by suggesting that the primary purpose of the fan was not extra downforce at all. Chapman had initiated the ground effect principle by ducting the air flow through radiators, and outflanking the legislators. He had not re-interpreted the regulations, nor even designed to the letter of the law; he had created something for which no law existed, and then raced it to establish the precedent. He could modify or develop it more or less as he pleased later—once the principle was accepted, it was difficult for the authorities to forbid it unless it was downright dangerous.

Ecclestone's approach was not so subtle. Had he started with a little fan, he might just have got away with describing it as primarily a means to force cooling air through the radiators. But every time the engine was switched on, the car settled noticeably on its springs. His claim that, without the fans, the engine would overheat was substantially true; what nobody could believe was the notion that they *had* to draw air from *underneath* the car.

The fan car's fate was sealed when Niki Lauda won the race. Ecclestone's fellow members of FOCA rebelled, and Colin Chapman entered his first formal protest in 20 years of racing. The drivers were opposed to the fan because of road debris and dust blown out of the back of the car. Chapman was backed by John Surtees, Ken Tyrrell, and Teddy Mayer, and although their protests were thrown out, the CSI did agree to meet and discuss the matter.

Unfortunately, the technical committee had already passed the car on a description given by Ecclestone in Spain a fortnight before. Rather shamefacedly therefore, realising their mistake, they met during the intervening two weeks before the French Grand Prix, and re-wrote the relevant rule. The car was henceforward banned, although the result of the Swedish Grand Prix was allowed to stand. It was an extraordinary procedure, but the ban stuck because it had the broad support of the competitors—with the exception of the Brabham team and Lauda, who saw little prospect of defeating the Lotus with the non-fan Brabham. The Alfa Romeo engine still suffered from unreliability and heavy fuel consumption.

Ronnie Peterson died from leg injuries received in an accident which highlighted the growing problem of opening-lap crashes. The ingredients of the tragedy had been present for a long time—the careless starting procedures at Monza, the narrow funnel of track into which the cars were forced by the unsatisfactory design of Monza's chicanes, themselves the product of compromise and indifference.

Ironically, Peterson's death came after he had achieved style and polish at the wheel—something he lacked in his early days, when he survived spectacular accidents, almost always walking away from the wreckage, then going out in another car and driving faster than ever.

He was born in Örebro, in 1944, and by the age of 19 won the first of five Swedish national Kart championships. He raced a home-built Formula 3 car in 1966, and the following year moved into motor racing professionally, giving up his career as a lift service engineer.

Peterson drove hard. His style was daring and entertaining, and in 1971 he scored four second places with March cars and finished runner-up in the world championship to Jackie Stewart. But like so many skilled drivers, Peterson never seemed to enjoy the gift of others such as Stewart, who always

complemented their skill with the worthiest cars. He was never able to get all the right ingredients of success—the right team, the best engineer—together. By the time he signed with Lotus (for the second time) for the 1978 season, his career had reached a critical stage.

He needed to restore his reputation, and agreed to play a subordinate role to Mario Andretti in the team. Andretti was to be the team leader and aim for the world championship. It was an arrangement which removed the threat of competition within the team from Andretti, and suited Peterson because it carried the prospect of re-establishing himself as one of the most important drivers of the decade. He had already succeeded, and found a new self-confidence not only as winner of a tough race in South Africa, and a rain-soaked Austrian Grand Prix, but also as a loyal and effective understudy to Andretti. Together they made the most formidable team in Grand Prix racing—with Chapman's brilliant engineering they were supreme.

Within a few weeks of Peterson's death, Gunnar Nilsson died from cancer in a London hospital. Sweden had lost two of her greatest sporting ambassadors in a tragically short time—two drivers of great skill, and two personalities of great warmth and humour as well. It was a sad ending for two careers which had promised so much, and led to a loss of support for the 1979 Swedish Grand Prix.

In the wake of Peterson's accident, the drivers held an undignified kangaroo court which laid the blame for some of the season's first lap collisions on Riccardo Patrese, an Italian in his first season of Formula 1. They contrived to ban him from the United States Grand Prix at Watkins Glen, but the sentence was as inappropriate as the indictment; few amongst Patrese's accusers were innocent of misjudgements or aggression during those highly-charged opening moments of Grand Prix races.

Patrese's team was already involved in a more formal legal battle. Arrows, founded by Alan Rees, Jackie Oliver, and Tony Southgate, following their defection from Shadow, were judged to have pirated the design of their car. In the High Court, Mr Justice Templeman granted Shadow an injunction preventing the Arrows running in Grand Prix races because 40 per cent of its components had been copied from the DN 9 Shadow, adding that Arrows had ' . . . inflicted humiliation and loss on the Shadow organisation', and awarded substantial damages. It was an inglorious episode in a season that would be remembered chiefly for intrigue and quarrels. It was a season whose saving graces were a technical *tour de force* by the most outstanding racing engineer of his generation, and a world champion, the first American since Phil Hill, who was first and foremost—a racer.

As seemingly indestructible as Jim Clark, Ronnie Peterson's loss prompted a re-examination of the values and philosophy of Grand Prix racing. The popularity of the talented Swede was secure, despite his never having won the title.

The winning team for 1978, world champion Mario Andretti talks to Colin Chapman, who designed more successful Grand Prix cars than anybody else.

Mario Andretti (b 1940)

In 1977 Mario Andretti became the first Italian-born driver to win the Italian Grand Prix for eleven years, and only the second for 25. In 1978 he became the first to win the world championship since his boyhood hero Alberto Ascari in 1953. For, while he invariably jetted back to Nazareth Pa. between races, playing the part of the American racing superstar with aplomb, scratching the surface of Andretti produced a certain amount of Latin.

Scoring his first Grand Prix success at the wheel of a Ferrari in 1971 was a pay-off for his boyhood enthusiasm, kindled in Italy when the family lived in Pisa and watched the Mille Miglia pass through. Andretti saw Fangio win at Monza in 1954. Then, in 1955, his parents emigrated to a new world of dirt track racing on the oval circuits of America, taking the twin brothers Mario and Aldo, aged 15, with them.

By 1965 Mario was United States Auto Club champion, and wealthy. American racing invariably paid better than Formula 1, and he was champion again in 1966 and 1969, when he hit the motor racing jackpot by winning the Indianapolis 500. Yet his heart was still in Grand Prix racing, and he accepted Colin Chapman's offer to drive for Lotus in the American Grand Prix of 1968, astonishing the Formula 1 establishment by setting fastest time in practice, and leading Jackie Stewart off the line.

Even Stewart was nervous of competition of such quality, but he never had to suffer it. Andretti's ambitions to take part in European-style world championship racing were still thwarted by the dollars he could earn racing in America. Occasional drives brought Ferrari the South African Grand Prix in 1971, and guaranteed Andretti a return to Lotus whenever he cared. He was bent on it, but America was an offer he could not afford to refuse.

Andretti's first consistent effort in Formula 1 was with an American team, Vel's Parnelli in 1975, but it was not a success. The following year he took up Chapman's offer despite Lotus being in an unaccustomed trough.

It was almost another year before the improved Lotus 77 won its first Grand Prix, the rain-soaked race at Fuji that made James Hunt world champion. Andretti never looked back.

His public persona typified the articulate, all-American expert in communications, with the practised, quotable, easily interviewable style that earned him the popularity of the international racing press. Yet he was a self-controlled extrovert. Underneath was an impatience that could be sparked off in a moment, and even lead him into one of his famous first-lap incidents, such as the one with John Watson at Zolder in 1977, or the angry collision with James Hunt at Zandvoort, or the spin in the wet at Zeltweg in 1978 when he threw away a likely victory on the first corner. Yet he could drive coolly, such as in the 1977 French Grand Prix at Dijon, a memorable race in which he drove the entire distance in the shadow of John Watson, ready to pounce on the final lap when the Brabham Alfa Romeo suddenly faltered.

Andretti, at 38, proved a popular champion; a racer's racer. One of the best all-round drivers in the history of the sport—besides USAC, and Formula 1, he drove in long-distance races for Ford and Ferrari, as well as Can-Am. His versatility and popularity made the world championship a fitting crown to a long and distinguished career.

1979

1979

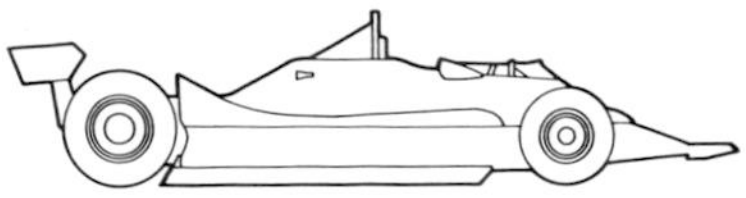

The world championship scoring system, that had been anomalous for nearly 30 years, was altered for 1979, but the result was more confusing than before, and very nearly appointed the wrong world champion. The Formula One Constructors' Association (FOCA) affirmed its embargo on drivers of whom it did not approve, but declared something of a truce in its running battle with the Fédération Internationale du Sport Automobile (FISA, lately the CSI). The season saw two world champions, the protagonists of 1976, James Hunt and Niki Lauda, retire dramatically. Each, having made his fortune, wanted no more of the ups and downs of Grand Prix racing—in particular the downs, with which both had unhappily become familiar.

For the first time in 18 years, the first *and* second placed drivers in the world championship were at the wheels of Ferraris, taking the Manufacturers' Cup to Maranello for the fifth time in four years. Once again the reigning champion failed to defend his title, and Jody Scheckter became the first South African to gain it. Gilles Villeneuve became the first Canadian to reach the first three places following a season in which there were some astonishing changes of fortune.

At first it looked as though Ligier were going to sweep the board, with Jacques Laffite winning the first two races—the Grands Prix of Argentina and Brazil. Run by former driver and international rugby player Guy Ligier, the team had at last discarded the Matra V-12 engine, and changed to Cosworth power. The results were immediate, and seemed to suggest that the car's chassis design had been advanced all along, and lacked only a reliable engine. Patrick Depailler, after years with Tyrrell, underlined the Ligier's superiority by finishing second to Laffite in Brazil, scoring the second Grand Prix victory of his career in the Spanish Grand Prix at the end of April.

But by then, the French challenge had been taken up. The oldest team in the business, Ferrari, had won the intervening Grands Prix of South Africa and Long Beach; Gilles Villeneuve and Jody Scheckter first and second both times. Lotus had gone into almost complete eclipse, Carlos Reutemann alone fighting a rearguard action to prevent it, Andretti no longer in the picture. It was not until the Belgian Grand Prix at Zolder in May that a new contender for the top honours became apparent.

This was Alan Jones, a 32-year-old Australian, driving for Frank Williams, the Grand Prix entrepreneur who had run cars for the ill-fated Piers Courage ten years before, and been scratching teams together ever since. Real success had eluded the energetic Williams, but with sponsorship from Saudia Airlines, and an encouraging season in 1978, he seemed, at last, on the point of winning. It was not to be at Zolder, however, for Scheckter took the lead, and won for Ferrari after Jones retired with electrical failure.

This put Scheckter into the lead for the world

championship, but throughout the season it was not easy to determine who was really at the head of the table. The system had been altered to the extent that drivers were allowed to count only their best four scores from each half of the season. The initiative for the change had come about because the sponsors of the tail-end races had felt put out over a championship that was decided, as often as not, by the end of the European season, at Monza in September.

The aim was worthy enough, but the means were ineffectual. The title was clinched, as usual, at Monza, and the new arrangement's principal shortcoming at once became obvious.

Alan Jones proved unable to score more than four points in the first half of the season, the result of breakdowns or misfortunes of one sort and another. Yet he could have won each of the remaining races in the second half without any chance of taking the title. As it was, he won four, one more than Jody Scheckter, and very nearly a fifth, the United States Grand Prix at the end of the year—yet to no avail. He was forced to disregard the three points he scored in France, and the six he scored in America, which would have given him a total of 49 points instead of the 40 he did earn. This was still fewer than Scheckter got, as things turned out; and had Scheckter been similarly unencumbered, his total would have soared to 60, but Jones could have been beaten by the system alone.

Mid-season occurred after the Monaco Grand Prix at the end of May, with the cancellation of the Swedish Grand Prix. There were thus no more races until the French Grand Prix at the beginning of July, and when the field lined up on the short circuit at Dijon-Prenois the table read as follows:

	Argentina	Brazil	South Africa	Long Beach	Spain	Belgium	Monaco	Total mid-season
Scheckter	—	1	6	6	3	9	9	30
Laffite	9	9	—	—	—	6	—	24
Villeneuve	—	2	9	9	—	—	—	20
Depailler	3	6	—	2	9	—	2	20
Reutemann	6	4	2	—	6	3	4	20
Andretti	2	—	3	3	4	—	—	12
Pironi	—	3	—	—	1	4	—	8
Watson	4	—	—	—	—	1	3	8
Jarier	—	—	4	1	2	—	—	7
Regazzoni	—	—	—	—	—	—	6	6
Jones	—	—	—	4	—	—	—	4
Patrese	—	—	—	—	—	2	—	2
Fittipaldi	1	—	—	—	—	—	—	1
Lauda	—	—	1	—	—	—	—	1
Mass	—	—	—	—	—	—	1	1

Jacky Ickx, who was to announce his retirement from Grand Prix racing at the end of the season, tries out the Ligier, advised by Jacques Laffite, who scored a sensational series of successes in the opening races of the season.

RENAULT elf MICHELIN
FACOM

The return of the supercharged car. Jean-Pierre Jabouille, the hero of France for winning the French Grand Prix convincingly for Renault. The Renault turbos very nearly finished first *and* second in a race which signalled a new era in Grand Prix racing.

Scheckter had to drop his scores in Brazil and Spain, Depailler his 2 for Monaco, and Reutemann his hard-earned fourth in Belgium and fifth in South Africa. Anyone who had scored single figures only, was obviously by now out of the picture.

The French Grand Prix was an historic and dramatic occasion. Jean-Pierre Jabouille gave Renault their long-awaited and popular victory, appropriately enough on their home ground. Renault very nearly took the first two places, their second turbocharged car driven by Rene Arnoux, only losing to Villeneuve's Ferrari after a hectic battle in which they exchanged places several times in the closing laps. The two were side by side, knocking their wheels together in a lively style of racing, characteristic of the other famous French Grand Prix duel between Fangio and Hawthorn at Rheims in 1953.

Yet in historical terms, this was more than the first victory for a supercharged car since Fangio's Spanish Grand Prix for Alfa Romeo in 1951. It was a replay of the very first Grand Prix of all, the 1906 French, in which the issue also lay between France and Italy, Renault and FIAT. Renault during the intervening years had passed from the hands of the pioneering motoring family and been nationalised in 1945. Fiat, on the other hand, had not made a Grand Prix car themselves since the $1\frac{1}{2}$-litre supercharged 12-cylinder 806 in 1927, but the connection with Ferrari was proudly acknowledged. Fiat cash had been behind them since 1956, although the name did not appear on the side of the car until 1977.

Renault may have thought of Dijon as a replay of 1906, and they also gained two second places in their best season so far, but the honours for the year went to Ferrari. It remained the name of which people tended to think when Grand Prix racing was mentioned. Yet Renault's intervention did perhaps signify a change in the mood of Grand Prix racing, and the initiative passing finally back to Continental Europe. FOCA only remained powerful so long as it controlled a clear majority of the cars ever likely to win the world championship. That gave them the confidence to threaten the authorities with the alternative of going off and running their own world championship series, unless the game was played their way.

After Dijon they no longer enjoyed such control. Although Ferrari and Renault were both nominally members of FOCA, neither had the same commitment to what Continental followers of Grand Prix racing knew as the English Mafia. More significantly, neither team was financed in the same way as the British, and it was mostly the financial advantages that kept FOCA together.

Bernie Ecclestone suddenly found means of accommodating Jean-Marie Balestre, and took a seat on the FISA sub-committee concerned with Grand Prix racing. There was talk of working out a future Grand Prix Formula to take account of fuel consumption, which would be more in tune with the times. Keith Duckworth, for one, welcomed the idea on the grounds that the technical challenge of a power unit for such a Formula would be more demanding than simply producing an engine which gave maximum power for two or three hours, and then had to be rebuilt at great expense. Talk of banning turbochargers because of cost found few supporters. Ferrari quickly made it clear they were thinking about a turbo, which would have served to isolate the British FOCA element further, so the idea was quickly dropped.

In the world championship's 30th year, despite the disarray of the scoring system, it was followed by millions on television. Despite also its air of theatrical unreality (or perhaps, who can tell, because of it) it remained a spectacle watched and adored by millions more. None of the participants have managed to find quite enough common cause to stage-manage the races, or manipulate the world championship—yet. It is as well, for therein lies its strength.

THE MAKE WITH THE MOST GRAND PRIX VICTORIES

Jody Scheckter, who brought Michelin their first world championship, brakes heavily for a corner.

1951	British GP Silverstone	F. Gonzalez	4494 cc	Ferarri Tipo 375F1
1951	German GP Nürburgring	A. Ascari	4494 cc	Ferrari Tipo 375F1
1951	Italian GP Monza	A. Ascari	4494 cc	Ferrari Tipo 375F1
1952	Swiss GP Bremgarten	P. Taruffi	1985 cc	Ferrari Tipo 500F2
1952	Belgian GP Spa-Francorchamps	A. Ascari	1985 cc	Ferrari Tipo 500F2
1952	French GP Rouen-les-Essarts	A. Ascari	1985 cc	Ferrari Tipo 500F2
1952	British GP Silverstone	A. Ascari	1985 cc	Ferrari Tipo 500F2
1952	German GP Nürburgring	A. Ascari	1985 cc	Ferrari Tipo 500F2
1952	Dutch GP Zandvoort	A. Ascari	1985 cc	Ferrari Tipo 500F2
1952	Italian GP Monza	A. Ascari	1985 cc	Ferrari Tipo 500F2
1953	Argentine GP Buenos Aires	A. Ascari	1985 cc	Ferrari Tipo 500F2
1953	Dutch GP Zandvoort	A. Ascari	1985 cc	Ferrari Tipo 500F2
1953	Belgian GP Spa-Francorchamps	A. Ascari	1985 cc	Ferrari Tipo 500F2
1953	French GP Rheims	J M Hawthorn	1985 cc	Ferrari Tipo 500F2
1953	British GP Silverstone	A. Ascari	1985 cc	Ferrari Tipo 500F2
1953	German GP Nürburgring	G. Farina	1985 cc	Ferrari Tipo 500F2
1953	Swiss GP Bremgarten	A. Ascari	1985 cc	Ferrari Tipo 500F2
1954	British GP Silverstone	F. Gonzalez	2498 cc	Ferrari Tipo 625
1954	Spanish GP Barcelona	J M Hawthorn	2498 cc	Ferrari Tipo 553
1955	Monaco GP Monte Carlo	M. Trintignant	2498 cc	Ferrari Tipo 625A
1956	Argentine GP Buenos Aires	L. Musso/J M Fangio	2487 cc	Lancia Ferrari D50
1956	Belgian GP Spa-Francorchamps	P. Collins	2487 cc	Lancia Ferrari D50
1956	French GP Rheims	P. Collins	2487 cc	Lancia Ferrari D50
1956	British GP Silverstone	J M Fangio	2487 cc	Lancia Ferrari D50
1956	German GP Nürburgring	J M Fangio	2487 cc	Lancia Ferrari D50
1958	French GP Rheims	J M Hawthorn	2417 cc	Ferrari Dino 246
1958	British GP Silverstone	P. Collins	2417 cc	Ferrari Dino 246
1959	French GP Rheims	C A S Brooks	2417 cc	Ferrari Dino 246
1959	German GP Avus	C A S Brooks	2417 cc	Ferrari Dino 246
1960	Italian GP Monza	P. Hill	2417 cc	Ferrari Dino 246
1961	Dutch GP Zandvoort	W. von Trips	1476 cc	Ferrari Dino 156
1961	Belgian GP Spa-Francorchamps	P. Hill	1476 cc	Ferrari Dino 156
1961	French GP Rheims	G. Baghetti	1476 cc	Ferrari Dino 156
1961	British GP Aintree	W. von Trips	1476 cc	Ferrari Dino 156
1961	Italian GP Monza	P. Hill	1476 cc	Ferrari Dino 156
1963	German GP Nürburgring	J. Surtees	1476 cc	Ferrari 156
1964	German GP Nürburgring	J. Surtees	1487 cc	Ferrari 158

Grand Prix Victories—continued

1964	Austrian GP Zeltweg	L. Bandini	1476 cc	Ferrari 156
1964	Italian GP Monza	J. Surtees	1487 cc	Ferrari 158
1966	Belgian GP Spa-Francorchamps	J. Surtees	2990 cc	Ferrari 312
1966	Italian GP Monza	L. Scarfiotti	2990 cc	Ferrari 312
1968	French GP Rouen-les-Essarts	J. Ickx	2990 cc	Ferrari 312
1970	Austrian GP Österreichring	J. Ickx	2999 cc	Ferrari 312B
1970	Italian GP Monza	C. Regazzoni	2999 cc	Ferrari 312B
1970	Canadian GP Ste Jovite	J. Ickx	2999 cc	Ferrari 312B
1970	Mexican GP Mexico City	J. Ickx	2999 cc	Ferrari 312B
1971	South African GP Kyalami	M. Andretti	2999 cc	Ferrari 312B
1971	Dutch GP Zandvoort	J. Ickx	2992 cc	Ferrari 312B/2
1972	German GP Nürburgring	J. Ickx	2992 cc	Ferrari 312B/2
1974	Spanish GP Jarama	N. Lauda	2992 cc	Ferrari 312B/3
1974	Dutch GP Zandvoort	N. Lauda	2992 cc	Ferrari 312B/3
1974	German GP Nürburgring	C. Regazzoni	2992 cc	Ferrari 312B/3
1975	Monaco GP Monte Carlo	N. Lauda	2992 cc	Ferrari 312T
1975	Belgian GP Zolder	N. Lauda	2992 cc	Ferrari 312T
1975	Swedish GP Anderstorp	N. Lauda	2992 cc	Ferrari 312T
1975	French GP Paul Ricard	N. Lauda	2992 cc	Ferrari 312T
1975	Italian GP Monza	C. Regazzoni	2992 cc	Ferrari 312T
1975	United States GP Watkins Glen	N. Lauda	2992 cc	Ferrari 312T
1976	Brazilian GP Interlagos	N. Lauda	2992 cc	Ferrari 312T
1976	United States GP West Long Beach	C. Regazzoni	2992 cc	Ferrari 312T
1976	South African GP Kyalami	N. Lauda	2992 cc	Ferrari 312T
1976	Belgian GP Zolder	N. Lauda	2992 cc	Ferrari 312T/2
1976	Monaco GP Monte Carlo	N. Lauda	2992 cc	Ferrari 312T/2
1976	British GP Brands Hatch	N. Lauda	2992 cc	Ferrari 312T/2
1977	Brazilian GP Interlagos	C. Reutemann	2992 cc	Ferrari 312T/2
1977	South African GP Kyalami	N. Lauda	2992 cc	Ferrari 312T/2
1977	German GP Hockenheim	N. Lauda	2992 cc	Ferrari 312T/2
1977	Dutch GP Zandvoort	N. Lauda	2992 cc	Ferrari 312T/2
1978	Brazilian GP Rio de Janeiro	C. Reutemann	2992 cc	Ferrari 312T/2
1978	United States GP West Long Beach	C. Reutemann	2992 cc	Ferrari 312T/3
1978	British Grand Prix Brands Hatch	C. Reutemann	2992 cc	Ferrari 312T/3
1978	United States GP Watkins Glen	C. Reutemann	2992 cc	Ferrari 312T/3
1978	Canadian GP Montreal	G. Villeneuve	2992 cc	Ferrari 312T/3
1979	South African GP Kyalami	G. Villeneuve	2992 cc	Ferrari 312T/4
1979	United States GP West Long Beach	G. Villeneuve	2992 cc	Ferrari 312T/4
1979	Belgian GP Zolder	J. Scheckter	2992 cc	Ferrari 312T/4
1979	Monaco GP Monte Carlo	J. Scheckter	2992 cc	Ferrari 312T/4
1979	Italian GP Monza	J. Scheckter	2992 cc	Ferrari 312T/4
1979	United States GP Watkins Glen	G. Villeneuve	2992 cc	Ferrari 312T/4

Jody Scheckter (b 1950)

For years, Jody Scheckter was a talent in search of a car. He had shown his aptitude from the age of eleven, first in karts, then on motor cycles, and raced cars from obtaining his driving licence at 17. He began in a Renault 8, taking part in local races in South Africa, graduating to Formula Ford, which brought him to Europe in 1971.

His progress was marked by an aggressive style of driving, but it was successful. Groomed by Ford, and encouraged by his fellow-countrymen to whom he became something of a national hero, he joined the McLaren team late the following year. His role was essentially a supporting one; most Grand Prix teams take on young chargers from time to time in the hope of discovering the talent of a Stewart or a Clark while it can still be bought cheaply.

In the French Grand Prix of 1973, Scheckter qualified for the front row of the starting grid alongside such established stars as Stewart and Fittipaldi. But his glory was short-lived, and he collided with Fittipaldi. Only two weeks later came the misjudgement on the opening lap of the British Grand Prix before not only the assembled ranks of spectators, the TV cameras of the world, and all his fellow drivers, but also all the team managers on whom his future career depended.

McLaren decided enough was enough, and released Scheckter at the end of the season before he did any more damage. Yet he was taken on by Ken Tyrrell, who had a reputation as one of the more conservative selectors. He drove for Tyrrell for the following three years, which included a season with the Project 34 six-wheeler. Scheckter alone managed to make it a winner.

Yet he could see that it would never provide him with the means to win the world championship, and he joined Wolf, with whom he had two reasonably fruitful years until its wealthy Canadian sponsor tired of it, and the team fell into disarray. For 1979 Scheckter took the unusual step, for a mature driver, of joining Ferrari with all the risks it implied for his career. His success came in the teeth of stiff opposition from Villeneuve who, despite his relatively tender years, displayed a determination and forcefulness that was at least a match for Scheckter's. In 1979, besides the most powerful and reliable car of the year, Ferrari also enjoyed the services of the two most competitive, and talented drivers in the field.

And in the long battle for the greatest number of world championship Grand Prix wins, Scheckter and Villeneuve kept Ferrari edging ahead, with a total of 79 victories against their closest rival, Lotus, with 71.

ANATOMY OF THE GRAND PRIX

WORLD CHAMPIONSHIP

1950

BRITISH GRAND PRIX

Silverstone; 13 May; 70 laps 202 miles/325 km
1 G. Farina (Alfa-Romeo) 2 hr 13 m 23.6 sec 90.95 mph/146.34 kph—2 L. Fagioli (Alfa-Romeo) 2 hr 13 min 26.2 sec—3 R. Parnell (Alfa-Romeo) 2 hr 14 min 15.6 sec—4 Y. Giraud-Cabantous (Lago-Talbot) 68 laps—5 L. Rosier (Lago-Talbot) 68 laps—6 F R Gerard (ERA) 67 laps—7 T C Harrison (ERA) 67 laps—8 P. Etancelin (Lago Talbot) 65 laps—9 D. Hampshire (Maserati) 64 laps—10 J G Fry, B N Shawe-Taylor (Maserati) 64 laps—11 J. Claes (Lago-Talbot) 64 laps—not classified as finishers J. Kelly (Alta) 57 laps—fastest lap, Farina 1 min 50.6 sec 94.02 mph/151.28 kph—retired L. Johnson (ERA) supercharger lap 2—P. Walker, A P R Rolt (ERA) gearbox lap 5—E. Martin (Lago-Talbot) oil pressure lap 9—L. Chiron (Maserati) clutch lap 24—E. de Graffenried (Maserati) con rod lap 34—G. Crossley (Alta) transmission lap 44—D. Murray (Maserati) engine lap 44—'B. Bira' (Maserati) fuel starvation lap 49—J M Fangio (Alfa Romeo) oil leak lap 62.

Starting grid, pattern 4-3-4

Farina 1 min 50.8 sec—Fagioli 1 min 51 sec—Fangio 1 min 51 sec—Parnell 1 min 52.2 sec—Bira 1 min 52.6 sec—Giraud-Cabantous 1 min 53.4 sec—Martin 1 min 55.4 sec—de Graffenried 1 min 55.8 sec—Rosier 1 min 56 sec—Walker 1 min 56.6 sec—Chiron 1 min 56.6 sec—Johnson 1 min 57.4 sec—Gerard 1 min 57.4 sec—Etancelin 1 min 57.8 sec—Harrison 1 min 58.4 sec—Hampshire 2 min 01 sec—Crossley 2 min 02.6 sec—Murray 2 min 05.6 sec—Kelly 2 min 06.2 sec—Fry 2 min 07 sec—Claes 2 min 08.8 sec—non starter F. Bonetto (Maserati).
(Maserati).
First world championship Grand Prix; 1950 Grand Prix d'Europe; attended by Their Majesties King George VI and Queen Elizabeth.

MONACO GRAND PRIX

Monte Carlo; 21 May; 100 laps 314 km/195 miles
1 J M Fangio (Alfa-Romeo) 3 hr 13 min 18.7 sec 98.68 kph/61.33 mph—2 A. Ascari (Ferrari) 99 laps—3 L. Chiron (Maserati) 98 laps—4 R. Sommer (Ferrari) 97 laps—5 'B. Bira' (Maserati) 95 laps—6 F R Gerard (ERA) 94 laps—fastest lap, Fangio 1 min 51.0 sec 103.12 kph/64.09 mph—retired G. Farina (Alfa-Romeo) accident lap 1—F. Gonzalez (Maserati) accident lap 1—L. Fagioli (Alfa-Romeo) accident lap 1—L. Rosier (Talbot) accident lap 1—M. Trintignant (Simca-Gordini) accident lap 1—F. Rol (Maserati) accident lap 1—E. de Graffenried (Maserati) accident lap 1—R. Manzon (Simca-Gordini) accident lap 1—C. Harrison (ERA) accident lap 1—H. Schell (Cooper JAP) accident lap 1—P. Etancelin (Lago-Talbot) oil pipe lap 36—L. Villoresi (Ferrari) back axle lap 63.

Starting grid; 3-2-3

Fangio 1 min 50.2 sec-Farina 1 min 52.8 sec—Gonzalez 1 min 53.7 sec—Etancelin 1 min 54.1 sec—Fagioli 1 min 54.2 sec—Villoresi 1 min 52.3 sec—Ascari 1 min 53.8 sec—Chiron 1 min 56.3 sec—Sommer 1 min 56.6 sec—Rosier 1 min 57.7 sec—Manzon 2 min 04.0 sec—de Graffenried 2 min 00.7 sec—Trintignant 2 min 00.9 sec—Harrison 2 min 01.6 sec—'B. Bira' 2 min 02.2 sec—Gerard 2 min 03.4 sec—Rol 2 min 04.5 sec—Claes 2 min 12.0 sec—Schell (no time)—non starters P. Whitehead (Ferrari)—A. Pian (Maserati).

SWISS GRAND PRIX

Bremgarten, Berne; 4 June; 42 laps 306 km/190 miles
1 G. Farina (Alfa-Romeo) 2 hr 2 min 53.7 sec 149.25 kph/92.76 mph—2 L. Fagioli (Alfa-Romeo) 2 hr 2 min 54.1 sec—3 L. Rosier (Lago-Talbot) 41 laps—4 'B. Bira' (Maserati) 40 laps—5 F. Bonetto (Maserati) 40 laps—6 E. de Graffenried (Maserati) 40 laps—7 N. Pagani (Maserati) 39 laps—8 H. Schell (Lago-Talbot) 39 laps—9 L. Chiron (Maserati) 39 laps—10 J. Claes (Lago-Talbot) 38 laps—11 A. Branca (Maserati) 35 laps—fastest lap, Farina, 2 min 41.6 sec 162.15 kph/100.78 mph—retired Y. Giraud-Cabantous (Lago-Talbot) accident lap 1—A. Ascari (Ferrari) oil pipe lap 5—L. Villoresi (Ferrari) transmission lap 10—E. Martin (Lago-Talbot) accident lap 20—R. Sommer (Ferrari) engine lap 20—P. Etancelin (Lago-Talbot) gearbox lap 26—J M Fangio (Alfa-Romeo) valve gear lap 35.

Starting grid 3-2-3

Fangio 2 min 42.1 sec—Farina 2 min 42.8 sec—Fagioli 2 min 45.2 sec—Villoresi 2 min 46.1 sec—Ascari 2 min 46.8 sec—Etancelin 2 min 51.1 sec—Giraud-Cabantous 2 min 52.7 sec—'B. Bira' 2 min 53.2 sec—non starters P. Whitehead (Ferrari)—R. Parnell (Maserati).

BELGIAN GRAND PRIX

Spa-Francorchamps; 18 June; 35 laps 494 km/307 miles
1 J M Fangio (Alfa-Romeo) 2 hr 47 min 26.0 sec 177.07 kph/110.05 mph—2 L. Fagioli (Alfa-Romeo) 2 hr 47 min 40 sec—3 L. Rosier (Lago-Talbot) 2 hr 49 min 45.0 sec—4 G. Farina (Alfa-Romeo) 2 hr 51 min 31 sec—5 A. Ascari (Ferrari) 34 laps—6 L. Villoresi (Ferrari) 33 laps—7 P. Levegh (Lago-Talbot) 33 laps—8 J. Claes (Lago-Talbot) 33 laps—9 G. Crossley (Alta) 30 laps—10 A. Branca (Maserati) 29 laps—fastest lap, Farina 4 min 34.1 sec 185.68 kph/115.4 mph—retired Y. Giraud-Cabantous (Lago-Talbot) engine lap 2—P. Etancelin (Lago-Talbot) overheating lap 15—R. Sommer (Lago-Talbot) engine lap 20—E. Chaboud (Lago-Talbot) lap 22.

Starting grid 3-2-3

Farina 4 min 37.0 sec—Fangio 4 min 37.0 sec—Fagioli 4 min 41.0 sec—Villoresi 4 min 47.0 sec—Sommer 4 min 47.0 sec—Etancelin 4 min 48.0 sec—Ascari 4 min 49.0 sec—Rosier 4 min 49.0 sec—Giraud-Cabantous—Levegh—Branca—Crossley—Chaboud—Claes.

FRENCH GRAND PRIX

Rheims; *Circuit de Reims*; 2 July; 64 laps 497 km/309 miles
1 J M Fangio (Alfa-Romeo) 2 hr 57 min 52.8 sec 168.69 kph/104.84 mph—2 L. Fagioli (Alfa-Romeo) 2 hr 58 min 18.5 sec—3 P. Whitehead (Ferrari) 61 laps—4 R. Manzon (Simca-Gordini) 61 laps—5 P. Etancelin. E. Chaboud (Lago-Talbot) 59 laps—6 C. Pozzi, L. Rosier (Lago-Talbot) 56 laps—7 G. Farina (Alfa-Romeo) 55 laps—8 Y. Giraud-Cabantous (Lago-Talbot) 52 laps—fastest lap, Fangio 2 min 35.6 sec 180.79 kph/112.36 mph—retired F. Gonzalez (Maserati) engine lap 4—R. Sommer (Lago-Talbot) overheating lap 5—D. Hampshire (Maserati) engine lap 6—L. Chiron (Maserati) engine lap 7—F. Rol (Maserati) engine lap 7—R. Parnell (Maserati) engine lap 10—L. Rosier (Lago-Talbot) overheating lap 11—J. Claes (Lago-Talbot) overheating lap 12—F. Bonetto (Maserati) engine lap 15—P. Levegh (Lago-Talbot) engine lap 37.

Starting grid 3-2-3

Fangio 2 min 30.6 sec—Farina 2 min 32.5 sec—Fagioli 2 min 34.7 sec—Etancelin 2 min 39.0 sec—Giraud-Cabantous 2 min 42.7 sec—Sommer 2 min 46.0 sec—Rol 2 min 46.7 sec—Gonzalez 2 min 48.0 sec—Levegh 2 min 49.0 sec—(vacant place on grid)—Parnell—Hampshire—Manzon—Chiron—Pozzi—Rosier—Claes—Bonetto—Whitehead.

ITALIAN GRAND PRIX

Monza; 3 September; 80 laps 504 km/313 miles
1 G. Farina (Alfa-Romeo) 2 hr 51 min 17.4 sec 174.39 kph/109.63 mph—2 D. Serafini, A. Ascari (Ferrari) 2 hr 52 min 36.0 sec—3 L. Fagioli (Alfa-Romeo) 2 hr 52 min 53.0 sec—4 L. Rosier (Lago-Talbot) 75 laps—5 P. Etancelin (Lago-Talbot) 75 laps—6 E. de Graffenried (Maserati) 72 laps—7 P N Whitehead (Ferrari) 72 laps—fastest lap, J M Fangio 2 min 00 sec 188.96 kph/117.44 mph—retired A. Ascari (Ferrari)

engine—C. Biondetti (Ferrari)—'B. Bira' (Maserati) engine 2 laps—L. Chiron (Maserati) oil pressure—J. Claes (Lago-Talbot) overheating—G. Comotti (Maserati-Milan)—J M Fangio (Alfa-Romeo) gearbox—C. Harrison (ERA) engine—P. Levegh (Lago-Talbot)—H. Louveau (Lago-Talbot)—G. Mairesse (Lago-Talbot)—R. Manzon (Simca-Gordini)—D. Murray (Maserati) gearbox—F. Rol (Maserati)—C. Sanesi (Alfa-Romeo) engine lap 12—R. Sommer (Lago-Talbot) gearbox lap 49—M. Trintignant (Simca-Gordini).

Starting grid

J M Fangio 1 min 58.6 sec—A. Ascari 1 min 58.8 sec.

1950 WORLD CHAMPIONSHIP

1 G. Farina 30—2 J M Fangio 27—3 L. Fagioli 24, 28—4 L. Rosier 13—5 A. Ascari 11—6 'B. Bira' 5—7 R. Parnell 4—7= P. Whitehead 4—7= L. Chiron 4—10 P. Etancelin 3—10= Y. Giraud-Cabantous 3—10= R. Sommer 3—10= R. Manzon 3—10= D. Serafini 3—15 F. Bonetto 2—16 E. Chaboud 1.

1951

SWISS GRAND PRIX

Bremgarten, Berne; 27 May; 42 laps 306 km/190 miles
1 J M Fangio (Alfa-Romeo) 2 hr 7 min 53.6 sec 143.28 kph/89.05 mph—2 P Taruffi (Ferrari) 2 hr 8 min 48.9 sec—3 G. Farina (Alfa-Romeo) 2 hr 9 min 12.9 sec—4 C. Sanesi (Alfa-Romeo) 41 laps—5 E. de Graffenried (Alfa-Romeo) 40 laps—6 A. Ascari (Ferrari) 40 laps—7 L. Chiron (Maserati) 40 laps—8 S. Moss (HWM) 40 laps—9 L. Rosier (Lago-Talbot) 39 laps—10 P. Etancelin (Lago-Talbot) 39 laps—11 R. Fischer (Ferrari) 39 laps—12 H. Schell (Maserati) 38 laps—13 J. Claes (Lago-Talbot) 35 laps—14 G. Mairesse (Lago-Talbot) 31 laps—fastest lap, Fangio 2 min 51.1 sec 153.18 kph/95.2 mph—retired F. Gonzalez (Lago-Talbot) oil pump lap 10—L. Villoresi (Ferrari) accident lap 12—Y. Giraud-Cabantous (Lago-Talbot) magneto lap 14—G. Abecassis (HWM) magneto lap 23—H. Louveau (Lago-Talbot) accident lap 30—P N Whitehead (Ferrari) accident lap 36.

Starting grid 3-2-3

Fangio—Farina—Villoresi—Sanesi—de Graffenried—Taruffi—Ascari—Rosier—Fischer—Whitehead—Gonzalez—Etancelin—Louveau—Moss—Giraud-Cabantous—Hirt—Schell—Claes—Chiron—Abecassis—Mairesse.

BELGIAN GRAND PRIX

Spa-Francorchamps; 17 June; 36 laps 507 km/315 miles
1 G. Farina (Alfa-Romeo) 2 hr 45 min 46.0 sec 183.91 kph/114.3 mph—2 A. Ascari (Ferrari) 2 hr 48 min 37.0 sec—3 L. Villoresi (Ferrari) 2 hr 50 min 8.0 sec—4 L. Rosier (Lago-Talbot) 34 laps—5 Y. Giraud-Cabantous (Lago-Talbot) 34 laps—6 A. Pilette (Lago-Talbot) 33 laps—7 J. Claes (Lago-Talbot) 33 laps—8 P. Levegh (Lago-Talbot) 32 laps—9 J M Fangio (Alfa-Romeo) 32 laps—fastest lap, J M Fangio 4 min 22.1 sec 193.88 kph/120.5 mph—retired P. Etancelin (Lago-Talbot) transmission lap 1—C. Sanesi (Alfa-Romeo) radiator lap 12—L. Chiron (Maserati) piston lap 28—P. Taruffi (Ferrari) transmission lap 9.

Starting grid 3-2-3

Fangio 4 min 25.0 sec—Farina 4 min 28.0 sec—Villoresi 4 min 29.0 sec—Ascari 4 min 30.0 sec—Taruffi 4 min 32.0 sec—Sanesi 4 min 36.0 sec—Rosier 4 min 45.0 sec—Giraud-Cabantous 4 min 52.0 sec—Chiron 5 min 01.0 sec—Etancelin 5 min 04.0 sec—Claes 5 min 09.0 sec—Pilette 5 min 16.0 sec—Levegh 5 min 17.0 sec.

FRENCH GRAND PRIX

Rheims, *Circuit de Reims*; 1 July; 77 laps 602 km/374 miles
1 J M Fangio, L. Fagioli (Alfa-Romeo) 3 hr 22 min 11.0 sec 178.55 kph/110.97 mph—2 A. Ascari, F. Gonzalez (Ferrari) 3 hr 23 min 9.2 sec—3 L. Villoresi (Ferrari) 74 laps—4 R. Parnell (Ferrari, Thinwall Spl) 73 laps—5 G. Farina (Alfa-Romeo) 73 laps—6 L. Chiron (Talbot) 71 laps—7 Y. Giraud-Cabantous (Lago-Talbot) 71 laps—8 E. Chaboud (Lago-Talbot) 69 laps—9 G. Mairesse (Lago-Talbot) 66 laps—10 C. Sanesi (Alfa-Romeo) 58 laps—11 L. Fagioli, J M Fangio (Alfa-Romeo) 55 laps—fastest lap, Fangio 2 min 27.8 sec 190.33 kph/118.29 mph—retired P. Whitehead (Ferrari) gasket lap 1—E. de Graffenried (Maserati) transmission lap 1—R. Manzon (Simca-Gordini) lap 3—A. Simon (Simca-Gordini) engine lap 7—A. Ascari (Ferrari) gearbox lap 10—M. Trintignant (Simca-Gordini) engine lap 11—H. Schell (Maserati) steering lap 24—A. Gordini (Simca-Gordini) lap 27—P. Etancelin (Lago-Talbot) engine lap 37—L. Rosier (Lago-Talbot) transmission lap 43—J. Claes (Lago-Talbot) accident lap 54.

Starting grid 3-2-3

Fangio 2 min 25.7 sec—Farina 2 min 27.4 sec—Ascari 2 min 28.1 sec—Villoresi 2 min 28.5 sec—Sanesi 2 min 28.9 sec—Gonzalez 2 min 30.8 sec—Fagioli 2 min 33.1 sec—Chiron 2 min 43.7 sec—Parnell 2 min 44.0 sec—Etancelin 2 min 44.8 sec—Giraud-Cabantous 2 min 45.7 sec—Claes 2 min 46.6 sec—Rosier 2 min 48.0 sec—Chaboud 2 min 49.6 sec—Marimon—de Graffenried 2 min 50.1 sec—Gordini 2 min 50.3 sec—Trintignant 2 min 50.3 sec—Mairesse 2 min 58.4 sec—Whitehead—Simon—Schell—Manzon
1951 Grand Prix d'Europe.

BRITISH GRAND PRIX

Silverstone; 14 July; 90 laps 260 miles/418 km
1 F. Gonzalez (Ferrari) 2 hr 42 min 18.2 sec 96.11 mph/154.64 kph—2 J M Fangio (Alfa-Romeo) 2 hr 43 min 9.2 sec—3 L. Villoresi (Ferrari) 88 laps—4 F. Bonetto (Alfa-Romeo) 87 laps—5 R. Parnell (BRM) 85 laps—6 C. Sanesi (Alfa-Romeo) 84 laps—7 P. Walker (BRM) 84 laps—8 B N Shawe-Taylor (ERA) 84 laps—9 P N Whitehead (Ferrari Thinwall Special) 83 laps—10 L. Rosier (Lago-Talbot) 83 laps—11 F R Gerard (ERA) 82 laps—12 D. Hamilton (Lago-Talbot) 82 laps—13 J. Claes (Lago-Talbot) 80 laps—not classified as finisher J. Kelly (Alta) 75 laps—fastest lap, Farina 1 min 44.0 sec 99.99 mph/160.88 kph—retired J. James (Maserati) radiator lap 22—L. Chiron (Talbot) brakes lap 41—D. Murray (Maserati) valve lap 45—P. Fotheringham-Parker (Maserati) oil pipe lap 46—A. Ascari (Ferrari) gearbox lap 56—G. Farina (Alfa-Romeo) clutch lap 75.

Starting grid 4-3-4

Gonzalez 1 min 43.4 sec—Fangio 1 min 44.4 sec—Farina 1 min 45.0 sec—Ascari 1 min 45.4 sec—Villoresi 1 min 45.8 sec—Sanesi 1 min 50.2 sec—Bonetto 1 min 52.0 sec—Whitehead 1 min 54.6 sec—Rosier 1 min 56.0 sec—Gerard 1 min 57.0 sec—Hamilton 1 min 57.2 sec—Shawe-Taylor 1 min 58.2 sec—Chiron 2 min 00.2 sec—Claes 2 min 05.8 sec—Murray 2 min 06.0 sec—Fotheringham-Parker 2 min 13.2 sec—James 2 min 17.0 sec—Kelly 2 min 18.4 sec—Walker—Parnell—non starters M. Trintignant (Simca-Gordini)—R. Manzon (Simca-Gordini)—A. Simon (Simca-Gordini)—P. Etancelin (Lago-Talbot). The BRMs of P D C Walker and R. Parnell did not practise.

GERMAN GRAND PRIX

Nürburgring; 29 July; 20 laps 455 km/283 miles
1 A. Ascari (Ferrari) 3 hr 23 min 3.3 sec 134.77 kph/83.76 mph—2 J M Fangio (Alfa-Romeo) 3 hr 23 min 33.8 sec—3 F. Gonzalez (Ferrari) 3 hr 27 min 42.3 sec—4 L. Villoresi (Ferrari) 3 hr 28 min 53.5 sec—5 P. Taruffi (Ferrari) 3 hr 30 min 52.4

GERMAN GRAND PRIX—*continued*

sec—6 R. Fischer (Ferrari) 19 laps—7 R. Manzon (Simca-Gordini) 19 laps—8 L. Rosier (Lago-Talbot) 19 laps—9 P. Levegh (Lago-Talbot) 18 laps—10 J. Swaters (Lago-Talbot) 18 laps—11 J. Claes (Lago-Talbot) 18 laps—fastest lap, Fangio 9 min 55.8 sec 137.79 kph/85.64 mph—retired E. de Graffenried (Maserati) engine lap 2—L. Chiron (Lago-Talbot) ignition lap 3—P. Etancelin (Lago-Talbot) gearbox lap 4—A. Branca (Maserati) engine lap 4—G. Farina (Alfa-Romeo) gearbox lap 8—P. Pietsch (Alfa-Romeo) accident lap 12—A. Simon (Simca-Gordini) engine lap 12—D. Hamilton (Lago-Talbot) oil pressure lap 12—F. Bonetto (Alfa-Romeo) supercharger lap 13—M. Trintignant (Simca-Gordini) engine lap 14—Y. Giraud-Cabantous (Lago-Talbot) accident lap 18.

Starting grid 4-3-4

Ascari 9 min 55.8 sec—Gonzalez 9 min 57.5 sec—Fangio 9 min 59.0 sec—Farina 10 min 01.0 sec—Villoresi 10 min 06.6 sec—Taruffi 10 min 12.9 sec—Pietsch 10 min 15.7 sec—Fischer 10 min 23.8 sec—Manzon 10 min 28.9 sec—Bonetto 10 min 46.1 sec—Giraud-Cabantous 10 min 52.8 sec—Simca 10 min 57.5 sec—Chiron 11 min 00.2 sec—Trintignant 11 min 07.5 sec—Rosier 11 min 08.2 sec—de Graffenried 11 min 25.6 sec—Branca 11 min 26.7 sec—Claes 11 min 33.6 sec—Levegh 11 min 41.9 sec—Hamilton 11 min 49.3 sec—Etancelin 11 min 52.9 sec—Swaters 12 min 09.1 sec—non starter D. Murray (Maserati).

ITALIAN GRAND PRIX

Monza; 16 September; 80 laps 502 km/312 miles
1 A. Ascari (Ferrari) 2 hr 42 min 39.3 sec 185.89 kph/115.53 mph—2 F. Gonzalez (Ferrari) 2 hr 43 min 23.9 sec—3 G. Farina, F. Bonetto (Alfa-Romeo) 79 laps—4 L. Villoresi (Ferrari) 79 laps—5 P. Taruffi (Ferrari) 78 laps—6 A. Simon (Simca-Gordini) 74 laps—7 L. Rosier (Lago-Talbot) 73 laps—8 Y. Giraud-Cabantous (Lago-Talbot) 72 laps—9 F. Rol (OSCA) 67 laps—fastest lap, Farina 1 min 56.7 sec 194.64 kph/120.97 mph—retired C. Landi (Ferrari) transmission lap 1—P. Whitehead (Ferrari) magneto lap 2—J. Claes (Lago-Talbot) engine lap 5—E. de Graffenried (Alfa-Romeo) supercharger lap 2—G. Farina (Alfa-Romeo) engine lap 7—J. Swaters (Lago-Talbot) engine lap 8—P. Levegh (Lago-Talbot) engine lap 10—L. Chiron (Lago-Talbot) ignition lap 23—M. Trintignant (Simca-Gordini) piston lap 30—R. Manzon (Simca-Gordini) engine lap 30—J M Fangio (Alfa-Romeo) engine lap 40.

Starting grid 4-3-3-3-3-1

Fangio 1 min 52.3 sec—Farina 1 min 53.9 sec—Ascari 1 min 55.1 sec—Gonzalez 1 min 55.9 sec—Villoresi 1 min 57.9 sec—Taruffi 1 min 58.2 sec—Bonetto 1 min 58.3 sec—de Graffenried 2 min 05.2 sec—Simon 2 min 08.0 sec—Trintignant 2 min 08.9 sec—Manzon 2 min 09.0 sec—Giraud-Cabantous 2 min 09.3 sec—Rosier 2 min 10.8 sec—Landi 2 min 11.3 sec—Chiron 2 min 12.1 sec—Rol 2 min 13.4 sec—Whitehead 2 min 16.0 sec—Levegh 2 min 16.5 sec—Claes 2 min 18.6 sec—Swaters 2 min 18.8 sec—non starter R. Parnell (BRM).

SPANISH GRAND PRIX

Pedralbes, Barcelona; 28 October; 70 laps 442 km/275 miles
1 J M Fangio (Alfa-Romeo) 2 hr 46 min 54.1 sec 158.81 kph/98.7 mph—2 F. Gonzalez (Ferrari) 2 hr 47 min 48.38 sec—3 G. Farina (Alfa-Romeo) 2 hr 48 min 39.64 sec—4 A. Ascari (Ferrari) 68 laps—5 F. Bonetto (Alfa-Romeo) 68 laps—6 E. de Graffenried (Alfa-Romeo) 66 laps—7 L. Rosier (Lago-Talbot) 65 laps—8 P. Etancelin (Lago-Talbot) 65 laps—9 R. Manzon (Simca-Gordini) 63 laps—10 F. Godia (Maserati) 60 laps—fastest lap, Fangio 2 min 14.3 sec 169.27 kph/105.2 mph—retired 'B. Bira' (OSCA) engine lap 1—L. Chiron (Lago-Talbot) ignition lap 4—Y. Giraud-Cabantous (Lago-Talbot) overheating lap 7—G. Grignard (Lago-Talbot) engine lap 24—M. Trintignant (Simca-Gordini) engine lap 25—P. Taruffi (Ferrari) suspension lap 30—J. Claes (Lago-Talbot) accident lap 37—L. Villoresi (Ferrari) ignition lap 48—A. Simon (Simca-Gordini) engine lap 49.

Starting grid 4-3-3-1-3-4-1

Ascari 2 min 10.59 sec—Fangio 2 min 12.27 sec—Gonzalez 2 min 14.1 sec—Farina 2 min 14.9 sec—Villoresi 2 min 16.4 sec—de Graffenried 2 min 16.4 sec—Taruffi 2 min 16.9 sec—Bonetto 2 min 21.8 sec—Manzon 2 min 23.81 sec—Simon 2 min 24.8 sec—Trintignant 2 min 25.3 sec—Chiron 2 min 30.32 sec—Etancelin 2 min 31.00 sec—Giraud-Cabantous 2 min 32.18 sec—Claes 2 min 34.46 sec—Grignard 2 min 36.58 sec—Godia 2 min 37.45 sec—'Bira' 2 min 45.99 sec—Rosier 2 min 46.78 sec—non starters A. Branca (Maserati)—P N Whitehead (Ferrari)—A. Jover (Maserati).

1951 WORLD CHAMPIONSHIP

1 J M Fangio 31, 37—2 A. Ascari 25, 28—3 F. Gonzalez 24, 27—4 G. Farina 19, 22—5 L. Villoresi 15, 18—6 P. Taruffi 10—7 F. Bonetto 6½—8 R. Parnell 5—9 L. Fagioli 4—10 L. Rosier 3—10= C. Sanesi 3—12 E. de Graffenried 2—12= Y. Giraud-Cabantous 2.

1952

SWISS GRAND PRIX

Bremgarten, Berne; 18 May; 62 laps 451 km/280 miles
1 P. Taruffi (Ferrari) 3 hr 1 min 46.1 sec 149.38 kph/92.78 mph—2 R. Fischer (Ferrari) 3 hr 4 min 23.3 sec—3 J. Behra (Gordini) 61 laps—4 K. Wharton (Frazer-Nash) 60 laps—5 A. Brown (Cooper-Bristol) 59 laps—6 E. de Graffenried (Maserati) 58 laps—7 P. Hirt (Ferrari) 56 laps—8 E. Brandon (Cooper-Bristol) 53 laps—fastest lap, Taruffi 2 min 49.1 sec 154.84 kph/86.25 mph—retired M. de Terra (Gordini) engine lap 1—L. Rosier (Ferrari) accident lap 2—T. Ulman (Veritas) lap 4—H. Stuck (AFM) lap 4—G. Abecassis (HWM) accident—P. Collins (HWM) drive shaft lap 12—G. Farina (Ferrari) magneto lap 16—R. Manzon (Gordini) radiator lap 20—S. Moss (HWM) L. Macklin (HWM) called in on lap 24 following the withdrawal of the other HWMs—H. Schell (Maserati) engine lap 24—A. Simon (Ferrari) gasket lap 51—'B. Bira' (Gordini) engine lap 52.

Starting grid 3-2-3

Farina 2 min 47.5 sec—Taruffi 2 min 50.0 sec—Manzon 2 min 52.1 sec—Simon 2 min 52.4 sec—Fischer 2 min 53.3 sec—Collins 2 min 55.9 sec—Behra 2 min 55.9 sec—de Graffenried 2 min 56.4 sec—Moss 2 min 56.4 sec—Abecassis 2 min 56.9 sec—'Bira' 2 min 59.3 sec—Macklin 3 min 00.2 sec—Wharton 3 min 00.9 sec—Stuck 3 min 01.7 sec—Brown 3 min 02.5 sec—Ulman 3 min 05.6 sec—Brandon 3 min 05.8 sec—Schell 3 min 07.6 sec—Hirt 3 min 10.2 sec—de Terra—Rosier—non starters J M Fangio (Maserati)—J F Gonzalez (Maserati).

BELGIAN GRAND PRIX

Spa-Francorchamps; 22 June; 36 laps 507 km/315 miles
1 A. Ascari (Ferrari) 3 hr 3 min 46.3 sec 165.94 kph/103.13 mph—2 G. Farina (Ferrari) 3 hr 5 min 41.5 sec—3 R. Manzon (Gordini) 3 hr 8 min 14.7 sec—4 J M Hawthorn (Cooper-Bristol) 35 laps—5 P. Frere (HWM) 34 laps—6 A. Brown (Cooper-Bristol) 34 laps—7 C. de Tornaco (Ferrari) 33 laps—8 J. Claes (Gordini) 33 laps—9 E. Brandon (Cooper-Bristol) 33 laps—10 'B. Bira' (Gordini) 32 laps—11 L. Macklin (HWM) 32 laps—12 R. Laurent (HWM) 32 laps—13 A. Legat (Veritas Meteor) 31 laps—14 R. O'Brien (Gordini) 30 laps—15 T. Gaze (HWM) 30 laps—fastest lap, Ascari 4 min 54.0 sec 172.87 kph/107.44 mph—retired S. Moss (ERA) engine and accident lap 1—P. Collins (HWM) axle tube lap 4—L. Rosier (Ferrari) engine lap 7—K. Wharton (Frazer-Nash) accident lap 11—J. Behra (Gordini) accident lap 14—P. Taruffi (Ferrari) accident

lap 14—R. Montgomery-Charrington (Aston Butterworth) fuel lap 18.

Starting grid 3-2-3

Ascari 4 min 37.0 sec—Farina 4 min 40.0 sec—Taruffi 4 min 46.0 sec—Manzon 4 min 52.0 sec—Behra 4 min 56.0 sec—Hawthorn 4 min 58.0 sec—Wharton 5 min 01.0 sec—Frere 5 min 05.0 sec—Brown—Moss—Collins—Brandon—de Tornaco—Macklin—Montgomery-Charrington—Gaze—Rosier—'Bira'—Claes—Laurent—Legat—O'Brien.

FRENCH GRAND PRIX

Rouen-Les Essarts; 6 July; three hours
1 A. Ascari (Ferrari) 386.48 km/240.2 miles 128.94 kph/80.14 mph 77 laps—2 G. Farina (Ferrari) 384.87 km/239.2 miles 76 laps—3 P. Taruffi (Ferrari) 377.64 km/234.7 miles 75 laps—4 R. Manzon (Gordini) 74 laps—5 M. Trintignant (Gordini) 73 laps—6 P. Collins (HWM) 72 laps—7 J. Behra (Gordini) 72 laps—8 P. Etancelin (Maserati) 71 laps—9 L. Macklin (HWM) 70 laps—10 Y. Giraud-Cabantous (HWM) 69 laps—11 R. Fischer, P. Hirt (Ferrari) 64 laps—12 G. Comotti (Ferrari) 64 laps—fastest lap, Farina 2 min 14.9 sec 136.03 kph (84.57 mph)—retired P. Carini (Ferrari) engine lap 2—H. Schell (Maserati) gearbox lap 7—J. Claes (Gordini) engine lap 15—L. Rosier (Ferrari) engine lap 17—P. Whitehead (Alta) clutch lap 26—E. de Graffenried, H. Schell (Maserati) brakes lap 34—J M Hawthorn (Cooper-Bristol) header tank lap 51—'B. Bira' (Gordini) rear axle lap 57.

Starting grid 3-2-3

Ascari 2 min 14.8 sec—Farina 2 min 16.2 sec—Taruffi 2 min 17.1 sec—Behra 2 min 19.3 sec—Manzon 2 min 20.4 sec—Trintignant 2 min 21.6 sec—'Bira' 2 min 23.0 sec—Collins 2 min 21.9 sec—Rosier 2 min 27.0 sec—Giraud-Cabantous 2 min 27.5 sec—Schell 2 min 29.0 sec—de Graffenried 2 min 28.6 sec—Whitehead 2 min 29.5 sec—Macklin 2 min 30.9 sec—Hawthorn 2 min 32.0 sec—Etancelin 2 min 33.7 sec—Fischer 2 min 34.6 sec—Comotti 2 min 36.0 sec—Carini 2 min 37.7 sec—Claes 2 min 39.6 sec—the grid was not assembled according to practice times.

BRITISH GRAND PRIX

Silverstone; 19 July; 85 laps 249 miles/401 km
1 A. Ascari (Ferrari) 2 hr 44 min 11.0 sec 90.92 mph/146.29 kph—2 P. Taruffi (Ferrari) 84 laps—3 J M Hawthorn (Cooper-Bristol) 83 laps—4 D. Poore (Connaught) 83 laps—5 E. Thompson (Connaught) 82 laps—6 G. Farina (Ferrari) 82 laps—7 R. Parnell (Cooper-Bristol) 82 laps—8 R. Salvadori (Ferrari) 82 laps—9 K H Downing (Connaught) 82 laps—10 P N Whitehead (Ferrari) 81 laps—11 'B. Bira' (Gordini) 81 laps—12 A G Whitehead (Alta) 80 laps—13 L. Macklin (HWM) 80 laps—14 R. Fischer (Ferrari) 80 laps—15 J. Claes (Gordini) 79 laps—16 K. McAlpine (Connaught) 79 laps—17 H. Schell (Maserati) 78 laps—18 G. Bianco (Maserati) 77 laps—19 E. de Graffenried (Maserati) 76 laps—20 E. Brandon (Cooper-Bristol) 76 laps—21 A. Crook (Frazer-Nash) 75 laps—22 A. Brown (Cooper-Bristol) 69 laps—fastest lap, Ascari 1 min 52.0 sec 94.08 mph/151.37 kph—retired D. Murray (Cooper-Bristol) engine—S. Moss (ERA) engine—P. Hirt (Ferrari) brakes—R. Manzon (Gordini) transmission—M. Trintignant (Gordini) transmission—F A O Gaze (HWM) gasket—P. Collins (HWM) ignition—J D Hamilton (HWM) engine—H. Cantoni (Maserati).

Starting grid 4-3-4

Farina 1 min 50.0 sec—Ascari 1 min 50.0 sec—Taruffi 1 min 53.0 sec—Manzon 1 min 55.0 sec—Downing 1 min 56.0 sec—Parnell 1 min 56.0 sec—Hawthorn 1 min 56.0 sec—Poore 1 min 56.0 sec—Thompson 1 min 57.0 sec—'Bira' 1 min 57.0 sec—Hamilton 1 min 57.0 sec—A G Whitehead 1 min 58.0 sec—Brown 1 min 58.0 sec—Collins 1 min 58.0 sec—Fischer 1 min 58.0 sec—Moss 1 min 59.0 sec—McAlpine 2 min 00 sec—Brandon 2 min 00 sec—Salvadori 2 min 00 sec—P N Whitehead 2 min 00 sec—Trintignant 2 min 00 sec—Murray 2 min 02.0 sec—Claes 2 min 02.0 sec—Hirt 2 min 03.0 sec—Crook 2 min 03.0 sec—Gaze 2 min 05.0 sec—Cantoni 2 min 06.0 sec—Bianco 2 min 07.0 sec—Macklin 2 min 08.0 sec—de Graffenried—Schell—non starters L. Rosier (Ferrari)—K. Wharton (Frazer-Nash)—B. Aston (Aston Butterworth).

GERMAN GRAND PRIX

Nürburgring; 3 August; 18 laps 410 km/255 miles
1 A. Ascari (Ferrari) 3 hr 06 min 13.3 sec 132.26 kph/82.2 mph—2 G. Farina (Ferrari) 3 hr 06 min 27.4 sec—3 R. Fischer (Ferrari) 3 hr 13 min 23.4 sec—4 P. Taruffi (Ferrari) 17 laps—5 J. Behra (Gordini) 17 laps—6 R. Laurent (Ferrari) 16 laps—7 F. Reiss (Veritas) 16 laps—fastest lap, Ascari 10 min 5.1 sec 135.64 kph/84.3 mph—retired Peters (Veritas) lap 1—P. Frere (HWM) gearbox lap 1—F. Bonetto (Maserati) disqualified lap 1—M. Trintignant (Gordini) gearbox lap 1—P. Carini (Ferrari) brakes lap 1—T. Helfrich (Veritas) lap 1—P. Pietsch (Veritas) gearbox lap 1—G. Bianco (Maserati) lap 1—B. Aston (Aston Butterworth) oil pressure lap 2—B. Krause (BMW Reif) lap 3—R. Schoeller (Ferrari) lap 3—H. Cantoni (Maserati) rear axle lap 4—M. Balsa (BMW) lap 5—Nacke (BMW) lap 5—A. Brudes (Veritas) lap 5—F A O Gaze (HWM) de Dion tube lap 6—W. Heeks (AFM) lap 7—R. Manzon (Gordini) wheel lap 8—Klodwig (BMW-Heck) lap 14—H. Klenk (Veritas) lap 14—J. Claes (HWM) lap 15—H. Niedermeyer (AFM) lap 15—T. Ulman (Veritas) lap 16.

Starting grid 4-3-4

Ascari—Farina—Trintignant—Manzon—Taruffi—Fischer—Pietsch—Klenk—Heeks—Bonetto—Behra—Reiss—Frere—Gaze—Ulman—Bianco—Laurent—Helfrich—Brudes—Peters—Aston—Niedermeyer—Krause—Schoeller—Balsa—Cantoni—Carini—Klodwig—Nacke—Claes.

DUTCH GRAND PRIX

Zandvoort; 17 August; 90 laps 376 km/234 miles
1 A. Ascari (Ferrari) 2 hr 53 min 28.5 sec 130.57 kph/81.15 mph—2 G. Farina (Ferrari) 2 hr 54 min 8.6 sec—3 L. Villoresi (Ferrari) 2 hr 55 min 2.9 sec—4 J M Hawthorn (Cooper-Bristol) 88 laps—5 R. Manzon (Gordini) 87 laps—6 M. Trintignant (Gordini) 87 laps—7 J D Hamilton (HWM) 85 laps—8 L. Macklin (HWM) 84 laps—9 C. Landi, J. Flinterman (Maserati) 83 laps—not classified as finishers A van der Lof (HWM)—fastest lap, Ascari 1 min 49.8 sec 137.47 kph/85.44 mph—retired G. Bianco (Maserati) rear axle lap 4—J. Flinterman (Maserati) rear axle lap 7—J. Behra (Gordini) magneto lap 10—P. Frere (Gordini) gearbox lap 15—C. de Tornaco (Ferrari) valve lap 19—K H Downing (Connaught) oil pressure lap 27—S. Moss (ERA) engine lap 73—K. Wharton (Frazer-Nash) rear axle lap 77.

Starting grid 3-2-3

Ascari 1 min 46.5 sec—Farina 1 min 48.6 sec—Hawthorn 1 min 51.6 sec—Villoresi 1 min 51.8 sec—Trintignant 1 min 53.0 sec—Behra 1 min 54.5 sec—Wharton 1 min 54.7 sec—Manzon 1 min 54.8 sec—Macklin 1 min 55.2 sec—Hamilton 1 min 55.8 sec—Frere 1 min 58.2 sec—Bianco 1 min 58.2 sec—Downing 1 min 58.6 sec—Van der Lof 1 min 59.4 sec—Flinterman 2 min 01.8 sec—Landi 2 min 02.1 sec—de Tornaco 2 min 03.7 sec—Moss.

ITALIAN GRAND PRIX

Monza; 7 September; 80 laps 502 km/312 miles
1 A. Ascari (Ferrari) 2 hr 50 min 45.6 sec 176.67 kph/109.8 mph—2 F. Gonzalez (Maserati) 2 hr 51 min 47.4 sec—3 L. Villoresi (Ferrari) 2 hr 52 min 52.8 sec—4 G. Farina (Ferrari) 2 hr 52 min 57.0 sec—5 F. Bonetto (Maserati) 79 laps—6 A. Simon (Ferrari) 79 laps—7 P. Taruffi (Ferrari) 77 laps—8 C. Landi (Maserati) 76 laps—9 K. Wharton (Cooper-Bristol) 76 laps—10 L. Rosier (Ferrari) 75 laps—11 H. Cantoni (Maserati) 75 laps—12 D. Poore (Connaught) 74 laps—13 E. Brandon (Cooper-Bristol) 73 laps—14 R. Manzon (Gordini) 69 laps—15 A. Brown (Cooper-Bristol) 68 laps—not classified as finisher

ITALIAN GRAND PRIX—*continued*

J M Hawthorn (Cooper-Bristol)—fastest lap, Ascari and Gonzalez 2 min 6.1 sec 179.84 kph/111.77 mph—retired E. Bayol (OSCA) gearbox 0 laps—R. Fischer (Ferrari) engine lap 3—K. McAlpine (Connaught) lap 5—M. Trintignant (Gordini) valve gear lap 5—F. Rol (Maserati) engine lap 24—J. Behra (Gordini) lap 43—G. Bianco (Maserati) lap 47—S. Moss (Connaught) pushrod lap 61.

Starting grid 4-4-4

Ascari 2 min 05.7 sec—Villoresi 2 min 06.6 sec—Farina 2 min 07.0 sec—Trintignant 2 min 07.2 sec—Gonzalez 2 min 07.6 sec—Taruffi 2 min 07.8 sec—Manzon 2 min 08.2 sec—Simon 2 min 09.1 sec—Moss 2 min 09.8 sec—Bayol 2 min 10.6 sec—Behra 2 min 10.8 sec—Hawthorn 2 min 11.2 sec—Bonetto 2 min 11.6 sec—Fischer 2 min 11.8 sec—Wharton 2 min 12.2 sec—Rod 2 min 12.7 sec—Rosier 2 min 12.7 sec—Landi 2 min 13.0 sec—Poore 2 min 14.0 sec—Brandon 2 min 14.0 sec—Brown 2 min 15.0 sec—McAlpine 2 min 15.1 sec—Cantoni 2 min 15.9 sec—Bianco 2 min 17.1 sec—failed to qualify B. Aston (Aston Butterworth)—H. Stuck (Ferrari)—P N Whitehead (Ferrari).

1952 WORLD CHAMPIONSHIP

1 A. Ascari 36, 52½—2 G. Farina 25, 28—3 P. Taruffi 22—4 R. Fischer 10—4= J M Hawthorn 10—6 R. Manzon 9—7 L. Villoresi 8—8 F. Gonzalez 6½—9 J. Behra 6—10 K. Wharton 3—10= D. Poore 3—12 F. Bonetto 2—12= A. Brown 2—12= P. Frere 2—12= M. Trintignant 2—12= E. Thompson 2.

1953

ARGENTINE GRAND PRIX

Buenos Aires; 18 January; 97 laps 386 km/240 miles
1 A. Ascari (Ferrari) 3 hr 1 min 4.6 sec 125.73 kph/78.14 mph—2 L. Villoresi (Ferrari) 96 laps—3 F. Gonzalez (Maserati) 96 laps—4 J M Hawthorn (Ferrari) 96 laps—5 O. Galvez (Maserati) 96 laps—6 J. Behra (Gordini) 91 laps—7 M. Trintignant (Gordini) 91 laps—8 J D Barber (Cooper-Bristol) 90 laps—9 A. Brown (Cooper-Bristol) 87 laps—fastest lap, Ascari 1 min 48.4 sec 129.28 kph/80.35 mph—retired Schwelm Cruz (Cooper) lost wheel lap 21—P. Birger (Gordini) crown wheel lap 22—C. Menditeguy (Gordini) gearbox lap 28—G. Farina (Ferrari) accident lap 32—J M Fangio (Maserati) universal joint lap 36—F. Bonetto (Maserati) transmission—R. Manzon (Gordini) lost wheel lap 68.

Starting grid 4-3-4

Ascari 1 min 55.4 sec—Fangio 1 min 56.1 sec—Villoresi 1 min 56.5 sec—Farina 1 min 57.1 sec—Gonzalez 1 min 58.4 sec—Hawthorn 1 min 59.4 sec—Trintignant 2 min 00.4 sec—Manzon 2 min 01.9 sec—Galvez—Menditeguy—Behra—Brown—Schwelm—Birger—Bonetto—Barber.

DUTCH GRAND PRIX

Zandvoort; 7 June; 90 laps 376 km/234 miles
1 A Ascari (Ferrari) 2 hr 53 min 35.7 sec 130.39 kph/81.04 mph—2 G. Farina (Ferrari) 2 hr 53 min 46.2 sec—3 F. Bonetto, F. Gonzalez (Maserati) 89 laps—4 J M Hawthorn (Ferrari) 89 laps—5 E. de Graffenried (Maserati) 88 laps—6 M. Trintignant (Gordini) 87 laps—7 L. Rosier (Ferrari) 86 laps—8 P. Collins (HWM) 84 laps—9 S. Moss (Connaught) 83 laps—not classified as finisher J. Claes (Connaught)—fastest lap, Villoresi 1 min 52.8 sec 133.79 kph/83.15 mph—retired L. Macklin (HWM) throttle lap 7—R. Salvadori (Connaught) valve lap 14—K. Wharton (Cooper-Bristol) suspension lap 17—F. Gonzalez (Maserati) rear axle lap 22—R. Mieres (Gordini) transmission lap 28—J M Fangio (Maserati) rear axle lap 36—H. Schell (Gordini) transmission lap 59—K. McAlpine (Connaught) engine lap 62—L. Villoresi (Ferrari) fumes lap 66.

Starting grid 3-2-3

Ascari 1 min 51.1 sec—Fangio 1 min 52.7 sec—Farina 1 min 53.0 sec—Villoresi 1 min 53.7 sec—Gonzalez 1 min 54.1 sec—Hawthorn 1 min 54.9 sec—de Graffenried 1 min 58.7 sec—Rosier 1 min 59.5 sec—Moss 2 min 00.0 sec—Schell 2 min 00.1 sec—Salvadori 2 min 00.5 sec—Trintignant 2 min 01.2 sec—Bonetto 2 min 01.5 sec—McAlpine 2 min 01.9 sec—Macklin 2 min 02.4 sec—Collins 2 min 03.1 sec—Claes 2 min 03.9 sec—Wharton 2 min 06.4 sec—Mieres 2 min 08.5 sec.

BELGIAN GRAND PRIX

Spa-Francorchamps; 21 June; 36 laps 507 km/315 miles
1 A. Ascari (Ferrari) 2 hr 48 min 30.4 sec 180.96 kph/112.47 mph—2 L. Villoresi (Ferrari) 2 hr 51 min 18.5 sec—3 O. Marimon (Maserati) 35 laps—4 E. de Graffenried (Maserati) 35 laps—5 M. Trintignant (Gordini) 35 laps—6 J M Hawthorn (Ferrari) 35 laps—7 H. Schell (Gordini) 33 laps—8 L. Rosier (Ferrari) 33 laps—9 F. Wacker (Gordini) 32 laps—10 P. Frere (HWM) 30 laps—11 A. Pilette (Connaught) 29 laps—fastest lap, Gonzalez 4 min 34.0 sec 185.47 kph/115.27 mph—retired A. Legat (Veritas Meteor) engine lap 1—G. Birger (Gordini) engine lap 4—L. Macklin (HWM) exhaust lap 5—J. Behra (Gordini) gasket lap 8—P. Collins (HWM) clutch lap 9—F. Gonzalez (Maserati) throttle lap 11—J M Fangio (Maserati) engine lap 13—G. Farina (Ferrari) engine lap 16—J M Fangio (Claes' Maserati) accident lap 35.

Starting grid 3-2-3

Fangio 4 min 30.0 sec—Ascari 4 min 32.0 sec—Gonzalez 4 min 32.0 sec—Farina 4 min 36.0 sec—Villoresi 4 min 39.0 sec—Marimon 4 min 40.0 sec—Hawthorn 4 min 42.0 sec—Trintignant 4 min 45.0 sec—de Graffenried 4 min 49.0 sec—Claes 4 min 50.0 sec—Frere 4 min 52.0 sec—Schell 4 min 53.0 sec—Rosier 4 min 56.0 sec—Behra 4 min 57.0 sec—Wacker 5 min 03.0 sec—Collins 5 min 03.0 sec—Macklin 5 min 14.0 sec—Pilette 5 min 23.0 sec—Legat 5 min 41.0 sec—Birger 5 min 58.0 sec.

FRENCH GRAND PRIX

Rheims; *Grand Circuit de Compétition de Reims*; 5 July; 60 laps 500 km/311 miles
1 J M Hawthorn (Ferrari) 2 hr 34 min 18.6 sec 182.86 kph/113.65 mph—2 J M Fangio (Maserati) 2 hr 44 min 19.6 sec—3 F. Gonzalez (Maserati) 2 hr 44 min 20.0 sec—4 A. Ascari (Ferrari) 2 hr 44 min 23.2 sec—5 G. Farina (Ferrari) 2 hr 45 min 26.2 sec—6 L. Villoresi (Ferrari) 2 hr 45 min 34.5 sec—7 E. de Graffenried (Maserati) 58 laps—8 L. Rosier (Ferrari) 56 laps—9 O. Marimon (Maserati) 55 laps—10 J. Behra (Gordini) 55 laps—11 F R Gerard (Cooper-Bristol) 55 laps—12 J. Claes (Connaught) 53 laps—13 P. Collins (HWM) 52 laps—14 Y. Giraud-Cabantous (HWM) 50 laps—15 L. Chiron (OSCA) 43 laps—fastest lap, Fangio 2 min 41.1 sec 186.5 kph/115.91 mph—retired R. Salvadori (Connaught) ignition lap 2—H. Schell (Gordini) engine lap 4—R. Mieres (Gordini) rear axle lap 4—L. Macklin (HWM) clutch lap 9—M. Trintignant (Gordini) transmission lap 14—K. Wharton (Cooper-Bristol) engine lap 17—E. Bayol (OSCA) lap 18—'B Bira' (Connaught) transmission lap 29—S. Moss (Cooper-Alta) clutch lap 38—F. Bonetto (Maserati) engine lap 42.

Starting grid 3-2-3

Ascari 2 min 41.2 sec—Bonetto 2 min 41.5 sec—Villoresi 2 min 41.9 sec—Fangio 2 min 42.0 sec—Gonzalez 2 min 42.4 sec—Farina 2 min 42.5 sec—Hawthorn 2 min 43.5 sec—Marimon 2 min 44.7 sec—de Graffenried 2 min 46.1 sec—Gerard 2 min 54.2 sec—Moss 2 min 55.7 sec—Wharton 2 min 55.8 sec—Bayol 2 min 56.9 sec—Macklin 2 min 57.2 sec—Collins 3 min 02.0 sec—Giraud-Cabantous 3 min 06.7 sec—Salvadori 3 min 23.0 sec—Schell 3 min 25.8 sec—Claes 4 min 08.8 sec—Behra—Trintignant—Mieres—Chiron.

BRITISH GRAND PRIX

Silverstone; 18 July; 90 laps 263 miles/423 km
1 A. Ascari (Ferrari) 2 hr 50 min 00 sec 92.97 mph/149.59 kph—2 J M Fangio (Maserati) 2 hr 51 min 00 sec—3 G. Farina (Ferrari) 88 laps—4 F. Gonzalez (Maserati) 88 laps—5 J M Hawthorn (Ferrari) 87 laps—6 F. Bonetto (Maserati) 82 laps—7 'B Bira' (Connaught) 82 laps—8 K. Wharton (Cooper-Bristol) 80 laps—9 P N Whitehead (Cooper-Alta) 79 laps—10 L. Rosier (Ferrari) 78 laps—fastest lap, Gonzalez and Ascari 1 min 50.0 sec 95.79 mph/154.13 kph—retired K. McAlpine (Connaught) 0 laps—A. Crook (Cooper-Alta) fuel feed 0 laps—F R Gerard (Cooper-Bristol) lap 8—J D Hamilton (HWM) clutch lap 14—M. Trintignant (Gordini) back axle lap 15—I M M Stewart (Connaught) ignition lap 26—J. Behra (Gordini) fuel feed lap 30—L. Macklin (HWM) clutch lap 31—R. Salvadori (Connaught) suspension lap 50—J. Fairman (HWM) clutch lap 54—P. Collins (HWM) accident lap 56—A. Brown (Cooper-Bristol) fan belt lap 61—O. Marimon (Maserati) engine lap 66—L. Villoresi (Ferrari) back axle lap 67—A P R Rolt (Connaught) half shaft lap 71—J R Stewart (Cooper-Bristol) accident lap 79.

Starting grid 4-3-4

Ascari 1 min 48.0 sec—Gonzalez 1 min 49.0 sec—Hawthorn 1 min 49.0 sec—Fangio 1 min 50.0 sec—Farina 1 min 50.0 sec—Villoresi 1 min 51.0 sec—Marimon 1 min 51.0 sec—Trintignant 1 min 52.0 sec—Schell 1 min 52.0 sec—Rolt 1 min 54.0 sec—Wharton 1 min 54.0 sec—Macklin 1 min 57.0 sec—McAlpine 1 min 57.0 sec—P. Whitehead 1 min 57.0 sec—J R Stewart 1 min 58.0 sec—Bonetto 1 min 58.0 sec—Hamilton 2 min 02.0 sec—Gerard 2 min 02.0 sec—'Bira' 2 min 04.0 sec—I M M Stewart 2 min 04.0 sec—Brown 2 min 04.0 sec—Behra 2 min 04.0 sec—Collins 2 min 06.0 sec—Rosier 2 min 07.0 sec—Crook 2 min 07.0 sec—de Graffenried 3 min 09.0 sec—Fairman 2 min 32.0 sec—Salvadori.

GERMAN GRAND PRIX

Nürburgring; 2 August; 18 laps 412 km/256 miles
1 G. Farina (Ferrari) 3 hr 2 min 25.0 sec 134.98 kph/83.89 mph—2 J M Fangio (Maserati) 3 hr 3 min 29.0 sec—3 J M Hawthorn (Ferrari) 3 hr 4 min 8.6 sec—4 F. Bonetto (Maserati) 3 hr 11 min 13.6 sec—5 E. de Graffenried (Maserati) 17 laps—6 S. Moss (Cooper-Alta) 17 laps—7 J. Swaters (Ferrari) 17 laps—8 A. Ascari, L. Villoresi (Ferrari) 17 laps—9 H. Herrmann (Veritas) 17 laps—10 L. Rosier (Ferrari) 17 laps—11 R. Nuckey (Cooper-Bristol) 16 laps—12 T. Helfrich (Veritas) 16 laps—13 K. McAlpine (Connaught) 16 laps—14 Krause (BMW) 16 laps—15 Klodwig (BMW-Heck) 15 laps—16 W. Seidel (Veritas) 14 laps—fastest lap, Ascari 9 min 56.0 sec 137.76 kph/85.62 mph—retired H. Stuck (AFM-Bristol) lap 1—E. Loof (Veritas) fuel pump lap 1—R. Salvadori (Connaught) rocker lap 1—M. Trintignant (Gordini) differential lap 1—G. Bechem (AFM) lap 3—K. Adolff (Ferrari) lap 4—Fitzau (AFM) lap 4—H. Schell (Gordini) gasket lap 7—'B. Bira' (Connaught) rocker lap 7—J. Behra (Gordini) gears lap 8—W. Heeks (Veritas) lap 9—Karch (Veritas) lap 11—J. Claes (Connaught) lap 13—O. Marimon (Maserati) lap 14—L. Villoresi, A. Ascari (Ferrari) lap 14—A. Brown (Cooper-Bristol) rear suspension lap 16—E. Barth (EMW)—E. Bauer (Veritas).

Starting grid 4-3-4

Ascari 9 min 59.8 sec—Fangio 10 min 03.7 sec—Farina 10 min 04.1 sec—Hawthorn 10 min 12.6 sec—Trintignant 10 min 21.7 sec—Villoresi 10 min 22.8 sec—Bonetto 10 min 40.8 sec—Marimon 10 min 41.0 sec—Behra 10 min 45.5 sec—Schell 10 min 46.2 sec—de Graffenried 10 min 46.6 sec—Moss 10 min 48.3 sec—Salvadori 10 min 57.5 sec—Herrmann 10 min 56.8 sec—Behra 11 min 02.1 sec—McAlpine 11 min 07.3 sec—Brown 11 min 08.7 sec—Heeks 11 min 18.0 sec—Swaters 11 min 18.9 sec—Nuckey 11 min 19.7 sec—Fitzau 11 min 23.4 sec—Rosier 11 min 27.4 sec—Stuck 11 min 37.2 sec—Barth 11 min 40.8 sec—Claes 11 min 45.5 sec—Krause 11 min 49.5 sec—Adolff 11 min 53.1 sec—Helfrich 11 min 56.3 sec—Seidel 11 min 59.3 sec—Bechem 12 min 13.3 sec—Loof 12 min 16.8 sec—Klodwig 12 min 24.6 sec—Bauer—Karch.

SWISS GRAND PRIX

Bremgarten, Berne; 23 August; 65 laps 473 km/294 miles
1 A. Ascari (Ferrari) 3 hr 1 min 34.4 sec 156.35 kph/97.17 mph—2 G. Farina (Ferrari) 3 hr 2 min 47.33 sec—3 J M Hawthorn (Ferrari) 3 hr 3 min 10.4 sec—4 F. Bonetto, J M Fangio (Maserati) 64 laps—5 H. Lang (Maserati) 62 laps—6 L. Villoresi (Ferrari) 62 laps—7 K. Wharton (Cooper-Bristol) 62 laps—8 M. de Terra (Ferrari) 51 laps—9 A. Scherrer (HWM) 49 laps—fastest lap, Ascari 2 min 41.3 sec 162.44 kph/100.96 mph—retired J. Swaters (Ferrari) accident lap 1—L. Rosier (Ferrari) lap 1—P. Frere (HWM) engine lap 2—P. Hirt (Ferrari) water pump lap 17—L. Macklin (HWM) oil pump lap 29—J M Fangio (Maserati) piston lap 29—J. Behra (Gordini) transmission lap 37—M. Trintignant (Gordini) transmission lap 43—O. Marimon (Maserati) oil pipe lap 46—E. de Graffenried (Maserati) transmission lap 49—C. Landi (Maserati) gearbox lap 54.

Starting grid 3-2-3

Fangio 2 min 40.1 sec—Ascari 2 min 40.7 sec—Farina 2 min 42.6 sec—Trintignant 2 min 43.8 sec—Marimon 2 min 44.5 sec—Villoresi 2 min 44.6 sec—Hawthorn 2 min 48.1 sec—de Graffenried 2 min 49.9 sec—Wharton 2 min 51.5 sec—Bonetto 2 min 52.3 sec—Lang 2 min 54.8 sec—Behra 2 min 55.0 sec—Swaters 2 min 55.1 sec—Rosier—Macklin 2 min 57.1 sec—Frere 2 min 57.3 sec—Hirt 3 min 01.5 sec—Scherrer 3 min 07.4 sec—de Terra 3 min 21.1 sec—Landi.

ITALIAN GRAND PRIX

Monza; 13 September; 80 laps 504 km/313 miles
1 J M Fangio (Maserati) 2 hr 49 min 45.9 sec 178.1 kph/110.69 mph—2 G. Farina (Ferrari) 2 hr 49 min 47.3 sec—3 L. Villoresi (Ferrari) 79 laps—J M Hawthorn (Ferrari) 79 laps—M. Trintignant (Gordini) 79 laps—6 R. Mieres (Gordini) 77 laps—7 S. Mantovani, L. Musso (Maserati) 76 laps—8 U. Maglioli (Ferrari) 76 laps—9 H. Schell (Gordini) 75 laps—10 L. Chiron (OSCA) 72 laps—11 'B. Bira' (Maserati) 72 laps—12 A. Brown (Cooper-Bristol) 70 laps—13 S. Moss (Cooper-Alta) 70 laps—14 H. Stuck (AFM-Bristol) 67 laps—15 Y. Giraud-Cabantous (HWM) 67 laps—16 L. Rosier (Ferrari) 65 laps—fastest lap, Fangio 2 min 4.5 sec 182.14 kph/113.2 mph—not classified as finishers J. Fairman (HWM)—K. Wharton (Cooper-Bristol)—K. McAlpine (Connaught)—retired L. Macklin (HWM) lap 7—J. Claes (Connaught) fuel line lap 8—J. Fitch (HWM) lap 15—C. Landi (Maserati) lap 19—E. Bayol (OSCA) lap 18—R. Salvadori (Connaught) lap 34—P. Carini (Ferrari) lap 41—E. de Graffenried (Maserati) lap 71—O. Marimon (Maserati) accident lap 76—F. Bonetto (Maserati) fuel lap 78—A. Ascari (Ferrari) accident lap 80.

Starting grid 3-3-3

Ascari 2 min 02.7 sec—Fangio 2 min 03.2 sec—Farina 2 min 03.9 sec—Marimon 2 min 04.1 sec—Villoresi 2 min 04.6 sec—Hawthorn 2 min 04.9 sec—Bonetto 2 min 05.1 sec—Trintignant 2 min 05.7 sec—de Graffenried 2 min 05.9 sec—Mantovani 2 min 07.5 sec—Bayol 2 min 07.8 sec—Salvadori 2 min 08.0 sec—Schell 2 min 08.0 sec—Mieres 2 min 08.7 sec—Rosier 2 min 09.3 sec—McAlpine 2 min 09.5 sec—Wharton 2 min 10.1 sec—Carini 2 min 11.2 sec—Landi 2 min 12.8 sec—Fairman 2 min 13.5 sec—'Bira' 2 min 13.6 sec—Brown 2 min 14.8 sec—Chiron 2 min 15.0 sec—Fitch 2 min 18.1 sec—Macklin 2 min 18.2 sec—Giraud-Cabantous 2 min 20.8 sec—Stuck 2 min 24.1 sec—Claes 2 min 28.2 sec.

1953 WORLD CHAMPIONSHIP

1 A. Ascari 34½, 46½—2 J M Fangio 28, 29½—3 G. Farina 26, 32—4 J M Hawthorn 19, 27—5 L. Villoresi 17—6 F. Gonzalez 15½, 16½—7 E. de Graffenried 7—8 F. Bonetto 6½—9 O. Marimon 4—9= M. Trintignant 4—11 O. Galvez 2—11= H. Lang 2.

1954

ARGENTINE GRAND PRIX

Buenos Aires; 17 January; 3 hours
1 J M Fangio (Maserati) 3 hr 00 min 55.8 sec 87 laps 112.84 kph/70.13 mph—2 G. Farina (Ferrari) 3 hr 02 min 14.8 sec 87 laps—3 F. Gonzalez (Ferrari) 3 hr 03 min 56.8 sec 87 laps—4 M. Trintignant (Ferrari) 86 laps—5 E. Bayol (Gordini) 86 laps—6 H. Schell (Maserati) 84 laps—7 'B. Bira' (Maserati) 83 laps—8 E. de Graffenried (Maserati) 83 laps—9 U. Maglioli (Maserati) 82 laps—fastest lap, Gonzalez 1 min 48.2 sec 129.85 kph/80.7 mph—retired L. Rosier (Maserati) accident lap 2—O. Marimon (Maserati) accident lap 5—J M Hawthorn (Ferrari) accident and disqualified—J. Behra (Gordini) push start and disqualified—J. Daponte (Maserati)—R. Loyer (Gordini)—R. Mieres (Maserati).

Starting grid 4-3-4

Farina 1 min 44.8 sec—Gonzalez 1 min 44.9 sec—Fangio 1 min 45.6 sec—Hawthorn 1 min 47.0 sec—Marimon 1 min 47.4 sec—Trintignant 1 min 47.4 sec—Musso 1 min 48.2 sec—Mieres 1 min 49.0 sec—'Bira' 1 min 49.3 sec—Schell 1 min 50.0 sec—Maglioli—Behra 1 min 50.7 sec—de Graffenried—Loyer—Rosier—Bayol—Daponte—non starter L. Musso (Ferrari).

BELGIAN GRAND PRIX

Spa-Francorchamps; 20 June; 36 laps 507 km/315 miles
1 J M Fangio (Maserati) 2 hr 44 min 42.4 sec 185.16 kph/115.08 mph—2 M. Trintignant (Ferrari) 2 hr 45 min 6.6 sec—3 S. Moss (Maserati) 35 laps—4 F. Gonzalez, J M Hawthorn (Ferrari) 35 laps—5 A. Pilette (Gordini) 35 laps—6 'B. Bira' (Maserati) 35 laps—7 S. Mantovani (Maserati) 34 laps—fastest lap, Fangio 4 min 25.5 sec 191.42 kph/118.97 mph—retired J. Swaters (Ferrari) engine lap 1—F. Gonzalez (Ferrari) piston lap 1—R. Mieres (Maserati) split fuel tank lap 1—O. Marimon (Maserati) engine lap 3—J. Behra (Gordini) rear suspension lap 12—G. Farina (Ferrari) rear axle lap 14—P. Frere (Gordini) engine lap 16.

Starting grid 3-2-3

Fangio 4 min 22.1 sec—Gonzalez 4 min 23.6 sec—Farina 4 min 26.0 sec—Marimon 4 min 27.6 sec—Hawthorn 4 min 29.4 sec—Trintignant 4 min 30.0 sec—Behra 4 min 34.5 sec—Pilette 4 min 40.0 sec—Moss 4 min 40.8 sec—Frere 4 min 42.0 sec—Mantovani 4 min 43.2 sec—Mieres 4 min 43.8 sec—'Bira' 4 min 46.5 sec—Swaters 4 min 54.2 sec.

FRENCH GRAND PRIX

Rheims, *Grand Circuit de Compétition de Reims*;
4 July; 61 laps 500 km/311 miles
1 J M Fangio (Mercedes-Benz) 2 hr 42 min 47.9 sec 186.11 kph/115.67 mph—2 K. Kling (Mercedes-Benz) 2 hr 42 min 48.0 sec—3 R. Manzon (Ferrari) 60 laps—4 'B. Bira' (Maserati) 60 laps—5 L. Villoresi (Maserati) 58 laps—6 J. Behra (Gordini) 56 laps—7 P. Frere (Gordini) 50 laps—fastest lap, Herrmann 2 min 32.9 sec 195.43 kph/121.46 mph—retired A. Ascari (Maserati) transmission lap 1—J. Pollet (Gordini) lap 8—J M Hawthorn (Ferrari) engine lap 9—G. Berger (Gordini) engine lap 9—L. Macklin (HWM) engine lap 10—F. Gonzalez (Ferrari) engine lap 12—R. Salvadori (Maserati) transmission lap 15—H. Hermann (Mercedes-Benz) engine lap 16—K. Wharton (Maserati) transmission lap 19—H. Schell (Maserati) fuel pump lap 19—R. Mieres (Maserati) engine lap 24—L. Rosier (Ferrari) lap 27—O. Marimon (Maserati) gearbox lap 28—M. Trintignant (Ferrari) engine lap 36.

Starting grid 3-2-3

Fangio 2 min 29.4 sec—Kling 2 min 30.4 sec—Ascari 2 min 30.5 sec—Gonzalez 2 min 30.6 sec—Marimon 2 min 31.6 sec—'Bira' 2 min 35.1 sec—Hermann 2 min 35.3 sec—Hawthorn 2 min 35.6 sec—Trintignant 2 min 36.1 sec—Salvadori 2 min 36.3 sec—Mieres 2 min 38.7 sec—Manzon 2 min 42.0 sec—Rosier 2 min 42.1 sec—Villoresi 2 min 42.7 sec—Macklin 2 min 52.5 sec—Wharton—Behra—Pollet—Frere—Berger—Schell.

BRITISH GRAND PRIX

Silverstone; 17 July; 90 laps 270 miles/434 km
1 F. Gonzalez (Ferrari) 2 hr 56 min 14.0 sec 89.69 mph/144.31 kph—2 J M Hawthorn (Ferrari) 2 hr 57 min 24.0 sec—3 O. Marimon (Maserati) 89 laps—4 J M Fangio (Mercedes-Benz) 89 laps—5 M. Trintignant (Ferrari) 87 laps—6 R. Mieres (Maserati) 87 laps—7 K. Kling (Mercedes-Benz) 87 laps—8 K. Wharton (Maserati) 86 laps—9 A. Pilette (Gordini) 86 laps—10 F R Gerard (Cooper-Bristol) 85 laps—11 D. Beauman (Connaught) 84 laps—12 H. Schell (Maserati) 83 laps—13 L. Marr (Connaught) 82 laps—14 L. Thorne (Connaught) 78 laps—15 H. Gould (Cooper-Bristol) 44 laps—fastest lap, Gonzales, Hawthorn, Moss, Ascari, Marimon, Behra, Fangio 1 min 50.0 sec 95.79 mph/154.13 kph—retired R. Nuckey (Cooper-Bristol) engine lap 2—L. Rosier (Ferrari) engine lap 3—P N Whitehead (Cooper-Alta) engine lap 3—R. Manzon (Ferrari) engine lap 16—P. Collins (Vanwall Special) gasket lap 17—C. Bucci (Gordini) accident lap 18—A. Ascari (Maserati) valve lap 21—R. Parnell (Ferrari) cylinder block lap 25—R. Risley-Pritchard (Connaught) steering lap 40—L. Villoresi, A. Ascari (Maserati) connecting rod lap 40—'B. Bira', R. Flockhart (Maserati) accident lap 44—R. Salvadori (Maserati) gearbox lap 53—J. Behra (Gordini) rear suspension lap 55—W J Whitehouse (Connaught) engine lap 64—S. Moss (Maserati) rear axle lap 80.

Starting grid 4-3-4

Fangio 1 min 45.0 sec—Gonzalez 1 min 46.0 sec—Hawthorn 1 min 46.0 sec—Moss 1 min 47.0 sec—Behra 1 min 48.0 sec—Kling 1 min 48.0 sec—Salvadori 1 min 48.0 sec—Trintignant 1 min 48.0 sec—Wharton 1 min 49.0 sec—'Bira' 1 min 49.0 sec—Collins 1 min 50.0 sec—Pilette 1 min 51.0 sec—Bucci 1 min 52.0 sec—Parnell 1 min 52.0 sec—Manzon 1 min 52.0 sec—Schell 1 min 53.0 sec—Beauman 1 min 55.0 sec—Gerard 1 min 55.0 sec—Whitehouse 1 min 56.0 sec—Gould 1 min 56.0 sec—Risley-Pritchard 1 min 58.0 sec—Marr 1 min 58.0 sec—Thorne 1 min 59.0 sec—Whitehead 2 min 00 sec—Brandon 2 min 05.0 sec reserve driver R. Nuckey—Villoresi—Marimon—Rosier—Ascari—Mieres.

GERMAN GRAND PRIX

Nürburgring; 1 August; 22 laps 502 km/312 miles
1 J M Fangio (Mercedes-Benz) 3 hr 45 min 45.8 sec 133.18 kph/82.77 mph—2 F. Gonzalez, J M Hawthorn (Ferrari) 3 hr 47 min 22.3 sec—3 M. Trintignant (Ferrari) 3 hr 50 min 54.4 sec—4 K. Kling (Mercedes-Benz) 3 hr 51 min 52.3 sec—5 S. Mantovani (Maserati) 3 hr 54 min 36.3 sec—6 P. Taruffi (Ferrari) 21 laps—7 H. Schell (Maserati) 21 laps—8 L. Rosier (Ferrari) 21 laps—9 R. Manzon (Ferrari) 20 laps—10 J. Behra (Gordini) 20 laps—fastest lap, Kling 9 min 55.1 sec 137.97 kph/85.75 mph—retired A. Pilette (Gordini) suspension lap 1—S. Moss (Maserati) big-end bearing lap 2—R. Mieres (Maserati) fuel leak lap 3—J M Hawthorn (Ferrari) rear axle lap 4—P. Frere (Gordini) wheel lap 5—H. Hermann (Mercedes-Benz) fuel pipe lap 8—T. Helfrich (Klenk Meteor) engine lap 9—C. Bucci (Gordini) wheel lap 9—H. Lang (Mercedes-Benz) stalled lap 11—'B. Bira' (Maserati) steering lap 19.

Starting grid 3-2-3

Fangio 9 min 50.1 sec—Hawthorn 9 min 53.3 sec—Moss 10 min 00.7 sec—Herrmann 10 min 01.5 sec—Gonzalez 10 min 01.8 sec—Frere 10 min 05.9 sec—Trintignant 10 min 07.5 sec—Behra 10 min 11.9 sec—Lang 10 min 13.1 sec—Manzon 10 min 16.0 sec—Taruffi 10 min 23.0 sec—Schell 10 min 28.7 sec—Mantovani 10 min 39.1 sec—Bucci 10 min 43.7 sec—Mieres 10 min 47.0 sec—Rosier 11 min 04.3 sec—'Bira' 11 min 10.3 sec—Pilette 11 min 13.4 sec—Helfrich 11 min 18.3 sec—Kling—non starter, O. Marimon (Maserati) following a fatal accident in practice. L. Villoresi withdrew.

SWISS GRAND PRIX

Bremgarten, Berne; 22 August; 66 laps 451 km/280 miles
1 J M Fangio (Mercedes-Benz) 3 hr 00 min 34.5 sec 159.56 kph/99.17 mph—2 F. Gonzalez (Ferrari) 3 hr 01 min 32.3

sec—3 H. Herrmann (Mercedes-Benz) 65 laps—4 R. Mieres (Maserati) 64 laps—5 S. Mantovani (Maserati) 64 laps—6 K. Wharton (Maserati) 64 laps—7 U. Maglioli (Ferrari) 62 laps—8 J. Swaters (Ferrari) 58 laps—fastest lap, Fangio 2 min 39.7 sec 163.96 kph/101.9 mph—retired J. Behra (Gordini) transmission lap 8—F. Wacker (Gordini) engine lap 10—S. Moss (Maserati) oil pressure lap 21—H. Schell (Maserati) oil pressure lap 23—J M Hawthorn (Ferrari) fuel pump lap 29—M. Trintignant (Ferrari) engine lap 33—K. Kling (Mercedes-Benz) engine lap 38.

Starting grid 3-2-3

Gonzalez 2 min 39.5 sec—Fangio 2 min 39.7 sec—Moss 2 min 41.4 sec—Trintignant 2 min 41.7 sec—Kling 2 min 41.9 sec—Hawthorn 2 min 43.2 sec—Herrmann 2 min 45.0 sec—Wharton 2 min 46.2 sec—Mantovani 2 min 56.9 sec—Maglioli 3 min 08.2 sec—Mieres 3 min 09.3 sec—Schell 3 min 12.1 sec—Behra 3 min 16.4 sec—Wacker 3 min 20.3 sec—Swaters 3 min 20.4 sec—non starters C. Bucci (Gordini)—R. Manzon (Ferrari)—R. Salvadori (Maserati)—E. de Graffenried (Maserati).

ITALIAN GRAND PRIX

Monza; 5 September; 80 laps 504 km/313 miles
1 J M Fangio (Mercedes-Benz) 2 hr 47 min 47.9 sec 180.17 kph/111.98 mph—2 J M Hawthorn (Ferrari) 79 laps—3 F. Gonzalez, U. Maglioli (Ferrari) 78 laps—4 H. Herrmann (Mercedes-Benz) 77 laps—5 M. Trintignant (Ferrari) 75 laps—6 F. Wacker (Gordini) 75 laps—7 P. Collins (Vanwall) 75 laps—8 L. Rosier (Maserati) 74 laps—9 S. Mantovani (Maserati) 74 laps—10 S. Moss (Maserati) 71 laps—11 G. Daponte (Maserati) 70 laps—fastest lap, Gonzalez 2 min 0.8 sec 187.61 kph/116.6 mph—retired J. Behra (Gordini) engine lap 3—C. Bucci (Gordini) lap 14—F. Gonzalez (Ferrari) engine lap 14—R. Manzon (Ferrari) engine lap 14—L. Musso (Maserati) lap 35—R. Mieres (Maserati) back axle lap 35—K. Kling (Mercedes-Benz) accident lap 38—L. Villoresi (Maserati) clutch lap 42—A. Ascari (Ferrari) engine lap 49—F. Gonzalez (Ferrari) overcome by fumes lap 59

Starting grid 3-3-3

Fangio 1 min 59.0 sec—Ascari 1 min 59.2 sec—Moss 1 min 59.3 sec—Kling 1 min 59.6 sec—Gonzalez 2 min 00.0 sec—Villoresi 2 min 00.2 sec—Hawthorn 2 min 00.2 sec—Herrmann 2 min 01.4 sec—Mantovani 2 min 01.6 sec—Mieres 2 min 01.7 sec—Trintignant 2 min 02.3 sec—Behra 2 min 02.4 sec—Maglioli 2 min 03.5 sec—Musso 2 min 03.5 sec—Manzon 2 min 04.7 sec—Collins 2 min 05.2 sec—Bucci 2 min 05.5 sec—Wacker 2 min 08.0 sec—Daponte 2 min 09.5 sec—Rosier 2 min 11.0 sec.

SPANISH GRAND PRIX

Pedralbes; 26 October; 80 laps 504 km/313 miles
1 J M Hawthorn (Ferrari) 3 hr 13 min 52.1 sec 157.57 kph/97.93 mph—2 L. Musso (Maserati) 3 hr 15 min 5.3 sec—3 J M Fangio (Mercedes-Benz) 79 laps—4 R. Mieres (Maserati) 79 laps—5 K. Kling (Mercedes-Benz) 79 laps—6 F. Godia (Maserati) 76 laps—7 L. Rosier (Maserati) 74 laps—8 K. Wharton (Maserati) 74 laps—9 'B. Bira' (Maserati) 68 laps—fastest lap, Ascari 2 min 20.4 sec 162.17 kph/100.79 mph—retired L. Villoresi (Lancia) transmission lap 2—R. Manzon (Ferrari) engine lap 3—A. Ascari (Lancia) clutch lap 10—J. Swaters (Ferrari) engine lap 16—J. Behra (Gordini) brakes lap 17—S. Moss (Maserati) oil pump drive lap 20—H. Schell (Maserati) accident lap 29—J. Pollet (Gordini) lap 37—M. Trintignant (Ferrari) gearbox lap 47—H. Herrmann (Mercedes-Benz) clutch lap 49—E. de Graffenried, O. Volunterio (Maserati) engine lap 57—S. Mantovani (Maserati) locked brake lap 58.

Starting grid 4-3-4

Ascari 2 min 18.1 sec—Fangio 2 min 19.1 sec—Hawthorn 2 min 20.6 sec—Schell 2 min 20.6 sec—Villoresi 2 min 21.0 sec—Moss 2 min 21.1 sec—Musso 2 min 21.5 sec—Trintignant 2 min 21.9 sec—Herrmann 2 min 21.9 sec—Mantovani 2 min 22.0 sec—Mieres 2 min 22.3 sec—Kling 2 min 23.4 sec—Godia 2 min 24.2 sec—Wharton 2 min 25.7 sec—'Bira' 2 min 26.1 sec—Pollet 2 min 27.4 sec—Manzon 2 min 27.5 sec—Behra 2 min 27.8 sec—Swaters 2 min 28.0 sec—Rosier 2 min 29.8 sec—de Graffenried 2 min 29.8 sec.

1954 WORLD CHAMPIONSHIP

1 J M Fangio 42, 57 1/7—2 F. Gonzalez 25 1/7, 26 9/14—3 J M Hawthorn 24 9/14—4 M. Trintignant 17—5 K. King 12—6 H. Herrmann 8—7 R. Mieres 6—7= L. Musso 6—7= G. Farina 6—10 S. Moss 4 1/7—10= O. Marimon 4 1/7—12 R. Manzon 4—12= S. Mantovani 4—14 'B. Bira' 3—15 L. Villoresi 2—15= U. Maglioli 2—15= A. Pilette 2—15= E. Bayol 2—19 A. Ascari 1 1/7—20 J. Behra 1/7.

1955

ARGENTINE GRAND PRIX

Buenos Aires; 16 January; 96 laps 375 km/233 miles
1 J M Fangio (Mercedes-Benz) 3 hr 0 min 8.6 sec 124.71 kph/77.51 mph—2 F. Gonzalez, G. Farina, M. Trintignant (Ferrari) 3 hr 2 min 8.2 sec—3 G. Farina, M. Trintignant, U. Maglioli (Ferrari) 94 laps—4 H. Herrmann, K. Kling, S. Moss (Mercedes-Benz) 94 laps—5 R. Mieres (Maserati) 91 laps—6 H. Schell, J. Behra (Maserati) 88 laps—7 L. Musso, J. Behra, S. Mantovani (Maserati) 86 laps—fastest lap, Fangio 1 min 48.3 sec 129.52 kph/80.5 mph—retired J. Behra (Maserati) accident lap 3—P. Birger (Gordini) accident lap 3—C. Menditeguy (Maserati) accident lap 3—L. Villoresi (Lancia) fuel feed lap 4—K. Kling (Mercedes-Benz) engine lap 4—E. Bayol (Gordini) engine lap 4—A. Ascari (Lancia) accident lap 20—S. Moss (Mercedes-Benz) heat exhaustion lap 28—J. Iglesias (Gordini) heat exhaustion—M. Trintignant (Ferrari) heat exhaustion lap 32—C. Bucci (Gordini) heat exhaustion—E. Castellotti (Lancia)—'Uria' (Gordini).

Starting grid 4-3-4

Gonzalez 1 min 43.1 sec—Ascari 1 min 43.6 sec—Fangio 1 min 43.6 sec—Behra 1 min 43.8 sec—Farina 1 min 43.8 sec—Kling 1 min 44.1 sec—Schell 1 min 44.3 sec—Moss 1 min 44.6 sec—Birger 1 min 44.8 sec—Herrmann 1 min 44.9 sec—Villoresi 1 min 45.2 sec—Castellotti 1 min 45.3 sec—Menditeguy 1 min 45.4 sec—Trintignant 1 min 45.8 sec—Bayol 1 min 46.1 sec—Mieres 1 min 46.2 sec—Iglesias 1 min 46.3 sec—Musso 1 min 46.4 sec—Mantovani 1 min 46.4 sec—Bucci 1 min 47.6 sec—'Uria' 1 min 52.3 sec—Maglioli 2 min 01.5 sec.

MONACO GRAND PRIX

Monte Carlo; 22 May; 100 laps 314 km/195 miles
1 M. Trintignant (Ferrari) 2 hr 58 min 09.8 sec 105.89 kph/65.81 mph—2 E. Castellotti (Lancia) 2 hr 58 min 30.0 sec—3 J. Behra, C. Perdisa (Maserati) 99 laps—4 G. Farina (Ferrari) 99 laps—5 L. Villoresi (Lancia) 99 laps—6 L. Chiron (Lancia) 95 laps—7 J. Pollet (Gordini) 91 laps—8 P. Taruffi, P. Frere (Ferrari) 86 laps—9 S. Moss (Mercedes-Benz) 81 laps—fastest lap, Fangio 1 min 42.4 sec 110.59 kph/68.73 mph—retired L. Musso (Maserati) transmission lap 8—L. Rosier (Maserati) split tank lap 9—J M Hawthorn (Vanwall) throttle lap 23—A. Simon (Mercedes-Benz) engine lap 25—R. Manzon (Gordini) gearbox lap 39—J M Fangio (Mercedes-Benz) transmission lap 50—E. Bayol (Gordini) rear axle lap 64—R. Mieres (Maserati) transmission lap 65—H. Schell (Ferrari) engine lap 69—A. Ascari (Lancia) accident lap 81—C. Perdisa, J. Behra (Maserati) accident lap 87.

MONACO GRAND PRIX—*continued*

Starting grid 3-2-3

Fangio 1 min 41.1 sec—Ascari 1 min 41.1 sec—Moss 1 min 41.2 sec—Castellotti 1 min 42.0 sec—Behra 1 min 42.6 sec—Mieres 1 min 43.7 sec—Villoresi 1 min 43.7 sec—Musso 1 min 44.3 sec—Trintignant 1 min 44.4 sec—Simon 1 min 45.5 sec—Perdisa 1 min 45.6 sec—Hawthorn 1 min 45.6 sec—Manzon 1 min 46.0 sec—Farina 1 min 46.0 sec—Taruffi 1 min 46.0 sec—Bayol 1 min 46.5 sec—Rosier 1 min 46.7 sec—Schell 1 min 46.8 sec—Chiron 1 min 47.3 sec—Pollet 1 min 49.4 sec—non starters E N Whiteway (HWM)—L. Macklin (Maserati).

BELGIAN GRAND PRIX

Spa-Francorchamps; 5 June; 36 laps 508 km/316 miles
1 J M Fangio (Mercedes-Benz) 2 hr 39 min 29.0 sec 191.21 kph/118.84 mph—2 S. Moss (Mercedes-Benz) 2 hr 39 min 37.1 sec—3 G. Farina (Ferrari) 2 hr 41 min 9.5 sec—4 P. Frere (Ferrari) 2 hr 42 min 54.5 sec—5 R. Mieres, J. Behra (Maserati) 35 laps—6 M. Trintignant (Ferrari) 35 laps—7 L. Musso (Maserati) 34 laps—8 C. Perdisa (Maserati) 33 laps—9 L. Rosier (Maserati) 33 laps—fastest lap, Fangio 4 min 20.6 sec 195.03 kph/121.21 mph—retired J. Behra (Maserati) accident lap 4—J M Hawthorn (Vanwall) oil leak lap 12—E. Castellotti (Lancia) engine lap 16—K. Kling (Mercedes-Benz) oil pipe lap 22.

Starting grid 3-2-3

Castellotti 4 min 18.1 sec—Fangio 4 min 18.6 sec—Moss 4 min 19.2 sec—Farina 4 min 20.9 sec—Behra 4 min 23.6 sec—Kling 4 min 24.0 sec—Musso 4 min 26.4 sec—Frere 4 min 29.7 sec—Hawthorn 4 min 33.1 sec—Trintignant 4 min 33.2 sec—Perdisa 4 min 50.4 sec—Rosier 4 min 54.7 sec—Mieres 5 min 09.0 sec—non starters H. Schell (Ferrari)—J. Claes (Maserati).

DUTCH GRAND PRIX

Zandvoort; 19 June; 100 laps 418 km/260 miles
1 J M Fangio (Mercedes Benz) 2 hr 54 min 23.8 sec 144.17 kph/89.6 mph—2 S. Moss (Mercedes-Benz) 2 hr 54 min 24.1 sec—3 L. Musso (Maserati) 2 hr 55 min 20.9 sec—4 R. Mieres (Maserati) 99 laps—5 E. Castellotti (Ferrari) 97 laps—6 J. Behra (Maserati) 97 laps—7 J M Hawthorn (Ferrari) 95 laps—8 H. da Silva Ramos (Gordini) 93 laps—9 L. Rosier (Maserati) 93 laps—10 J. Pollet (Gordini) 92 laps—11 J. Claes (Ferrari) 88 laps—fastest lap, R. Mieres 1 min 40.9 sec 149.57 kph/92.96 mph—retired P. Walker (Maserati) wheel lap 3—K. Kling (Mercedes-Benz) accident lap 22—H. Gould (Maserati) transmission lap 24—R. Manzon (Gordini) transmission lap 24—M. Trintignant (Ferrari) transmission lap 65.

Starting grid 3-2-3

Fangio 1 min 40.0 sec—Moss 1 min 40.4 sec—Kling 1 min 41.1 sec—Musso 1 min 41.2 sec—Hawthorn 1 min 41.5 sec—Behra 1 min 41.5 sec—Mieres 1 min 42.1 sec—Trintignant 1 min 42.4 sec—Castellotti 1 min 42.7 sec—Walker 1 min 44.9 sec—Manzon 1 min 46.0 sec—Pollet 1 min 48.6 sec—Rosier 1 min 49.2 sec—da Silva Ramos 1 min 50.2 sec—Gould 1 min 50.4 sec—Claes 1 min 53.3 sec.

BRITISH GRAND PRIX

Aintree; 16 July; 90 laps 270 miles/434 km
1 S. Moss (Mercedes-Benz) 3 hr 7 min 21.2 sec 86.47 mph/139.13 kph—2 J M Fangio (Mercedes-Benz) 3 hr 7 min 21.4 sec—3 K. Kling (Mercedes-Benz) 3 hr 8 min 33.0 sec—4 P. Taruffi (Mercedes-Benz) 89 laps—5 L. Musso (Maserati) 89 laps—6 J M Hawthorn, E. Castellotti (Ferrari) 87 laps—7 M. Sparken (Gordini) 81 laps—8 L. Macklin (Maserati) 79 laps—9 H. Schell, K. Wharton (Vanwall) 72 laps—fastest lap, Moss 2 min 0.4 sec 89.7 mph/144.33 kph—retired R. Manzon (Gordini) transmission lap 5—J. Behra (Maserati) oil pipe lap 10—A. Simon (Maserati) gearbox lap 10—E. Castellotti (Ferrari) transmission lap 17—L. Marr (Connaught) brakes lap 18—A P R Rolt, P. Walker (Connaught) throttle lap 19—H. Schell (Vanwall) throttle lap 21—H. Gould (Maserati) brakes lap 22—R. Salvadori (Maserati) oil pressure lap 24—H da Silva Ramos (Gordini) engine lap 27—P. Collins (Maserati) clutch lap 29—K. McAlpine (Connaught) oil pressure lap 31—J. Brabham (Cooper) valve lap 31—R. Mieres (Maserati) piston lap 48—M. Trintignant (Ferrari) cylinder head lap 60.

Starting grid 3-2-3

Moss 2 min 0.4 sec—Fangio 2 min 0.6 sec—Behra 2 min 1.4 sec—Kling 2 min 2.0 sec—Taruffi 2 min 3.0 sec—Mieres 2 min 3.2 sec—Schell 2 min 3.8 sec—Simon 2 min 4.0 sec—Musso 2 min 4.2 sec—Castellotti 2 min 5.0 sec—Manzon 2 min 5.0 sec—Hawthorn 2 min 5.4 sec—Trintignant 2 min 5.4 sec—Rolt 2 min 6.6 sec—Wharton 2 min 8.4 sec—Macklin 2 min 8.4 sec—McAlpine 2 min 9.8 sec—da Silva Ramos 2 min 10.6 sec—Marr 2 min 11.6 sec—Salvadori 2 min 11.6 sec—Gould 2 min 11.8 sec—Sparken 2 min 12.6 sec—Collins 2 min 13.4 sec—Brabham 2 min 27.4 sec—non starter J. Fairman (Connaught).

ITALIAN GRAND PRIX

Monza banked track; 11 September; 50 laps 502 km/312 miles
1 J M Fangio (Mercedes-Benz) 2 hr 25 min 4.4 sec 206.63 kph/128.42 mph—2 P. Taruffi (Mercedes-Benz) 2 hr 25 min 5.1 sec—3 E. Castellotti (Ferrari) 2 hr 25 min 50.6 sec—4 J. Behra (Maserati) 2 hr 29 min 1.9 sec—5 C. Menditeguy (Maserati) 49 laps—6 U. Maglioli (Ferrari) 49 laps—7 R. Mieres (Maserati) 48 laps—8 M. Trintignant (Ferrari) 47 laps—9 J. Fitch (Maserati) 46 laps—fastest lap, Moss 2 min 46.9 sec 215.67 kph/134.04 mph—retired K. Wharton (Vanwall) transmission lap 1—H. Schell (Vanwall) de Dion tube lap 8—J. Lucas (Gordini) engine lap 8—P. Collins (Maserati) rear suspension lap 23—H. da Silva Ramos (Gordini) lap 24—J. Pollet (Gordini) lap 27—S. Moss (Mercedes-Benz) transmission lap 28—L. Musso (Maserati) gearbox lap 32—K. Kling (Mercedes-Benz) gearbox lap 33—H. Gould (Maserati) engine lap 33—J M Hawthorn (Ferrari) gearbox mounts lap 39.

Starting grid 3-2-3

Fangio 2 min 46.5 sec—Moss 2 min 46.8 sec—Kling 2 min 48.3 sec—Castellotti 2 min 49.6 sec—Behra 2 min 50.1 sec—Mieres 2 min 51.1 sec—Taruffi 2 min 51.8 sec—Musso 2 min 52.2 sec—Collins 2 min 55.3 sec—Maglioli 2 min 55.4 sec—Schell 2 min 55.5 sec—Hawthorn 2 min 56.2 sec—Trintignant 2 min 56.6 sec—Menditeguy 2 min 58.4 sec—Wharton 2 min 59.5 sec—da Silva Ramos 2 min 59.8 sec—Pollet 2 min 59.9 sec—Fitch 3 min 03.1 sec—Gould 3 min 05.2 sec—Lucas 3 min 15.9 sec—non starters G. Farina (Lancia)—L. Villoresi (Lancia).

1955 WORLD CHAMPIONSHIP

1 J M Fangio 40, 41—2 S. Moss 23—3 E. Castellotti 12—4 M. Trintignant 11 1/3—5 G. Farina 10 1/3—6 P. Taruffi 9—7 R. Mieres 7—8 J. Behra 6—8= L. Musso 6—10 K. Kling 5—11 P. Frere 3—12 F. Gonzalez 2—12= C. Perdisa 2—12= L. Villoresi 2—12= C. Menditeguy 2—16 U. Maglioli 1 1/3—17 H. Herrmann 1.

1956

ARGENTINE GRAND PRIX

Buenos Aires; 22 January; 98 laps 383 km/238 miles
1 J M Fangio, L. Musso (Ferrari) 3 hr 00 min 3.7 sec 127.72 kph/79.38 mph—2 J. Behra (Maserati) 3 hr 00 min 28.1 sec—3 J M Hawthorn (Maserati) 96 laps—4 C. Landi, G. Gerini (Maserati) 92 laps—5 O. Gendebien (Ferrari) 91 laps—6 O. Gonzalez, 'Uria' (Maserati) 88 laps—fastest lap, Fangio 1 min 45.3 sec 133.72 kph/83.11 mph—retired J M Fangio (Ferrari) carburation lap 23—F. Gonzalez (Maserati) valve lap 25—E. Castellotti (Ferrari) gearbox lap 41—C. Menditeguy (Maserati) accident lap 43—L. Piotti (Maserati) accident lap 58—P. Collins (Ferrari) accident lap 59—S. Moss (Maserati) engine lap 82.

Starting grid 4-3-4

Fangio 1 min 42.5 sec—Castellotti 1 min 44.7 sec—Musso 1 min 44.7 sec—Behra 1 min 45.1 sec—F. Gonzalez 1 min 45.2 sec—Menditeguy 1 min 45.6 sec—Moss 1 min 45.9 sec—Hawthorn 1 min 47.4 sec—Collins 1 min 47.7 sec—Gendebien 1 min 50.4 sec—Landi, Gerini 1 min 52.1 sec—Piotti 1 min 57.9 sec—O. Gonzalez, 'Uria'.

MONACO GRAND PRIX

Monte Carlo; 13 May; 100 laps 314 km/195 miles
1 S. Moss (Maserati) 3 hr 00 min 32.9 sec 104.5 kph/64.95 mph—2 P. Collins, J M Fangio (Ferrari) 3 hr 00 min 39.0 sec—3 J. Behra (Maserati) 99 laps—4 J M Fangio, E. Castellotti (Ferrari) 94 laps—5 H. da Silva Ramos (Gordini) 93 laps—6 E. Bayol, A. Pilette (Gordini) 88 laps—7 C. Perdisa (Maserati) 86 laps—8 H. Gould (Maserati) 85 laps—fastest lap, Fangio 1 min 44.4 sec 108.43 kph/67.39 mph—retired L. Musso (Ferrari) accident lap 2—H. Schell (Vanwall) accident lap 2—M. Trintignant (Vanwall) overheating lap 11—E. Castellotti (Ferrari) clutch lap 15—L. Rosier (Maserati) engine lap 73—R. Manzon (Gordini) accident lap 91.

Starting grid 3-2-3

Fangio 1 min 44.0 sec—Moss 1 min 44.6 sec—Castellotti 1 min 44.9 sec—Behra 1 min 45.3 sec—Schell 1 min 45.6 sec—Trintignant 1 min 45.6 sec—Perdisa 1 min 46.0 sec—Musso 1 min 46.8 sec—Collins 1 min 47.0 sec—da Silva Ramos 1 min 50.0 sec—Manzon 1 min 50.3 sec—Bayol 1 min 50.6 sec—Rosier 1 min 51.6 sec—Gould 1 min 51.7 sec—non starters G. Scarlatti (Ferrari)—L. Chiron (Maserati)—J M Hawthorn (BRM)—C A S Brooks (BRM).

BELGIAN GRAND PRIX

Spa-Francorchamps; 3 June; 36 laps 510 km/317 miles
1 P. Collins (Ferrari) 2 hr 40 min 00.3 sec 190.55 kph/118.43 mph—2 P. Frere (Ferrari) 2 hr 41 min 51.6 sec—3 S. Moss, C. Perdisa (Maserati) 2 hr 43 min 16.9 sec—4 H. Schell (Vanwall) 35 laps—5 L. Villoresi (Maserati) 34 laps—6 A. Pilette (Ferrari) 33 laps—7 J. Behra (Maserati) 33 laps—8 L. Rosier (Maserati) 33 laps—fastest lap, Moss 4 min 14.7 sec 199.54 kph/124.01 mph—retired F. Godia (Maserati) accident lap 1—H. Gould (Maserati) gearbox lap 3—P. Scotti (Connaught) engine lap 9—S. Moss (Maserati) rear wheel lap 10—M. Trintignant (Vanwall) fuel line lap 10—E. Castellotti (Ferrari) transmission lap 10—J M Fangio (Ferrari) transmission lap 24.

Starting grid 3-2-3

Fangio 4 min 09.8 sec—Moss 4 min 14.7 sec—Collins 4 min 15.3 sec—Behra 4 min 16.7 sec—Castellotti 4 min 16.7 sec—Schell 4 min 19.0 sec—Trintignant 4 min 22.8 sec—Frere 4 min 32.8 sec—Perdisa 4 min 35.7 sec—Rosier 4 min 35.9 sec—Villoresi 4 min 37.7 sec—Scotti 4 min 41.9 sec—Godia 4 min 49.8 sec—Gould 4 min 50.4 sec—Pilette 4 min 51.9 sec.

FRENCH GRAND PRIX

Rheims, *Grand Circuit de Compétition de Reims*; 1 July; 61 laps 506 km/315 miles
1 P. Collins (Ferrari) 2 hr 34 min 23.4 sec 196.63 kph/122 .21 mph—2 E. Castellotti (Ferrari) 2 hr 34 min 23.7 sec—3 J. Behra (Maserati) 2 hr 35 min 53.3 sec—4 J M Fangio (Ferrari) 2 hr 35 min 58.5 sec—5 C. Perdisa, S. Moss (Maserati) 59 laps—6 L. Rosier (Maserati) 58 laps—7 F. Godia (Maserati) 57 laps—8 H. da Silva Ramos (Gordini) 57 laps—9 R. Manzon (Gordini) 56 laps—10 J M Hawthorn, H Schell (Vanwall) 56 laps—11 A Pilette (Gordini) 55 laps—fastest lap, Fangio 2 min 25.8 sec 204.94 kph/127.37 mph—retired H. Schell (Vanwall) engine lap 6—S. Moss (Maserati) gear lever lap 11—M. Trintignant (Bugatti) throttle lap 18—A de Portago (Ferrari) gearbox lap 20—L. Villoresi (Maserati) brakes lap 22—O. Gendebien (Ferrari) clutch lap 33—P. Taruffi (Maserati) lap 39—A. Simon (Maserati) lap 46.

Starting grid 3-2-3

Fangio 2 min 23.3 sec—Castellotti 2 min 24.6 sec—Collins 2 min 25.6 sec—Schell 2 min 26.1 sec—Hawthorn 2 min 27.0 sec—Behra 2 min 27.8 sec—Moss 2 min 29.9 sec—de Portago 2 min 30.9 sec—Villoresi 2 min 33.3 sec—Gendebien 2 min 34.5 sec—Taruffi 2 min 34.5 sec—Rosier 2 min 35.3 sec—da Silva Ramos 2 min 35.9 sec—Manzon 2 min 36.0 sec—Perdisa 2 min 36.4 sec—Godia 2 min 40.4 sec—Trintignant 2 min 41.9 sec—Pilette 2 min 46.8 sec—Simon 2 min 47.9 sec.

BRITISH GRAND PRIX

Silverstone; 14 July; 101 laps 303 miles/488 km
1 J M Fangio (Ferrari) 2 hr 59 min 47.0 sec 98.65 mph/158.73 kph—2 A de Portago, P. Collins (Ferrari) 100 laps—3 J. Behra (Maserati) 99 laps—4 J. Fairman (Connaught) 98 laps—5 H. Gould (Maserati) 97 laps—6 L. Villoresi (Maserati) 96 laps—7 C. Perdisa (Maserati) 95 laps—8 F. Godia (Maserati) 94 laps—9 R. Manzon (Gordini) 94 laps—10 E. Castellotti, A de Portago (Ferrari) 92 laps—11 F R Gerard (Cooper-Bristol) 88 laps—fastest lap, Moss 1 min 43.2 sec 102.1 mph/164.28 kph—retired F. Gonzalez (Vanwall) axle lap 1—R. Flockhart (BRM) engine lap 2—J. Brabham (Maserati) lap 4—P. Emery (Emeryson) ignition lap 13—A. Scott-Brown (Connaught) stub axle lap 17—U. Maglioli (Maserati) gearbox lap 22—B. Halford (Maserati) piston lap 24—J M Hawthorn (BRM) transmission lap 24—L. Rosier (Maserati) magneto lap 24—C A S Brooks (BRM) accident lap 41—R. Salvadori (Maserati) fuel lap 60—P. Collins (Ferrari) oil pressure lap 64—H. da Silva Ramos (Gordini) rear axle lap 72—M. Trintignant (Vanwall) fuel line lap 75—D. Titterington (Connaught) con rod lap 75—H. Schell (Vanwall) fuel line lap 87—S. Moss (Maserati) rear axle lap 95.

Starting grid 4-3-4

Moss 1 min 41.0 sec—Fangio 1 min 42.0 sec—Hawthorn 1 min 43.0 sec—Collins 1 min 43.0 sec—Schell 1 min 44.0 sec—Gonzalez 1 min 44.0 sec—Salvadori 1 min 44.0 sec—Castellotti 1 min 44.0 sec—Brooks 1 min 45.0 sec—Scott-Brown 1 min 45.0 sec—Titterington 1 min 46.0 sec—de Portago 1 min 47.0 sec—Behra 1 min 47.0 sec—Gould 1 min 48.0 sec—Perdisa 1 min 49.0 sec—Trintignant 1 min 49.0 sec—Flockhart 1 min 49.0 sec—Manzon 1 min 49.0 sec—Villoresi 1 min 50.0 sec—Halford 1 min 51.0 sec—Fairman 1 min 51.0 sec—Gerard 1 min 53.0 sec—Emery 1 min 54.0 sec—Maglioli 1 min 54.0 sec—Godia 1 min 55.0 sec—da Silva Ramos 1 min 56.0 sec—Rosier 1 min 59.0 sec—Brabham 2 min 01.0 sec—non starters O. Gendebien (Ferrari)—O Volonterio (Maserati)—M. Oliver (Connaught).

GERMAN GRAND PRIX

Nürburgring; 5 August; 22 laps 502 km/312 miles
1 J M Fangio (Ferrari) 3 hr 38 min 43.7 sec 137.76 kph/85.62 mph—2 S. Moss (Maserati) 3 hr 39 min 30.1 sec—3 J. Behra (Maserati) 3 hr 46 min 22.0 sec—4 F. Godia (Maserati) 20 laps—5 L. Rosier (Maserati) 19 laps—fastest lap, Fangio 9 min 41.6 sec 141.17 kph/87.74 mph—retired L. Piotti

GERMAN GRAND PRIX—*continued*

(Maserati) engine lap 1—G. Scarlatti (Ferrari) engine lap 1—R. Manzon (Gordini) front suspension lap 1—R. Salvadori (Maserati) rear suspension lap 3—H. Gould (Maserati) oil pressure lap 4—U. Maglioli (Maserati) steering lap 4—E. Castellotti (Ferrari) magneto lap 6—P. Collins (Ferrari) fuel tank lap 9—L. Musso, E. Castellotti (Ferrari) accident lap 13—H. Schell (Maserati) overheating lap 13—L. Villoresi (Maserati) engine lap 14—A. de Portago, P. Collins (Ferrari) accident lap 15—A. Milhoux (Gordini) engine lap 16—B. Halford (Maserati) disqualified—O. Volonterio (Maserati) disqualified.

Starting grid 4-3-4

Fangio 9 min 51.2 sec—Collins 9 min 51.5 sec—Castellotti 9 min 54.4 sec—Moss 10 min 03.4 sec—Musso 10 min 20.3 sec—Maglioli 10 min 26.7 sec—Behra 10 min 31.6 sec—Salvadori 10 min 32.4 sec—de Portago 10 min 37.1 sec—Halford 11 min 04.1 sec—Schell 11 min 16.5 sec—Gould 11 min 32.2 sec—Rosier 11 min 39.0 sec—Manzon 11 min 55.8 sec—Godia 11 min 57.6 sec—Scarlatti 13 min 05.2 sec—Piotti 13 min 50.1 sec—Volonterio 14 min 17.1 sec—Milhoux—Villoresi—non starters A. Pilette (Gordini)—C. Perdisa (Maserati).

ITALIAN GRAND PRIX

Monza banked track; 2 September; 50 laps 499 km/310 miles
1 S. Moss (Maserati) 2 hr 23 min 41.3 sec 208.73 kph/129.73 mph—2 P. Collins, J M Fangio (Ferrari) 2 hr 23 min 47.0 sec—3 R. Flockhart (Connaught) 49 laps—4 F. Godia (Maserati) 49 laps—5 J. Fairman (Connaught) 47 laps—6 L. Piotti (Maserati) 47 laps—7 E. de Graffenried (Maserati) 46 laps—8 E. Castellotti, J M Fangio (Ferrari) 46 laps—9 A. Simon (Gordini) 45 laps—10 G. Gerini (Maserati) 42 laps—11 R. Salvadori (Maserati) 41 laps—fastest lap, Moss 2 min 45.5 sec 218.02 kph/135.5 mph—retired H. da Silva Ramos (Gordini) engine lap 3—A. de Portago (Ferrari) suspension lap 6—L. Leston (Connaught) torsion bar lap 6—R. Manzon (Gordini) gearbox lap 7—L. Villoresi (Maserati) valve lap 7—E. Castellotti (Ferrari) steering lap 9—P. Taruffi (Vanwall) suspension lap 12—M. Trintignant (Vanwall) suspension lap 13—B. Halford (Maserati) engine lap 16—J M Fangio (Ferrari) engine lap 20—J. Behra (Maserati) ignition lap 23—H. Schell (Vanwall) suspension lap 32—J. Behra (in Maglioli's Maserati) steering lap 42—L. Musso (Ferrari) steering lap 37.

Starting grid 3-3-3

Fangio 2 min 42.6 sec—Castellotti 2 min 43.4 sec—Musso 2 min 43.7 sec—Taruffi 2 min 45.4 sec—Behra 2 min 45.6 sec—Moss 2 min 45.9 sec—Collins 2 min 46.0 sec—Villoresi 2 min 47.7 sec—de Portago 2 min 47.8 sec—Schell 2 min 50.1 sec—Trintignant 2 min 51.6 sec—Maglioli 2 min 52.7 sec—Salvadori 2 min 54.6 sec—Piotti 2 min 58.4 sec—Fairman 2 min 59.2 sec—Gerini 3 min 02.6 sec—Godia 3 min 02.9 sec—de Graffenried 3 min 03.3 sec—Leston 3 min 04.3 sec—da Silva Ramos 3 min 04.8 sec—Halford 3 min 05.0 sec—Manzon 3 min 06.6 sec—Flockhart 3 min 08.1 sec—Simon 3 min 13.3 sec—non starter—W. von Trips (Ferrari).

1956 WORLD CHAMPIONSHIP

1 J M Fangio 30, 33—2 S. Moss 27, 28—3 P. Collins 25—4 J. Behra 22—5 E. Castellotti 7½—6 P. Frere 6—6= F. Godia 6—8 J. Fairman 5—9 L. Musso 4—9= J M Hawthorn 4—9= R. Flockhart 4—12 C. Perdisa 3—12= H. Schell 3—12= A. de Portago 3—15 O. Gendebien 2—15= H. da Silva Ramos 2—15= L. Villoresi 2—15= H. Gould 2—15= L. Rosier 2—20 C. Landi 1½—20= G. Gerini 1½.

1957

ARGENTINE GRAND PRIX

Buenos Aires; 13 January; three hours
1 J M Fangio (Maserati) 3 hr 0 min 55.9 sec 100 laps 129.48 kph/80.47 mph—2 J. Behra (Maserati) 3 hr 1 min 14.2 sec—3 C. Menditeguy (Maserati) 99 laps—4 H. Schell (Maserati) 98 laps—5 F. Gonzalez, A. de Portago (Ferrari) 98 laps—6 W. von Trips, P. Collins, C. Perdisa (Ferrari) 98 laps—7 J. Bonnier (Maserati) 95 laps—8 S. Moss (Maserati) 93 laps—9 A. de Tomaso (Ferrari) 91 laps—10 L. Piotti (Maserati) 90 laps—fastest lap, S. Moss 1 min 44.7 sec 133.55 kph/83.0 mph—retired P. Collins (Ferrari) clutch lap 26—L. Musso (Ferrari) clutch lap 31—J M Hawthorn (Ferrari) clutch lap 35—E. Castellotti (Ferrari) rear wheel lap 75.

Starting grid 4-3-4

Moss 1 min 42.6 sec—Fangio 1 min 43.7 sec—Behra 1 min 44.0 sec—Castellotti 1 min 44.2 sec—Collins 1 min 44.6 sec—Musso 1 min 44.8 sec—Hawthorn 1 min 44.8 sec—Menditeguy 1 min 45.1 sec—Schell 1 min 46.6 sec—Gonzalez 1 min 46.8 sec—Perdisa 1 min 48.6 sec—de Tomaso 1 min 56.1 sec—Bonnier 1 min 58.2 sec—Piotti 1 min 58.2 sec.

MONACO GRAND PRIX

Monte Carlo; 19 May; 105 laps 330 km/205 miles
1 J M Fangio (Maserati) 3 hr 10 min 12.8 sec 104.13 kph/64.72 mph—2 C A S Brooks (Vanwall) 3 hr 10 min 38.0 sec—3 M. Gregory (Maserati) 103 laps—4 S. Lewis-Evans (Connaught) 102 laps—5 M. Trintignant (Ferrari) 100 laps—6 J. Brabham (Cooper-Climax) 100 laps—fastest lap, Fangio 1 min 45.6 sec 107.21 kph/66.63 mph—retired S. Moss (Vanwall) accident lap 3—P. Collins (Ferrari) accident lap 3—J M Hawthorn (Ferrari) accident lap 3—H. Gould (Maserati) oil tank lap 9—H. Schell (Maserati) suspension lap 22—I. Bueb (Connaught) fuel tank lap 46—C. Menditeguy (Maserati) accident lap 50—R. Flockhart (BRM) engine lap 59—G. Scarlatti, H. Schell (Maserati) oil leak lap 64—W. von Trips, J M Hawthorn (Ferrari) engine lap 95.

Starting grid 3-2-3

Fangio 1 min 42.7 sec—Collins 1 min 43.3 sec—Moss 1 min 43.6 sec—Brooks 1 min 44.4 sec—Hawthorn 1 min 44.6 sec—Menditeguy 1 min 46.7 sec—Trintignant 1 min 46.7 sec—Schell 1 min 47.3 sec—von Trips 1 min 47.9 sec—Gregory 1 min 48.4 sec—Flockhart 1 min 48.6 sec—Gould 1 min 48.7 sec—Lewis-Evans 1 min 49.1 sec—Scarlatti 1 min 49.2 sec—Brabham 1 min 49.3 sec—Bueb 1 min 49.4 sec—failed to qualify R. Salvadori (BRM) 1 min 50.9 sec—L. Piotti (Maserati) 1 min 54.3 sec—A. Simon (Maserati) 1 min 51.7 sec—L. Leston (Cooper) 1 min 58.9 sec.

FRENCH GRAND PRIX

Rouen-les-Essarts; 7 July; 77 laps 503 km/313 miles
1 J M Fangio (Maserati) 3 hr 7 min 46.4 sec 160.93 kph/100.02 mph—2 L. Musso (Ferrari) 3 hr 8 min 37.2 sec—3 P. Collins (Ferrari) 3 hr 9 min 52.4 sec—4 J M Hawthorn (Ferrari) 76 laps—5 H. Schell (Maserati) 70 laps—6 J. Behra (Maserati) 69 laps—7 M. McDowell, J. Brabham (Cooper-Climax) 68 laps—fastest lap, Musso 2 min 22.4 sec 165.55 kph/102.87 mph—retired R. Flockhart (BRM) accident lap 3—H. Gould (Maserati) axle lap 4—J. Brabham (Cooper-Climax) suspension lap 4—M. Trintignant (Ferrari) ignition lap 23—H. Mackay Fraser (BRM) transmission lap 24—R. Salvadori (Vanwall) engine lap 25—S. Lewis-Evans (Vanwall) steering lap 30—C. Menditeguy (Maserati) radiator lap 30.

Starting grid 3-2-3

Fangio 2 min 21.5 sec—Behra 2 min 22.6 sec—Musso 2 min 22.7 sec—Schell 2 min 23.2 sec—Collins 2 min 23.3 sec—Salvadori 2 min 25.1 sec—Hawthorn 2 min 25.6 sec—Trintignant 2 min 25.9 sec—Menditeguy 2 min 26.1 sec—Lewis-Evans 2 min 27.6 sec—Flockhart 2 min 27.8 sec—Fraser 2 min 29.9 sec—Brabham 2 min 30.9 sec—Gould 2 min 35.0 sec—McDowall 2 min 38.6 sec.

BRITISH GRAND PRIX

Aintree; 20 July; 90 laps 270 miles/434 km
1 S. Moss, C A S Brooks (Vanwall) 3 hr 6 min 37.8 sec 86.8 mph/139.66 kph—2 L. Musso (Ferrari) 3 hr 7 min 3.4 sec—3 J M Hawthorn (Ferrari) 3 hr 7 min 20.6 sec—4 M. Trintignant (Ferrari) 88 laps—5 R. Salvadori (Cooper-Climax) 85 laps—6 F R Gerard (Cooper-Bristol) 82 laps—7 S. Lewis-Evans (Vanwall) 82 laps—8 I. Bueb (Maserati) 71 laps—fastest lap, Moss 1 min 59.2 sec 90.6 mph/145.77 kph—retired J. Bonnier (Maserati) gearbox lap 18—C. Menditeguy (Maserati) transmission lap 35—H. Schell (Maserati) water pump lap 39—L. Leston (BRM) engine lap 45—J. Fairman (BRM) engine lap 48—J M Fangio (Maserati) engine lap 49—C A S Brooks (Vanwall) fuel pump lap 51—P. Collins (Ferrari) cooling lap 53—J. Behra (Maserati) clutch lap 69—J. Brabham (Cooper-Climax) clutch lap 75.

Starting grid 3-2-3

Moss 2 min 00.2 sec—Behra 2 min 00.4 sec—Brooks 2 min 00.4 sec—Fangio 2 min 00.6 sec—Hawthorn 2 min 01.2 sec—Lewis-Evans 2 min 01.2 sec—Schell 2 min 01.4 sec—Collins 2 min 01.8 sec—Trintignant 2 min 03.2 sec—Musso 2 min 03.4 sec—Menditeguy 2 min 05.4 sec—Leston 2 min 05.6 sec—Brabham 2 min 07.0 sec—Salvadori 2 min 07.4 sec—Fairman 2 min 08.6 sec—Bonnier 2 min 12.6 sec—Gerard 2 min 12.6 sec—Bueb 2 min 15.4 sec—non starter H. Gould (Maserati) 2 min 07.0 sec.

GERMAN GRAND PRIX

Nürburgring; 4 August; 22 laps 502 km/312 miles
1 J M Fangio (Maserati) 3 hr 30 min 38.3 sec 142.72 kph/88.7 mph—2 J M Hawthorn (Ferrari) 3 hr 30 min 41.9 sec—3 P. Collins (Ferrari) 3 hr 31 min 13.9 sec—4 L. Musso (Ferrari) 3 hr 34 min 15.9 sec—5 S. Moss (Vanwall) 3 hr 35 min 15.8 sec—6 J. Behra (Maserati) 3 hr 35 min 16.8 sec—7 H. Schell (Maserati) 3 hr 37 min 25.8 sec—8 M. Gregory (Maserati) 21 laps—9 C A S Brooks (Vanwall) 21 laps—10 G. Scarlatti (Maserati) 21 laps—11 B. Halford (Maserati) 21 laps—fastest lap, Fangio 9 min 17.4 sec 147.27 kph/91.53 mph—retired H. Gould (Maserati) rear axle lap 3—S. Lewis-Evans (Vanwall) gearbox lap 11—F. Godia (Maserati) steering lap 12—H. Herrmann (Maserati) chassis lap 15.

Starting grid 4-3-4

Fangio 9 min 25.6 sec—Hawthorn 9 min 28.4 sec—Behra 9 min 30.5 sec—Collins 9 min 34.7 sec—Brooks 9 min 36.1 sec—Schell 9 min 39.2 sec—Moss 9 min 41.2 sec—Musso 9 min 43.1 sec—Lewis-Evans 9 min 45.0 sec—Gregory 9 min 51.5 sec—Herrmann 10 min 00.0 sec—Scarlatti 10 min 04.9 sec—Halford 10 min 14.5 sec—Gould 10 min 20.8 sec—Godia 10 min 32.3 sec.

PESCARA GRAND PRIX

Circuit Pescara; 18 August; 18 laps 465 km/289 miles
1 S. Moss (Vanwall) 2 hr 59 min 22.7 sec 153.74 kph/95.55 mph—2 J M Fangio (Maserati) 3 hr 02 min 36.6 sec—3 H. Schell (Maserati) 3 hr 06 min 9.5 sec—4 M. Gregory (Maserati) 3 hr 07 min 39.2 sec—5 S. Lewis-Evans (Vanwall) 17 laps—6 G. Scarlatti (Maserati) 17 laps—7 J. Brabham (Cooper-Climax) 16 laps—fastest lap, Moss 5 min 44.6 sec 157.47 kph/97.87 mph—retired C A S Brooks (Vanwall) engine lap 1—L. Piotti (Maserati) transmission lap 1—H. Gould (Maserati) accident lap 1—R. Salvadori (Cooper-Climax) suspension lap 4—J. Behra (Maserati) engine lap 5—J. Bonnier (Maserati) engine lap 7—B. Halford (Maserati) differential lap 9—L. Musso (Ferrari) oil tank lap 9—F. Godia (Maserati) engine lap 9.

Starting grid 3-2-3

Fangio 9 min 44.6 sec—Moss 9 min 54.7 sec—Musso 10 min 00.0 sec—Behra 10 min 03.1 sec—Schell 10 min 04.6 sec—Brooks 10 min 08.8 sec—Gregory 10 min 26.1 sec—Lewis-Evans 10 min 29.6 sec—Bonnier 10 min 36.2 sec—Scarlatti 10 min 36.6 sec—Gould 10 min 49.6 sec—Godia 11 min 09.8 sec—Piotti 11 min 10.6 sec—Halford 11 min 16.3 sec—Salvadori 11 min 24.2 sec—Brabham 11 min 35.2 sec.

ITALIAN GRAND PRIX

Monza; 8 September; 87 laps 500 km/311 miles
1 S. Moss (Vanwall) 2 hr 35 min 3.9 sec 193.53 kph/120.28 mph—2 J M Fangio (Maserati) 2 hr 35 min 45.1 sec—3 W. von Trips (Ferrari) 85 laps—4 M. Gregory (Maserati) 84 laps—5 G. Scarlatti, H. Schell (Maserati) 84 laps—6 J M Hawthorn (Ferrari) 83 laps—7 C A S Brooks (Vanwall) 82 laps—8 L. Musso (Ferrari) 82 laps—9 F. Godia (Maserati) 81 laps—10 H. Gould (Maserati) 78 laps—11 A. Simon, O. Volonterio (Maserati) 72 laps—fastest lap, Brooks 1 min 43.7 sec 199.58 kph/124.04 mph—retired L. Piotti (Maserati) engine lap 3—J. Bonnier (Maserati) overheating lap 31—H. Schell (Maserati) water pump lap 34—B. Halford (Maserati) engine lap 47—S. Lewis-Evans (Vanwall) engine lap 49—J. Behra (Maserati) engine lap 50—P. Collins (Ferrari) cylinder block lap 62.

Starting grid 4-3-4

Lewis-Evans 1 min 42.4 sec—Moss 1 min 42.7 sec—Brooks 1 min 42.9 sec—Fangio 1 min 43.1 sec—Behra 1 min 43.9 sec—Schell 1 min 45.1 sec—Collins 1 min 45.3 sec—von Trips 1 min 45.5 sec—Musso 1 min 45.7 sec—Hawthorn 1 min 46.1 sec—Gregory 1 min 48.9 sec—Scarlatti 1 min 49.2 sec—Bonnier 1 min 49.7 sec—Halford 1 min 51.6 sec—Godia 1 min 52.2 sec—Simon 1 min 52.8 sec—Piotti 1 min 52.9 sec—Gould 1 min 53.7 sec.

1957 WORLD CHAMPIONSHIP

1 J M Fangio 40, 46—2 S. Moss 25—3 L. Musso 16—4 J M Hawthorn 13—5 C A S Brooks 11—6 H. Schell 10—6= M. Gregory 10—8 P. Collins 8—9 J. Behra 6—10 S. Lewis-Evans 5—10= M. Trintignant 5—12 W. von Trips 4—12= C. Menditeguy 4—14 R. Salvadori 2—15 G. Scarlatti 1—15= F. Gonzalez 1—15= A. de Portago 1.

1958

ARGENTINE GRAND PRIX

Buenos Aires; 19 January; 80 laps 314 km/195 miles
1 S. Moss (Cooper) 2 hr 19 min 33.7 sec 134.53 kph/83.61 mph—2 L. Musso (Ferrari) 2 hr 19 min 36.4 sec—3 J M Hawthorn (Ferrari) 2 hr 19 min 46.3 sec—4 J M Fangio (Maserati) 2 hr 20 min 26.7 sec—5 J. Behra (Maserati) 78 laps—6 H. Schell (Maserati) 77 laps—7 C. Menditeguy (Maserati) 76 laps—8 F. Godia (Maserati) 75 laps—9 H. Gould (Maserati) 71 laps—fastest lap, Fangio 1 min 41.8 sec 138.33 kph/85.97 mph—retired P. Collins (Ferrari) axle lap 1.

Starting grid 4-3-4

Fangio 1 min 42.0 sec—Hawthorn 1 min 42.6 sec—Collins 1 min 42.6 sec—Behra 1 min 42.7 sec—Musso 1 min 42.9 sec—Menditeguy 1 min 43.7 sec—Moss 1 min 44.0 sec—Schell 1 min 44.2 sec—Godia 1 min 49.3 sec—Gould 1 min 51.7 sec.

MONACO GRAND PRIX

Monte Carlo; 18 May; 100 laps 314 km/195 miles
1 M. Trintignant (Cooper) 2 hr 52 min 27.9 sec 109.25 kph/67.9 mph—2 L. Musso (Ferrari) 2 hr 52 min 48.2 sec—3 P. Collins (Ferrari) 2 hr 53 min 06.7 sec—4 J. Brabham (Cooper) 97 laps—5 H. Schell (BRM) 91 laps—6 C. Allison (Lotus) 87 laps—fastest lap, J M Hawthorn 1 min 40.6 sec 112.53 kph/69.94 mph—retired S. Lewis-Evans (Vanwall) steering lap 12—C A S Brooks (Vanwall) plugs lap 21—G. Scarlatti (Maserati) engine lap 26—J. Behra (BRM) brakes lap 28—S. Moss (Vanwall) valve lap 38—J M Hawthorn (Ferrari)

MONACO GRAND PRIX—*continued*

fuel pump lap 46—R. Salvadori (Cooper) gearbox lap 55 G. Hill (Lotus) transmission lap 69—J. Bonnier (Maserati) accident lap 71—W. von Trips (Ferrari) engine lap 90.

Starting grid: 3-2-3

Brooks 1 min 39.8 sec—Behra 1 min 40.8 sec—Brabham 1 min 41.0 sec—Salvadori 1 min 41.0 sec—Trintignant 1 min 41.1 sec—Hawthorn 1 min 41.5 sec—Lewis-Evans 1 min 41.8 sec—Moss 1 min 42.3 sec—Collins 1 min 42.4 sec—Musso 1 min 42.6 sec—Schell 1 min 43.8 sec—von Trips 1 min 44.3 sec—Allison 1 min 44.6 sec—Scarlatti 1 min 44.7 sec—Hill 1 min 45.0 sec—Bonnier 1 min 45.0 sec—non starters G. Cabianca (OSCA)—L. Piotti (OSCA)—F. Godia (Maserati)—G. Gerini (Maserati)—M T de Fillipis (Maserati)—A. Testut (Maserati)—L. Chiron (Maserati)—L. Tarmazzo (Maserati).

DUTCH GRAND PRIX

Zandvoort 25 May; 75 laps; 314 km/195 miles
1 S. Moss (Vanwall) 2 hr 4 min 49.2 sec 151.16 kph/93.95 mph—2 H. Schell (BRM) 2 hr 5 min 37.1 sec—3 J. Behra (BRM) 2 hr 6 min 31.5 sec—4 R. Salvadori (Cooper) 74 laps—5 J M Hawthorn (Ferrari) 74 laps—6 C. Allison (Lotus) 73 laps—7 L. Musso (Ferrari) 73 laps—8 J. Brabham (Cooper) 73 laps—9 M. Trintignant (Cooper) 72 laps—10 J. Bonnier (Maserati) 71 laps—11 C G de Beaufort (Porsche) 69 laps—fastest lap, Moss 1 min 38.5 sec 152.5 kph/94.78 mph—retired C A S Brooks (Vanwall) axle lap 14—M. Gregory (Maserati) fuel pump lap 17—P. Collins (Ferrari) gearbox lap 33—G. Hill (Lotus) engine lap 41—S. Lewis-Evans (Vanwall) engine lap 47—G. Scarlatti (Maserati) rear axle lap 51.

Starting grid 3-2-3

Lewis-Evans 1 min 37.1 sec—Moss 1 min 38.0 sec—Brooks 1 min 38.1 sec—Behra 1 min 38.4 sec—Brabham 1 min 38.5 sec—Hawthorn 1 min 39.1 sec—Schell 1 min 39.2 sec—Trintignant 1 min 39.2 sec—Salvadori 1 min 39.2 sec—Collins 1 min 39.3 sec—Allison 1 min 39.4 sec—Musso 1 min 39.5 sec—Hill 1 min 39.8 sec—Gregory 1 min 42.0 sec—Bonnier 1 min 42.3 sec—Scarlatti 1 min 44.6 sec—de Beaufort 1 min 46.7 sec.

BELGIAN GRAND PRIX

Spa-Francorchamps; 15 June; 24 laps 341 km/212 miles
1 C A S Brooks (Vanwall) 1 hr 37 min 6.3 sec 209.04 kph/129.92 mph—2 J M Hawthorn (Ferrari) 1 hr 37 min 27.00 sec—3 S. Lewis-Evans (Vanwall) 1 hr 40 min 7.2 sec—4 C. Allison (Lotus) 1 hr 41 min 21.8 sec—5 H. Schell (BRM) 23 laps—6 O. Gendebien (Ferrari) 23 laps—7 M. Trintignant (Maserati) 23 laps—8 R. Salvadori (Cooper) 23 laps—9 J. Bonnier (Maserati) 22 laps—10 M T de Fillipis (Maserati) 22 laps—fastest lap, Hawthorn 3 min 58.3 sec 212.97 kph/132.36 mph—retired M. Gregory (Maserati) engine lap 1—S. Moss (Vanwall) valve lap 2—W. Seidel (Maserati) rear axle lap 5—J. Behra (BRM) oil pressure lap 6—P. Collins (Ferrari) overheating lap 6—L. Musso (Ferrari) accident lap 6—G. Hill (Lotus) engine lap 11—J. Brabham (Cooper) overheating lap 17—F. Godia (Maserati) engine lap 22

Starting grid 3-2-3

Hawthorn 3 min 57.1 sec—Musso 3 min 57.5 sec—Moss 3 min 57.6 sec—Collins 3 min 57.7 sec—Brooks 3 min 59.1 sec—Gendebien 3 min 59.3 sec—Schell 4 min 04.5 sec—Brabham 4 min 05.1 sec—Gregory 4 min 05.4 sec—Behra 4 min 06.2 sec—Lewis-Evans 4 min 07.2 sec—Allison 4 min 07.7 sec—Salvadori 4 min 15.6 sec—Bonnier 4 min 15.7 sec—G. Hill 4 min 17.8 sec—Trintignant 4 min 21.7 sec—Seidel 4 min 21.9 sec—Godia 4 min 24.5 sec—de Fillipis 4 min 31.0 sec—non starter K. Kavanagh (Maserati)

FRENCH GRAND PRIX

Rheims 6 July; 50 Laps 415 km/258 miles
1 J M Hawthorn (Ferrari) 2 hr 3 min 21.3 sec 201.86 kph/125.46 mph—2 S. Moss (Vanwall) 2 hr 3 min 45.9 sec—3 W. von Trips (Ferrari) 2 hr 4 min 21.0 sec—4 J M Fangio (Maserati) 2 hr 5 min 51.9 sec—5 P. Collins (Ferrari) 2 hr 8 min 46.2 sec—6 J. Brabham (Cooper) 49 laps—7 P. Hill (Maserati) 49 laps—8 J. Bonnier (Maserati) 48 laps—9 G. Gerini (Maserati) 47 laps—10 T. Ruttman (Maserati) 45 laps—11 R. Salvadori (Cooper) 37 laps—fastest lap, Hawthorn 2 min 24.9 sec 206.26 kph/128.19 mph—retired C. Allison (Lotus) engine lap 7—C. Shelby (Maserati) engine lap 8—L. Musso (Ferrari) fatal accident lap 9—C A S Brooks (Vanwall) gearbox lap 16—M. Trintignant (BRM) oil pipe lap 24—F. Godia (Maserati) accident lap 29—G. Hill (Lotus) lap 33—C A S Brooks, S. Lewis-Evans (Vanwall) engine lap 35—J. Behra (BRM) fuel pump lap 41—H. Schell (BRM) fuel pump lap 41.

Starting grid 3-2-3

Hawthorn 2 min 21.7 sec—Musso 2 min 22.4 sec—Schell 2 min 23.1 sec—Collins 2 min 23.3 sec—Brooks 2 min 23.4 sec—Moss 2 min 23.7 sec—Trintignant 2 min 23.7 sec—Fangio 2 min 24.0 sec—Behra 2 min 24.2 sec—Lewis-Evans 2 min 25.3 sec—Godia 2 min 27.1 sec—Brabham 2 min 27.3 sec—P. Hill 2 min 29.5 sec—Salvadori 2 min 30.0 sec—Gerini 2 min 30.7 sec—Bonnier 2 min 30.9 sec—Shelby 2 min 32.0 sec—Ruttman 2 min 36.0 sec—G. Hill 2 min 40.9 sec—Allison 2 min 49.7 sec—von Trips.

BRITISH GRAND PRIX

Silverstone; 19 July; 75 laps 225 miles/410 km
1 P. Collins (Ferrari) 2 hr 9 min 4.2 sec 102.05 mph/164.2 kph—2 J M Hawthorn (Ferrari) 2 hr 9 min 28.4 sec—3 R. Salvadori (Cooper) 2 hr 9 min 54.8 sec—4 S. Lewis-Evans (Vanwall) 2 hr 9 min 55.0 sec—5 H. Schell (BRM) 2 hr 10 min 19.0 sec—6 J. Brabham (Cooper) 2 hr 10 min 27.4 sec—7 C A S Brooks (Vanwall) 74 laps—8 M. Trintignant (Cooper) 73 laps—9 C. Shelby (Maserati) 72 laps—fastest lap, Hawthorn 1 min 40.8 sec 104.54 mph/168.2 kph—retired J. Fairman (Connaught) ignition lap 8—G. Hill (Lotus) oil pressure lap 18—J. Behra (BRM) suspension lap 20—A. Stacey (Lotus) oil pressure lap 20—I. Bueb (Connaught) gearbox lap 20—C. Allison (Lotus) engine lap 22—S. Moss (Vanwall) engine lap 26—I. Burgess (Cooper) clutch lap 41—G. Gerini (Maserati) gearbox lap 44—J. Bonnier (Maserati) transmission lap 50—W. von Trips (Ferrari) engine lap 60.

Starting grid 4-3-4

Moss 1 min 39.4 sec—Schell 1 min 39.8 sec—Salvadori 1 min 40.0 sec—Hawthorn 1 min 40.4 sec—Allison 1 min 40.4 sec—Collins 1 min 40.6 sec—Lewis-Evans 1 min 41.4 sec—Behra 1 min 41.4 sec—Brooks 1 min 41.6 sec—Brabham 1 min 42.0 sec—von Trips 1 min 42.0 sec—Trintignant 1 min 42.6 sec—Bonnier 1 min 43.0 sec—G. Hill 1 min 43.0 sec—Shelby 1 min 44.2 sec—Burgess 1 min 45.4 sec—Bueb 1 min 51.4 sec—Gerini 1 min 53.0 sec—Fairman 1 min 58.8 sec—Stacey 1 min 58.8 sec.

GERMAN GRAND PRIX

Nürburgring; 3 August; 15 laps 341 km/212 miles
1 C A S Brooks (Vanwall) 2 hr 21 min 15.0 sec 145.29 kph/90.3 mph—2 R. Salvadori (Cooper) 2 hr 24 min 44.7 sec—3 M. Trintignant (Cooper) 2 hr 26 min 26.2 sec—4 W. von Trips (Ferrari) 2 hr 27 min 31.3 sec—5 C. Allison (Lotus) 13 laps—fastest lap, Moss 9 min 9.2 sec 148.83 kph/92.9 mph—retired J. Bonnier (Maserati) engine lap 2—S. Moss (Vanwall) magneto lap 4—J. Behra (BRM) suspension lap 4—H. Herrmann (Maserati) engine lap 4—H. Schell (BRM) brakes lap 9—P. Collins (Ferrari) fatal accident lap 11—J M Hawthorn (Ferrari) clutch lap 12.

Starting grid 4-3-4

Hawthorn 9 min 14.0 sec—Brooks 9 min 15.0 sec—Moss 9 min 19.1 sec—Collins 9 min 21.9 sec—von Trips 9 min 24.7 sec—Salvadori 9 min 35.3 sec—Trintignant 9 min 36.9 sec—Schell 9 min 39.6 sec—Behra 9 min 46.8 sec—Herrmann 10 min 13.5 sec—Bonnier 9 min 42.7 sec—Allison 9 min 44.0 sec.

PORTUGUESE GRAND PRIX

Oporto; 24 August; 50 laps 370 km/230 miles
1 S. Moss (Vanwall) 2 hr 11 min 27.8 sec—168.99 kph/105.3 mph—2 J M Hawthorn (Ferrari) 2 hr 16 min 40.6 sec—3 S. Lewis-Evans (Vanwall) 49 laps—4 J. Behra (BRM) 49 laps—5 W. von Trips (Ferrari) 49 laps—6 H. Schell (BRM) 49 laps—7 J. Brabham (Cooper) 48 laps—8 M. Trintignant (Cooper) 48 laps—9 R. Salvadori (Cooper) 46 laps—fastest lap, Hawthorn 2 min 32.37 sec 178.20 kph/110.75 mph—retired M T de Fillipis (Maserati) lap 7—J. Bonnier (Maserati) illness lap 8—C. Allison (Maserati) lap 16—G. Hill (Lotus) accident lap 25—C A S Brooks (Vanwall) accident lap 38—C. Shelby (Maserati) brakes lap 47.

Starting grid 3-2-3

Moss 2 min 34.2 sec—Hawthorn 2 min 34.2 sec—Lewis-Evans 2 min 34.6 sec—Behra 2 min 34.9 sec—Brooks 2 min 35.9 sec—von Trips 2 min 37.0 sec—Schell 2 min 37.0 sec—Brabham 2 min 37.4 sec—Trintignant 2 min 37.9 sec—Shelby 2 min 40.4 sec—Salvadori 2 min 43.0 sec—G. Hill 2 min 46.2 sec—Allison 2 min 46.2 sec—Bonnier 2 min 46.6 sec—de Fillipis 3 min 01.9 sec.

ITALIAN GRAND PRIX

Monza; 7 September; 70 laps 439 km/273 miles
1 C A S Brooks (Vanwall) 2 hr 3 min 47.8 sec 195.03 kph/121.21 mph—2 J M Hawthorn (Ferrari) 2 hr 4 min 12.0 sec—3 P. Hill (Ferrari) 2 hr 4 min 16.1 sec—4 M. Gregory, C. Shelby (Maserati) 69 laps—5 R. Salvadori (Cooper) 62 laps—6 G. Hill (Lotus) 62 laps—7 C. Allison (Lotus) 61 laps—fastest lap, P. Hill 1 min 42.9 sec 201.12 kph/125.0 mph—retired J. Brabham (Cooper) axle lap 1—G. von Trips (Ferrari) accident lap 1—H. Schell (BRM) accident lap 1—C. Shelby (Maserati) wheel lap 2—G. Gerini (Maserati) lap 3—O. Gendebien (Ferrari) axle lap 5—J. Bonnier (BRM) fire lap 15—S. Moss (Vanwall) gearbox lap 18—M. Trintignant (Cooper) gearbox lap 25—S. Lewis-Evans (Vanwall) cylinder head lap 31—H. Herrmann (Maserati) valve lap 33—J. Behra (BRM) clutch lap 43—G. Cabianca (Maserati) fuel pipe lap 52—M T de Fillipis (Maserati) engine lap 58.

Starting grid 4-3-4

Moss 1 min 40.5 sec—Brooks 1 min 41.4 sec—Hawthorn 1 min 41.8 sec—Lewis-Evans 1 min 42.4 sec—Gendebien 1 min 42.5 sec—von Trips 1 min 42.6 sec—P. Hill 1 min 42.7 sec—Behra 1 min 43.2 sec—Schell 1 min 43.2 sec—Bonnier 1 min 44.7 sec—Gregory 1 min 44.9 sec—G. Hill 1 min 46.0 sec—Trintignant 1 min 46.4 sec—Salvadori 1 min 47.0 sec—Brabham 1 min 47.3 sec—Allison 1 min 47.8 sec—Shelby 1 min 48.0 sec—Herrmann 1 min 49.8 sec—Gerini 1 min 50.1 sec—Cablanca 1 min 54.6 sec—de Fillipis 1 min 55.9 sec.

MOROCCAN GRAND PRIX

Ain Diab Casablanca; 19 October; 53 laps 402 km/250 miles
1 S. Moss (Vanwall) 2 hr 9 min 15.1 sec 186.96 kph/116.2 mph—2 J M Hawthorn (Ferrari) 2 hr 10 min 39.8 sec—3 P. Hill (Ferrari) 2 hr 10 min 40.6 sec—4 J. Bonnier (BRM) 2 hr 11 min 1.8 sec—5 H. Schell (BRM) 2 hr 11 min 48.8 sec—6 M. Gregory (Maserati) 52 laps—7 R. Salvadori (Cooper) 51 laps—8 J. Fairman (Cooper) 50 laps—9 H. Herrmann (Maserati) 50 laps—10 C. Allison (Lotus) 49 laps—11 J. Brabham (Cooper) 49 laps—12 B. McLaren (Cooper) 48 laps—13 G. Gerini (Maserati) 48 laps—14 R. La Caze (Cooper) 48 laps—15 A. Guelfi (Cooper) 48 laps—16 G. Hill (Lotus) 46 laps—fastest lap, Moss 2 min 22.5 sec 189.64 kph/117.86 mph—retired M. Trintignant (Cooper) final drive lap 10—R. Flockhart (BRM) camshaft lap 16—W. Seidel (Maserati) accident lap 16—J. Behra (BRM) lap 27—C A S Brooks (Vanwall) engine lap 29—O. Gendebien (Ferrari) accident lap 29—T. Bridger (Cooper) accident lap 29—F. Picard (Cooper) accident lap 29—S. Lewis-Evans (Vanwall) fatal accident lap 42.

Starting grid 3-2-3

Hawthorn 2 min 23.1 sec—Moss 2 min 23.2 sec—Lewis-Evans 2 min 23.7 sec—Behra 2 min 23.8 sec—P. Hill 2 min 24.1 sec—Gendebien 2 min 24.3 sec—Brooks 2 min 24.4 sec—Bonnier 2 min 24.9 sec—Trintignant 2 min 26.1 sec—Schell 2 min 26.4 sec—Fairman 2 min 27.0 sec—G. Hill 2 min 27.1 sec—Gregory 2 min 27.6 sec—Salvadori 2 min 28.6 sec—Flockhart 2 min 29.8 sec—Allison 2 min 33.7 sec—Gerini 2 min 35.1 sec—Herrmann 2 min 35.1 sec—Brabham 2 min 36.6 sec—Siedel 2 min 38.2 sec—McLaren 2 min 41.2 sec—Bridger 2 min 42.5 sec—La Caze 2 min 43.1 sec—Picard 2 min 46.0 sec—Guelfi 2 min 47.0 sec.

1958 WORLD CHAMPIONSHIP

1 J M Hawthorn 42, 49—2 S. Moss 41—3 C A S Brooks 24—4 R. Salvadori 15—5 H. Schell 14—5= P. Collins 14—7 M. Trintignant 12—7= L. Musso 12—9 S. Lewis-Evans 11—10 P. Hill 9—10= W. von Trips 9—10= J. Behra 9—13 J M Fangio 7—14 J. Brabham 3—14= C. Allison 3—14= J. Bonnier 3—14= M. Gregory 3.

1959

MONACO GRAND PRIX

Monte Carlo; 10 May; 100 laps 314 km/195 miles
1 J. Brabham (Cooper) 2 hr 55 min 51.3 sec 107.32 kph/66.7 mph—2 C A S Brooks (Ferrari) 2 hr 56 min 11.7 sec—3 M. Trintignant (Cooper) 98 laps—4 P. Hill (Ferrari) 97 laps—5 B. McLaren (Cooper) 96 laps—6 R. Salvadori (Cooper) 83 laps—fastest lap, Brabham 1 min 40.4 sec 112.74 kph/70.07 mph—retired W. von Trips (Porsche) accident lap 1—C. Allison (Ferrari) accident lap 1—B. Halford (Lotus) accident lap 1—M. Gregory (Cooper) gearbox lap 6—G. Hill (Lotus) fire lap 21—J. Behra (Ferrari) engine lap 24—J. Bonnier (BRM) brakes lap 45—H. Schell (BRM) accident lap 48—R. Flockhart (BRM) accident lap 64—S. Moss (Cooper) transmission lap 81.

Starting grid 3-2-3

Moss 1 min 39.6 sec—Behra 1 min 40.0 sec—Brabham 1 min 40.1 sec—Brooks 1 min 41.0 sec—P. Hill 1 min 41.3 sec—Trintignant 1 min 41.7 sec—Bonnier 1 min 42.3 sec—Salvadori 1 min 42.4 sec—Schell 1 min 43.0 sec—Flockhart 1 min 43.1 sec—Gregory 1 min 43.2 sec—von Trips 1 min 43.8 sec—McLaren 1 min 43.9 sec—G. Hill 1 min 43.9 sec—Allison 1 min 44.4 sec—Halford 1 min 44.8 sec—non starters I. Bueb (Cooper)—G. Scarlatti (Maserati)—L. Bianchi (Cooper)—de Changy (Cooper)—P. Lovely (Lotus)—M T de Fillipis (Porsche)—Lucienbonnet (Cooper)—A. Testut (Maserati).

DUTCH GRAND PRIX

Zandvoort; 31 May; 75 laps 314 km/195 miles
1 J. Bonnier (BRM) 2 hr 5 min 26.8 sec 150.38 kph/93.46 mph—2 J. Brabham (Cooper) 2 hr 5 min 41.0 sec—3 M. Gregory (Cooper) 2 hr 6 min 49.8 sec—4 I. Ireland (Lotus) 74 laps—5 J. Behra (Ferrari) 74 laps—6 P. Hill (Ferrari) 74 laps—7 G. Hill (Lotus) 73 laps —8 M. Trintignant (Cooper) 73 laps—9 C. Allison (Ferrari) 71 laps—10 C G de Beaufort (Porsche) 68 laps—fastest lap S. Moss (Cooper) 1 min 36.6 sec 156.23 kph/97.1 mph—retired R. Salvadori (Aston Martin) engine lap 4—C. Shelby (Aston Martin) engine lap 26—C A S Brooks (Ferrari) oil leak lap 44—H. Schell (BRM) gearbox lap 47—S. Moss (Cooper) gearbox lap 64.

Starting grid 3-2-3

Bonnier 1 min 36.0 sec—Brabham 1 min 36.0 sec—Moss 1 min 36.2 sec—Behra 1 min 36.6 sec—G. Hill 1 min 36.7 sec—Schell 1 min 37.3 sec—Gregory 1 min 37.6 sec—Brooks 1 min 37.9 sec—Ireland 1 min 38.3 sec—Shelby 1 min 38.5 sec—Trintignant 1 min 38.7 sec—P. Hill 1 min 39.2 sec—Salvadori 1 min 39.7 sec—de Beaufort 1 min 44.5 sec—Allison.

FRENCH GRAND PRIX

Rheims; 3 July; 50 laps 415 km/258 miles
1 C A S Brooks (Ferrari) 2 hr 1 min 26.5 sec 205.03 kph/127.43 mph—2 P. Hill (Ferrari) 2 hr 1 min 54.0 sec—3 J. Brabham (Cooper) 2 hr 3 min 4.2 sec—4 O. Gendebien (Ferrari) 2 hr 3 min 14.0 sec—5 B. McLaren (Cooper) 2 hr 3 min 14.2 sec—6 R. Flockhart (BRM) 2 hr 3 min 32.2 sec—7 H. Schell (BRM) 47 laps—8 G. Scarlatti (Maserati) 41 laps—9 C G de Beaufort (Maserati) 40 laps—10 F. d'Orey (Maserati) 40 laps—11 M. Trintignant (Cooper) 36 laps—fastest lap S. Moss (BRM) 2 min 22.8 sec 209.25 kph/130.05 mph—retired J. Bonnier (BRM) engine lap 6—C. Davis (Cooper) oil pipe lap 7—G. Hill (Lotus) damaged radiator lap 7—M. Gregory (Cooper) illness lap 9—I. Ireland (Lotus) wheel lap 13—I. Burgess (Cooper) engine lap 13—D. Gurney (Ferrari) damaged radiator lap 19—R. Salvadori (Cooper) engine lap 20—J. Behra (Ferrari) engine lap 31—S. Moss (BRM) disqualified lap 43.

Starting grid 4-3-4

Brooks 2 min 19.4 sec—Brabham 2 min 19.7 sec—P. Hill 2 min 19.8 sec—Moss 2 min 19.9 sec—Behra 2 min 20.2 sec—Bonnier 2 min 20.6 sec—Gregory 2 min 20.8 sec—Trintignant 2 min 21.3 sec—Schell 2 min 21.5 sec—McLaren 2 min 21.5 sec—Gendebien 2 min 21.5 sec—Gurney 2 min 21.9 sec—Flockhart 2 min 23.4 sec—G. Hill 2 min 23.7 sec—Ireland 2 min 24.2 sec—Salvadori 2 min 26.4 sec—Davis 2 min 32.3 sec—d'Orey 2 min 34.0 sec—Burgess 2 min 35.2 sec—de Beaufort 2 min 35.4 sec—Scarlatti 2 min 35.6 sec—non starter Bayardo (Maserati).

BRITISH GRAND PRIX

Aintree; 18 July; 75 laps 225 miles/362 km
1 J. Brabham (Cooper) 2 hr 30 min 11.6 sec 89.88 mph/144.62 kph—2 S. Moss (BRM) 2 hr 30 min 33.8 sec—3 B. McLaren (Cooper) 2 hr 30 min 34.0 sec—4 H. Schell (BRM) 74 laps—5 M. Trintignant (Cooper) 74 laps—6 R. Salvadori (Aston Martin) 74 laps—7 M. Gregory (Cooper) 73 laps—8 A. Stacey (Lotus) 71 laps—9 G. Hill (Lotus) 70 laps—fastest lap, Moss, McLaren 1 min 57.0 sec 92.31 mph/148.53 kph—retired C A S Brooks (Vanwall) ignition lap 12—B. Naylor (JBW) transmission lap 17—H. Herrmann (Cooper) clutch lap 20—I. Burgess (Cooper) transmission lap 31—J. Fairman (Cooper) gearbox lap 36—J. Bonnier (BRM) brakes lap 37—R. Flockhart (BRM) accident lap 54—F. d'Orey (Maserati) accident lap 57—C. Shelby (Aston Martin) ignition lap 68.

Starting grid 3-2-3

Brabham 1 min 58.0 sec—Salvadori 1 min 58.0 sec—Schell 1 min 59.2 sec—Trintignant 1 min 59.2 sec—Gregory 1 min 59.4 sec—Shelby 1 min 59.6 sec—Moss 1 min 59.6 sec—McLaren 1 min 59.6 sec—G. Hill 2 min 00.0 sec—Bonnier 2 min 00.0 sec—Flockhart 2 min 00.2 sec—Ireland 2 min 02.8 sec (Stacey's race car)—Burgess 2 min 03.0 sec—Naylor 2 min 03.0 sec—Fairman 2 min 04.2 sec—Brooks 2 min 04.6 sec—Herrmann 2 min 05.6 sec—d'Orey 2 min 05.6 sec.

GERMAN GRAND PRIX

Avus; 2 August; 2 heats, 30 laps each 249 km/155 miles, final order decided on aggregate
1 C A S Brooks (Ferrari) 2 hr 9 min 31.6 sec 230.65 kph/143.35 mph—2 D. Gurney (Ferrari) 2 hr 9 min 33.5 sec—3 P. Hill (Ferrari) 2 hr 10 min 36.4 sec—4 M. Trintignant (Cooper) 59 laps—5 J. Bonnier (BRM) 58 laps—6 I. Burgess (Cooper) 56 laps—7 H. Schell (BRM) 49 laps—fastest lap, Brooks 2 min 4.5 sec 239.97 kph/149.14 mph—heat 1: 1 Brooks—2 Gurney—3 P. Hill—4 McLaren—5 Schell—6 Trintignant—7 Bonnier—8 Herrmann—9 Burgess—heat 2: 1 Brooks—2 P. Hill—3 Gurney—4 Trintignant—5 Bonnier—6 Burgess—7 Schell—retired heat 1: S. Moss (Cooper) transmission lap 2—C. Allison (Ferrari) clutch lap 3—I. Ireland (Lotus) final drive lap 8—G. Hill (Lotus) gearbox lap 11—J. Brabham (Cooper) transmission lap 16—M. Gregory (Cooper) engine lap 24—retired heat 2: H. Herrmann (BRM) accident lap 7—B. McLaren (Cooper) transmission lap 7.

Starting grid heat 1: 4-3-4

Brooks 2 min 05.9 sec—Moss 2 min 06.8 sec—Gurney 2 min 07.2 sec—Brabham 2 min 07.4 sec—Gregory 2 min 07.5 sec—P. Hill 2 min 07.6 sec—Bonnier 2 min 10.3 sec—Schell 2 min 10.3 sec—McLaren 2 min 10.4 sec—G. Hill 2 min 10.8 sec—Herrmann 2 min 11.4 sec—Trintignant 2 min 12.7 sec—Ireland 2 min 14.6 sec—Allison 2 min 15.8 sec—Burgess 2 min 18.9 sec—**starting grid heat 2: 4-3-4**—Brooks—Gurney—P. Hill—McLaren—Schell—Trintignant—Bonnier—Herrmann—Burgess.

PORTUGUESE GRAND PRIX

Monsanto; 23 August; 62 laps 336 km/209 miles
1 S. Moss (Cooper) 2 hr 11 min 55.4 sec 153.37 kph/95.32 mph—2 M. Gregory (Cooper) 61 laps—3 D. Gurney (Ferrari) 61 laps—4 M. Trintignant (Cooper) 60 laps—5 H. Schell (BRM) 59 laps—6 R. Salvadori (Aston Martin) 59 laps—7 R. Flockhart (BRM) 59 laps—8 C. Shelby (Aston Martin) 58 laps—9 C A S Brooks (Ferrari) 57 laps—10 M. Cabral (Cooper) 56 laps—fastest lap, Moss 2 min 5.1 sec 156.55 kph/97.3 mph—retired I. Ireland (Lotus) gearbox lap 4—P. Hill (Ferrari) accident lap 6—G. Hill (Lotus) accident lap 6—J. Bonnier (BRM) fuel pump lap 11—J. Brabham (Cooper) accident lap 24—B. McLaren (Cooper) clutch lap 39.

Starting grid 3-2-3

Moss 2 min 02.89 sec—Brabham 2 min 04.95 sec—Gregory 2 min 06.33 sec—Trintignant 2 min 07.38 sec—Bonnier 2 min 07.86 sec—Gurney 2 min 07.9 sec—P. Hill 2 min 08.2 sec—McLaren 2 min 08.2 sec—Schell 2 min 09.8 sec—Brooks 2 min 10.96 sec—Flockhart 2 min 10.98 sec—Salvadori 2 min 13.38 sec—Shelby 2 min 13.58 sec—Cabral 2 min 15.25 sec—G. Hill 2 min 15.55 sec—Ireland 2 min 18.47 sec.

ITALIAN GRAND PRIX

Monza; 13 September; 72 laps 414 km/257 miles
1 S. Moss (Cooper) 2 hr 4 min 5.4 sec 200.14 kph/124.39 mph—2 P. Hill (Ferrari) 2 hr 4 min 52.1 sec—3 J. Brabham (Cooper) 2 hr 5 min 17.9 sec—4 D. Gurney (Ferrari) 2 hr 5 min 25.0 sec—5 C. Allison (Ferrari) 71 laps—6 O. Gendebien (Ferrari) 71 laps—7 H. Schell (BRM) 70 laps—8 J. Bonnier (BRM) 70 laps—9 M. Trintignant (Cooper) 70 laps—10 C. Shelby (Aston Martin) 70 laps—11 C. Davis (Cooper) 68 laps—13 G. Scarlatti (Cooper) 68 laps—13 R. Flockhart (BRM) 67 laps—14 I. Burgess (Cooper) 67 laps—15 G. Cabianca (Maserati) 64 laps—fastest lap, P. Hill 1 min 40.4 sec 206.11 kph/128.1 mph.

Starting grid 3-2-3

Moss 1 min 39.7 sec—Brooks 1 min 39.8 sec—Brabham 1 min 40.2 sec—Gurney 1 min 40.8 sec—P. Hill 1 min 41.2 sec—Gendebien 1 min 41.4 sec—Schell 1 min 41.6 sec—Allison 1 min 41.8 sec—McLaren 1 min 42.0 sec—G. Hill 1 min 42.9 sec—Bonnier 1 min 43.1 sec—Scarlatti 1 min 43.3 sec—Trintignant 1 min 43.4 sec—Ireland 1 min 43.5 sec—Flockhart 1 min 43.6 sec—Burgess 1 min 44.6 sec—Salvadori 1 min 44.7 sec—Davis 1 min 44.9 sec—Shelby 1 min 46.4 sec—Fairman 1 min 49.4 sec—Cabianca 1 min 51.5 sec.

UNITED STATES GRAND PRIX

Sebring; 12 December; 42 laps 218 miles/351 km
1 B. McLaren (Cooper) 2 hr 12 min 35.7 sec 98.83 mph/159.02 kph—2 M. Trintignant (Cooper) 2 hr 12 min 36.6 sec—3 C A S Brooks (Ferrari) 2 hr 15 min 36.6 sec—4 J. Brabham (Cooper) 2 hr 17 min 33.0 sec—5 I. Ireland (Lotus) 39 laps—6 W. von Trips (Ferrari) 38 laps—7 H. Blanchard (Porsche) 38 laps—fastest lap, Trintignant 3 min 5.0 sec 101.13 mph/162.72 kph—retired B. Said (Connaught) accident lap 2—A. Stacey (Lotus) clutch lap 3—S. Moss (Cooper) transmission lap 6—H. Schell (Cooper) clutch lap 7—G. Constantine (Cooper) overheating lap 7—F. d'Orey (Tec-Mec) oil leak lap 8—P. Hill (Ferrari) clutch lap 10—A. de Tomaso (Cooper) brakes lap 15—R. Ward (Kurtis Kraft) clutch lap 22—C. Allison (Ferrari) clutch lap 24—R. Salvadori (Cooper) transmission lap 25.

Starting grid: 3-2-3

Moss 3 min 00.0 sec—Brabham 3 min 03.0 sec—Schell 3 min 05.2 sec—Brooks 3 min 05.9 sec—Trintignant 3 min 06.0 sec—von Trips 3 min 06.2 sec—Allison 3 min 06.8 sec—P. Hill 3 min 07.2 sec—Ireland 3 min 08.2 sec—McLaren 3 min 08.6 sec—Salvadori 3 min 12.0 sec—Stacey 3 min 13.8 sec—Said 3 min 27.3 sec—de Tomaso 3 min 28.0 sec—Constantine 3 min 30.6 sec—Blanchard 3 min 32.7 sec—d'Orey 3 min 33.4 sec—Ward 3 min 43.8 sec—non starter P. Cade (Maserati).

1959 WORLD CHAMPIONSHIP

1 J. Brabham 31, 34—2 C A S Brooks 27—3 S. Moss 25½—4 P. Hill 20—5 M. Trintignant 19—6 B. McLaren 16½—7 D. Gurney 13—8 J. Bonnier 10—8= M. Gregory 10—10 H. Schell 5—10= I. Ireland 5—12 O. Gendebien 3—13 C. Allison 2—13= J. Behra 2.

1960

ARGENTINE GRAND PRIX

Buenos Aires: 7 February; 80 laps 312 km/194 miles
1 B. McLaren (Cooper) 2 hr 17 min 49.5 sec 132.74 kph/82.8 mph—2 C. Allison (Ferrari) 2 hr 18 min 15.8 sec—3 M. Trintignant, S. Moss (Cooper) 2 hr 18 min 26.4 sec—4 C. Menditeguy (Cooper) 2 hr 18 min 42.8 sec—5 W. von Trips (Ferrari) 79 laps—6 I. Ireland (Lotus) 79 laps—7 J. Bonnier (BRM) 79 laps—8 P. Hill (Ferrari) 77 laps—9 R. Larreta (Lotus) 77 laps—10 F. Gonzalez (Ferrari) 77 laps—11 R. Bonomi (Cooper) 76 laps—12 M. Gregory (Porsche) 76 laps—13 G. Munaron (Maserati) 72 laps—14 M. Stefano (Maserati) 70 laps—fastest lap, Moss 1 min 38.9 sec 140.38 kph/87.25 mph—retired G. Scarlatti (Maserati) overheating lap 11—A. Creus (Maserati) lap 17—E. Chimeri (Maserati) lap 24—A. Stacey (Lotus) lap 25—G. Hill (BRM) valve spring lap 38—S. Moss (Cooper) suspension lap 41—J. Brabham (Cooper) transmission lap 43—H. Schell (Cooper) fuel pump lap 62.

Starting grid 4-3-4

Moss 1 min 36.9 sec—Ireland 1 min 38.5 sec—G. Hill 1 min 38.9 sec—Bonnier 1 min 39.9 sec—von Trips 1 min 39.2 sec—P. Hill 1 min 39.3 sec—Allison 1 min 39.7 sec—Trintignant 1 min 39.9 sec—Schell 1 min 40.3 sec—Brabham 1 min 40.6 sec—Gonzalez 1 min 41.0 sec—Menditeguy 1 min 41.8 sec—McLaren 1 min 41.8 sec—Stacey 1 min 43.5 sec—Larreta 1 min 45.0 sec—Gregory 1 min 45.5 sec—Bonomi 1 min 46.1 sec—Scarlatti 1 min 46.1 sec—Munaron 1 min 49.0 sec—Stefano 1 min 50.1 sec—Chimen 1 min 50.5 sec—Creus 1 min 52.8 sec.

MONACO GRAND PRIX

Monte Carlo; 19 May; 100 laps 314 km/195 miles
1 S. Moss (Lotus) 2 hr 53 min 45.5 sec 108.54 kph/67.46 mph—2 B. McLaren (Cooper) 2 hr 54 min 37.6 sec—3 P. Hill (Ferrari) 2 hr 54 min 47.4 sec—4 C A S Brooks (Cooper) 99 laps—5 J. Bonnier (BRM) 83 laps—6 R. Ginther (Ferrari) 70 laps—7 G. Hill (BRM) 66 laps—8 W. von Trips (Ferrari) 61 laps—9 I. Ireland (Lotus) 56 laps—fastest lap, McLaren 1 min 36.2 sec 116.06 kph/72.13 mph—retired M. Trintignant (Cooper) gearbox lap 5—C. Bristow (Cooper) gearbox lap 17—J. Surtees (Lotus) transmission lap 18—A. Stacey (Lotus) engine mountings lap 23—R. Salvadori (Cooper) overheating lap 39—J. Brabham (Cooper) disqualified lap 42—D. Gurney (BRM) suspension lap 45.

Starting grid 3-2-3

Moss 1 min 36.3 sec—Brabham 1 min 37.3 sec—Brooks 1 min 37.7 sec—Bristow 1 min 37.7 sec—Bonnier 1 min 37.7 sec—G. Hill 1 min 38.0 sec—Ireland 1 min 38.2 sec—von Trips 1 min 38.3 sec—Ginther 1 min 38.6 sec—P. Hill 1 min 38.6 sec—McLaren 1 min 38.6 sec—Salvadori 1 min 38.7 sec—Stacey 1 min 38.9 sec—Gurney 1 min 38.9 sec—Surtees 1 min 39.0 sec—Trintignant 1 min 39.1 sec—non starters L. Reventlow (Scarab)—C. Daigh (Scarab)—B. Naylor (JBW)—G. Scarlatti (Cooper)—M. Gregory (Cooper)—I. Burgess (Cooper)—G. Munaron (Cooper)—B. Halford (Cooper).

DUTCH GRAND PRIX

Zandvoort; 6 June; 75 laps 314 km/195 miles
1 J. Brabham (Cooper) 2 hr 1 min 47.2 sec 154.9 kph/96.27 mph—2 I. Ireland (Lotus) 2 hr 2 min 11.2 sec—3 G. Hill (BRM) 2 hr 2 min 43.8 sec—4 S. Moss (Lotus) 2 hr 2 min 44.9 sec—5 W. von Trips (Ferrari) 74 laps—6 R. Ginther (Ferrari) 74 laps—7 H. Taylor (Cooper) 70 laps—8 C. G de Beaufort (Cooper) 69 laps—fastest lap, Moss 1 min 33.8 sec 160.87 kph/99.98 mph—retired C A S Brooks (Cooper) gearbox lap 5—B. McLaren (Cooper) transmission lap 9—C. Bristow (Cooper) engine lap 10—D. Gurney (BRM) brakes lap 12—M. Trintignant (Cooper) gearbox lap 40—J. Clark (Lotus) gearbox lap 43—J. Bonnier (BRM) engine lap 55—P. Hill (Ferrari) engine lap 56—A. Stacey (Lotus) transmission lap 59.

Starting grid 3-2-3

Moss 1 min 33.2 sec—Brabham 1 min 33.4 sec—Ireland 1 min 33.9 sec—Bonnier 1 min 34.3 sec—G. Hill 1 min 35.1 sec—Gurney 1 min 35.2 sec—Bristow 1 min 35.3 sec—Stacey 1 min 35.4 sec—McLaren 1 min 35.7 sec—Brooks 1 min 36.0 sec—Clark 1 min 36.3 sec—Ginther 1 min 36.3 sec—P. Hill 1 min 36.4 sec—H. Taylor 1 min 36.4 sec—von Trips 1 min 36.7 sec—Trintignant 1 min 38.5 sec—de Beaufort 1 min 41.7 sec—non starters R. Salvadori (Aston Martin)—L. Reventlow (Scarab)—C. Daigh (Scarab)—M. Gregory (Cooper).

BELGIAN GRAND PRIX

Spa-Francorchamps; 19 June; 36 laps 507 km/315 miles
1 J. Brabham (Cooper) 2 hr 21 min 37.3 sec 215.01 kph/133.63 mph—2 B. McLaren (Cooper) 2 hr 22 min 40.6 sec—3 O. Gendebien (Cooper) 35 laps—4 P. Hill (Ferrari) 35 laps—5 J. Clark (Lotus) 34 laps—6 L. Bianchi (Cooper) 28 laps—fastest lap, Brabham, P. Hill, Ireland 3 min 51.9 sec 217.91 kph/135.43 mph—retired L. Reventlow (Scarab) engine lap 2—C A S Brooks (Cooper) gearbox lap 4—D. Gurney (BRM) engine lap 5—I. Ireland (Lotus) accident lap 14—J. Bonnier (BRM) engine lap 15—C. Daigh (Scarab) engine lap 17—C. Bristow (Cooper) fatal accident lap 20—W. von Trips (Ferrari) clutch lap 23—A. Stacey (Lotus) fatal accident lap 25—W. Mairesse (Ferrari) engine lap 25—G. Hill (BRM) engine lap 36.

Starting grid 3-2-3

Brabham 3 min 50.0 sec—Brooks 3 min 52.5 sec—P. Hill 3 min 53.3 sec—Gendebien 3 min 53.5 sec—G. Hill 3 min 54.2 sec—Bonnier 3 min 54.8 sec—Ireland 3 min 55.4 sec—Bristow 3 min 56.3 sec—Clark 3 min 57.5 sec—von Trips 3 min 57.8 sec—Gurney 3 min 58.3 sec—Mairesse 3 min 58.9 sec—McLaren 4 min 00.0 sec—Bianchi 4 min 00.6 sec—Reventlow 4 min 09.7 sec—Stacey 4 min 17.6 sec—Daigh 4 min 18.5 sec—non starters S. Moss (Lotus)—M. Taylor (Lotus).

FRENCH GRAND PRIX

Rheims; 3 July; 50 laps 415 km/258 miles
1 J. Brabham (Cooper) 1 hr 57 min 24.9 sec 212.69 kph/132.19 mph—2 O. Gendebien (Cooper) 1 hr 58 min 13.2 sec—3 B. McLaren (Cooper) 1 hr 58 min 16.8 sec—4 H. Taylor (Cooper) 49 laps—5 J. Clark (Lotus) 49 laps—6 R. Flockhart (Lotus) 49

FRENCH GRAND PRIX—*continued*

laps—7 I. Ireland (Lotus) 43 laps—8 B. Halford (Cooper) 40 laps—9 M. Gregory (Cooper) 37 laps—10 I. Burgess (Cooper) 36 laps—11 W. von Trips (Ferrari) 31 laps—12 P. Hill (Ferrari) 29 laps—fastest lap, Brabham 2 min 17.5 sec 217.31 kph/135.06 mph—retired G. Hill (BRM) accident, start—M. Trintignant (Cooper) accident lap 1—C A S Brooks (Vanwall) accident lap 8—W. Mairesse (Ferrari) transmission lap 15—G. Munaron (Cooper) transmission lap 16—D. Gurney (BRM) engine lap 17—L. Bianchi (Cooper) transmission lap 18—J. Bonnier (BRM) engine lap 22.

Starting grid 3-2-3

Brabham 2 min 16.8 sec—P. Hill 2 min 18.2 sec—G. Hill 2 min 18.4 sec—Ireland 2 min 18.5 sec—Mairesse 2 min 19.3 sec—von Trips 2 min 19.4 sec—Gurney 2 min 19.4 sec—Flockhart 2 min 19.5 sec—McLaren 2 min 19.6 sec—Bonnier 2 min 19.8 sec—Gendebien 2 min 20.0 sec—Clark 2 min 20.3 sec—H. Taylor 2 min 22.8 sec—Brooks 2 min 23.3 sec—Bianchi 2 min 23.6 sec—Halford 2 min 23.6 sec—Gregory 2 min 24.3 sec—Trintignant 2 min 24.7 sec—Munaron 2 min 31.3 sec—Burgess 2 min 36.7 sec.

BRITISH GRAND PRIX

Silverstone; 16 July; 77 laps 225 miles/362 km
1 J. Brabham (Cooper) 2 hr 4 min 24.6 sec 108.69 mph/174.88 kph—2 J. Surtees (Lotus) 2 hr 5 min 14.2 sec—3 I. Ireland (Lotus) 2 hr 5 min 54.2 sec—4 B. McLaren (Cooper) 76 laps—5 C A S Brooks (Cooper) 76 laps—6 W. von Trips (Ferrari) 75 laps—7 P. Hill (Ferrari) 75 laps—8 H. Taylor (Cooper) 74 laps—9 O. Gendebien (Cooper) 74 laps—10 D. Gurney (BRM) 74 laps—11 M. Trintignant (Aston Martin) 72 laps—12 D. Piper (Lotus) 72 laps—13 B. Naylor (Cooper) 72 laps—14 M. Gregory (Cooper) 71 laps—15 G. Munaron (Cooper) 70 laps—16 J. Clark (Lotus) 70 laps—fastest lap, G. Hill 1 min 34.4 sec 111.62 mph/179.6 kph—retired K. Greene (Cooper) overheating lap 12—R. Salvadori (Aston Martin) steering lap 46—J. Fairman (Cooper) fuel pump lap 46—C. Daigh (Cooper) engine lap 58—I. Burgess (Cooper) valves lap 58—J. Bonnier (BRM) suspension lap 61—L. Bianchi (Cooper) engine lap 63—G. Hill (BRM) accident lap 72.

Starting grid 4-3-4

Brabham 1 min 34.6 sec—G. Hill 1 min 35.6 sec—McLaren 1 min 36.0 sec—Bonnier 1 min 36.2 sec—Ireland 1 min 36.2 sec—Gurney 1 min 36.6 sec—von Trips 1 min 37.0 sec—Clark 1 min 37.0 sec—Brooks 1 min 37.6 sec—P. Hill 1 min 37.8 sec—Surtees 1 min 38.6 sec—Gendebien 1 min 39.2 sec—Salvadori 1 min 39.4 sec—Gregory 1 min 39.8 sec—Fairman 1 min 39.8 sec—H. Taylor 1 min 40.0 sec—Bianchi 1 min 40.2 sec—Naylor 1 min 41.2 sec—Daigh 1 min 42.4 sec—Burgess 1 min 42.6 sec—Trintignant 1 min 43.8 sec—Greene 1 min 45.8 sec—Piper 2 min 05.6 sec—Munaron

PORTUGUESE GRAND PRIX

Oporto; 14 August; 55 laps 407 km/253 miles
1 J. Brabham (Cooper) 2 hr 19 min 00.3 sec 175.81 kph/109.27 mph—2 B. McLaren (Cooper) 2 hr 19 min 58.0 sec—3 J. Clark (Lotus) 2 hr 20 min 53.3 sec—4 W. von Trips (Ferrari) 2 hr 20 min 58.8 sec—5 C A S Brooks (Cooper) 49 laps—6 I. Ireland (Lotus) 48 laps—7 O. Gendebien (Cooper) 46 laps—fastest lap, Surtees 2 min 27.5 sec 180.67 kph/112.29 mph—retired J. Bonnier (BRM) engine lap 7—G. Hill (BRM) gearbox lap 9—M. Gregory (Cooper) gearbox lap 22—D. Gurney (BRM) engine lap 26—P. Hill (Ferrari) clutch lap 31—J. Surtees (Lotus) split radiator lap 37—M. Cabral (Cooper) clutch lap 38—S. Moss (Lotus) disqualified lap 51.

Starting grid 3-2-3

Surtees 2 min 25.6 sec—Gurney 2 min 25.6 sec—Brabham 2 min 26.0 sec—Moss 2 min 26.2 sec—G. Hill 2 min 27.1 sec—McLaren 2 min 27.4 sec—Ireland 2 min 27.5 sec—Clark 2 min 28.4 sec—von Trips 2 min 28.4 sec—P. Hill 2 min 28.4 sec—Gregory 2 min 29.2 sec—Brooks 2 min 32.1 sec—Bonnier 2 min 33.3 sec—Gendebien 2 min 33.7 sec—Cabral 2 min 35.8 sec—non starter H. Taylor (Cooper).

ITALIAN GRAND PRIX

Monza banked track; 4 September; 50 laps 500 km/311 miles
1 P. Hill (Ferrari) 2 hr 21 min 9.2 sec 212.5 kph/132.07 mph—2 R. Ginther (Ferrari) 2 hr 23 min 36.8 sec—3 W. Mairesse (Ferrari) 49 laps—4 G. Cabianca (Cooper) 48 laps—5 W. von Trips (Ferrari) 48 laps—6 H. Herrmann (Porsche) 47 laps—7 E. Barth (Porsche) 47 laps—8 P. Drogo (Cooper) 45 laps—9 W. Seidel (Cooper) 44 laps—10 F. Gamble (Porsche) 41 laps—fastest lap, P. Hill 2 min 43.6 sec 219.95 kph/136.7 mph—retired A. Owen (Cooper) accident lap 1—V. Wilson (Cooper) lap 25—G. Scarlatti (Cooper) throttle lap 27—G. Munaron (Cooper) oil pipe lap 28—A. Thiele (Cooper) gearbox lap 33—B. Naylor (Cooper) transmission lap 42.

Starting grid 3-2-3

P. Hill 2 min 41.4 sec—Ginther 2 min 43.3 sec—Mairesse 2 min 43.9 sec—Cabianca 2 min 49.3 sec—Scarlatti 2 min 49.7 sec—von Trips 2 min 51.9 sec—Naylor 2 min 52.4 sec—Munaron 2 min 53.1 sec—Thiele 2 min 55.6 sec—Herrmann 2 min 58.3 sec—Owen 3 min 01.5 sec—Barth 3 min 02.1 sec—Seidel 3 min 07.0 sec—Gamble 3 min 10.6 sec—Drogo 3 min 11.9 sec—Wilson 3 min 16.5 sec.

UNITED STATES GRAND PRIX

Riverside; 20 November; 75 laps 246 miles/396 km
1 S. Moss (Lotus) 2 hr 28 min 52.2 sec 99.0 mph/159.29 kph—2 I. Ireland (Lotus) 2 hr 29 min 30.2 sec—3 B. McLaren (Cooper) 2 hr 29 min 44.2 sec—4 J. Brabham (Cooper) 74 laps—5 J. Bonnier (BRM) 74 laps—6 P. Hill (Cooper) 74 laps—7 J. Hall (Lotus) 73 laps—8 R. Salvadori (Cooper) 73 laps—9 W. von Trips (Cooper) 72 laps—10 C. Daigh (Scarab) 70 laps—11 P. Lovely (Cooper) 69 laps—12 O. Gendebien (Cooper) 69 laps—13 P. Drake (Maserati) 68 laps—14 H. Taylor (Cooper) 68 laps—15 M. Trintignant (Cooper) 66 laps—16 J. Clark (Lotus) 61 laps—fastest lap, Brabham 1 min 56.3 sec 100.9 mph/162.35 kph—retired J. Surtees (Lotus) accident lap 4—C A S Brooks (Cooper) ignition lap 7—R. Flockhart (Cooper) transmission lap 12—D. Gurney (BRM) cooling lap 19—B. Naylor (Maserati) engine lap 21—I. Burgess (Cooper) ignition lap 30—G. Hill (BRM) engine lap 35.

Starting grid 3-2-3

Moss 1 min 54.4 sec—Brabham 1 min 55.0 sec—Gurney 1 min 55.2 sec—Bonnier 1 min 55.6 sec—Clark 1 min 55.6 sec—Surtees 1 min 55.6 sec—Ireland 1 min 57.0 sec—Gendebien 1 min 57.2 sec—Brooks 1 min 57.2 sec—McLaren 1 min 57.4 sec—G. Hill 1 min 57.6 sec—Hall 1 min 58.2 sec—P. Hill 1 min 58.8 sec—H. Taylor 1 min 59.0 sec—Salvadori 1 min 59.6 sec—von Trips 2 min 01.4 sec—Naylor 2 min 02.2 sec—Daigh 2 min 02.6 sec—Trintignant 2 min 03.2 sec—Lovely 2 min 03.4 sec—Flockhart 2 min 04.4 sec—Drake 2 min 05.4 sec—Burgess 2 min 06.6 sec.

1960 WORLD CHAMPIONSHIP

1 J. Brabham 43—2 B. McLaren 34, 37—3 S. Moss 19—4 I. Ireland 18—5 P. Hill 16—6 W. von Trips 10—6= O.Gendebien 10—8 R. Ginther 8—8= J. Clark 8—10 C A S Brooks 7—11 C. Allison 6—11= J. Surtees 6—13 J. Bonnier 4—13= G. Hill 4—13= W. Mairesse 4—16 C. Menditeguy 3—16= G. Cabianca 3—16= H. Taylor 3—19 L. Bianchi 1—19= R. Flockhart 1—19= H. Herrmann 1.

1961

MONACO GRAND PRIX

Monte Carlo; 14 May; 100 laps 314 km/195 miles
1 S. Moss (Lotus) 2 hr 45 min 50.1 sec 113.76 kph/70.7 mph—2 R. Ginther (Ferrari) 2 hr 45 min 53.7 sec—3 P. Hill (Ferrari) 2 hr 46 min 31.4 sec—4 W. von Trips (Ferrari) 98 laps—5 D. Gurney (Porsche) 98 laps—6 B. McLaren (Cooper) 95 laps—7 M. Trintignant (Cooper) 95 laps—8 C. Allison (Lotus) 93 laps—9 H. Herrmann (Porsche) 91 laps—10 J. Clark (Lotus) 89 laps—11 J. Surtees (Cooper) 68 laps—12 J. Bonnier (Porsche) 59 laps—13 C A S Brooks (BRM) 54 laps—fastest lap, Ginther, Moss 1 min 36.3sec/115.93kph/72.05 mph—retired G. Hill (BRM) fuel pump lap 11—J. Brabham (Cooper) engine lap 38—M. May (Lotus) gearbox lap 41.

Starting grid 3-2-3

Moss 1 min 39.1 sec—Ginther 1 min 39.3 sec—Clark 1 min 39.6 sec—G. Hill 1 min 39.6 sec—P. Hill 1 min 39.8 sec—von Trips 1 min 39.8 sec—McLaren 1 min 39.8 sec—Brooks 1 min 40.1 sec—Bonnier 1 min 40.3 sec—Gurney 1 min 40.6 sec—Surtees 1 min 41.1 sec—Herrmann 1 min 41.1 sec—May 1 min 42.0 sec—Allison 1 min 42.3 sec—Trintignant 1 min 42.4 sec—Brabham 1 min 44.0 sec—non starters H. Taylor (Lotus)—L. Bianchi (Emeryson)—O. Gendebien (Emeryson)—I. Ireland (Lotus)—M. Gregory (Cooper)—I. Burgess (Lotus).

DUTCH GRAND PRIX

Zandvoort; 22 May; 75 laps 314 km/195 miles
1 W. von Trips (Ferrari) 2 hr 52.1 sec 154.8 kph/96.21 mph—2 P. Hill (Ferrari) 2 hr 53.0 sec—3 J. Clark (Lotus) 2 hr 2 min 5.2 sec—4 S. Moss (Lotus) 2 hr 2 min 14.3 sec—5 R. Ginther (Ferrari) 2 hr 2 min 14.4 sec—6 J. Brabham (Cooper) 2 hr 3 min 12.2 sec—7 J. Surtees (Cooper) 2 hr 3 min 18.8 sec—8 G. Hill (BRM) 2 hr 3 min 21.9 sec—9 C A S Brooks (BRM) 74 laps—10 D. Gurney (Porsche) 74 laps—11 J. Bonnier (Porsche) 73 laps—12 B. McLaren (Cooper) 73 laps—13 T. Taylor (Lotus) 73 laps—14 C G de Beaufort (Porsche) 72 laps—15 H. Herrmann (Porsche) 72 laps—fastest lap, Clark 1 min 35.5 sec 158.0 kph/98.2 mph—none retired.

Starting grid 3-2-3

P. Hill 1 min 35.7 sec—von Trips 1 min 35.7 sec—Ginther 1 min 35.9 sec—Moss 1 min 36.2 sec—G. Hill 1 min 36.3 sec—Gurney 1 min 36.4 sec—Brabham 1 min 36.6 sec—Brooks 1 min 36.8 sec—Surtees 1 min 36.8 sec—Clark 1 min 36.9 sec—Bonnier 1 min 37.1 sec—Herrmann 1 min 38.0 sec—McLaren 1 min 38.2 sec—T. Taylor 1 min 39.5 sec—de Beaufort 1 min 39.8 sec—non starters I. Burgess (Lotus)—M. Gregory (Cooper).

BELGIAN GRAND PRIX

Spa-Francorchamps; 18 June; 30 laps 423 km/263 miles
1 P. Hill (Ferrari) 2 hr 3 min 3.8 sec 206.19 kph/128.15 mph—2 W. von Trips (Ferrari) 2 hr 3 min 4.5 sec—3 R. Ginther (Ferrari) 2 hr 3 min 23.3 sec—4 O. Gendebien (Ferrari) 2 hr 3 min 49.4 sec—5 J. Surtees (Cooper) 2 hr 4 min 30.6 sec—6 D. Gurney (Porsche) 2 hr 4 min 34.8 sec—7 J. Bonnier (Porsche) 2 hr 5 min 50.9 sec—8 S. Moss (Lotus) 2 hr 6 min 59.4 sec—9 J. Lewis (Cooper) 29 laps—10 M. Gregory (Cooper) 29 laps—11 C G de Beaufort (Porsche) 28 laps—12 J. Clark (Lotus) 24 laps—13 C A S Brooks (BRM) 24 laps—fastest lap, Ginther 3 min 59.8 sec 211.58 kph/131.5 mph—retired W. Mairesse (Lotus) engine lap 8—B. McLaren (Cooper) fuel feed lap 9—I. Ireland (Lotus) engine lap 10—L. Bianchi (Lotus) oil pipe lap 10—J Brabham (Cooper) engine lap 12—L. Bandini (Cooper) engine lap 20—M. Trintignant (Cooper) transmission lap 23—G. Hill (BRM) engine lap 24.

Starting grid 3-2-3

P.Hill 3 min 59.3 sec—von Trips 4 min 00.1 sec—Gendebien 4 min 03.0 sec—Surtees 4 min 06.0 sec—Ginther 4 min 06.1 sec—G. Hill 4 min 07.6 sec—Brooks 4 min 07.9 sec—Moss 4 min 08.2 sec—Bonnier 4 min 08.3 sec—Gurney 4 min 08.4 sec—Brabham 4 min 08.6 sec—Gregory 4 min 10.2 sec—Lewis 4 min 11.1 sec—de Beaufort 4 min 16.7 sec—McLaren 4 min 17.4 sec—Clark 4 min 17.7 sec—Bandini 4 min 19.0 sec—Ireland 4 min 20.0 sec—Mairesse 4 min 20.6 sec—Trintignant 4 min 21.4 sec—Bianchi 4 min 27.3 sec—non starters—H. Taylor, C. Allison (Lotus)—A. Marsh (Lotus)—W. Seidel (Lotus)—I. Burgess (Lotus).

FRENCH GRAND PRIX

Rheims; 2 July; 52 laps 432 km/268 miles
1 G. Baghetti (Ferrari) 2 hr 14 min 17.5 sec 192.82 kph/119.84 mph—2 D. Gurney (Porsche) 2 hr 14 min 17.6 sec—3 J. Clark (Lotus) 2 hr 15 min 18.6 sec—4 I. Ireland (Lotus) 2 hr 15 min 27.8 sec—5 B. McLaren (Cooper) 2 hr 15 min 59.3 sec—6 G. Hill (BRM) 2 hr 15 min 59.4 sec—7 J. Bonnier (Porsche) 2 hr 17 min 32.9 sec—8 R. Salvadori (Cooper) 51 laps—9 P. Hill (Ferrari) 50 laps—10 H. Taylor (Lotus) 49 laps—11 M. May (Lotus) 48 laps—12 M. Gregory (Cooper) 43 laps—13 M. Trintignant (Cooper) 42 laps—14 I. Burgess (Lotus) 42 laps—15 R. Ginther (Ferrari) 40 laps—fastest lap, P. Hill 2 min 29.9 sec 199.32 kph/123.88 mph—retired J. Lewis (Cooper) engine lap 4—J. Surtees (Cooper) suspension lap 4—C A S Brooks (BRM) engine lap 4—B. Collomb (Cooper) engine lap 7—J. Brabham (Cooper) engine lap 14—W. von Trips (Ferrari) engine lap 18—L. Bianchi (Lotus) clutch lap 21—C G de Beaufort (Porsche) engine lap 23—G. Scarlatti (de Tomaso) engine lap 24—W. Mairesse (Lotus) fuel lap 25—S. Moss (Lotus) suspension lap 31.

Starting grid 3-2-3

P. Hill 2 min 24.9 sec—von Trips 2 min 26.4 sec—Ginther 2 min 26.8 sec—Moss 2 min 27.6 sec—Clark 2 min 29.0 sec—G. Hill 2 min 29.1 sec—Surtees 2 min 29.1 sec—McLaren 2 min 29.4 sec—Gurney 2 min 29.6 sec—Ireland 2 min 29.8 sec—Brooks 2 min 29.9 sec—Baghetti 2 min 30.5 sec—Bonnier 2 min 30.5 sec—Brabham 2 min 31.0 sec—Salvadori 2 min 31.2 sec—Gregory 2 min 31.3 sec—de Beaufort 2 min 31.8 sec—Lewis 2 min 32.0 sec—Bianchi 2 min 33.4 sec—Mairesse 2 min 35.8 sec—Collomb 2 min 36.8 sec—May 2 min 37.9 sec—Trintignant 2 min 38.8 sec—Burgess 2 min 39.7 sec—H. Taylor 2 min 40.3 sec—Scarlatti2 min 47.1 sec.

BRITISH GRAND PRIX

Aintree; 15 July; 75 laps 225 miles/362 km
1 W. von Trips (Ferrari) 2 hr 40 min 53.6 sec 83.91 mph/135.01 kph—2 P. Hill (Ferrari) 2 hr 41 min 39.6 sec—3 R. Ginther (Ferrari) 2 hr 41 min 40.4 sec—4 J. Brabham (Cooper) 2 hr 42 min 02.2 sec—5 J. Bonnier (Porsche) 2 hr 42 min 09.8 sec—6 R. Salvadori (Cooper) 2 hr 42 min 19.8 sec—7 D. Gurney (Porsche) 74 laps—8 B. McLaren (Cooper) 74 laps—9 C A S Brooks (BRM) 73 laps—10 I. Ireland (Lotus) 72 laps—11 M. Gregory (Cooper) 71 laps—12 L. Bandini (Cooper) 71 laps—13 T. Maggs (Cooper) 69 laps—14 I. Burgess (Lotus) 69 laps—15 K. Greene (Gilby) 69 laps—16 C G de Beaufort (Porsche) 69 laps—17 W. Seidel (Lotus) 58 laps—fastest lap, Brooks 1 min 57.8 sec 91.00 mph/146.42 kph—retired N. Natili (Cooper) transmission lap 1—H. Taylor (Lotus) accident lap 6—G. Ashmore (Lotus) engine lap 8—J. Lewis (Cooper) suspension lap 8—T. Parnell (Lotus) clutch lap 13—J. Surtees (Cooper) differential lap 24—A. Marsh (Lotus) misfiring—G. Baghetti (Ferrari) accident lap 29—G. Hill (BRM) valve springs lap 44—S. Moss (Lotus) brakes lap 45—L. Bianchi (Lotus) gearbox lap 46—J. Fairman, S. Moss (Ferguson) disqualified lap 57—J. Clark (Lotus) oil pipe lap 63.

Starting grid 3-2-3

P. Hill 1 min 58.8 sec—Ginther 1 min 58.8 sec—Bonnier 1 min 58.8 sec—von Trips 1 min 58.8 sec—Moss 1 min 59.0 sec—Brooks 1 min 59.0 sec—Ireland 1 min 59.2 sec—Clark 1 min 59.2 sec—Brabham 1 min 59.4 sec—Surtees 1 min 59.6 sec—G. Hill 2 min 00.0 sec—Gurney 2 min 00.2 sec—Salvadori 2 min 00.8 sec—McLaren 2 min 01.0 sec—Lewis 2 min 01.0 sec—Gregory 2 min 01.4 sec—H. Taylor 2 min 01.8 sec—de Beaufort 2 min 02.0 sec—Baghetti

BRITISH GRAND PRIX—*continued*

2 min 02.0 sec—Fairman 2 min 03.4 sec—Bandini 2 min 03.6 sec—Seidel 2 min 04.2 sec—Greene 2 min 06.0 sec—Maggs 2 min 06.4 sec—Burgess 2 min 06.6 sec—Ashmore 2 min 08.2 sec—Marsh 2 min 09.6 sec—Natili 2 min 10.2 sec—Parnell 2 min 16.8 sec—Bianchi 2 min 18.8 sec.

GERMAN GRAND PRIX

Nürburgring; 6 August; 15 laps 340 km/211 miles
1 S. Moss (Lotus) 2 hr 18 min 12.4 sec 148.57 kph/92.34 mph—2 W von Trips (Ferrari) 2 hr 18 min 33.8 sec—3 P. Hill (Ferrari) 2 hr 18 min 34.9 sec—4 J. Clark (Lotus) 2 hr 19 min 29.5 sec—5 J. Surtees (Cooper) 2 hr 20 min 5.5 sec—6 B. McLaren (Cooper) 2 hr 20 min 53.8 sec—7 D. Gurney (Porsche) 2 hr 21 min 33.0 sec—8 R. Ginther (Ferrari) 2 hr 23 min 35.5 sec—9 J. Lewis (Cooper) 2 hr 23 min 36.1 sec—10 R. Salvadori (Cooper) 2 hr 30 min 23.9 sec—11 T. Maggs (Lotus) 14 laps—12 I. Burgess (Lotus) 14 laps—13 H. Herrmann (Porsche) 14 laps—14 C G de Beaufort (Porsche) 14 laps—15 A. Marsh (Lotus) 13 laps—16 G. Ashmore (Lotus) 13 laps—17 M. Trintignant (Cooper) 12 laps—fastest lap, P. Hill 8 min 57.8 sec 152.53 kph/94.8 mph—retired J. Brabham (Cooper) accident lap 1—G. Hill (BRM) accident lap 2—I. Ireland (Lotus) fire lap 3—W. Seidel (Lotus) steering lap 4—J. Bonnier (Porsche) engine lap 5—C A S Brooks (BRM) engine lap 7—L. Bandini (Cooper) engine lap 10—B. Collomb (Cooper) transmission lap 12—W. Mairesse (Ferrari) accident lap 14.

Starting grid 4-3-4

P. Hill 8 min 55.2 sec—Brabham 9 min 01.4 sec—Moss 9 min 01.7 sec—Bonnier 9 min 04.8 sec—von Trips 9 min 05.5 sec—G. Hill 9 min 06.4 sec—Gurney 9 min 06.6 sec—Clark 9 min 08.1 sec—Brooks 9 min 09.3 sec—Surtees 9 min 11.2 sec—Herrmann 9 min 12.7 sec—McLaren 9 min 13.0 sec—Mairesse 9 min 15.9 sec—Ginther 9 min 16.6 sec—Salvadori 9 min 22.0 sec—Ireland 9 min 22.9 sec—de Beaufort 9 min 28.4 sec—Lewis 9 min 31.4 sec—Bandini 9 min 35.4 sec—Marsh 9 min 37.7 sec—Trintignant 9 min 38.5 sec—Maggs 9 min 45.5 sec—Seidel 9 min 59.9 sec—Burgess 10 min 01.4 sec—Ashmore 10 min 06.0 sec—Collomb 10 min 23.0 sec—non starter M. May (Lotus).

Italian Grand Prix

Monza; 10 September; 43 laps 430 km/267 miles
1 P. Hill (Ferrari) 2 hr 3 min 13.0 sec 209.3 kph/130.06 mph—2 D. Gurney (Porsche) 2 hr 3 min 44.2 sec—3 B. McLaren (Cooper) 2 hr 5 min 41.4 sec—4 J. Lewis (Cooper) 2 hr 5 min 53.4 sec—5 C A S Brooks (BRM) 2 hr 5 min 53.5 sec—6 R. Salvadori (Cooper) 42 laps—7 C G de Beaufort (Porsche) 41 laps—8 L. Bandini (Cooper) 41 laps—9 M. Trintignant (Cooper) 40 laps—10 T. Parnell (Lotus) 40 laps—11 H. Taylor (Lotus) 39 laps—12 R. Pirocchi (Cooper) 38 laps—fastest lap, Baghetti 2 min 48.4 sec 213.74 kph/132.84 mph retired G. Ashmore (Lotus) accident lap 1—R. Bussinello (de Tomaso) lap 1—W. Seidel (Lotus) lap 1—W. von Trips (Ferrari) fatal accident lap 2—J. Clark (Lotus) lap 2—R. Lippi (de Tomaso) engine lap 3—J. Surtees (Cooper) suspension lap 3—J. Fairman (Cooper) lap 6—B. Naylor (JBW) lap 7—J. Brabham (Cooper) engine lap 9—G. Hill (BRM) engine lap 11—M. Gregory (Lotus) suspension lap 12—R. Rodriguez (Ferrari) engine lap 14—G. Baghetti (Ferrari) engine lap 14—N. Vaccarella (de Tomaso) engine lap 15—J. Bonnier (Porsche)—I. Ireland (Lotus) suspension lap 15—R. Ginther (Ferrari) engine lap 24—S. Moss (Lotus) suspension lap 37—G. Starrabba (Lotus).

Starting grid 2-2-2

von Trips 2 min 46.3 sec—R. Rodriguez 2 min 46.4 sec—Ginther 2 min 46.8 sec—P. Hill 2 min 47.2 sec—G. Hill 2 min 48.7 sec—Baghetti 2 min 49.0 sec—Clark 2 min 49.2 sec—Bonnier 2 min 49.6 sec—Ireland 2 min 50.3—Brabham 2 min 51.6 sec—Moss 2 min 51.8 sec—Gurney 2 min 52.0 sec—Brooks 2 min 52.2 sec—McLaren 2 min 53.4 sec—de Beaufort 2 min 53.8 sec—Lewis 2 min 54.0 sec—Gregory 2 min 55.2 sec—Salvadori 2 min 55.2 sec—Surtees 2 min 55.6 sec—Vaccarella 2 min 56.0 sec—Bandini 2 min 57.7 sec—Trintignant 2 min 58.7 sec—H. Taylor 3 min 00.6 sec—Bussinello 3 min 01.7 sec—Ashmore 3 min 03.0 sec—Fairman 3 min 04.8 sec—Parnell 3 min 05.7 sec—Seidel 3 min 06.0 sec—Pirocchi 3 min 06.5 sec—Starrabba 3 min 07.9 sec—Naylor 3 min 08.1 sec—Lippi 3 min 08.9 sec—non starter A. Pilette.

UNITED STATES GRAND PRIX

Watkins Glen; 8 October; 100 laps 230 miles/370 km
1 I. Ireland (Lotus) 2 hr 13 min 45.8 sec 103.17 mph/166.04 kph—2 D. Gurney (Porsche) 2 hr 13 min 50.1 sec—3 C A S Brooks (BRM) 2 hr 14 min 34.8 sec—4 B. McLaren (Cooper) 2 hr 14 min 43.8 sec—5 G. Hill (BRM) 99 laps—6 J. Bonnier (Porsche) 98 laps—7 J. Clark (Lotus) 96 laps—8 R. Penske (Cooper) 96 laps—9 P. Ryan (Lotus) 95 laps—10 H. Sharp (Cooper) 93 laps—11 O. Gendebien, M. Gregory (Lotus) 92 laps—fastest lap, Moss 1 min 18.2 sec 105.8 mph/170.23 kph—retired J. Surtees (Cooper) con-rod lap 1—W. Hansgen (Cooper) engine lap 14—M. Gregory (Lotus) gearbox lap 23—J. Brabham (Cooper) water leak lap 57—S. Moss (Lotus) engine lap 59—L. Ruby (Lotus) magneto lap 76—J. Hall (Lotus) lap 76—R. Salvadori (Cooper) con-rod lap 97.

Starting grid 2-2-2

Brabham 1 min 17.0 sec—G. Hill 1 min 18.1 sec—Moss 1 min 18.2 sec—McLaren 1 min 18.2 sec—Brooks 1 min 18.3 sec—Clark 1 min 18.3 sec—Gurney 1 min 18.6 sec—Ireland 1 min 18.8 sec—Surtees 1 min 18.9 sec—Bonnier 1 min 18.9 sec—Gregory 1 min 19.1 sec—Salvadori 1 min 19.2 sec—Ryan 1 min 20.0 sec—Hansgen 1 min 20.4 sec—Gendebien 1 min 20.5 sec—Sharp 1 min 21.0 sec—Penske 1 min 21.6 sec—Hall 1 min 21.8 sec—Ruby 1 min 21.8 sec.

1961 WORLD CHAMPIONSHIP

1 P. Hill 34, 38—2 W. von Trips 33—3 S. Moss 21—3= D. Gurney 21—5 R. Ginther 16—6 I. Ireland 12—7 J. Clark 11—7= B. McLaren 11—9 G. Baghetti 9—10 C A S Brooks 6—11 J. Brabham 4—11= J. Surtees 4—13 O. Gendebien 3—13= J. Bonnier 3—13= G. Hill 3—13= J. Lewis 3—17 R. Salvadori 2.

1962

DUTCH GRAND PRIX

Zandvoort; 20 May; 80 laps 335 km/208 miles
1 G. Hill (BRM) 2 hr 11 min 2.1 sec 153.56 kph/95.44 mph—2 T. Taylor (Lotus) 2 hr 11 min 29.3 sec—3 P. Hill (Ferrari) 2 hr 12 min 23.2 sec—4 G. Baghetti (Ferrari) 79 laps—5 T. Maggs (Cooper) 78 laps—6 C G de Beaufort (Porsche) 76 laps—7 J. Bonnier (Porsche) 75 laps—8 J. Lewis (Cooper) 70 laps—9 J. Clark (Lotus) 70 laps—not classified W. Seidel (Emeryson) 52 laps—fastest lap, McLaren 1 min 34.4 sec 159.87 kph/99.36 mph—retired B. Pon (Porsche) accident lap 3—J. Brabham (Lotus) accident lap 5—J. Surtees (Lola) accident lap 9—R. Salvadori (Lola) transmission lap 12—B. McLaren (Cooper) gearbox lap 22—D. Gurney (Porsche) gearbox lap 48—M. Gregory (Lotus) gearbox lap 55—I. Ireland (Lotus) accident lap 62—R. Ginther (BRM) accident lap 72—R. Rodriguez (Ferrari) accident lap 74.

Starting grid 3-2-3

Surtees 1 min 32.5 sec—G. Hill 1 min 32.6 sec—Clark 1 min 33.2 sec—Brabham 1 min 33.3 sec—McLaren 1 min 33.9 sec—Ireland 1 min 34.1 sec—Ginther 1 min 34.5 sec—Gurney 1 min 34.7 sec—P. Hill 1 min 35.0 sec—T. Taylor 1 min 35.4 sec—R. Rodriguez 1 min 36.1 sec—Baghetti 1 min 36.3 sec—Bonnier 1 min 37.0 sec—de Beaufort 1 min 37.4 sec—Maggs 1 min 37.5 sec—Gregory 1 min 38.0 sec—Salvadori 1 min 38.8 sec—Pon 1 min 40.9 sec—Lewis 1 min 43.2 sec—Seidel 1 min 46.0 sec.

MONACO GRAND PRIX

Monte Carlo; 3 June; 100 laps 314 km/195 miles
1 B. McLaren (Cooper) 2 hr 46 min 29.7 sec 113.37 kph/70.46 mph—2 P. Hill (Ferrari) 2 hr 46 min 31.0 sec—3 L. Bandini (Ferrari) 2 hr 47 min 53.8 sec—4 J. Surtees (Lola) 99 laps—5 J. Bonnier (Porsche) 93 laps—6 G. Hill (BRM) 92 laps—7 W. Mairesse (Ferrari) 90 laps—8 J. Brabham (Lotus) 77 laps—fastest lap, Clark 1 min 35.5 sec 118.53 kph/73.67 mph—retired R. Ginther (BRM) accident lap 1—M. Trintignant (Lotus) accident lap 1—D. Gurney (Porsche) accident lap 1—T. Taylor (Lotus) oil leak lap 24—T. Maggs (Cooper) gearbox lap 43—R. Salvadori (Lola) suspension lap 44—J. Clark (Lotus) clutch lap 55—I. Ireland (Lotus) fuel pump lap 63.

Starting grid 3-2-3

Clark 1 min 35.4 sec—G. Hill 1 min 35.8 sec—McLaren 1 min 36.4 sec—Mairesse 1 min 36.4 sec—Gurney 1 min 36.4 sec—Brabham 1 min 36.5 sec—Trintignant 1 min 36.8 sec—Ireland 1 min 37.0 sec—P. Hill 1 min 37.1 sec—Bandini 1 min 37.2 sec—Surtees 1 min 37.9 sec—Salvadori 1 min 38.5 sec—Ginther 1 min 39.0 sec—T. Taylor 1 min 40.0 sec—Bonnier 1 min 42.4 sec—Maggs 1 min 42.7 sec—non starters N. Vaccarella (Lotus) —J. Siffert (Lotus)—C G de Beaufort (Porsche)—J. Lewis (BRM)—M. Gregory (Lotus)—R. Rodriguez (Ferrari).

BELGIAN GRAND PRIX

Spa-Francorchamps; 17 June; 32 laps 450 km/280 miles
1 J. Clark (Lotus) 2 hr 7 min 32.5 sec 212.21 kph/131.89 mph—2 G. Hill (BRM) 2 hr 8 min 16.4 sec—3 P. Hill (Ferrari) 2 hr 9 min 38.8 sec—4 R. Rodriguez (Ferrari) 2 hr 9 min 38.9 sec—5 J. Surtees (Lola) 31 laps—6 J. Brabham (Lotus) 30 laps—7 C G de Beaufort (Porsche) 30 laps—8 M. Trintignant (Lotus) 30 laps—9 L. Bianchi (Lotus) 29 laps—10 J. Siffert (Lotus) 29 laps—11 J. Campbell-Jones (Lotus) 16 laps—fastest lap, Clark 3 min 55.6 sec 215.57 kph/133.98 mph—retired G. Baghetti (Ferrari) ignition lap 4—I. Ireland (Lotus) suspension lap 9—M. Gregory (Lotus) engine lap 13—B. McLaren (Cooper) engine lap 20—T. Maggs (Cooper) gearbox lap 22—R. Ginther (BRM) transmission lap 23—T. Taylor (Lotus) accident lap 26—W. Mairesse (Ferrari) accident lap 26.

Starting grid 3-2-3

G. Hill 3 min 57.0 sec—McLaren 3 min 58.8 sec—Taylor 3 min 59.3 sec—P. Hill 3 min 59.6 sec—Ireland 3 min 59.8 sec—Mairesse 3 min 59.8 sec—R. Rodriguez 4 min 01.0 sec—Gregory 4 min 01.0 sec—Ginther 4 min 01.4 sec—Maggs 4 min 03.6 sec—Surtees 4 min 04.4 sec—Clark 4 min 04.9 sec—de Beaufort 4 min 07.7 sec—Baghetti 4 min 08.0 sec—Brabham 4 min 08.2 sec—Trintignant 4 min 09.2 sec—Siffert 4 min 11.6 sec—Bianchi 4 min 18.0 sec—Campbell-Jones 4 min 26.9 sec.

FRENCH GRAND PRIX

Rouen-les-Essarts; 8 July; 54 laps 353 km/219 miles
1 D. Gurney (Porsche) 2 hr 7 min 35.5 sec 163.94 kph/101.89 mph—2 T. Maggs (Cooper) 53 laps—3 R. Ginther (BRM) 52 laps—4 B. McLaren (Cooper) 51 laps—5 J. Surtees (Lola) 51 laps—6 C G de Beaufort (Porsche) 51 laps—7 M. Trintignant (Lotus) 50 laps—8 T. Taylor (Lotus) 48 laps—9 G. Hill (BRM) 44 laps—10 J. Bonnier (Porsche) 42 laps—fastest lap, G. Hill 2 min 16.9 sec 172.00 kph/106.9 mph—retired I. Ireland (Lotus) wheel lap 1—J. Siffert (Lotus) clutch lap 5—J. Brabham (Lotus) rear suspension lap 11—M. Gregory (Lotus) engine lap 15—R. Salvadori (Lola) engine lap 20—J. Lewis (Cooper) brakes lap 28—J. Clark (Lotus) front suspension lap 34.

Starting grid 3-2-3

Clark 2 min 14.8 sec—G. Hill 2 min 15.0 sec—McLaren 2 min 15.4 sec—Brabham 2 min 16.1 sec—Surtees 2 min 16.3 sec—Gurney 2 min 16.5 sec—Gregory 2 min 17.3 sec—Ireland 2 min 17.5 sec—Bonnier 2 min 17.9 sec—Ginther 2 min 18.2 sec—Maggs 2 min 18.6 sec—T. Taylor 2 min 19.1 sec—Trintignant 2 min 20.8 sec—Salvadori 2 min 21.3 sec—Siffert 2 min 23.4 sec—Lewis 2 min 25.5 sec—de Beaufort 2 min 26.5 sec.

BRITISH GRAND PRIX

Aintree; 21 July; 75 laps 225 miles/362 km
1 J. Clark (Lotus) 2 hr 26 min 20.8 sec 92.25 mph/148.43 kph—2 J. Surtees (Lola) 2 hr 27 min 10.0 sec—3 B. McLaren (Cooper) 2 hr 28 min 5.6 sec—4 G. Hill (BRM) 2 hr 28 min 17.6 sec—5 J. Brabham (Lotus) 74 laps—6 T. Maggs (Cooper) 74 laps—7 M. Gregory (Lotus) 74 laps—8 T. Taylor (Lotus) 74 laps—9 D. Gurney (Porsche) 73 laps—10 J. Lewis (Cooper) 72 laps—11 T. Settember (Emeryson) 71 laps—12 I. Burgess (Cooper) 71 laps—13 R. Ginther (BRM) 70 laps—14 C G de Beaufort (Porsche) 69 laps—15 J. Chamberlain (Lotus) 64 laps—16 I. Ireland (Lotus) 61 laps—fastest lap, Clark 1 min 55.0 sec 93.9 mph/151.08 kph—retired T. Shelley (Lotus) overheating lap 6—W. Seidel (Lotus) brakes lap 11—J. Bonnier (Porsche) gearbox lap 27—R. Salvadori (Lola) ignition lap 35—P. Hill (Ferrari) ignition lap 47.

Starting grid 3-2-3

Clark 1 min 53.6 sec—Surtees 1 min 54.2 sec—Ireland 1 min 54.4 sec—McLaren 1 min 54.6 sec—G. Hill 1 min 54.6 sec—Gurney 1 min 54.8 sec—Bonnier 1 min 55.2 sec—Ginther 1 min 55.2 sec—Brabham 1 min 55.4 sec—T. Taylor 1 min 56.0 sec—Salvadori 1 min 56.2 sec—P. Hill 1 min 56.2 sec—Maggs 1 min 57.0 sec—Gregory 1 min 57.2 sec—Lewis 1 min 59.4 sec—Burgess 2 min 00.6 sec—de Beaufort 2 min 01.4 sec—Shelley 2 min 02.4 sec—Settember 2 min 02.4 sec—Chamberlain 2 min 03.4 sec—Seidel 2 min 11.6 sec.

GERMAN GRAND PRIX

Nürburgring; 5 August; 15 laps 339 km/211 miles
1 G. Hill (BRM) 2 hr 38 min 45.3 sec 129.17 kph/80.28 mph—2 J. Surtees (Lola) 2 hr 38 min 47.8 sec—3 D. Gurney (Porsche) 2 hr 38 min 49.7 sec—4 J. Clark (Lotus) 2 hr 39 min 27.4 sec—5 B. McLaren (Cooper) 2 hr 40 min 4.9 sec—6 R. Rodriguez (Ferrari) 2 hr 40 min 9.1 sec—7 J. Bonnier (Porsche) 2 hr 43 min 22.6 sec—8 R. Ginther (BRM) 2 hr 43 min 45.4 sec—9 T. Maggs (Cooper) 2 hr 43 min 52.1 sec—10 G. Baghetti (Ferrari) 2 hr 47 min 00.0 sec—11 I. Burgess (Cooper) 2 hr 47 min 00.6 sec—12 J. Siffert (Lotus) 2 hr 47 min 03.8 sec—13 C G de Beaufort (Porsche) 2 hr 47 min 57.1 sec—14 H. Walter (Porsche) 14 laps—15 N. Vaccarella (Porsche) 14 laps—16 L. Bianchi (ENB Maserati) 14 laps—17 J. Lewis (Cooper) 10 laps—fastest lap, G. Hill 10 min 12.2 sec 134.03 kph/83.3 mph—retired T. Taylor (Lotus) accident lap 1—B. Collomb (Cooper) gearbox lap 3—H. Schiller (Lotus) engine lap 4—L. Bandini (Ferrari) accident lap 4—R. Salvadori (Lola) gearbox lap 4—M. Trintignant (Lotus) gearbox lap 4—K. Greene (Gilby) suspension lap 8—P. Hill (Ferrari) suspension lap 9—J. Brabham (Brabham) throttle linkage lap 9.

Starting grid 4-3-4

Gurney 8 min 47.2 sec—G. Hill 8 min 50.2 sec—Clark 8 min 51.2 sec—Surtees 8 min 57.5 sec—McLaren 9 min 00.7 sec—Bonnier 9 min 04.0 sec—Ginther 9 min 05.9 sec—de Beaufort 9 min 12.9 sec—Salvadori 9 min 14.1 sec—Rodriguez 9 min 14.2 sec—Trintignant 9 min 19.0 sec—P. Hill 9 min 24.7 sec—Baghetti 9 min 28.1 sec—Walter 9 min 30.0 sec—Vaccarella 9 min 33.8 sec—Burgess 9 min 39.2 sec—Siffert 9 min 39.3 sec—Bandini 9 min 39.7 sec—Greene 9 min 47.1 sec—Schiller 9 min 51.5 sec—Lewis 9 min 58.0 sec—Collomb 10 min 09.7 sec—Maggs 10 min 21.2 sec—Brabham 10 min 21.6 sec—Bianchi 10 min 40.7 sec—Taylor 9 min 57.0 sec—non starters T. Shelley (Lotus)—J. Chamberlain (Lotus)—W. Seidel (Lotus).

ITALIAN GRAND PRIX

Monza; 16 September; 86 laps 494 km/307 miles
1 G. Hill (BRM) 2 hr 29 min 8.4 sec 198.9 kph/123.62 mph—2 R. Ginther (BRM) 2 hr 29 min 38.2 sec—3 B. McLaren (Cooper) 2 hr 30 min 6.2 sec—4 W. Mairesse (Ferrari) 2 hr 30

ITALIAN GRAND PRIX—*continued*

min 6.6 sec—5 G. Baghetti (Ferrari) 2 hr 30 min 39.7 sec—6 J. Bonnier (Porsche) 85 laps—7 T. Maggs (Cooper) 85 laps—8 L. Bandini (Ferrari) 84 laps—9 N. Vaccarella (Lotus) 84 laps—10 C G de Beaufort (Porsche) 81 laps—11 P. Hill (Ferrari) 81 laps—12 M. Gregory (Lotus) 77 laps—fastest lap, G. Hill 1 min 42.3 sec 202.3 kph/125.73 mph—retired J. Clark (Lotus) transmission lap 13—M. Trintignant (Lotus) electrics lap 18—T. Settember (Emeryson) head gasket lap 21—T. Taylor (Lotus) transmission lap 26—R. Salvadori (Lola) engine lap 42—J. Surtees (Lola) engine lap 43—I. Ireland (Lotus) suspension lap 46—R. Rodriguez (Ferrari) ignition lap 64—D. Gurney (Porsche) transmission lap 67.

Starting grid 2-2-2

Clark 1 min 40.3 sec—G. Hill 1 min 40.4 sec—Ginther 1 min 41.1 sec—McLaren 1 min 41.8 sec—Ireland 1 min 41.8 sec—Gregory 1 min 41.9 sec—Gurney 1 min 41.9 sec—Surtees 1 min 42.4 sec—Bonnier 1 min 42.6 sec—Mairesse 1 min 42.8 sec—Rodriguez 1 min 43.1 sec—Maggs 1 min 43.2 sec—Salvadori 1 min 43.3 sec—Vaccarella 1 min 43.4 sec—P. Hill 1 min 43.4 sec—T. Taylor 1 min 44.2 sec—Bandini 1 min 44.3 sec—Baghetti 1 min 44.4 sec—Trintignant 1 min 44.4 sec—de Beaufort 1 min 46.8 sec—Settember 1 min 49.1 sec—non starters I. Burgess (Cooper)—K. Greene (Gilby)—W. Seidel (Lotus)—T. Shelley (Lotus)—J. Siffert (Lotus)—E. Prinoth (Lotus)—K. Kuhnke (Lotus)—E. Nasif (de Tomaso)—R. Lippi (de Tomaso).

UNITED STATES GRAND PRIX

Watkins Glen; 7 October; 100 laps 230 miles/370 km
1 J. Clark (Lotus) 2 hr 7 min 13.0 sec 108.61 mph/174.75 kph—2 G. Hill (BRM) 2 hr 7 min 22.2 sec—3 B. McLaren (Cooper) 99 laps—4 J. Brabham (Brabham) 99 laps—5 D. Gurney (Porsche) 99 laps—6 M. Gregory (Lotus) 99 laps—7 T. Maggs (Cooper) 97 laps—8 I. Ireland (Lotus) 96 laps—9 R. Penske (Lotus) 96 laps—10 B. Schroeder (Lotus) 93 laps—11 H. Sharp (Cooper) 91 laps—12 T. Taylor (Lotus) 85 laps—13 J. Bonnier (Porsche) 79 laps—fastest lap, Clark 1 min 15.0 sec 110.4 mph/177.63 kph—retired C G de Beaufort (Porsche) accident lap 10—J. Surtees (Lola) oil leak lap 20—T. Mayer (Cooper) engine lap 32—M. Trintignant (Lotus) brakes lap 33—R. Ginther (BRM) engine lap 36.

Starting grid 2-2-2

Clark 1 min 15.8 sec—Ginther 1 min 16.6 sec—G. Hill 1 min 16.7 sec—Gurney 1 min 16.9 sec—Brabham 1 min 16.9 sec—McLaren 1 min 17.1 sec—Gregory 1 min 17.9 sec—T. Taylor 1 min 18.0 sec—Bonnier 1 min 19.0 sec—Maggs 1 min 19.7 sec—Mayer 1 min 20.7 sec—Penske 1 min 21.3 sec—de Beaufort 1 min 21.8 sec—Sharp 1 min 22.4 sec—Ireland 1 min 24.0 sec—Schroeder 1 min 24.0 sec—Trintignant 1 min 25.8 sec—Surtees 1 min 29.2 sec—non starters J. Hall (Lotus)—R. Salvadori (Lola).

SOUTH AFRICAN GRAND PRIX

East London; 29 December; 82 laps 200 miles/322 km
1 G. Hill (BRM) 2 hr 8 min 3.3 sec 93.57 mph/150.55 kph—2 B. McLaren (Cooper) 2 hr 8 min 53.1 sec—3 T. Maggs (Cooper) 2 hr 8 min 53.6 sec—4 J. Brabham (Brabham) 2 hr 8 min 57.1 sec—5 I. Ireland (Lotus) 81 laps—6 N. Lederie (Lotus) 78 laps—7 R. Ginther (BRM) 78 laps—8 J. Love (Cooper) 78 laps—9 B. Johnston (BRM) 76 laps—10 E. Pieterse (Lotus) 71 laps—11 C G de Beaufort (Porsche) 70 laps—fastest lap, Clark 1 min 31.0 sec 96.35 mph/155.03 kph—retired T. Taylor (Lotus) gearbox lap 12—J. Surtees (Lola) valve lap 27—Harris (Cooper) engine lap 32—R. Salvadori (Lola) fuel tank lap 57—D. Serrurier (LDS) radiator lap 61—J. Clark (Lotus) oil leak lap 63.

Starting grid 2-2-2

Clark 1 min 29.3 sec—G. Hill 1 min 29.6 sec—Brabham 1 min 31.0 sec—Ireland 1 min 31.1 sec—Surtees 1 min 31.5 sec—Maggs 1 min 31.7 sec—Ginther 1 min 31.7 sec—McLaren 1 min 31.7 sec—T. Taylor 1 min 32.7 sec—Lederfe 1 min 33.6 sec—Salvadori 1 min 35.4 sec—Love 1 min 36.4 sec—Pieterse 1 min 36.8 sec—Serrurier 1 min 36.8 sec—Harris 1 min 39.1 sec—de Beaufort 1 min 39.2 sec—Johnston.

1962 WORLD CHAMPIONSHIP

1 G. Hill 42, 52—2 J. Clark 30—3 B. McLaren 27, 32—4 J. Surtees 19—5 D. Gurney 15—6 P. Hill 14—7 T. Maggs 13—8 R. Ginther 10—9 J. Brabham 9—10 T. Taylor 6—11 G. Baghetti 5—12 R. Rodriguez 4—12= L. Bandini 4—14 W. Mairesse 3—14= J. Bonnier 3—16 I. Ireland 2—16= C G de Beaufort 2—18 M. Gregory 1—18= N. Lederie 1.

1963

MONACO GRAND PRIX

Monte Carlo; 26 May; 100 laps 314 km/195 miles
1 G. Hill (BRM) 2 hr 41 min 49.7 sec 116.55 kph/72.43 mph—2 R. Ginther (BRM) 2 hr 41 min 54.3 sec—3 B. McLaren (Cooper) 2 hr 42 min 02.5 sec—4 J. Surtees (Ferrari) 2 hr 42 min 03.8 sec—5 T. Maggs (Cooper) 98 laps—6 T. Taylor (Lotus) 98 laps—7 J. Bonnier (Cooper) 94 laps—8 J. Clark (Lotus) 78 laps—9 J. Brabham (Brabham) 77 laps—fastest lap, Surtees 1 min 34.5 sec 119.81 kph/74.45 mph—retired J. Siffert (Lotus) engine lap 3—J. Hall (Lotus) drop gears lap 20—D. Gurney (Brabham) gearbox lap 25—M. Trintignant (Lola) oil lap 34—W. Mairesse (Ferrari) clutch lap 37—I. Ireland (Lotus) gear selector lap 40.

Starting grid 2-2-2

Clark 1 min 34.3 sec—G. Hill 1 min 35.0 sec—Surtees 1 min 35.2 sec—Ginther 1 min 35.2 sec—Ireland 1 min 35.5 sec—Gurney 1 min 35.8 sec—Mairesse 1 min 35.9 sec—McLaren 1 min 36.0 sec—Taylor 1 min 37.2 sec—Maggs 1 min 37.9 sec—Bonnier 1 min 38.6 sec—Siffert 1 min 39.4 sec—Hall 1 min 41.0 sec—Trintignant 1 min 41.3 sec—Brabham 1 min 44.7 sec.

BELGIAN GRAND PRIX

Spa-Francorchamps; 9 June; 32 laps 451 km/280 miles
1 J. Clark (Lotus) 2 hr 27 min 47.6 sec 183.63 kph/114.1 mph—2 B. McLaren (Cooper) 2 hr 32 min 41.6 sec—3 D. Gurney (Brabham) 31 laps—4 R. Ginther (BRM) 31 laps—5 J. Bonnier (Cooper) 30 laps—6 C G de Beaufort (Porsche) 30 laps—7 T. Maggs (Cooper) 27 laps—8 T. Settember (Scirocco) 25 laps—fastest lap, Clark 3 min 58.1 sec 213.19 kph/132.47 mph—retired T. Taylor (Lotus) practice injury lap 5—W. Mairesse (Ferrari) dropped valve lap 7—I. Ireland (BRP) gearbox lap 9 —C. Amon (Lola) oil pressure lap 10—J. Brabham (Brabham) fuel lap 12—P. Hill (ATS) gearbox lap 13—J. Siffert (Lotus) engine lap 16—J. Hall (Lotus) accident lap 16—L. Bianchi (Lola) accident lap 17—G. Hill (BRM) gearbox lap 17—J. Surtees (Ferrari) fuel lap 19.

Starting grid 3-2-3

G. Hill 3 min 54.1 sec—Gurney 3 min 55.0 sec—Mairesse 3 min 55.3 sec—Maggs 3 min 56.0 sec—Brabham 3 min 56.6 sec—Ireland 3 min 56.9 sec—Clark 3 min 57.1 sec—Ginther 3 min 57.6 sec—Surtees 3 min 57.9 sec—Taylor 3 min 58.1 sec—McLaren 3 min 58.2 sec—Hall 4 min 00.1 sec—Bonnier 4 min 00.1 sec—Siffert 4 min 02.3 sec—Amon 4 min 04.9 sec—P. Hill 4 min 06.7 sec—Bianchi 4 min 08.5 sec—de Beaufort 4 min 14.6 sec—Settember 4 min 25.2 sec—Baghetti 4 min 31.7 sec.

DUTCH GRAND PRIX

Zandvoort; 23 June; 80 laps 335 km/208 miles
1 J. Clark (Lotus) 2 hr 8 min 13.07 sec 156.96 kph/97.53 mph—2 D. Gurney (Brabham) 79 laps—3 J. Surtees (Ferrari) 79 laps—4 I. Ireland (BRP) 79 laps—5 R. Ginther (BRM) 79 laps—6 L. Scarfiotti (Ferrari) 78 laps—7 J. Siffert (BRM) 77 laps—8 J. Hall (BRP) 77 laps—9 C G de Beaufort (Porsche) 75 laps—10 T. Taylor (Lotus) 66 laps—11 J. Bonnier (Cooper) 56 laps—fastest lap, Clark 1 min 33.7 sec 161.09 kph/100.1 mph—retired G. Mitter (Porsche) clutch lap 2—B. McLaren (Cooper) transmission lap 7—T. Maggs (Cooper) overheating lap 14—P. Hill (ATS) rear hub lap 15—G. Baghetti (ATS) engine lap 17—C. Amon (Lola) water pump lap 29—J. Brabham (Brabham) rear suspension lap 68—G. Hill (BRM) lap 69.

Starting grid 3-2-3

Clark 1 min 31.6 sec—G. Hill 1 min 32.2 sec—McLaren 1 min 32.3 sec—Brabham 1 min 32.4 sec—Surtees 1 min 33.0 sec—Ginther 1 min 33.3 sec—Ireland 1 min 33.3 sec—Bonnier 1 min 34.1 sec—Maggs 1 min 34.3 sec—Taylor 1 min 35.2 sec—Scarfiotti 1 min 35.6 sec—Amon 1 min 35.9 sec—P. Hill 1 min 36.0 sec—Gurney 1 min 36.2 sec—Baghetti 1 min 37.8 sec—Miller 1 min 38.8 sec—Siffert 1 min 39.0 sec—Hall 1 min 39.0 sec—de Beaufort 1 min 39.0 sec.

FRENCH GRAND PRIX

Rheims; 30 June; 53 laps 440 km/273 miles
1 J. Clark (Lotus) 2 hr 10 min 54.3 sec 201.67 kph/125.32 mph—2 T. Maggs (Cooper) 2 hr 11 min 59.2 sec—3 G. Hill (BRM) 2 hr 12 min 08.2 sec—4 J. Brabham (Brabham) 2 hr 13 min 09.5 sec—5 D. Gurney (Brabham) 2 hr 13 min 27.7 sec—6 J. Siffert (Lotus) 52 laps—7 C. Amon (Lola) 51 laps—8 M. Trintignant (Lotus) 50 laps—9 I. Ireland (BRP) 49 laps—10 L. Bandini (BRM) 45 laps—11 J. Hall (Lotus) 45 laps—12 B. McLaren (Cooper) 42 laps—13 T. Taylor (Lotus) 41 laps—fastest lap, Clark 2 min 21.6 sec 211.06 kph/131.15 mph—retired R. Ginther (BRM) holed radiator lap 4—T. Settember (Scirocco) rear hub lap 5—J. Surtees (Ferrari) fuel pump lap 12—M. Gregory (Lotus) transmission lap 30—J. Bonnier (Cooper) ignition lap 32—P. Hill (Lotus) fuel pump lap 34.

Starting grid 3-2-3

Clark 2 min 20.2 sec—G. Hill 2 min 20.9 sec—Gurney 2 min 21.7 sec—Surtees 2 min 21.9 sec—Brabham 2 min 21.9 sec—McLaren 2 min 22.5 sec—Taylor 2 min 23.7 sec—Maggs 2 min 24.4 sec—Ireland 2 min 25.1 sec—Siffert 2 min 25.2 sec—Bonnier 2 min 25.7 sec—Ginther 2 min 25.9 sec—P. Hill 2 min 27.7 sec—Trintignant 2 min 28.3 sec—Amon 2 min 30.5 sec—Hall 2 min 30.9 sec—Gregory 2 min 33.2 sec—Settember 2 min 36.7 sec—Bandini 2 min 37.8 sec.

BRITISH GRAND PRIX

Silverstone; 20 July; 82 laps 238 miles/383 km
1 J. Clark (Lotus) 2 hr 14 min 09.6 sec 107.75 mph/172.75 kph—2 J. Surtees (Ferrari) 2 hr 14 min 35.4 sec—3 G. Hill (BRM) 2 hr 14 min 47.2 sec—4 R. Ginther (BRM) 81 laps—5 L. Bandini (BRM) 81 laps—6 J. Hall (Lotus) 80 laps—7 C. Amon (Lola) 80 laps—8 M. Hailwood (Lotus) 78 laps—9 T. Maggs (Cooper) 78 laps—10 C G de Beaufort (Porsche) 76 laps —11 M. Gregory (Lotus) 75 laps—12 B. Anderson (Lola) 75 laps—13 J. Campbell-Jones (Lola) 74 laps—fastest lap, Surtees 1 min 36.0 sec 109.76 mph/176.65 kph—retired B. McLaren (Cooper) engine lap 6—T. Settember (Scirocco) gearbox lap 20—T. Taylor (Lotus) gearbox lap 23—I. Ireland (BRP) disqualified lap 26—J. Brabham (Brabham) engine lap 27—I. Burgess (Scirocco) ignition lap 36—D. Gurney (Brabham) engine lap 59—I. Raby (Gilby) gearbox lap 59—J. Bonnier (Cooper) oil pressure lap 65—J. Siffert (Lotus) gearbox lap 66.

Starting grid 4-3-4

Clark 1 min 34.4 sec—Gurney 1 min 34.6 sec—G. Hill 1 min 34.8 sec—Brabham 1 min 35.0 sec—Surtees 1 min 35.2 sec—McLaren 1 min 35.4 sec—Maggs 1 min 36.0 sec—Bandini 1 min 36.0 sec—Ginther 1 min 36.0 sec—Taylor 1 min 36.8 sec—Ireland 1 min 36.8 sec—Bonnier 1 min 36.8 sec—Hall 1 min 37.0 sec—Amon 1 min 37.2 sec—Siffert 1 min 38.4 sec—Anderson 1 min 39.0 sec—Hailwood 1 min 39.8 sec—Settember 1 min 40.8 sec—Raby 1 min 42.4 sec—Burgess 1 min 42.6 sec—de Beaufort 1 min 43.4 sec—Gregory 1 min 44.2 sec—Campbell-Jones 1 min 48.8 sec.

GERMAN GRAND PRIX

Nürburgring; 4 August; 15 laps 342 km/212 miles
1 J. Surtees (Ferrari) 2 hr 13 min 06.8 sec 154.2 kph/95.8 mph—2 J. Clark (Lotus) 2 hr 14 min 24.3 sec—3 R. Ginther (BRM) 2 hr 15 min 51.7 sec—4 G. Mitter (Porsche) 2 hr 21 min 18.3 sec—5 J. Hall (Lotus) 14 laps—6 J. Bonnier (Cooper) 14 laps—7 J. Brabham (Brabham) 14 laps—8 T. Taylor (Lotus) 14 laps—9 J. Siffert (Lotus) 10 laps—10 B. Collomb (Lotus) 10 laps—fastest lap, Surtees 8 min 47.0 sec 155.8 kph/96.8 mph—retired L. Bandini (Ferrari) accident 0 laps—I. Ireland (Lotus) accident lap 1—W. Mairesse (Ferrari) accident lap 1—G. Hill (BRM) transmission lap 2—C. Amon (Lola) accident lap 2—B. McLaren (Cooper) accident lap 3—I. Burgess (Scirocco) accident lap 5—T. Settember (Scirocco) accident lap 5—M. Cabral (Cooper) gearbox lap 6—D. Gurney (Brabham) gearbox lap 6—T. Maggs (Cooper) engine lap 7—C G de Beaufort (Porsche) lost wheel lap 9.

Starting grid 4-3-4

Clark 8 min 45.8 sec—Surtees 8 min 46.7 sec—Bandini 8 min 54.3 sec—G. Hill 8 min 57.2 sec—McLaren 8 min 57.3 sec—Ginther 9 min 02.8 sec—Mairesse 9 min 03.5 sec—Brabham 9 min 04.2 sec—Siffert 9 min 11.1 sec—Maggs 9 min 11.6 sec—Ireland 9 min 14.6 sec—Bonnier 9 min 16.0 sec—Gurney 9 min 17.2 sec—Amon 9 min 20.1 sec—Mitter 9 min 20.9 sec—Hall 9 min 22.7 sec—de Beaufort 9 min 25.1 sec—Taylor 9 min 33.8 sec—Burgess 9 min 52.2 sec—Cabral 9 min 53.1 sec—Collomb 10 min 01.1 sec—Settember 10 min 02.0 sec.

ITALIAN GRAND PRIX

Monza; 8 September; 86 laps 494 km/307 miles
1 J. Clark (Lotus) 2 hr 24 min 19.6 sec 205.53 kph/127.74 mph—2 R. Ginther (BRM) 2 hr 25 min 54.6 sec—3 B. McLaren (Cooper) 85 laps—4 I. Ireland (BRP) 84 laps—5 J. Brabham (Brabham) 84 laps—6 T. Maggs (Cooper) 84 laps—7 J. Bonnier (Cooper) 84 laps—8 J. Hall (Lotus) 84 laps—9 M. Trintignant (BRM) 83 laps—10 M. Hailwood (Lola) 82 laps—11 P. Hill (ATS) 79 laps—12 B. Anderson (Lola) 79 laps—13 M. Spence (Lotus) 73 laps—14 D. Gurney (Brabham) 64 laps—15 G. Baghetti (ATS) 63 laps—16 G. Hill (BRM) 59 laps—fastest lap, Clark 1 min 38.9 sec 209.26 kph/130.05 mph—retired J. Surtees (Ferrari) engine lap 16—M. Gregory (Lotus) engine lap 26—L. Bandini (Ferrari) gearbox lap 37—J. Siffert (Lotus) transmission lap 40.

Starting grid 2-2-2

Surtees 1 min 37.3 sec—G. Hill 1 min 38.5 sec—Clark 1 min 39.0 sec—Ginther 1 min 39.2 sec—Gurney 1 min 39.2 sec—Bandini 1 min 40.1 sec—Brabham 1 min 40.4 sec—McLaren 1 min 40.5 sec—Spence 1 min 40.9 sec—Ireland 1 min 41.6 sec—Bonnier 1 min 41.9 sec—Gregory 1 min 42.1 sec—Maggs 1 min 42.2 sec—P. Hill 1 min 42.7 sec—Siffert 1 min 43.3 sec—Hall 1 min 43.8 sec—Hailwood 1 min 43.9 sec—Anderson 1 min 44.2 sec—Trintignant 1 min 44.4 sec—Baghetti 1 min 45.8 sec.

UNITED STATES GRAND PRIX

Watkins Glen; 6 October; 110 laps 253 miles/407 km
1 G. Hill (BRM) 2 hr 9 min 22.1 sec 109.91 mph/176.84 kph—2 R. Ginther (BRM) 2 hr 19 min 56.4 sec—3 J. Clark (Lotus) 109 laps—4 J. Brabham (Brabham) 108 laps—5 L. Bandini (Ferrari) 106 laps—6 C G de Beaufort (Porsche) 99 laps—7 P. Broeker (Stebro) 88 laps—8 J. Bonnier (Cooper) 85 laps—9 J. Surtees (Ferrari) 82 laps—10 J. Hall (Lotus) 76 laps—11 B. McLaren (Cooper) 74 laps—fastest lap, Clark 1 min 14.5 sec

UNITED STATES GRAND PRIX—*continued*

111.14 mph/178.82 kph—retired G. Baghetti (ATS) engine 0 laps—P. Hill (ATS) engine lap 4—H. Sharp (Lotus) tappet lap 6—M. Gregory (Lola) overheating lap 14—T. Taylor (Lotus) ignition lap 24—P. Rodriguez (Lotus) engine lap 36—D. Gurney (Brabham) fuel lap 42—T. Maggs (Cooper) engine lap 44—R. Ward (Lotus) gearbox lap 44—J. Siffert (Lotus) gearbox lap 56.

Starting grid 2-2-2

G. Hill 1 min 13.4 sec—Clark 1 min 13.5 sec—Surtees 1 min 13.7 sec—Ginther 1 min 14.0 sec—Brabham 1 min 14.2 sec—Gurney 1 min 14.5 sec—Taylor 1 min 15.6 sec—Gregory 1 min 15.6 sec—Bandini 1 min 15.8 sec—Maggs 1 min 15.8 sec—McLaren 1 min 15.9 sec—Bonnier 1 min 16.3 sec—Rodriguez 1 min 16.5 sec—Siffert 1 min 16.5 sec—P. Hill 1 min 17.1 sec—Hall 1 min 17.7 sec—Ward 1 min19.2 sec—Sharp 1 min 20.0 sec—de Beaufort 1 min 22.3 sec—Baghetti 1 min 25.2 sec—Broeker 1 min 28.6 sec.

MEXICAN GRAND PRIX

Mexico City; 20 October; 65 laps 208 miles/335 km
1 J. Clark (Lotus) 2 hr 9 min 52.1 sec 93.3 mph/150.12 kph—2 J. Brabham (Brabham) 2 hr 11 min 33.2 sec—3 R. Ginther (BRM) 2 hr 11 min 46.8 sec—4 G. Hill (BRM) 64 laps—5 J. Bonnier (Cooper) 62 laps—6 D. Gurney (Brabham) 62 laps—7 H. Sharp (Lotus) 61 laps—8 J. Hall (Lotus) 60 laps—9 J. Siffert (Lotus) 59 laps—10 C G de Beaufort (Porsche) 58 laps—11 M. Solana (BRM) 57 laps—fastest lap, Clark 1 min 58.1 sec 94.65 mph/152.29 kph—retired T. Maggs (Cooper) bearings lap 7—C. Amon (Lotus) gearbox lap 9—G. Baghetti (ATS) misfiring lap 12—J. Surtees (Ferrari) disqualified lap 19—T. Taylor (Lotus) gearbox lap 19—M. Gregory (Lola) suspension lap 23—P. Rodriguez (Lotus) suspension lap 26—B. McLaren (Cooper) engine lap 30—L. Bandini (Ferrari) misfiring lap 36—P. Hill (ATS) suspension lap 40.

Starting grid 2-2-2

Clark 1 min 58.8 sec—Surtees 2 min 00.5 sec—G. Hill 2 min 00.6 sec—Gurney 2 min 01.6 sec—Ginther 01.8 sec—McLaren 2 min 02.3 sec—Bandini 2 min 02.4 sec—Bonnier 2 min 02.6 sec—Siffert 2 min 03.3 sec—Brabham 2 min 03.6 sec—Solana 2 min 04.1 sec—Taylor 2 min 04.9 sec—Maggs 2 min 05.2 sec—Gregory 2 min 05.5 sec—Hall 2 min 06.1 sec—Sharp 2 min 07.7 sec—P. Hill 2 min 13.6 sec—de Beaufort 2 min 14.1 sec—Amon 2 min 14.7 sec—Rodriguez 2 min 15.3 sec—Baghetti 2 min 14.7 sec.

SOUTH AFRICAN GRAND PRIX

East London; 28 December; 85 laps 206 miles/332 km
1 J. Clark (Lotus) 2 hr 10 min 36.9 sec 95.5 mph/153.66 kph—2 D. Gurney (Brabham) 2 hr 11 min 43.7 sec—3 G. Hill (BRM) 84 laps—4 B. McLaren (Cooper) 84 laps—5 L. Bandini (Ferrari) 84 laps—6 J. Bonnier (Cooper) 83 laps—7 T. Maggs (Cooper) 82 laps—8 T. Taylor (Lotus) 81 laps—9 J. Love (Cooper) 80 laps—10 C G de Beaufort (Porsche) 79 laps—11 L. Serrurier (LDS) 78 laps—12 T. Blokdyk (Cooper) 77 laps—13 J. Brabham (Brabham) 70 laps—14 B. Niemann (Lotus) 66 laps—fastest lap, Gurney 1 min 29.1 sec 98.41 mph/158.34 kph—retired S. Tingle (LDS) half shaft lap 2—E. Pieterse (Lotus) engine lap 3—J. Surtees (Ferrari) engine lap 43—R. Ginther (BRM) transmission lap 43—D. Prophet (Brabham) oil pressure lap 49—P. de Klerk (Alfa Special) gearbox lap 53.

Starting grid 3-2-3

Clark 1 min 28.9 sec—Brabham 1 min 29.0 sec—Gurney 1 min 29.1 sec—Surtees 1 min 29.8 sec—Bandini 1 min 30.2 sec—G. Hill 1 min 30.3 sec—Ginther 1 min 30.4 sec—Taylor 1 min 30.4 sec—McLaren 1 min 31.2 sec—Maggs 1 min 31.5 sec—Bonnier 1 min 32.0 sec—Pieterse 1 min 34.5 sec—Love 1 min 34.6 sec—Prophet 1 min 35.5 sec—Niemann 1 min 35.6 sec—de Klerk 1 min 35.7 sec—Tingle 1 min 35.8 sec—Serrurier 1 min 36.4 sec—Blokdyk 1 min 36.5 sec—de Beaufort 1 min 36.6 sec—non starter P. Driver (Lotus).

1963 WORLD CHAMPIONSHIP

1 J. Clark 54, 73—2 G. Hill 29—3 R. Ginther 29, 34—4 J. Surtees 22—5 D. Gurney 19—6 B. McLaren 17—7 J. Brabham 14—8 T. Maggs 9—9 I. Ireland 6—9= L. Bandini 6—9= J. Bonnier 6—12 G. Mitter 3—12= J. Hall 3—14 C G de Beaufort 2—15 T. Taylor 1—15= L. Scarfiotti 1—15= J. Siffert 1.

1964

MONACO GRAND PRIX

Monte Carlo; 10 May; 100 laps 314 km/195 miles
1 G. Hill (BRM) 2 hr 41 min 19.5 sec 116.88 kph/72.64 mph—2 R. Ginther (BRM) 99 laps—3 P. Arundell (Lotus) 97 laps—4 J. Clark (Lotus) 96 laps—5 J. Bonnier (Cooper) 96 laps—6 M. Hailwood (Lotus) 96 laps—7 B. Anderson (Brabham) 86 laps—8 J. Siffert (Lotus) 78 laps—9 P. Hill (Cooper) 70 laps—10 L. Bandini (Ferrari) 68 laps—fastest lap, G. Hill 1 min 33.9 sec 120.55 kph/74.92 mph—retired T. Taylor (BRP) fuel tank lap 9—J. Surtees (Ferrari) gearbox lap 16—B. McLaren (Cooper) oil leak lap 18—J. Brabham (Brabham) final drive lap 29—M. Trintignant (BRM) overheating lap 54—D. Gurney (Brabham) transmission lap 63.

Starting grid 2-2-2

Clark 1 min 34.0 sec—Brabham 1 min 34.1 sec—G. Hill 1 min 34.5 sec—Surtees 1 min 34.5 sec—Gurney 1 min 34.7 sec—Arundell 1 min 35.5 sec—Bandini 1 min 35.5 sec—Ginther 1 min 35.9 sec—P. Hill 1 min 35.9 sec—McLaren 1 min 36.6 sec—Bonnier 1 min 37.4 sec—Anderson 1 min 38.0 sec—Trintignant 1 min 38.1 sec—Taylor 1 min 38.1 sec—Hailwood 1 min 38.5 sec—Siffert 1 min 38.7 sec.

DUTCH GRAND PRIX

Zandvoort; 24 May; 80 laps 335 km/208 miles
1 J. Clark (Lotus) 2 hr 7 min 35.4 sec 157.71 kph/98.02 mph—2 J. Surtees (Ferrari) 2 hr 8 min 29.0 sec—3 P. Arundell (Lotus) 79 laps—4 G. Hill (BRM) 79 laps—5 C. Amon (Lotus) 79 laps—6 B. Anderson (Brabham) 78 laps—7 B. McLaren (Cooper) 78 laps—8 P. Hill (Cooper) 76 laps—9 J. Bonnier (Brabham) 76 laps—10 G. Baghetti (BRM) 74 laps—11 R. Ginther (BRM) 64 laps—12 M. Hailwood (Lotus) 57 laps—13 J. Siffert (Brabham) 55 laps—fastest lap, Clark 1 min 32.8 sec 162.62 kph/101.07 mph—retired C G de Beaufort (Porsche) valve lap 9—L. Bandini (Ferrari) fuel injection lap 21—D. Gurney (Brabham) broken steering wheel lap 23—J. Brabham (Brabham) fuel pump drive lap 44.

Starting grid 3-2-3

Gurney 1 min 31.2 sec—Clark 1 min 31.3 sec—G. Hill 1 min 31.4 sec—Surtees 1 min 32.8 sec—McLaren 1 min 33.3 sec—Arundell 1 min 33.5 sec—Brabham 1 min 33.8 sec—Ginther 1 min 34.0 sec—P. Hill 1 min 34.8 sec—Bandini 1 min 35.0 sec—Anderson 1 min 35.4 sec—Bonnier 1 min 35.4 sec—Amon 1 min 35.9 sec—Hailwood 1 min 36.1 sec—Baghetti 1 min 38.0 sec—de Beaufort 1 min 39.5 sec—Siffert 1 min 44.0 sec.

BELGIAN GRAND PRIX

Spa-Francorchamps; 14 June; 32 laps 450 km/280 miles
1 J. Clark (Lotus) 2 hr 6 min 40.5 sec 213.66 kph/132.79 mph—2 B. McLaren (Cooper) 2 hr 6 min 43.9 sec—3 J. Brabham (Brabham) 2 hr 7 min 28.6 sec—4 R. Ginther (BRM) 2 hr 8 min 39.1 sec—5 G. Hill (BRM) 31 laps—6 D. Gurney (Brabham) 31 laps—7 T. Taylor (BRP) 31 laps—8 G. Baghetti

(BRM) 31 laps—9 P. Arundell (Lotus) 28 laps—10 I. Ireland (BRP) 28 laps—fastest lap, Gurney 3 min 49.2 sec 221.41 kph/137.61 mph—retired J. Surtees (Ferrari) engine bearing lap 4—C. Amon (Lotus) engine lap 4—J. Bonnier (Brabham) ill lap 8—A. Pilette (Scirocco) engine lap 11—L. Bandini (Ferrari) transmission lap 12—P. Hill (Cooper) engine lap 13—J. Siffert (Brabham) piston lap 14—P. Revson (Lotus) disqualified lap 28.

Starting grid 3-2-3

Gurney 3 min 50.9 sec—G. Hill 3 min 52.7 sec—Brabham 3 min 52.8 sec—Arundell 3 min 52.8 sec—Surtees 3 min 55.2 sec—Clark 3 min 56.2 sec—McLaren 3 min 56.2 sec—Ginther 3 min 57.2 sec—Bandini 3 min 58.8 sec—Revson 59.9 sec—Amon 4 min 00.1 sec—Taylor 4 min 00.2 sec—Siffert 4 min 2.7 sec—Bonnier 4 min 2.7 sec—P. Hill 4 min 2.8 sec—Ireland 4 min 4.0 sec—Baghetti 4 min 7.6 sec—Pilette 4 min 22.9 sec.

FRENCH GRAND PRIX

Rouen-les-Essarts; 28 June; 57 laps 373 km/232 miles
1 D. Gurney (Brabham) 2 hr 7 min 49.1 sec 175.01 kph/108.77 mph—2 G. Hill (BRM) 2 hr 8 min 13.2 sec—3 J. Brabham (Brabham) 2 hr 8 min 14.0 sec—4 P. Arundell (Lotus) 2 hr 8 min 59.7 sec—5 R. Ginther (BRM) 2 hr 10 min 01.2 sec—6 B. McLaren (Cooper) 56 laps—7 P. Hill (Cooper) 56 laps—8 M. Hailwood (Lotus) 56 laps—9 L. Bandini (Ferrari) 55 laps—10 C. Amon (Lotus) 53 laps—11 M. Trintignant (BRM) 52 laps—12 B. Anderson (Brabham) 50 laps—fastest lap, Brabham 2 min 11.4 sec 179.19 kph/111.37 mph—retired J. Siffert (Brabham) engine lap 5—J. Surtees (Ferrari) engine lap 7—T. Taylor (BRP) accident lap 7—J. Clark (Lotus) engine lap 32—I. Ireland (BRP) accident lap 33.

Starting grid 3-2-3

Clark 2 min 09.6 sec—Gurney 2 min 10.1 sec—Surtees 2 min 11.1 sec—Arundell 2 min 11.6 sec—Brabham 2 min 11.8 sec—G. Hill 2 min 12.1 sec—McLaren 2 min 12.4 sec—Bandini 2 min 12.8 sec—Ginther 2 min 13.9 sec—P. Hill 2 min 14.5 sec—Ireland 2 min 14.8 sec—Taylor 2 min 14.9 sec—Hailwood 2 min 16.2 sec—Amon 2 min 16.4 sec—Anderson 2 min 16.9 sec—Trintignant 2 min 21.5 sec—Siffert 2 min 23.6 sec.

BRITISH GRAND PRIX

Brands Hatch; 11 July; 80 laps 212 miles/341 km
1 J. Clark (Lotus) 2 hr 15 min 07.0 sec 94.14 mph/151.47 kph—2 G. Hill (BRM) 2 hr 15 min 09.8 sec—3 J. Surtees (Ferrari) 2 hr 16 min 27.6 sec—4 J. Brabham (Brabham) 79 laps—5 L. Bandini (Ferrari) 78 laps—6 P. Hill (Cooper) 78 laps—7 B. Anderson (Brabham) 78 laps—8 R. Ginther (BRM) 77 laps—9 M. Spence (Lotus) 77 laps—10 I. Ireland (BRP) 77 laps—11 J. Siffert (Brabham) 76 laps—12 G. Baghetti (BRM) 76 laps—13 D. Gurney (Brabham) 75 laps—14 J. Taylor (Cooper) 56 laps—fastest lap, Clark 1 min 38.8 sec 96.56 mph/155.36 kph—retired F. Gardner (Brabham) rear suspension 0 laps—B. McLaren (Cooper) gearbox lap 7—C. Amon (Lotus) clutch lap 9—M. Hailwood (Lotus) engine lap 17—T. Taylor (Lotus) ill lap 23—T. Maggs (BRM) gearbox lap 37—I. Raby (Brabham) accident lap 37—P. Revson (Lotus) plugs lap 43—J. Bonnier (Brabham) brakes lap 46.

Starting grid 3-2-3

Clark 1 min 38.1 sec—G. Hill 1 min 38.3 sec—Gurney 1 min 38.4 sec—Brabham 1 min 38.5 sec—Surtees 1 min 38.7 sec—McLaren 1 min 39.6 sec—Anderson 1 min 39.8 sec—Bandini 1 min 40.2 sec—Bonnier 1 min 40.2 sec—Ireland 1 min 40.8 sec—Amon 1 min 41.2 sec—Hailwood 1 min 41.4 sec—Spence 1 min 41.4 sec—Ginther 1 min 41.6 sec—P. Hill 1 min 42.6 sec—Siffert 1 min 42.8 sec—Raby 1 min 42.8 sec—T. Taylor 1 min 42.8 sec—Gardner 1 min 43.0 sec—J. Taylor 1 min 43.2 sec—Baghetti 1 min 43.4 sec—Revson 1 min 43.4 sec—Maggs 1 min 45.0 sec.

GERMAN GRAND PRIX

Nürburgring; 2 August; 15 laps 341 km/212 miles
1 J. Surtees (Ferrari) 2 hr 12 min 04.8 sec 155.38 kph/96.56 mph—2 G. Hill (BRM) 2 hr 13 min 20.4 sec—3 L. Bandini (Ferrari) 2 hr 16 min 57.6 sec—4 J. Siffert (Brabham) 2 hr 17 min 27.9 sec—5 M. Trintignant (BRM) 14 laps—6 T. Maggs (BRM) 14 laps—7 R. Ginther (BRM) 14 laps—8 M. Spence (Lotus) 14 laps—9 G. Mitter (Lotus) 14 laps—10 D. Gurney (Brabham) 14 laps—11 C. Amon (Lotus) 12 laps—12 J. Brabham (Brabham) 11 laps—13 R. Bucknum (Honda) 11 laps—14 P. Revson (Lotus) 10 laps—fastest lap, Surtees 8 min 39.0 sec 158.16 kph/98.3 mph—retired M. Hailwood (Lotus) engine lap 1—J. Bonnier (Brabham) engine lap 1—P. Hill (Cooper) engine lap 2—G. Baghetti (BRM) throttle lap 3—E. Barth (Cooper) clutch lap 3—B. McLaren (Cooper) engine lap 4—B. Anderson (Brabham) suspension lap 5—J. Clark (Lotus) engine lap 7.

Starting grid 3-2-3

Surtees 8 min 38.4 sec—Clark 8 min 38.8 sec—Gurney 8 min 39.3 sec—Bandini 8 min 42.6 sec—G. Hill 8 min 43.8 sec—Brabham 8 min 46.6 sec—McLaren 8 min 47.1 sec—P. Hill 8 min 52.7 sec—Amon 8 min 54.0 sec—Siffert 8 min 56.9 sec—Ginther 8 min 57.9 sec—Bonnier 9 min 01.3 sec—Hailwood 9 min 01.9 sec—Trintignant 9 min 06.8 sec—Anderson 9 min 07.5 sec—Maggs 9 min 09.6 sec—Spence 9 min 09.9 sec—Revson 9 min 13.0 sec—Mitter 9 min 14.1 sec—Barth 9 min 14.2 sec—Baghetti 9 min 14.6 sec—Bucknum 9 min 34.3 sec.

AUSTRIAN GRAND PRIX

Zeltweg; 23 August; 105 laps 322 km/200 miles
1 L. Bandini (Ferrari) 2 hr 6 min 18.2 sec 159.61 kph/99.2 mph—2 R. Ginther (BRM) 2 hr 6 min 24.4 sec—3 B. Anderson (Brabham) 102 laps—4 T. Maggs (BRM) 102 laps—5 I. Ireland (BRP) 102 laps—6 J. Bonnier (Brabham) 101 laps—7 G. Baghetti (BRM) 98 laps—8 M. Hailwood (Lotus) 95 laps—9 J. Brabham (Brabham) 73 laps—fastest lap, Gurney 1 min 10.56 sec 163.31 kph/101.5 mph—retired G. Hill (BRM) distributor drive lap 5—J. Surtees (Ferrari) rear suspension lap 8—C. Amon (Lotus) engine lap 8—Siffert (Brabham) accident lap 19—T. Taylor (BRP) rear suspension lap 22—J. Clark (Lotus) drive shaft lap 41—M. Spence (Lotus) drive shaft lap 42—B. McLaren (Cooper) engine lap 44—D. Gurney (Brabham) suspension mountings lap 47—P. Hill (Cooper) fire lap 58—J. Rindt (Brabham) steering lap 58.

Starting grid 4-3-4

G. Hill 1 min 09.8 sec—Surtees 1 min 10.1 sec—Clark 1 min 10.2 sec—Gurney 1 min 10.4 sec—Ginther 1 min 10.4 sec—Brabham 1 min 10.6 sec—Bandini 1 min 10.6 sec—Spence 1 min 11.0 sec—McLaren 1 min 11.2 sec—Bonnier 1 min 11.6 sec—Ireland 1 min 11.6 sec—Siffert 1 min 11.8 sec—Rindt 1 min 12.0 sec—Anderson 1 min 12.0 sec—Baghetti 1 min 12.1 sec—Taylor 1 min 12.2 sec—Amon 1 min 12.3 sec—Hailwood 1 min 12.4 sec—Maggs 1 min 12.4 sec—P. Hill 1 min 13.1 sec.

ITALIAN GRAND PRIX

Monza; 6 September; 78 laps 449 km/279 miles
1 J. Surtees (Ferrari) 2 hr 10 min 51.8 sec 205.6 kph/127.78 mph—2 B. McLaren (Cooper) 2 hr 11 min 57.8 sec—3 L. Bandini (Ferrari) 77 laps—4 R. Ginther (BRM) 77 laps—5 I. Ireland (BRP) 77 laps—6 M. Spence (Lotus) 77 laps—7 J. Siffert (Brabham) 77 laps—8 G. Baghetti (BRM) 77 laps—9 L. Scarfiotti (Ferrari) 77 laps—10 D. Gurney (Brabham) 75 laps—11 B. Anderson (Brabham) 75 laps—12 J. Bonnier (Brabham) 74 laps—13 P. Revson (Lotus) 72 laps—14 J. Brabham (Brabham) 59 laps—fastest lap, Surtees 1 min 38.8 sec 209.5 kph/130.18 mph—retired G. Hill (BRM) clutch 0 laps—M. Hailwood (Lotus) engine lap 5—R. Bucknum (Honda) brakes lap 13—M. Trintignant (BRM) engine lap 22—M. Cabral (ATS) ignition lap 25—J. Clark (Lotus) engine lap 28.

ITALIAN GRAND PRIX—*continued*

Starting grid 3-2-3

Surtees 1 min 37.4 sec—Gurney 1 min 38.2 sec—G. Hill 1 min 38.7 sec—Clark 1 min 39.1 sec—McLaren 1 min 39.4 sec—Siffert 1 min 39.7 sec—Bandini 1 min 39.8 sec—Spence 1 min 40.3 sec—Ginther 1 min 40.4 sec—Bucknam 1 min 40.4 sec—Brabham 1 min 40.8 sec—Bonnier 1 min 41.0 sec—Ireland 1 min 41.0 sec—Anderson 1 min 41.3 sec—Baghetti 1 min 41.4 sec—Scarfiotti 1 min 41.6 sec—Hailwood 1 min 41.6 sec—Revson 1 min 42.0 sec—Cabral 1 min 42.6 sec—Trintignant 1 min 43.3 sec.

UNITED STATES GRAND PRIX

Watkins Glen; 4 October; 110 laps 253 miles/407 km
1 G. Hill (BRM) 2 hr 16 min 38.0 sec 111.1 mph/178.76 kph—2 J. Surtees (Ferrari) 2 hr 17 min 08.5 sec—3 J. Siffert (Brabham) 109 laps—4 R. Ginther (BRM) 107 laps—5 W. Hansgen (Lotus) 107 laps—6 T. Taylor (BRP) 106 laps—7 M. Spence, J. Clark (Lotus) 102 laps—8 M. Hailwood (Lotus) 101 laps—fastest lap, Clark 1 min 12.7 sec 113.89 mph/183.25 kph—retired I. Ireland (BRP) broken gear lever lap 2—P. Hill (Cooper) ignition lap 4—J. Brabham (Brabham) engine lap 14—B. McLaren (Cooper) fuel pump lap 27—J. Bonnier (Brabham) stub axle lap 37—C. Amon (Lotus) starter motor bracket lap 47—R. Bucknum (Honda) overheating lap 50—J. Clark, M Spence (Lotus) fuel injection lap 54—L. Bandini (Ferrari) engine lap 58—H. Sharp (Brabham) lap 68—D. Gurney (Brabham) engine lap 69.

Starting grid 2-2-2

Clark 1 min 12.6 sec—Surtees 1 min 12.8 sec—Gurney 1 min 12.9 sec—G. Hill 1 min 12.9 sec—McLaren 1 min 13.1 sec—Spence 1 min 13.3 sec—Brabham 1 min 13.6 sec—Bandini 1 min 13.8 sec—Bonnier 1 min 14.1 sec—Ireland 1 min 14.3 sec—Amon 1 min 14.4 sec—Siffert 1 min 14.6 sec—Ginther 1 min 14.7 sec—Bucknum 1 min 14.9 sec—T. Taylor 1 min 15.3 sec—Hailwood 1 min 15.6 sec—Hansgen 1 min 15.9 sec—Sharp 1 min 18.2 sec—P. Hill 1 min 19.6 sec.

MEXICAN GRAND PRIX

Mexico City; 20 October; 65 laps 202 miles/325 km
1 D. Gurney (Brabham) 2 hr 9 min 50.3 sec 93.32 mph/150.15 kph—2 J. Surtees (Ferrari) 2 hr 10 min 59.3 sec—3 L. Bandini (Ferrari) 2 hr 10 min 59.9 sec—4 M. Spence (Lotus) 2 hr 11 min 12.2 sec—5 J. Clark (Lotus) 64 laps—6 P. Rodriguez (Ferrari) 64 laps—7 B. McLaren (Cooper) 64 laps—8 R. Ginther (BRM) 64 laps—9 P. Hill (Cooper) 63 laps—10 M. Solana (Lotus) 63 laps—11 G. Hill (BRM) 63 laps—12 I. Ireland (BRP) 61 laps—13 H. Sharp (Brabham) 60 laps—14 J. Brabham (Brabham) 44 laps—fastest lap, Gurney 1 min 58.4 sec 94.56 mph/152.15 kph—retired T. Taylor (BRP) overheating lap 6—J. Bonnier (Brabham) suspension lap 10—J. Siffert (Brabham) fuel pump lap 11—M. Hailwood (Lotus) overheating lap 12—C. Amon (Lotus) gearbox lap 46.

Starting grid 2-2-2

Clark 1 min 57.2 sec—Gurney 1 min 58.1 sec—Bandini 1 min 58.6 sec—Surtees 1 min 58.7 sec—Spence 1 min 59.2 sec—G. Hill 1 min 59.8 sec—Brabham 2 min 00.0 sec—Bonnier 2 min 00.2 sec—Rodriguez 2 min 00.9 sec—McLaren 2 min 01.1 sec—Ginther 2 min 01.1 sec—Amon 2 min 01.2 sec—Siffert 2 min 01.4 sec—Solana 2 min 01.4 sec—P. Hill 2 min 02.0 sec—Ireland 2 min 02.3 sec—Hailwood 2 min 04.1 sec—Taylor 2 min 04.9 sec—Sharp 2 min 06.9 sec.

1964 WORLD CHAMPIONSHIP

1 J. Surtees 40—2 G. Hill 39, 41—3 J. Clark 32—4 L. Bandini 23—4= R. Ginther 23—6 D. Gurney 19—7 B. McLaren 13—8 J. Brabham 11—8= P. Arundell 11—10 J. Siffert 7—11 B. Anderson 5—12 T. Maggs 4—12= M. Spence 4—12= I. Ireland 4—15 J. Bonnier 3—16 C. Amon 2—16= W. Hansgen 2—16= M. Trintignant 2—19 T. Taylor 1—19= M. Hailwood 1—19= P. Hill 1—19= P. Rodriguez 1.

1965

SOUTH AFRICAN GRAND PRIX

East London; 1 January; 85 laps 206 miles/331 km
1 J. Clark (Lotus) 2 hr 6 min 46.0 sec 97.97 mph/157.63 kph—2 J. Surtees (Ferrari) 2 hr 7 min 15.0 sec—3 G. Hill (BRM) 2 hr 7 min 17.8 sec—4 M. Spence (Lotus) 2 hr 7 min 40.4 sec—5 B. McLaren (Cooper) 84 laps—6 J Y Stewart (BRM) 84 laps—7 J. Siffert (Brabham) 83 laps—8 J. Brabham (Brabham) 81 laps—9 P. Hawkins (Brabham) 81 laps—10 P. de Klerk (Alfa Special) 79 laps—11 T. Maggs (Lotus) 77 laps—12 F. Gardner (Brabham) 75 laps—13 S. Tingle (LDS) 73 laps—14 D. Prophet (Brabham) 71 laps—15 L. Bandini (Ferrari) 66 laps—B. Anderson (Brabham) not classified 50 laps—fastest lap, Clark 1 min 27.4 sec 100.1 mph/161.06 kph—retired D. Gurney (Brabham) ignition lap 12—J. Love (Cooper) broken half shaft lap 21—J. Rindt (Cooper) electrics lap 40—J. Bonnier (Brabham) transmission lap 43.

Starting grid 3-2-3

Clark 1 min 27.2 sec—Surtees 1 min 28.1 sec—Brabham 1 min 28.3 sec—Spence 1 min 28.3 sec—G. Hill 1 min 28.6 sec—Bandini 1 min 29.3 sec—Bonnier 1 min 29.3 sec—McLaren 1 min 29.4 sec—Gurney 1 min 29.5 sec—Rindt 1 min 30.4 sec—Stewart 1 min 30.5 sec—Anderson 1 min 31.0 sec—Maggs 1 min 31.3 sec—Siffert 1 min 31.8 sec—Gardner 1 min 32.3 sec—Hawkins 1 min 33.1 sec—de Klerk 1 min 33.3 sec—Love 1 min 33.8 sec—Prophet 1 min 33.9 sec—Tingle 1 min 34.6 sec—non starters D. Serrurier (LDS)—E. Pieterse (Lotus)—N. Lederle (Lotus)—B. Niemann (Lotus)—T. Blokdyk (Cooper).

MONACO GRAND PRIX

Monte Carlo; 30 May; 100 laps 314 km/195 miles
1 G. Hill (BRM) 2 hr 37 min 39.6 sec 119.55 kph/74.3 mph—2 L. Bandini (Ferrari) 2 hr 38 min 43.6 sec—3 J Y Stewart (BRM) 2 hr 39 min 21.5 sec—4 J. Surtees (Ferrari) 99 laps—5 B. McLaren (Cooper) 98 laps—6 J. Siffert (Brabham) 98 laps—7 J. Bonnier (Brabham) 97 laps—8 D. Hulme (Brabham) 92 laps—9 B. Anderson (Brabham) 85 laps—10 P. Hawkins (Lotus) 79 laps—fastest lap, Hill 1 min 31.7 sec 123.44 kph/76.72 mph—retired R. Ginther (Honda) final drive lap 1—M. Hailwood (Lotus) gearbox lap 12—F. Gardner (Brabham) oil pipe lap 30—R. Bucknum (Honda) gear linkage lap 33—J. Brabham (Brabham) oil pipe lap 43—R. Attwood (Lotus) accident lap 44.

Starting grid 2-2-2

G. Hill 1 min 32.5 sec—Brabham 1 min 32.8 sec—Stewart 1 min 32.9 sec—Bandini 1 min 33.0 sec—Surtees 1 min 33.2 sec—Attwood 1 min 33.9 sec—McLaren 1 min 34.3 sec—Hulme 1 min 34.8 sec—Anderson 1 min 35.5 sec—Siffert 1 min 36.0 sec—Gardner 1 min 36.0 sec—Hailwood 1 min 36.5 sec—Bonnier 1 min 36.5 sec—Hawkins 1 min 37.0 sec—Bucknum 1 min 37.5 sec—Ginther 1 min 39.7 sec—non starters J. Rindt (Cooper)—M. Spence (Lotus)—P. Rodriguez (Lotus).

BELGIAN GRAND PRIX

Spa-Francorchamps; 13 June; 32 laps 450 km/280 miles
1 J. Clark (Lotus) 2 hr 23 min 34.8 sec 188.51 kph/117.16 mph—2 J Y Stewart (BRM) 2 hr 24 min 19.6 sec—3 B. McLaren (Cooper) 31 laps—4 J. Brabham (Brabham) 31 laps—5 G. Hill (BRM) 31 laps—6 R. Ginther (Honda) 31 laps—7 M. Spence (Lotus) 31 laps—8 J. Siffert (Brabham) 31 laps—9 L. Bandini (Ferrari) 30 laps—10 D. Gurney (Brabham) 30 laps—11 J. Rindt (Cooper) 29 laps—12 L. Bianchi (BRM) 29 laps—13 I. Ireland (Lotus) 27 laps—14 R. Attwood (Lotus) 26 laps—fastest lap, Clark 4 min 12.9 sec 200.67 kph/124.72 mph—retired F. Gardner (Brabham) ignition lap 3—J. Surtees

(Ferrari) engine lap 6—R. Bucknum (Honda) transmission lap 10—J. Bonnier (Brabham) ignition lap 10—M. Gregory (BRM) fuel pump lap 13.

Starting grid 3-2-3

G. Hill 3 min 45.4 sec—Clark 3 min 47.5 sec—Stewart 3 min 48.8 sec—Ginther 3 min 49.0 sec—Gurney 3 min 49.2 sec—Surtees 3 min 49.5 sec—Bonnier 3 min 49.7 sec—Siffert 3 min 50.7 sec—McLaren 3 min 51.3 sec—Brabham 3 min 51.5 sec—Bucknum 3 min 52.3 sec—Spence 3 min 52.6 sec—Attwood 3 min 53.2 sec—Rindt 3 min 53.3 sec—Bandini 3 min 54.0 sec—Ireland 3 min 57.4 sec—Bianchi 3 min 59.0 sec—Gardner 3 min 59.4 sec—Gregory 4 min 02.8 sec—non starters B. Anderson (Brabham)—W. Mairesse (BRM).

FRENCH GRAND PRIX

Clermont-Ferrand; 27 June; 40 laps 322 km/200 miles
1 J. Clark (Lotus) 2 hr 14 min 38.4 sec 143.52 kph/89.2 mph—2 J Y Stewart (BRM) 2 hr 15 min 4.7 sec—3 J. Surtees (Ferrari) 2 hr 17 min 11.9 sec—4 D. Hulme (Brabham) 2 hr 17 min 31.5 sec—5 G. Hill (BRM) 39 laps—6 J. Siffert (Brabham) 39 laps—7 M. Spence (Lotus) 39 laps—8 L. Bandini (Ferrari) 36 laps—9 B. Anderson (Brabham) 34 laps—fastest lap, Clark 3 min 18.9 sec 158.63 kph/98.59 mph—retired J. Rindt (Cooper) accident lap 3—R. Bucknum (Honda) engine lap 4—R. Ginther (Honda) electrics lap 9—D. Gurney (Brabham) engine lap 16—C. Amon (Lotus) engine lap 18—I. Ireland (Lotus) gearbox lap 19—J. Bonnier (Brabham) ignition lap 21—B. McLaren (Cooper) suspension lap 23.

Starting grid 3-2-3

Clark 3 min 18.3 sec—Stewart 3 min 18.8 sec—Bandini 3 min 19.1 sec—Surtees 3 min 19.1 sec—Gurney 3 min 19.8 sec—Hulme 3 min 20.5 sec—Ginther 3 min 21.4 sec—Amon 3 min 23.0 sec—McLaren 3 min 23.2 sec—Spence 3 min 23.4 sec—Bonnier 3 min 23.4 sec—Rindt 3 min 23.6 sec—G. Hill 3 min 23.7 sec—Siffert 3 min 25.2 sec—Anderson 3 min 26.0 sec—Bucknum 3 min 26.3 sec—Ireland 3 min 30.5 sec.

BRITISH GRAND PRIX

Silverstone; 10 July; 80 laps 234 miles/376 km
1 J. Clark (Lotus) 2 hr 5 min 25.4 sec 112.02 mph/180.24 kph—2 G. Hill (BRM) 2 hr 5 min 28.6 sec—3 J. Surtees (Ferrari) 2 hr 5 min 53.6 sec—4 M. Spence (Lotus) 2 hr 6 min 5.0 sec—5 J Y Stewart (BRM) 2 hr 6 min 40.0 sec—6 D. Gurney (Brabham) 79 laps—7 J. Bonnier (Brabham) 79 laps—8 F. Gardner (Brabham) 78 laps—9 J. Siffert (Brabham) 78 laps—10 B. McLaren (Cooper) 77 laps—11 I. Raby (Brabham) 73 laps—12 M. Gregory (BRM) 70 laps—13 R. Attwood (Lotus) 63 laps—14 J. Rindt (Cooper) 62 laps—fastest lap, G. Hill 1 min 32.2 sec 114.29 mph/183.89 kph—retired L. Bandini (Ferrari) engine lap 3—R. Ginther (Honda) ignition lap 27—D. Hulme (Brabham) alternator belt lap 30—B. Anderson (Brabham) gearbox lap 34—J. Rhodes (Cooper) ignition lap 39—I. Ireland (Lotus) engine lap 42.

Starting grid 4-3-4

Clark 1 min 30.8 sec—G. Hill 1 min 31.0 sec—Ginther 1 min 31.3 sec—Stewart 1 min 31.3 sec—Surtees 1 min 31.3 sec—Spence 1 min 31.7 sec—Gurney 1 min 32.5 sec—Bandini 1 min 32.7 sec—Hulme 1 min 32.7 sec—McLaren 1 min 32.8 sec—Rindt 1 min 32.9 sec—Gardner 1 min 33.4 sec—Bonnier 1 min 33.5 sec—Ireland 1 min 33.6 sec—Attwood 1 min 33.8 sec—Anderson 1 min 34.1 sec—Siffert 1 min 34.2 sec—Gregory 1 min 35.9 sec—Raby 1 min 36.0 sec—Rhodes 1 min 39.4 sec—(Gurney started in a different car; his practice time with it was 1 min 31.9 sec)—non starters B. Gubby (Lotus)—A. Rollinson (Cooper)—C. Amon (Brabham).

DUTCH GRAND PRIX

Zandvoort; 18 July; 80 laps 355 km/221 miles
1 J. Clark (Lotus) 2 hr 3 min 59.1 sec 162.3 kph/100.87 mph—2 J Y Stewart (BRM) 2 hr 4 min 07.1 sec—3 D. Gurney (Brabham) 2 hr 4 min 12.1 sec—4 G. Hill (BRM) 2 hr 4 min 44.2 sec—5 D. Hulme (Brabham) 79 laps—6 R. Ginther (Honda) 79 laps—7 J. Surtees (Ferrari) 79 laps—8 M. Spence (Lotus) 79 laps—9 L. Bandini (Ferrari) 79 laps—10 I. Ireland (Lotus) 78 laps—11 F. Gardner (Brabham) 77 laps—12 R. Attwood (Lotus) 77 laps—13 J. Siffert (Brabham) 55 laps—fastest lap, Clark 1 min 30.6 sec 166.56 kph/103.52 mph—retired B. Anderson (Brabham) head gasket lap 12—J. Bonnier (Brabham) ignition lap 17—B. McLaren (Cooper) gearbox lap 37—J. Rindt (Cooper) engine lap 49.

Starting grid 3-2-3

G. Hill 1 min 30.7 sec—Clark 1 min 31.0 sec—Ginther 1 min 31.0 sec—Surtees 1 min 31.0 sec—Gurney 1 min 31.2 sec—Stewart 1 min 31.4 sec—Hulme 1 min 32.0 sec—Spence 1 min 32.2 sec—McLaren 1 min 32.6 sec—Siffert 1 min 32.9 sec—Gardner 1 min 32.9 sec—Bandini 1 min 33.1 sec—Ireland 1 min 33.4 sec—Rindt 1 min 33.7 sec—Bonnier 1 min 33.8 sec—Anderson 1 min 34.1 sec—Attwood 1 min 34.6 sec.

GERMAN GRAND PRIX

Nürburgring; 31 July; 15 laps 341 km/212 miles
1 J. Clark (Lotus) 2 hr 7 min 52.4 sec 160.56 kph/99.79 mph—2 G. Hill (BRM) 2 hr 8 min 08.3 sec—3 D. Gurney (Brabham) 2 hr 8 min 13.8 sec—4 J. Rindt (Cooper) 2 hr 11 min 22.0 sec—5 J. Brabham (Brabham) 2 hr 12 min 33.6 sec—6 L. Bandini (Ferrari) 2 hr 13 min 01.0 sec—7 J. Bonnier (Brabham) 2 hr 13 min 50.9 sec—8 M. Gregory (BRM) 14 laps—fastest lap, Clark 8 min 24.1 sec 162.86 kph/101.22 mph—retired F. Gardner (Brabham) transmission lap 1—J. Y Stewart (BRM) suspension lap 2—P. Hawkins (Lotus) oil leak lap 3—D. Hulme (Brabham) steering lap 5—B. McLaren (Cooper) gearbox lap 7—M. Spence (Lotus) drive shaft lap 9—G. Mitter (Lotus) water leak lap 9—R. Attwood (Lotus) water leak lap 9—C. Amon (Lotus) ignition lap 10—J. Siffert (Brabham) engine lap 10—J. Surtees (Ferrari) gearbox lap 11.

Starting grid 4-3-4

Clark 8 min 22.7 sec—Stewart 8 min 26.1 sec—G. Hill 8 min 26.8 sec—Surtees 8 min 27.0 sec—Gurney 8 min 29.0 sec—Spence 8 min 33.4 sec—Bandini 8 min 33.8 sec—Rindt 8 min 37.5 sec—Bonnier 8 min 37.9 sec—McLaren 8 min 39.0 sec—Siffert 8 min 39.6 sec—Mitter 8 min 40.4 sec—Hulme 8 min 42.3 sec—Brabham 8 min 44.9 sec—Amon 8 min 50.5 sec—Attwood 8 min 57.7 sec—Gardner 8 min 59.3 sec—Gregory 9 min 14.3 sec—Hawkins 9 min 16.8 sec—non starters I. Raby (Brabham)—B. Anderson (Brabham)—R. Bussinello (BRM).

ITALIAN GRAND PRIX

Monza; 12 September; 76 laps 438 km/272 miles
1 J Y Stewart (BRM) 2 hr 4 min 52.8 sec 209.91 kph/130.46 mph—2 G. Hill (BRM) 2 hr 4 min 56.1 sec—3 D. Gurney (Brabham) 2 hr 5 min 09.3 sec—4 L. Bandini (Ferrari) 2 hr 6 min 08.7 sec—5 B. McLaren (Cooper) 75 laps—6 R. Attwood (Lotus) 75 laps—7 J. Bonnier (Brabham) 74 laps—8 J. Rindt (Cooper) 74 laps—9 I. Ireland (Lotus) 74 laps—10 J. Clark (Lotus) 63 laps—11 M. Spence (Lotus) 62 laps—12 N. Vaccarella (Ferrari) 58 laps—13 R. Bussinello (BRM) 58 laps—14 R. Ginther (Honda) 56 laps—fastest lap, Clark 1 min 36.4 sec 214.69 kph/133.43 mph—retired G. Bassi (BRM) engine lap 9—G. Baghetti (Brabham) engine lap 13—M. Gregory (BRM) transmission lap 22—R. Bucknum (Honda) engine lap 27—J. Surtees (Ferrari) clutch lap 35—'Geki' Russo (Lotus) gearbox lap 38—J. Siffert (Brabham) transmission lap 44—F. Gardner (Brabham) ignition lap 47—D. Hulme (Brabham) suspension lap 47.

Starting grid 3-2-3

Clark 1 min 35.9 sec—Surtees 1 min 36.1 sec—Stewart 1 min 36.6 sec—G. Hill 1 min 37.1 sec—Bandini 1 min 37.2 sec—Bucknum 1 min 37.3 sec—Rindt 1 min 37.7 sec—Spence 1 min 37.8 sec—Gurney 1 min 38.1 sec—Siffert 1 min 38.1 sec—McLaren 1 min 38.3 sec—Hulme 1 min 38.3 sec—Attwood 1 min 38.8 sec—Bonnier 1 min 38.9

ITALIAN GRAND PRIX—*continued*

sec—Vaccarella 1 min 38.9 sec—Gardner 1 min 39.0 sec—Ginther 1 min 39.6 sec—Ireland 1 min 39.8 sec—Baghetti 1 min 40.9 sec—'Geki' 1 min 41.7 sec—Bussinello 1 min 41.8 sec—Bassi 1 min 45.4 sec—Gregory 1 min 45.6 sec.

UNITED STATES GRAND PRIX

Watkins Glen; 3 October; 110 laps 253 miles/407 km
1 G. Hill (BRM) 2 hr 20 min 36.1 sec 107.98 mph/173.74 kph—2 D. Gurney (Brabham) 2 hr 20 min 48.6 sec—3 J. Brabham (Brabham) 2 hr 21 min 33.6 sec—4 L. Bandini (Ferrari) 109 laps—5 P. Rodriguez (Ferrari) 109 laps—6 J. Rindt (Cooper) 108 laps—7 R. Ginther (Honda) 108 laps—8 J. Bonnier (Brabham) 107 laps—9 B. Bondurant (Ferrari) 106 laps—10 R. Attwood (Lotus) 101 laps—11 J. Siffert (Brabham) 99 laps—12 M. Solana (Lotus) 95 laps—13 R. Bucknum (Honda) 92 laps—fastest lap, G. Hill 1 min 11.9 sec 115.16 mph/185.29 kph—retired M. Spence (Lotus) engine lap 9—I. Ireland (Lotus) ill lap 9—J. Clark (Lotus) engine lap 11—B. McLaren (Cooper) oil pressure lap 11—J Y Stewart (BRM) suspension lap 12.

Starting grid 2-2-2

G. Hill 1 min 11.2 sec—Clark 1 min 11.3 sec—Ginther 1 min 11.4 sec—Spence 1 min 11.5 sec—Bandini 1 min 11.7 sec—Stewart 1 min 11.8 sec—Brabham 1 min 12.2 sec—Gurney 1 min 12.2 sec—McLaren 1 min 12.4 sec—Bonnier 1 min 12.4 sec—Siffert 1 min 12.5 sec—Bucknum 1 min 12.7 sec—Rindt 1 min 12.9 sec—Bondurant 1 min 12.9 sec—Rodriguez 1 min 13.0 sec—Attwood 1 min 13.7 sec—Solana 1 min 13.7 sec—Ireland 1 min 15.0 sec.

MEXICAN GRAND PRIX

Mexico City; 24 October; 65 laps 208 miles/335 km
1 R. Ginther (Honda) 2 hr 8 min 32.1 sec 94.26 mph/151.66 kph—2 D. Gurney (Brabham) 2 hr 8 min 35.0 sec—3 M. Spence (Lotus) 2 hr 9 min 32.2 sec—4 J. Siffert (Brabham) 2 hr 10 min 26.5 sec—5 R. Bucknum (Honda) 64 laps—6 R. Attwood (Lotus) 64 laps—7 P. Rodriguez (Ferrari) 62 laps—8 L. Bandini (Ferrari) 62 laps—fastest lap, Gurney 1 min 55.8 sec 96.59 mph/155.41 kph—retired J. Clark (Lotus) engine lap 9—B. McLaren (Cooper) gear selector lap 25—B. Bondurant (Lotus) suspension lap 29—J Y Stewart (BRM) clutch lap 35—J. Brabham (Brabham) oil leak lap 38—J. Rindt (Cooper) ignition lap 39—J. Bonnier (Brabham) chassis lap 43—M. Solana (Lotus) electrics lap 55—G. Hill (BRM) engine lap 56.

Starting grid 2-2-2

Clark 1 min 56.2 sec—Gurney 1 min 56.2 sec—Ginther 1 min 56.5 sec—Brabham 1 min 56.8 sec—G. Hill 1 min 57.1 sec—Spence 1 min 57.2 sec—Bandini 1 min 57.3 sec—Stewart 1 min 57.5 sec—Solana 1 min 57.5 sec—Bucknum 1 min 57.9 sec—Siffert 1 min 57.9 sec—Bonnier 1 min 58.2 sec—Rodriguez 1 min 59.1 sec—McLaren 1 min 59.1 sec—Rindt 1 min 59.3 sec—Attwood 2 min 00.6 sec—Bondurant 2 min 00.8 sec—non starters I. Ireland (Lotus)—L. Scarfiotti (Ferrari).

1965 WORLD CHAMPIONSHIP

1 J. Clark 54—2 G. Hill 40, 47—3 J Y Stewart 33, 34—4 D. Gurney 25—5 J. Surtees 17—6 L. Bandini 13—7 R. Ginther 11—8 B. McLaren 10—8= M. Spence 10—10 J. Brabham 9—11 D. Hulme 5—11= J. Siffert 5—13 J. Rindt 4—14 P. Rodriguez 2—14= R. Attwood 2—14= R. Bucknum 2.

1966

MONACO GRAND PRIX

Monte Carlo; 22 May; 100 laps 314km/195 miles
1 J Y Stewart (BRM) 2 hr 33 min 10.5 sec 123.09 kph/76.5 mph—2 L. Bandini (Ferrari) 2 hr 33 min 50.7 sec—3 G. Hill (BRM) 99 laps—4 B. Bondurant (BRM) 95 laps—not classified G. Ligier (Cooper) 75 laps—J. Bonnier (Cooper) 73 laps—fastest lap, Bandini 1 min 29.8 sec 126.05 kph/78.34 mph—retired B. Anderson (Brabham) engine lap 4—B. McLaren (McLaren) oil leak lap 10—D. Hulme (Brabham) drive shaft lap 16—J. Surtees (Ferrari) rear axle lap 17—J. Brabham (Brabham) gearbox lap 18—M. Spence (Lotus) suspension lap 35—J. Siffert (Brabham) clutch lap 36—J. Rindt (Cooper) engine lap 56—J. Clark (Lotus) suspension lap 61—R. Ginther (Cooper) drive shaft lap 81.

Starting grid 2-2-2

Clark 1 min 29.9 sec—Surtees 1 min 30.1 sec—Stewart 1 min 30.3 sec—Hill 1 min 30.4 sec—Bandini 1 min 30.5 sec—Hulme 1 min 31.1 sec—Rindt 1 min 32.2 sec—Anderson 1 min 32.5 sec—Ginther 1 min 32.6 sec—McLaren 1 min 32.8 sec—Brabham 1 min 32.8 sec—Spence 1 min 33.5 sec—Siffert 1 min 34.4 sec—Bonnier 1 min 35.0 sec—Ligier 1 min 35.2 sec—Bondurant 1 min 37.3 sec—non starters C. Amon (McLaren)—P. Arundell (Lotus)—R. Attwood (Lotus)—D. Gurney (Eagle).

BELGIAN GRAND PRIX

Spa-Francorchamps; 12 June; 28 laps 394 km/245 miles
1 J. Surtees (Ferrari) 2 hr 9 min 11.3 sec 182.44 kph/113.39 mph—2 J. Rindt (Cooper) 2 hr 9 min 53.4 sec—3 L. Bandini (Ferrari) 27 laps—4 J. Brabham (Brabham) 26 laps—5 R. Ginther (Cooper) 25 laps—not classified G. Ligier (Cooper) 24 laps—D. Gurney (Eagle) 23 laps—fastest lap, Surtees 4 min 18.7 sec 196.15 kph/121.91 mph—retired J. Clark (Lotus) engine lap 1—J. Siffert (Cooper) accident lap 1—M. Spence (Lotus) accident lap 1—J Y Stewart (BRM) accident lap 1—G. Hill (BRM) accident lap 1—J. Bonnier (Cooper) accident lap 1—D. Hulme (Brabham) accident lap 1—B. Bondurant (BRM) accident lap 1.

Starting grid 3-2-3

Surtees 3 min 38.0 sec—Rindt 3 min 41.2 sec—Stewart 3 min 41.5 sec—Brabham 3 min 41.8 sec—Bandini 3 min 43.8 sec—Bonnier 3 min 44.3 sec—Spence 3 min 45.2 sec—Ginther 3 min 45.4 sec—Hill 3 min 45.6 sec—Clark 3 min 45.8 sec—Bondurant 3 min 50.5 sec—Ligier 3 min 51.1 sec—Hulme 3 min 51.4 sec—Siffert 3 min 53.8 sec—Gurney 3 min 57.6 sec—non starters P. Arundell (BRM)—B. McLaren (McLaren).

FRENCH GRAND PRIX

Rheims; 3 July; 48 laps 397 km/247 miles
1 J. Brabham (Brabham) 1 hr 48 min 31.3 sec 220.27 kph/136.9 mph—2 M Parkes (Ferrari) 1 hr 48 min 40.8 sec—3 D. Hulme (Brabham) 46 laps—4 J. Rindt (Cooper) 46 laps—5 D. Gurney (Eagle) 45 laps—6 J. Taylor (Brabham) 45 laps—7 B. Anderson (Brabham) 44 laps—8 C. Amon (Cooper) 44 laps—not classified G. Ligier (Cooper) 42 laps—P. Rodriguez (Lotus) 40 laps—L. Bandini (Ferrari) 37 laps—J. Bonnier (Brabham) 32 laps—fastest lap, Bandini 2 min 11.3 sec 227.58 kph/141.44 mph—retired P. Arundell (Lotus) gearbox lap 2—J. Surtees (Cooper) fuel system lap 5—M. Spence (Lotus) clutch lap 8—J. Siffert (Cooper) fuel lap 10—G. Hill (BRM) engine lap 12.

Starting grid 3-2-3

Bandini 2 min 07.8 sec—Surtees 2 min 08.4 sec—Parkes 2 min 09.1 sec—Brabham 2 min 10.2 sec—Rindt 2 min 10.9 sec—Siffert 2 min 12.2 sec—Amon 2 min 12.4 sec—Hill 2 min 12.8 sec—Hulme 2 min 13.3 sec—Spence 2 min 14.2 sec—Ligier 2 min 15.4 sec—Rodriguez 2 min 15.6 sec—Anderson 2 min 15.6 sec—Gurney 2 min 17.9 sec—Taylor 2 min 19.2 sec—Arundell 2 min 19.6 sec—Bonnier 2 min 23.5 sec.

BRITISH GRAND PRIX

Brands Hatch; 16 July; 80 laps 202 miles/325 km
1 J. Brabham (Brabham) 2 hr 13 min 13.4 sec 95.48 mph/153.63 kph—2 D. Hulme (Brabham) 2 hr 13 min 23.0 sec—3 G. Hill (BRM) 79 laps—4 J. Clark (Lotus) 79 laps—5 J. Rindt (Cooper) 79 laps—6 B. McLaren (McLaren) 78 laps—7 C. Irwin (Brabham) 78 laps—8 J. Taylor (Brabham) 76 laps—9 B. Bondurant (BRM) 76 laps—10 G. Ligier (Cooper) 75 laps —11 C. Lawrence (Cooper) 73 laps—12 J. Siffert (Cooper) 70 laps—13 B. Anderson (Brabham) 70 laps—fastest lap, Brabham 1 min 37.0 sec 98.35 mph/158.24 kph—retired T. Taylor (Shannon) split fuel tank lap 2—D. Gurney (Eagle) engine lap 9—M. Spence (Lotus) oil pipe lap 15—J. Bonnier (Brabham) clutch lap 42—P. Arundell (Lotus) gear linkage lap 17—J Y Stewart (BRM) engine lap 17—J. Surtees (Cooper) transmission lap 67.

Starting grid 3-2-3

Brabham 1 min 34.5 sec—Hulme 1 min 34.8 sec—Gurney 1 min 35.8 sec—Hill 1 min 36.0 sec—Clark 1 min 36.1 sec—Surtees 1 min 36.4 sec—Rindt 1 min 36.6 sec—Stewart 1 min 36.9 sec—Spence 1 min 37.3 sec—Anderson 1 min 37.5 sec—Siffert 1 min 38.0 sec—Irwin 1 min 38.1 sec—McLaren 1 min 38.5 sec—Bondurant 1 min 38.9 sec—Bonnier 1 min 39.3 sec—J. Taylor 1 min 40.0 sec—Ligier 1 min 41.4 sec—T. Taylor 1 min 41.6 sec—Lawrence 1 min 43.8 sec—Arundell 1 min 54.3 sec.

DUTCH GRAND PRIX

Zandvoort; 24 July; 90 laps 376 km/234 miles
1 J. Brabham (Brabham) 2 hr 10 min 32.5 sec 161.06 kph/100.1 mph—2 G. Hill (BRM) 89 laps—3 J. Clark (Lotus) 88 laps—4 J Y Stewart (BRM) 88 laps—5 M. Spence (Lotus) 87 laps—6 L. Bandini (Ferrari) 67 laps—7 J. Bonnier (Cooper) 84 laps—8 J. Taylor (Brabham) 84 laps—9 G. Ligier (Cooper) 84 laps—fastest lap, Hulme 1 min 30.6 sec 166.58 kph/103.53 mph—retired J. Rindt (Cooper) accident lap 2—M. Parkes (Ferrari) accident lap 10—D. Gurney (Eagle) engine lap 24—P. Arundell (Lotus) ignition lap 28—D. Hulme (Brabham) ignition lap 37—J. Surtees (Cooper) ignition lap 43—B. Anderson (Brabham) engine lap 73—J. Siffert (Cooper) engine lap 73.

Starting grid 3-2-3

Brabham 1 min 28.1 sec—Hulme 1 min 28.7 sec—Clark 1 min 28.7 sec—Gurney 1 min 28.8 sec—Parkes 1 min 29.0 sec—Rindt 1 min 29.2 sec—Hill 1 min 29.7 sec—Stewart 1 min 29.8 sec—Bandini 1 min 30.0 sec—Surtees 1 min 30.6 sec—Siffert 1 min 31.1 sec—Spence 1 min 31.4 sec—Bonnier 1 min 31.7 sec—Anderson 1 min 32.0 sec—Arundell 1 min 32.0 sec—Ligier 1 min 35.0 sec—J. Taylor 1 min 35.7 sec—non starter B. McLaren (McLaren).

GERMAN GRAND PRIX

Nürburgring; 7 August; 15 laps 343 km/213 miles
1 J. Brabham (Brabham) 2 hr 27 min 3.0 sec 139.58 kph/86.75 mph—2 J. Surtees (Cooper) 2 hr 27 min 47.4 sec—3 J. Rindt (Cooper) 2 hr 29 min 35.6 sec—4 G. Hill (BRM) 2 hr 33 min 44.4 sec—5 J Y Stewart (BRM) 2 hr 35 min 31.9 sec—6 L. Bandini (Ferrari) 2 hr 37 min 59.4 sec—7 D. Gurney (Eagle) 14 laps—8 P. Arundell (Lotus) 14 laps—fastest lap, Surtees 8 min 48.0 sec 155.17 kph/96.44 mph—retired J. Taylor (Brabham) accident 0 laps—B. Bondurant (BRM) engine lap 3—B. Anderson (Brabham) engine lap 3—J. Bonnier (Cooper) clutch lap 4—D. Hulme (Brabham) ignition lap 5—M. Parkes (Ferrari) engine lap 8—L. Scarfiotti (Ferrari) battery lap 8—C. Lawrence (Cooper) engine lap 10—J. Clark (Lotus) accident lap 11—M. Spence (Lotus) ignition lap 12.

Starting grid 4-3-4

Clark 8 min 16.5 sec—Surtees 8 min 18.0 sec—Stewart 8 min 18.8 sec—Scarfiotti 8 min 20.2 sec—Brabham 8 min 20.8 sec—Bandini 8 min 21.1 sec—Parkes 8 min 21.7 sec—Gurney 8 min 22.8 sec—Rindt 8 min 27.7 sec—Hill 8 min 26.6 sec—Bondurant 8 min 33.0 sec—Bonnier 8 min 35.3 sec—Spence 8 min 38.6 sec—Anderson 8 min 42.5 sec—Hulme 8 min 49.3 sec—Arundell 8 min 52.7 sec—Taylor 9 min 08.9 sec—Lawrence 9 min 10.9 sec—non starter G. Ligier (Cooper).

ITALIAN GRAND PRIX

Monza; 4 September; 68 laps 391 km/243 miles
1 L. Scarfiotti (Ferrari) 1 hr 47 min 14.8 sec 218.71 kph/135.93 mph—2 M. Parkes (Ferrari) 1 hr 47 min 20.6 sec—3 D. Hulme (Brabham) 1 hr 47 min 20.9 sec—4 J. Rindt (Cooper) 67 laps—5 M. Spence (Lotus) 67 laps—6 B. Anderson (Brabham) 66 laps—7 B. Bondurant (BRM) 65 laps—8 P. Arundell (Lotus) 63 laps—9 'Geki' Russo (Lotus) 63 laps—fastest lap, Scarfiotti 1 min 32.4 sec 223.89 kph/139.19 mph—retired G. Hill (BRM) engine lap 1—J. Bonnier (Cooper) engine lap 4—J Y Stewart (BRM) fuel tank lap 6—J. Brabham (Brabham) engine lap 8—D. Gurney (Eagle) engine lap 17—R. Ginther (Honda) accident lap 17—J. Surtees (Cooper) fuel tank lap 32—L. Bandini (Ferrari) ignition lap 34—J. Siffert (Cooper) engine lap 47—J. Clark (Lotus) gearbox lap 59.

Starting grid 3-2-3

Parkes 1 min 31.3 sec—Scarfiotti 1 min 31.6 sec—Clark 1 min 31.8 sec—Surtees 1 min 31.9 sec—Bandini 1 min 32.0 sec—Brabham 1 min 32.2 sec—Ginther 1 min 32.4 sec—Rindt 1 min 32.7 sec—Stewart 1 min 32.8 sec—Hulme 1 min 32.8 sec—Hill 1 min 33.4 sec—Bonnier 1 min 33.7 sec—Arundell 1 min 34.1 sec—Spence 1 min 35.0 sec—Anderson 1 min 35.3 sec—Baghetti 1 min 35.5 sec—Siffert 1 min 36.3 sec—Bondurant 1 min 36.9 sec—Gurney 1 min 39.1 sec—'Geki' 1 min 39.3 sec—non starters P. Hill (Eagle)—C. Amon (BRM).

UNITED STATES GRAND PRIX

Watkins Glen; 2 October; 108 laps 248 miles/399 km
1 J. Clark (Lotus) 2 hr 9 min 40.1 sec 114.94 mph/184.94 kph—2 J. Rindt (Cooper) 2 hr 10 min 26.9 sec—3 J. Surtees (Cooper) 107 laps—4 J. Siffert (Cooper) 105 laps—5 B. McLaren (McLaren) 105 laps—6 P. Arundell (Lotus) 101 laps—7 I. Ireland (BRM) 96 laps—8 R. Ginther (Honda) 81 laps—9 M. Spence (Lotus) 74 laps—not classified J. Bonnier (Cooper) 57 laps—fastest lap, Surtees 1 min 09.7 sec 118.85 mph/191.23 kph—retired B. Bondurant (Eagle) rear suspension lap 5—P. Rodriguez (Lotus) suspension lap 15—D. Gurney (Eagle) distributor drive lap 15—D. Hulme (Brabham) oil pressure lap 18—L. Bandini (Ferrari) gasket lap 35—G. Hill (BRM) gearbox lap 52—J Y Stewart (BRM) engine lap 53—J. Brabham (Brabham) camshaft drive lap 55—R. Bucknum (Honda) transmission lap 58.

Starting grid 2-2-2

Brabham 1 min 08.4 sec—Clark 1 min 08.5 sec—Bandini 1 min 08.6 sec—Surtees 1 min 08.7 sec—Hill 1 min 08.9 sec—Stewart 1 min 09.2 sec—Hulme 1 min 09.3 sec—Ginther 1 min 09.4 sec—Rindt 1 min 09.6 sec—Rodriguez 1 min 10.4 sec—McLaren 1 min 10.6 sec—Spence 1 min 10.7 sec—Siffert 1 min 11.0 sec—Gurney 1 min 11.0 sec—Bonnier 1 min 11.4 sec—Bondurant 1 min 12.4 sec—Ireland 1 min 12.6 sec—Bucknum 1 min 12.7 sec—Arundell.

MEXICAN GRAND PRIX

Mexico City; 23 October; 65 laps 202 miles/325 km
1 J. Surtees (Cooper) 2 hr 6 min 35.3 sec 95.72 mph/154.01 kph—2 J. Brabham (Brabham) 2 hr 6 min 43.22 sec—3 D. Hulme (Brabham) 64 laps—4 R. Ginther (Honda) 64 laps—5 D. Gurney (Eagle) 64 laps—6 J. Bonnier (Cooper) 63 laps—7 P. Arundell (Lotus) 61 laps—8 R. Bucknum (Honda) 60 laps—fastest lap, Ginther 1 min 53.7 sec 98.3 mph/158.16 kph—retired J. Clark (Lotus) gear selectors lap 9—M. Solana (Cooper) overheating lap 9—G. Hill (BRM) engine lap 18—B. Bondurant (Eagle) engine lap 24—J Y Stewart (BRM) engine lap 26—I. Ireland (BRM) differential lap 28—J. Rindt (Cooper) lost wheel lap 32—J. Siffert (Cooper) front suspension lap 33—B. McLaren (McLaren) engine lap 40—P. Rodriguez (Lotus) final drive lap 49.

MEXICAN GRAND PRIX—*continued*

Starting grid 2-2-2

Surtees 1 min 53.2 sec—Clark 1 min 53.5 sec—Ginther 1 min 53.6 sec—Brabham 1 min 54.0 sec—Rindt 1 min 54.2 sec—Hulme 1 min 54.2 sec—Hill 1 min 54.6 sec—Rodriguez 1 min 54.8 sec—Gurney 1 min 54.9 sec—Stewart 1 min 55.9 sec—Siffert 1 min 56.0 sec—Bonnier 1 min 56.5 sec—Bucknum 1 min 56.6 sec—McLaren 1 min 56.8 sec—Solana 1 min 57.4 sec—Ireland 1 min 57.5 sec—Arundel 2 min 00.8 sec—Bondurant 2 min 02.9 sec—non starter M. Spence (Lotus).

1966 WORLD CHAMPIONSHIP

1 J. Brabham 42, 45—2 J. Surtees 28—3 J. Rindt 22, 24—4 D. Hulme 18—5 G. Hill 17—6 J. Clark 16—7 J Y Stewart 14—8 L. Bandini 12—8= M. Parkes 12—10 L. Scarfiotti 9—11 R. Ginther 5—12 M. Spence 4—12= D. Gurney 4—14 B. Bondurant 3—14= J. Siffert 3—14= B. McLaren 3—17 J. Taylor 1—17= B. Anderson 1—17= P. Arundell 1—17= J. Bonnier 1.

1967

SOUTH AFRICAN GRAND PRIX

Kyalami; 2 January; 80 laps 204 miles/328 km
1 P. Rodriguez (Cooper) 2 hr 5 min 45.9 sec 97.09 mph/156.22 kph—2 J. Love (Cooper) 2 hr 6 min 12.3 sec—3 J. Surtees (Honda) 79 laps—4 D. Hulme (Brabham) 78 laps—5 B. Anderson (Brabham) 78 laps—6 J. Brabham (Brabham) 76 laps—not classified D. Charlton (Brabham) 62 laps—L. Botha (Brabham) 60 laps—fastest lap, Hulme 1 min 29.9 sec 101.88 mph/163.92 kph—retired J Y Stewart (BRM) engine lap 2—G. Hill (Lotus) suspension lap 6—J. Clark (Lotus) fuel system lap 22—J. Bonnier (Cooper) ignition lap 30—M. Spence (BRM) oil pipe lap 31—J. Rindt (Cooper) engine lap 38—J. Siffert (Cooper) engine lap 41—D. Gurney (Eagle) chassis lap 44—P. Courage (Lotus) oil pipe lap 51—S. Tingle (LDS) wheel lap 56.

Starting grid 2-2-2

Brabham 1 min 28.3 sec—Hulme 1 min 28.9 sec—Clark 1 min 29.0 sec—Rodriguez 1 min 29.1 sec—Love 1 min 29.5 sec—Surtees 1 min 29.8 sec—Gurney 1 min 29.8 sec—Rindt 1 min 30.2 sec—Charlton 1 min 30.2 sec—Stewart 1 min 30.3 sec—Anderson 1 min 30.6 sec—Bonnier 1 min 31.8 sec—Spence 1 min 32.1 sec—Tingle 1 min 32.4 sec—Hill 1 min 32.6 sec—Siffert 1 min 32.8 sec—Botha 1 min 33.1 sec—Courage 1 min 33.8 sec.

MONACO GRAND PRIX

Monte Carlo; 7 May; 100 laps 314 km/195 miles
1 D. Hulme (Brabham) 2 hr 34 min 34.3 sec 120.5 kph/75.89 mph—2 G. Hill (Lotus) 99 laps—3 C. Amon (Ferrari) 98 laps—4 B. McLaren (McLaren) 97 laps—5 P. Rodriguez (Cooper) 96 laps—6 M. Spence (BRM) 96 laps—fastest lap, Clark 1 min 29.5 sec 126.47 kph/78.6 mph—retired J. Brabham (Brabham) con-rod lap 1—J. Servoz-Gavin (Matra) metering unit lap 1—D. Gurney (Eagle) metering unit lap 4—J. Y Stewart (BRM) transmission lap 14—J. Rindt (Cooper) gearbox lap 14—J. Siffert (Cooper) radiator lap 32—J. Surtees (Honda) piston lap 33—J. Clark (Lotus) accident lap 43—P. Courage (BRM) accident lap 63—L. Bandini (Ferrari) fatal accident lap 82.

Starting grid 2-2-2

Brabham 1 min 27.6 sec—Bandini 1 min 28.3 sec—Surtees 1 min 28.4 sec—Hulme 1 min 28.8 sec—Clark 1 min 28.8 sec—Stewart 1 min 29.0 sec—Gurney 1 min 29.3 sec—Hill 1 min 29.9 sec—Siffert 1 min 30.0 sec—McLaren 1 min 30.0 sec—Servoz-Gavin 1 min 30.4 sec—Spence 1 min 30.6 sec—Courage 1 min 30.6 sec—Amon 1 min 30.7 sec—Rindt 1 min 30.8 sec—Rodriguez 1 min 32.4 sec—non starters J-P Beltoise (Matra)—B. Anderson (Brabham)—R. Ginther (Eagle)—G. Ligier (Cooper).

DUTCH GRAND PRIX

Zandvoort; 4 June; 90 laps 376 km/234 miles
1 J. Clark (Lotus) 2 hr 14 min 45.1 sec 168.12 kph/104.49 mph—2 J. Brabham (Brabham) 2 hr 15 min 08.7 sec—3 D. Hulme (Brabham) 2 hr 15 min 10.8 sec—4 C. Amon (Ferrari) 2 hr 15 min 12.4 sec—5 M. Parkes (Ferrari) 89 laps—6 L. Scarfiotti (Ferrari) 89 laps—7 C. Irwin (Lotus) 88 laps—8 M. Spence (BRM) 87 laps—9 B. Anderson (Brabham) 86 laps—10 J. Siffert (Cooper) 83 laps—fastest lap, Clark 1 min 28.1 sec 171.34 kph/106.49 mph—retired B. McLaren (McLaren) accident lap 2—D. Gurney (Eagle) metering unit drive lap 7—G. Hill (Lotus) camshaft gears lap 11—P. Rodriguez (Cooper) gearbox lap 40—J. Rindt (Cooper) suspension lap 44—J Y Stewart (BRM) brakes lap 51—J. Surtees (Honda) throttle slides lap 73.

Starting grid 3-2-3

Hill 1 min 24.6 sec—Gurney 1 min 25.1 sec—Brabham 1 min 25.6 sec—Rindt 1 min 26.5 sec—Rodriguez 1 min 26.6 sec—Surtees 1 min 26.7 sec—Hulme 1 min 26.7 sec—Clark 1 min 26.8 sec—Amon 1 min 26.9 sec—Parkes 1 min 27.0 sec—Stewart 1 min 27.2 sec—Spence 1 min 27.4 sec—Irwin 1 min 27.5 sec—McLaren 1 min 27.7 sec—Scarfiotti 1 min 27.9 sec—Siffert 1 min 28.8 sec—Anderson 1 min 29.0 sec.

BELGIAN GRAND PRIX

Spa-Francorchamps; 18 June; 28 laps 394 km/245 miles
1 D. Gurney (Eagle) 1 hr 40 min 49.4 sec 234.49 kph/145.74 mph—2 J Y Stewart (BRM) 1 hr 41 min 52.4 sec—3 C. Amon (Ferrari) 1 hr 42 min 29.4 sec—4 J. Rindt (Cooper) 1 hr 43 min 03.3 sec—5 M. Spence (BRM) 27 laps—6 J. Clark (Lotus) 27 laps—7 J. Siffert (Cooper) 27 laps—8 B. Anderson (Brabham) 26 laps—9 P. Rodriguez (Cooper) 75 laps—10 G. Ligier (Cooper) 25 laps—not classified L. Scarfiotti (Ferrari) 24 laps—fastest lap, Gurney 3 min 31.9 sec 239.5 kph/148.85 mph—retired M. Parkes (Ferrari) accident lap 1—J. Surtees (Honda) engine lap 1—C. Irwin (BRM) engine lap 1—G. Hill (Lotus) clutch lap 3—J. Bonnier (Cooper) engine lap 10—D. Hulme (Brabham) engine lap 14—J. Brabham (Brabham) engine lap 15.

Starting grid 3-2-3

Clark 3 min 28.1 sec—Gurney 3 min 31.2 sec—Hill 3 min 32.9 sec—Rindt 3 min 34.3 sec—Amon 3 min 34.3 sec—Stewart 3 min 34.8 sec—Brabham 3 min 35.0 sec—Parkes 3 min 36.6 sec—Scarfiotti 3 min 37.7 sec—Surtees 3 min 38.4 sec—Spence 3 min 38.5 sec—Bonnier 3 min 39.1 sec—Rodriguez 3 min 39.5 sec—Hulme 3 min 40.3 sec—Irwin 3 min 44.3 sec—Siffert 3 min 45.4 sec—Anderson 3 min 49.5 sec—Ligier 4 min 01.2 sec.

FRENCH GRAND PRIX

Le Mans; 2 July; 80 laps 360 km/224 miles
1 J. Brabham (Brabham) 2 hr 13 min 21.3 sec 159.13 kph/98.9 mph—2 D. Hulme (Brabham) 2 hr 14 min 10.8 sec—3 J Y Stewart (BRM) 79 laps—4 J. Siffert (Cooper) 77 laps—5 C. Irwin (BRM) 76 laps—6 P. Rodriguez (Cooper) 76 laps—7 G. Ligier (Cooper) 68 laps—fastest lap, Hill 1 min 36.7 sec 164.59 kph/102.3 mph—retired M. Spence (BRM) half shaft lap 9—G. Hill (Lotus) gearbox lap 14—B. Anderson (Brabham) ignition lap 17—J. Clark (Lotus) final drive lap 23—B. McLaren (Eagle) ignition lap 26—J. Rindt (Cooper) engine lap 33—D. Gurney (Eagle) fuel pipe lap 40—C. Amon (Ferrari) throttle cable lap 47.

Starting grid 3-2-3

Hill 1 min 36.2 sec—Brabham 1 min 36.3 sec—Gurney 1 min 37.0 sec—Clark 1 min 37.5 sec—McLaren 1 min 37.6 sec—Hulme 1 min 37.9 sec—Amon 1 min 38.0 sec—Rindt 1 min 38.9 sec—Irwin 1 min 39.4 sec—Stewart 1 min 39.6 sec—Siffert 1 min 40.1 sec—Spence 1 min 40.3 sec—Rodriguez 1 min 40.5 sec—Anderson 1 min 44.9 sec—Ligier 1 min 45.2 sec.

BRITISH GRAND PRIX

Silverstone; 15 July; 80 laps 240 miles/386 km
1 J. Clark (Lotus) 1 hr 59 min 25.6 sec 117.64 mph/189.28 kph—2 D. Hulme (Brabham) 1 hr 59 min 38.4 sec—3 C. Amon (Ferrari) 1 hr 59 min 42.2 sec—4 J. Brabham (Brabham) 1 hr 59 min 47.4 sec—5 P. Rodriguez (Cooper) 79 laps—6 J. Surtees (Honda) 78 laps—7 C. Irwin (BRM) 77 laps—8 D. Hobbs (BRM) 77 laps—9 A. Rees (Cooper) 76 laps—10 G. Ligier (Brabham) 76 laps—fastest lap, Hulme 1 min 27.0 sec 121.12 mph/194.88 kph—retired J. Bonnier (Cooper) engine lap 1—J. Siffert (Cooper) engine lap 10—B. McLaren (Eagle) engine lap 14—J Y Stewart (BRM) transmission lap 20—J. Rindt (Cooper) gearbox lap 26—S. Moser (Cooper) oil pressure lap 29—D. Gurney (Eagle) fuel feed lap 34—M. Spence (BRM) ignition lap 44—G. Hill (Lotus) engine lap 64—B. Anderson (Brabham) engine lap 67.

Starting grid 4-3-4

Clark 1 min 25.3 sec—Hill 1 min 26.0 sec—Brabham 1 min 26.2 sec—Hulme 1 min 26.3 sec—Gurney 1 min 26.4 sec—Amon 1 min 26.9 sec—Surtees 1 min 27.2 sec—Rindt 1 min 27.4 sec—Rodriguez 1 min 27.9 sec—McLaren 1 min 28.1 sec—Spence 1 min 28.3 sec—Stewart 1 min 28.7 sec—Irwin 1 min 29.6 sec—Hobbs 1 min 30.1 sec—Rees 1 min 30.3 sec—Anderson 1 min 30.7 sec—Siffert 1 min 31.0 sec—Bonnier 1 min 32.0 sec—Moser 1 min 32.9 sec—Ligier 1 min 34.8 sec—non starter P. Courage (BRM).

GERMAN GRAND PRIX

Nürburgring; 6 August; 15 laps 343 km/213 miles
1 D. Hulme (Brabham) 2 hr 5 min 55.7 sec 262.69 kph/101.47 mph—2 J. Brabham (Brabham) 2 hr 6 min 34.2 sec—3 C. Amon (Ferrari) 2 hr 6 min 34.7 sec—4 J. Surtees (Honda) 2 hr 8 min 21.4 sec—5 J. Bonnier (Cooper) 2 hr 14 min 37.8 sec—6 G. Ligier (Brabham) 14 laps—7 C. Irwin (BRM) 13 laps—8 P. Rodriguez (Cooper) 13 laps—fastest lap, Gurney 8 min 15.1 sec 165.97 kph/103.15 mph—retired M. Spence (BRM) gearbox lap 3—J. Clark (Lotus) suspension lap 4—J. Rindt (Cooper) engine lap 4—B. McLaren (Eagle) engine lap 4—J Y Stewart (BRM) final drive lap 5—G. Hill (Lotus) suspension lap 6—H. Hahne (Lola) suspension lap 6—D. Gurney (Eagle) engine lap 12—J. Siffert (Cooper) fuel pump lap 12.

Starting grid 4-3-4

Clark 8 min 04.1 sec—Hulme 8 min 13.5 sec—Stewart 8 min 15.2 sec—Gurney 8 min 16.9 sec—McLaren 8 min 17.7 sec—Surtees 8 min 18.2 sec—Brabham 8 min 18.9 sec—Amon 8 min 20.4 sec—Rindt 8 min 20.9 sec—Rodriguez 8 min 22.2 sec—Spence 8 min 26.5 sec—Siffert 8 min 31.7 sec—Hill 8 min 31.7 sec—Hahne 8 min 32.8 sec—Irwin 8 min 41.6 sec—Bonnier 8 min 47.8 sec—Ligier 9 min 14.4 sec.

CANADIAN GRAND PRIX

Mosport; 27 August; 90 laps 220 miles/354 km
1 J. Brabham (Brabham) 2 hr 40 min 40.0 sec 82.65 mph/132.98 kph—2 D. Hulme (Brabham) 2 hr 41 min 41.9 sec—3 D. Gurney (Eagle) 89 laps—4 G. Hill (Lotus) 88 laps—5 M. Spence (BRM) 87 laps—6 C. Amon (Ferrari) 87 laps—7 B. McLaren (McLaren) 86 laps—8 J. Bonnier (Cooper) 85 laps—9 D. Hobbs (BRM) 85 laps—10 R. Attwood (Cooper) 84 laps—11 M. Fisher (Lotus) 81 laps—12 A. Pease (Eagle) 47 laps—fastest lap, Clark 1 min 23.1 sec 106.53 mph/171.41 kph—retired J. Rindt (Cooper) ignition lap 4—C. Irwin (BRM) accident—J Y Stewart (BRM) accident lap 65—E. Wietzes (Lotus) ignition lap 69—J. Clark (Lotus) ignition lap 69.

Starting grid 3-2-3

Clark 1 min 22.4 sec—Hill 1 min 22.7 sec—Hulme 1 min 23.2 sec—Amon 1 min 23.3 sec—Gurney 1 min 23.4 sec—McLaren 1 min 23.5 sec—Brabham 1 min 24.7 sec—Rindt 1 min 24.9 sec—Stewart 1 min 25.4 sec—Spence 1 min 25.8 sec—Irwin 1 min 26.0 sec—Hobbs 1 min 26.2 sec—Attwood 1 min 27.1 sec—Bonnier 1 min 27.3 sec—Pease 1 min 30.1 sec—Wietzes 1 min 30.8 sec—Fisher 1 min 31.9 sec—non starters J. Siffert (Cooper)—T. Jones (Cooper).

ITALIAN GRAND PRIX

Monza; 10 September; 68 laps 391 km/243 miles
1 J. Surtees (Honda) 1 hr 43 min 45.0 sec 226.06 kph/140.5 mph—2 J. Brabham (Brabham) 1 hr 43 min 45.2 sec—3 J. Clark (Lotus) 1 hr 44 min 08.1 sec—4 J. Rindt (Cooper) 1 hr 44 min 41.6 sec—5 M. Spence (BRM) 67 laps—6 J. Ickx (Cooper) 66 laps—7 C. Amon (Ferrari) 64 laps—fastest lap, Clark 1 min 28.5 sec 233.79 kph/145.3 mph—retired D. Gurney (Eagle) engine lap 5—L. Scarfiotti (Eagle) engine lap 6—C. Irwin (BRM) injection pump lap 17—G. Ligier (Brabham) engine lap 27—D. Hulme (Brabham) engine lap 31—J Y Stewart (BRM) engine lap 46—J. Bonnier (Cooper) engine lap 47—B. McLaren (McLaren) engine lap 47—J. Siffert (Cooper) accident lap 51—G. Baghetti (Lotus) engine lap 51—G. Hill Lotus) engine lap 59.

Starting grid 3-2-3

Clark 1 min 28.5 sec—Brabham 1 min 28.8 sec—McLaren 1 min 29.3 sec—Amon 1 min 29.3 sec—Gurney 1 min 29.4 sec—Hulme 1 min 29.5 sec—Stewart 1 min 29.6 sec—Hill 1 min 29.7 sec—Surtees 1 min 30.3 sec—Scarfiotti 1 min 30.8 sec—Rindt 1 min 31.3 sec—Spence 1 min 32.1 sec—Siffert 1 min 32.3 sec—Bonnier 1 min 32.5 sec—Ickx 1 min 33.0 sec—Irwin 1 min 33.2 sec—Baghetti 1 min 35.2 sec—Ligier 1 min 37.3 sec—non starter A. de Adamich (Cooper).

UNITED STATES GRAND PRIX

Watkins Glen; 1 October; 108 laps 248 miles/399 km
1 J. Clark (Lotus) 2 hr 3 min 13.2 sec 120.95 mph/194.61 kph—2 G. Hill (Lotus) 2 hr 3 min 19.5 sec—3 D. Hulme (Brabham) 107 laps—4 J. Siffert (Cooper) 106 laps—5 J. Brabham (Brabham) 104 laps—6 J. Bonnier (Cooper) 101 laps—7 J-P Beltoise (Matra) 101 laps—fastest lap, Hill 1 min 06.0 sec 125.5 mph/201.93 kph—retired M. Solana (Lotus) electrics lap 7—B. McLaren (McLaren) water hose lap 16—D. Gurney (Eagle) suspension lap 24—J. Rindt (Cooper) piston lap 33—M. Spence (BRM) con-rod lap 35—C. Irwin (BRM) con-rod lap 41—G. Ligier (Brabham) camshaft lap 43—J. Ickx (Cooper) piston lap 45—J Y Stewart (BRM) metering unit lap 72—C. Amon (Ferrari) engine lap 95—J. Surtees (Honda) battery lap 96.

Starting grid 2-2-2

Hill 1 min 05.5 sec—Clark 1 min 06.1 sec—Gurney 1 min 06.6 sec—Amon 1 min 06.6 sec—Brabham 1 min 06.7 sec—Hulme 1 min 07.4 sec—Solana 1 min 07.9 sec—Rindt 1 min 08.0 sec—McLaren 1 min 08.0 sec—Stewart 1 min 08.1 sec—Surtees 1 min 08.1 sec—Siffert 1 min 08.2 sec—Spence 1 min 09.0 sec—Irwin 1 min 09.6 sec—Bonnier 1 min 09.8 sec—Ickx 1 min 09.9 sec—Ligier 1 min 11.3 sec—Beltoise 1 min 12.0 sec.

MEXICAN GRAND PRIX

Mexico City; 22 October; 65 laps 202 miles/325 km
1 J. Clark (Lotus) 1 hr 59 min 28.7 sec 101.42 mph/163.18 kph—2 J. Brabham (Brabham) 2 hr 0 min 54.1 sec—3 D. Hulme (Brabham) 64 laps—4 J. Surtees (Honda) 64 laps—5 M. Spence (BRM) 63 laps—6 P. Rodriguez (Cooper) 63 laps—7 J-P Beltoise (Matra) 63 laps—8 J. Williams (Ferrari) 63 laps—9 C. Amon (Ferrari) 62 laps—10 J. Bonnier (Cooper)

MEXICAN GRAND PRIX—*continued*

61 laps—11 G. Ligier (Brabham) 61 laps—12 J. Siffert (Cooper) 59 laps—13 B. McLaren (McLaren) 45 laps—fastest lap, Clark 1 min 48.1 sec 103.44 mph/166.43 kph—retired D. Gurney (Eagle) radiator lap 4—M. Solana (Lotus) suspension lap 12—G. Hill (Lotus) drive shaft lap 18—J Y Stewart (BRM) vibration lap 24—C. Irwin (BRM) oil pressure lap 33.

Starting grid 2-2-2

Clark 1 min 47.6 sec—Amon 1 min 48.0 sec—Gurney 1 min 48.1 sec—Hill 1 min 48.7 sec—Brabham 1 min 49.1 sec—Hulme 1 min 49.5 sec—Surtees 1 min 49.8 sec—McLaren 1 min 50.1 sec—Solana 1 min 50.5 sec—Siffert 1 min 51.9 sec—Spence 1 min 52.2 sec—Stewart 1 min 52.3 sec—Rodriguez 1 min 52.8 sec—Beltoise 1 min 53.1 sec—Irwin 1 min 54.4 sec—Williams 1 min 54.8 sec—Bonnier 1 min 55.6 sec—Ligier 1 min 58.4 sec—non starter M. Fisher (Lotus).

1967 WORLD CHAMPIONSHIP

1 D. Hulme 51—2 J. Brabham 46, 48—3 J. Clark 41—4 J. Surtees 20—4= C. Amon 20—6 P. Rodriguez 15—6= G. Hill 15—8 D. Gurney 13—9 J Y Stewart 10—10 M. Spence 9—11 J. Love 6—11= J. Rindt 6—11= J. Siffert 6—14 B. McLaren 3—14= J. Bonnier 3—16 C. Irwin 2—16= M. Parkes 2—16= B. Anderson 2—19 L. Scarfiotti 1—19= G. Ligier 1—19= J. Ickx 1.

1968

SOUTH AFRICAN GRAND PRIX

Kyalami; 1 January; 80 laps 204 miles/328 km
1 J. Clark (Lotus) 1 hr 53 min 56.6 sec 107.42 mph/172.84 kph—2 G. Hill (Lotus) 1 hr 54 min 21.9 sec—3 J. Rindt (Brabham) 1 hr 54 min 27.0 sec—4 C. Amon (Ferrari) 78 laps—5 D. Hulme (McLaren) 78 laps—6 J-P Beltoise (Matra-Cosworth) 77 laps—7 J. Siffert (Cooper) 77 laps—8 J. Surtees (Honda) 75 laps—9 J. Love (Brabham) 75 laps—not classified J. Pretorius (Brabham) 70 laps—fastest lap, Clark 1 min 23.7 sec 109.68 mph/176.47 kph—retired L. Scarfiotti (Cooper) radiator lap 2—D. Charlton (Brabham) final drive lap 3—B. Redman (Cooper) engine lap 5—M. Spence (BRM) boiling fuel lap 8—A. de Adamich (Ferrari) accident lap 13—J. Brabham (Brabham) engine lap 17—B. van Rooyen (Cooper) engine lap 20—P. Rodriguez (BRM) fuel vaporised lap 20—J Y Stewart (Matra-Ford) engine lap 38—S. Tingle (LDS) ignition lap 38—J Bonnier (Cooper) overheating lap 47—J. Ickx (Ferrari) oil tank lap 51—D. Gurney (Eagle) oil leak lap 58.

Starting grid 3-2-3

Clark 1 min 21.6 sec—Hill 1 min 22.6 sec—Stewart 1 min 22.7 sec—Rindt 1 min 23.0 sec—Brabham 1 min 23.2 sec—Surtees 1 min 23.5 sec—de Adamich 1 min 23.6 sec—Amon 1 min 23.8 sec—Hulme 1 min 24.0 sec—Rodriguez 1 min 24.9 sec—Ickx 1 min 24.9 sec—Gurney 1 min 25.6 sec—Spence 1 min 25.9 sec—Charlton 1 min 26.2 sec—Scarfiotti 1 min 26.3 sec—Siffert 1 min 26.4 sec—Love 1 min 27.0 sec—Beltoise 1 min 27.2 sec—Bonnier 1 min 27.3 sec—van Rooyen 1 min 27.8 sec—Redman 1 min 28.0 sec—Tingle 1 min 28.6 sec—Pretorius 1 min 29.0 sec—non starter T. Jeffries (Cooper).

SPANISH GRAND PRIX

Jarama; 12 May; 90 laps 306 km/190 miles
1 G. Hill (Lotus) 2 hr 15 min 20.1 sec 130.99 kph/84.41 mph—2 D. Hulme (McLaren) 2 hr 15 min 36.0 sec—3 B. Redman (Cooper) 89 laps—4 L. Scarfiotti (Cooper) 89 laps—5 J-P Beltoise (Matra-Ford) 81 laps—fastest lap, Beltoise 1 min 28.3 sec 138.78 kph/86.25 mph—retired J. Rindt (Brabham) overheating lap 11—J. Ickx (Ferrari) ignition lap 14—P. Rodriguez (BRM) accident lap 28—P. Courage (BRM) metering unit lap 53—C. Amon (Ferrari) fuel pump lap 58—J. Siffert (Lotus) transmission lap 63—J. Surtees (Honda) gear linkage lap 75—B. McLaren (McLaren) oil lap 78.

Starting grid 3-2-3

Amon 1 min 27.9 sec—Rodriguez 1 min 28.1 sec—Hulme 1 min 28.3 sec—McLaren 1 min 28.3 sec—Beltoise 1 min 28.3 sec—Hill 1 min 28.4 sec—Surtees 1 min 28.8 sec—Ickx 1 min 29.6 sec—Rindt 1 min 29.7 sec—Siffert 1 min 29.7 sec—Courage 1 min 29.9 sec—Scarfiotti 1 min 30.8 sec—Redman 1 min 31.0 sec—non starter J. Brabham (Brabham).

MONACO GRAND PRIX

Monte Carlo; 26 May; 80 laps 251 km/156 miles
1 G. Hill (Lotus) 2 hr 0 min 32.3 sec 125.21 kph/77 .82 mph—2 R. Attwood (BRM) 2 hr 0 min 34.5 sec—3 L. Bianchi (Cooper) 76 laps—4 L. Scarfiotti (Cooper) 76 laps—5 D. Hulme (McLaren) 73 laps—fastest lap, Attwood 1 min 28.1 sec 128.2 kph/79.68 mph—retired B. McLaren (McLaren) accident lap 1—J. Oliver (Lotus) accident lap 1—J. Servoz-Gavin (Matra-Ford) drive shaft lap 4—J. Brabham (Brabham) suspension lap 8—J. Rindt (Brabham) accident lap 9—D. Gurney (Eagle) oil pressure lap 10—J. Siffert (Lotus) final drive lap 11—P. Courage (BRM) sub-frame lap 12—J-P Beltoise (Matra) accident lap 12—J. Surtees (Honda) gearbox lap 17—P. Rodriguez (BRM) accident lap 17.

Starting grid 2-2-2

Hill 1 min 28.2 sec—Servoz-Gavin 1 min 28.8 sec—Siffert 1 min 28.8 sec—Surtees 1 min 29.1 sec—Rindt 1 min 29.2 sec—Attwood 1 min 29.6 sec—McLaren 1 min 29.6 sec—Beltoise 1 min 29.7 sec—Rodriguez 1 min 30.4 sec—Hulme 1 min 30.4 sec—Courage 1 min 30.6 sec—Brabham 1 min 31.2 sec—Oliver 1 min 31.7 sec—Bianchi 1 min 31.9 sec—Scarfiotti 1 min 32.9 sec—Gurney 1 min 32.9 sec—non starters J. Bonnier (McLaren)—S. Moser (Brabham)—K. St John (McLaren).

BELGIAN GRAND PRIX

Spa-Francorchamps; 9 June; 28 laps 394 km/245 miles
1 B. McLaren (McLaren) 1 hr 40 min 02.1 sec 236.75 kph/147.14 mph—2 P. Rodriguez (BRM) 1 hr 40 min 14.2 sec—3 J. Ickx (Ferrari) 1 hr 40 min 41.7 sec—4 J Y Stewart (Matra-Ford) 27 laps—5 J. Oliver (Lotus) 26 laps—6 L. Bianchi (Cooper) 26 laps—7 J-P Beltoise (Matra) 25 laps—fastest lap, Surtees 3 min 30.5 sec 241.09 kph/149.84 mph—retired J. Bonnier (McLaren) wheel stud lap 1—G. Hill (Lotus) universal joint lap 6—J. Brabham (Brabham) throttle lap 6—R. Attwood (BRM) accident lap 6—B. Redman (Cooper) accident lap 6—J. Rindt (Brabham) engine lap 6—C. Amon (Ferrari) radiator lap 8—J. Surtees (Honda) wishbone lap 11—D. Hulme (McLaren) half shaft lap 18—P. Courage (BRM) cracked liner lap 23—J. Siffert (Lotus) oil pressure lap 26.

Starting grid 3-2-3

Amon 3 min 28.6 sec—Stewart 3 min 32.3 sec—Ickx 3 min 34.3 sec—Surtees 3 min 35.0 sec—Hulme 3 min 35.4 sec—McLaren 3 min 37.1 sec—Courage 3 min 37.2 sec—Rodriguez 3 min 37.8 sec—Siffert 3 min 39.0 sec—Redman 3 min 41.4 sec—Attwood 3 min 45.2 sec—Bianchi 3 min 45.9 sec—Beltoise 3 min 52.9 sec—Hill 4 min 06.1 sec—Oliver 4 min 30.8 sec—Bonnier 4 min 34.3 sec—Rindt 4 min 46.7 sec—Brabham.

DUTCH GRAND PRIX

Zandvoort; 23 June; 90 laps 376 km/234 miles
1 J Y Stewart (Matra-Ford) 2 hr 46 min 11.3 sec 136.22 kph/84.66 mph—2 J-P Beltoise (Matra) 2 hr 47 min 45.2

sec—3 P. Rodriguez (BRM) 89 laps—4 J. Ickx (Ferrari) 88 laps—5 S. Moser (Brabham) 87 laps—6 C. Amon (Ferrari) 85 laps—7 R. Attwood (BRM) 85 laps—8 J. Bonnier (McLaren) 82 laps—9 G. Hill (Lotus) 81 laps—10 J. Oliver (Lotus) 80 laps—fastest lap, Beltoise 1 min 45.9 sec 140.88 kph/87.56 mph—retired L. Bianchi (Cooper) accident lap 10—D. Hulme (McLaren) ignition lap 11—B. McLaren (McLaren) accident lap 20—J. Brabham (Brabham) spun lap 23—J. Rindt (Brabham) ignition lap 40—J. Surtees (Honda) alternator drive lap 51—P. Courage (BRM) accident lap 52—J. Siffert (Lotus) gear selector lap 56—D. Gurney (Brabham) throttle slide lap 64.

Starting grid 3-2-3

Amon 1 min 23.5 sec—Rindt 1 min 23.7 sec—Hill 1 min 23.8 sec—Brabham 1 min 23.9 sec—Stewart 1 min 24.4 sec—Ickx 1 min 24.4 sec—Hulme 1 min 24.4 sec—McLaren 1 min 24.6 sec—Surtees 1 min 25.2 sec—Oliver 1 min 25.5 sec—Rodriguez 1 min 25.5 sec—Gurney 1 min 25.8 sec—Siffert 1 min 25.9 sec—Courage 1 min 26.1 sec—Attwood 1 min 26.7 sec—Beltoise 1 min 26.8 sec—Moser 1 min 28.3 sec—Bianchi 1 min 28.3 sec—Bonnier 1 min 28.4 sec.

FRENCH GRAND PRIX

Rouen-les-Essarts; 7 July; 60 laps 392 km/244 miles
1 J. Ickx (Ferrari) 2 hr 25 min 40.9 sec 161.62 kph/100.45 mph—2 J. Surtees (Honda) 2 hr 27 min 39.5 sec—3 J Y Stewart (Matra-Ford) 59 laps—4 V. Elford (Cooper) 58 laps—5 D. Hulme (McLaren) 58 laps—6 P. Courage (BRM) 57 laps—7 R. Attwood (BRM) 57 laps—8 B. McLaren (McLaren) 56 laps—9 J-P Beltoise (Matra) 56 laps—10 C. Amon (Ferrari) 55 laps—11 J. Siffert (Lotus) 54 laps—12 P. Rodriguez (BRM) 53 laps—fastest lap, Rodriguez 2 min 11.5 sec 179.05 kph/111.28 mph—retired J. Schlesser (Honda) fatal accident lap 3—G. Hill (Lotus) drive shaft lap 15—J. Servoz-Gavin (Cooper) accident lap 15—J. Brabham (Brabham) fuel pump lap 16—J. Rindt (Brabham) fuel leak lap 46.

Starting grid 3-2-3

Rindt 1 min 56.1 sec—Stewart 1 min 57.3 sec—Ickx 1 min 57.7 sec—Hulme 1 min 57.7 sec—Amon 1 min 57.8 sec—McLaren 1 min 58.0 sec—Surtees 1 min 58.2 sec—Beltoise 1 min 58.9 sec—Hill 1 min 59.1 sec—Rodriguez 1 min 59.3 sec—Siffert 2 min 00.3 sec—Attwood 2 min 00.8 sec—Brabham 2 min 00.8 sec—Courage 2 min 01.1 sec—Servoz-Gavin 2 min 01.2 sec—Schlesser 2 min 04.5 sec—Elford 2 min 05.5 sec—non starter J. Oliver (Lotus).

BRITISH GRAND PRIX

Brands Hatch; 20 July; 80 laps 212 miles/341 km
1 J. Siffert (Lotus) 2 hr 1 min 20.3 sec 104.83 mph/168.67 kph—2 C. Amon (Ferrari) 2 hr 1 min 24.7 sec—3 J. Ickx (Ferrari) 79 laps—4 D. Hulme (McLaren) 79 laps—5 J. Surtees (Honda) 78 laps—6 J Y Stewart (Matra-Ford) 78 laps—7 B. McLaren (McLaren) 77 laps—8 P. Courage (BRM) 72 laps—not classified S. Moser (Brabham) 52 laps—fastest lap, Siffert 1 min 29.7 sec 171.12 mph/106.35 kph—retired J. Brabham (Brabham) exhaust camshaft lap 1—J. Bonnier (McLaren) engine lap 7—D. Gurney (Eagle) fuel pump lap 8—R. Attwood (BRM) radiator lap 11—J-P Beltoise (Matra) oil pressure lap 12—G. Hill (Lotus) universal joint lap 27—V. Elford (Cooper) engine lap 27—R. Widdows (Cooper) ignition lap 36—J. Oliver (Lotus) gearbox lap 44—P. Rodriguez (BRM) timing chain lap 53—J. Rindt (Brabham) fuel system lap 56.

Starting grid 3-2-3

Hill 1 min 28.9 sec—Oliver 1 min 29.4 sec—Amon 1 min 29.5 sec—Siffert 1 min 29.7 sec—Rindt 1 min 29.9 sec—Gurney 1 min 30.0 sec—Stewart 1 min 30.0 sec—Brabham 1 min 30.2 sec—Surtees 1 min 30.3 sec—McLaren 1 min 30.4 sec—Hulme 1 min 30.4 sec—Ickx 1 min 31.0 sec—Rodriguez 1 min 31.6 sec—Beltoise 1 min 31.6 sec—Attwood 1 min 31.7 sec—Courage 1 min 32.3 sec—Elford 1 min 33.0 sec—Widdows 1 min 34.0 sec—Moser 1 min 35.4 sec—Bonnier 1 min 36.8 sec—non starters T. Lanfranchi (BRM)—L. Bianchi (Cooper)—T. Jones (Cooper).

GERMAN GRAND PRIX

Nürburgring; 4 August; 14 laps 320 km/199 miles
1 J Y Stewart (Matra-Ford) 2 hr 19 min 03.2 sec 139.76 kph/86.86 mph—2 G. Hill (Lotus) 2 hr 23 min 06.4 sec—3 J. Rindt (Brabham) 2 hr 23 min 12.6 sec—4 J. Ickx (Ferrari) 2 hr 24 min 58.4 sec—5 J. Brabham (Brabham) 2 hr 25 min 24.3 sec—6 P. Rodriguez (BRM) 2 hr 25 min 28.2 sec—7 D. Hulme (McLaren) 2 hr 25 min 34.2 sec—8 P. Courage (BRM) 2 hr 26 min 59.6 sec—9 D. Gurney (Eagle) 2 hr 27 min 16.9 sec—10 H. Hahne (BMW) 2 hr 29 min 14.6 sec—11 J. Oliver (Lotus) 13 laps—12 K. Ahrens (Brabham) 13 laps—13 B. McLaren (McLaren) 13 laps—14 R. Attwood (BRM) 13 laps—fastest lap, Stewart 9 min 36.0 sec 142.67 kph/88.67 mph—retired V. Elford (Cooper) accident lap 1—J. Surtees (Honda) engine lap 4—J. Siffert (Lotus) ignition lap 7—L. Bianchi (Cooper) fuel tank lap 7—J-P Beltoise (Matra) accident lap 9—C. Amon (Ferrari) accident lap 12.

Starting grid 3-2-3

Ickx 9 min 04.0 sec—Amon 9 min 14.9 sec—Rindt 9 min 31.9 sec—Hill 9 min 46.0 sec—Elford 9 min 53.0 sec—Stewart 9 min 54.2 sec—Surtees 9 min 57.8 sec—Courage 10 min 00.1 sec—Siffert 10 min 03.4 sec—Gurney 10 min 13.9 sec—Hulme 10 min 16.0 sec—Beltoise 10 min 17.3 sec—Oliver 10 min 18.7 sec—Rodriguez 10 min 19.7 sec—Brabham 10 min 23.1 sec—McLaren 10 min 33.0 sec—Ahrens 10 min 37.3 sec—Hahne 10 min 42.9 sec—Bianchi 10 min 46.6 sec—Attwood 10 min 48.2 sec—non starters S. Moser (Brabham)—J. Bonnier (McLaren).

ITALIAN GRAND PRIX

Monza; 8 September; 68 laps 389 km/242 miles
1 D. Hulme (McLaren) 1 hr 40 min 14.8 sec 233.96 kph/145.41 mph—2 J. Servoz-Gavin (Matra-Ford) 1 hr 41 min 43.2 sec—3 J. Ickx (Ferrari) 1 hr 41 min 43.4 sec—4 P. Courage (BRM) 67 laps—5 J-P Beltoise (Matra) 66 laps—6 J. Bonnier (McLaren) 64 laps—fastest lap, Oliver 1 min 26.5 sec 239.24 kph/148.69 mph—retired V. Elford (Cooper) accident lap 2—D. Bell (Ferrari) fuel pump lap 2—C. Amon (Ferrari) accident lap 9—J. Surtees (Honda) accident lap 9—G. Hill (Lotus) wheel lap 11—D. Gurney (Eagle) oil pressure lap 18—P. Rodriguez (BRM) engine lap 18—B. McLaren (McLaren) oil lap 34—J. Rindt (Brabham) dropped valve lap 34—J. Oliver (Lotus) gearbox lap 40—D. Hobbs (Honda) engine lap 40—J Y Stewart (Matra-Ford) engine lap 40—J. Brabham (Brabham) oil pressure lap 57—J. Siffert (Lotus) suspension lap 50.

Starting grid 3-2-3

Surtees 1 min 26.1 sec—McLaren 1 min 26.1 sec—Amon 1 min 26.1 sec—Ickx 1 min 26.4 sec—Hill 1 min 26.6 sec—Stewart 1 min 26.6 sec—Hulme 1 min 26.6 sec—Bell 1 min 26.9 sec—Siffert 1 min 27.0 sec—Rindt 1 min 27.3 sec—Oliver 1 min 27.4 sec—Gurney 1 min 27.6 sec—Servoz-Gavin 1 min 27.6 sec—Hobbs 1 min 27.7 sec—Rodriguez 1 min 28.2 sec—Brabham 1 min 28.8 sec—Courage 1 min 29.1 sec—Beltoise 1 min 29.3 sec—Bonnier 1 min 30.5 sec—Elford 1 min 31.3 sec—non starters M. Andretti (Lotus)—B. Unser (BRM)—F. Gardner (BRM)—S. Moser (Brabham)—L. Bianchi (Cooper)—R. Widdows (Cooper).

CANADIAN GRAND PRIX

Mont Tremblant; 22 September; 90 laps 238 miles/383 km
1 D. Hulme (McLaren) 2 hr 27 min 11.2 sec 97.25 mph/156.47 kph—2 B. McLaren (McLaren) 89 laps—3 P. Rodriguez (BRM) 88 laps—4 G. Hill (Lotus) 86 laps—5 V. Elford (Cooper) 86 laps—6 J Y Stewart (Matra-Ford) 83 laps—7 L. Bianchi (Cooper) 56 laps—fastest lap, Siffert 1 min 35.1 sec 100.32 mph/161.41 kph—retired J. Bonnier (McLaren) metering unit lap 1—J. Surtees (Honda) gearbox lap 11—W. Brack (Lotus) drive shaft lap 19—P. Courage (BRM) gearbox lap 23—D. Gurney (McLaren) radiator lap 30—J. Siffert (Lotus) engine lap 30—J. Brabham (Brabham) exhaust studs lap 32—J. Oliver (Lotus) drive shaft lap 33—J. Rindt (Brabham) engine lap 40—H. Pescarolo (Matra) oil pressure lap 55—J. Servoz-Gavin (Matra-Ford) accident lap 71—C. Amon (Ferrari) transmission lap 73—J-P Beltoise (Matra) gearbox lap 78.

CANADIAN GRAND PRIX—*continued*

Starting grid 3-2-3

Rindt 1 min 33.8 sec—Amon 1 min 33.8 sec—Siffert 1 min 34.5 sec—Gurney 1 min 34.5 sec—Hill 1 min 34.8 sec—Hulme 1 min 34.9 sec—Surtees 1 min 34.9 sec—McLaren 1 min 35.0 sec—Oliver 1 min 35.2 sec—Brabham 1 min 35.4 sec—Stewart 1 min 35.4 sec—Rodriguez 1 min 35.7 sec—Servoz-Gavin 1 min 36.6 sec—Courage 1 min 37.3 sec—Beltoise 1 min 38.7 sec—Elford 1 min 39.4 sec—Bonnier 1 min 39.6 sec—Bianchi 1 min 40.5 sec—Pescarolo 1 min 41.2 sec—Brack 1 min 41.2 sec—non starter A. Pease (Eagle).

UNITED STATES GRAND PRIX

Watkins Glen; 6 October; 108 laps 248 miles/400 km
1 J Y Stewart (Matra-Ford) 1 hr 59 min 20.3 sec 124.89 mph/200.95 kph—2 G. Hill (Lotus) 1 hr 59 min 45.0 sec—3 J. Surtees (Honda) 107 laps—4 D. Gurney (McLaren) 107 laps—5 J. Siffert (Lotus) 105 laps—6 B. McLaren (McLaren) 103 laps—not classified L. Bianchi (Cooper) 88 laps—fastest lap, Stewart 1 min 05.2 sec 126.96 mph/204.28 kph—retired D. Bell (Ferrari) engine lap 15—M. Andretti (Lotus) clutch lap 33—B. Unser (BRM) engine lap 36—J-P Beltoise (Matra) drive shaft lap 45—C. Amon (Ferrari) water pump lap 60—J. Bonnier (McLaren) ignition lap 63—P. Rodriguez (BRM) suspension lap 67—V. Elford (Cooper) camshaft lap 72—J. Rindt (Brabham) engine lap 74—J. Brabham (Brabham) cam follower lap 78—D. Hulme (McLaren) accident lap 93—P. Courage (BRM) fuel lap 94.

Starting grid 2-3-2

Andretti 1 min 04.2 sec—Stewart 1 min 04.3 sec—Hill 1 min 04.3 sec—Amon 1 min 04.4 sec—Hulme 1 min 04.5 sec—Rindt 1 min 04.8 sec—Gurney 1 min 05.2 sec—Brabham 1 min 05.2 sec—Surtees 1 min 05.3 sec—McLaren 1 min 05.7 sec—Rodriguez 1 min 06.1 sec—Siffert 1 min 06.2 sec—Beltoise 1 min 07.0 sec—Courage 1 min 07.0 sec—Bell 1 min 07.1 sec—Elford 1 min 08.5 sec—Bonnier 1 min 08.9 sec—Unser 1 min 09.6 sec—Bianchi 1 min 09.8 sec—non starters H. Pescarolo (Matra)—J. Oliver (Lotus).

MEXICAN GRAND PRIX

Mexico City; 3 November; 65 laps 202 miles/325 km
1 G. Hill (Lotus) 1 hr 56 min 43.9 sec 103.81 mph/167.02 kph—2 B. McLaren (McLaren) 1 hr 58 min 03.3 sec—3 J. Oliver (Lotus) 1 hr 58 min 24.6 sec—4 P. Rodriguez (BRM) 1 hr 58 min 25.0 sec—5 J. Bonnier (Honda) 64 laps—6 J. Siffert (Lotus) 64 laps—7 J Y Stewart (Matra-Ford) 64 laps—8 V. Elford (Cooper) 63 laps—9 H. Pescarolo (Matra) 62 laps—fastest lap, Siffert 1 min 44.2 sec 107.32 mph/172.67 kph—retired J. Rindt (Brabham) engine lap 2—J. Ickx (Ferrari) engine lap 3—D. Hulme (McLaren) accident lap 10—J-P Beltoise (Matra) rear suspension lap 10—J Surtees (Honda) overheating lap 19—M. Solana (Lotus) wing lap 15—C. Amon (Ferrari) water pump lap 21—P. Courage (BRM) engine lap 26—L. Bianchi (Cooper) engine lap 22—D. Gurney (McLaren) suspension lap 28—J. Servoz-Gavin (Matra-Ford) engine lap 57—J. Brabham (Brabham) oil pressure lap 59.

Starting grid 2-2-2

Siffert 1 min 45.2 sec—Amon 1 min 45.6 sec—Hill 1 min 46.0 sec—Hulme 1 min 46.0 sec—Gurney 1 min 46.3 sec—Surtees 1 min 46.5 sec—Stewart 1 min 46.7 sec—Brabham 1 min 46.8 sec—McLaren 1 min 47.0 sec—Rindt 1 min 47.1 sec—Solana 1 min 47.7 sec—Rodriguez 1 min 47.8 sec—Beltoise 1 min 48.4 sec—Oliver 1 min 48.4 sec—Ickx 1 min 49.2 sec—Servoz-Gavin 1 min 49.3 sec—Elford 1 min 49.5 sec—Bonnier 1 min 50.0 sec—Courage 1 min 50.3 sec—Pescarolo 1 min 50.4 sec—Bianchi 1 min 50.6 sec.

1968 WORLD CHAMPIONSHIP

1 G. Hill 48—2 J Y Stewart 36—3 D. Hulme 33—4 J. Ickx 27—5 B. McLaren 22—6 P. Rodriguez 18—7 J. Siffert 12—7= J. Surtees 12—9 J-P Beltoise 11—10 C. Amon 10—11 J. Clark 9—12 J. Rindt 8—13 L. Scarfiotti 6—13= R. Attwood 6—13= J. Servoz-Gavin 6—13= J. Oliver 6—17 V. Elford 5—17= L. Bianchi 5—19 B. Redman 4—19= P. Courage 4—21 D. Gurney 3—21= J. Bonnier 3—23 S. Moser 2—23= J. Brabham 2.

1969

SOUTH AFRICAN GRAND PRIX

Kyalami; 1 March; 80 laps 203 miles/327 km
1 J Y Stewart (Matra-Ford) 1 hr 50 min 39.1 sec 110.62 mph/177.99 kph—2 G. Hill (Lotus) 1 hr 50 min 57.9 sec—3 D. Hulme (McLaren) 1 hr 51 min 10.9 sec—4 J. Siffert (Lotus) 1 hr 51 min 28.3 sec—5 B. McLaren (McLaren) 79 laps—6 J-P Beltoise (Matra-Ford) 78 laps—7 J. Oliver (BRM) 77 laps—8 S. Tingle (Brabham) 73 laps—9 P. de Klerk (Brabham) 67 laps—fastest lap, Stewart 1 min 21.6 sec 112.5 mph/181.01 kph—retired B. van Rooyen (McLaren) brakes lap 12—J. Ickx (Brabham) engine lap 20—M. Andretti (Lotus) gearbox lap 31—J. Love (Lotus) ignition lap 31—J. Brabham (Brabham) wing lap 32—C. Amon (Ferrari) engine lap 34—P. Rodriguez (BRM) clutch lap 38—J. Surtees (BRM) valve lap 14—J. Rindt (Lotus) fuel pump lap 44.

Starting grid 3-2-3

Brabham 1 min 20.0 sec—Rindt 1 min 20.2 sec—Hulme 1 min 20.3 sec—Stewart 1 min 20.4 sec—Amon 1 min 20.5 sec—Andretti 1 min 20.8 sec—Hill 1 min 21.1 sec—McLaren 1 min 21.1 sec—van Rooyen 1 min 21.8 sec—Love 1 min 22.1 sec—Beltoise 1 min 22.2 sec—Siffert 1 min 22.2 sec—Ickx 1 min 23.1 sec—Oliver 1 min 24.1 sec—Rodriguez 1 min 25.2 sec—de Klerk 1 min 27.2 sec—Tingle 1 min 50.4 sec—Surtees.

SPANISH GRAND PRIX

Barcelona; Montjuich Park; 4 May; 90 laps 341 km/212 miles
1 J Y Stewart (Matra-Ford) 2 hr 16 min 54.0 sec 151.07 kph/93.89 mph—2 B. McLaren (McLaren) 88 laps—3 J-P Beltoise (Matra-Ford) 87 laps—4 D. Hulme (McLaren) 87 laps—5 J. Surtees (BRM) 84 laps—J. Ickx (Brabham) 83 laps—7 P. Rodriguez (BRM) 73 laps—fastest lap, Rindt 1 min 28.3 sec 154.51 kph/96.03 mph—retired J. Oliver (BRM) oil pipe lap 2—G. Hill (Lotus) accident lap 9—P. Courage (Brabham) engine lap 19—J. Rindt (Lotus) accident lap 20—J. Siffert (Lotus) engine lap 31—J. Brabham (Brabham) engine lap 52—C. Amon (Ferrari) engine lap 57—P. Rodriguez (BRM) engine lap 74—J. Ickx (Brabham) suspension lap 84.

Starting grid 3-2-3

Rindt 1 min 25.7 sec—Amon 1 min 26.2 sec—Hill 1 min 26.6 sec—Stewart 1 min 26.9 sec—Brabham 1 min 27.8 sec—Siffert 1 min 28.2 sec—Ickx 1 min 28.4 sec—Hulme 1 min 28.6 sec—Surtees 1 min 28.9 sec—Oliver 1 min 29.2 sec—Courage 1 min 29.3 sec—Beltoise 1 min 29.5 sec—McLaren 1 min 29.7 sec—Rodriguez 1 min 34.1 sec.

MONACO GRAND PRIX

Monte Carlo; 18 May; 80 laps 251 km/156 miles
1 G. Hill (Lotus) 1 hr 56 min 59.4 sec 129.01 kph/80.18 mph—2 P. Courage (Brabham) 1 hr 57 min 16.7 sec—3 J. Siffert (Lotus) 1 hr 57 min 34.0 sec—4 R. Attwood (Lotus) 1 hr 57 min 52.3 sec—5 B. McLaren (McLaren) 79 laps—6 D. Hulme (McLaren) 78 laps—7 V. Elford (Cooper) 74 laps—fastest lap, Stewart 1 min 25.1 sec 133.02 kph/82.67 mph—retired J. Oliver (BRM) accident lap 1—J. Surtees (BRM) accident lap 10—J. Brabham (Brabham) accident lap 10—P. Rodriguez (BRM) engine lap 16—C. Amon (Ferrari)

differential lap 17—S. Moser (Brabham) rear upright lap 17—J-P Beltoise (Matra-Ford) rear upright lap 22—J Y Stewart (Matra-Ford) rear upright lap 23—J. Ickx (Brabham) rear upright lap 49.

Starting grid 2-2-2

Stewart 1 min 24.6 sec—Amon 1 min 25.0 sec—Beltoise 1 min 25.4 sec—Hill 1 min 25.8 sec—Siffert 1 min 26.0 sec—Surtees 1 min 26.0 sec—Ickx 1 min 26.3 sec—Brabham 1 min 26.4 sec—Courage 1 min 26.4 sec—Attwood 1 min 26.5 sec—McLaren 1 min 26.7 sec—Hulme 1 min 26.8 sec—Oliver 1 min 28.4 sec—Rodriguez 1 min 30.5 sec—Moser 1 min 30.5 sec—Elford 1 min 32.8 sec.

DUTCH GRAND PRIX

Zandvoort; 21 June; 90 laps 378 km/235 miles
1 J Y Stewart (Matra-Ford) 2 hr 6 min 42.1 sec 178.66 kph/111.04 mph—2 J. Siffert (Lotus) 2 hr 7 min 06.6 sec—3 C. Amon (Ferrari) 2 hr 7 min 12.6 sec—4 D. Hulme (McLaren) 2 hr 7 min 19.2 sec—5 J. Ickx (Brabham) 2 hr 7 min 19.7 sec—6 J. Brabham (Brabham) 2 hr 7 min 52.9 sec—7 G. Hill (Lotus) 88 laps—8 J-P Beltoise (Matra-Ford) 87 laps—9 J. Surtees (BRM) 87 laps—10 V. Elford (McLaren) 84 laps—fastest lap, Stewart 1 min 22.9 sec 181.94 kph/113.08 mph—retired J. Oliver (BRM) gearbox lap 10—P. Courage (Brabham) clutch lap 13—J. Rindt (Lotus) drive shaft lap 17—B. McLaren (McLaren) stub axle lap 25—S. Moser (Brabham) steering lap 55.

Starting grid 3-2-3

Rindt 1 min 20.8 sec—Stewart 1 min 21.1 sec—Hill 1 min 22.0 sec—Amon 1 min 22.7 sec—Ickx 1 min 22.8 sec—McLaren 1 min 22.9 sec—Hulme 1 min 23.1 sec—Brabham 1 min 23.1 sec—Courage 1 min 23.4 sec—Siffert 1 min 23.9 sec—Beltoise 1 min 24.4 sec—Surtees 1 min 25.1 sec—Oliver 1 min 25.1 sec—Moser 1 min 26.5 sec—Elford 1 min 28.5 sec.

FRENCH GRAND PRIX

Clermont-Ferrand; 6 July; 38 laps 306 km/190 miles
1 J Y Stewart (Matra-Ford) 1 hr 56 min 47.4 sec 157.21 kph/97.71 mph—2 J P Beltoise (Matra-Ford) 1 hr 57 min 44.5 sec—3 J. Ickx (Brabham) 1 hr 57 min 44.7 sec—4 B. McLaren (McLaren) 37 laps—5 V. Elford (McLaren) 37 laps—6 G. Hill (Lotus) 37 laps—7 S. Moser (Brabham) 36 laps—8 D. Hulme (McLaren) 35 laps—9 J. Siffert (Lotus) 34 laps—10 C. Amon (Ferrari) 30 laps—fastest lap, Stewart 3 min 02.7 sec 158.68 kph/98.62 mph—retired J. Miles (Lotus) fuel pump lap 2—P. Courage (Brabham) loose bodywork lap 22—J. Rindt (Lotus) ill lap 23—C. Amon (Ferrari) engine lap 31.

Starting grid 2-2-2

Stewart 3 min 00.6 sec—Hulme 3 min 02.4 sec—Rindt 3 min 02.5 sec—Ickx 3 min 02.6 sec—Beltoise 3 min 02.9 sec—Amon 3 min 04.2 sec—McLaren 3 min 05.5 sec—Hill 3 min 05.9 sec—Siffert 3 min 06.3 sec—Elford 3 min 08.0 sec—Courage 3 min 09.9 sec—Miles 3 min 12.8 sec—Moser 3 min 14.6 sec.

BRITISH GRAND PRIX

Silverstone; 19 July; 84 laps 246 miles/396 km
1 J Y Stewart (Matra-Ford) 1 hr 55 min 55.6 sec 127.25 mph/204.74 kph—2 J. Ickx (Brabham) 83 laps—3 B. McLaren (McLaren) 83 laps—4 J. Rindt (Lotus) 83 laps—5 P. Courage (Brabham) 83 laps—6 V. Elford (McLaren) 82 laps—7 G. Hill (Lotus) 82 laps—8 J. Siffert (Lotus) 81 laps—9 J-P Beltoise (Matra-Ford) 78 laps—10 J. Miles (Lotus) 75 laps—fastest lap, Stewart 1 min 21.3 sec 129.61 mph/208.54 kph—retired J. Surtees (BRM) front suspension lap 1—D. Bell (McLaren) suspension lap 5—J. Bonnier (Lotus) engine lap 6—J. Oliver (BRM) transmission lap 20—D. Hulme (McLaren) ignition lap 27—C. Amon (Ferrari) gearbox lap 45—P. Rodriguez (Ferrari) engine lap 61.

Starting grid 3-2-3

Rindt 1 min 20.8 sec—Stewart 1 min 21.2 sec—Hulme 1 min 21.5 sec—Ickx 1 min 21.6 sec—Amon 1 min 21.9 sec—Surtees 1 min 22.2 sec—McLaren 1 min 22.6 sec—Rodriguez 1 min 22.6 sec—Siffert 1 min 22.7 sec—Courage 1 min 22.9 sec—Elford 1 min 23.3 sec—Hill 1 min 23.6 sec—Oliver 1 min 23.7 sec—Miles 1 min 25.1 sec—Bell 1 min 26.1 sec—Bonnier 1 min 28.2 sec—Beltoise 1 min 31.2 sec—non starters D. Gurney (Brabham)—B. Redman (Cosworth).

GERMAN GRAND PRIX

Nürburgring; 3 August; 14 laps 320 km/199 miles
1 J. Ickx (Brabham) 1 hr 49 min 55.4 sec 174.46 kph/108.43 mph—2 J Y Stewart (Matra-Ford) 1 hr 50 min 53.1 sec—3 B. McLaren (McLaren) 1 hr 53 min 17.0 sec—4 G. Hill (Lotus) 1 hr 53 min 54.2 sec—5 J. Siffert (Lotus) 12 laps—6 J-P Beltoise (Matra-Ford) 12 laps—fastest lap, Ickx 7 min 43.8 sec 177.2 kph/110.13 mph—retired M. Andretti (Lotus) accident lap 1—V. Elford (McLaren) accident lap 1—P. Courage (Brabham) accident lap 2—J. Bonnier (Lotus) fuel leak lap 5—J. Rindt (Lotus) ignition lap 11—D. Hulme (McLaren) transmission lap 12—J. Oliver (BRM) damaged sump lap 12—J-P Beltoise (Matra-Ford) front upright lap 13—J. Siffert (Lotus) accident lap 13.

Starting grid 3-2-3

Ickx 7 min 42.1 sec—Stewart 7 min 42.4 sec—Rindt 7 min 48.0 sec—Siffert 7 min 50.3 sec—Hulme 7 min 52.8 sec—Elford 7 min 54.8 sec—Courage 7 min 56.1 sec—McLaren 7 min 56.5 sec—Hill 7 min 57.0 sec—Beltoise 8 min 00.3 sec—Andretti 8 min 15.4 sec—Oliver 8 min 16.2 sec—Bonnier 8 min 35.0 sec—non starter J. Surtees (BRM).

ITALIAN GRAND PRIX

Monza; 7 September; 58 laps 391 km/243 miles
1 J Y Stewart (Matra-Ford) 1 hr 39 min 11.26 sec 236.46 kph/146.96 mph—2 J Rindt (Lotus) 1 hr 39 min 11.34 sec—3 J-P Beltoise (Matra-Ford) 1 hr 39 min 11.43 sec—4 B. McLaren (McLaren) 1 hr 39 min 11.45 sec—5 P. Courage (Brabham) 1 hr 39 min 44.7 sec—6 P. Rodriguez (Ferrari) 66 laps—7 D. Hulme (McLaren) 66 laps—8 J. Siffert (Lotus) 64 laps—9 G. Hill (Lotus) 63 laps—10 J. Ickx (Brabham) 61 laps—11 J. Surtees (BRM) 60 laps—fastest lap, Beltoise 1 min 25.2 sec 242.09 kph/150.06 mph—retired J. Miles (Lotus) engine lap 4—J. Brabham (Brabham) fuel pipe lap 7—S. Moser (Brabham) fuel leaks lap 10—J. Oliver (BRM) oil pressure lap 49.

Starting grid 2-2-2

Rindt 1 min 25.5 sec—Hulme 1 min 25.7 sec—Stewart 1 min 25.8 sec—Courage 1 min 26.5 sec—McLaren 1 min 26.5 sec—Beltoise 1 min 26.7 sec—Brabham 1 min 26.9 sec—Siffert 1 min 27.0 sec—Hill 1 min 27.3 sec—Surtees 1 min 27.4 sec—Oliver 1 min 28.4 sec—Rodriguez 1 min 28.5 sec—Moser 1 min 28.5 sec—Miles 1 min 30.6 sec—Ickx 1 min 38.0 sec—non starters V. Brambilla (Ferrari)—C. Amon (Ferrari)—J. Servoz-Gavin (Matra-Ford)—J. Bonnier (Lotus).

CANADIAN GRAND PRIX

Mosport; 20 September; 90 laps 221 miles/356 km
1 J. Ickx (Brabham) 1 hr 59 min 25.7 sec 112.76 mph/181.43 kph—2 J. Brabham (Brabham) 2 hr 0 min 11.9 sec—3 J. Rindt (Lotus) 2 hr 0 min 17.7 sec—4 J-P Beltoise (Matra-Ford) 89 laps—5 B. McLaren (McLaren) 87 laps—6 J. Servoz-Gavin (Matra-Ford) 84 laps—7 P. Lovely (Lotus) 81 laps—8 W. Brack (BRM) 80 laps—fastest lap, Ickx 1 min 18.1 sec 114.78 mph/184.68 kph—retired S. Moser (Brabham) accident lap 1—J. Oliver (BRM) engine lap 3—D. Hulme (McLaren) distributor lap 10—J. Cordts (Brabham) oil leak lap 11—P. Courage (Brabham) fuel leak lap 14—J. Surtees (BRM) engine lap 16—A Pease (Eagle) black flagged lap 23—J Y Stewart (Matra-Ford) accident lap 33—P. Rodriguez (Ferrari) oil pressure lap 38—J. Miles (Lotus) gearbox lap 41—J. Siffert (Lotus) drive shaft lap 41—G. Hill (Lotus) camshaft lap 43.

CANADIAN GRAND PRIX—*continued*

Starting grid 3-2-3

Ickx 1 min 17.4 sec—Beltoise 1 min 17.9 sec—Rindt 1 min 17.9 sec—Stewart 1 min 17.9 sec—Hulme 1 min 18.0 sec—Brabham 1 min 18.0 sec—Hill 1 min 18.3 sec—Siffert 1 min 18.5 sec—McLaren 1 min 18.5 sec—Courage 1 min 19.5 sec—Miles 1 min 20.0 sec—Oliver 1 min 20.2 sec—Rodriguez 1 min 20.5 sec—Surtees 1 min 20.6 sec—Servoz-Gavin 1 min 21.4 sec—Lovely 1 min 22.9 sec—Pease 1 min 28.5 sec—Brack 1 min 28.7 sec—Cordts 1 min 29.7 sec—Moser 1 min 41.4 sec.

UNITED STATES GRAND PRIX

Watkins Glen; 5 October; 108 laps 248 miles/400 km
1 J. Rindt (Lotus) 1 hr 57 min 56.8 sec 126.36 mph/203.31 kph—2 P. Courage (Brabham) 1 hr 58 min 43.8 sec—3 J. Surtees (BRM) 106 laps—4 J. Brabham (Brabham) 106 laps—5 P. Rodriguez (Ferrari) 101 laps—6 S. Moser (Brabham) 98 laps—7 J. Servoz-Gavin (Matra-Ford) 92 laps—fastest lap, Rindt 1 min 04.3 sec 128.69 mph/207.06 kph—retired J. Siffert (Lotus) metering unit lap 4—M. Andretti (Lotus) rear suspension lap 4—J. Oliver (BRM) engine lap 24—P. Lovely (Lotus) drive shaft lap 26—J Y Stewart (Matra-Ford) engine lap 36—D. Hulme (McLaren) gear selector lap 53—J-P Beltoise (Matra-Ford) engine lap 73—G. Eaton (BRM) engine lap 77—J. Ickx (Brabham) engine lap 78—G. Hill (Lotus) accident lap 91.

Starting grid 2-2-2

Rindt 1 min 03.6 sec—Hulme 1 min 03.6 sec—Stewart 1 min 03.8 sec—Hill 1 min 04.0 sec—Siffert 1 min 04.1 sec—Beltoise 1 min 04.3 sec—Ickx 1 min 04.3 sec—Courage 1 min 04.6 sec—Brabham 1 min 04.8 sec—Surtees 1 min 05.1 sec—Rodriguez 1 min 05.9 sec—Andretti 1 min 06.5 sec—Oliver 1 min 06.5 sec—Servoz-Gavin 1 min 07.1 sec—Lovely 1 min 07.5 sec—Moser 1 min 08.2 sec—Eaton 1 min 11.3 sec—non starter B. McLaren (McLaren).

MEXICAN GRAND PRIX

Mexico City; 19 October; 65 laps 202 miles/325 km
1 D. Hulme (McLaren) 1 hr 54 min 08.8 sec 106.15 mph/170.79 kph—2 J. Ickx (Brabham) 1 hr 54 min 11.4 sec—3 J. Brabham (Brabham) 1 hr 54 min 47.3 sec—4 J Y Stewart (Matra-Ford) 1 hr 54 min 55.8 sec—5 J-P Beltoise (Matra-Ford) 1 hr 55 min 47.3 sec—6 J. Oliver (BRM) 63 laps—7 P. Rodriguez (Ferrari) 63 laps—8 J. Servoz-Gavin (Matra-Ford) 63 laps—9 P. Lovely (Lotus) 62 laps—10 P. Courage (Brabham) 61 laps—11 S. Moser (Brabham) 60 laps—fastest lap, Ickx 1 min 43.0 sec 108.53 mph/174.62 kph—retired B. McLaren (McLaren) fuel injection drive belt, warming-up lap—J. Miles (Lotus) fuel pump lap 4—J. Siffert (Lotus) accident lap 5—G. Eaton (BRM) gearbox lap 7—J. Rindt (Lotus) wishbone lap 22—J. Surtees (BRM) gearbox lap 54—S. Moser (Brabham) fuel leak lap 61.

Starting grid 2-2-2

Brabham 1 min 42.9 sec—Ickx 1 min 43.6 sec—Stewart 1 min 43.7 sec—Hulme 1 min 43.7 sec—Siffert 1 min 43.8 sec—Rindt 1 min 43.9 sec—McLaren 1 min 44.7 sec—Beltoise 1 min 45.6 sec—Courage 1 min 47.2 sec—Surtees 1 min 47.3 sec—Miles 1 min 47.8 sec—Oliver 1 min 48.0 sec—Moser 1 min 48.2 sec—Servoz-Gavin 1 min 48.7 sec—Rodriguez 1 min 49.5 sec—Lovely 1 min 50.3 sec—Eaton 1 min 52.3 sec.

1969 WORLD CHAMPIONSHIP

1 J Y Stewart 63—2 J. Ickx 37—3 B. McLaren 26—4 J. Rindt 22—5 J-P Beltoise 21—6 D. Hulme 20—7 G. Hill 19—8 P. Courage 16—9 J. Siffert 15—10 J. Brabham 14—11 J. Surtees 6—12 C. Amon 4—13 R. Attwood 3—13= V. Elford 3—13= P. Rodriguez 3—16 J. Servoz-Gavin 1—16= S. Moser 1—16= J. Oliver 1.

1970

SOUTH AFRICAN GRAND PRIX

Kyalami; 7 March; 80 laps 204 miles/328 km
1 J. Brabham (Brabham) 1 hr 49 min 34.6 sec 111.7 mph/179.72 kph—2 D. Hulme (McLaren) 1 hr 49 min 42.7 sec—3 J Y Stewart (March) 1 hr 49 min 51.7 sec—4 J-P Beltoise (Matra) 1 hr 50 min 47.7 sec—5 J. Miles (Lotus) 79 laps—6 G. Hill (Lotus) 79 laps--7 H. Pescarolo (Matra) 78 laps—8 J. Love (Lotus) 78 laps—9 P. Rodriguez (BRM) 76 laps—10 J. Siffert (March) 75 laps—11 P. de Klerk (Brabham) 75 laps—12 D. Charlton (Lotus) 73 laps—13 J. Rindt (Lotus) 72 laps—fastest lap, Surtees, Brabham, 1 min 20.8 sec 113.61 mph/182.8 kph—retired C. Amon (March) overheating lap 14—J. Oliver (BRM) gear selector lap 22—R. Stommelen (Brabham) engine lap 23—M. Andretti (March) overheating lap 26—B. McLaren (McLaren) engine lap 39—P. Courage (de Tomaso) suspension lap 39—J. Servoz-Gavin (March) engine lap 57—G. Eaton (BRM) engine lap 57—J. Surtees (McLaren) engine lap 59—J. Ickx (Ferrari) engine lap 60.

Starting grid 3-2-3

Stewart 1 min 19.3 sec—Amon 1 min 19.3 sec—Brabham 1 min 19.6 sec—Rindt 1 min 19.9 sec—Ickx 1 min 20.0 sec—Hulme 1 min 20.1 sec—Surtees 1 min 20.2 sec—Beltoise 1 min 20.2 sec—Siffert 1 min 20.2 sec—McLaren 1 min 20.3 sec—Andretti 1 min 20.5 sec—Oliver 1 min 20.9 sec—Charlton 1 min 20.9 sec—Miles 1 min 21.0 sec—Stommelen 1 min 21.2 sec—Rodriguez 1 min 21.3 sec—Servoz-Gavin 1 min 21.4 sec—Pescarolo 1 min 21.5 sec—Hill 1 min 21.6 sec—Courage 1 min 22.0 sec—de Klerk 1 min 22.7 sec—Love 1 min 23.1 sec—Eaton 1 min 24.4 sec.

SPANISH GRAND PRIX

Jarama; 19 April; 90 laps 306 km/190 miles
1 J Y Stewart (March) 2 hr 10 min 58.2 sec 140.32 kph/87.21 mph—2 B. McLaren (McLaren) 89 laps—3 M. Andretti (March)—89 laps—4 G. Hill (Lotus) 89 laps—5 J. Servoz-Gavin (March) 88 laps—fastest lap, Brabham 1 min 24.3 sec 145.34 kph/90.33 mph—retired J. Icks (Ferrari) accident lap 1—J. Oliver (BRM) accident lap 1—P Rodriguez (BRM) withdrawn lap 5—J. Rindt (Lotus) engine lap 10—D. Hulme (McLaren) rotor arm lap 11—C. Amon (March) clutch lap 11—J-P Beltoise (Matra) engine lap 32—H. Pescarolo (Matra) con-rod lap 34—R. Stommelen (Brabham) engine lap 44—J. Brabham (Brabham) engine lap 62—J. Surtees (McLaren) gearbox lap 77.

Starting grid 3-2-3

Rindt 1 min 23.9 sec—Hulme 1 min 24.1 sec—Stewart 1 min 24.2 sec—Beltoise 1 min 24.5 sec—Rodriguez 1 min 24.5 sec—Amon 1 min 24.6 sec—Ickx 1 min 24.7 sec—Rindt 1 min 24.8 sec—Pescarolo 1 min 24.9 sec—Oliver 1 min 25.0 sec—McLaren 1 min 25.0 sec—Surtees 1 min 25.2 sec—Courage 1 min 25.4 sec—Servoz-Gavin 1 min 25.5 sec—Hill 1 min 25.5 sec—Andretti 1 min 25.7 sec—Stommelen—non starters P. Courage (de Tomaso)—A de Adamich (McLaren)—G. Eaton (BRM)—J. Miles (Lotus)—J. Siffert (March)—A. Soler-Roig (Lotus).

MONACO GRAND PRIX

Monte Carlo; 10 May; 80 laps 251 km/156 miles
1 J. Rindt (Lotus) 1 hr 54 min 36.6 sec 131.68 kph/81.84 mph—2 J. Brabham (Brabham) 1 hr 54 min 59.7 sec—3 H. Pescarolo (Matra) 1 hr 55 min 28.0 sec—4 D. Hulme (McLaren) 1 hr 56 min 04.9 sec—5 G. Hill (Lotus) 79 laps—6 P. Rodriguez (BRM) 78 laps—7 R. Peterson (March) 78 laps—8 J. Siffert (March) 76 laps—not classified P. Courage

(de Tomaso) 58 laps—fastest lap, Rindt 1 min 23.2 sec 136.06 kph/84.56 mph—retired J. Ickx (Ferrari) drive shaft lap 12—J. Surtees (McLaren) oil pressure lap 15—B. McLaren (McLaren) accident lap 20—J-P Beltoise (Matra) final drive lap 22—J. Oliver (BRM) engine lap 43—J Y Stewart (March) engine lap 59—C. Amon (March) suspension lap 61.

Starting grid 2-2-2

Stewart 1 min 24.0 sec—Amon 1 min 24.6 sec—Hulme 1 min 25.1 sec—Brabham 1 min 25.4 sec—Ickx 1 min 25.5 sec—Beltoise 1 min 25.6 sec—Pescarolo 1 min 25.7 sec—Rindt 1 min 25.9 sec—Courage 1 min 26.1 sec—McLaren 1 min 26.1 sec—Siffert 1 min 26.2 sec—Peterson 1 min 26.8 sec—Surtees 1 min 27.4 sec—Oliver 1 min 27.5 sec—Rodriguez 1 min 27.8 sec—Hill 1 min 26.8 sec—non starters R. Stommelen (Brabham)—J. Servoz-Gavin (March) —J. Miles (Lotus)—A. de Adamich (McLaren)—G. Eaton (BRM).

BELGIAN GRAND PRIX

Spa—Francorchamps; 7 June; 28 laps 395 km/245 miles
1 P. Rodriguez (BRM) 1 hr 38 min 09.9 sec 241.25 kph/149.94 mph—2 C. Amon (March) 1 hr 38 min 11.0 sec—3 J-P Beltoise (Matra) 1 hr 39 min 53.6 sec—4 I. Giunti (Ferrari) 1 hr 40 min 48.4 sec—5 R. Stommelen (Brabham) 1 hr 41 min 41.7 sec—6 H. Pescarolo (Matra) 27 laps—7 J. Siffert (March) 26 laps—8 J. Ickx (Ferrari) 26 laps—not classified R. Peterson (March) 20 laps—fastest lap, Amon 3 min 27.4 sec/244.68 kph/152.07 mph—retired D. Bell (Brabham) gearchange lap 1—P. Courage (de Tomaso) oil pressure lap 4—J. Oliver (BRM) engine lap 7—J. Rindt (Lotus) engine lap 11—J. Miles (Lotus) tyre lap 13—J Y Stewart (March) engine lap 14—J. Brabham (Brabham) clutch lap 19—G. Hill (Lotus) engine lap 20.

Starting grid 3-2-3

Stewart 3 min 28.0 sec—Rindt 3 min 30.1 sec—Amon 3 min 30.3 sec—Ickx 3 min 30.7 sec—Brabham 3 min 31.5 sec—Rodriguez 3 min 31.6 sec—Stommelen 3 min 32.0 sec—Giunti 3 min 32.4 sec—Peterson 3 min 32.8 sec—Siffert 3 min 32.9 sec—Beltoise 3 min 32.9 sec—Courage 3 min 33.0 sec—Miles 3 min 33.8 sec—Oliver 3 min 34.2 sec—Bell 3 min 36.2 sec—Hill 3 min 37.0 sec—Pescarolo 3 min 37.1 sec—non starters A Soler-Roig (Lotus)—G. Eaton (BRM)—S. Moser (Bellasi)—J. Surtees (McLaren).

DUTCH GRAND PRIX

Zandvoort; 21 June; 80 laps 540 km/209 miles
1 J. Rindt (Lotus) 1 hr 50 min 43.4 sec 181.74 kph/112.95 mph—2 J Y Stewart (March) 1 hr 51 min 13.4 sec—3 J. Ickx (Ferrari) 79 laps—4 C. Regazzoni (Ferrari) 79 laps—5 J-P Beltoise (Matra) 79 laps—6 J. Surtees (McLaren) 79 laps—7 J. Miles (Lotus) 78 laps—8 H. Pescarolo (Matra) 78 laps—9 R. Peterson (March) 78 laps—10 P. Rodriguez (BRM) 77 laps—11 J. Brabham (Brabham) 76 laps—not classified G. Hill (Lotus) 71 laps—fastest lap, Ickx 1 min 19.2 sec 190.47 kph/118.38 mph—retired C. Amon (March) clutch 0 laps—D. Gurney (McLaren) timing gear lap 3—P. Gethin (McLaren) accident lap 19—J. Siffert (March) engine lap 23—P. Courage (de Tomaso) fatal accident lap 23—J. Oliver (BRM) con-rod lap 24—G. Eaton (BRM) oil tank lap 27—F. Cevert (March) con-rod lap 32.

Starting grid 3-2-3

Rindt 1 min 18.5 sec—Stewart 1 min 18.7 sec—Ickx 1 min 18.9 sec—Amon 1 min 19.2 sec—Oliver 1 min 19.3 sec—Regazzoni 1 min 19.5 sec—Rodriguez 1 min 20.1 sec—Miles 1 min 20.2 sec—Courage 1 min 20.3 sec—Beltoise 1 min 20.4 sec—Gethin 1 min 20.4 sec—Brabham 1 min 20.8 sec—Pescarolo 1 min 20.9 sec—Surtees 1 min 21.2 sec—Cevert 1 min 21.2 sec—Peterson 1 min 21.2 sec—Siffert 1 min 21.3 sec—Eaton 1 min 21.3 sec—Gurney 1 min 21.4 sec—Hill 1 min 21.7 sec—non starters R. Stommelen (Brabham)—A. de Adamich (McLaren)—S. Moser (Bellasi)—P. Lovely (Lotus).

FRENCH GRAND PRIX

Clermont-Ferrand; 5 July; 38 laps 306 km/190 miles
1 J. Rindt (Lotus) 1 hr 55 min 57.0 sec 158.36 kph/98.42 mph—2 C. Amon (March) 1 hr 56 min 04.6 sec—3 J. Brabham (Brabham) 1 hr 56 min 41.8 sec—4 D. Hulme (McLaren) 1 hr 56 min 42.7 sec—5 H. Pescarolo (Matra) 1 hr 57 min 16.4 sec—6 D. Gurney (McLaren) 1 hr 57 min 16.6 sec—7 R. Stommelen (Brabham) 1 hr 58 min 17.2 sec—8 J. Miles (Lotus) 1 hr 58 min 44.2 sec—9 J Y Stewart (March) 1 hr 59 min 06.6 sec—10 G. Hill (Lotus) 37 laps—11 F. Cevert (March) 37 laps—12 G. Eaton (BRM) 36 laps—13 J-P Beltoise (Matra) 35 laps—14 I. Giunti (Ferrari) 35 laps—15 A. de Adamich (McLaren) 29 laps—fastest lap, Brabham 3 min 00.7 sec 160.38 kph/99.68 mph—retired J. Oliver (BRM) engine lap 6—P. Rodriguez (BRM) gearbox lap 7—J. Ickx (Ferrari) valve lap 17—R. Peterson (March) final drive lap 18—J. Siffert (March) accident lap 24.

Starting grid 2-2-2

Ickx 2 min 58.2 sec—Beltoise 2 min 58.7 sec—Amon 2 min 59.1 sec—Stewart 2 min 59.2 sec—Brabham 2 min 59.7 sec—Rindt 2 min 29.7 sec—Hulme 3 min 00.4 sec—Pescarolo 3 min 00.6 sec—Peterson 3 min 01.2 sec—Rodriguez 3 min 01.3 sec—Giunti 3 min 01.8 sec—Oliver 3 min 02.8 sec—Cevert 3 min 02.9 sec—Stommelen 3 min 03.4 sec—de Adamich 3 min 03.5 sec—Siffert 3 min 03.8 sec—Gurney 3 min 04.0 sec—Miles 3 min 04.2 sec—Eaton 3 min 04.9 sec—Hill 3 min 07.8 sec—non starters A. Soler-Roig (Lotus)—S. Moser (Bellasi)—P. Lovely (Lotus).

BRITISH GRAND PRIX

Brands Hatch; 19 July; 80 laps 212 miles/341 km
1 J. Rindt (Lotus) 1 hr 57 min 2.0 sec 108.69 mph/174.88 kph—2 J. Brabham (Brabham) 1 hr 57 min 34.9 sec—3 D. Hulme (McLaren) 1 hr 57 min 56.4 sec—4 C. Regazzoni (Ferrari) 1 hr 57 min 56.8 sec—5 C. Amon (March) 79 laps—6 G. Hill (Lotus) 79 laps—7 F. Cevert (March) 79 laps—8 E. Fittipaldi (Lotus) 78 laps—9 R. Peterson (March) 72 laps—10 P. Lovely (Lotus) 69 laps—fastest lap, Brabham 1 min 25.9 sec 111.06 mph/178.69 kph—retired J. Ickx (Ferrari) final drive lap 7—G. Eaton (BRM) oil pressure lap 11—J. Miles (Lotus) engine lap 16—J. Siffert (March) rear suspension bracket lap 20—M. Andretti (March) rear suspension bracket lap 22—J-P Beltoise (Matra) front wheel lap 25—H. Pescarolo (Matra) accident lap 42—J. Surtees (Surtees) oil pressure lap 52—J Y Stewart (March) clutch lap 53—J. Oliver (BRM) engine lap 55—P. Rodriguez (BRM) accident lap 59—D. Gurney (McLaren) overheating lap 61.

Starting grid 2-3-2

Rindt 1 min 24.8 sec—Brabham 1 min 24.8 sec—Ickx 1 min 25.1 sec—Oliver 1 min 25.6 sec—Hulme 1 min 25.8 sec—Regazzoni 1 min 25.8 sec—Miles 1 min 25.9 sec—Stewart 1 min 26.0 sec—Andretti 1 min 26.2 sec—Beltoise 1 min 26.5 sec—Gurney 1 min 26.6 sec—Pescarolo 1 min 26.7 sec—Peterson 1 min 26.8 sec—Cevert 1 min 26.8 sec—Rodriguez 1 min 26.9 sec—Eaton 1 min 26.9 sec—Amon 1 min 27.0 sec—Surtees 1 min 27.7 sec—Siffert 1 min 28.0 sec—Fittipaldi 1 min 28.1 sec—Hill 1 min 28.4 sec—Lovely 1 min 30.3 sec—non starters R. Stommelen (Brabham)—B. Redman (de Tomaso)—A. de Adamich (McLaren).

GERMAN GRAND PRIX

Hockenheim; 2 August; 50 laps 339 km/211 miles
1 J. Rindt (Lotus) 1 hr 42 min 00.3 sec 199.35 kph/123.9 mph—2 J. Ickx (Ferrari) 1 hr 42 min 01.0 sec—3 D. Hulme (McLaren) 1 hr 43 min 22.1 sec—4 E. Fittipaldi (Lotus) 1 hr 43 min 55.4 sec—5 R. Stommelen (Brabham) 49 laps—6 H. Pescarolo (Matra) 49 laps—7 F. Cevert (March) 49 laps—8 J. Siffert (March) 47 laps—9 J. Surtees (Surtees) 46 laps—fastest lap, Ickx 2 min 00.5 sec 202.77 kph/126.02 mph—retired P. Gethin (McLaren) engine lap 4—J-P Beltoise (Matra) wishbone lap 5—J. Brabham (Brabham) oil union lap 5—J. Oliver (BRM) engine lap 6—P. Rodriguez (BRM) engine

GERMAN GRAND PRIX—*continued*

lap 8—R. Peterson (March) engine lap 12—M. Andretti (March) gearbox lap 16—J Y Stewart (March) engine lap 21—J. Miles (Lotus) engine lap 25—C. Regazzoni (Ferrari) gearbox lap 31—C. Amon (March) engine lap 35—G. Hill (Lotus) engine lap 38.

Starting grid 2-2-2

Ickx 1 min 59.5 sec—Rindt 1 min 59.7 sec—Regazzoni 1 min 59.8 sec—Siffert 2 min 00.0 sec—Pescarolo 2 min 00.5 sec—Amon 2 min 00.9 sec—Stewart 2 min 01.0 sec—Rodriguez 2 min 01.1 sec—Andretti 2 min 01.5 sec—Miles 2 min 01.6 sec—Stommelen 2 min 01.6 sec—Brabham 2 min 02.0 sec—Fittipaldi 2 min 02.0 sec—Cevert 2 min 02.1 sec—Surtees 2 min 02.1 sec—Hulme 2 min 02.1 sec—Gethin 2 min 02.2 sec—Oliver 2 min 02.3 sec—Peterson 2 min 02.4 sec—Hill 2 min 03.0 sec—Beltoise 2 min 05.2 sec—non starters A. de Adamich (McLaren)—B. Redman (de Tomaso)—H. Hahne (March)—S. Moser (Bellasi).

AUSTRIAN GRAND PRIX

Österreichring; 16 August; 60 laps 354 km/220 miles
1 J. Ickx (Ferrari) 1 hr 42 min 17.3 sec 207.99 kph/129.27 mph—2 C. Regazzoni (Ferrari) 1 hr 42 min 17.9 sec—3 R. Stommelen (Brabham) 1 hr 43 min 45.2 sec—4 P. Rodriguez (BRM) 59 laps—5 J. Oliver (BRM) 59 laps—6 J-P Beltoise (Matra) 59 laps—7 I. Giunti (Ferrari) 59 laps—8 C. Amon (March) 59 laps—9 J. Siffert (March) 59 laps—10 P. Gethin (McLaren) 59 laps—11 G. Eaton (BRM) 58 laps—12 A. de Adamich (McLaren) 57 laps—13 J. Brabham (Brabham) 56 laps—14 H. Pescarolo (Matra) 56 laps—15 E. Fittipaldi (Lotus) 55 laps—fastest lap, Ickx, Regazzoni 1 min 40.4 sec 211.9 kph/131.7 mph—retired F. Cevert (March) engine lap 1—J. Miles (Lotus) brake shaft lap 5—J Y Stewart (March) fuel line lap 8—M. Andretti (March) accident lap 14—S. Moser (Bellasi) radiator lap 14—J. Rindt (Lotus) engine lap 22—T. Schenken (de Tomaso) engine lap 26—J. Surtees (Surtees) engine lap 28—D. Hulme (McLaren) engine lap 31.

Starting grid 2-2-2

Rindt 1 min 39.2 sec—Regazzoni 1 min 39.7 sec—Ickx 1 min 39.9 sec—Stewart 1 min 40.1 sec—Giunti 1 min 40.2 sec—Amon 1 min 40.6 sec—Beltoise 1 min 40.8 sec—Brabham 1 min 40.8 sec—Cevert 1 min 40.9 sec—Miles 1 min 41.5 sec—Hulme 1 min 41.5 sec—Surtees 1 min 41.5 sec—Pescarolo 1 min 41.7 sec—Oliver 1 min 41.7 sec—de Adamich 1 min 41.8 sec—Fittipaldi 1 min 41.9 sec—Stommelen 1 min 42.1 sec—Andretti 1 min 42.3 sec—Schenken 1 min 42.4 sec—Siffert 1 min 42.6 sec—Gethin 1 min 42.8 sec—Rodriguez 1 min 43.2 sec—Eaton 1 min 45.0 sec—Moser 1 min 45.6 sec.

ITALIAN GRAND PRIX

Monza; 6 September; 68 laps 389 km/242 miles

1 C. Regazzoni (Ferrari) 1 hr 39 min 06.9 sec 236.63 kph/147.07 mph—2 J Y Stewart (March) 1 hr 39 min 12.6 sec—3 J-P Beltoise (Matra) 1 hr 39 min 12.7 sec—4 D. Hulme (McLaren) 1 hr 39 min 13.0 sec—5 R. Stommelen (Brabham) 1 hr 39 min 13.3 sec—6 F. Cevert (March) 1 hr 40 min 10.34 sec—7 C. Amon (March) 67 laps—8 A. de Adamich (McLaren) 61 laps—9 P. Gethin (McLaren) 60 laps—fastest lap, Regazzoni 1 min 25.2 sec 242.89 kph/150.96 mph—retired J. Surtees (Surtees) electrics lap 1—J. Siffert (March) engine lap 3—P. Rodriguez (BRM) engine lap 13—H. Pescarolo (Matra) engine lap 15—I. Giunti (Ferrari) overheating lap 15—T. Schenken (de Tomaso) engine lap 18—G. Eaton (BRM) overheating lap 22—J. Ickx (Ferrari) transmission lap 26—J. Brabham (Brabham) accident lap 32—R. Peterson (March) engine lap 36—J. Oliver (BRM) engine lap 37.

Starting grid 2-2-2

Ickx 1 min 24.1 sec—Rodriguez 1 min 24.4 sec—Regazzoni 1 min 24.4 sec—Stewart 1 min 24.7 sec—Giunti 1 min 24.7 sec—Oliver 1 min 24.8 sec—Siffert 1 min 25.1 sec—Brabham 1 min 25.4 sec—Hulme 1 min 25.5 sec—Surtees 1 min 25.6 sec—Cevert 1 min 25.6 sec—de Adamich 1 min 25.9 sec—Peterson 1 min 25.9 sec—Beltoise 1 min 26.0 sec—Pescarolo 1 min 26.0 sec—Gethin 1 min 26.2 sec—Stommelen 1 min 26.8 sec—Amon 1 min 26.7 sec—Schenken 1 min 28.7 sec—Eaton 1 min 27.1 sec—non starters J. Rindt (Lotus) fatal accident in practice—J. Miles (Lotus)—E. Fittipaldi (Lotus)—G. Hill (Lotus)—J Y Stewart (Tyrrell)—J. Bonnier (McLaren)—'Nanni Galli' (McLaren)—S. Moser (Belfast).

CANADIAN GRAND PRIX

Mont Tremblant; 20 September; 90 laps 238 miles/383 km
1 J. Ickx (Ferrari) 2 hr 21 min 18.4 sec 101.27 mph/162.94 kph—2 C. Regazzoni (Ferrari) 2 hr 21 min 33.2 sec—3 C. Amon (March) 2 hr 22 min 16.3 sec—4 P. Rodriguez (BRM) 89 laps—5 J. Surtees (Surtees) 89 laps—6 P. Gethin (McLaren) 88 laps—7 H. Pescarolo (Matra) 87 laps—8 J-P Beltoise (Matra) 85 laps—9 F. Cevert (March) 85 laps—10 G. Eaton (BRM) 85 laps—not classified T. Schenken (de Tomaso) 79 laps—G. Hill (Lotus) 77 laps—R. Peterson (March) 65 laps—J. Oliver (BRM) 52 laps—fastest lap, Regazzoni 1 min 32.2 sec 103.47 mph/166.48 kph—retired J. Siffert (March) engine lap 22—R. Stommelen (Brabham) steering lap 23—J Y Stewart (Tyrrell) stub axle lap 31—J. Brabham (Brabham) oil leak lap 57—D. Hulme (McLaren) flywheel lap 59—A. de Adamich (McLaren) oil pressure lap 69.

Starting grid 2-2-2

Stewart 1 min 31.5 sec—Ickx 1 min 31.6 sec—Regazzoni 1 min 31.9 sec—Cevert 1 min 32.4 sec—Surtees 1 min 32.6 sec—Amon 1 min 32.6 sec—Rodriguez 1 min 32.7 sec—Pescarolo 1 min 32.9 sec—Eaton 1 min 32.9 sec—Oliver 1 min 33.1 sec—Gethin 1 min 33.2 sec—de Adamich 1 min 33.2 sec—Beltoise 1 min 33.4 sec—Siffert 1 min 33.5 sec—Hulme 1 min 33.9 sec—Peterson 1 min 34.4 sec—Schenken 1 min 34.6 sec—Stommelen 1 min 34.7 sec—Brabham 1 min 35.4 sec—Hill 1 min 35.8 sec.

UNITED STATES GRAND PRIX

Watkins Glen; 4 October; 108 laps 248 miles/399 km
1 E. Fittipaldi (Lotus) 1 hr 57 min 32.8 sec 126.79 mph/204.0 kph—2 P. Rodriguez (BRM) 1 hr 58 min 09.2 sec—3 R. Wisell (Lotus) 1 hr 58 min 18.0 sec—4 J. Ickx (Ferrari) 107 laps—5 C. Amon (March) 107 laps—6 D. Bell (Surtees) 107 laps—7 D. Hulme (McLaren) 106 laps—8 H. Pescarolo (Matra) 105 laps—9 J. Siffert (March) 105 laps—10 J. Brabham (Brabham) 105 laps—11 R. Peterson (March) 104 laps—12 R. Stommelen (Brabham) 104 laps—13 C. Regazzoni (Ferrari) 101 laps—14 P. Gethin (McLaren) 100 laps—fastest lap, Ickx 1 min 02.7 sec 131.97 mph/212.34 kph—retired J. Surtees (Surtees) engine lap 7—G. Eaton (BRM) engine lap 11—J. Oliver (BRM) engine lap 15—G. Hutchison (Brabham) fuel tank lap 22—J-P Beltoise (Matra) handling lap 28—J. Bonnier (McLaren) water pipe lap 51—T. Schenken (de Tomaso) rear suspension lap 62—F. Cevert (March) rear wheel lap 63—G. Hill (Lotus) clutch lap 73—J Y Stewart (Tyrrell) engine lap 83.

Starting grid 2-2-2

Ickx 1 min 03.1 sec—Stewart 1 min 03.6 sec—Fittipaldi 1 min 03.7 sec—Rodriguez 1 min 04.2 sec—Amon 1 min 04.2 sec—Regazzoni 1 min 04.3 sec—Oliver 1 min 04.4 sec—Surtees 1 min 04.5 sec—Wisell 1 min 04.8 sec—Hill 1 min 04.8 sec—Hulme 1 min 04.8 sec—Pescarolo 1 min 05.0 sec—Bell 1 min 05.0 sec—Eaton 1 min 05.1 sec—Peterson 1 min 05.2 sec—Brabham 1 min 05.3 sec—Cevert 1 min 05.3 sec—Beltoise 1 min 05.4 sec—Stommelen 1 min 05.8 sec—Schenkan 1 min 08.1 sec—Gethin 1 min 06.1 sec—Hutchison 1 min 08.2 sec—Siffert 1 min 06.2 sec—Bonnier 1 min 06.5 sec—non starters P. Westbury (BRM)—P. Lovely (Lotus)—A. de Adamich (McLaren).

MEXICAN GRAND PRIX

Mexico City; 25 October; 65 laps 202 miles/325 km
1 J. Ickx (Ferrari) 1 hr 53 min 28.4 sec 106.78 mph/171.81 kph—2 C. Regazzoni (Ferrari) 1 hr 53 min 53.0 sec—3 D.

Hulme (McLaren) 1 hr 54 min 14.3 sec—4 C. Amon (March) 1 hr 54 min 15.4 sec—5 J-P Beltoise (Matra) 1 hr 54 min 18.5 sec—6 P. Rodriguez (BRM) 1 hr 54 min 53.1 sec—7 J. Oliver (BRM) 64 laps—8 J. Surtees (Surtees) 64 laps—9 H. Pescarolo (Matra) 61 laps—10 R. Wisell (Lotus) 56 laps—fastest lap, Ickx 1 min 43.1 sec 108.49 mph/174.56 kph—retired E. Fittipaldi (Lotus) engine lap 1—J. Siffert (March) engine lap 3—G. Hill (Lotus) overheating lap 4—F. Cevert (March) engine lap 8—R. Stommelen (Brabham) fuel system lap 15—P. Gethin (McLaren) engine lap 27—J Y Stewart (Tyrrell) front suspension lap 33—J Brabham (Brabham) engine lap 52.

Starting grid 2-2-2

Regazzoni 1 min 41.9 sec—Stewart 1 min 41.9 sec—Ickx 1 min 42.4 sec—Brabham 1 min 43.6 sec—Amon 1 min 43.7 sec—Beltoise 1 min 43.8 sec—Rodriguez 1 min 44.0 sec—Hill 1 min 44.1 sec—Cevert 1 min 44.2 sec—Gethin 1 min 44.5 sec—Pescarolo 1 min 44.5 sec—Wisell 1 min 44.6 sec—Oliver 1 min 44.7 sec—Hulme 1 min 44.9 sec—Surtees 1 min 45.0 sec—Siffert 1 min 46.1 sec—Stommelen 1 min 46.3 sec—Fittipaldi 1 min 48.1 sec.

1970 WORLD CHAMPIONSHIP

1 J. Rindt 45—2 J. Ickx 40—3 C. Regazzoni 33—4 D. Hulme 27—5 J. Brabham 25—5= J Y Stewart 25—7 C. Amon 23—7= P. Rodriguez 23—9 J-P Beltoise 16—10 E. Fittipaldi 12—11 R. Stommelen 10—12 H. Pescarolo 8—13 G. Hill 7—14 B. McLaren 6—15 M. Andretti 4—15= R. Wisell 4—17 I. Giunti 3—17= J. Surtees 3—19 J. Miles 2—19= J. Oliver 2—19= J. Servoz-Gavin 2—22 D. Bell 1—22= F. Cevert 1—22= P. Gethin 1—22= D. Gurney 1.

1971

SOUTH AFRICAN GRAND PRIX

Kyalami; 6 March; 79 laps 201 miles/324 km
1 M. Andretti (Ferrari) 1 hr 47 min 35.5 sec 112.36 mph/180.79 kph—2 J Y Stewart (Tyrrell) 1 hr 47 min 56.4 sec—3 C. Regazzoni (Ferrari) 1 hr 48 min 06.9 sec—4 R. Wisell (Lotus) 1 hr 48 min 44.9 sec—5 C. Amon (Matra) 78 laps—6 D. Hulme (McLaren) 78 laps—7 B. Redman (Surtees) 78 laps—8 J. Ickx (Ferrari) 78 laps—9 G. Hill (Brabham) 77 laps—10 R. Peterson (March) 77 laps—11 H. Pescarolo (March) 77 laps—12 R. Stommelen (Surtees) 77 laps—13 A. de Adamich (March) 75 laps—Fastest lap, Andretti 1 min 20.3 sec 114.32 mph/183.9 kph—retired A. Soler-Roig (March) engine lap 5—J. Bonnier (McLaren) suspension lap 5—P. Gethin (McLaren) fuel lap 7—J. Pretorius (Brabham) engine lap 22—J. Siffert (BRM) engine lap 31—D. Charlton (Brabham) engine lap 31—J. Love (March) transmission lap 33—P. Rodriguez (BRM) overheating lap 33—H. Ganley (BRM) heat exhaustion lap 42—F. Cevert (Tyrrell) accident lap 47—E. Fittipaldi (Lotus) engine lap 58—J. Surtees (Surtees) transmission lap 58.

Starting grid 3-2-3

Stewart 1 min 17.8 sec—Amon 1 min 18.4 sec—Regazzoni 1 min 18.7 sec—Andretti 1 min 19.0 sec—Fittipaldi 1 min 19.1 sec—Surtees 1 min 19.1 sec—Hulme 1 min 19.1 sec—Ickx 1 min 19.2 sec—Cevert 1 min 19.2 sec—Rodriguez 1 min 19.3 sec—Gethin 1 min 19.6 sec—Charlton 1 min 19.8 sec—Peterson 1 min 19.9 sec—Wisell 1 min 19.9 sec—Stommelen 1 min 20.1 sec—Siffert 1 min 20.2 sec—Redman 1 min 20.2 sec—Pescarolo 1 min 20.2 sec—Hill 1 min 20.5 sec—Pretorius 1 min 21.7 sec—Love 1 min 21.9 sec—de Adamich 1 min 22.2 sec—Bonnier 1 min 22.3 sec—Ganley 1 min 23.7 sec—Soler-Roig 1 min 25.8 sec.

SPANISH GRAND PRIX

Montjuich; 18 April; 75 laps 284 km/177 miles
1 J Y Stewart (Tyrrell) 1 hr 49 min 03.4 sec 156.38 kph/97.19 mph—2 J. Ickx (Ferrari) 1 hr 49 min 06.8 sec—3 C. Amon (Matra) 1 hr 50 min 1.5 sec—4 P. Rodriguez (BRM) 1 hr 50 min 21.3 sec—5 D. Hulme (McLaren) 1 hr 50 min 30.4 sec—6 J-P Beltoise (Matra) 74 laps—7 F. Cevert (Tyrrell) 74 laps—8 P. Gethin (McLaren) 73 laps—9 T. Schenken (Brabham) 72 laps—10 H. Ganley (BRM) 71 laps—11 J. Surtees (Surtees) 67 laps—12 R. Wisell (Lotus) 58 laps—fastest lap, Ickx 1 min 25.1 sec 160.32 kph/99.64 mph—retired G. Hill (Brabham) accident lap 6—J. Siffert (BRM) gear linkage lap 6—R. Stommelen (Surtees) fuel pressure lap 10—C. Regazzoni (Ferrari) engine lap 14—R. Peterson (March) ignition lap 25—A. de Adamich (March) ignition lap 27—A. Soler-Roig (March) fuel line lap 47—M. Andretti (Ferrari) fuel pump lap 51—H. Pescarolo (March) wing lap 54—E. Fittipaldi (Lotus) suspension lap 55.

Starting grid 3-2-3

Ickx 1 min 25.9 sec—Regazzoni 1 min 26.0 sec—Amon 1 min 26.0 sec—Stewart 1 min 26.2 sec—Rodriguez 1 min 26.5 sec—Beltoise 1 min 26.6 sec—Gethin 1 min 26.8 sec—Andretti 1 min 26.9 sec—Hulme 1 min 27.1 sec—Siffert 1 min 27.3 sec—Pescarolo 1 min 27.5 sec—Cevert 1 min 27.7 sec—Peterson 1 min 27.8 sec—Fittipaldi 1 min 27.9 sec—Hill 1 min 28.4 sec—Wisell 1 min 28.6 sec—Ganley 1 min 28.6 sec—de Adamich 1 min 29.5 sec—Stommelen 1 min 29.6 sec—Soler-Roig 1 min 29.8 sec—Schenken 1 min 30.6 sec—Surtees 1 min 30.8 sec.

MONACO GRAND PRIX

Monte Carlo; 23 May; 80 laps 252 km/156 miles
1 J Y Stewart (Tyrrell) 1 hr 52 min 21.3 sec 134.33 kph/83.49 mph—2 R Peterson (March) 1 hr 52 min 46.9 sec—3 J. Ickx (Ferrari) 1 hr 53 min 14.6 sec—4 D. Hulme (McLaren) 1 hr 53 min 28.0 sec—5 E. Fittipaldi (Lotus) 79 laps—6 R. Stommelen (Surtees) 79 laps—7 J. Surtees (Surtees) 79 laps—8 H. Pescarolo (March) 77 laps—9 P. Rodriguez (BRM) 76 laps—10 T. Schenken (Brabham) 76 laps—fastest lap, Stewart 1 min 22.2 sec 137.7 kph/85.58 mph—retired G. Hill (Brabham) accident lap 2—F. Cevert (Tyrrell) accident lap 6—R. Wisell (Lotus) rear hub lap 22—P. Gethin (McLaren) accident lap 23—C. Regazzoni (Ferrari) accident lap 25—C. Amon (Matra) final drive lap 46—J-P Beltoise (Matra) final drive lap 48—J. Siffert (BRM) engine lap 59.

Starting grid 2-2-2

Stewart 1 min 23.2 sec—Ickx 1 min 24.4 sec—Siffert 1 min 24.8 sec—Amon 1 min 24.8 sec—Rodriguez 1 min 25.1 sec—Hulme 1 min 25.3 sec—Beltoise 1 min 25.6 sec—Peterson 1 min 25.8 sec—Hill 1 min 26.0 sec—Surtees 1 min 26.0 sec—Regazzoni 1 min 26.1 sec—Wisell 1 min 26.7 sec—Pescarolo 1 min 26.7 sec—Gethin 1 min 26.9 sec—Cevert 1 min 27.2 sec—Stommelen 1 min 27.2 sec—Fittipaldi 1 min 27.7 sec—Schenken 1 min 28.3 sec—non starters H. Ganley (BRM)—M. Andretti (Ferrari)—'N Galli' (March)—A. Soler-Roig (March)—S. Barber (March).

DUTCH GRAND PRIX

Zandvoort; 20 June; 70 laps 294 km/183 miles
1 J. Ickx (Ferrari) 1 hr 56 min 20.1 sec 151.34 kph/94.06 mph—2 P. Rodriguez (BRM) 1 hr 56 min 28.1 sec—3 C. Regazzoni (Ferrari) 69 laps—4 R. Peterson (March) 68 laps—5 J. Surtees (Surtees) 68 laps—6 J. Siffert (BRM) 68 laps—7 H. Ganley (BRM) 66 laps—8 G. van Lennep (Surtees) 65 laps—9 J-P Beltoise (Matra) 65 laps—10 G. Hill (Brabham) 65 laps—11 J Y Stewart (Tyrrell) 65 laps—12 D. Hulme (McLaren) 63 laps—13 H. Pescarolo (March) 62 laps—14 S. Barber (March) 60 laps—15 P. Gethin (McLaren) 60 laps—fastest lap, Ickx 1 min 34.9 sec 158.94 kph/98.78 mph—retired C. Amon (Matra) accident lap 2—M. Andretti (Ferrari) fuel pump lap 44—D. Walker (Lotus) accident lap 6—'N Galli' (March) accident lap 8—R. Wisell (Lotus) disqualified lap 17—R. Stommelen (Surtees) disqualified lap 19—F. Cevert (Tyrrell) suspension lap 29—T. Schenken (Brabham) suspension lap 39—A. Soler-Roig (March) engine lap 58.

DUTCH GRAND PRIX—*continued*

Starting grid 3-2-3

Ickx 1 min 17.4 sec—Rodriguez 1 min 17.5 sec—Stewart 1 min 17.6 sec—Regazzoni 1 min 18.0 sec—Amon 1 min 18.5 sec—Wisell 1 min 18.7 sec—Surtees 1 min 18.7 sec—Siffert 1 min 18.9 sec—Ganley 1 min 19.1 sec—Stommelen 1 min 19.1 sec—Beltoise 1 min 19.2 sec—Cevert 1 min 19.5 sec—Peterson 1 min 19.7 sec—Hulme 1 min 19.7 sec—Pescarolo 1 min 20.0 sec—Hill 1 min 20.1 sec—Soler-Roig 1 min 20.3 sec—Andretti 1 min 20.3 sec—Schenken 1 min 20.3 sec—'Galli' 1 min 20.6 sec—van Lennep 1 min 20.8 sec—Walker 1 min 21.8 sec—Gethin 1 min 22.1 sec—Barber 1 min 22.2 sec.

FRENCH GRAND PRIX

Paul Ricard; 4 July; 55 laps 319 km/198 miles
1 J Y Stewart (Tyrrell) 1 hr 46 min 41.7 sec 179.66 kph/111.66 mph—2 F. Cevert (Tyrrell) 1 hr 47 min 09.8 sec—3 E. Fittipaldi (Lotus) 1 hr 47 min 15.7 sec—4 J. Siffert (BRM) 1 hr 47 min 18.8 sec—5 C. Amon (Matra) 1 hr 47 min 22.8 sec—6 R. Wisell (Lotus) 1 hr 47 min 57.7 sec—7 J-P Beltoise (Matra) 1 hr 47 min 58.6 sec—8 J. Surtees (Surtees) 1 hr 48 min 06.6 sec—9 P. Gethin (McLaren) 54 laps—10 H. Ganley (BRM) 54 laps—11 R. Stommelen (Surtees) 53 laps—12 T. Schenken (Brabham) 50 laps—13 F. Mazet (March) 50 laps—14 J. Max (March) 46 laps—fastest lap, Stewart 1 min 54.1 sec 183.28 kph/113.9 mph—retired A. Soler-Roig (March) fuel pump lap 4—J. Ickx (Ferrari) engine lap 5—D. Hulme (McLaren) ignition lap 16—R. Peterson (March) engine lap 20—C. Regazzoni (Ferrari) accident lap 21—P. Rodriguez (BRM) ignition lap 28—A. de Adamich (March) engine lap 32—G. Hill (Brabham) engine lap 35—H. Pescarolo (March) gearbox lap 45—T. Schenken (Brabham) engine lap 50.

Starting grid 3-2-3

Stewart 1 min 50.7 sec—Regazzoni 1 min 51.5 sec—Ickx 1 min 51.9 sec—Hill 1 min 52.3 sec—Rodriguez 1 min 52.5 sec—Siffert 1 min 52.5 sec—Cevert 1 min 52.7 sec—Beltoise 1 min 52.9 sec—Amon 1 min 52.9 sec—Stommelen 1 min 53.1 sec—Hulme 1 min 53.2 sec—Peterson 1 min 53.4 sec—Surtees 1 min 53.6 sec—Schenken 1 min 53.6 sec—Wisell 1 min 53.7 sec—Ganley 1 min 53.8 sec—Fittipaldi 1 min 54.2 sec—Pescarolo 1 min 54.3 sec—Gethin 1 min 54.9 sec—de Adamich 1 min 56.2 sec—Soler-Roig 1 min 57.1 sec—Max 1 min 59.8 sec—Mazet 2 min 00.5 sec—non starter 'N. Galli' (March).

BRITISH GRAND PRIX

Silverstone; 17 July; 68 laps 199 miles/320 km
1 J Y Stewart (Tyrrell) 1 hr 31 min 31.5 sec 130.48 mph/209.94 kph—2 R. Peterson (March) 1 hr 32 min 07.6 sec—3 E. Fittipaldi (Lotus) 1 hr 32 min 22.0 sec—4 H. Pescarolo (March) 67 laps—5 R. Stommelen (Surtees) 67 laps—6 J. Surtees (Surtees) 67 laps—7 J-P Beltoise (Matra) 66 laps—8 H. Ganley (BRM) 66 laps—9 J. Siffert (BRM) 66 laps—10 F. Cevert (Tyrrell) 65 laps—11 'N. Galli' (March) 65 laps—12 T. Schenken (Brabham) 63 laps—not classified R. Wisell (Lotus) 57 laps—A. de Adamich (March) 56 laps—fastest lap, Stewart 1 min 19.9 sec 131.88 mph/212.19 kph—retired G. Hill (Brabham) accident 0 laps—J Oliver (McLaren) accident 0 laps—D. Charlton (Lotus) engine lap 2—M. Beuttler (March) engine lap 22—D. Bell (Surtees) suspension lap 24—D. Hulme (McLaren) engine lap 32—C. Amon (Matra) engine lap 36—C. Regazzoni (Ferrari) engine lap 49—J. Ickx (Ferrari) engine lap 52—P. Gethin (McLaren) engine lap 54—T. Schenken (Brabham) gearbox lap 63.

Starting grid 3-2-3

Regazzoni 1 min 18.1 sec—Stewart 1 min 18.1 sec—Siffert 1 min 18.2 sec—Fittipaldi 1 min 18.3 sec—Peterson 1 min 19.0 sec—Ickx 1 min 19.5 sec—Schenken 1 min 19.5 sec—Hulme 1 min 19.6 sec—Amon 1 min 19.7 sec—Cevert 1 min 19.8 sec—Ganley 1 min 19.8 sec—Stommelen 1 min 19.9 sec—Charlton 1 min 20.0 sec—Gethin 1 min 20.1 sec—Beltoise 1 min 20.2 sec—Hill 1 min 20.3 sec—Pescarolo 1 min 20.5 sec—Surtees 1 min 20.6 sec—Wisell 1 min 20.7 sec—Beuttler 1 min 20.7 sec—'Galli' 1 min 20.9 sec—Oliver 1 min 21.0 sec—Bell 1 min 22.3 sec—de Adamich 1 min 23.2.

GERMAN GRAND PRIX

Nürburgring; 1 August; 12 laps 274 km/170 miles
1 J Y Stewart (Tyrrell) 1 hr 29 min 15.7 sec 184.17 kph/114.46 mph—2 F. Cevert (Tyrrell) 1 hr 29 min 45.8 sec—3 C. Regazzoni (Ferrari) 1 hr 29 min 52.8 sec—4 M. Andretti (Ferrari) 1 hr 31 min 20.7 sec—5 R. Peterson (March) 1 hr 31 min 44.8 sec—6 T. Schenken (Brabham) 1 hr 32 min 14.3 sec—7 J. Surtees (Surtees) 1 hr 32 min 34.7 sec—8 R. Wisell (Lotus) 1 hr 35 min 47.4 sec—9 G. Hill (Brabham) 1 hr 35 min 52.7 sec—10 R. Stommelen (Surtees) 11 laps—11 V. Elford (BRM) 11 laps—12 'N. Galli' (March) 10 laps—fastest lap, Cevert 7 min 20.1 sec 186.76 kph/116.07 mph—retired J. Ickx (Ferrari) accident lap 2—H. Ganley (BRM) engine lap 3—A. de Adamich (March) fuel injection lap 3—M. Beuttler (March) disqualified lap 4—D. Hulme (McLaren) fuel leak lap 4—H. Pescarolo (March) suspension lap 6—P. Gethin (McLaren) accident lap 6—J. Siffert (BRM) coil lap 7—C. Amon (Matra) accident lap 7—E. Fittipaldi (Lotus) oil leak lap 9.

Starting grid 2-2-2

Stewart 7 min 19.0 sec—Ickx 7 min 19.2 sec—Siffert 7 min 22.4 sec—Regazzoni 7 min 22.7 sec—Cevert 7 min 23.4 sec—Hulme 7 min 26.0 sec—Peterson 7 min 16.5 sec—Fittipaldi 7 min 27.5 sec—Schenken 7 min 29.8 sec—Pescarolo 7 min 30.3 sec—Andretti 7 min 31.7 sec—Stommelen 7 min 34.7 sec—Hill 7 min 36.1 sec—Ganley 7 min 36.6 sec—Surtees 7 min 36.7 sec—Amon 7 min 37.3 sec—Wisell 7 min 40.0 sec—Elford 7 min 40.0 sec—Gethin 7 min 41.4 sec—de Adamich 7 min 41.7 sec—'Galli' 7 min 47.6 sec—Beuttler 7 min 52.6 sec—non starter J. Bonnier (McLaren).

AUSTRIAN GRAND PRIX

Österreichring; 15 August; 54 laps 319 km/198 miles
1 J. Siffert (BRM) 1 hr 30 min 23.9 sec 212.87 kph/132.3 mph—2 E. Fittipaldi (Lotus) 1 hr 30 min 28.0 sec—3 T. Schenken (Brabham) 1 hr 30 min 43.7 sec—4 R. Wisell (Lotus) 1 hr 30 min 55.8 sec—5 G. Hill (Brabham) 1 hr 31 min 12.3 sec—6 H. Pescarolo (March) 1 hr 31 min 48.4 sec—7 R. Stommelen (Surtees) 1 hr 32 min 01.3 sec—8 R. Peterson (March) 53 laps—9 J. Oliver (McLaren) 53 laps—10 P. Gethin (BRM) 52 laps—11 H. Marko (BRM) 52 laps—12 'N Galli' (March) 51 laps—not classified M. Beuttler (March) 44 laps—fastest lap, Siffert 1 min 38.5 sec 216.23 kph/134.39 mph—retired D. Hulme (McLaren) engine lap 6—H. Ganley (BRM) electrics lap 6—C. Regazzoni (Ferrari) engine lap 9—J. Surtees (Surtees) engine lap 12—N. Lauda (March) handling lap 20—J. Ickx (Ferrari) engine lap 31—J Y Stewart (Tyrrell) accident lap 35—F. Cevert (Tyrrell) engine lap 42.

Starting grid 2-2-2

Siffert 1 min 37.4 sec—Stewart 1 min 37.6 sec—Cevert 1 min 37.9 sec—Regazzoni 1 min 37.9 sec—Fittipaldi 1 min 37.9 sec—Ickx 1 min 38.3 sec—Schenken 1 min 38.6 sec—Hill 1 min 38.7 sec—Hulme 1 min 38.9 sec—Wisell 1 min 38.9 sec—Peterson 1 min 39.0 sec—Stommelen 1 min 39.1 sec—Pescarolo 1 min 39.1 sec—Ganley 1 min 39.5 sec—'Galli' 1 min 39.5 sec—Gethin 1 min 39.7 sec—Marko 1 min 39.8 sec—Surtees 1 min 40.4 sec—Beuttler 1 min 41.5 sec—Lauda 1 min 43.7 sec—Oliver 1 min 44.2 sec—non starter J. Bonnier (McLaren).

ITALIAN GRAND PRIX

Monza; 5 September; 55 laps 316 km/196 miles
1 P. Gethin (BRM) 1 hr 18 min 12.6 sec 242.57 kph/150.76 mph—2 R. Peterson (March) 1 hr 18 min 12.61 sec—3 F. Cevert (Tyrrell) 1 hr 18 min 12.69 sec—4 M. Hailwood (Surtees) 1 hr 18 min 12.78 sec—5 H. Ganley (BRM) 1 hr 18 min 13.21 sec—6 C. Amon (Matra) 1 hr 18 min 44.96 sec—7 J. Oliver (McLaren) 1 hr 19 min 37.43 sec—8 E. Fittipaldi (Lotus) 54 laps—9 J. Siffert (BRM) 53 laps—10 J. Bonnier (McLaren) 51 laps—11 G. Hill (Brabham) 47 laps—12 J-P Jarier (March) 47 laps—fastest lap, Pescarolo 1 min 23.8 sec

246.96 kph/153.49 mph—retired H. Marko (BRM) engine lap 3—J. Surtees (Surtees) engine lap 3—T. Schenken (Brabham) suspension lap 5—S. Moser (Bellasi) suspension lap 5—'N Galli' (March) electrics lap 11—J. Ickx (Ferrari) engine lap 15—J Y Stewart (Tyrrell) con-rod lap 15—C. Regazzoni (Ferrari) engine lap 17—A. de Adamich (March) engine lap 33—H. Pescarolo (March) suspension lap 40—M. Beuttler (March) engine lap 41—G. Hill (Brabham) gearbox lap 47.

Starting grid 2-2-2

Amon 1 min 22.4 sec—Ickx 1 min 22.8 sec—Siffert 1 min 23.0 sec—Ganley 1 min 23.1 sec—Cevert 1 min 23.4 sec—Peterson 1 min 23.5 sec—Stewart 1 min 23.5 sec—Regazzoni 1 min 23.7 sec—Schenken 1 min 23.7 sec—Pescarolo 1 min 23.8 sec—Gethin 1 min 23.9 sec—Marko 1 min 24.0 sec—Oliver 1 min 24.1 sec—Hill 1 min 24.3 sec—Surtees 1 min 24.4 sec—Beuttler 1 min 25.0 sec—Hailwood 1 min 25.2 sec—Fittipaldi 1 min 25.2 sec—'Galli' 1 min 25.2 sec—de Adamich 1 min 25.8 sec—Bonnier 1 min 26.1 sec—Moser 1 min 26.5 sec—Jarier 1 min 28.2 sec—non starters C. Pace (March)—H. Muller (Lotus)—R. Stommelen (Surtees).

CANADIAN GRAND PRIX

Mosport; 19 September; 64 laps 157 miles/253 km
1 J Y Stewart (Tyrrell) 1 hr 55 min 12.9 sec 81.97 mph/131.89 kph—2 R. Peterson (March) 1 hr 55 min 51.2 sec—3 M. Donohue (McLaren) 1 hr 56 min 48.7 sec—D. Hulme (McLaren) 63 laps—5 R. Wisell (Lotus) 63 laps—6 F. Cevert (Tyrrell) 62 laps—7 E. Fittipaldi (Lotus) 62 laps—8 J. Ickx (Ferrari) 62 laps—9 J. Siffert (BRM) 61 laps—10 C. Amon (Matra) 61 laps—11 J. Surtees (Surtees) 60 laps—12 H. Marko (BRM) 60 laps—13 M. Andretti (Ferrari) 60 laps—14 P. Gethin (BRM) 59 laps—15 G. Eaton (BRM) 59 laps—16 'N. Galli' (March) 57 laps—not classified M. Beuttler (March) 56 laps—P. Lovely (Lotus) 55 laps—fastest lap, Hulme 1 min 43.5 sec 85.53 mph/137.62 kph—retired H. Ganley (BRM) accident 0 laps—T. Schenken (Brabham) ignition lap 1—G. Hill (Brabham) accident lap 2—C. Regazzoni (Ferrari) accident lap 7—S. Barber (March) engine lap 14—J-P Beltoise (Matra) accident lap 15—R. Stommelen (Surtees) engine lap 26.

Starting grid 3-2-3

Stewart 1 min 15.3 sec—Siffert 1 min 15.5 sec—Cevert 1 min 15.7 sec—Fittipaldi 1 min 16.1 sec—Amon 1 min 16.1 sec—Peterson 1 min 16.2 sec—Wisell 1 min 16.3 sec—Donohue 1 min 16.3 sec—Ganley 1 min 16.3 sec—Hulme 1 min 18.4 sec—Beltoise 1 min 16.5 sec—Ickx 1 min 16.5 sec—Andretti 1 min 16.9 sec—Surtees 1 min 17.1 sec—Hill 1 min 17.2 sec—Gethin 1 min 17.2 sec—Schenken 1 min 17.4 sec—Regazzoni 1 min 17.5 sec—Marko 1 min 17.8 sec—'Galli' 1 min 18.2 sec—Eaton 1 min 18.4 sec—Beuttler 1 min 18.5 sec—Stommelen 1 min 18.8 sec—Barber 1 min 19.8 sec—Lovely 1 min 21.1 sec—non starters H. Pescarolo (March)—C. Craft (Brabham).

UNITED STATES GRAND PRIX

Watkins Glen; 3 October; 59 laps 199 miles/321 km
1 F. Cevert (Tyrrell) 1 hr 43 min 52.0 sec 115.09 mph/185.18 kph—2 J. Siffert (BRM) 1 hr 44 min 32.0 sec—3 R. Peterson (March) 1 hr 44 min 36.1 sec—4 H. Ganley (BRM) 1 hr 44 min 48.7 sec—5 J Y Stewart (Tyrrell) 1 hr 44 min 52.0 sec—6 C. Regazzoni (Ferrari) 1 hr 45 min 08.4 sec—7 G. Hill (Brabham) 58 laps—8 J-P Beltoise (Matra) 58 laps—9 P. Gethin (BRM) 58 laps—10 D. Hobbs (McLaren) 58 laps—11 A. de Adamich (March) 57 laps—12 C. Amon (Matra) 57 laps—13 H. Marko (BRM) 57 laps—14 J. Cannon (BRM) 56 laps—15 M. Hailwood (Surtees) 54 laps—16 J. Bonnier (McLaren) 54 laps—17 J. Surtees (Surtees) 54 laps—18 S. Barber (March) 52 laps—19 E. Fittipaldi (Lotus) 49 laps—20 P. Lovely (Lotus) 49 laps—fastest lap, Ickx 1 min 43.5 sec 117.49 mph/189.05 kph—retired P. Revson (Tyrrell) clutch lap 1—R. Wisell (Lotus) accident lap 5—'N. Galli' (March) suspension lap 11—S. Posey (Surtees) engine lap 15—H. Pescarolo (March) engine lap 23—C. Craft (Brabham) tyres lap 30—T. Schenken (Brabham) engine lap 41—D. Hulme (McLaren) accident lap 47—J. Ickx (Ferrari) electrics lap 49—J. Bonnier (McLaren) engine lap 54—M. Hailwood (Surtees) accident lap 54.

Starting grid 3-2-3

Stewart 1 min 42.6 sec—Fittipaldi 1 min 42.7 sec—Hulme 1 min 42.9 sec—Regazzoni 1 min 43.0 sec—Cevert 1 min 43.1 sec—Siffert 1 min 43.5 sec—Ickx 1 min 43.8 sec—Amon 1 min 44.0 sec—Wisell 1 min 44.0 sec—Beltoise 1 min 44.1 sec—Peterson 1 min 44.2 sec—Ganley 1 min 44.4 sec—Surtees 1 min 44.9 sec—Hailwood 1 min 45.1 sec—Schenken 1 min 45.1 sec—Marko 1 min 45.2 sec—Posey 1 min 45.3 sec—Hill 1 min 45.4 sec—Revson 1 min 45.5 sec—Pescarolo 1 min 45.6 sec—Gethin 1 min 46.7 sec—Cannon 1 min 47.5 sec—Barber 1 min 47.7 sec—de Adamich 1 min 47.9 sec—Craft 1 min 48.7 sec—Bonnier 1 min 49.4 sec—Lovely 1 min 52.1 sec—non starters G. van Lennep (Surtees)—M. Donohue (McLaren)—M. Andretti (Ferrari).

1971 WORLD CHAMPIONSHIP

1 J Y Stewart 62—2 R. Peterson 33—3 F. Cevert 26—4 J. Ickx 19—4= J. Siffert 19—6 E. Fittipaldi 16—7 C. Regazzoni 13—8 M. Andretti 12—9 P. Gethin 9—9= P. Rodriguez 9—9= C. Amon 9—9= R. Wisell 9—9= D. Hulme 9—14 T. Schenken 5—14= H. Ganley 5—16 M. Donohue 4—16= H. Pescarolo 4—18 M. Hailwood 3—18= J. Surtees 3—18= R. Stommelen 3—21 G. Hill 2—22 J-P Beltoise 1.

1972

ARGENTINE GRAND PRIX

Buenos Aires; 23 January; 95 laps 324 km/201 miles
1 J Y Stewart (Tyrrell) 1 hr 57 min 58.8 sec 161.43 kph/100.33 mph—2 D. Hulme (McLaren) 1 hr 58 min 24.8 sec—3 J. Ickx (Ferrari) 1 hr 58 min 58.2 sec—4 C. Regazzoni (Ferrari) 1 hr 59 min 05.5 sec—5 T. Schenken (Surtees) 1 hr 59 min 07.9 sec—6 R. Peterson (March) 94 laps—7 C. Reutemann (Brabham) 93 laps—8 H. Pescarolo (March) 93 laps—9 H. Ganley (BRM) 93 laps—10 H. Marko (BRM) 93 laps—11 N. Lauda (March) 93 laps—fastest lap, Stewart 1 min 13.7 sec 163.46 kph/101.59 mph—retired C. Amon (Matra) gearbox 0 laps—A. Soler-Roig (BRM) accident lap 1—P. Gethin (BRM) accident lap 1—D. Walker (Lotus) disqualified lap 8—G. Hill (Brabham) puncture lap 11—A. de Adamich (Surtees) fuel line lap 11—M. Andretti (Ferrari) engine lap 20—P. Revson (McLaren) engine lap 49—R. Wisell (BRM) water hose lap 59—F. Cevert (Tyrrell) gearbox lap 59—E. Fittipaldi (Lotus) rear radius rod lap 60.

Starting grid 2-2-2

Reutemann 1 min 12.5 sec—Stewart 1 min 12.7 sec—Revson 1 min 12.7 sec—Hulme 1 min 13.0 sec—Fittipaldi 1 min 13.3 sec—Regazzoni 1 min 13.3 sec—Cevert 1 min 13.4 sec—Ickx 1 min 13.5 sec—Andretti 1 min 13.6 sec—Peterson 1 min 14.1 sec—Schenken 1 min 14.2 sec—Amon 1 min 14.3 sec—Ganley 1 min 14.3 sec—de Adamich 1 min 14.3 sec—Pescarolo 1 min 14.5 sec—Hill 1 min 14.5 sec—Wisell 1 min 14.5 sec—Gethin 1 min 15.1 sec—Marko 1 min 15.5 sec—Walker 1 min 15.5 sec—Soler-Roig 1 min 15.7 sec—Lauda 1 min 15.9 sec.

SOUTH AFRICAN GRAND PRIX

Kyalami; 4 March; 79 laps 201 miles/324 km
1 D. Hulme (McLaren) 1 hr 45 min 49.1 sec 114.23 mph/183.8 kph—2 E. Fittipaldi (Lotus) 1 hr 46 min 03.2 sec—3 P. Revson (McLaren) 1 hr 46 min 14.9 sec—4 M. Andretti (Ferrari) 1 hr 46 min 27.6 sec—5 R. Peterson (March) 1 hr 46 min 38.1 sec—6 G. Hill (Brabham) 78 laps—7 N. Lauda (March) 78 laps—8 J. Ickx (Ferrari) 78 laps—9 F. Cevert (Tyrrell) 78 laps—10 D. Walker (Lotus) 78 laps—11 H.

SOUTH AFRICAN GRAND PRIX—*continued*

Pescarolo (March) 78 laps—12 C. Regazzoni (Ferrari) 77 laps—13 R. Stommelen (March) 77 laps—14 H. Marko (BRM) 76 laps—15 C. Amon (Matra) 76 laps—16 J. Love (Surtees) 73 laps—17 C. Pace (March) 73 laps—not classified H. Ganley (BRM) 69 laps—A. de Adamich (Surtees) 69 laps—P. Gethin (BRM) 65 laps—fastest lap, Hailwood 1 min 18.9 sec 116.35 mph/187.21 kph—retired D. Charlton (Lotus) fuel pump lap 2—T. Schenken (Surtees) engine lap 9—C. Reutemann (Brabham) fuel line lap 27—M. Hailwood (Surtees) suspension lap 28—J Y Stewart (Tyrrell) gearbox lap 45—J-P Beltoise (BRM) engine lap 61.

Starting grid 3-2-3

Stewart 1 min 17.0 sec—Regazzoni 1 min 17.3 sec—Fittipaldi 1 min 17.4 sec—Hailwood 1 min 17.4 sec—Hulme 1 min 17.4 sec—Andretti 1 min 17.5 sec—Ickx 1 min 17.7 sec—Cevert 1 min 17.8 sec—Peterson 1 min 17.8 sec—Schenken 1 min 17.8 sec—Beltoise 1 min 17.9 sec—Revson 1 min 18.0 sec—Amon 1 min 18.0 sec—Hill 1 min 18.1 sec—Reutemann 1 min 18.2 sec—Ganley 1 min 18.3 sec—Charlton 1 min 18.5 sec—Gethin 1 min 18.7 sec—Walker 1 min 18.7 sec—de Adamich 1 min 18.9 sec—Lauda 1 min 18.9 sec—Pescarolo 1 min 19.0 sec—Marko 1 min 19.1 sec—Pace 1 min 20.3 sec—Stommelen 1 min 20.4 sec—Love 1 min 21.0 sec.

SPANISH GRAND PRIX

Jarama; 1 May; 90 laps 306 km/190 miles
1 E. Fittipaldi (Lotus) 2 hr 3 min 41.2 sec 148.59 kph/92.35 mph—2 J. Ickx (Ferrari) 2 hr 4 min 00.1 sec—3 C. Regazzoni (Ferrari) 89 laps—4 A. de Adamich (Surtees) 89 laps—5 P. Revson (McLaren) 89 laps—6 C. Pace (March) 89 laps—7 W. Fittipaldi (Brabham) 88 laps—8 T. Schenken (Surtees) 88 laps—9 D. Walker (Lotus) 87 laps—10 G. Hill (Brabham) 86 laps—11 H. Pescarolo (March) 86 laps—fastest lap, Ickx 1 min 21.0 sec 151.25 kph/94.00 mph—retired A. Soler-Roig (BRM) accident lap 6—N. Lauda (March) throttle lap 7—J-P Beltoise (BRM) transmission lap 9—R. Stommelen (March) accident lap 15—R. Peterson (March) accident lap 16—M. Hailwood (Surtees) electrics lap 20—M. Andretti (Ferrari) engine lap 23—R. Wisell (BRM) accident lap 24—H. Ganley (BRM) engine lap 38—D. Hulme (McLaren) gearbox lap 48—P. Gethin (BRM) engine lap 65—F. Cevert (Tyrrell) engine lap 65—C. Amon (Matra) gearbox lap 66—J Y Stewart (Tyrrell) accident lap 69.

Starting grid 3-2-3

Ickx 1 min 18.4 sec—Hulme 1 min 19.2 sec—Fittipaldi 1 min 19.3 sec—Stewart 1 min 19.3 sec—Andretti 1 min 19.4 sec—Amon 1 min 19.5 sec—Beltoise 1 min 19.6 sec—Regazzoni 1 min 19.7 sec—Peterson 1 min 19.9 sec—Wisell 1 min 19.9 sec—Revson 1 min 20.1 sec—Cevert 1 min 20.5 sec—de Adamich 1 min 20.8 sec—W. Fittipaldi 1 min 20.8 sec—Hailwood 1 min 21.0 sec—Pace 1 min 21.0 sec—Stommelen 1 min 21.0 sec—Schenken 1 min 21.1 sec—Pescarolo 1 min 21.2 sec—Ganley 1 min 21.4 sec—Gethin 1 min 22.4 sec—Soler-Roig 1 min 22.6 sec—Hill 1 min 22.6 sec—Walker 1 min 22.7 sec—Lauda 1 min 25.0 sec—non starter M. Beuttler (March).

MONACO GRAND PRIX

Monte Carlo; 14 May; 80 laps 251 km/156 miles
1 J-P Beltoise (BRM) 2 hr 26 min 54.7 sec 102.73 kph/63.85 mph—2 J. Ickx (Ferrari) 2 hr 27 min 32.9 sec—3 E. Fittipaldi (Lotus) 79 laps—4 J Y Stewart (Tyrrell) 78 laps—5 B. Redman (McLaren) 77 laps—6 C. Amon (Matra) 77 laps—7 A. de Adamich (Surtees) 77 laps—8 H. Marko (BRM) 77 laps—9 W. Fittipaldi (Brabham) 77 laps—10 R. Stommelen (March) 77 laps—11 R. Peterson (March) 76 laps—12 G. Hill (Brabham) 76 laps—13 M. Beuttler (March) 76 laps—14 D. Walker (Lotus) 75 laps—15 D. Hulme (McLaren) 74 laps—16 N. Lauda (March) 74 laps—17 C. Pace (March) 72 laps—not classified F. Cevert (Tyrrell) 70 laps—fastest lap, Beltoise 1 min 40.0 sec 113.19 kph/70.35 mph—retired R. Wisell (BRM) engine lap 16—P. Gethin (BRM) accident lap 27—T. Sckenken (Surtees) accident lap 31—H. Ganley (BRM) suspension lap 47—M. Hailwood (Surtees) accident lap 48—C. Regazzoni (Ferrari) accident lap 51—H. Pescarolo (March) accident lap 58.

Starting grid 2-2-2

E. Fittipaldi 1 min 21.4 sec—Ickx 1 min 21.6 sec—Regazzoni 1 min 21.9 sec—Beltoise 1 min 22.5 sec—Gethin 1 min 22.6 sec—Amon 1 min 22.6 sec—Hulme 1 min 22.7 sec—Stewart 1 min 22.9 sec—Pescarolo 1 min 22.9 sec—Redman 1 min 23.1 sec—Hailwood 1 min 23.7 sec—Cevert 1 min 23.8 sec—Schenken 1 min 23.9 sec—Walker 1 min 24.0 sec—Peterson 1 min 24.1 sec—Wisell 1 min 24.4 sec—Marko 1 min 24.6 sec—de Adamich 1 min 24.7 sec—Hill 1 min 24.7 sec—Ganley 1 min 24.7 sec—W. Fittipaldi 1 min 25.2 sec—Lauda 1 min 25.6 sec—Beuttler 1 min 26.5 sec—Pace 1 min 26.6 sec—Stommelen 1 min 29.5 sec.

BELGIAN GRAND PRIX

Nivelles; 4 June; 85 laps 316 km/197 miles
1 E. Fittipaldi (Lotus) 1 hr 44 min 06.7 sec 182.38/113.35 mph—2 F. Cevert (Tyrrell) 1 hr 44 min 33.3 sec—3 D. Hulme (McLaren) 1 hr 45 min 04.8 sec—4 M. Hailwood (Surtees) 1 hr 45 min 18.7 sec—5 C. Pace (March) 84 laps—6 C. Amon (Matra) 84 laps—7 P. Revson (McLaren) 83 laps—8 H. Ganley (BRM) 83 laps—9 R. Peterson (March) 83 laps—10 H. Marko (BRM) 83 laps—11 R. Stommelen (March) 83 laps—12 N. Lauda (March) 82 laps—13 C. Reutemann (Brabham) 81 laps—14 D. Walker (Lotus) 79 laps—not classified H. Pescarolo (March) 59 laps—fastest lap, Amon 1 min 12.1 sec 185.65 kph/115.38 mph—retired T. Schenken (Surtees) engine lap 11—J-P Beltoise (BRM) engine lap 15—P. Gethin (BRM) engine lap 27—W. Fittipaldi (Brabham) gearbox lap 28—M. Beuttler (March) transmission lap 31—J. Ickx (Ferrari) fuel injection lap 47—'N. Galli' (Tecno) accident lap 54—A. de Adamich (Surtees) engine lap 55—C. Regazzoni (Ferrari) accident lap 57—G. Hill (Brabham) suspension lap 73.

Starting grid 3-2-3

E. Fittipaldi 1 min 11.4 sec—Regazzoni 1 min 11.6 sec—Hulme 1 min 11.8 sec—Ickx 1 min 11.8 sec—Cevert 1 min 11.9 sec—Beltoise 1 min 12.1 sec—Revson 1 min 12.2 sec—Hailwood 1 min 12.3 sec—Reutemann 1 min 12.5 sec—de Adamich 1 min 12.5 sec—Pace 1 min 12.6 sec—Walker 1 min 12.8 sec—Amon 1 min 12.8 sec—Peterson 1 min 13.0 sec—Ganley 1 min 13.0 sec—Hill 1 min 13.1 sec—Gethin 1 min 13.1 sec—W. Fittipaldi 1 min 13.2 sec—Pescarolo 1 min 13.4 sec—Stommelen 1 min 13.4 sec—Schenken 1 min 13.6 sec—Beuttler 1 min 13.7 sec—Marko 1 min 14.1 sec—'Galli' 1 min 14.6 sec—Lauda 1 min 16.5 sec—non starter V. Schuppan (BRM).

FRENCH GRAND PRIX

Clermont-Ferrand; 4 July; 38 laps 306 km/190 miles
1 J Y Stewart (Tyrrell) 1 hr 52 min 21.5 sec 163.41 kph/101.56 mph—2 E. Fittipaldi (Lotus) 1 hr 52 min 49.2 sec—3 C. Amon (Matra) 1 hr 52 min 53.4 sec—4 F. Cevert (Tyrrell) 1 hr 53 min 10.8 sec—5 R. Peterson (March) 1 hr 53 min 18.3 sec—6 M. Hailwood (Surtees) 1 hr 53 min 57.6 sec—7 D. Hulme (McLaren) 1 hr 54 min 09.6 sec—8 W. Fittipaldi (Brabham) 1 hr 54 min 46.6 sec—9 B. Redman (McLaren) 1 hr 55 min 17.0 sec—10 G. Hill (Brabham) 1 hr 55 min 21.0 sec—11 J. Ickx (Ferrari) 37 laps—12 C. Reutemann (Brabham) 37 laps—13 'N Galli' (Ferrari) 37 laps—14 A. de Adamich (Surtees) 37 laps—15 J-P Beltoise (BRM) 37 laps—16 R. Stommelen (March) 37 laps—17 T. Schenken (Surtees) 36 laps—18 D. Walker (Lotus) 34 laps—not classified P. Depailler (Tyrrell) 33 laps—fastest lap, Amon 2 min 53.9 sec 166.71 kph/103.61 mph—retired N. Lauda (March) drive shaft lap 4—H. Marko (BRM) accident lap 8—C. Pace (March) engine lap 18—R. Wisell (BRM) gear linkage lap 25—M. Beuttler (March) fuel lap 33.

Starting grid 2-2-2

Amon 2 min 53.4 sec—Hulme 2 min 54.2 sec—Stewart 2 min 55.0 sec—Ickx 2 min 55.1 sec—Schenken 2 min 57.2 sec—Marko 2 min 57.3 sec—Cevert 2 min 58.1 sec—E. Fittipaldi 2 min 58.1 sec—Peterson 2 min 58.2 sec—Hailwood 2 min 58.3 sec—Pace 2 min 58.6 sec—de Adamich 2 min 59.1 sec—Redman 2 min 59.4 sec—W. Fittipaldi 2 min 59.5 sec—Stommelen 2 min 59.6 sec—Depailler 2 min 59.6 sec—Reutemann 3 min 00.7

sec—Wisell 3 min 00.7 sec—'Galli' 3 min 00.7 sec—Hill 3 min 03.0 sec—Lauda 3 min 03.1 sec—Walker 3 min 04.7 sec—Beuttler 3 min 05.9 sec—Beltoise—non starters H. Pescarolo (March)—H. Ganley (BRM)—P. Gethin (BRM)—D. Bell (Tecno)—D. Charlton (Lotus).

BRITISH GRAND PRIX

Brands Hatch; 17 July; 76 laps 201 miles/324 km
1 E. Fittipaldi (Lotus) 1 hr 47 min 50.2 sec 112.06 mph/180.3 kph—2 J Y Stewart (Tyrrell) 1 hr 47 min 54.3 sec—3 P. Revson (McLaren) 1 hr 49 min 02.7 sec—4 C. Amon (Matra) 75 laps—5 D. Hulme (McLaren) 75 laps—6 A. Merzario (Ferrari) 75 laps—7 R. Peterson (March) 74 laps—8 C. Reutemann (Brabham) 73 laps—9 N. Lauda (March) 73 laps—10 R. Stommelen (March) 71 laps—11 J-P Beltoise (BRM) 70 laps—12 W. Fittipaldi (Brabham) 69 laps—13 M. Beuttler (March) 69 laps—fastest lap, Stewart 1 min 24.0 sec 113.57 mph/182.73 kph—retired A. de Adamich (Surtees) accident lap 3—P. Gethin (BRM) engine lap 5—H. Pescarolo (Williams) accident lap 7—'N. Galli' (Tecno) accident lap 9—D. Charlton (Lotus) gearbox lap 21—M. Hailwood (Surtees) gearbox lap 31—J. Oliver (BRM) suspension lap 36—C. Pace (March) final drive lap 39—G. Hill (Brabham) accident lap 47—J. Ickx (Ferrari) engine lap 49—D. Walker (Lotus) suspension lap 59—F. Cevert (Tyrrell) accident lap 60—T. Schenken (Surtees) suspension lap 64.

Starting grid 2-2-2

Ickx 1 min 22.2 sec—E. Fittipaldi 1 min 22.6 sec—Revson 1 min 22.7 sec—Stewart 1 min 22.9 sec—Schenken 1 min 23.2 sec—Beltoise 1 min 23.4 sec—Hailwood 1 min 23.5 sec—Peterson 1 min 23.7 sec—Merzario 1 min 23.7 sec—Reutemann 1 min 23.8 sec—Hulme 1 min 23.9 sec—Cevert 1 min 23.9 sec—Pace 1 min 24.0 sec—Oliver 1 min 24.4 sec—Walker 1 min 24.4 sec—Gethin 1 min 24.5 sec—Amon 1 min 24.6 sec—'Galli' 1 min 25.1 sec—Lauda 1 min 25.1 sec—de Adamich 1 min 25.2 sec—Hill 1 min 25.2 sec—W. Fittipaldi 1 min 25.5 sec—Beuttler 1 min 25.6 sec—Charlton 1 min 25.6 sec—Stommelen 1 min 26.3 sec—Pescarolo 1 min 27.4 sec—non starter F. Migault (Connew).

GERMAN GRAND PRIX

Nürburgring; 1 August; 14 laps 320 km/199 miles
1 J. Ickx (Ferrari) 1 hr 42 min 12.3 sec 187.66 kph/116.63 mph—2 C. Regazzoni (Ferrari) 1 hr 43 min 00.6 sec—3 R. Peterson (March) 1 hr 43 min 19.0 sec—4 H. Ganley (BRM) 1 hr 44 min 32.5 sec—5 B. Redman (McLaren) 1 hr 44 min 48.0 sec—6 G. Hill (Brabham) 1 hr 45 min 11.9 sec—7 W. Fittipaldi (Brabham) 1 hr 45 min 12.4 sec—8 M. Beuttler (March) 1 hr 47 min 23.0 sec—9 J-P Beltoise (BRM) 1 hr 47 min 32.5 sec—10 F. Cevert (Tyrrell) 1 hr 47 min 56.0 sec—11 J Y Stewart (Tyrrell) 13 laps—12 A. Merzario (Ferrari) 13 laps—13 A. de Adamich (Surtees) 13 laps—14 T. Schenken (Surtees) 13 laps—15 C. Amon (Matra) 13 laps—not classified C. Pace (March) 11 laps—fastest lap, Ickx 7 min 13.6 sec 189.56 kph/117.81 mph—retired R. Wisell (BRM) engine lap 3—D. Charlton (Lotus) ill lap 4—N. Lauda (March) oil tank lap 4—D. Bell (Tecno) engine lap 4—D. Walker (Lotus) oil tank lap 6—R. Stommelen (March) electrical lap 6—C. Reutemann (Brabham) transmission lap 6—M. Hailwood (Surtees) suspension lap 8—D. Hulme (McLaren) engine lap 8—E. Fittipaldi (Lotus) gearbox fire lap 10—H. Pescarolo (March) accident lap 10.

Starting grid 2-2-2

Ickx 7 min 07.0 sec—Stewart 7 min 08.7 sec—E. Fittipaldi 7 min 09.9 sec—Peterson 7 min 11.6 sec—Cevert 7 min 12.2 sec—Reutemann 7 min 12.4 sec—Regazzoni 7 min 13.4 sec—Amon 7 min 13.9 sec—Pescarolo 7 min 14.4 sec—Hulme 7 min 14.5 sec—Pace 7 min 16.6 sec—Schenken 7 min 17.2 sec—Beltoise 7 min 17.3 sec—Stommelen 7 min 17.5 sec—Hill 7 min 18.4 sec—Hailwood 7 min 21.0 sec—Wisell 7 min 21.4 sec—Ganley 7 min 22.3 sec—Redman 7 min 23.2 sec—de Adamich 7 min 23.7 sec—W. Fittipaldi 7 min 24.8 sec—Merzario 7 min 25.9 sec—Walker 7 min 29.5 sec—Lauda 7 min 32.2 sec—Bell 7 min 33.3 sec—Charlton 7 min 34.1 sec—Beuttler 7 min 35.9 sec.

AUSTRIAN GRAND PRIX

Österreichring; 13 August; 54 laps 319 km/198 miles
1 E. Fittipaldi (Lotus) 1 hr 29 min 16.7 sec 214.51 kph/133.32 mph—2 D. Hulme (McLaren) 1 hr 29 min 17.8 sec—3 P. Revson (McLaren) 1 hr 29 min 53.2 sec—4 M. Hailwood (Surtees) 1 hr 30 min 01.4 sec—5 C. Amon (Matra) 1 hr 30 min 02.3 sec—6 H. Ganley (BRM) 1 hr 30 min 17.8 sec—7 J Y Stewart (Tyrrell) 1 hr 30 min 25.7 sec—8 J-P Beltoise (BRM) 1 hr 30 min 38.1 sec—9 F. Cevert (Tyrrell) 53 laps—10 N. Lauda (March) 53 laps—11 T. Schenken (Surtees) 52 laps—12 R. Peterson (March) 52 laps—13 P. Gethin (BRM) 51 laps—not classified A. de Adamich (Surtees) 51 laps—R. Stommelen (March) 48 laps—C. Pace (March) 46 laps—'N Galli' (Tecno) 45 laps—fastest lap, Hulme 1 min 38.3 sec 216.41 kph/134.5 mph—retired D. Walker (Lotus) con-rod lap 6—C. Regazzoni (Ferrari) fuel vaporisation lap 13—C. Reutemann (Brabham) fuel system lap 14—J. Ickx (Ferrari) fuel vaporisation lap 20—F. Migault (Connew) suspension lap 22—M. Beuttler (March) fuel system lap 24—W. Fittipaldi (Brabham) brakes lap 31—G. Hill (Brabham) fuel system lap 36.

Starting grid 2-2-2

E. Fittipaldi 1 min 36.0 sec—Regazzoni 1 min 36.0 sec—Stewart 1 min 36.3 sec—Revson 1 min 36.6 sec—Reutemann 1 min 37.1 sec—Amon 1 min 37.2 sec—Hulme 1 min 37.2 sec—Schenken 1 min 37.2 sec—Ickx 1 min 37.3 sec—Ganley 1 min 37.5 sec—Peterson 1 min 37.6 sec—Hailwood 1 min 37.8 sec—de Adamich 1 min 38.1 sec—Hill 1 min 38.1 sec—W. Fittipaldi 1 min 38.3 sec—Gethin 1 min 38.5 sec—Stommelen 1 min 38.6 sec—Pace 1 min 38.6 sec—Walker 1 min 38.8 sec—Cevert 1 min 38.8 sec—Beltoise 1 min 38.9 sec—Lauda 1 min 39.0 sec—'Galli' 1 min 39.1 sec—Beuttler 1 min 39.9 sec—Migault 1 min 43.9 sec—non starter H. Pescarolo (March).

ITALIAN GRAND PRIX

Monza; 10 September; 55 laps 316 km/196 miles
1 E. Fittipaldi (Lotus) 1 hr 29 min 58.4 sec 340.72 kph/131.61 mph—2 M. Hailwood (Surtees) 1 hr 30 min 12.9 sec—3 D. Hulme (McLaren) 1 hr 30 min 22.2 sec—4 P. Revson (McLaren) 1 hr 30 min 34.1 sec—5 G. Hill (Brabham) 1 hr 31 min 04.0 sec—6 P. Gethin (BRM) 1 hr 31 min 20.3 sec—7 M. Andretti (Ferrari) 54 laps—8 J-P Beltoise (BRM) 54 laps—9 R. Peterson (March) 54 laps—10 M. Beuttler (March) 54 laps—11 H. Ganley (BRM) 52 laps—12 R. Wisell (BRM) 51 laps—13 N. Lauda (March) 50 laps—fastest lap, Ickx 1 min 36.3 sec 215.83 kph/134.14 mph—retired J Y Stewart (Tyrrell) clutch 0 laps—'N Galli' (Tecno) engine lap 6—F. Cevert (Tyrrell) engine lap 14—C. Reutemann (Brabham) accident lap 14—C. Pace (March) accident lap 15—C. Regazzoni (Ferrari) accident lap 16—J. Surtees (Surtees) fuel vaporisation lap 20—W. Fittipaldi (Brabham) suspension lap 20—T. Schenken (Surtees) accident lap 20—A. de Adamich (Surtees) brakes lap 33—C. Amon (Matra) brakes lap 38—J. Ickx (Ferrari) electrics lap 46.

Starting grid 2-2-2

Ickx 1 min 35.6 sec—Amon 1 min 35.7 sec—Stewart 1 min 35.8 sec—Regazzoni 1 min 35.8 sec—Hulme 1 min 36.0 sec—E. Fittipaldi 1 min 36.3 sec—Andretti 1 min 36.3 sec—Revson 1 min 36.4 sec—Hailwood 1 min 36.5 sec—Wisell 1 min 36.7 sec—Reutemann 1 min 37.1 sec—Gethin 1 min 37.2 sec—Hill 1 min 37.6 sec—Cevert 1 min 37.8 sec—W. Fittipaldi 1 min 37.8 sec—Beltoise 1 min 37.9 sec—Ganley 1 min 37.9 sec—Pace 1 min 38.0 sec—Surtees 1 min 38.3 sec—Lauda 1 min 38.5 sec—de Adamich 1 min 38.6 sec—Schenken 1 min 38.6 sec—'Galli' 1 min 38.6 sec—Peterson 1 min 38.7 sec—Beuttler 1 min 39.7 sec—non starters H. Pescarolo (March)—D. Bell (Tecno).

CANADIAN GRAND PRIX

Mosport; 24 September; 80 laps 197 miles/316 km
1 J Y Stewart (Tyrrell) 1 hr 43 min 16.9 sec 114.28 mph/183.88 kph—2 P. Revson (McLaren) 1 hr 44 min 05.1 sec—3 D.

CANADIAN GRAND PRIX—*continued*

Hulme (McLaren) 1 hr 44 min 11.5 sec—4 C. Reutemann (Brabham) 1 hr 44 min 17.6 sec—5 C. Regazzoni (Ferrari) 1 hr 44 min 23.8 sec—6 C. Amon (Matra) 79 laps—7 T. Schenken (Surtees) 79 laps—8 G. Hill (Brabham) 79 laps—9 C. Pace (March) 78 laps—10 H. Ganley (BRM) 78 laps—11 E. Fittipaldi (Lotus) 78 laps—12 J. Ickx (Ferrari) 76 laps—13 H. Pescarolo (March) 73 laps—not classified M. Beuttler (March) 59 laps—S. Barber (March) 24 laps—fastest lap, Stewart 1 min 15.7 sec 117.57 mph/189.17 kph—retired N. Lauda (March) disqualified 0 laps—A. de Adamich (Surtees) gearbox lap 2—W. Fittipaldi (Brabham) gearbox lap 5—B. Brack (BRM) accident lap 20—J-P Beltoise (BRM) oil cooler lap 21—P. Gethin (BRM) suspension lap 25—F. Cevert (Tyrrell) gearbox lap 51—R. Peterson (March) disqualified lap 54—R. Wisell (Lotus) engine lap 65.

Starting grid 3-2-3

Revson 1 min 13.6 sec—Hulme 1 min 13.9 sec—Peterson 1 min 14.0 sec—E. Fittipaldi 1 min 14.4 sec—Stewart 1 min 14.4 sec—Cevert 1 min 14.5 sec—Regazzoni 1 min 14.5 sec—Ickx 1 min 14.7 sec—Reutemann 1 min 14.9 sec—Amon 1 min 15.4 sec—W. Fittipaldi 1 min 15.6 sec—Gethin 1 min 15.7 sec—Schenken 1 min 15.7 sec—Ganley 1 min 15.7 sec—de Adamich 1 min 15.9 sec—Wisell 1 min 16.0 sec—Hill 1 min 16.2 sec—Pace 1 min 16.4 sec—Lauda 1 min 16.8 sec—Beltoise 1 min 16.8 sec—Pescarolo 1 min 17.0 sec—Barber 1 min 17.1 sec—Brack 1 min 17.9 sec—Beuttler 1 min 18.4 sec—non starter D. Bell (Tecno).

UNITED STATES GRAND PRIX

Watkins Glen; 8 October; 59 laps 199 miles/321 km
1 J Y Stewart (Tyrrell) 1 hr 41 min 45.3 sec 117.48 mph/189.03 kph—2 F. Cevert (Tyrrell) 1 hr 42 min 17.6 sec—3 D. Hulme (McLaren) 1 hr 42 min 22.9 sec—4 R. Peterson (March) 1 hr 43 min 07.9 sec—5 J. Ickx (Ferrari) 1 hr 43 min 08.5 sec—6 M. Andretti (Ferrari) 58 laps—7 P. Depailler (Tyrrell) 58 laps—8 C. Regazzoni (Ferrari) 58 laps—9 J. Scheckter (McLaren) 58 laps—10 R. Wisell (Lotus) 57 laps—11 G. Hill (Brabham) 57 laps—12 S. Posey (Surtees) 57 laps—13 M. Beuttler (March) 57 laps—14 H. Pescarolo (March) 57 laps—15 C. Amon (Matra) 57 laps—16 S. Barber (March) 57 laps—17 M. Hailwood (Surtees) 56 laps—18 P. Revson (McLaren) 54 laps—not classified N. Lauda (March) 49 laps—fastest lap, Stewart 1 min 41.6 sec 119.61 mph/192.45 kph—retired D. Bell (Tecno) engine lap 8—E. Fittipaldi (Lotus) tyres lap 17—T. Schenken (Surtees) suspension lap 22—A. de Adamich (Surtees) accident lap 25—C. Reutemann (Brabham) engine lap 31—B. Redman (BRM) engine lap 34—J-P Beltoise (BRM) ignition lap 40—W. Fittipaldi (Brabham) engine lap 43—H. Ganley (BRM) engine lap 44—D. Walker (Lotus) engine lap 44—P. Gethin (BRM) engine lap 47—C. Pace (March) fuel injection lap 48.

Starting grid 3-2-3

Stewart 1 min 40.5 sec—Revson 1 min 40.5 sec—Hulme 1 min 41.1 sec—Cevert 1 min 41.4 sec—Reutemann 1 min 41.7 sec—Regazzoni 1 min 41.9 sec—Scheckter 1 min 42.1 sec—E. Fittipaldi 1 min 42.4 sec—Andretti 1 min 42.5 sec—Depailler 1 min 42.5 sec—Ickx 1 min 42.6 sec—W. Fittipaldi 1 min 42.8 sec—Hailwood 1 min 43.2 sec—Pace 1 min 43.3 sec—Wisell 1 min 43.5 sec—Ganley 1 min 44.1 sec—Beltoise 1 min 44.2 sec—de Adamich 1 min 44.3 sec—Barber 1 min 44.3 sec—Beuttler 1 min 44.4 sec—Pescarolo 1 min 44.4 sec—Posey 1 min 44.5 sec—Redman 1 min 44.9 sec—Lauda 1 min 45.3 sec—Peterson 1 min 46.1 sec—Hill 1 min 46.3 sec—Gethin 1 min 46.6 sec—Bell 1 min 47.0 sec—Walker 1 min 50.6 sec—Schenken 1 min 57.7 sec—Amon 1 min 42.0 sec.

1972 WORLD CHAMPIONSHIP

1 E. Fittipaldi 61—2 J Y Stewart 45—3 D. Hulme 39—4 J. Ickx 27—5 P. Revson 23—6 F. Cevert 15—7 C. Regazzoni 15—8 M. Hailwood 13—9 R. Peterson 12—10 C. Amon 12—11 J-P Beltoise 9—12 M. Andretti 4—12= H. Ganley 4—14 B. Redman 4—15 G. Hill 4—16 A. de Adamich 3—16= C. Reutemann 3—18 C. Pace 3—19 T. Schenken 2—20 A. Merzario 1—20= P. Gethin 1.

1973

ARGENTINE GRAND PRIX

Buenos Aires; 28 January; 96 laps; 321 km/200 miles
1 E. Fittipaldi (Lotus) 1 hr 56 min 18.2 sec 165.65 kph/102.95 mph—2 F. Cevert (Tyrrell) 1 hr 56 min 22.9 sec—3 J Y Stewart (Tyrrell) 1 hr 56 min 51.4 sec—4 J. Ickx (Ferrari) 1 hr 57 min 00.8 sec—5 D. Hulme (McLaren) 95 laps—6 W. Fittipaldi (Brabham) 95 laps—7 C. Regazzoni (BRM) 93 laps—8 P. Revson (McLaren) 92 laps—9 A. Merzario (Ferrari) 92 laps—10 M. Beuttler (March) 90 laps—not classified H. Ganley (Williams) 79 laps—fastest lap, E. Fittipaldi 1 min 11.2 sec 169.07 mph/105.08 mph—retired 'N Galli' (Williams) fuel system 0 laps—M. Hailwood (Surtees) drive shaft lap 10—C. Pace (Surtees) suspension lap 10—C. Reutemann (Brabham) gearbox lap 16—N. Lauda (BRM) engine lap 66—R. Peterson (Lotus) engine lap 67—J-P Beltoise (BRM) engine lap 79—J-P Jarier (March) gear linkage lap 84.

Starting grid 2-2-2

Regazzoni 1 min 10.5 sec—E. Fittipaldi 1 min 10.8 sec—Ickx 1 min 11.0 sec—Stewart 1 min 11.0 sec—Peterson 1 min 11.1 sec—Cevert 1 min 11.5 sec—Beltoise 1 min 11.5 sec—Hulme 1 min 11.7 sec—Reutemann 1 min 12.1 sec—Hailwood 1 min 12.1 sec—Revson 1 min 12.2 sec—W. Fittipaldi 1 min 12.3 sec—Lauda 1 min 12.4 sec—Merzario 1 min 12.5 sec—Pace 1 min 12.8 sec—'Galli' 1 min 14.0 sec—Jarier 1 min 14.3 sec—Beuttler 1 min 15.1 sec—Ganley 1 min 15.3 sec.

BRAZILIAN GRAND PRIX

Interlagos; 11 February; 40 laps 318 km/198 miles
1 E. Fittipaldi (Lotus) 1 hr 43 min 55.6 sec 183.78 kph/114.22 mph—2 J Y Stewart (Tyrrell) 1 hr 44 min 09.1 sec—3 D. Hulme (McLaren) 1 hr 45 min 42.0 sec—4 A. Merzario (Ferrari) 39 laps—5 J. Ickx (Ferrari) 39 laps—6 C. Regazzoni (BRM) 39 laps—7 H. Ganley (Williams) 39 laps—8 N. Lauda (BRM) 38 laps—9 'N. Galli' (Williams) 38 laps—10 F. Cevert (Tyrrell) 38 laps—11 C. Reutemann (Brabham) 38 laps—12 L. Bueno (Surtees) 36 laps—fastest lap, Fittipaldi, Hulme 2 min 35.0 sec 184.84 kph/114.88 mph—retired P. Revson (McLaren) gearbox lap 3—W. Fittipaldi (Brabham) engine lap 5—R. Peterson (Lotus) rear wheel lap 5—J-P Jarier (March) gearbox lap 6—M. Hailwood (Surtees) gearbox lap 6—C. Pace (Surtees) suspension lap 9—M. Beuttler (March) overheating lap 18—J-P Beltoise (BRM) electrics lap 23.

Starting grid 3-2-3

Peterson 2 min 30.5 sec—E. Fittipaldi 2 min 30.7 sec—Ickx 2 min 32.0 sec—Regazzoni 2 min 32.4 sec—Hulme 2 min 32.7 sec—Pace 2 min 32.7 sec—Reutemann 2 min 32.9 sec—Stewart 2 min 33.3 sec—Cevert 2 min 33.4 sec—Beltoise 2 min 33.5 sec—W. Fittipaldi 2 min 34.3 sec—Revson 2 min 34.3 sec—Lauda 2 min 35.1 sec—Hailwood 2 min 35.5 sec—Jarier 2 min 37.6 sec—Ganley 2 min 37.6 sec—Merzario 2 min 37.7 sec—'Galli' 2 min 38.7 sec—Beuttler 2 min 39.9 sec—Bueno 2 min 42.5 sec.

SOUTH AFRICAN GRAND PRIX

Kyalami; 3 March; 79 laps 201 miles/324 km
1 J Y Stewart (Tyrrell) 1 hr 43 min 11.1 sec 117.14 mph/188.48 kph—2 P. Revson (McLaren) 1 hr 43 min 35.6 sec—3 E. Fittipaldi (Lotus) 1 hr 43 min 36.1 sec—4 A. Merzario (Ferrari) 78 laps—5 D. Hulme (McLaren) 77 laps—6 G. Follmer (Shadow) 77 laps—7 C. Reutemann (Brabham) 77 laps—8 A. de Adamich (Surtees) 77 laps—9 J. Scheckter (McLaren) 75 laps—10 H. Ganley (Williams) 73 laps—11 R.

Peterson (Lotus) 73 laps—not classified E. Keizan (Tyrrell) 67 laps—J-P Jarier (March) 66 laps—F. Cevert (Tyrrell) 66 laps—M. Beuttler (March) 65 laps—fastest lap, E. Fittipaldi 1 min 17.1 sec 119.07 mph/191.58 kph—retired M. Hailwood (Surtees) accident lap 2—J. Ickx (Ferrari) accident lap 2—C. Regazzoni (BRM) accident lap 2—D. Charlton (Lotus) accident lap 3—J-P Beltoise (BRM) clutch lap 4—J. Oliver (Shadow) engine lap 14—N. Lauda (BRM) engine lap 26—J. Pretorius (Williams) overheating lap 35—W. Fittipaldi (Brabham) gear selectors lap 52—C. Pace (Surtees) accident lap 69.

Starting grid 3-2-3

Hulme 1 min 16.3 sec—E. Fittipaldi 1 min 16.4 sec—Scheckter 1 min 16.4 sec—Peterson 1 min 16.4 sec—Regazzoni 1 min 16.5 sec—Revson 1 min 16.7 sec—Beltoise 1 min 16.8 sec—Reutemann 1 min 16.9 sec—Pace 1 min 17.1 sec—Lauda 1 min 17.1 sec—Ickx 1 min 17.2 sec—Hailwood 1 min 17.2 sec—Charlton 1 min 17.2 sec—Oliver 1 min 17.6 sec—Merzario 1 min 17.6 sec—Stewart 1 min 17.6 sec—W. Fittipaldi 1 min 17.9 sec—Jarier 1 min 18.0 sec—Ganley 1 min 18.1 sec—de Adamich 1 min 18.7 sec—Follmer 1 min 18.8 sec—Keizan 1 min 18.9 sec—Beuttler 1 min 20.4 sec—Pretorius 1 min 20.5 sec—Cevert.

SPANISH GRAND PRIX

Montjuich; 29 April; 75 laps 284 km/177 miles
1 E. Fittipaldi (Lotus) 1 hr 48 min 18.7 sec 157.46 kph/97.86 mph—2 F. Cevert (Tyrrell) 1 hr 49 min 01.4 sec—3 G. Follmer (Shadow) 1 hr 49 min 31.8 sec—4 P. Revson (McLaren) 74 laps—5 J-P Beltoise (BRM) 74 laps—6 D. Hulme (McLaren) 74 laps—7 M. Beuttler (March) 74 laps—8 H. Pescarolo (March) 73 laps—9 C. Regazzoni (BRM) 69 laps—10 W. Fittipaldi (Brabham) 69 laps—11 'N. Galli' (Williams) 69 laps—12 J. Ickx (Ferrari) 69 laps—fastest lap, Peterson 1 min 23.8 sec 162.8 kph/101.18 mph—retired C. Pace (Surtees) drive shaft lap 13—A. de Adamich (Brabham) accident lap 17—Oliver (Shadow) engine lap 23—M. Hailwood (Surtees) oil pipe lap 25—G. Hill (Shadow) brakes lap 27—N. Lauda (BRM) tyres lap 28—J Y Stewart (Tyrrell) brakes lap 47—R. Peterson (Lotus) gearbox lap 56—H. Ganley (Williams) fuel lap 63—C. Reutemann (Brabham) drive shaft lap 66.

Starting grid 2-3-2

Peterson 1 min 21.8 sec—Hulme 1 min 22.5 sec—Cevert 1 min 22.7 sec—Stewart 1 min 23.2 sec—Revson 1 min 23.4 sec—Ickx 1 min 23.5 sec—E. Fittipaldi 1 min 23.7 sec—Regazzoni 1 min 23.7 sec—Hailwood 1 min 24.2 sec—Beltoise 1 min 24.2 sec—Lauda 1 min 24.4 sec—W. Fittipaldi 1 min 24.5 sec—Oliver 1 min 24.6 sec—Follmer 1 min 24.7 sec—Reutemann 1 min 24.7 sec—Pace 1 min 25.0 sec—de Adamich 1 min 25.2 sec—Pescarolo 1 min 26.1 sec—Beuttler 1 min 26.2 sec—'Galli' 1 min 26.3 sec—Ganley 1 min 26.5 sec—Hill 1 min 30.3 sec.

BELGIAN GRAND PRIX

Zolder; 20 May; 70 laps 295 km/184 miles
1 J Y Stewart (Tyrrell) 1 hr 42 min 13.4 sec 173.35 kph/107.74 mph—2 F. Cevert (Tyrrell) 1 hr 42 min 45.3 sec—3 E. Fittipaldi (Lotus) 1 hr 44 min 16.2 sec—4 A. de Adamich (Brabham) 69 laps—5 N. Lauda (BRM) 69 laps—6 C. Amon (Tecno) 67 laps—7 D. Hulme (McLaren) 67 laps—8 C. Pace (Surtees) 66 laps—9 G. Hill (Shadow) 65 laps—10 C. Regazzoni (BRM) 63 laps—11 M. Beuttler (March) 63 laps—fastest lap, Cevert 1 min 25.4 sec 177.81 kph/110.51 mph—retired M. Hailwood (Surtees) accident lap 4—'N. Galli' (Williams) engine lap 6—J. Ickx (Ferrari) engine lap 6—J. Oliver (Shadow) accident lap 11—G. Follmer (Shadow) throttle slides lap 13—C. Reutemann (Brabham) oil leak lap 14—H. Ganley (Williams) accident lap 16—P. Revson (McLaren) accident lap 33—R. Peterson (Lotus) accident lap 42—W. Fittipaldi (Brabham) engine lap 46—J-P Beltoise (BRM) engine lap 56—J-P Jarier (March) accident lap 60.

Starting grid 2-2-2

Peterson 1 min 22.5 sec—Hulme 1 min 23.0 sec—Ickx 1 min 23.1 sec—Cevert 1 min 23.2 sec—Beltoise 1 min 23.2 sec—Stewart 1 min 23.3 sec—Reutemann 1 min 23.3 sec—Pace 1 min 23.3 sec—E. Fittipaldi 1 min 23.4 sec—Revson 1 min 23.5 sec—Follmer 1 min 23.9 sec—Regazzoni 1 min 23.9 sec—Hailwood 1 min 24.0 sec—Lauda 1 min 24.5 sec—Amon 1 min 24.8 sec—Jarier 1 min 24.8 sec—'Galli' 1 min 24.9 sec—de Adamich 1 min 25.3 sec—W. Fittipaldi 1 min 25.6 sec—Beuttler 1 min 25.8 sec—Ganley 1 min 26.7 sec—Oliver 1 min 28.1 sec—Hill 1 min 30.4 sec.

MONACO GRAND PRIX

Monte Carlo; 3 June; 78 laps 256 km/159 miles
1 J Y Stewart (Tyrrell) 1 hr 57 min 44.3 sec 130.26 kph/80.96 mph—2 E. Fittipaldi (Lotus) 1 hr 57 min 45.6 sec—3 R. Peterson (Lotus) 77 laps—4 F. Cevert (Tyrrell) 77 laps—5 P. Revson (McLaren) 76 laps—6 D. Hulme (McLaren) 76 laps—7 A. de Adamich (Brabham) 75 laps—8 M. Hailwood (Surtees) 75 laps—9 J. Hunt (March) 73 laps—10 J. Oliver (Shadow) 72 laps—11 W. Fittipaldi (Brabham) 71 laps—fastest lap, Fittipaldi 1 min 28.1 sec 133.92 kph/83.23 mph—retired M. Beuttler (March) engine lap 3—C. Regazzoni (BRM) brakes lap 15—C. Amon (Tecno) overheating lap 22—N. Lauda (BRM) gearbox lap 24—'N. Galli' (Williams) drive shaft lap 30—C. Pace (Surtees) drive shaft lap 31—D. Purley (March) air intake lap 31—J-P Beltoise (BRM) accident lap 39—H. Ganley (Williams) drive shaft lap 41—J. Ickx (Ferrari) drive shaft lap 44—C. Reutemann (Brabham) gearbox lap 46—A. Merzario (Ferrari) oil pressure lap 58—G. Hill (Shadow) suspension lap 62—J-P Jarier (March) gearbox lap 67.

Starting grid 2-2-2

Stewart 1 min 27.5 sec—Peterson 1 min 27.7 sec—Hulme 1 min 27.8 sec—Cevert 1 min 27.9 sec—E. Fittipaldi 1 min 28.1 sec—Lauda 1 min 28.5 sec—Ickx 1 min 28.7 sec—Regazzoni 1 min 28.9 sec—W. Fittipaldi 1 min 28.9 sec—Ganley 1 min 29.0 sec—Beltoise 1 min 29.0 sec—Amon 1 min 29.3 sec—Hailwood 1 min 29.4 sec—Jarier 1 min 29.4 sec—Revson 1 min 29.4 sec—Merzario 1 min 29.5 sec—Pace 1 min 29.6 sec—Hunt 1 min 29.9 sec—Reutemann 1 min 30.1 sec—Beuttler 1 min 31.0 sec—'Galli' 1 min 31.1 sec—Oliver 1 min 31.2 sec—Purley 1 min 31.9 sec—Hill 1 min 31.9 sec—de Adamich 1 min 32.1 sec—non starter G. Follmer (Shadow).

SWEDISH GRAND PRIX

Anderstorp; 17 June; 80 laps 321 km/200 miles
1 D. Hulme (McLaren) 1 hr 56 min 46.0 sec 165.13 kph/102.63 mph—2 R. Peterson (Lotus) 1 hr 56 min 50.1 sec—3 F. Cevert (Tyrrell) 1 hr 57 min 00.7 sec—4 C. Reutemann (Brabham) 1 hr 57 min 04.1 sec—5 J Y Stewart (Tyrrell) 1 hr 57 min 12.0 sec—6 J. Ickx (Ferrari) 79 laps—7 P. Revson (McLaren) 79 laps—8 M. Beuttler (March) 78 laps—7 P. Revson (McLaren) 79 laps—8 M. Beuttler (March) 78 laps—9 C. Regazzoni (BRM) 77 laps—10 C. Pace (Surtees) 77 laps—11 H. Ganley (Williams) 77 laps—12 E. Fittipaldi (Lotus) 76 laps—13 N. Lauda (BRM) 75 laps—14 G. Follmer (Shadow) 74 laps—fastest lap, Hulme 1 min 26.1 sec 167.87 kph/104.33 mph—retired W. Fittipaldi (Brabham) accident 0 laps—G. Hill (Shadow) ignition lap 16—J-P Jarier (March) throttle lap 38—M. Hailwood (Surtees) tyres lap 41—J. Oliver (Shadow) suspension lap 50—J-P Beltoise (BRM) engine lap 57.

Starting grid 2-3-2

Peterson 1 min 23.8 sec—Cevert 1 min 23.9 sec—Stewart 1 min 23.9 sec—E. Fittipaldi 1 min 24.1 sec—Reutemann 1 min 24.5 sec—Hulme 1 min 24.6 sec—Revson 1 min 24.9 sec—Ickx 1 min 25.6 sec—Beltoise 1 min 25.7 sec—Hailwood 1 min 25.8 sec—Ganley 1 min 25.8 sec—Regazzoni 1 min 26.0 sec—W. Fittipaldi 1 min 26.1 sec—Lauda 1 min 26.2 sec—Pace 1 min 26.2 sec—Oliver 1 min 26.3 sec—Hill 1 min 26.4 sec—Follmer 1 min 26.6 sec—Jarier 1 min 26.9 sec—Beuttler 1 min 25.6 sec—non starters R. Wisell (March)—T. Belso (Williams).

FRENCH GRAND PRIX

Paul Ricard; 1 July; 54 laps 314 km/195 miles
1 R. Peterson (Lotus) 1 hr 41 min 36.5 sec 185.23 kph/115.12 mph—2 F. Cevert (Tyrrell) 1 hr 42 min 17.4 sec—3 C. Reutemann (Brabham) 1 hr 42 min 23.0 sec—4 J Y Stewart (Tyrrell) 1 hr 42 min 23.4 sec—5 J. Ickx (Ferrari) 1 hr 42 min 25.4 sec—6 J. Hunt (March) 1 hr 42 min 59.1 sec—7 A. Merzario (Ferrari) 1 hr 43 min 05.7 sec—8 D. Hulme (McLaren) 1 hr 43 min 06.0 sec—9 N. Lauda (BRM) 1 hr 43 min 22.3 sec—10 G. Hill (Shadow) 53 laps—11 J-P Beltoise (BRM) 53 laps—12 C. Regazzoni (BRM) 53 laps—13 C. Pace (Surtees) 51 laps—14 H. Ganley (Williams) 51 laps—15 R. von Opel (Ensign) 51 laps—16 W. Fittipaldi (Brabham) 50 laps—fastest lap, Hulme 1 min 51.0 sec 188.41 kph/117.1 mph—retired J. Oliver (Shadow) clutch 0 laps—J-P Jarier (March) drive shaft lap 7—H. Pescarolo (Williams) overheating lap 16—G. Follmer (Shadow) vapour lock lap 16—R. Wisell (March) engine lap 20—A. de Adamich (Brabham) drive shaft lap 28—M. Hailwood (Surtees) engine lap 30—E. Fittipaldi (Lotus) accident lap 41—J. Scheckter (McLaren) accident lap 43.

Starting grid 3-2-3

Stewart 1 min 48.4 sec—Scheckter 1 min 49.2 sec—E. Fittipaldi 1 min 49.4 sec—Cevert 1 min 49.4 sec—Peterson 1 min 49.4 sec—Hulme 1 min 49.7 sec—Jarier 1 min 50.7 sec—Reutemann 1 min 50.7 sec—Regazzoni 1 min 51.0 sec—Merzario 1 min 51.2 sec—Hailwood 1 min 51.2 sec—Icks 1 min 51.4 sec—de Adamich 1 min 51.5 sec—Hunt 1 min 51.6 sec—Beltoise 1 min 51.7 sec—Hill 1 min 51.7 sec—Lauda 1 min 51.8 sec—Pace 1 min 51.9 sec—W. Fittipaldi 1 min 52.1 sec—Follmer 1 min 52.3 sec—Oliver 1 min 52.9 sec—Wisell 1 min 53.2 sec—Pescarolo 1 min 53.6 sec—Ganley 1 min 53.9 sec—von Opel 1 min 55.5 sec.

BRITISH GRAND PRIX

Silverstone; 14 July; 67 laps 196 miles/315 km
1 P. Revson (McLaren) 1 hr 29 min 18.5 sec 131.75 mph/211.98 kph—2 R. Peterson (Lotus) 1 hr 29 min 21.3 sec—3 D. Hulme (McLaren) 1 hr 29 min 21.5 sec—4 J. Hunt (March) 1 hr 29 min 21.9 sec—5 F. Cevert (Tyrrell) 1 hr 29 min 55.1 sec—6 C. Reutemann (Brabham) 1 hr 30 min 03.2 sec—7 C. Regazzoni (BRM) 1 hr 30 min 30.2 sec—8 J. Ickx (Ferrari) 1 hr 30 min 35.9 sec—9 H. Ganley (Williams) 66 laps—10 J Y Stewart (Tyrrell) 66 laps—11 M. Beuttler (March) 65 laps—12 N. Lauda (BRM) 63 laps—13 R. von Opel (Ensign) 61 laps—fastest lap, Hunt 1 min 18.6 sec 134.06 mph/215.7 kph—retired J. Oliver (Shadow) accident 0 laps—J. Scheckter (McLaren) accident lap 1—A. de Adamich (Brabham) accident lap 1—R. Williamson (March) accident lap 1—G. Follmer (Shadow) accident lap 1—J-P Beltoise (BRM) accident lap 1—M. Hailwood (Surtees) accident lap 1—C. Pace (Surtees) accident lap 1—J. Mass (Surtees) accident lap 1—(after restart) G. McRae (Williams) throttle slide 0 laps—C. Amon (Tecno) fuel pressure lap 6—G. Hill (Shadow) sub-frame lap 24—J. Watson (Brabham) fuel system lap 36—E. Fittipaldi (Lotus) transmission lap 36—W. Fittipaldi (Brabham) oil pipe lap 44.

Starting grid 3-2-3

Peterson 1 min 16.3 sec—Hulme 1 min 16.5 sec—Revson 1 min 16.5 sec—Stewart 1 min 16.7 sec—E. Fittipaldi 1 min 16.7 sec—Scheckter 1 min 16.9 sec—Cevert 1 min 17.3 sec—Reutemann 1 min 17.4 sec—Lauda 1 min 17.4 sec—Regazzoni 1 min 17.5 sec—Hunt 1 min 17.6 sec—Hailwood 1 min 18.0 sec—W. Fittipaldi 1 min 18.1 sec—Mass 1 min 18.3 sec—Pace 1 min 18.3 sec—Beltoise 1 min 18.4 sec—Ganley 1 min 18.6 sec—Ickx 1 min 18.9 sec—de Adamich 1 min 19.1 sec—von Opel 1 min 19.2 sec—Williamson 1 min 19.5 sec—Watson 1 min 20.1 sec—Beuttler 1 min 20.1 sec—Follmer 1 min 20.3 sec—Oliver 1 min 20.3 sec—Hill 1 min 20.5 sec—McRae 1 min 20.8 sec—Amon 1 min 21.0 sec—non starter D. Purley (March).

DUTCH GRAND PRIX

Zandvoort; 29 July; 72 laps 304 km/189 miles
1 J Y Stewart (Tyrrell) 1 hr 39 min 12.4 sec 183.99 kph/114.35 mph—2 F. Cevert (Tyrrell) 1 hr 39 min 28.3 sec—3 J. Hunt (March) 1 hr 40 min 15.5 sec—4 P. Revson (McLaren) 1 hr 40 min 21.6 sec—5 J-P Beltoise (BRM) 1 hr 40 min 25.8 sec—6 G. van Lennep (Williams) 70 laps—7 C. Pace (Surtees) 69 laps—8 C. Regazzoni (BRM) 68 laps—9 H. Ganley (Williams) 68 laps—10 G. Follmer (Shadow) 67 laps—11 R. Peterson (Lotus) 66 laps—not classified G. Hill (Shadow) 56 laps—fastest lap, Peterson 1 min 20.3 sec 189.39 kph/117.71 mph—retired J. Oliver (Shadow) accident lap 1—M. Beuttler (March) electrics lap 2—E. Fittipaldi (Lotus) ill lap 2—R. Williamson (March) fatal accident lap 7—D. Purley (March) withdrawn lap 8—C. Reutemann (Brabham) puncture lap 9—C. Amon (Tecno) fuel pressure lap 22—W. Fittipaldi (Brabham) accident lap 27—D. Hulme (McLaren) engine lap 31—N. Lauda (BRM) tyre lap 51—M. Hailwood (Surtees) electrics lap 52.

Starting grid 3-2-3

Peterson 1 min 19.5 sec—Stewart 1 min 20.0 sec—Cevert 1 min 20.1 sec—Hulme 1 min 20.3 sec—Reutemann 1 min 20.6 sec—Revson 1 min 20.6 sec—Hunt 1 min 20.7 sec—Pace 1 min 21.0 sec—Beltoise 1 min 21.1 sec—Oliver 1 min 21.2 sec—Lauda 1 min 21.4 sec—Regazzoni 1 min 21.6 sec—W. Fittipaldi 1 min 21.8 sec—Ganley 1 min 22.1 sec—E. Fittipaldi 1 min 22.2 sec—Hill 1 min 22.5 sec—Williamson 1 min 22.7 sec—Amon 1 min 22.7 sec—van Lennep 1 min 22.9 sec—Purley 1 min 22.1 sec—Follmer 1 min 24.1 sec—Beuttler 1 min 24.4 sec—Hailwood 1 min 32.3 sec—non starter R. von Opel (Ensign).

GERMAN GRAND PRIX

Nürburgring; 5 August; 14 laps 320 km/199 miles
1 J Y Stewart (Tyrrell) 1 hr 42 min 03.0 sec 187.91 kph/116.79 mph—2 F. Cevert (Tyrrell) 1 hr 42 min 46.0 sec—3 J. Ickx (McLaren) 1 hr 42 min 44.2 sec—4 C. Pace (Surtees) 1 hr 42 min 56.8 sec—5 W. Fittipaldi (Brabham) 1 hr 43 min 22.9 sec—6 E. Fittipaldi (Lotus) 1 hr 43 min 27.3 sec—7 J. Mass (Surtees) 1 hr 43 min 28.2 sec—8 J. Oliver (Shadow) 1 hr 43 min 28.7 sec—9 P. Revson (McLaren) 1 hr 44 min 14.8 sec—10 H. Pescarolo (Williams) 1 hr 44 min 25.5 sec—11 R. Stommelen (Brabham) 1 hr 45 min 30.3 sec—12 D. Hulme (McLaren) 1 hr 45 min 41.7 sec—13 G. Hill (Shadow) 1 hr 45 min 45.2 sec—14 M. Hailwood (Surtees) 13 laps—15 D. Purley (March) 13 laps—16 M. Beuttler (March) 13 laps—fastest lap, Pace 7 min 11.4 sec 190.55 kph /118.43 mph—retired R. Peterson (Lotus) distributor 0 laps—N. Lauda (BRM) accident lap 1—J-P Beltoise (BRM) puncture lap 4—G. Follmer (Shadow) accident lap 5—C. Regazzoni (BRM) engine lap 7—C. Reutemann (Brabham) engine lap 7.

Starting grid 2-2-2

Stewart 7 min 07.8 sec—Peterson 7 min 08.3 sec—Cevert 7 min 09.3 sec—Ickx 7 min 09.7 sec—Lauda 7 min 09.9 sec—Reutemann 7 min 15.1 sec—Revson 7 min 15.9 sec—Hulme 7 min 16.5 sec—Beltoise 7 min 18.1 sec—Regazzoni 7 min 18.2 sec—Pace 7 min 18.8 sec—Pescarolo 7 min 18.8 sec—W. Fittipaldi 7 min 19.1 sec—E. Fittipaldi 7 min 19.7 sec—Mass 7 min 20.4 sec—Stommelen 7 min 22.2 sec—Oliver 7 min 22.3 sec—Hailwood 7 min 22.3 sec—Hill 7 min 27.1 sec—Beuttler 7 min 26.6 sec—Follmer 7 min 28.3 sec—Purley 7 min 54.2 sec—non starter H. Ganley (Williams).

AUSTRIAN GRAND PRIX

Österreichring; 19 August; 54 laps 319 km/198 miles
1 R. Peterson (Lotus) 1 hr 28 min 48.8 sec 215.59 kph/133.99 mph—2 J Y Stewart (Tyrrell) 1 hr 28 min 57.8 sec—3 C. Pace (Surtees) 1 hr 29 min 35.4 sec—4 C. Reutemann

(Brabham) 1 hr 29 min 36.7 sec—5 J-P Beltoise (BRM) 1 hr 30 min 10.4 sec—6 C. Regazzoni (BRM) 1 hr 30 min 27.2 sec—7 A. Merzario (Ferrari) 53 laps—8 D. Hulme (McLaren) 53 laps—9 G. van Lennep (Williams) 52 laps—10 M. Hailwood (Surtees) 49 laps—11 E. Fittipaldi (Lotus) 48 laps—not classified H. Ganley (Williams) 44 laps—fastest lap, Pace 1 min 37.3 sec 218.68 kph/135.91 mph—retired P. Revson (McLaren) clutch 0 laps—M. Beuttler (March) accident 0 laps—J. Hunt (March) fuel system lap 3—F. Cevert (Tyrrell) accident lap 3—J. Oliver (Shadow) fuel leak lap 9—R. Stommelen (Brabham) wheel bearing lap 21—G. Follmer (Shadow) final drive lap 23—G. Hill (Shadow) suspension lap 28—W. Fittipaldi (Brabham) fuel system lap 31—R. von Opel (Ensign) fuel pressure lap 34—J-P Jarier (March) engine lap 37.

Starting grid 2-2-2

E. Fittipaldi 1 min 35.0 sec—Peterson 1 min 35.4 sec—Hulme 1 min 35.7 sec—Revson 1 min 35.9 sec—Reutemann 1 min 36.0 sec—Merzario 1 min 36.4 sec—Stewart 1 min 36.4 sec—Pace 1 min 36.5 sec—Hunt 1 min 36.6 sec—Cevert 1 min 36.8 sec—Beuttler 1 min 36.8 sec—Jarier 1 min 36.9 sec—Beltoise 1 min 37.5 sec—Regazzoni 1 min 37.5 sec—Hailwood 1 min 37.6 sec—W. Fittipaldi 1 min 37.8 sec—Stommelen 1 min 37.8 sec—Oliver 1 min 38.0 sec—von Opel 1 min 38.2 sec—Follmer 1 min 38.3 sec—Ganley 1 min 39.4 sec—Hill 1 min 39.5 sec—van Lennep 1 min 41.0 sec—non starters C. Amon (Tecno)—N. Lauda (BRM).

ITALIAN GRAND PRIX

Monza; 9 September; 55 laps 316 km/196 miles
1 R. Peterson (Lotus) 1 hr 29 min 17.0 sec 213.4 kph/132.63 mph—2 E. Fittipaldi (Lotus) 1 hr 29 min 17.8 sec—3 P. Revson (McLaren) 1 hr 29 min 45.8 sec—4 J Y Stewart (Tyrrell) 1 hr 29 min 50.2 sec—5 F. Cevert (Tyrrell) 1 hr 30 min 03.2 sec—6 C. Reutemann (Brabham) 1 hr 30 min 16.8 sec—7 M. Hailwood (Surtees) 1 hr 30 min 45.7 sec—8 J. Ickx (Ferrari) 54 laps—9 D. Purley (March) 54 laps—10 G. Follmer (Shadow) 54 laps—11 J. Oliver (Shadow) 54 laps—12 R. Stommelen (Brabham) 54 laps—13 J-P Beltoise (BRM) 54 laps—14 G. Hill (Shadow) 54 laps—15 D. Hulme (McLaren) 53 laps—not classified H. Ganley (Williams) 44 laps—fastest lap, Stewart 1 min 35.3 sec 218.1 kph/135.55 mph—retired A. Merzario (Ferrari) accident lap 2—W. Fittipaldi (Brabham) brakes lap 6—R. von Opel (Ensign) overheating lap 10—G. van Lennep (Williams) overheating lap 14—C. Pace (Surtees) puncture lap 17—C. Regazzoni (BRM) coil lap 31—N. Lauda (BRM) accident lap 33—M. Beuttler (March) gear lever lap 34.

Starting grid 2-2-2

Peterson 1 min 34.8 sec—Revson 1 min 35.2 sec—Hulme 1 min 35.4 sec—E. Fittipaldi 1 min 35.7 sec—Pace 1 min 36.1 sec—Stewart 1 min 36.1 sec—Merzario 1 min 36.4 sec—Hailwood 1 min 36.4 sec—Stommelen 1 min 36.5 sec—Reutemann 1 min 36.5 sec—Cevert 1 min 36.6 sec—Beuttler 1 min 36.7 sec—Beltoise 1 min 36.9 sec—Ickx 1 min 37.0 sec—Lauda 1 min 37.3 sec—W. Fittipaldi 1 min 37.3 sec—von Opel 1 min 37.4 sec—Regazzoni 1 min 37.6 sec—Oliver 1 min 37.8 sec—Ganley 1 min 38.1 sec—Follmer 1 min 38.7 sec—Hill 1 min 38.8 sec—van Lennep 1 min 39.2 sec—Purley 1 min 39.3 sec—non starter J. Hunt (March).

CANADIAN GRAND PRIX

Mosport; 23 September; 80 laps 197 miles/316 km
1 P. Revson (McLaren) 1 hr 59 min 04.1 sec 99.13 mph/159.5 kph—2 E. Fittipaldi (Lotus) 1 hr 59 min 36.8 sec—3 J. Oliver (Shadow) 1 hr 59 min 38.6 sec—4 J-P Beltoise (BRM) 1 hr 59 min 40.6 sec—5 J Y Stewart (Tyrrell) 79 laps—6 H. Ganley (Williams) 79 laps—7 J. Hunt (March) 78 laps—8 C. Reutemann (Brabham) 78 laps—9 M. Hailwood (Surtees) 78 laps—10 C. Amon (Tyrrell) 77 laps—11 W. Fittipaldi (Brabham) 77 laps—12 R. Stommelen (Brabham) 76 laps—13 D. Hulme (McLaren) 75 laps—14 T. Schenken (Williams) 75 laps—15 A. Merzario (Ferrari) 75 laps—16 G. Hill (Shadow) 73 laps—17 G. Follmer (Shadow) 73 laps—18 C. Pace (Surtees) 72 laps—not classified J-P Jarier (March) 71 laps—R. von Opel (Ensign) 68 laps—fastest lap, Fittipaldi 1 min 15.5 sec 117.27 mph/188.69 kph—retired P. Gethin (BRM) oil pump lap 5—R. Peterson (Lotus) accident lap 16—M. Beuttler (March) engine lap 20—F. Cevert (Tyrrell) accident lap 32—J. Scheckter (McLaren) accident lap 32—N. Lauda (BRM) transmission lap 62.

Starting grid 2-2-2

Peterson 1 min 13.7 sec—Revson 1 min 14.7 sec—Scheckter 1 min 14.8 sec—Reutemann 1 min 14.6 sec—Fittipaldi 1 min 15.0 sec—Cevert 1 min 15.1 sec—Hulme 1 min 15.4 sec—Lauda 1 min 15.4 sec—Stewart 1 min 15.6 sec—W. Fittipaldi 1 min 16.1 sec—Amon 1 min 16.2 sec—Hailwood 1 min 16.3 sec—Follmer 1 min 16.4 sec—Oliver 1 min 16.4 sec—Hunt 1 min 16.6 sec—Beltoise 1 min 16.6 sec—Hill 1 min 16.7 sec—Stommelen 1 min 16.8 sec—Pace 1 min 17.0 sec—Merzario 1 min 17.3 sec—Beuttler 1 min 17.4 sec—Ganley 1 min 17.6 sec—Jarier 1 min 17.7 sec—Schenken 1 min 18.4 sec—Gethin 1 min 18.5 sec—von Opel 1 min 18.7 sec.

UNITED STATES GRAND PRIX

Watkins Glen; 7 October; 59 laps 199 miles/321 km
1 R. Peterson (Lotus) 1 hr 41 min 15.8 sec 118.05 mph/189.94 kph—2 J. Hunt (March) 1 hr 41 min 16.5 sec—3 C. Reutemann (Brabham) 1 hr 41 min 38.7 sec—4 D. Hulme (McLaren) 1 hr 42 min 06.0 sec—5 P. Revson (McLaren) 1 hr 42 min 36.2 sec—6 E. Fittipaldi (McLaren) 1 min 43 min 03.7 sec—7 J. Ickx (Williams) 58 laps—8 C. Regazzoni (BRM) 58 laps—9 J-P Beltoise (BRM) 58 laps—10 M. Beuttler (March) 58 laps—11 J-P Jarier (March) 57 laps—12 H. Ganley (Williams) 57 laps—13 G. Hill (Shadow) 57 laps—14 G. Follmer (Shadow) 57 laps—15 J. Oliver (Shadow) 55 laps—16 A. Merzario (Ferrari) 55 laps—not classified W. Fittipaldi (Brabham) 52 laps—fastest lap, Hunt 1 min 41.6 sec 119.6 mph/192.44 kph—retired R. von Opel (Ensign) throttle 0 laps—B. Redman (Shadow) disqualified lap 5—J. Watson (Brabham) engine lap 7—C. Pace (Surtees) suspension lap 32—M. Hailwood (Surtees) suspension lap 34—N. Lauda (BRM) fuel pump lap 35—J. Mass (Surtees) engine lap 35—J. Scheckter (McLaren) suspension lap 39.

Starting grid 2-2-2

Peterson 1 min 39.7 sec—Reutemann 1 min 40.0 sec—E. Fittipaldi 1 min 40.4 sec—Hunt 1 min 40.5 sec—Hailwood 1 min 40.8 sec—Revson 1 min 40.9 sec—Hulme 1 min 40.9 sec—Pace 1 min 41.1 sec—Scheckter 1 min 41.3 sec—Merzario 1 min 41.4 sec—Redman 1 min 42.2 sec—Beltoise 1 min 42.4 sec—Regazzoni 1 min 42.5 sec—Mass 1 min 42.5 sec—Jarier 1 min 42.7 sec—Hill 1 min 42.8 sec—Ganley 1 min 43.2 sec—Follmer 1 min 43.4 sec—Lauda 1 min 43.5 sec—Oliver 1 min 43.6 sec—Ickx 1 min 43.9 sec—Watson 1 min 43.9 sec—W. Fittipaldi 1 min 44.5 sec—Beuttler 1 min 45.0 sec—von Opel 1 min 45.4 sec—non starter F. Cevert (Tyrrell) fatal accident in practice—J Y Stewart (Tyrrell) withdrawn—C. Amon (Tyrrell) withdrawn.

1973 WORLD CHAMPIONSHIP

1 J Y Stewart 71—2 E. Fittipaldi 55—3 R. Peterson 52—4 F. Cevert 47—5 P. Revson 38—6 D. Hulme 26—7 C. Reutemann 16—8 J. Hunt 14—9 J. Ickx 12—10 J-P Beltoise 9—11 C. Pace 7—12 A. Merzario 6—13 G. Follmer 5—14 J. Oliver 4—15 A. de Adamich 3—16 W. Fittipaldi 3—17 N. Lauda 2—18 C. Regazzoni 2—19 C. Amon 1—19= G. van Lennep 1—19= H. Ganley 1.

1974

ARGENTINE GRAND PRIX

Buenos Aires; 13 January; 53 laps 316 km/196 miles
1 D. Hulme (McLaren) 1 hr 41 min 02.0 sec 187.81 kph/116.72 mph—2 N. Lauda (Ferrari) 1 hr 41 min 11.3 sec—3 C. Regazzoni (Ferrari) 1 hr 41 min 22.4 sec—4 M. Hailwood (McLaren) 1 hr 41 min 33.8 sec—5 J-P Beltoise (BRM) 1 hr 41 min 53.8 sec—6 P. Depailler (Tyrrell) 1 hr 42 min 54.5 sec—7 C. Reutemann (Brabham) 52 laps—8 H. Ganley (March) 52 laps—9 H. Pescarolo (BRM) 52 laps—10 E. Fittipaldi (McLaren) 52 laps—11 G. Edwards (Lola) 51 laps—12 J. Watson (Brabham) 49 laps—13 R. Peterson (Lotus) 48 laps—fastest lap, Regazzoni 1 min 52.1 sec 191.62 kph/119.09 mph—retired J-P Jarier (Shadow) accident 0 laps—P. Revson (Shadow) accident lap 1—J. Mass (Surtees) engine lap 10—J. Hunt (March) overheating lap 11—A. Merzario (Williams) engine lap 19—C. Pace (Surtees) engine lap 21—J. Scheckter (Tyrrell) cylinder head gasket lap 25—F. Migault (BRM) water leak lap 31—H-J Stuck (March) transmission lap 31—R. Robarts (Brabham) gearbox lap 35—J. Ickx (Lotus) transmission lap 35—G. Hill (Lola) engine lap 45.

Starting grid 2-2-2

Peterson 1 min 50.8 sec—Regazzoni 1 min 51.0 sec—Fittipaldi 1 min 51.1 sec—Revson 1 min 51.3 sec—Hunt 1 min 51.5 sec—Reutemann 1 min 51.5 sec—Ickx 1 min 51.7 sec—Lauda 1 min 51.8 sec—Hailwood 1 min 51.9 sec—Hulme 1 min 52.1 sec—Pace 1 min 52.2 sec—Scheckter 1 min 52.5 sec—Merzario 1 min 53.1 sec—Beltoise 1 min 53.2 sec—Depailler 1 min 53.3 sec—Jarier 1 min 53.7 sec—Hill 1 min 53.9 sec—Mass 1 min 53.9 sec—Ganley 1 min 54.2 sec—Wilson 1 min 54.4 sec—Pescarolo 1 min 54.7 sec—Robarts 1 min 54.7 sec—Stuck 1 min 55.2 sec—Migault 1 min 55.4 sec—Edwards 1 min 56.4 sec—non starter R. von Opel (Ensign).

BRAZIL GRAND PRIX

Interlagos; 27 January; 32 laps 255 km/158 miles
1 E. Fittipaldi (McLaren) 1 hr 24 min 37.1 sec 180.58 kph/112.23 mph—2 C. Regazzoni (Ferrari) 1 hr 24 min 50.6 sec—3 J. Ickx (Lotus) 31 laps—4 C. Pace (Surtees) 31 laps—5 M. Hailwood (McLaren) 31 laps—6 R. Peterson (Lotus) 31 laps—7 C. Reutemann (Brabham) 31 laps—8 P. Depailler (Tyrrell) 31 laps—9 J. Hunt (March) 31 laps—10 J-P Beltoise (BRM) 31 laps—11 G. Hill (Lola) 31 laps—12 D. Hulme (McLaren) 31 laps—13 J. Scheckter (Tyrrell) 31 laps—14 H. Pescarolo (BRM) 30 laps—15 R. Robarts (Brabham) 30 laps—16 F. Migault (BRM) 30 laps—17 J. Mass (Surtees) 30 laps—fastest lap, Regazzoni 2 min 36.0 sec 183.59 kph/114.1 mph—retired G. Edwards (Lola) engine lap 3—N. Lauda (Ferrari) wing lap 3—H. Ganley (March) ignition lap 9—P. Revson (Shadow) overheating lap 11—A. Merzario (Williams) throttle slides lap 20—J-P Jarier (Shadow) brakes lap 22—H-J Stuck (March) transmission lap 24—J. Watson (Brabham) clutch lap 27.

Starting grid 2-2-2

Fittipaldi 2 min 33.0 sec—Reutemann 2 min 33.2 sec—Lauda 2 min 33.8 sec—Peterson 2 min 33.8 sec—Ickx 2 min 34.6 sec—Revson 2 min 34.7 sec—Hailwood 2 min 34.9 sec—Regazzoni 2 min 35.0 sec—Mass 2 min 35.4 sec—Hulme 2 min 35.5 sec—Pace 2 min 35.6 sec—Stuck 2 min 35.6 sec—Scheckter 2 min 35.8 sec—Watson 2 min 36.1 sec—Depailler 2 min 36.2 sec—Beltoise 2 min 36.5 sec—Hunt 2 min 37.2 sec—Jarier 2 min 37.6 sec—Ganley 2 min 37.6 sec—Hill 2 min 38.6 sec—Pescarolo 2 min 38.8 sec—Migault 2 min 39.2 sec—Robarts 2 min 39.8 sec—Edwards 2 min 42.1 sec—late starter Merzario 2 min 35.1 sec.

SOUTH AFRICAN GRAND PRIX

Kyalami; 30 March; 78 laps 199 miles/320 km
1 C. Reutemann (Brabham) 1 hr 42 min 41.0 sec 116.22 mph/187.00 kph—2 J-P Beltoise (BRM) 1 hr 43 min 14.9 sec—3 M. Hailwood (McLaren) 1 hr 43 min 23.1 sec—4 P. Depailler (Tyrrell) 1 hr 43 min 25.1 sec—5 H-J Stuck (March) 1 hr 43 min 27.2 sec—6 A. Merzario (Williams) 1 hr 43 min 37.0 sec—7 E. Fittipaldi (McLaren) 1 hr 43 min 49.3 sec—8 J. Scheckter (Tyrrell) 1 hr 43 min 51.5 sec—9 D. Hulme (McLaren) 77 laps—10 V. Brambilla (March) 77 laps—11 C. Pace (Surtees) 77 laps—12 G. Hill (Lola) 77 laps—13 I. Scheckter (Lotus) 76 laps—14 E. Keizan (Tyrrell) 76 laps—15 F. Migault (BRM) 75 laps—16 N. Lauda (Ferrari) 74 laps—17 R. Robarts (Brabham) 74 laps—18 H. Pescarolo (BRM) 72 laps—19 D. Charlton (McLaren) 71 laps—fastest lap, Reutemann 1 min 18.2 sec 117.45 mph/188.98 kph—retired T. Belso (Williams) clutch 0 laps—R. Peterson (Lotus) accident lap 2—P. Driver (Lotus) clutch lap 6—J. Mass (Surtees) accident lap 11—J. Hunt (Hesketh) transmission lap 13—J. Ickx (Lotus) brakes lap 31—J. Watson (Brabham) fuel system lap 55—C. Regazzoni (Ferrari) oil pressure lap 65.

Starting grid 2-2-2

Lauda 1 min 16.6 sec—Pace 1 min 16.6 sec—Merzario 1 min 16.8 sec—Reutemann 1 min 16.8 sec—Fittipaldi 1 min 16.8 sec—Regazzoni 1 min 16.8 sec—Stuck 1 min 17.0 sec—Scheckter 1 min 17.0 sec—Hulme 1 min 17.1 sec—Ickx 1 min 17.2 sec—Beltoise 1 min 17.3 sec—Hailwood 1 min 17.3 sec—Watson 1 min 17.4 sec—Hunt 1 min 17.4 sec—Depailler 1 min 17.7 sec—Peterson 1 min 18.0 sec—Mass 1 min 18.2 sec—Hill 1 min 18.2 sec—Brambilla 1 min 18.3 sec—Charlton 1 min 18.4 sec—Pescarolo 1 min 18.4 sec—Scheckter 1 min 18.6 sec—Robarts 1 min 18.6 sec—Kelzan 1 min 19.0 sec—Migault 1 min 19.1 sec—Driver 1 min 19.5 sec—Belso 1 min 19.8 sec.

SPANISH GRAND PRIX

Jarama; 28 April; 84 laps 286 km/178 miles
1 N. Lauda (Ferrari) 2 hr 0 min 29.6 sec 142.35 kph/88.47 mph—2 C. Regazzoni (Ferrari) 2 hr 1 min 05.2 sec—3 E. Fittipaldi (McLaren) 83 laps—4 H-J Stuck (March) 82 laps—5 J. Scheckter (Tyrrell) 82 laps—6 D. Hulme (McLaren) 82 laps—7 B. Redman (Shadow) 81 laps—8 P. Depailler (Tyrrell) 81 laps—9 M. Hailwood (McLaren) 81 laps—10 J. Hunt (Hesketh) 81 laps—11 J. Watson (Brabham) 80 laps—12 H. Pescarolo (BRM) 80 laps—13 C. Pace (Surtees) 78 laps—14 T. Schenken (Trojan) 76 laps—not classified J-P Jarier (Shadow) 73 laps—fastest lap, Lauda 1 min 20.8 sec 151.57 kph/94.2 mph—retired J-P Beltoise (BRM) engine lap 2—C. Reutemann (Brabham) accident lap 12—R. von Opel (Brabham) oil leak lap 14—C. Amon (Amon) brake shaft lap 22—R. Peterson (Lotus) overheating lap 23—J. Ickx (Lotus) brakes lap 26—F. Migault (BRM) engine lap 27—J. Mass (Surtees) gearbox lap 35—A. Merzario (Williams) accident lap 37—G. Hill (Lola) engine lap 43.

Starting grid 2-2-2

Lauda 1 min 18.4 sec—Peterson 1 min 18.5 sec—Regazzoni 1 min 18.8 sec—Fittipaldi 1 min 19.2 sec—Ickx 1 min 19.3 sec—Reutemann 1 min 19.4 sec—Merzario 1 min 19.5 sec—Hulme 1 min 19.7 sec—Scheckter 1 min 19.9 sec—Hunt 1 min 19.9 sec—Beltoise 1 min 20.0 sec—Jarier 1 min 20.2 sec—Stuck 1 min 20.5 sec—Pace 1 min 20.5 sec—Watson 1 min 20.5 sec—Depailler 1 min 20.6 sec—Hailwood 1 min 20.6 sec—Mass 1 min 20.8 sec—Hill 1 min 21.0 sec—Pescarolo 1 min 21.3 sec—Redman 1 min 21.3 sec—Migault 1 min 21.4 sec—Amon 1 min 21.8 sec—von Opel 1 min 21.8 sec—Schenken 1 min 21.9 sec—non starters V. Brambilla (March)—G. Edwards (Lola)—T. Belso (Williams).

BELGIAN GRAND PRIX

Nivelles; 12 May; 85 laps 316 km/197 miles
1 E. Fittipaldi (McLaren) 1 hr 44 min 20.6 sec 181.98 kph/113.1 mph—2 N. Lauda (Ferrari) 1 hr 44 min 20.9 sec—3 J. Scheckter (Tyrrell) 1 hr 45 min 06.2 sec—4 C. Regazzoni (Ferrari) 1 hr 45 min 12.6 sec—5 J-P Beltoise (BRM) 1 hr 45 min 28.6 sec—6 D. Hulme (McLaren) 1 hr 45 min 31.1 sec—7 M. Hailwood (McLaren) 84 laps—8 G. Hill (Lola) 83 laps—9 V. Brambilla (March) 83 laps—10 T. Schenken

(Trojan) 83 laps—11 J. Watson (Brabham) 83 laps—12 G. Edwards (Lola) 82 laps—13 J-P Jarier (Shadow) 82 laps—14 G. van Lennep (Williams) 82 laps—15 V. Schuppan (Ensign) 82 laps—16 F. Migault (BRM) 82 laps—17 T. Pilette (Brabham) 81 laps—18 B. Redman (Shadow) 80 laps—fastest lap, Hulme 1 min 11.3 sec 187.96 kph/116.82 mph—retired H-J Stuck (March) clutch lap 6—H. Pescarolo (BRM) accident lap 12—A. Merzario (Williams) transmission lap 29—J. Hunt (Hesketh) suspension lap 45—R. von Opel (Brabham) oil pressure lap 49—C. Pace (Surtees) tyres lap 50—G. Larrousse (Brabham) tyres lap 53—J. Mass (Surtees) suspension lap 53—P. Depailler (Tyrrell) brakes lap 53—R. Peterson (Lotus) fuel tank lap 56—C. Reutemann (Brabham) fuel line lap 62—T. Pryce (Token) accident lap 66—J. Ickx (Lotus) brakes lap 72.

Starting grid 2-2-2

Regazzoni 1 min 09.8 sec—Scheckter 1 min 10.9 sec—Lauda 1 min 11.0 sec—Fittipaldi 1 min 11.1 sec—Peterson 1 min 11.2 sec—Merzario 1 min 11.3 sec—Beltoise 1 min 11.4 sec—Pace 1 min 11.5 sec—Hunt 1 min 11.5 sec—Stuck 1 min 11.6 sec—Depailler 1 min 11.6 sec—Hulme 1 min 11.6 sec—Hailwood 1 min 12.0 sec—Schuppen 1 min 12.0 sec—Pescarolo 1 min 12.3 sec—Ickx 1 min 12.4 sec—Jarier 1 min 12.5 sec—Redman 1 min 12.7 sec—Watson 1 min 12.8 sec—Pryce 1 min 12.8 sec—Edwards 1 min 13.3 sec—von Opel 1 min 13.3 sec—Schenken 1 min 13.4 sec—Reutemann 1 min 13.5 sec—Migault 1 min 13.5 sec—Mass 1 min 13.8 sec—Pilette 1 min 14.0 sec—Larrousse 1 min 14.2 sec—Hill 1 min 14.3 sec—van Lennep 1 min 15.6 sec—Brambilla 1 min 23.8 sec—non starter L. Kinnunen (Surtees).

MONACO GRAND PRIX

Monte Carlo; 26 May; 78 laps 256 km/159 miles
1 R. Peterson (Lotus) 1 hr 58 min 03.7 sec 129.91 kph/80.74 mph—2 J. Scheckter (Tyrrell) 1 hr 58 min 32.5 sec—3 J-P Jarier (Shadow) 1 hr 58 min 52.6 sec—4 C. Regazzoni (Ferrari) 1 hr 59 min 06.8 sec—5 E. Fittipaldi (McLaren) 77 laps—6 J. Watson (Brabham) 77 laps—7 G. Hill (Lola) 76 laps—8 G. Edwards (Lola) 75 laps—9 P. Depailler (Tyrrell) 74 laps—fastest lap, Peterson 1 min 27.9 sec 134.22 kph/83.42 mph—retired T. Schenken (Trojan) accident 0 laps—C. Pace (Surtees) accident 0 laps—B. Redman (Shadow) accident 0 laps—A. Merzario (Williams) accident 0 laps—D. Hulme (McLaren) accident 0 laps—J-P Beltoise (BRM) accident lap 1—V. Brambilla (March) accident lap 1—H-J Stuck (March) accident lap 3—V. Schuppan (Ensign) accident lap 4—F. Migault (BRM) accident lap 5—C. Reutemann (Brabham) accident lap 5—M. Hailwood (McLaren) accident lap 11—J. Hunt (Hesketh) drive shaft lap 28—N. Lauda (Ferrari) ignition lap 32—J. Ickx (Lotus) gearbox lap 34—H. Pescarolo (BRM) gearbox lap 62.

Starting grid 2-2-2

Lauda 1 min 26.3 sec—Regazzoni 1 min 26.6 sec—Peterson 1 min 26.8 sec—Scheckter 1 min 27.1 sec—Jarier 1 min 27.5 sec—Hunt 1 min 27.8 sec—Reutemann 1 min 27.8 sec—Stuck 1 min 28.0 sec—Hailwood 1 min 28.1 sec—Beltoise 1 min 28.1 sec—Hulme 1 min 28.2 sec—Fittipaldi 1 min 28.2 sec—Merzario 1 min 28.5 sec—Brambilla 1 min 28.7 sec—Redman 1 min 28.8 sec—Pace 1 min 29.1 sec—Ickx 1 min 29.4 sec—Hill 1 min 30.0 sec—Migault 1 min 30.0 sec—Watson 1 min 30.0 sec—Schenken 1 min 30.2 sec—Schuppan 1 min 30.3 sec—Edwards 1 min 30.4 sec—Pescarolo 1 min 30.7 sec—Depailler 1 min 27.1 sec—non starters J. Mass (Surtees)—C. Amon (Amon)—von Opel (Brabham).

SWEDISH GRAND PRIX

Anderstorp; 9 June; 80 laps 321 km/200 miles
1 J. Scheckter (Tyrrell) 1 hr 58 min 31.4 sec 162.68 kph/101.11 mph—2 P. Depailler (Tyrrell) 1 hr 58 min 31.8 sec—3 J. Hunt (Hesketh) 1 hr 58 min 34.7 sec—4 E. Fittipaldi (McLaren) 1 hr 59 min 24.9 sec—5 J-P Jarier (Shadow) 1 hr 59 min 47.8 sec—6 G. Hill (Lola) 79 laps—7 G. Edwards (Lola) 79 laps—8 T. Belso (Williams) 79 Laps—9 R. von Opel (Brabham) 79 laps—10 V. Brambilla (March) 78 laps—11 J. Watson (Brabham) 77 laps—fastest lap, Depailler 1 min 27.3 sec 165.73 kph/103.0 mph—retired H. Pescarolo (BRM) fire 0 laps—B. Roos (Shadow) transmission lap 1—J-P Beltoise (BRM) engine lap 2—M. Hailwood (McLaren) fuel line lap 5—L. Kinnunen (Surtees) electrics lap 8—R. Peterson (Lotus) drive shaft lap 8—C. Pace (Surtees) handling lap 14—C. Regazzoni (Ferrari) transmission lap 23—J. Ickx (Lotus) oil pressure lap 27—C. Reutemann (Brabham) oil leak lap 29—J. Mass (Surtees) suspension lap 53—D. Hulme (McLaren) suspension lap 56—R. Wisell (March) suspension lap 59—N. Lauda (Ferrari) transmission lap 69—V. Schuppan (Ensign) disqualified lap 77.

Starting grid 2-2-2

Depailler 1 min 24.8 sec—Scheckter 1 min 25.1 sec—Lauda 1 min 25.2 sec—Regazzoni 1 min 25.3 sec—Peterson 1 min 25.4 sec—Hunt 1 min 25.6 sec—Ickx 1 min 25.6 sec—Jarier 1 min 25.7 sec—Fittipaldi 1 min 25.9 sec—Reutemann 1 min 26.0 sec—Hailwood 1 min 26.0 sec—Hulme 1 min 26.5 sec—Beltoise 1 min 26.8 sec—Watson 1 min 27.1 sec—Hill 1 min 27.2 sec—Wisell 1 min 27.4 sec—Brambilla 1 min 27.4 sec—Edwards 1 min 27.4 sec—Pescarolo 1 min 27.5 sec—von Opel 1 min 27.7 sec—Belso 1 min 27.9 sec—Mass 1 min 28.1 sec—Roos 1 min 28.3 sec—Pace 1 min 28.6 sec—Kinnunen 1 min 29.4 sec—Schuppan 1 min 29.5 sec—non starter R. Robarts (Williams).

DUTCH GRAND PRIX

Zandvoort; 23 June; 75 laps 317 km/197 miles
1 N. Lauda (Ferrari) 1 hr 43 min 00.3 sec 184.58 kph/114.72 mph—2 C. Regazzoni (Ferrari) 1 hr 43 min 08.6 sec—3 E. Fittipaldi (McLaren) 1 hr 43 min 30.6 sec—4 M. Hailwood (McLaren) 1 hr 43 min 31.6 sec—5 J. Scheckter (Tyrrell) 1 hr 43 min 34.6 sec—6 P. Depailler (Tyrrell) 1 hr 43 min 51.9 sec—7 J. Watson (Brabham) 1 hr 44 min 14.3 sec—8 R. von Opel (Brabham) 73 laps—9 J. Ickx (Lotus) 72 laps—10 R. Peterson (Lotus) 72 laps—11 V. Brambilla (March) 72 laps—12 C. Reutemann (Brabham) 71 laps—fastest lap, Peterson 1 min 21.4 sec 186.77 kph/116.08 mph—retired H-J Stuck (March) accident 0 laps—T. Pryce (Shadow) accident 0 laps—J. Hunt (Hesketh) suspension lap 2—J. Mass (Surtees) transmission lap 8—H. Pescarolo (BRM) handling lap 15—G. Hill (Lola) clutch lap 16—J-P Beltoise (BRM) gearbox lap 18—J-P Jarier (Shadow) clutch lap 27—G. Edwards (Lola) fuel system lap 36—A. Merzario (Williams) gearbox lap 54—F. Migault (BRM) gear linkage lap 60—D. Hulme (McLaren) ignition lap 65—V. Schuppan (Ensign) disqualified lap 69.

Starting grid 2-2-2

Lauda 1 min 18.3 sec—Regazzoni 1 min 18.9 sec—Fittipaldi 1 min 19.6 sec—Hailwood 1 min 19.7 sec—Scheckter 1 min 19.9 sec—Hunt 1 min 19.9 sec—Jarier 1 min 20.1 sec—Depailler 1 min 20.1 sec—Hulme 1 min 20.1 sec—Peterson 1 min 20.2 sec—Pryce 1 min 20.4 sec—Reutemann 1 min 20.4 sec—Watson 1 min 20.8 sec—Edwards 1 min 21.0 sec—Brambilla 1 min 21.0 sec—Beltoise 1 min 21.0 sec—Schuppan 1 min 21.1 sec—Ickx 1 min 21.2 sec—Hill 1 min 21.2 sec—Mass 1 min 21.3 sec—Merzario 1 min 21.5 sec—Stuck 1 min 21.5 sec—von Opel 1 min 21.6 sec—Pescarolo 1 min 21.8 sec—Migault 1 min 22.3 sec—non starters T. Schenken (Trojan)—G. van Lennep (Williams).

FRENCH GRAND PRIX

Dijon-Prenois; 7 July; 80 laps 263 km/163 miles
1 R. Peterson (Lotus) 1 hr 21 min 55.0 sec 192.68 kph/119.75 mph—2 N. Lauda (Ferrari) 1 hr 22 min 15.4 sec—3 C. Regazzoni (Ferrari) 1 hr 22 min 22.9 sec—4 J. Scheckter (Tyrrell) 1 hr 22 min 23.1 sec—5 J. Ickx (Lotus) 1 hr 22 min 32.6 sec—6 D. Hulme (McLaren) 1 hr 22 min 33.2 sec—7 M. Hailwood (McLaren) 79 laps—8 P. Depailler (Tyrrell) 79 laps—9 A. Merzario (Williams) 79 laps—10 J-P Beltoise (BRM) 79 laps—11 V. Brambilla (March) 79 laps—12 J-P Jarier (Shadow) 79 laps—13 G. Hill (Lola) 78 laps—14 F. Migault (BRM) 78 laps—15 G. Edwards (Lola) 77 laps—16 J. Watson (Brabham) 76 laps—fastest lap, Scheckter 1 min 00.0 sec 197.3 kph/122.62 mph—retired H. Pescarolo (BRM) clutch 0 laps—J. Hunt (Hesketh) accident 0 laps—T. Pryce

FRENCH GRAND PRIX—*continued*

(Shadow) accident 0 laps—J. Mass (Surtees) clutch lap 4—C. Reutemann (Brabham) handling lap 24—E. Fittipaldi (McLaren) engine lap 27.

Starting grid 2-2-2

Lauda 0 min 58.8 sec—Peterson 0 min 59.1 sec—Pryce 0 min 59.1 sec—Regazzoni 0 min 59.1 sec—Fittipaldi 0 min 59.2 sec—Hailwood 0 min 59.2 sec—Scheckter 0 min 59.3 sec—Reutemann 0 min 59.4 sec—Depailler 0 min 59.4 sec—Hunt 0 min 59.5 sec—Hulme 0 min 59.5 sec—Jarier 0 min 59.6 sec—Ickx 1 min 00.0 sec—Watson 1 min 00.0 sec—Merzario 1 min 00.2 sec—Brambilla 1 min 00.3 sec—Beltoise 1 min 00.4 sec—Mass 1 min 00.5 sec—Pescarolo 1 min 00.7 sec—Edwards 1 min 00.7 sec—Hill 1 min 00.7 sec—Migault 1 min 00.9 sec—non starters V. Schuppan (Ensign)—C. Pace (Brabham)—J-P Jabouille (Williams)—H-J Stuck (March)—J. Dolhem (Surtees)—R. von Opel (Brabham)—L. Kinnunen (Surtees)—G. Larrousse (Brabham).

BRITISH GRAND PRIX

Brands Hatch; 20 July; 75 laps 199 miles/320 km
1 J. Scheckter (Tyrrell) 1 hr 43 min 02.2 sec 117.73 mph/189.43 kph—2 E. Fittipaldi (McLaren) 1 hr 43 min 17.5 sec—3 J. Ickx (Lotus) 1 hr 44 min 03.7 sec—4 C. Regazzoni (Ferrari) 1 hr 44 min 09.4 sec—5 N. Lauda (Ferrari) 74 laps—6 C. Reutemann (Brabham) 74 laps—7 D. Hulme (McLaren) 74 laps—8 T. Pryce (Shadow) 74 laps—9 C. Pace (Brabham) 74 laps—10 R. Peterson (Lotus) 73 laps—11 J. Watson (Brabham) 73 laps—12 J-P Beltoise (BRM) 72 laps—13 G. Hill (Lola) 69 laps—14 J. Mass (Surtees) 68 laps—not classified F. Migault (BRM) 63 laps—fastest lap, Lauda 1 min 21.1 sec 117.63 mph/189.27 kph—retired P. Gethin (Lola) puncture 0 laps—J. Hunt (Hesketh) suspension lap 2—T. Schenken (Trojan) suspension lap 6—V. Brambilla (March) fuel pressure lap 17—A. Merzario (Williams) engine lap 26—P. Depailler (Tyrrell) engine lap 35—H-J Stuck (March) accident lap 36—J-P Jarier (Shadow) suspension lap 45—M. Hailwood (McLaren) accident lap 57—H. Pescarolo (BRM) engine lap 64.

Starting grid 2-2-2

Lauda 1 min 19.7 sec—Peterson 1 min 19.7 sec—Scheckter 1 min 20.1 sec—Reutemann 1 min 20.2 sec—Pryce 1 min 20.3 sec—Hunt 1 min 20.3 sec—Regazzoni 1 min 20.3 sec—Fittipaldi 1 min 20.5 sec—Stuck 1 min 20.7 sec—Depailler 1 min 20.8 sec—Hailwood 1 min 21.2 sec—Ickx 1 min 21.2 sec—Watson 1 min 21.3 sec—Migault 1 min 21.4 sec—Merzario 1 min 21.6 sec—Jarier 1 min 21.6 sec—Mass 1 min 21.6 sec—Brambilla 1 min 21.6 sec—Hulme 1 min 21.7 sec—Pace 1 min 21.7 sec—Gethin 1 min 21.7 sec—Hill 1 min 21.9 sec—Beltoise 1 min 22.1 sec—Pescarolo 1 min 22.2 sec—Schenken 1 min 22.4 sec—non starters D. Purley (Token)—D. Bell (Surtees)—T. Belso (Williams)—L. Lombardi (Brabham)—V. Schuppan (Ensign)—J. Nicholson (Lyncar)—H. Ganley (Maki)—M. Wilds (March)—L. Kinnunen (Surtees).

GERMAN GRAND PRIX

Nürburgring; 4 August; 14 laps 320 km/199 miles
1 C. Regazzoni (Ferrari) 1 hr 41 min 35.0 sec 188.78 kph/117.33 mph—2 J. Scheckter (Tyrrell) 1 hr 42 min 25.7 sec—3 C. Reutemann (Brabham) 1 hr 42 min 58.2 sec—4 R. Peterson (Lotus) 1 hr 42 min 59.2 sec—5 J. Ickx (Lotus) 1 hr 43 min 00.0 sec—6 T. Pryce (Shadow) 1 hr 43 min 53.1 sec—7 H-J Stuck (March) 1 hr 44 min 33.7 sec—8 J-P Jarier (Shadow) 1 hr 45 min 00.9 sec—9 G. Hill (Lola) 1 hr 45 min 01.4 sec—10 H. Pescarolo (BRM) 1 hr 45 min 52.7 sec—11 D. Bell (Surtees) 1 hr 46 min 52.7 sec—12 C. Pace (Brabham) 1 hr 48 min 01.3 sec—13 V. Brambilla (March) 1 hr 50 min 18.1 sec—14 I. Ashley (Token) 13 laps—fastest lap, Scheckter 7 min 11.1 sec 190.65 kph/118.49 mph—retired D. Hulme (McLaren) accident 0 laps—N. Lauda (Ferrari) accident 0 laps—J. Watson (Brabham) accident lap 1—D. Hulme (McLaren) disqualified lap 2—E. Fittipaldi (McLaren) accident lap 2—J. Laffite (Williams) accident lap 2—V. Schuppan (Ensign) transmission lap 4—J-P Beltoise (BRM) engine lap 4—A. Merzario (Williams) throttle lap 5—P. Depailler (Tyrrell) accident lap 5—J. Mass (Surtees) engine lap 10—J. Hunt (Hesketh) transmission lap 11—M. Hailwood (McLaren) accident lap 12.

Starting grid 2-2-2

Lauda 7 min 00.8 sec—Regazzoni 7 min 01.1 sec—Fittipaldi 7 min 02.3 sec—Scheckter 7 min 03.4 sec—Depailler 7 min 06.2 sec—Reutemann 7 min 07.2 sec—Hulme 7 min 08.8 sec—Peterson 7 min 09.0 sec—Ickx 7 min 09.1 sec—Mass 7 min 09.8 sec—Pryce 7 min 09.9 sec—Hailwood 7 min 10.1 sec—Hunt 7 min 10.4 sec—Watson 7 min 10.5 sec—Beltoise 7 min 10.5 sec—Merzario 7 min 11.2 sec—Pace 7 min 12.7 sec—Jarier 7 min 14.9 sec—Hill 7 min 15.5 sec—Stuck 7 min 16.0 sec—Laffite 7 min 17.6 sec—Schuppan 7 min 20.8 sec—Brambilla 7 min 20.9 sec—Pescarolo 7 min 20.9 sec—Bell 7 min 22.0 sec—Ashley 7 min 24.6 sec—non starters F. Migault (BRM)—T. Schenken (Trojan)—G. Edwards (Lola)—L. Perkins (Amon)—C. Amon (Amon)—H. Ganley (Maki).

AUSTRIAN GRAND PRIX

Österreichring; 18 August; 54 laps 319 km/198 miles
1 C. Reutemann (Brabham) 1 hr 28 min 44.7 sec 215.76 kph/134.1 mph—2 D. Hulme (McLaren) 1 hr 29 min 27.6 sec—3 J. Hunt (Hesketh) 1 hr 29 min 46.3 sec—4 J. Watson (Brabham) 1 hr 29 min 54.1 sec—5 C. Regazzoni (Ferrari) 1 hr 29 min 57.8 sec—6 V. Brambilla (March) 1 hr 29 min 58.5 sec—7 D. Hobbs (McLaren) 53 laps—8 J-P Jarier (Shadow) 52 laps—9 D. Quester (Surtees) 51 laps—10 T. Schenken (Trojan) 50 laps—11 H-J Stuck (March) 48 laps—not classified G. Hill (Lola) 48 laps—I. Ashley (Token) 46 laps—J. Laffite (Williams) 37 laps—fastest lap, Regazzoni 1 min 37.2 sec 218.83 kph/136.01 mph—retired J. Scheckter (Tyrrell) engine lap 8—R. Stommelen (Lola) accident lap 14—N. Lauda (Ferrari) engine lap 17—T. Pryce (Shadow) accident lap 22—J-P Beltoise (BRM) engine lap 22—A. Merzario (Williams) fuel pressure lap 24—E. Fittipaldi (McLaren) engine lap 37—C. Pace (Brabham) fuel system lap 41—P. Depailler (Tyrrell) accident lap 42—J. Ickx (Lotus) accident lap 43—R. Peterson (Lotus) transmission lap 45.

Starting grid 2-2-2

Lauda 1 min 35.4 sec—Reutemann 1 min 35.6 sec—Fittipaldi 1 min 35.8 sec—Pace 1 min 35.9 sec—Scheckter 1 min 35.9 sec—Peterson 1 min 36.0 sec—Hunt 1 min 36.1 sec—Regazzoni 1 min 36.3 sec—Merzario 1 min 36.3 sec—Hulme 1 min 36.4 sec—Watson 1 min 36.5 sec—Laffite 1 min 36.9 sec—Stommelen 1 min 37.2 sec—Depailler 1 min 37.2 sec—Stuck 1 min 37.4 sec—Pryce 1 min 37.4 sec—Hobbs 1 min 37.4 sec—Beltoise 1 min 37.4 sec—Schenken 1 min 37.4 sec—Brambilla 1 min 37.5 sec—Hill 1 min 37.5 sec—Ickx 1 min 38.1 sec—Quester 1 min 38.9 sec—non starters—I. Scheckter (Hesketh)—L. Kinnunen (Surtees)—D. Bell (Surtees)—M. Wilds (Ensign)—J-P Jabouille (Surtees)—H. Koinigg (Brabham).

ITALIAN GRAND PRIX

Monza; 8 September; 52 laps 300 km/187 miles
1 R. Peterson (Lotus) 1 hr 22 min 56.6 sec 217.37 kph/135.1 mph—2 E. Fittipaldi (McLaren) 1 hr 22 min 57.4 sec—3 J. Scheckter (Tyrrell) 1 hr 23 min 21.3 sec—4 A. Merzario (Williams) 1 hr 24 min 24.3 sec—5 C. Pace (Brabham) 51 laps—6 D. Hulme (McLaren) 51 laps—7 J. Watson (Brabham) 51 laps—8 G. Hill (Lola) 51 laps—9 D. Hobbs (McLaren) 51 laps—10 T. Pryce (Shadow) 50 laps—11 P. Depailler (Tyrrell) 50 laps—fastest lap, Pace, 1 min 34.2 sec 220.84 kph/137.25 mph—retired J-P Beltoise (BRM) electrics 0 laps—F. Migault (BRM) gearbox 0 laps—J. Hunt (Hesketh) engine lap 2—H. Pescarolo (BRM) engine lap 3—H-J Stuck (March) engine mountings lap 10—C. Reutemann (Brabham) gearbox lap 11—T. Schenken (Trojan) gear selector lap 14—V. Brambilla (March) accident lap 16—J-P Jarier (Shadow) engine lap 19—J. Laffite (Williams) engine lap 21—R. Stommelen (Lola) suspension lap 24—J. Ickx (Lotus) throttle lap 30—N. Lauda (Ferrari) engine lap 31—C. Regazzoni (Ferrari) engine lap 40.

Starting grid 2-2-2

Lauda 1 min 33.2 sec—Reutemann 1 min 33.3 sec—Pace 1 min 33.5 sec—Watson 1 min 33.6 sec—Regazzoni 1 min 33.7 sec—Fittipaldi 1 min 33.9 sec—Peterson 1 min 34.2 sec—Hunt 1 min 34.3 sec—Jarier 1 min 34.6 sec—Depailler 1 min 34.6 sec—Beltoise 1 min 34.6 sec—Scheckter 1 min 34.7 sec—Brambilla 1 min 34.8 sec—Stommelen 1 min 34.8 sec—Merzario 1 min 35.0 sec—Ickx 1 min 35.2 sec—Laffite 1 min 35.2 sec—Stuck 1 min 35.2 sec—Hulme 1 min 35.6 sec—Schenken 1 min 35.7 sec—Hill 1 min 35.8 sec—Pryce 1 min 36.3 sec—Hobbs 1 min 36.3 sec—Migault 1 min 36.4 sec—Pescarolo 1 min 36.6 sec—non starters J. Dolhem (Surtees)—C. Facetti (Brabham)—D. Bell (Surtees)—M. Wilds (Ensign)—C. Amon (Amon)—L. Kinnunen (Surtees).

CANADIAN GRAND PRIX

Mosport; 22 September; 80 laps 197 miles/316 km
1 E. Fittipaldi (McLaren) 1 hr 40 min 26.1 sec 117.52 mph/189.09 kph—2 C. Regazzoni (Ferrari) 1 hr 40 min 39.2 sec—3 R. Peterson (Lotus) 1 hr 40 min 40.6 sec—4 J. Hunt (Hesketh) 1 hr 40 min 41.8 sec—5 P. Depailler (Tyrrell) 1 hr 41 min 21.5 sec—6 D. Hulme (McLaren) 79 laps—7 M. Andretti (Parnelli) 79 laps—8 C. Pace (Brabham) 79 laps—9 C. Reutemann (Brabham) 79 laps—10 H. Koinigg (Surtees) 78 laps—11 R. Stommelen (Lola) 78 laps—12 M. Donohue (Penske) 78 laps—13 J. Ickx (Lotus) 78 laps—14 G. Hill (Lola) 77 laps—15 J. Laffite (Williams) 74 laps—16 J. Mass (McLaren) 72 laps—not classified C. Amon (BRM) 70 laps—J-P Beltoise (BRM) 60 laps—fastest lap, Lauda 1 min 13.7 sec 120.18 mph/193.37 kph—retired H-J Stuck (March) engine lap 12—E. Wietzes (Brabham) transmission lap 33—A. Merzario (Williams) handling lap 40—J-P Jarier (Shadow) drive shaft lap 46—J. Scheckter (Tyrrell) accident lap 48—J. Watson (Brabham) accident lap 61—T. Pryce (Shadow) engine lap 65—N. Lauda (Ferrari) accident lap 67.

Starting grid 2-2-2

Fittipaldi 1 min 13.2 sec—Lauda 1 min 13.2 sec—Scheckter 1 min 13.3 sec—Reutemann 1 min 13.5 sec—Jarier 1 min 13.5 sec—Regazzoni 1 min 13.5 sec—Depailler 1 min 13.6 sec—Hunt 1 min 13.7 sec—Pace 1 min 14.1 sec—Peterson 1 min 14.3 sec—Stommelen 1 min 14.4 sec—Mass 1 min 14.5 sec—Pryce 1 min 14.6 sec—Hulme 1 min 14.7 sec—Watons 1 min 14.8 sec—Andretti 1 min 14.9 sec—Beltoise 1 min 15.0 sec—Laffite 1 min 15.2 sec—Merzario 1 min 15.3 sec—Hill 1 min 15.5 sec—Ickx 1 min 15.7 sec—Koinigg 1 min 15.7 sec—Stuck 1 min 15.7 sec—Donohue 1 min 15.7 sec—Amon 1 min 15.8 sec—Wietzes 1 min 16.3 sec—non starters D. Bell (Surtees)—M. Wilds (Ensign)—V. Brambilla (March)—I. Ashley (Brabham).

UNITED STATES GRAND PRIX

Watkins Glen; 6 October; 59 laps 199 miles/321 km
1 C. Reutemann (Brabham) 1 hr 40 min 21.4 sec 119.12 mph/191.66 kph—2 C. Pace (Brabham) 1 hr 40 min 32.2 sec—3 J. Hunt (Hesketh) 1 hr 41 min 31.8 sec—4 E. Fittipaldi (McLaren) 1 hr 41 min 39.2 sec—5 J. Watson (Brabham) 1 hr 41 min 47.2 sec—6 P. Depailler (Tyrrell) 1 hr 41 min 48.9 sec—7 J. Mass (McLaren) 1 hr 41 min 51.4 sec—8 G. Hill (Lola) 58 laps—9 C. Amon (BRM) 57 laps—10 J-P Jarier (Shadow) 57 laps—11 C. Regazzoni (Ferrari) 55 laps—12 R. Stommelen (Lola) 54 laps—13 R. Peterson (Lotus) 52 laps—not classified M. Wilds (Ensign) 50 laps—T. Pryce (Shadow) 47 laps—fastest lap, Pace 1 min 40.6 sec 120.84 mph/194.43 kph—retired M. Andretti (Parnelli) disqualified lap 4—D. Hulme (McLaren) engine lap 4—T. Schenken (Lotus) disqualified lap 6—J. Ickx (Lotus) accident lap 7—H. Koinigg (Surtees) fatal accident lap 9—V. Brambilla (March) fuel metering unit lap 21—J. Dolhem (Surtees) withdrawn lap 25—M. Donohue (Penske) suspension lap 27—J. Laffite (Williams) wheel lap 31—N. Lauda (Ferrari) suspension lap 38—A. Merzario (Williams) fire extinguisher discharge lap 43—J. Scheckter (Tyrrell) fuel pipe lap 44.

Starting grid 2-2-2

Reutemann 1 min 38.98 sec—Hunt 1 min 38.99 sec—Andretti 1 min 39.2 sec—Pace 1 min 39.3 sec—Lauda 1 min 39.3 sec—Scheckter 1 min 39.5 sec—Watson 1 min 39.5 sec—Fittipaldi 1 min 39.5 sec—Regazzoni 1 min 39.6 sec—Jarier 1 min 40.3 sec—Laffite 1 min 40.6 sec—Amon 1 min 40.7 sec—Depailler 1 min 40.7 sec—Donohue 1 min 40.8 sec—Merzario 1 min 40.8 sec—Ickx 1 min 40.9 sec—Hulme 1 min 41.0 sec—Pryce 1 min 41.2 sec—Peterson 1 min 41.2 sec—Mass 1 min 41.3 sec—Stommelen 1 min 41.4 sec—Wilds 1 min 41.5 sec—Koinigg 1 min 41.8 sec—Hill 1 min 41.9 sec—Brambilla 1 min 42.0 sec—Dolhem 1 min 42.9 sec—Schenken 1 min 43.2 sec—non starters H-J Stuck (March)—I. Ashley (Brabham).

1974 WORLD CHAMPIONSHIP

1 E. Fittipaldi 55—2 C. Regazzoni 52—3 J. Scheckter 45—4 N. Lauda 38—5 R. Peterson 35—6 C. Reutemann 32—7 D. Hulme 20—8 J. Hunt 15—9 P. Depailler 14—10 M. Hailwood 12—10= J. Ickx 12—12 C. Pace 11—13 J-P Beltoise 10—14 J-P Jarier 6—14= J. Watson 6—16 H-J Stuck 5—17 A. Merzario 4—18 G. Hill 1—18= T. Pryce 1—18= V. Brambilla 1.

1975

ARGENTINE GRAND PRIX

Buenos Aires; 12 January; 53 laps 316 km/197 miles
1 E. Fittipaldi (McLaren) 1 hr 39 min 26.3 sec 190.82 kph/118.59 mph—2 J. Hunt (Hesketh) 1 hr 39 min 32.2 sec—3 C. Reutemann (Brabham) 1 hr 39 min 43.3 sec—4 C. Regazzoni (Ferrari) 1 hr 40 min 02.1 sec—5 P. Depailler (Tyrrell) 1 hr 40 min 20.5 sec—6 N. Lauda (Ferrari) 1 hr 40 min 45.9 sec—7 M. Donohue (Penske) 52 laps—6 J. Ickx (Lotus) 52 laps—9 V. Brambilla (March) 52 laps—10 G. Hill (Lola) 52 laps—11 J. Scheckter (Tyrrell) 52 laps—12 T. Pryce (Shadow) 51 laps—13 R. Stommelen (Lola) 51 laps—14 J. Mass (McLaren) 50 laps—not classified A. Merzario (Williams) 44 laps—fastest lap, Hunt 1 min 50.9 sec 193.68 kph/120.37 mph—retired J-P Jarier (Shadow) final drive 0 laps—J. Watson (Surtees) disqualified lap 6—W. Fittipaldi (Fittipaldi) accident lap 12—J. Laffite (Williams) gearbox lap 15—R. Peterson (Lotus) brakes lap 15—M. Wilds (BRM) oil scavenge pump lap 24—M. Andretti (Parnelli) transmission lap 27—C. Pace (Brabham) engine lap 46.

Starting grid 2-2-2

Pace 1 min 49.6 sec—Reutemann 1 min 49.8 sec—Lauda 1 min 50.0 sec—Fittipaldi 1 min 50.0 sec—Hunt 1 min 50.3 sec—Regazzoni 1 min 50.7 sec—Depailler 1 min 50.8 sec—Scheckter 1 min 50.8 sec—Andretti 1 min 51.1 sec—Peterson 1 min 51.4 sec—Brambilla 1 min 51.8 sec—Mass 1 min 51.8 sec—Pryce 1 min 51.9 sec—Watson 1 min 52.1 sec—Donohue 1 min 52.4 sec—Laffite 1 min 52.9 sec—Ickx 1 min 52.9 sec—Stommelen 1 min 53.1 sec—Merzario 1 min 53.4 sec—Hill 1 min 54.0 sec—Wilds 1 min 54.5 sec—W. Fittipaldi 2 min 00.2 sec—non starter J-P Jarier (Shadow).

BRAZIL GRAND PRIX

Sao Paulo; 26 January; 40 laps 318 km/198 miles
1 C. Pace (Brabham) 1 hr 44 min 41.2 sec 182.45 kph/113.39 mph—2 E. Fittipaldi (McLaren) 1 hr 44 min 47.0 sec—3 J. Mass (McLaren) 1 hr 45 min 17.8 sec—4 C. Regazzoni (Ferrari) 1 hr 45 min 24.4 sec—5 N. Lauda (Ferrari) 1 hr 45 min 43.0 sec—6 J. Hunt (Hesketh) 1 hr 45 min 46.3 sec—7 M. Andretti (Parnelli) 1 hr 45 min 48.0 sec—8 C. Reutemann

BRAZIL GRAND PRIX—*continued*

(Brabham) 1 hr 46 min 20.8 sec—9 J. Ickx (Lotus) 1 hr 46 min 33.0 sec—10 J. Watson (Surtees) 1 hr 47 min 10.8 sec—11 J. Laffite (Williams) 39 laps—12 G. Hill (Lola) 39 laps—13 W. Fittipaldi (Fittipaldi) 39 laps—14 R. Stommelen (Lola) 39 laps—15 R. Peterson (Lotus) 38 laps—fastest lap, Jarier 2 min 34.2 sec 185.84 kph/115.5 mph—retired V. Brambilla (March) engine lap 1—J. Scheckter (Tyrrell) oil tank lap 18—M. Donohue (Penske) handling lap 22—M. Wilds (BRM) electrics lap 22—A. Merzario (Williams) fuel system lap 24—T. Pryce (Shadow) accident lap 31—P. Depailler (Tyrrell) accident lap 31—J-P Jarier (Shadow) fuel system lap 32.

Starting grid 2-2-2

Jarier 2 min 29.9 sec—Fittipaldi 2 min 30.7 sec—Reutemann 2 min 31.0 sec—Lauda 2 min 31.1 sec—Regazzoni 2 min 31.2 sec—Pace 2 min 31.6 sec—Hunt 2 min 31.7 sec—Scheckter 2 min 31.7 sec—Depailler 2 min 32.9 sec—Mass 2 min 33.1 sec—Merzario 2 min 33.2 sec—Ickx 2 min 33.2 sec—Watson 2 min 33.2 sec—Pryce 2 min 33.2 sec—Donohue 2 min 33.3 sec—Peterson 2 min 33.9 sec—Brambilla 2 min 34.4 sec—Andretti 2 min 34.6 sec—Laffite 2 min 34.8 sec—Hill 2 min 35.5 sec—W. Fittipaldi 2 min 36.5 sec—Wilds 2 min 37.1 sec—Stommelen 2 min 38.0 sec.

SOUTH AFRICAN GRAND PRIX

Kyalami; 1 March; 78 laps 199 miles/320 km
1 J. Scheckter (Tyrrell) 1 hr 43 min 16.9 sec 115.55 mph/185.9 kph—2 C. Reutemann (Brabham) 1 hr 43 min 20.6 sec—3 P. Depailler (Tyrrell) 1 hr 43 min 33.8 sec—4 C. Pace (Brabham) 1 hr 43 min 34.2 sec—5 N. Lauda (Ferrari) 1 hr 43 min 45.5 sec—6 J. Mass (McLaren) 1 hr 44 min 20.2 sec—7 R. Stommelen (Lola) 1 hr 44 min 29.8 sec—8 M. Donohue (Penske) 77 laps—9 T. Pryce (Shadow) 77 laps—10 R. Peterson (Lotus) 77 laps—11 G. Tunmer (Lotus) 76 laps—12 J. Ickx (Lotus) 76 laps—13 E. Keizan (Lotus) 76 laps—14 D. Charlton (McLaren) 76 laps—15 B. Evans (BRM) 76 laps—16 C. Regazzoni (Ferrari) 71 laps—17 M. Andretti (Parnelli) 70 laps—not classified J. Laffite (Williams) 69 laps—E. Fittipaldi (McLaren) 65 laps—fastest lap, Pace 1 min 17.2 sec 118.91 mph/191.33 kph—retired V. Brambilla (March) oil cooler lap 16—J. Watson (Surtees) clutch lap 19—A. Merzario (Williams) engine lap 22—L. Lombardi (March) engine lap 23—J-P Jarier (Shadow) engine lap 37—J. Hunt (Hesketh) fuel system lap 53—I. Scheckter (Tyrrell) accident lap 55.

Starting grid 2-2-2

Pace 1 min 16.4 sec—Reutemann 1 min 16.5 sec—Scheckter 1 min 16.6 sec—Lauda 1 min 16.8 sec—Depailler 1 min 16.8 sec—Andretti 1 min 16.9 sec—Brambilla 1 min 17.0 sec—Peterson 1 min 17.1 sec—Regazzoni 1 min 17.2 sec—Watson 1 min 17.2 sec—Fittipaldi 1 min 17.2 sec—Hunt 1 min 17.3 sec—Jarier 1 min 17.3 sec—Stommelen 1 min 17.5 sec—Merzario 1 min 17.5 sec—Mass 1 min 17.8 sec—I. Scheckter 1 min 18.0 sec—Donohue 1 min 18.3 sec—Pryce 1 min 18.4 sec—Charlton 1 min 18.5 sec—Ickx 1 min 18.7 sec—Keizan 1 min 19.0 sec—Laffite 1 min 19.1 sec—Evans 1 min 19.2 sec—Tunmer 1 min 19.5 sec—Lombardi 1 min 19.7 sec.

SPANISH GRAND PRIX

Montjuich; 27 April; 29 laps 110 km/68 miles
1 J. Mass (McLaren) 42 min 53.7 sec 153.73 kph/95.54 mph—2 J. Ickx (Lotus) 42 min 54.8 sec—3 C. Reutemann (Brabham) 28 laps—4 J-P Jarier (Shadow) 28 laps—5 V. Brambilla (March) 28 laps—6 L. Lombardi (March) 27 laps—7 T. Brise (Williams) 27 laps—8 J. Watson (Surtees) 26 laps—not classified C. Regazzoni (Ferrari) 25 laps—F. Migault (Hill) 18 laps—fastest lap Andretti 1 min 25.1 sec 160.32 kph/99.64 mph—retired N. Lauda (Ferrari) accident 0 laps—W. Fittipaldi (Fittipaldi) withdrew lap 1—A. Merzario (Williams) withdrew lap 1—P. Depailler (Tyrrell) accident lap 1—A. Jones (Hesketh) accident lap 3—M. Donohue (Penske) accident lap 3—J. Scheckter (Tyrrell) engine lap 3—J. Hunt (Hesketh) accident lap 6—B. Evans (BRM) fuel system lap 7—M. Andretti (Parnelli) accident lap 16—R. Wunderink (Ensign) drive shaft lap 20—T. Pryce (Shadow) accident lap 23—R. Peterson (Lotus) accident lap 23—C. Pace (Brabham) accident lap 25—R. Stommelen (Hill) accident lap 25.

Starting grid 2-2-2

Lauda 1 min 23.4 sec—Regazzoni 1 min 23.5 sec—Hunt 1 min 23.8 sec—Andretti 1 min 23.9 sec—Brambilla 1 min 24.2 sec—Watson 1 min 24.3 sec—Depailler 1 min 24.4 sec—Pryce 1 min 24.5 sec—Stommelen 1 min 24.7 sec—Jarier 1 min 25.0 sec—Mass 1 min 25.2 sec—Peterson 1 min 25.3 sec—Scheckter 1 min 25.4 sec—Pace 1 min 25.8 sec—Reutemann 1 min 25.8 sec—Ickx 1 min 26.3 sec—Donohue 1 min 26.3 sec—Brise 1 min 26.4 sec—Wunderink 1 min 26.6 sec—Jone 1 min 26.7 sec—W. Fittipaldi 1 min 27.2 sec—Migault 1 min 27.9 sec—Evans 1 min 28.8 sec—Lombardi 1 min 30.3 sec—Merzario 1 min 54.3 sec—non starter E. Fittipaldi (McLaren).

MONACO GRAND PRIX

Monte Carlo; 11 May; 75 laps 246 km/153 miles
1 N. Lauda (Ferrari) 2 hr 1 min 21.3 sec 121.53 kph/75.53 mph—2 E. Fittipaldi (McLaren) 2 hr 1 min 24.1 sec—3 C. Pace (Brabham) 2 hr 1 min 39.1 sec—4 R. Peterson (Lotus) 2 hr 1 min 59.8 sec—5 P. Depailler (Tyrrell) 2 hr 2 min 02.2 sec—6 J. Mass (McLaren) 2 hr 2 min 03.4 sec—7 J. Scheckter (Tyrrell) 74 laps—8 J. Ickx (Lotus) 74 laps—9 C. Reutemann (Brabham) 73 laps—fastest lap, Depailler 1 min 28.7 sec133.06 kph/82.7 mph—retired J-P Jarier (Shadow) accident 0 laps—M. Andretti (Parnelli) fire lap 9—C. Regazzoni (Ferrari) accident lap 36—J. Watson (Surtees) accident lap 36—T. Pryce (Shadow) accident lap 39—V. Brambilla (March) accident lap 48—A. Jones (Hesketh) wheel lap 61—J. Hunt (Hesketh) accident lap 63—M. Donohue (Penske) accident lap 66.

Starting grid 1-1-1

Lauda 1 min 26.4 sec—Pryce 1 min 27.1 sec—Jarier 1 min 27.2 sec—Peterson 1 min 27.4 sec—Brambilla 1 min 27.5 sec—Regazzoni 1 min 27.5 sec—Scheckter 1 min 27.6 sec—Pace 1 min 27.7 sec—Fittipaldi 1 min 27.8 sec—Reutemann 1 min 27.9 sec—Hunt 1 min 27.9 sec—Depailler 1 min 27.9 sec—Andretti 1 min 28.1 sec—Ickx 1 min 28.3 sec—Mass 1 min 28.5 sec—Donohue 1 min 28.8 sec—Watson 1 min 28.9 sec—Jones 1 min 29.1 sec—non starters J. Laffite (Williams)—A. Merzario (Williams)—G. Hill (Hill)—B. Evans (BRM)—R. Wunderink (Ensign)—T. Palm (Hesketh)—L. Lombardi (March)—W. Fittipaldi (Fittipaldi).

BELGIAN GRAND PRIX

Zolder; 25 May; 70 laps 298 km/185 miles
1 N. Lauda (Ferrari) 1 hr 43 min 54.0 sec 172.25 kph/107.05 mph—2 J. Scheckter (Tyrrell) 1 hr 44 min 13.2 sec—3 C. Reutemann (Brabham) 1 hr 44 min 35.8 sec—4 P. Depailler (Tyrrell) 1 hr 44 min 54.1 sec—5 C. Regazzoni (Ferrari) 1 hr 44 min 57.8 sec—6 T. Pryce (Shadow) 1 hr 45 min 22.4 sec—7 E. Fittipaldi (McLaren) 69 laps—8 C. Pace (Brabham) 69 laps—9 B. Evans (BRM) 68 laps—10 J. Watson (Surtees) 68 laps—11 M. Donohue (Penske) 67 laps—12 W. Fittipaldi (Fittipaldi) 67 laps—fastest lap, Regazzoni 1 min 26.8 sec 176.81 kph/109.89 mph—retired J. Mass (McLaren) accident 0 laps—A. Jones (Hesketh) accident lap 1—A. Merzario (Williams) clutch lap 2—J-P Jarier (Shadow) accident lap 13—J. Hunt (Hesketh) gear linkage lap 15—T. Brise (Hill) engine lap 17—J. Laffite (Williams) gearbox lap 18—L. Lombardi (March) engine lap 18—R. Peterson (Lotus) accident lap 36—J. Ickx (Lotus) front brake shaft lap 52—V. Brambilla (March) brakes lap 54—F. Migault (Hill) suspension lap 57.

Starting grid 2-2-2

Lauda 1 min 25.4 sec—Pace 1 min 25.5 sec—Brambilla 1 min 25.7 sec—Regazzoni 1 min 25.8 sec—Pryce 1 min 25.9 sec—Reutemann 1 min 26.1 sec—Brise 1 min 26.2 sec—Fittipaldi 1 min 26.3 sec—Scheckter 1 min 26.4

sec—Jarier 1 min 26.4 sec—Hunt 1 min 26.5 sec—Depailler 1 min 26.7 sec—Jones 1 min 27.0 sec—Peterson 1 min 27.2 sec—Mass 1 min 27.4 sec—Ickx 1 min 27.4 sec—Laffite 1 min 27.7 sec—Watson 1 min 28.0 sec—Merzario 1 min 28.2 sec—Evans 1 min 28.6 sec—Donohue 1 min 28.6 sec—Migault 1 min 29.6 sec—Lombardi 1 min 29.7 sec—W. Fittipaldi 1 min 30.3 sec.

SWEDISH GRAND PRIX

Anderstorp; 8 June; 80 laps 321 km/200 miles
1 N. Lauda (Ferrari) 1 hr 59 min 18.3 sec 161.62 kph/100.45 mph—2 C. Reutemann (Brabham) 1 hr 59 min 24.6 sec—3 C. Regazzoni (Ferrari) 1 hr 59 min 47.4 sec—4 M. Andretti (Parnelli) 2 hr 0 min 02.7 sec—5 M. Donohue (Penske) 2 hr 0 min 49.1 sec—6 T. Brise (Hill) 79 laps—7 J. Scheckter (Tyrrell) 79 laps—8 E. Fittipaldi (McLaren) 79 laps—9 R. Peterson (Lotus) 79 laps—10 T. Palm (Hesketh) 78 laps—11 A. Jones (Hesketh) 78 laps—12 P. Depailler (Tyrrell) 78 laps—13 B. Evans (BRM) 78 laps—14 D. Magee (Williams) 78 laps—15 J. Ickx (Lotus) 77 laps—16 J. Watson (Surtees) 77 laps—17 W. Fittipaldi (Fittipaldi) 74 laps—fastest lap, Lauda 1 min 28.3 sec 163.84 kph/101.83 mph—retired L. Lombardi (March) fuel metering lap 10—J. Hunt (Hesketh) brakes lap 21—J. Mass (McLaren) water leak lap 34—V. Brambilla (March) transmission lap 36—J-P Jarier (Shadow) engine lap 38—C. Pace (Brabham) accident lap 41—V. Schuppan (Hill) tranmission lap 47—I. Scheckter (Williams) accident lap 49—T. Pryce (Shadow) accident lap 53.

Starting grid 2-2-2

Brambilla 1 min 24.6 sec—Depailler 1 min 25.0 sec—Jarier 1 min 25.1 sec—Reutemann 1 min 25.2 sec—Lauda 1 min 25.5 sec—Pace 1 min 25.8 sec—Pryce 1 min 25.9 sec—Scheckter 1 min 25.9 sec—Peterson 1 min 26.0 sec—Watson 1 min 26.1 sec—Fittipaldi 1 min 26.1 sec—Regazzoni 1 min 26.3 sec—Hunt 1 min 26.5 sec—Mass 1 min 26.8 sec—Andretti 1 min 26.8 sec—Donohue 1 min 27.1 sec—Brise 1 min 27.3 sec—Ickx 1 min 27.3 sec—Jones 1 min 27.4 sec—I. Scheckter 1 min 27.5 sec—Palm 1 min 27.6 sec—Magee 1 min 27.7 sec—Evans 1 min 28.4 sec—Lombardi 1 min 28.7 sec—W. Fittipaldi 1 min 28.8 sec—Schuppan 1 min 29.0 sec.

DUTCH GRAND PRIX

Zandvoort; 22 June; 75 laps 317 km/197 miles
1 J. Hunt (Hesketh) 1 hr 46 min 57.4 sec 177.76 kph/110.48 mph—2 N. Lauda (Ferrari) 1 hr 46 min 58.5 sec—3 C. Regazzoni (Ferrari) 1 hr 47 min 52.5 sec—C. Reutemann (Brabham) 74 laps—5 C. Pace (Brabham) 74 laps—6 T. Pryce (Shadow) 74 laps—7 T. Brise (Hill) 74 laps—8 M. Donohue (Penske) 74 laps—9 P. Depailler (Tyrrell) 73 laps—10 G. van Lennep (Ensign) 71 laps—11 W. Fittipaldi (Fittipaldi) 71 laps—12 I. Scheckter (Williams) 70 laps—13 A. Jones (Hill) 70 laps—14 L. Lombardi (March) 70 laps—15 R. Peterson (Lotus) 69 laps—16 J. Scheckter (Tyrrell) 67 laps—fastest lap, Lauda 1 min 21.5 sec 186.54 kph/115.93 mph—retired V. Brambilla (March) accident 0 laps—J. Ickx (Lotus) engine lap 6—B. Evans (BRM) transmission lap 23—E. Fittipaldi (McLaren) engine lap 40—J. Watson (Surtees) vibration lap 43—J-P Jarier (Shadow) accident lap 44—J. Mass (McLaren) accident lap 61—J. Laffite (Williams) engine lap 65.

Starting grid 2-2-2

Lauda 1 min 20.3 sec—Regazzoni 1 min 20.6 sec—Hunt 1 min 20.7 sec—Scheckter 1 min 20.7 sec—Reutemann 1 min 20.9 sec—Fittipaldi 1 min 20.9 sec—Brise 1 min 20.9 sec—Mass 1 min 21.0 sec—Pace 1 min 21.1 sec—Jarier 1 min 21.1 sec—Brambilla 1 min 21.1 sec—Pryce 1 min 21.2 sec—Depailler 1 min 21.2 sec—Watson 1 min 21.2 sec—Laffite 1 min 21.3 sec—Peterson 1 min 21.5 sec—Jones 1 min 22.0 sec—Donohue 1 min 22.3 sec—I. Scheckter 1 min 22.8 sec—Evans 1 min 23.0 sec—Ickx 1 min 23.2 sec—van Lennep 1 min 23.3 sec—Lombardi 1 min 24.0 sec—W. Fittipaldi 1 min 24.1 sec—non starter H. Fushida (Maki).

FRENCH GRAND PRIX

Paul Ricard; 6 July; 54 laps 314 km/195 miles
1 N. Lauda (Ferrari) 1 hr 40 min 18.8 sec 187.61 kph/116.6 mph—2 J. Hunt (Hesketh) 1 hr 40 min 20.4 sec—3 J. Mass (McLaren) 1 hr 40 min 21.1 sec—4 E. Fittipaldi (McLaren) 1 hr 40 min 58.6 sec—5 M. Andretti (Parnelli) 1 hr 41 min 20.9 sec—6 P. Depailler (Tyrrell) 1 hr 41 min 26.2 sec—7 T. Brise (Hill) 1 hr 41 min 28.4 sec—8 J-P Jarier (Shadow) 1 hr 41 min 38.6 sec—9 J. Scheckter (Tyrrell) 1 hr 41 min 50.5 sec—10 R. Peterson (Lotus) 1 hr 41 min 54.9 sec—11 J. Laffite (Williams) 1 hr 41 min 55.6 sec—12 J-P Jabouille (Tyrrell) 1 hr 41 min 56.0 sec—13 J. Watson (Surtees) 53 laps—14 C. Reutemann (Brabham) 53 laps—15 G. van Lennep (Ensign) 53 laps—16 A. Jones (Hill) 53 laps—17 B. Evans (BRM) 52 laps—18 L. Lombardi (March) 50 laps—fastest lap, Mass 1 min 50.6 sec 189.07 kph/117.51 mph—retired T. Pryce (Shadow) transmission lap 2—C. Regazzoni (Ferrari) engine lap 6—V. Brambilla (March) suspension lap 6—M. Donohue (Penske) transmission lap 6—W. Fittipaldi (Fittipaldi) engine lap 14—J. Ickx (Lotus) brake shaft lap 17—C. Pace (Brabham) drive shaft lap 26.

Starting grid 2-2-2

Lauda 1 min 47.8 sec—Scheckter 1 min 48.2 sec—Hunt 1 min 48.2 sec—Jarier 1 min 48.4 sec—Pace 1 min 48.5 sec—Pryce 1 min 48.5 sec—Mass 1 min 48.5 sec—Brambilla 1 min 48.6 sec—Regazzoni 1 min 48.7 sec—Fittipaldi 1 min 48.7 sec—Reutemann 1 min 48.8 sec—Brise 1 min 49.2 sec—Depailler 1 min 49.3 sec—Watson 1 min 49.7 sec—Andretti 1 min 49.7 sec—Laffite 1 min 49.7 sec—Peterson 1 min 50.0 sec—Donohue 1 min 50.1 sec—Ickx 1 min 50.9 sec—Jones 1 min 51.0 sec—Jabouille 1 min 51.1 sec—van Lennep 1 min 51.2 sec—W. Fittipaldi 1 min 51.6 sec—Evans 1 min 51.8 sec—Lombardi 1 min 53.0 sec—non starter F. Migault (Williams).

BRITISH GRAND PRIX

Silverstone; 19 July; 56 laps 164 miles/264 km
1 E. Fittipaldi (McLaren) 1 hr 22 min 05.0 sec 120.02 mph/193.11 kph—2 C. Pace (Brabham) 55 laps—3 J. Scheckter (Tyrrell) 55 laps—4 J. Hunt (Hesketh) 55 laps—5 M. Donohue (March) 55 laps—6 V. Brambilla (March) 55 laps—7 J. Mass (McLaren) 55 laps—8 N. Lauda (Ferrari) 54 laps—9 P. Depailler (Tyrrell) 54 laps—10 A. Jones (Hill) 54 laps—11 J. Watson (Surtees) 54 laps—12 M. Andretti (Parnelli) 54 laps—13 C. Regazzoni (Ferrari) 54 laps—14 J-P Jarier (Shadow) 53 laps—15 T. Brise (Hill) 53 laps—16 B. Henton (Lotus) 53 laps—17 J. Nicholson (Lyncar) 51 laps—not classified D. Morgan (Surtees) 50 laps—W. Fittipaldi (Fittipaldi) 50 laps—fastest lap, Regazzoni 1 min 20.9 sec 130.47 mph/209.93 kph—retired C. Reutemann (Brabham) engine lap 4—J. Laffite (Williams) gearbox lap 5—R. Peterson (Lotus) engine lap 7—L. Lombardi (March) ignition lap 18—T. Pryce (Shadow) accident lap 20—J. Crawford (Lotus) accident lap 28—H-J Stuck (March) accident lap 45.

Starting grid 2-2-2

Pryce 1 min 19.4 sec—Pace 1 min 19.5 sec—Lauda 1 min 19.5 sec—Regazzoni 1 min 19.5 sec—Brambilla 1 min 19.6 sec—Scheckter 1 min 19.8 sec—Fittipaldi 1 min 19.9 sec—Reutemann 1 min 20.0 sec—Hunt 1 min 20.1 sec—Mass 1 min 20.2 sec—Jarier 1 min 20.3 sec—Andretti 1 min 20.4 sec—Brise 1 min 20.4 sec—Stuck 1 min 20.5 sec—Donohue 1 min 20.5 sec—Peterson 1 min 20.6 sec—Depailler 1 min 20.6 sec—Watson 1 min 20.8 sec—Laffite 1 min 21.0 sec—Jones 1 min 21.2 sec—Henton 1 min 21.4 sec—Lombardi 1 min 21.6 sec—Morgan 1 min 21.6 sec—W. Fittipaldi 1 min 21.7 sec—Crawford 1 min 21.9 sec—Nicholson 1 min 22.9 sec—non starters R. Wunderink (Ensign)—H. Fushida (Maki).

GERMAN GRAND PRIX

Nürburgring; 3 August; 14 laps 320 km/199 miles
1 C. Reutemann (Brabham) 1 hr 41 min 14.1 sec 189.43 kph/117.73 mph—2 J. Laffite (Williams) 1 hr 42 min 51.8

GERMAN GRAND PRIX—*continued*

sec—3 N. Lauda (Ferrari) 1 hr 43 min 37.4 sec—4 T. Pryce (Shadow) 1 hr 44 min 45.5 sec—5 A. Jones (Hill) 1 hr 45 min 04.4 sec—6 G. van Lennep (Ensign) 1 hr 46 min 19.6 sec—7 L. Lombardi (March) 1 hr 48 min 44.5 sec—8 H. Ertl (Hesketh) 1 hr 48 min 55.0 sec—9 P. Depailler (Tyrrell) 13 laps—10 M. Andretti (Parnelli) 12 laps—fastest lap, Regazzoni 7 min 06.4 sec 192.75 kph/119.79 mph—retired J. Mass (McLaren) accident 0 laps—M. Donohue (March) puncture lap 1—R. Peterson (Lotus) clutch lap 1—J. Watson (Lotus) suspension lap 2—V. Brambilla (March) suspension lap 3—H-J Stuck (March) engine lap 3—E. Fittipaldi (McLaren) puncture lap 3—W. Fittipaldi (Fittipaldi) engine lap 4—C. Pace (Brabham) rear upright lap 5—J-P Jarier (Shadow) puncture lap 7—J. Scheckter (Tyrrell) accident lap 7—T. Brise (Hill) accident lap 9—C. Regazzoni (Ferrari) engine lap 9—J. Hunt (Hesketh) rear hub lap 10.

Starting grid 2-2-2

Lauda 6 min 58.6 sec—Pace 7 min 00.0 sec—Scheckter 7 min 01.3 sec—Depailler 7 min 01.4 sec—Regazzoni 7 min 01.6 sec—Mass 7 min 01.8 sec—Stuck 7 min 02.1 sec—Fittipaldi 7 min 02.7 sec—Reutemann 7 min 04.0 sec—Brambilla 7 min 06.0 sec—Jarier 7 min 07.1 sec—Andretti 7 min 08.2 sec—Watson 7 min 09.4 sec—Laffite 7 min 10.0 sec—Pryce 7 min 10.1 sec—Brise 7 min 10.9 sec—Peterson 7 min 11.6 sec—Donohue 7 min 11.8 sec—Jones 7 min 18.6 sec—W. Fittipaldi 7 min 19.1 sec—Ertl 7 min 19.5 sec—van Lennep 7 min 20.4 sec—Lombardi 7 min 36.4 sec—non starters I. Ashley (Williams)—T. Trimmer (Maki).

AUSTRIAN GRAND PRIX

Österreichring; 17 August; 29 laps 171 km/107 miles
1 V. Brambilla (March) 57 min 56.7 sec 177.47 kph/110.3 mph—2 J. Hunt (Hesketh) 58 min 23.7 sec—3 T. Pryce (Shadow) 58 min 31.5 sec—4 J. Mass (McLaren) 59 min 09.3 sec—5 R. Peterson (Lotus) 59 min 20.0 sec—6 N. Lauda (Ferrari) 59 min 27.0 sec—7 C. Regazzoni (Ferrari) 59 min 35.8 sec—8 J. Scheckter (Tyrrell) 28 laps—9 E. Fittipaldi (McLaren) 28 laps—10 J. Watson (Surtees) 28 laps—11 P. Depailler (Tyrrell) 28 laps—12 C. Amon (Ensign) 28 laps—13 B. Lunger (Hesketh) 28 laps—14 C. Reutemann (Brabham) 28 laps—15 T. Brise (Hill) 28 laps—16 R. Stommelen (Hill) 27 laps—17 L. Lombardi (March) 26 laps—not classified R. Wunderink (Ensign) 25 laps—fastest lap, Brambilla 1 min 53.9 sec 186.8 kph/116.1 mph—retired M. Andretti (Parnelli) accident lap 1—B. Evans (BRM) engine lap 2—J-P Jarier (Shadow) fuel system lap 10—H-J Stuck (March) accident lap 10—J. Vonlanthen (Williams) engine lap 14—C. Pace (Brabham) engine lap 17—J. Laffite (Williams) handling lap 21—H. Ertl (Hesketh) electrics lap 23.

Starting grid 2-2-2

Lauda 1 min 34.8 sec—Hunt 1 min 35.0 sec—Fittipaldi 1 min 35.2 sec—Stuck 1 min 35.4 sec—Regazzoni 1 min 35.4 sec—Pace 1 min 35.7 sec—Depailler 1 min 35.8 sec—Brambilla 1 min 35.8 sec—Mass 1 min 36.1 sec—Scheckter 1 min 36.1 sec—Reutemann 1 min 36.4 sec—Laffite 1 min 37.6 sec—Peterson 1 min 37.6 sec—Jarier 1 min 37.6 sec—Pryce 1 min 37.6 sec—Brise 1 min 37.7 sec—Lunger 1 min 37.9 sec—Watson 1 min 38.0 sec—Andretti 1 min 38.0 sec—Lombardi 1 min 38.4 sec—Amon 1 min 38.7 sec—Evans 1 min 39.5 sec—Stommelen 1 min 39.6 sec—Ertl 1 min 40.7 sec—Wunderink 1 min 42.6 sec—Vontanthen 1 min 42.8 sec—non starters W. Fittipaldi(Fittipaldi)—M. Donohue (March) fatal accident in practice—B. Henton (Lotus)—T. Trimmer (Maki).

ITALIAN GRAND PRIX

Monza; 7 September; 52 laps 300 km/187 miles
1 C. Regazzoni (Ferrari) 1 hr 22 min 42.6 sec 217.99 kph/135.48 mph—2 E. Fittipaldi (McLaren) 1 hr 22 min 59.2 sec—3 N. Lauda (Ferrari) 1 hr 23 min 05.8 sec—4 C. Reutemann (Brabham) 1 hr 23 min 37.7 sec—5 J. Hunt (Hesketh) 1 hr 23 min 39.7 sec—6 T. Pryce (Shadow) 1 hr 23 min 58.5 sec—7 P. Depailler (Tyrrell) 51 laps—8 J. Scheckter (Tyrrell) 51 laps—9 H. Ertl (Hesketh) 51 laps—10 B. Lunger (Hesketh) 50 laps—11 A. Merzario (Fittipaldi) 48 laps—12 C. Amon (Ensign) 48 laps—13 J. Crawford (Lotus) 46 laps—R. Zorzi (Williams) 46 laps—fastest lap, Regazzoni 1 min 33.1 sec 223.45 kph/138.88 mph—retired B. Evans (BRM) electrics 0 laps—R. Peterson (Lotus) engine lap 1—T. Brise (Hill) accident lap 1—M. Andretti (Parnelli) accident lap 1—V. Brambilla (March) clutch lap 1—J. Mass (McLaren) accident lap 2—R. Stommelen (Hill) accident lap 3—C. Pace (Brabham) throttle linkage lap 6—J. Laffite (Williams) gearbox lap 7—H-J Stuck (March) accident lap 15—L. Lombardi (March) accident lap 21—J-P Jarier (Shadow) fuel pump lap 32.

Starting grid 2-2-2

Lauda 1 min 32.2 sec—Regazzoni 1 min 32.7 sec—Fittipaldi 1 min 33.1 sec—Scheckter 1 min 33.3 sec—Mass 1 min 33.3 sec—Brise 1 min 33.3 sec—Reutemann 1 min 33.4 sec—Hunt 1 min 33.7 sec—Brambilla 1 min 33.9 sec—Pace 1 min 34.2 sec—Peterson 1 min 34.2 sec—Depailler 1 min 34.4 sec—Jarier 1 min 34.6 sec—Pryce 1 min 34,7 sec—Andretti 1 min 34.7 sec—Stuck 1 min 35.3 sec—Ertl 1 min 35.4 sec—Laffite 1 min 35.5 sec—Amon 1 min 35.6 sec—Evans 1 min 35.6 sec—Lunger 1 min 36.1 sec—Zorzi 1 min 36.2 sec—Stommelen 1 min 36.4 sec—Lombardi 1 min 37.1 sec—Crawford 1 min 37.1 sec—Merzario 1 min 37.3 sec—non starters R. Wunderink (Ensign)—T. Trimmer (Maki).

UNITED STATES GRAND PRIX

Watkins Glen; 5 October; 59 laps 199 miles/321 km
1 N. Lauda (Ferrari) 1 hr 42 min 58.2 sec 116.1 mph/186.8 kph—2 E. Fittipaldi (McLaren) 1 hr 43 min 03.1 sec—3 J. Mass (McLaren) 1 hr 43 min 45.8 sec—4 J. Hunt (Hesketh) 1 hr 43 min 47.6 sec—5 R. Peterson (Lotus) 1 hr 43 min 48.2 sec—6 J. Scheckter (Tyrrell) 1 hr 43 min 48.5 sec—7 V. Brambilla (March) 1 hr 44 min 42.2 sec—8 H-J Stuck (March) 58 laps—9 J. Watson (Penske) 57 laps—10 W. Fittipaldi (Fittipaldi) 55 laps—not classified T. Pryce (Shadow) 52 laps—B. Henton (Lotus) 49 laps—fastest lap, Fittipaldi 1 min 43.4 sec 117.6 mph/189.22 kph—retired L. Lombardi (Williams) ignition 0 laps—C. Pace (Brabham) accident lap 2—P. Depailler (Tyrrell) accident lap 2—M. Leclere (Tyrrell) engine lap 5—T. Brise (Hill) accident lap 5—M. Andretti (Parnelli) suspension lap 9—C. Reutemann (Brabham) engine lap 9—J-P Jarier (Shadow) wheel bearing lap 19—C. Regazzoni (Ferrari) withdrawn lap 28—R. Wunderink (Ensign) gearbox lap 41—B. Lunger (Hesketh) accident lap 46.

Starting grid 2-2-2

Lauda 1 min 42.0 sec—Fittipaldi 1 min 42.4 sec—Reutemann 1 min 42.7 sec—Jarier 1 min 42.8 sec—Andretti 1 min 42.8 sec—Brambilla 1 min 42.8 sec—Pryce 1 min 43.0 sec—Depailler 1 min 43.0 sec—Mass 1 min 43.1 sec—Scheckter 1 min 43.1 sec—Regazzoni 1 min 43.2 sec—Stuck 1 min 43.4 sec—Peterson 1 min 43.6 sec—Hunt 1 min 43.8 sec—Pace 1 min 44.0 sec—Brise 1 min 44.1 sec—Lunger 1 min 45.2 sec—Henton 1 min 45.2 sec—Leclere 1 min 46.0 sec—Wunderink 1 min 47.2 sec—W. Fittipaldi 1 min 48.2 sec—Watson—non starters J. Laffite (Williams)—L. Lombardi (Williams).

1975 WORLD CHAMPIONSHIP

1 N. Lauda 64½—2 E. Fittipaldi 45—3 C. Reutemann 37—4 J. Hunt 33—5 C. Regazzoni 25—6 C. Pace 24—7 J. Scheckter 20—7= J. Mass 20—9 P. Depailler 12—10 T. Pryce 8—11 V. Brambilla 6½—12 J. Laffite 6—12= R. Peterson 6—14 M. Andretti 5—15 M. Donohue 4—16 J. Ickx 3—17 A. Jones 2—18 J-P Jarier 1½—19 T. Brise 1—19= G. van Lennep 1—21 L. Lombardi ½.

1976

BRAZIL GRAND PRIX

Interlagos; 25 January; 40 laps 318 km/198 miles
1 N. Lauda (Ferrari) 1 hr 45 min 16.8 sec 181.5 kph/112.7 mph—2 P. Depailler (Tyrrell) 1 hr 45 min 38.2 sec—3 T. Pryce (Shadow) 1 hr 45 min 40.6 sec—4 H-J Stuck (March) 1 hr 46 min 44.9 sec—5 J. Scheckter (Tyrrell) 1 hr 47 min 13.2 sec—6 J. Mass (McLaren) 1 hr 47 min 15.0 sec—7 C. Regazzoni (Ferrari) 1 hr 47 min 32.0 sec—8 J. Ickx (Williams) 39 laps—9 R. Zorzi (Williams) 39 laps—10 C. Pace (Brabham) 39 laps—11 I. Hoffmann (Fittipaldi) 39 laps—12 C. Reutemann (Brabham) 37 laps—13 E. Fittipaldi (Fittipaldi) 37 laps—14 L. Lombardi (March) 36 laps—fastest lap, Jarier 2 min 35.1 sec 184.76 kph/114.83 mph—retired I. Ashley (BRM) oil pump lap 2—J. Watson (Penske) fire lap 2—M. Andretti (Lotus) accident lap 6—R. Peterson (Lotus) accident lap 10—J. Laffite (Ligier) gear linkage lap 14—V. Brambilla (March) oil leak lap 15—J. Hunt (McLaren) accident lap 32—J-P Jarier (Shadow) accident lap 33.

Starting grid 2-2-2

Hunt 2 min 32.5 sec—Lauda 2 min 32.5 sec—Jarier 2 min 32.7 sec—Regazzoni 2 min 33.2 sec—Fittipaldi 2 min 33.3 sec—Mass 2 min 33.6 sec—Brambilla 2 min 33.8 sec—Watson 2 min 33.9 sec—Depailler 2 min 34.5 sec—Pace 2 min 34.5 sec—Laffite 2 min 34.7 sec—Pryce 2 min 34.8 sec—Scheckter 2 min 35.0 sec—Stuck 2 min 35.4 sec—Reutemann 2 min 36.0 sec—Andretti 2 min 36.0 sec—Zorzi 2 min 37.1 sec—Peterson 2 min 37.2 sec—Ickx 2 min 37.6 sec—Hoffman 2 min 40.2 sec—Ashley 2 min 40.9 sec—Lombardi 2 min 40.9 sec.

SOUTH AFRICAN GRAND PRIX

Kyalami; 6 March; 78 laps 199 miles/320 km
1 N. Lauda (Ferrari) 1 hr 42 min 18.4 sec 116.65 mph/187.73 kph—2 J. Hunt (McLaren) 1 hr 42 min 19.7 sec—3 J. Mass (McLaren) 1 hr 43 min 04.3 sec—4 J. Scheckter (Tyrrell) 1 hr 43 min 26.8 sec—5 J. Watson (Penske) 77 laps—6. M. Andretti (Parnelli) 77 laps—7 T. Pryce (Shadow) 77 laps—8 V. Brambilla (March) 77 laps—9 P. Depailler (Tyrrell) 77 laps—10 B. Evans (Lotus) 77 laps—11 B. Lunger (Surtees) 77 laps—12 H-J Stuck (March) 76 laps—13 M. Leclere (Williams) 76 laps—14 C. Amon (Ensign) 76 laps—15 H. Ertl (Hesketh) 74 laps—16 J. Ickx (Williams) 73 laps—17 E. Fittipaldi (Fittipaldi) 70 laps—fastest lap, Lauda 1 min 18.0 sec 117.74 mph/189.48 kph—retired I. Scheckter (Tyrrell) collision 0 laps—R. Peterson (March) accident lap 15—C. Reutemann (Brabham) engine lap 16—G. Nilsson (Lotus) clutch lap 18—C. Pace (Brabham) engine lap 22—J-P Jarier (Shadow) radiator lap 28—J. Laffite (Ligier) engine lap 49—C. Regazzoni (Ferrari) engine lap 52.

Starting grid 2-2-2

Lauda 1 min 16.2 sec—Hunt 1 min 16.1 sec—Mass 1 min 16.4 sec—Watson 1 min 16.4 sec—Brambilla 1 min 16.6 sec—Depailler 1 min 16.8 sec—Pryce 1 min 16.8 sec—Laffite 1 min 16.9 sec—Regazzoni 1 min 16.9 sec—Peterson 1 min 17.0 sec—Reutemann 1 min 17.1 sec—Scheckter 1 min 17.2 sec—Andretti 1 min 17.2 sec—Pace 1 min 17.3 sec—Jarier 1 min 17.3 sec—I. Scheckter 1 min 17.4 sec—Stuck 1 min 17.4 sec—Amon 1 min 17.7 sec—Ickx 1 min 18.1 sec—Lunger 1 min 18.4 sec—Fittipaldi 1 min 18.4 sec—Leclere 1 min 18.8 sec—Evans 1 min 19.3 sec—Ertl 1 min 22.1 sec—Nilsson 1 min 22.7 sec.

UNITED STATES GRAND PRIX WEST

Long Beach; 28 March; 80 laps 162 miles/260 km
1 C. Regazzoni (Ferrari) 1 hr 53 min 18.5 sec 85.57 mph/137.71 kph—2 N. Lauda (Ferrari) 1 hr 54 min 00.9 sec—3 P. Depailler (Tyrrell) 1 hr 54 min 08.4 sec—4 J. Laffite (Ligier) 1 hr 54 min 31.3 sec—5 J. Mass (McLaren) 1 hr 54 min 40.8 sec—6 E. Fittipaldi (Fittipaldi) 79 laps—7 J-P Jarier (Shadow) 79 laps—8 C. Amon (Ensign) 78 laps—9 C. Pace (Brabham) 77 laps—10 R. Peterson (March) 77 laps—not classified A Jones (Surtees) 70 laps—J. Watson (Penske) 69 laps—fastest lap, Regazzoni 1 min 23.1 sec 87.53 mph/140.87 kph—retired V. Brambilla (March) accident 0 laps—C. Reutemann (Brabham) accident 0 laps—G. Nilsson (Lotus) accident 0 laps—H-J Stuck (March) accident lap 2—J. Hunt (McLaren) accident lap 3—M. Andretti (Parnelli) water leak lap 15—T. Pryce (Shadow) drive shaft lap 32—J. Scheckter (Tyrrell) suspension lap 34.

Starting grid 1-1-1

Regazzoni 1 min 23.1 sec—Depailler 1 min 23.3 sec—Hunt 1 min 23.4 sec—Lauda 1 min 23.6 sec—Pryce 1 min 23.7 sec—Peterson 1 min 24.2 sec—Jarier 1 min 24.2 sec—Brambilla 1 min 24.2 sec—Watson 1 min 24.2 sec—Reutemann 1 min 24.3 sec—Scheckter 1 min 24.3 sec—Laffite 1 min 24.4 sec—Pace 1 min 24.5 sec—Mass 1 min 24.5 sec—Andretti 1 min 24.6 sec—Fittipaldi 1 min 24.8 sec—Amon 1 min 24.8 sec—Stuck 1 min 25.1 sec—Jones 1 min 25.2 sec—Nilsson 1 min 25.3 sec—non starters M. Leclere (Williams)—I. Hoffman (Fittipaldi)—A. Merzario (March)—B. Evans (Lotus)—J. Ickx (Williams)—H. Ertl (Hesketh)—B. Lunger (Surtees).

SPANISH GRAND PRIX

Jarama; 2 May; 75 laps 255 km/159 miles
1 J. Hunt (McLaren) 1 hr 42 min 20.4 sec 149.69 kph/93.01 mph—2 N. Lauda (Ferrari) 1 hr 42 min 51.4 sec—3 G. Nilsson (Lotus) 1 hr 43 min 08.4 sec—4 C. Reutemann (Brabham) 74 laps—5 C. Amon (Ensign) 74 laps—6 C. Pace (Brabham) 74 laps—7 J. Ickx (Williams) 74 laps—8 T. Pryce (Shadow) 74 laps—9 A. Jones (Surtees) 74 laps—10 M. Leclere (Williams) 73 laps—11 C. Regazzoni (Ferrari) 72 laps—12 J. Laffite (Ligier) 72 laps—13 L. Perkins (Boro) 72 laps—fastest lap, Mass 1 min 20.9 sec 151.43 kph/94.1 mph—retired E. Fittipaldi (Fittipaldi) gear linkage lap 3—R. Peterson (March) transmission lap 11—H-J Stuck (March) gearbox lap 16—V. Brambilla (March) accident lap 21—P. Depailler (Tyrrell) accident lap 25—M. Andretti (Lotus) gear selector lap 34—A. Merzario (March) gear linkage lap 36—J. Watson (Penske) engine lap 51—J. Scheckter (Tyrrell) engine lap 53—J-P Jarier (Shadow) electrics lap 61—J. Mass (McLaren) engine lap 65.

Starting grid 2-2-2

Hunt 1 min 18.5 sec—Lauda 1 min 18.8 sec—Depailler 1 min 19.1 sec—Mass 1 min 19.1 sec—Regazzoni 1 min 19.1 sec—Brambilla 1 min 19.3 sec—Nilsson 1 min 19.3 sec—Laffite 1 min 19.4 sec—Andretti 1 min 19.6 sec—Amon 1 min 19.8 sec—Pace 1 min 19.9 sec—Reutemann 1 min 20.1 sec—Watson 1 min 20.2 sec—Scheckter 1 min 20.2 sec—Jarier 1 min 20.2 sec—Peterson 1 min 20.3 sec—Stuck 1 min 20.4 sec—Merzario 1 min 20.6 sec—Fittipaldi 1 min 20.7 sec—Jones 1 min 20.9 sec—Ickx 1 min 21.1 sec—Pryce 1 min 21.2 sec—Leclere 1 min 21.3 sec—Perkins 1 min 21.5 sec—non starters B. Lunger (Surtees)—L. Kessel (Brabham)—E. Zapico (Williams)—E. Villota (Brabham) H. Ertl (Hesketh)—I. Hoffman (Fittipaldi).

BELGIAN GRAND PRIX

Zolder; 16 May; 70 laps 298 km/185 miles
1 N. Lauda (Ferrari) 1 hr 42 min 53.2 sec 173.98 kph/108.11 mph—2 C. Regazzoni (Ferrari) 1 hr 42 min 56.7 sec—3 J. Laffite (Ligier) 1 hr 43 min 28.6 sec—4 J. Scheckter (Tyrrell) 1 hr 44 min 24.3 sec—5 A. Jones (Surtees) 69 laps—6 J. Mass (McLaren) 69 laps—7 J. Watson (Penske) 69 laps—8 L. Perkins (Boro) 69 laps—9 J-P Jarier (Shadow) 69 laps—10 T. Pryce (Shadow) 68 laps—11 M. Leclere (Williams) 68 laps—12 L. Kessel (Brabham) 63 laps—fastest lap, Lauda 1 min 26.0 sec 178.45 kph/110.88 mph retired V. Brambilla (March) drive shaft lap 6—G. Nilsson (Lotus) accident lap 7—R. Peterson (March) accident lap 16—C. Reutemann (Brabham) engine lap 17—A. Merzario (March) engine lap 21—P. Neve (Brabham) drive shaft lap 24—M. Andretti (Lotus) drive shaft lap 28—P. Depailler (Tyrrell) engine lap 29—H. Ertl (Hesketh) engine lap 31—H-J Stuck (March)

BELGIAN GRAND PRIX—*continued*

suspension lap 33—J. Hunt (McLaren) transmission lap 35—C. Amon (Ensign) accident lap 51—C. Pace (Brabham) electrics lap 58—B. Lunger (Surtees) electrics lap 62.

Starting grid 2-2-2

Lauda 1 min 26.5 sec—Regazzoni 1 min 26.6 sec—Hunt 1 min 26.7 sec—Depailler 1 min 26.9 sec—Brambilla 1 min 26.9 sec—Laffite 1 min 27.1 sec—Scheckter 1 min 27.2 sec—Amon 1 min 27.5 sec—Pace 1 min 27.7 sec—Peterson 1 min 27.7 sec—Andretti 1 min 27.7 sec—Reutemann 1 min 28.3 sec—Pryce 1 min 28.4 sec—Jarier 1 min 28.4 sec—Stuck 1 min 28.4 sec—Jones 1 min 28.4 sec—Watson 1 min 28.4 sec—Mass 1 min 28.5 sec—Neve 1 min 28.8 sec—Perkins 1 min 28.8 sec—Merzario 1 min 28.8 sec—Nilsson 1 min 29.0 sec—Kessel 1 min 29.1 sec—Ertl 1 min 29.4 sec—Leclere 1 min 29.5 sec—Lunger 1 min 29.8 sec—non starters E. Fittipaldi (Fittipaldi)—J. Ickx (Williams)—G. Edwards (Hesketh).

MONACO GRAND PRIX

Monte Carlo; 30 May; 78 laps 258 km/160 miles
1 N. Lauda (Ferrari) 1 hr 59 min 51.5 sec 129.32 kph/80.36 mph—2 J. Scheckter (Tyrrell) 2 hr 0 min 02.6 sec—3 P. Depailler (Tyrrell) 2 hr 0 min 56.3 sec—4 H-J Stuck (March) 77 laps—5 J. Mass (McLaren) 77 laps—6 E. Fittipaldi (Fittipaldi) 77 laps—7 T. Pryce (Shadow) 77 laps—8 J-P Jarier (Shadow) 76 laps—9 C. Pace (Brabham) 76 laps—10 J. Watson (Penske) 76 laps—11 M. Leclere (Williams) 76 laps—12 J. Laffite (Ligier) 75 laps—13 C. Amon (Ensign) 74 laps—fastest lap, Regazzoni 1 min 30.3 sec 132.07 kph/82.06 mph—retired C. Reutemann (Brabham) accident 0 laps—A. Jones (Surtees) accident lap 1—V. Brambilla (March) suspension lap 9—J. Hunt (McLaren) engine lap 24—R. Peterson (March) accident lap 26—G. Nilsson (Lotus) engine lap 39—C. Regazzoni (Ferrari) accident lap 73.

Starting grid 1-1-1

Lauda 1 min 29.6 sec—Regazzoni 1 min 29.9 sec—Peterson 1 min 30.1 sec—Depailler 1 min 30.3 sec—Scheckter 1 min 30.5 sec—Stuck 1 min 30.6 sec—Fittipaldi 1 min 31.4 sec—Laffite 1 min 31.5 sec—Brambilla 1 min 31.5 sec—Jarier 1 min 31.6 sec—Mass 1 min 31.7 sec—Amon 1 min 31.7 sec—Pace 1 min 31.8 sec—Hunt 1 min 31.9 sec—Pryce 1 min 32.0 sec—Nilsson 1 min 32.1 sec—Watson 1 min 32.1 sec—Leclere 1 min 32.2 sec—Jones 1 min 32.3 sec—Reutemann 1 min 32.4 sec—non starters J. Ickx (Williams)—H. Pescarolo (Surtees)—L. Perkins (Boro)—H. Ertl (Hesketh)—A. Merzario (March).

SWEDISH GRAND PRIX

Anderstorp; 13 June; 72 laps 289 km/180 miles
1 J. Scheckter (Tyrrell) 1 hr 46 min 53.7 sec 162.38 kph/100.9 mph—2 P. Depailler (Tyrrell) 1 hr 47 min 13.5 sec—3 N. Lauda (Ferrari) 1 hr 47 min 27.6 sec—4 J. Laffite (Ligier) 1 hr 47 min 49.5 sec—5 J. Hunt (McLaren) 1 hr 47 min 53.2 sec—6 C. Regazzoni (Ferrari) 1 hr 47 min 54.1 sec—7 R. Peterson (March) 1 hr 47 min 57.2 sec—8 C. Pace (Brabham) 1 hr 48 min 05.3 sec—9 T. Pryce (Shadow) 71 laps—10 V. Brambilla (March) 71 laps—11 J. Mass (McLaren) 71 laps—12 J-P Jarier (Shadow) 71 laps—13 A. Jones (Surtees) 71 laps—14 A. Merzario (March) 70 laps—15 B. Lunger (Surtees) 70 laps—fastest lap, Andretti 1 min 28.0 sec 164.37 kph/102.13 mph—retired J. Watson (Penske) accident 0 laps—C. Reutemann (Brabham) engine lap 2—G. Nilsson (Lotus) accident lap 2—L. Kessel (Brabham) accident lap 5—E. Fittipaldi (Fittipaldi) handling lap 10—L. Perkins (Boro) engine lap 18—M. Leclere (Williams) engine lap 20—C. Amon (Ensign) accident lap 38—M. Andretti (Lotus) engine lap 45—H-J Stuck (March) engine lap 52—H. Ertl (Hesketh) accident lap 54.

Starting grid 2-2-2

Scheckter 1 min 25.7 sec—Andretti 1 min 26.0 sec—Amon 1 min 26.2 sec—Depailler 1 min 26.4 sec—Lauda 1 min 26.4 sec—Nilsson 1 min 26.6 sec—Laffite 1 min 26.8 sec—Hunt 1 min 27.0 sec—Peterson 1 min 27.0 sec—Pace 1 min 27.1 sec—Regazzoni 1 min 27.2 sec—Pryce 1 min 27.5 sec—Mass 1 min 27.6 sec—Jarier 1 min 27.6 sec—Brambilla 1 min 27.6 sec—Reutemann 1 min 27.8 sec—Watson 1 min 28.1 sec—Jones 1 min 28.2 sec—Merzario 1 min 28.2 sec—Stuck 1 min 28.2 sec—Fittipaldi 1 min 28.7 sec—Perkins 1 min 28.8 sec—Ertl 1 min 28.9 sec—Lunger 1 min 29.3 sec—Leclere 1 min 29.6 sec—Kessel 1 min 30.0 sec—non starter J. Nelleman (Brabham).

FRENCH GRAND PRIX

Paul Ricard; 4 July; 54 laps 314 km/195 miles
1 J. Hunt (McLaren) 1 hr 40 min 58.6 sec 186.42 kph/115.84 mph—2 P. Depailler (Tyrrell) 1 hr 41 min 11.3 sec—3 J. Watson (Penske) 1 hr 41 min 22.1 sec—4 C. Pace (Brabham) 1 hr 41 min 23.4 sec—5 M. Andretti (Lotus) 1 hr 41 min 42.5 sec—6 J. Scheckter (Tyrrell) 1 hr 41 min 53.7 sec—7 H-J Stuck (March) 1 hr 42 min 20.1 sec—8 T. Pryce (Shadow) 1 hr 42 min 29.3 sec—9 A. Merzario (March) 1 hr 42 min 52.2 sec—10 J. Ickx (Williams) 53 laps—11 C. Reutemann (Brabham) 53 laps—12 J-P Jarier (Shadow) 53 laps—13 M. Leclere (Williams) 53 laps—14 J. Laffite (Ligier) 53 laps—15 J. Mass (McLaren) 53 laps—16 B. Lunger (Surtees) 53 laps—17 G. Edwards (Hesketh) 53 laps—18 P. Neve (Ensign) 53 laps—19 R. Peterson (March) 51 laps—fastest lap, Lauda 1 min 51.0 sec 188.43 kph/117.09 mph—retired H. Ertl (Hesketh) drive shaft lap 4—G. Nilsson (Lotus) transmission lap 8—N. Lauda (Ferrari) engine lap 8—C. Regazzoni (Ferrari) engine lap 17—H. Pescarolo (Surtees) suspension lap 19—E. Fittipaldi (Fittipaldi) engine lap 21—V. Brambilla (March) engine lap 28—A. Jones (Surtees) suspension lap 44.

Starting grid 2-2-2

Hunt 1 min 47.9 sec—Lauda 1 min 48.2 sec—Depailler 1 min 48.6 sec—Regazzoni 1 min 48.7 sec—Pace 1 min 48.7 sec—Peterson 1 min 49.1 sec—Andretti 1 min 49.2 sec—Watson 1 min 49.2 sec—Scheckter 1 min 49.6 sec—Reutemann 1 min 49.8 sec—Brambilla 1 min 49.8 sec—Nilsson 1 min 49.8 sec—Laffite 1 min 50.1 sec—Mass 1 min 50.1 sec—Jarier 1 min 50.1 sec—Pryce 1 min 50.3 sec—Stuck 1 min 50.3 sec—Jones 1 min 51.1 sec—Ickx 1 min 51.4 sec—Merzario 1 min 51.8 sec—Fittipaldi 1 min 52.1 sec—Leclere 1 min 52.3 sec—Lunger 1 min 52.4 sec—Pescarolo 1 min 52.6 sec—Edwards 1 min 52.6 sec—Neve 1 min 52.8 sec—Ertl 1 min 54.0 sec—non starters D. Magee (Brabham)—I. Hoffman (Fittipaldi)—L. Kessel (Brabham).

BRITISH GRAND PRIX

Brands Hatch; 18 July; 76 laps 198 miles/320 km
1 N. Lauda (Ferrari) 1 hr 44 min 19.7 sec 114.24 mph/183.84 kph—2 J. Scheckter (Tyrrell) 1 hr 44 min 35.8 sec—3 J. Watson (Penske) 75 laps—4 T. Pryce (Shadow) 75 laps—5 A. Jones (Surtees) 75 laps—6 E. Fittipaldi (Fittipaldi) 74 laps—7 H. Ertl (Hesketh) 73 laps—8 C. Pace (Brabham) 73 laps—9 J-P Jarier (Shadow) 70 laps—fastest lap, Lauda 1 min 19.9 sec 117.74 mph/189.49 kph—retired G. Edwards (Hesketh) accident 0 laps—H-J Stuck (March) accident 0 laps—J. Mass (McLaren) clutch lap 1—M. Andretti (Lotus) engine lap 4—C. Amon (Ensign) water leak lap 8—H. Pescarolo (Surtees) fuel pressure lap 16—V. Brambilla (March) accident lap 22—B. Evans (Brabham) gearbox lap 24—A. Merzario (March) engine lap 39—C. Reutemann (Brabham) oil pressure lap 46—P. Depailler (Tyrrell) engine lap 47—B. Lunger (Surtees) gearbox lap 55—R. Peterson (March) fuel pressure lap 60—G. Nilsson (Lotus) engine lap 67—J. Laffite (Ligier) disqualified lap 31—C. Regazzoni (Ferrari) disqualified lap 36—J. Hunt (McLaren) disqualified lap 76.

Starting grid 2-2-2

Lauda 1 min 19.3 sec—Hunt 1 min 19.4 sec—Andretti 1 min 19.8 sec—Regazzoni 1 min 20.0 sec—Depailler 1 min 20.1 sec—Amon 1 min 20.3 sec—Peterson 1 min 20.3 sec—Scheckter 1 min 20.3 sec—Merzario 1 min 20.3

sec—Brambilla 1 min 20.4 sec—Watson 1 min 20.4 sec—Mass 1 min 20.6 sec—Laffite 1 min 20.7 sec—Nilsson 1 min 20.7 sec—Reutemann 1 min 21.0 sec—Pace 1 min 21.0 sec—Stuck 1 min 21.2 sec—Lunger 1 min 21.3 sec—Jones 1 min 21.4 sec—Pryce 1 min 21.8 sec—Fittipaldi 1 min 22.1 sec—Evans 1 min 22.5 sec—Ertl 1 min 22.7 sec—Jarier 1 min 22.7 sec—Edwards 1 min 22.8 sec—Pescarolo 1 min 22.8 sec—non starters J. Ickx (Williams)—D. Galica (Surtees)—M. Wilds (Shadow)—L. Lombardi (Brabham).

GERMAN GRAND PRIX

Nürburgring; 1 August; 14 laps 320 km/199 miles
1 J. Hunt (McLaren) 1 hr 41 min 42.7 sec 188.59 kph/117.18 mph—2 J. Scheckter (Tyrrell) 1 hr 42 min 10.4 sec—3 J. Mass (McLaren) 1 hr 42 min 35.1 sec—4 C. Pace (Brabham) 1 hr 42 min 36.9 sec—5 G. Nilsson (Lotus) 1 hr 43 min 40.0 sec—6 R. Stommelen (Brabham) 1 hr 44 min 13.0 sec—7 J. Watson (Penske) 1 hr 44 min 16.6 sec—8 T. Pryce (Shadow) 1 hr 44 min 30.9 sec—9 C. Regazzoni (Ferrari) 1 hr 45 min 28.7 sec—10 A. Jones (Surtees) 1 hr 45 min 30.0 sec—11 J-P Jarier (Shadow) 1 hr 46 min 34.4 sec—12 M. Andretti (Lotus) 1 hr 46 min 40.8 sec—13 E. Fittipaldi (Fittipaldi) 1 hr 47 min 07.9 sec—14 A. Pesenti-Rossi (Tyrrell) 13 laps—15 G. Edwards (Hesketh) 13 laps—fastest lap, Scheckter 7 min 10.8 sec 190.82 kph/118.57 mph—retired R. Peterson (March) accident 0 laps—C. Reutemann (Brabham) engine 0 laps—P. Depailler (Tyrrell) accident 0 laps—V. Brambilla (March) accident lap 1—A. Merzario (Williams) brakes lap 3. Retired before restart N. Lauda (Ferrari) accident lap 1—B. Lunger (Surtees) accident lap 1—H. Ertl (Hesketh) accident lap 1—H-J Stuck (March) clutch lap 1—J. Laffite (Ligier) gearbox lap 1—C. Amon (Ensign) withdrew lap 1.

Starting grid 2-2-2

Hunt 7 min 06.5 sec—Lauda 7 min 07.4 sec—Depailler 7 min 08.8 sec—Stuck 7 min 09.1 sec—Regazzoni 7 min 09.3 sec—Laffite 7 min 11.3 sec—Pace 7 min 12.0 sec—Scheckter 7 min 12.2 sec—Mass 7 min 13.0 sec—Reutemann 7 min 14.9 sec—Peterson 7 min 14.9 sec—Andretti 7 min 16.1 sec—Brambilla 7 min 17.7 sec—Jones 7 min 19.9 sec—Stommelen 7 min 21.6 sec—Nilsson 7 min 23.0 sec—Amon 7 min 23.1 sec—Pryce 7 min 23.3 sec—Watson 7 min 23.5 sec—Fittipaldi 7 min 28.0 sec—Merzario 7 min 28.8 sec—Ertl 7 min 30.0 sec—Jarier 7 min 30.9 sec—Lunger 7 min 32.7 sec—Edwards 7 mins 38.6 sec—Pesenti-Rossi 7 min 48.5 sec—non starters L. Lombardi (Brabham)—H. Pescarolo (Surtees).

AUSTRIAN GRAND PRIX

Österreichring; 15 August; 54 laps 319 km/198 miles
1 J. Watson (Penske) 1 hr 30 min 07.9 sec 212.43 kph/132.0 mph—2 J. Laffite (Ligier) 1 hr 30 min 18.6 sec—3 G. Nilsson (Lotus) 1 hr 30 min 19.8 sec—4 J. Hunt (McLaren) 1 hr 30 min 20.3 sec—5 M. Andretti (Lotus) 1 hr 30 min 29.3 sec—6 R. Peterson (March) 1 hr 30 min 42.2 sec—7 J. Mass (McLaren) 1 hr 31 min 07.3 sec—8 H. Ertl (Hesketh) 53 laps—9 H. Pescarolo (Surtees) 52 laps—10 B. Lunger (Surtees) 51 laps—11 A. Pesenti-Rossi (Tyrrell) 51 laps—12 L. Lombardi (Brabham) 50 laps—not classified L. Kessel (Brabham) 44 laps—fastest lap, Hunt 1 min 35.9 sec 221.81 kph/137.83 mph—retired C. Reutemann (Brabham) clutch 0 laps—J. Scheckter (Tyrrell) accident lap 14—T. Pryce (Shadow) brakes lap 14—A. Merzario (Williams) accident lap 17—P. Depailler (Tyrrell) suspension lap 24—H-J Stuck (March) fuel pressure lap 26—A. Jones (Surtees) accident lap 40—C. Pace (Brabham) accident lap 40—J-P Jarier (Shadow) fuel pump lap 40—E. Fittipaldi (Fittipaldi) accident lap 43—V. Brambilla (March) accident lap 43—H. Binder (Ensign) throttle lap 47.

Starting grid 2-2-2

Hunt 1 min 35.0 sec—Watson 1 min 35.8 sec—Peterson 1 min 36.3 sec—Nilsson 1 min 36.5 sec—Laffite 1 min 36.5 sec—Pryce 1 min 36.6 sec—Brambilla 1 min 36.6 sec—Pace 1 min 36.7 sec—Andretti 1 min 36.7 sec—Scheckter 1 min 36.9 sec—Stuck 1 min 36.9 sec—Mass 1 min 37.2 sec—Depailler 1 min 37.2 sec—Reutemann 1 min 37.2 sec—Jones 1 min 37.6 sec—Lunger 1 min 37.6 sec—Fittipaldi 1 min 37.8 sec—Jarier 1 min 37.9 sec—Binder 1 min 38.4 sec—Ertl 1 min 39.1 sec—Merzario 1 min 39.3 sec—Pescarolo 1 min 39.8 sec—Pesenti-Rossi 1 min 40.7 sec—Lombardi 1 min 42.2 sec—Kessel 1 min 56.0 sec.

DUTCH GRAND PRIX

Zandvoort; 29 August; 75 laps 317 km/197 miles
1 J. Hunt (McLaren) 1 hr 44 min 52.1 sec 181.34 kph/112.68 mph—2 C. Regazzoni (Ferrari) 1 hr 44 min 53.0 sec—3 M. Andretti (Lotus) 1 hr 44 min 54.2 sec—4 T. Pryce (Shadow) 1 hr 44 min 59.0 sec—5 J. Scheckter (Tyrrell) 1 hr 45 min 14.5 sec—6 V. Brambilla (March) 1 hr 45 min 37.1 sec—7 P. Depailler (Tyrrell) 1 hr 45 min 48.4 sec—8 A. Jones (Surtees) 74 laps—9 J. Mass (McLaren) 74 laps—10 J-P Jarier (Shadow) 74 laps—11 H. Pescarolo (Surtees) 74 laps—12 R. Stommelen (Hesketh) 72 laps—fastest lap, Regazzoni 1 min 22.6 sec 184.21 kph/114.46 mph—retired A. Merzario (Williams) accident lap 5—H-J Stuck (March) engine lap 9—C. Andersson (Surtees) engine lap 9—G. Nilsson (Lotus) accident lap 10—C. Reutemann (Brabham) clutch lap 11—E. Fittipaldi (Fittipaldi) electrics lap 40—L. Perkins (Boro) accident lap 44—J. Watson (Penske) gearbox lap 47—H. Ertl (Hesketh) accident lap 49—R. Peterson (March) engine lap 52—J. Laffite (Ligier) engine lap 53—C. Pace (Brabham) oil leak lap 53—B. Hayje (Penske) drive shaft lap 63—J. Ickx (Ensign) electrics lap 66.

Starting grid 2-2-2

Peterson 1 min 21.3 sec—Hunt 1 min 21.4 sec—Pryce 1 min 21.5 sec—Watson 1 min 21.6 sec—Regazzoni 1 min 21.8 sec—Andretti 1 min 21.9 sec—Brambilla 1 min 21.9 sec—Scheckter 1 min 21.9 sec—Pace 1 min 22.0 sec—Laffite 1 min 22.1 sec—Ickx 1 min 22.1 sec—Reutemann 1 min 22.2 sec—Nilsson 1 min 22.2 sec—Depailler 1 min 22.3 sec—Mass 1 min 22.5 sec—Jones 1 min 22.5 sec—Fittipaldi 1 min 22.5 sec—Stuck 1 min 22.6 sec—Perkins 1 min 23.1 sec—Jarier 1 min 23.2 sec—Hayje 1 min 23.3 sec—Pescarolo 1 min 23.5 sec—Merzario 1 min 24.1 sec—Ertl 1 min 24.4 sec—Stommelen 1 min 24.7 sec—Andersson 1 min 24.7 sec—non starter A. Pesenti-Rossi (Tyrrell).

ITALIAN GRAND PRIX

Monza; 12 September; 52 laps 302 km/187 miles
1 R. Peterson (March) 1 hr 30 min 35.6 sec 199.75 kph/124.12 mph—2 C. Regazzoni (Ferrari) 1 hr 30 min 37.9 sec—3 J. Laffite (Ligier) 1 hr 30 min 38.6 sec—4 N. Lauda (Ferrari) 1 hr 30 min 55.0 sec—5 J. Scheckter (Tyrrell) 1 hr 30 min 55.1 sec—6 P. Depailler (Tyrrell) 1 hr 31 min 11.3 sec—7 V. Brambilla (March) 1 hr 31 min 19.5 sec—8 T. Pryce (Shadow) 1 hr 31 min 28.5 sec—9 C. Reutemann (Ferrari) 1 hr 31 min 33.1 sec—10 J. Ickx (Ensign) 1 hr 31 min 48.0 sec—11 J. Watson (Penske) 1 hr 32 min 17.8 sec—12 A. Jones (Surtees) 51 laps—13 G. Nilsson (Lotus) 51 laps—14 B. Lunger (Surtees) 50 laps—15 E. Fittipaldi (Fittipaldi) 50 laps—16 H. Ertl (Hesketh) 49 laps—17 H. Pescarolo (Surtees) 49 laps—18 A. Pesenti-Rossi (Tyrrell) 49 laps—19 J-P Jarier (Shadow) 47 laps—fastest lap, Peterson 1 min 41.3 sec 206.12 kph/128.08 mph—retired J. Mass (McLaren) engine lap 2—C. Pace (Brabham) engine lap 4—L. Perkins (Boro) con-rod lap 8—J. Hunt (McLaren) accident lap 11—M. Andretti (Lotus) accident lap 23—H-J Stuck (March) accident lap 23—R. Stommelen (Brabham) engine lap 41.

Starting grid 2-2-2

Laffite 1 min 41.3 sec—Scheckter 1 min 41.4 sec—Pace 1 min 41.5 sec—Depailler 1 min 42.1 sec—Lauda 1 min 42.1 sec—Stuck 1 min 42.2 sec—Reutemann 1 min 42.4 sec—Peterson 1 min 42.6 sec—Regazzoni 1 min 43.0 sec—Ickx 1 min 43.3 sec—Stommelen 1 min 43.3 sec—Nilsson 1 min 43.3 sec—Perkins 1 min 43.3 sec—Andretti 1 min 43.3 sec—Pryce 1 min 43.6 sec—Brambilla 1 min 43.9 sec—Jarier 1 min 44.0 sec—Jones 1 min 44.4 sec—Ertl 1 min 44.6 sec—Fittipaldi

ITALIAN GRAND PRIX—*continued*

1 min 44.6 sec—Pesenti-Rossi 1 min 44.6 sec—Pescarolo 1 min 45.1 sec—Lunger 1 min 46.5 sec—Hunt 2 min 08.8 sec—Mass 2 min 11.1 sec—Watson 2 min 13.9 sec—non starters G. Edwards (Hesketh)—A. Merzario (Williams)—O. Stuppacher (Tyrrell).

CANADIAN GRAND PRIX

Mosport; 3 October; 80 laps 197 miles/317 km
1 J. Hunt (McLaren) 1 hr 40 min 09.6 sec 117.84 mph/189.65 kph—2 P. Depailler (Tyrrell) 1 hr 40 min 16.0 sec—3 M. Andretti (Lotus) 1 hr 40 min 20.0 sec—4 J. Scheckter (Tyrrell) 1 hr 40 min 29.4 sec—5 J. Mass (McLaren) 1 hr 40 min 51.4 sec—6 C. Regazzoni (Ferrari) 1 hr 40 min 55.9 sec—7 C. Pace (Brabham) 1 hr 40 min 56.1 sec—8 N. Lauda (Ferrari) 1 hr 41 min 22.6 sec—9 R. Peterson (March) 79 laps—10 J. Watson (Penske) 79 laps—11 T. Pryce (Shadow) 79 laps—12 G. Nilsson (Lotus) 79 laps—13 J. Ickx (Ensign) 79 laps—14 V. Brambilla (March) 79 laps—15 B. Lunger (Surtees) 78 laps—16 A. Jones (Surtees) 78 laps—17 L. Perkins (Brabham) 78 laps—18 J-P Jarier (Shadow) 77 laps—19 H. Pescarolo (Surtees) 77 laps—20 G. Edwards (Hesketh) 75 laps—fastest lap, Depailler 1 min 13.8 sec 119.92 mph/193.0 kph—retired A. Merzario (Williams) accident lap 3—H-J Stuck (March) handling lap 36—E. Fittipaldi (Fittipaldi) exhaust lap 41—J. Laffite (Ligier) oil pressure lap 43.

Starting grid 2-2-2

Hunt 1 min 12.4 sec—Peterson 1 min 12.8 sec—Brambilla 1 min 12.8 sec—Depailler 1 min 12.8 sec—Andretti 1 min 13.0 sec—Lauda 1 min 13.1 sec—Scheckter 1 min 13.2 sec—Stuck 1 min 13.3 sec—Laffite 1 min 13.4 sec—Pace 1 min 13.4 sec—Mass 1 min 13.4 sec—Regazzoni 1 min 13.5 sec—Pryce 1 min 13.7 sec—Watson 1 min 14.0 sec—Nilsson 1 min 14.4 sec—Ickx 1 min 14.5 sec—Fittipaldi 1 min 14.5 sec—Jarier 1 min 15.1 sec—Perkins 1 min 15.6 sec—Jones 1 min 15.6 sec—Pescarolo 1 min 15.8 sec—Lunger 1 min 16.2 sec—Edwards 1 min 17.2 sec—Merzario 1 min 17.3 sec—non starters H. Ertl (Hesketh)—C. Amon (Williams)—O. Stuppacher (Tyrell).

UNITED STATES GRAND PRIX

Watkins Glen; 10 October; 59 laps 199 miles/321 km
1 J. Hunt (McLaren) 1 hr 42 min 40.7 sec 116.43 mph/187.37 kph—2 J. Scheckter (Tyrrell) 1 hr 42 min 48.8 sec—3 N. Lauda (Ferrari) 1 hr 43 min 43.1 sec—4 J. Mass (McLaren) 1 hr 43 min 43.2 sec—5 H-J Stuck (March) 1 hr 43 min 48.7 sec—6 J. Watson (Penske) 1 hr 43 min 48.9 sec—7 C. Regazzoni (Ferrari) 58 laps—8 A. Jones (Surtees) 58 laps—9 E. Fittipaldi (Fittipaldi) 57 laps—10 J-P Jarier (Shadow) 57 laps—11 B. Lunger (Surtees) 57 laps—12 A. Ribeiro (Hesketh) 57 laps—13 H. Ertl (Hesketh) 54 laps—14 W. Brown (Williams) 54 laps—not classified H. Pescarolo (Surtees) 48 laps—fastest lap, Hunt 1 min 42.8 sec 118.2 mph/190.23 kph—retired P. Depailler (Tyrrell) fuel line lap 7—A. Merzario (Williams) accident lap 9—R. Peterson (March) front suspension lap 12—G. Nilsson (Lotus) engine lap 13—J. Ickx (Ensign) accident lap 14—M. Andretti (Lotus) suspension lap 23—L. Perkins (Brabham) suspension lap 30—C. Pace (Brabham) accident lap 31—V. Brambilla (March) puncture lap 34—J. Laffite (Ligier) puncture lap 34—T. Pryce (Shadow) engine lap 45.

Starting grid 2-2-2

Hunt 1 min 43.6 sec—Scheckter 1 min 43.9 sec—Peterson 1 min 43.9 sec—Brambilla 1 min 44.2 sec—Lauda 1 min 44.3 sec—Stuck 1 min 44.3 sec—Depailler 1 min 44.5 sec—Watson 1 min 44.7 sec—Pryce 1 min 45.1 sec—Pace 1 min 45.3 sec—Andretti 1 min 45.3 sec—Laffite 1 min 45.3 sec—Perkins 1 min 45.3 sec—Regazzoni 1 min 45.5 sec—Fittipaldi 1 min 45.6 sec—Jarier 1 min 46.0 sec—Mass 1 min 46.1 sec—Jones 1 min 46.4 sec—Ickx 1 min 46.6 sec—Nilsson 1 min 46.8 sec—Ertl 1 min 49.4 sec—Ribeiro 1 min 49.7 sec—Brown 1 min 51.1 sec—Lunger 1 min 51.4 sec—Merzario 2 min 00.9 sec—Pescarolo 2 min 05.2 sec—non starter O. Stuppacher (Tyrrell).

JAPANESE GRAND PRIX

Fuji; 24 October; 73 laps 198 miles/318 km
1 M. Andretti (Lotus) 1 hr 43 min 58.9 sec 114.09 mph/183.61 kph—2 P. Depailler (Tyrrell) 72 laps—3 J. Hunt (McLaren) 72 laps—4 A. Jones (Surtees) 72 laps—5 C. Regazzoni (Ferrari) 72 laps—6 G. Nilsson (Lotus) 72 laps—7 J. Laffite (Ligier) 72 laps—8 H. Ertl (Hesketh) 72 laps—9 N. Takahara (Surtees) 70 laps—10 J-P Jarier (Shadow) 69 laps—11 M. Hasemi (Kojima) 66 laps—fastest lap, Hasemi 1 min 18.2 sec 124.64 mph/200.59 kph—retired R. Peterson (March) engine 0 laps—L. Perkins (Brabham) withdrew lap 1—N. Lauda (Ferrari) withdrew lap 2—C. Pace (Brabham) withdrew lap 7—E. Fittipaldi (Fittipaldi) withdrew lap 9—A. Merzario (Williams) gearbox lap 23—K. Hoshino (Tyrrell) tyres lap 27—J. Watson (Penske) engine lap 33—J. Mass (McLaren) accident lap 35—H-J Stuck (March) electrics lap 37—V. Brambilla (March) engine lap 38—T. Pryce (Shadow) engine lap 46—H. Binder (Williams) wheel bearing lap 49—J. Scheckter (Tyrrell) engine lap 58.

Starting grid 2-2-2

Andretti 1 min 12.8 sec—Hunt 1 min 12.8 sec—Lauda 1 min 13.1 sec—Watson 1 min 13.3 sec—Scheckter 1 min 13.3 sec—Pace 1 min 13.4 sec—Regazzoni 1 min 13.6 sec—Brambilla 1 min 13.7 sec—Peterson 1 min 13.8 sec—Hasemi 1 min 13.9 sec—Laffite 1 min 13.9 sec—Mass 1 min 14.0 sec—Depailler 1 min 14.1 sec—Pryce 1 min 14.2 sec—Jarier 1 min 14.3 sec—Nilsson 1 min 14.3 sec—Perkins 1 min 14.4 sec—Stuck 1 min 14.4 sec—Merzario 1 min 14.4 sec—Jones 1 min 14.6 sec—Hoshino 1 min 14.6 sec—Ertl 1 min 15.3 sec—Fittipaldi 1 min 15.3 sec—Takahara 1 min 15.8 sec—Binder 1 min 17.4 sec—non starters M. Kuwashima (Williams)—T. Trimmer (Maki).

1976 WORLD CHAMPIONSHIP

1 J. Hunt 69—2 N. Lauda 68—3 J. Scheckter 49—4 P. Depailler 39—5 C. Regazzoni 31—6 M. Andretti 22—7 J. Laffite 20—7= J. Watson 20—9 J. Mass 19—10 G. Nilsson 11—11 R. Peterson 10—11= T. Pryce 10—13 H-J Stuck 8—14 C. Pace 7—14= A. Jones 7—16 C. Reutemann 3—16= E. Fittipaldi 3—18 C. Amon 2—19 R. Stommelen 1—19= V. Brambilla 1.

1977

ARGENTINE GRAND PRIX

Buenos Aires; 9 January; 53 laps 316 km/197 miles
1 J. Scheckter (Wolf) 1 hr 40 min 11.2 sec 189.43 kph/117.71 mph—2 C. Pace (Brabham) 1 hr 40 min 54.4 sec—3 C. Reutemann (Ferrari) 1 hr 40 min 57.2 sec—4 E. Fittipaldi (Fittipaldi) 1 hr 41 min 06.7 sec—5 M. Andretti (Lotus) 51 laps—6 C. Regazzoni (Ensign) 51 laps—7 V. Brambilla (Surtees) 48 laps—not classified T. Pryce (Shadow) 45 laps—J. Laffite (Ligier) 37 laps—fastest lap, Hunt 1 min 51.1 sec 193.46 kph/120.21 mph—retired R. Zorzi (Shadow) gearbox lap 2—H. Binder (Surtees) damage lap 18—N. Lauda (Ferrari) fuel metering unit lap 20—I. Hoffman (Fittipaldi) engine lap 22—R. Peterson (Tyrrell) accident lap 28—J. Mass (McLaren) accident lap 28—J. Hunt (McLaren) suspension lap 31—P. Depailler (Tyrrell) overheating lap 32—A. Ribeiro (March) broken gear lever lap 39—J. Watson (Brabham) suspension lap 41—I. Scheckter (March) battery lap 45.

Starting grid 2-2-2

Hunt 1 min 48.7 sec—Watson 1 min 49.0 sec—Depailler 1 min 49.1 sec—Lauda 1 min 49.7 sec—Mass 1 min 49.8 sec—Pace 1 min 50.0 sec—Reutemann 1 min 50.0 sec—Andretti 1 min 50.1 sec—Pryce 1 min 50.6 sec—Scheckter 1 min 50.8 sec—Regazzoni 1 min 51.0 sec—Brambilla 1 min 51.0 sec—Peterson 1 min 51.3 sec—Laffite 1 min 51.5 sec—Fittipaldi 1 min 51.5 sec—I. Scheckter 1 min 52.4 sec—Binder 1 min 53.1 sec—Hoffman 1 min 53.3 sec—Ribeiro 1 min 53.5 sec—Zorzi 1 min 54.2 sec—non starter Nilsson (Lotus).

BRAZIL GRAND PRIX

Interlagos; 23 January; 40 laps 318 km/198 miles
1 C. Reutemann (Ferrari) 1 hr 45 min 07.7 sec 181.72 kph/112.92 mph—2 J. Hunt (McLaren) 1 hr 45 min 18.4 sec—3 N. Lauda (Ferrari) 1 hr 46 min 55.2 sec—4 E. Fittipaldi (Fittipaldi) 39 laps—5 G. Nilsson (Lotus) 39 laps—6 R. Zorzi (Shadow) 39 laps—7 I. Hoffman (Fittipaldi) 38 laps—fastest lap, Hunt 2 min 34.5 sec 185.42 kph/115.22 mph—retired L. Perkins (BRM) engine lap 1—I. Scheckter (March) transmission lap 1—V. Brambilla (Surtees) accident lap 11—J. Scheckter (Wolf) engine lap 11—R. Peterson (Tyrrell) accident lap 12—C. Regazzoni (Ensign) accident lap 12—J. Mass (McLaren) accident lap 12—A. Ribeiro (March) engine lap 16—M. Andretti (Lotus) electrics lap 19—P. Depailler (Tyrrell) accident lap 23—J. Laffite (Ligier) accident lap 26—J. Watson (Brabham) accident lap 30—H. Binder (Surtees) suspension lap 32—C. Pace (Brabham) accident lap 33—T. Pryce (Shadow) engine lap 33.

Starting grid 2-2-2

Hunt 2 min 30.1 sec—Reutemann 2 min 30.2 sec—Andretti 2 min 30.3 sec—Mass 2 min 30.4 sec—Pace 2 min 30.6 sec—Depailler 2 min 30.7 sec—Watson 2 min 31.1 sec—Peterson 2 min 31.6 sec—Regazzoni 2 min 31.7 sec—Nilsson 2 min 32.1 sec—Brambilla 2 min 32.2 sec—Pryce 2 min 32.2 sec—Lauda 2 min 32.4 sec—Laffite 2 min 32.4 sec—Scheckter 2 min 32.8 sec—Fittipaldi 2 min 32.9 sec—I. Scheckter 2 min 33.5 sec—Zorzi 2 min 34.6 sec—Hoffman 2 min 35.6 sec—Binder 2 min 35.8 sec—Ribeiro 2 min 36.2 sec—Perkins 2 min 42.2 sec.

SOUTH AFRICAN GRAND PRIX

Kyalami; 5 March; 78 laps 199 miles/320 km
1 N. Lauda (Ferrari) 1 hr 42 min 21.6 sec 116.59 mph/187.63 kph—2 J. Scheckter (Wolf) 1 hr 42 min 26.8 sec—3 P. Depailler (Tyrrell) 1 hr 42 min 27.3 sec—4 J. Hunt (McLaren) 1 hr 42 min 31.1 sec—5 J. Mass (McLaren) 1 hr 42 min 41.5 sec—6 J. Watson (Brabham) 1 hr 42 min 41.8 sec—7 V. Brambilla (Surtees) 1 hr 42 min 45.2 sec—8 C. Reutemann (Ferrari) 1 hr 42 min 48.3 sec—9 C. Regazzoni (Ensign) 1 hr 43 min 07.8 sec—10 E. Fittipaldi (Fittipaldi) 1 hr 43 min 33.3 sec—11 H. Binder (Surtees) 77 laps—12 G. Nilsson (Lotus) 77 laps—13 C. Pace (Brabham) 76 laps—14 B. Lunger (March) 76 laps—15 L. Perkins (BRM) 73 laps—fastest lap, Watson 1 min 17.6 sec 118.25 mph/190.31 kph—retired R. Peterson (Tyrrell) fuel pressure lap 5—R. Zorzi (Shadow) engine lap 21—J. Laffite (Matra) accident lap 22—T. Pryce (Shadow) fatal accident lap 22—B. Hayje (March) gearbox lap 33—M. Andretti (Lotus) accident lap 43—H-J Stuck (March) engine lap 55—A. Ribeiro (March) engine lap 66.

Starting grid 2-2-2

Hunt 1 min 16.0 sec—Pace 1 min 16.0 sec—Lauda 1 min 16.3 sec—Depailler 1 min 16.3 sec—Scheckter 1 min 16.3 sec—Andretti 1 min 16.4 sec—Peterson 1 min 16.4 sec—Reutemann 1 min 16.5 sec—Fittipaldi 1 min 16.6 sec—Nilsson 1 min 16.6 sec—Watson 1 min 16.7 sec—Laffite 1 min 16.7 sec—Mass 1 min 17.0 sec—Brambilla 1 min 17.1 sec—Pryce 1 min 17.1 sec—Regazzoni 1 min 17.2 sec—Ribeiro 1 min 17.4 sec—Stuck 1 min 17.5 sec—Binder 1 min 18.1 sec—Zorzi 1 min 18.4 sec—Hayje 1 min 19.6 sec—Perkins 1 min 21.8 sec—Lunger 1 min 24.3 sec.

UNITED STATES GRAND PRIX WEST

Long Beach; 3 April; 80 laps 162 miles/258 km
1 M. Andretti (Lotus) 1 hr 51 min 35.5 sec 86.89 mph/139.83 kph—2 N. Lauda (Ferrari) 1 hr 51 min 36.2 sec—3 J. Scheckter (Wolf) 1 hr 51 min 40.3 sec—4 P. Depailler (Tyrrell) 1 hr 52 min 50.0 sec—5 E. Fittipaldi (Fittipaldi) 1 hr 52 min 56.4 sec—6 J-P Jarier (Penske) 79 laps—7 J. Hunt (McLaren) 79 laps—8 G. Nilsson (Lotus) 79 laps—9 J. Laffite (Ligier) 78 laps—10 B. Henton (March) 77 laps—11 H. Binder (Surtees) 77 laps—fastest lap, Lauda 1 min 22.7 sec 87.88 mph/141.42 kph—retired V. Brambilla (Surtees) accident 0 laps—B. Lunger (March) accident lap 4—C. Reutemann (Ferrari) accident lap 5—A. Ribeiro (March) gearbox lap 15—R. Zorzi (Shadow) gearbox lap 27—J. Watson (Brabham) disqualified lap 33—J. Mass (McLaren) vibration lap 39—A. Jones (Shadow) gearbox lap 40—H-J Stuck (Brabham) brakes lap 53—C. Regazzoni (Ensign) gearbox lap 57—R. Peterson (Tyrrell) fuel line lap 62.

Starting grid 2-2-2

Lauda 1 min 21.6 sec—Andretti 1 min 21.9 sec—Scheckter 1 min 21.9 sec—Reutemann 1 min 22.3 sec—Laffite 1 min 22.3 sec—Watson 1 min 22.4 sec—Fittipaldi 1 min 22.4 sec—Hunt 1 min 22.5 sec—Jarier 1 min 22.6 sec—Peterson 1 min 22.6 sec—Brambilla 1 min 22.7 sec—Depailler 1 min 22.7 sec—Regazzoni 1 min 22.8 sec—Jones 1 min 23.1 sec—Mass 1 min 23.2 sec—Nilsson 1 min 23.4 sec—Stuck 1 min 23.8 sec—Henton 1 min 24.0 sec—Binder 1 min 24.2 sec—Zorzi 1 min 24.4 sec—Lunger 1 min 25.0 sec—Ribeiro 1 min 25.1 sec.

SPANISH GRAND PRIX

Jarama; 8 May; 75 laps 255 km/159 miles
1 M. Andretti (Lotus) 1 hr 42 min 52.2 sec—2 C. Reutemann (Ferrari) 1 hr 43 min 08.1 sec—3 J. Scheckter (Wolf) 1 hr 43 min 16.7 sec—4 J. Mass (McLaren) 1 hr 43 min 17.1 sec—5 G. Nilsson (Lotus) 1 hr 43 min 58.0 sec—6 H-J Stuck (Brabham) 74 laps—7 J. Laffite (Ligier) 74 laps—8 R. Peterson (Tyrrell) 74 laps—9 H. Binder (Surtees) 73 laps—10 B. Lunger (March) 72 laps—11 I. Scheckter (March) 72 laps—12 P. Neve (March) 71 laps—13 E. Villota (McLaren) 70 laps—14 E. Fittipaldi (Fittipaldi) 70 laps—fastest lap, Laffite 1 min 20.8 sec 151.66 kph/94.24 mph—retired V. Brambilla (Surtees) accident lap 9—C. Regazzoni (Ensign) accident lap 9—J. Hunt (McLaren) engine lap 10—P. Depailler (Tyrrell) engine lap 12—A. Merzario (March) damaged suspension lap 16—R. Zorzi (Shadow) engine lap 25—H. Ertl (Hesketh) radiators lap 29—R. Keegan (Hesketh) accident lap 32—A. Jones (Shadow) accident lap 56—J. Watson (Brabham) fuel metering unit lap 64.

Starting grid 2-2-2

Andretti 1 min 18.7 sec—Laffite 1 min 19.4 sec—Reutemann 1 min 19.5 sec—Scheckter 1 min 19.8 sec—Watson 1 min 19.9 sec—Hunt 1 min 20.1 sec—Regazzoni 1 min 20.1 sec—Mass 1 min 20.1 sec—Depailler 1 min 20.2 sec—Brambilla 1 min 20.3 sec—Nilsson 1 min 20.4 sec—Stuck 1 min 20.5 sec—Jones 1 min 20.7 sec—Peterson 1 min 21.0 sec—Keegan 1 min 21.0 sec—I. Scheckter 1 min 21.0 sec—Ertl 1 min 21.2 sec—Fittipaldi 1 min 21.6 sec—Binder 1 min 21.7 sec—Merzario 1 min 21.8 sec—Neve 1 min 21.9 sec—Vilotta 1 min 22.0 sec—Zorzi 1 min 22.1 sec—Lunger 1 min 22.2 sec—non starters Lauda (Ferrari)—Jarrier (Penske)—Ribeiro (March)—Hayje (March)—Henton (March)—Purley (Lec)—Andersson (BRM).

MONACO GRAND PRIX

Monte Carlo; 22 May; 76 laps 252 km/156 miles
1 J. Scheckter (Wolf) 1 hr 57 min 52.8 sec 128.12 kph/79.61 mph—2 N. Lauda (Ferrari) 1 hr 57 min 53.7 sec—3 C. Reutemann (Ferrari) 1 hr 58 min 25.6 sec—4 J. Mass (McLaren) 1 hr 58 min 27.4 sec—5 M. Andretti (Lotus) 1 hr 58 min 28.3 sec—6 A. Jones (Shadow) 1 hr 58 min 29.4 sec—7 J. Laffite (Ligier) 1 hr 58 min 57.2 sec—8 V. Brambilla (Surtees) 1 hr 59 min 01.4 sec—9 R. Patrese (Shadow) 75 laps—10 J. Ickx (Ensign) 75 laps—11 J-P Jarier

MONACO GRAND PRIX—*continued*

(Penske) 74 laps—12 R. Keegan (Hesketh) 73 laps—fastest lap, Scheckter 1 min 31.1 sec 130.92 kph/81.35 mph—retired R. Peterson (Tyrrell) brakes lap 10—H-J Stuck (Brabham) fire lap 19—J. Hunt (McLaren) engine valve lap 25—E. Fittipaldi (Fittipaldi) engine lap 37—H. Binder (Surtees) fuel injection lap 41—P. Depailler (Tyrrell) brakes lap 46—J. Watson (Brabham) gearbox lap 48—G. Nilsson (Lotus) gearbox lap 51.

Starting grid 1-1-1

Watson 1 min 29.9 sec—Scheckter 1 min 30.3 sec—Reutemann 1 min 30.4 sec—Peterson 1 min 30.7 sec—Stuck 1 min 30.7 sec—Lauda 1 min 30.8 sec—Hunt 1 min 30.8 sec—Depailler 1 min 31.2 sec—Mass 1 min 31.4 sec—Andretti 1 min 31.5 sec—Jones 1 min 32.0 sec—Jarier 1 min 32.3 sec—Nilsson 1 min 32.4 sec—Brambilla 1 min 32.4 sec—Patrese 1 min 32.5 sec—Laffite 1 min 32.6 sec—Ickx 1 min 33.2 sec—Fittipaldi 1 min 33.4 sec—Binder 1 min 33.5 sec—Keegan 1 min 33.8 sec—non starters Merzario (March)—Hayje (March)—Ertl (Hesketh)—Regazzoni (Ensign)—Ribeiro (March)—I. Scheckter (March).

BELGIAN GRAND PRIX

Zolder; 5 June; 70 laps 298 km/185 miles
1 G. Nilsson (Lotus) 1 hr 55 min 05.7 sec 155.53 kph/96.64 mph—2 N. Lauda (Ferrari) 1 hr 55 min 19.9 sec—3 R. Peterson (Tyrrell) 1 hr 55 min 25.7 sec—4 V. Brambilla (Surtees) 1 hr 55 min 30.7 sec—5 A. Jones (Shadow) 1 hr 56 min 21.2 sec—6 H-J Stuck (Brabham) 69 laps—7 J. Hunt (McLaren) 69 laps—8 P. Depailler (Tyrrell) 69 laps—9 H. Ertl (Hesketh) 69 laps—10 P. Neve (March) 68 laps—11 J-P Jarier (Penske) 68 laps—12 L. Perkins (Surtees) 67 laps—13 D. Purley (Lec) 67 laps—14 A. Merzario (March) 65 laps—not classified B. Hayje (March) 63 laps—fastest lap, Nilsson 1 min 27.4 sec 175.63 kph/109.13 mph—retired J. Watson (Brabham) accident 0 laps—M. Andretti (Lotus) accident 0 laps—E. Fittipaldi (Fittipaldi) ignition lap 2—I. Scheckter (March) accident lap 8—R. Patrese (Shadow) accident lap 12—C. Reutemann (Ferrari) accident lap 14—R. Keegan (Hesketh) accident lap 14—C. Regazzoni (Ensign) engine lap 29—J. Laffite (Ligier) engine lap 32—J. Mass (McLaren) accident lap 39—J. Scheckter (Wolf) engine lap 62.

Starting grid 2-2-2

Andretti 1 min 24.6 sec—Watson 1 min 26.2 sec—Nilsson 1 min 26.4 sec—Scheckter 1 min 26.5 sec—Depailler 1 min 26.7 sec—Mass 1 min 26.8 sec—Reutemann 1 min 26.8 sec—Peterson 1 min 26.9 sec—Hunt 1 min 27.0 sec—Laffite 1 min 27.0 sec—Lauda 1 min 27.1 sec—Brambilla 1 min 27.2 sec—Regazzoni 1 min 27.3 sec—Merzario 1 min 27.3 sec—Patrese 1 min 27.3 sec—Fittipaldi 1 min 27.5 sec—Jones 1 min 27.5 sec—Stuck 1 min 27.7 sec—Keegan 1 min 28.0 sec—Purley 1 min 28.1 sec—I. Scheckter 1 min 28.5 sec—Perkins 1 min 28.5 sec—Neve 1 min 28.7 sec—Ertl 1 min 29.0 sec—Jarier 1 min 29.1 sec—Hayje 1 min 29.5 sec.

SWEDISH GRAND PRIX

Anderstorp; 19 June; 72 laps 289 km/180 miles
1 J. Laffite (Ligier) 1 hr 46 min 55.5 sec 162.33 kph/100.87 mph—2 J. Mass (McLaren) 1 hr 47 min 04.0 sec—3 C. Reutemann (Ferrari) 1 hr 47 min 09.9 sec—4 P. Depailler (Tyrrell) 1 hr 47 min 11.8 sec—5 J. Watson (Brabham) 1 hr 47 min 14.2 sec—6 M. Andretti (Lotus) 1 hr 47 min 20.8 sec—7 C. Regazzoni (Ensign) 1 hr 47 min 26.8 sec—8 J-P Jarier (Penske) 1 hr 48 min 00.1 sec—9 J. Oliver (Shadow) 1 hr 48 min 18.0 sec—10 H-J Stuck (Brabham) 71 laps—11 B. Lunger (McLaren) 71 laps—12 J. Hunt (McLaren) 71 laps—13 R. Keegan (Hesketh) 71 laps—14 D. Purley (Lec) 70 laps—15 P. Neve (March) 69 laps—16 H. Ertl (Hesketh) 68 laps—17 A. Jones (Shadow) 67 laps—fastest lap, Andretti 1 min 27.6 sec 165.11 kph/102.59 mph—retired R. Peterson (Tyrrell) ignition lap 7—J. Scheckter (Wolf) accident lap 29—N. Lauda (Ferrari) handling lap 47—V. Brambilla (Surtees) engine lap 52—I. Scheckter (March) drive shaft lap 61—G. Nilsson (Lotus) wheel bearing lap 64—E. Fittipaldi (Fittipaldi) engine lap 66.

Starting grid 2-2-2

Andretti 1 min 25.4 sec—Watson 1 min 25.5 sec—Hunt 1 min 25.6 sec—Scheckter 1 min 25.7 sec—Stuck 1 min 26.1 sec—Depailler 1 min 26.2 sec—Nilsson 1 min 26.2 sec—Laffite 1 min 26.3 sec—Mass 1 min 26.4 sec—Peterson 1 min 26.4 sec—Jones 1 min 26.5 sec—Reutemann 1 min 26.5 sec—Brambilla 1 min 26.6 sec—Regazzoni 1 min 26.6 sec—Lauda 1 min 26.8 sec—Oliver 1 min 27.5 sec—Jarier 1 min 27.5 sec—Fittipaldi 1 min 27.6 sec—Purley 1 min 27.7 sec—Neve 1 min 27.8 sec—I. Scheckter 1 min 27.8 sec—Lunger 1 min 28.2 sec—Ertl 1 min 28.4 sec—Keegan 1 min 28.4 sec—non starters Ribeiro (March)—Villota (McLaren)—Perkins (Surtees)—Hayje (March)—Rebaque (Hesketh)—Andersson (BRM)—Kozarowitsky (March).

FRENCH GRAND PRIX

Dijon-Prenois; 80 laps 304 km/189 miles
1 M. Andretti (Lotus) 1 hr 39 min 40.1 sec 183.01 kph/113.71 mph—2 J. Watson (Brabham) 1 hr 39 min 41.7 sec—3 J. Hunt (McLaren) 1 hr 40 min 14.0 sec—4 G. Nilsson (Lotus) 1 hr 40 min 51.2 sec—5 N. Lauda (Ferrari) 1 hr 40 min 54.6 sec—6 C. Reutemann (Ferrari) 79 laps—7 C. Regazzoni (Ensign) 79 laps—8 J. Laffite (Ligier) 78 laps—9 J. Mass (McLaren) 78 laps—10 R. Keegan (Hesketh) 78 laps—11 E. Fittipaldi (Fittipaldi) 77 laps—12 R. Peterson (Tyrrell) 77 laps—13 V. Brambilla (Surtees) 77 laps—not classified I. Scheckter (March) 69 laps—fastest lap, Andretti 1 min 13.7 sec 185.49 kph/115.26 mph—retired J-P Jarier (Penske) accident lap 4—D. Purley (Lec) accident lap 5—R. Patrese (Shadow) clutch lap 6—P. Depailler (Tyrrell) accident lap 21—A. Merzario (March) gearbox lap 27—A. Jones (Shadow) drive shaft lap 60—H-J Stuck (Brabham) accident lap 64—J. Scheckter (Wolf) accident lap 66.

Starting grid 2-2-2

Andretti 1 min 12.2 sec—Hunt 1 min 12.7 sec—Nilsson 1 min 12.8 sec—Watson 1 min 12.8 sec—Laffite 1 min 13.3 sec—Reutemann 1 min 13.4 sec—Mass 1 min 13.4 sec—Scheckter 1 min 13.4 sec—Lauda 1 min 13.5 sec—Jones 1 min 13.6 sec—Brambila 1 min 13.6 sec—Depailler 1 min 13.7 sec—Stuck 1 min 13.7 sec—Keegan 1 min 13.7 sec—Patrese 1 min 13.9 sec—Regazzoni 1 min 13.9 sec—Peterson 1 min 13.9 sec—Merzario 1 min 13.9 sec—Jarier 1 min 14.2 sec—I. Scheckter 1 min 14.2 sec—Purley 1 min 14.4 sec—Fittipaldi 1 min 14.4 sec—non starters Ribeiro (March)—Neve (March)—Lunger (McLaren)—Ertl (Hesketh)—Perkins (Surtees)-Rebaque (Hesketh)—Tambay (Surtees)—Andersson (BRM).

BRITISH GRAND PRIX

Silverstone; 16 July; 68 laps 199 miles/321 km
1 J. Hunt (McLaren) 1 hr 31 min 46.1 sec 130.36 mph/209.79 kph—2 N. Lauda (Ferrari) 1 hr 32 min 04.4 sec—3 G. Nilsson (Lotus) 1 hr 32 min 05.6 sec—4 J. Mass (McLaren) 1 hr 32 min 33.8 sec—5 H-J Stuck (Brabham) 1 hr 32 min 57.8 sec—6 J. Laffite (Ligier) 67 laps—7 A. Jones (Shadow) 67 laps—8 V. Brambilla (Surtees) 67 laps—9 J-P Jarier (Penske) 67 laps—10 P. Neve (March) 66 laps—11 G. Villeneuve (McLaren) 66 laps—12 V. Schuppan (Surtees) 66 laps—13 B. Lunger (McLaren) 64 laps—14 C. Reutemann (Ferrari) 62 laps—fastest lap, Hunt 1 min 19.6 sec 132.6 mph/213.4 kph—retired R. Keegan (Hesketh) accident 0 laps—R. Peterson (Tyrrell) engine lap 3—P. Tambay (Ensign) electrics lap 3—I. Scheckter (March) accident lap 6—J-P Jabouille (Renault) turbocharger lap 16—P. Depailler (Tyrrell) accident lap 16—R. Patrese (Shadow) fuel pressure lap 20—A. Merzario (March) drive shaft lap 28—E. Fittipaldi (Fittipaldi) engine lap 42—J. Scheckter (Wolf) engine lap 59—J. Watson (Brabham) fuel feed lap 60—M. Andretti (Lotus) engine lap 62.

Starting grid 2-2-2

Hunt 1 min 18.5 sec—Watson 1 min 18.8 sec—Lauda 1 min 18.8 sec—Scheckter 1 min 18.8 sec—Nilsson 1 min 18.9 sec—Andretti 1 min 19.1 sec—Stuck 1 min 19.2 sec—Brambilla 1 min 19.2 sec—Villeneuve 1 min 19.3

sec—Peterson 1 min 19.4 sec—Mass 1 min 19.5 sec—Jones 1 min 19.6 sec—Keegan 1 min 19.6 sec—Reutemann 1 min 19.6 sec—Laffite 1 min 19.7 sec—Tambay 1 min 19.8 sec—Merzario 1 min 19.9 sec—Depailler 1 min 19.9 sec—Lunger 1 min 20.1 sec—Jarier 1 min 20.1 sec—Jabouille 1 min 20.1 sec—Fittipaldi 1 min 20.2 sec—Schuppan 1 min 20.2 sec—I. Scheckter 1 min 20.3 sec—Patrese 1 min 20.3 sec—Neve 1 min 20.4 sec—non starters Ribeiro (March)—Regazzoni (Ensign)—Henton (March)—Villota (McLaren).

GERMAN GRAND PRIX

Hockenheim; 31 July; 47 laps 320 km/198 miles
1 N. Lauda (Ferrari) 1 hr 31 min 48.6 sec 208.53 kph/129.57 mph—2 J. Scheckter (Wolf) 1 hr 32 min 02.9 sec—3 H-J Stuck (Brabham) 1 hr 32 min 09.5 sec—4 C. Reutemann (Ferrari) 1 hr 32 min 48.9 sec—5 V. Brambilla (Surtees) 1 hr 33 min 16.0 sec—6 P. Tambay (Ensign) 1 hr 33 min 18.4 sec—7 V. Schuppan (Surtees) 46 laps—8 A. Ribeiro (March) 46 laps—9 R. Peterson (Tyrrell) 42 laps—10 R. Patrese (Shadow) 42 laps—fastest lap, Lauda 1 min 56.0 sec 210.71 kph/130.93 mph—retired C. Regazzoni (Ensign) accident 0 laps—A. Jones (Shadow) accident 0 laps—J-P Jarier (Penske) accident lap 5—J. Watson (Brabham) engine lap 8—I. Scheckter (March) clutch lap 9—B. Lunger (McLaren) accident lap 14—H. Rebaque (Hesketh) battery lap 20—J. Laffite (Ligier) engine lap 21—P. Depailler (Tyrrell) engine lap 22—J. Mass (McLaren) gearbox lap 26—G. Nilsson (Lotus) engine lap 31—J. Hunt (McLaren) fuel pump lap 32—M. Andretti (Lotus) engine lap 34—R. Keegan (Hesketh) accident lap 40.

Starting grid 2-2-2

Scheckter 1 min 53.1 sec—Watson 1 min 53.3 sec—Lauda 1 min 53.5 sec—Hunt 1 min 53.7 sec—Stuck 1 min 53.9 sec—Laffite 1 min 54.0 sec—Andretti 1 min 54.0 sec—Reutemann 1 min 54.3 sec—Nilsson 1 min 54.4 sec—Brambilla 1 min 54.5 sec—Tambay 1 min 54.8 sec—Jarier 1 min 55.2 sec—Mass 1 min 55.2 sec—Peterson 1 min 55.7 sec—Depailler 1 min 55.9 sec—Patrese 1 min 56.1 sec—Jones 1 min 56.2 sec—I. Scheckter 1 min 56.3 sec—Schuppan 1 min 56.5 sec—Ribeiro 1 min 56.6 sec—Lunger 1 min 56.6 sec—Regazzoni 1 min 56.7 sec—Keegan 1 min 56.9 sec—Rebaque 1 min 57.2 sec—H. Heyer (Penske) started illegally 1 min 57.6 sec—non starters Neve (March)—Villota (McLaren)—Fittipaldi (Fittipaldi)—Merzario (March) Pilotte (BRM).

AUSTRIAN GRAND PRIX

Österreichring; 14 August; 54 laps 321 km/199 miles
1 A. Jones (Shadow) 1 hr 37 min 16.5 sec 197.93 kph/122.99 mph—2 N. Lauda (Ferrari) 1 hr 37 min 36.6 sec—3 H-J Stuck (Brabham) 1 hr 37 min 51.0 sec—4 C. Reutemann (Ferrari) 1 hr 37 min 51.2 sec—5 R. Peterson (Tyrrell) 1 hr 38 min 18.6 sec—6 J. Mass (McLaren) 53 laps—7 R. Keegan (Hesketh) 53 laps—8 J. Watson (Brabham) 53 laps—9 P. Neve (March) 53 laps—10 B. Lunger (McLaren) 53 laps—11 E. Fittipaldi (Fittipaldi) 53 laps—12 H. Binder (Penske) 53 laps—13 P. Depailler (Tyrrell) 53 laps—14 J-P Jarier (Penske) 52 laps—15 V. Brambilla (Surtees) 52 laps—16 V. Schuppan (Surtees) 52 laps—17 E. Villota (McLaren) 50 laps—fastest lap, Watson 1 min 41.0 sec 211.89 kph/131.66 mph—retired C. Regazzoni (Ensign) accident 0 laps—I. Scheckter (March) accident lap 2—M. Andretti (Lotus) engine lap 11—J. Laffite (Ligier) oil leak lap 21—A. Merzario (Shadow) gear linkage lap 29—G. Nilsson (Lotus) engine lap 38—P. Tambay (Ensign) engine lap 41—J. Hunt (McLaren) engine lap 43—J. Scheckter (Wolf) accident lap 45.

Starting grid 2-2-2

Lauda 1 min 39.3 sec—Hunt 1 min 39.4 sec—Andretti 1 min 39.7 sec—Stuck 1 min 40.0 sec—Reutemann 1 min 40.1 sec—Laffite 1 min 40.2 sec—Tambay 1 min 40.3 sec—Scheckter 1 min 40.4 sec—Mass 1 min 40.4 sec—Depailler 1 min 40.6 sec—Regazzoni 1 min 40.7 sec—Watson 1 min 40.9 sec—Brambilla 1 min 40.9 sec—Jones 1 min 41.0 sec—Peterson 1 min 41.1 sec—Nilsson 1 min 41.2 sec—Lunger 1 min 41.4 sec—Jarier 1 min 41.7 sec—Keegan 1 min 41.9 sec—Merzario 1 min 41.9 sec—Neve 1 min 42.0 sec—Fittipaldi 1 min 42.1 sec—I. Scheckter 1 min 42.2 sec—Schuppan 1 min 42.3 sec—Villota 1 min 42.4 sec—Binder 1 min 41.7 sec—started from pit road—non starters Henton (March)—Ashley (Hesketh)—Rebaque (Hesketh)—Ribeiro (March).

DUTCH GRAND PRIX

Zandvoort; 28 August; 75 laps 317 km/197 miles
1 N. Lauda (Ferrari) 1 hr 41 min 45.9 sec 186.87 kph/116.12 mph—2 J. Laffite (Ligier) 1 hr 41 min 47.8 sec—3 J. Scheckter (Wolf) 74 laps—4 E. Fittipaldi (Fittipaldi) 74 laps—5 P. Tambay (Ensign) 73 laps—6 C. Reutemann (Ferrari) 73 laps—7 H-J Stuck (Brabham) 73 laps—8 H. Binder (Penske) 73 laps—9 B. Lunger (McLaren) 73 laps—10 I. Scheckter (March) 73 laps—11 A. Ribeiro (March) 72 laps—12 V. Brambilla (Surtees) 67 laps—13 R. Patrese (Shadow) 67 laps—fastest lap, Lauda 1 min 20.0 sec 190.19 kph/118.18 mph—retired J. Mass (McLaren) accident 0 laps—J. Watson (Brabham) accident lap 2—J-P Jarier (Penske) engine lap 4—J. Hunt (McLaren) accident lap 5—R. Keegan (Hesketh) accident lap 8—M. Andretti (Lotus) engine lap 14—C. Regazzoni (Ensign) throttle cable lap 17—R. Peterson (Tyrrell) ignition lap 18—P. Depailler (Tyrrell) engine lap 31—A. Jones (Shadow) engine lap 32—G. Nilsson (Lotus) accident lap 34—J-P Jabouille (Renault) suspension lap 39—B. Henton (Ensign) disqualified lap 52.

Starting grid 2-2-2

Andretti 1 min 18.6 sec—Laffite 1 min 19.3 sec—Hunt 1 min 19.5 sec—Lauda 1 min 19.5 sec—Nilsson 1 min 19.6 sec—Reutemann 1 min 19.7 sec—Peterson 1 min 19.8 sec—Watson 1 min 19.9 sec—Regazzoni 1 min 19.9 sec—Jabouille 1 min 20.1 sec—Depailler 1 min 20.1 sec—Tambay 1 min 20.2 sec—Jones 1 min 20.2 sec—Mass 1 min 20.2 sec—Scheckter 1 min 20.2 sec—Patrese 1 min 20.4 sec—Fittipaldi 1 min 20.5 sec—Binder 1 min 20.8 sec—Stuck 1 min 20.9 sec—Lunger 1 min 20.9 sec—Jarier 1 min 21.1 sec—Brambilla 1 min 21.1 sec—Henton 1 min 21.1 sec—Ribeiro 1 min 21.2 sec—I. Scheckter 1 min 21.2 sec—Keegan 1 min 21.5 sec—non starters Neve (March)—Merzario (March)—Schuppan (Surtees)—Ashley (Hesketh)—Hayje (March)—Rebaque (Hesketh)—Pilette (BRM)—Bleekemolen (March).

ITALIAN GRAND PRIX

Monza; 11 September; 52 laps 302 km/187 miles
1 M. Andretti (Lotus) 1 hr 27 min 50.3 sec 206.01 kph/128.01 mph—2 N. Lauda (Ferrari) 1 hr 28 min 07.3 sec—3 A. Jones (Shadow) 1 hr 28 min 13.9 sec—4 J. Mass (McLaren) 1 hr 28 min 18.8 sec—5 C. Regazzoni (Ensign) 1 hr 28 min 21.4 sec—6 R. Peterson (Tyrrell) 1 hr 29 min 09.5 sec—7 P. Neve (March) 50 laps—8 J. Laffite (Ligier) 50 laps—9 R. Keegan (Hesketh) 48 laps—fastest lap, Andretti 1 min 39.1 sec 210.7 kph/130.92 mph—retired J. Watson (Brabham) accident lap 3—G. Nilsson (Lotus) front upright lap 4—B. Lunger (McLaren) engine lap 4—P. Tambay (Ensign) engine lap 9—V. Brambilla (Surtees) accident lap 5—J-P Jarier (Penske) engine lap 19—J-P Jabouille (Renault) engine lap 23—J. Scheckter (Wolf) engine lap 23—P. Depailler (Tyrrell) engine lap 24—J. Hunt (McLaren) accident lap 26—H-J Stuck (Brabham) engine lap 31—R. Patrese (Shadow) accident lap 38—B. Giacomelli (McLaren) engine lap 38—C. Reutemann (Ferrari) accident lap 39—I. Scheckter (March) transmission lap 41.

Starting grid 2-2-2

Hunt 1 min 38.1 sec—Reutemann 1 min 38.1 sec—Scheckter 1 min 38.3 sec—Andretti 1 min 38.4 sec—Lauda 1 min 38.5 sec—Patrese 1 min 38.7 sec—Regazzoni 1 min 38.7 sec—Laffite 1 min 38.8 sec—Mass 1 min 38.9 sec—Brambilla 1 min 38.9 sec—Stuck 1 min 39.0 sec—Peterson 1 min 39.2 sec—Depailler 1 min 39.2 sec—Watson 1 min 39.2 sec—Giacomelli 1 min 39.4 sec—Jones 1 min 39.5 sec—I. Scheckter 1 min 39.6 sec—Jarier 1 min 39.6 sec—Nilsson 1 min 39.8 sec—Jabouille 1 min 40.0 sec—Tambay 1 min 40.2

ITALIAN GRAND PRIX—*continued*

sec—Lunger 1 min 40.3 sec—Keegan 1 min 40.3 sec—Neve 1 min 40.5 sec—non starters Ribeiro (March)—Fittipaldi (Fittipaldi)—Leoni (Surtees)—Henton (Boro-Ensign)—Villota (McLaren)—Ashley (Hesketh)—Pilette (BRM)—Binder (Penske)—Kessel (Williams)—Francia (Brabham).

UNITED STATES GRAND PRIX

Watkins Glen; 2 October; 59 laps 199 miles/321 km
1 J. Hunt (McLaren) 1 hr 58 min 23.3 sec 100.98 mph/162.51 kph—2 M. Andretti (Lotus) 1 hr 58 min 25.3 sec—3 J. Scheckter (Wolf) 1 hr 59 min 42.1 sec—4 N. Lauda (Ferrari) 2 hr 0 min 03.9 sec—5 C. Regazzoni (Ensign) 2 hr 0 min 11.4 sec—6 C. Reutemann (Ferrari) 58 laps—7 J. Laffite (Ligier) 58 laps—8 R. Keegan (Hesketh) 58 laps—9 J-P Jarier (Shadow) 58 laps—10 B. Lunger (McLaren) 57 laps—11 H. Binder (Surtees) 57 laps—12 J. Watson (Brabham) 57 laps—13 E. Fittipaldi (Fittipaldi) 57 laps—14 P. Depailler (Tyrrell) 56 laps—15 A. Ribeiro (March) 56 laps—16 R. Peterson (Tyrrell) 56 laps—17 I. Ashley (Hesketh) 55 laps—18 P. Neve (March) 55 laps—19 V. Brambilla (Surtees) 54 laps—fastest lap, Peterson 1 min 51.8 sec 108.69 mph/174.92 kph—retired A. Jones (Shadow) accident lap 3—D. Ongais (Penske) accident lap 6—J. Mass (McLaren) fuel pump lap 8—I. Scheckter (March) accident lap 10—H-J Stuck (Brabham) accident lap 14—G. Nilsson (Lotus) accident lap 17—J-P Jabouille (Renault) alternator lap 30.

Starting grid 2-2-2

Hunt 1 min 40.9 sec—Stuck 1 min 41.1 sec—Watson 1 min 41.2 sec—Andretti 1 min 41.5 sec—Peterson 1 min 41.9 sec—Reutemann 1 min 41.9 sec—Lauda 1 min 42.1 sec—Depailler 1 min 42.2 sec—Scheckter 1 min 42.3 sec—Laffite 1 min 42.6 sec—Brambilla 1 min 42.8 sec—Nilsson 1 min 42.8 sec—Jones 1 min 43.0 sec—Jabouille 1 min 43.1 sec—Mass 1 min 43.2 sec—Jarier 1 min 43.5 sec—Lunger 1 min 43.7 sec—Fittipaldi 1 min 43.9 sec—Regazzoni 1 min 44.2 sec—Keegan 1 min 44.5 sec—I. Scheckter 1 min 44.7 sec—Ashley 1 min 45.1 sec—Ribeiro 1 min 45.5 sec—Neve 1 min 45.8 sec—Binder 1 min 45.9 sec—Ongais 1 min 46.1 sec—non starter Tambay (Ensign).

CANADIAN GRAND PRIX

Mosport; 9 October; 80 laps 197 miles/317 km
1 J. Scheckter (Wolf) 1 hr 40 min 00.0 sec 118.03 mph/ 189.95 kph—2 P. Depailler (Tyrrell) 1 hr 40 min 06.8 sec—3 J. Mass (McLaren) 1 hr 40 min 15.8 sec—4 A. Jones (Shadow) 1 hr 40 min 46.7 sec—5 P. Tambay (Ensign) 1 hr 41 min 03.3 sec—6 V. Brambilla (Surtees) 78 laps—7 D. Ongais (Penske) 78 laps—8 A. Ribeiro (March) 78 laps—9 M. Andretti (Lotus) 77 laps—10 R. Patrese (Shadow) 76 laps—11 B. Lunger (McLaren) 76 laps—12 G. Villeneuve (Ferrari) 76 laps—fastest lap, Andretti 1 min 13.3 sec 120.77 mph/194.36 kph—retired C. Regazzoni (Ensign) accident 0 laps—J. Watson (Brabham) accident lap 1—J. Laffite (Ligier) drive shaft lap 12—G. Nilsson (Lotus) accident lap 17—H-J Stuck (Brabham) engine lap 19—C. Reutemann (Ferrari) fuel pressure lap 20—I. Scheckter (March) engine lap 29—E. Fittipaldi (Fittipaldi) engine lap 29—H. Binder (Surtees) accident lap 31—R. Keegan (Hesketh) accident lap 32—R. Peterson (Tyrrell) fuel leak lap 34—P. Neve (March) engine lap 56—J. Hunt (McLaren) accident lap 61.

Starting grid 2-2-2

Andretti 1 min 11.4 sec—Hunt 1 min 11.9 sec—Peterson 1 min 12.7 sec—Nilsson 1 min 13.0 sec—Mass 1 min 13.1 sec—Depailler 1 min 13.2 sec—Jones 1 min 13.3 sec—Patrese 1 min 13.4 sec—Scheckter 1 min 13.5 sec—Watson 1 min 13.5 sec—Laffite 1 min 13.7 sec—Reutemann 1 min 13.9 sec—Stuck 1 min 13.9 sec—Regazzoni 1 min 14.0 sec—Brambilla 1 min 14.2 sec—Tambay 1 min 14.5 sec—Villeneuve 1 min 14.5 sec—I. Scheckter 1 min 14.8 sec—Fittipaldi 1 min 14.9 sec—Lunger 1 min 14.9 sec—Neve 1 min 15.5 sec—Ongais 1 min 15.6 sec—Ribeiro 1 min 15.8 sec—Binder 1 min 16.6 sec—Keegan 1 min 17.0 sec—non starters Ashley (Hesketh)—Jabouille (Renault).

JAPANESE GRAND PRIX

Fuji; 23 October; 73 laps 198 miles/318 km
1 J. Hunt (McLaren) 1 hr 31 min 51.7 sec 129.14 mph/207.84 kph—2 C. Reutemann (Ferrari) 1 hr 32 min 54.1 sec—3 P. Depailler (Tyrrell) 1 hr 32 min 58.1 sec—4 A. Jones (Shadow) 1 hr 32 min 58.3 sec—5 J. Laffite (Ligier) 72 laps—6 R. Patrese (Shadow) 72 laps—7 H-J Stuck (Brabham) 72 laps—8 V. Brambilla (Surtees) 71 laps—9 K. Takahashi (Tyrrell) 71 laps—10 J. Scheckter (Wolf) 71 laps—11 K. Hoshino (Kojima) 71 laps—12 A. Ribeiro (March) 69 laps—fastest lap, Scheckter 1 min 14.3 sec 131.23 mph/211.2 kph—retired M. Andretti (Lotus) accident lap 1—N. Takahara (Kojima) accident lap 1—H. Binder (Surtees) accident lap 1—J-P Jarier (Ligier) engine lap 3—G. Villeneuve (Ferrari) accident lap 5—R. Peterson (Tyrrell) accident lap 5—P. Tambay (Ensign) engine lap 14—J. Mass (McLaren) engine lap 28—J. Watson (Brabham) gearbox lap 29—C. Regazzoni (Ensign) engine lap 43—G. Nilsson (Lotus) gearbox lap 63.

Starting grid 2-2-2

Andretti 1 min 12.2 sec—Hunt 1 min 12.4 sec—Watson 1 min 12.5 sec—Stuck 1 min 13.0 sec—Laffite 1 min 13.1 sec—Scheckter 1 min 13.1 sec—Reutemann 1 min 13.3 sec—Mass 1 min 13.4 sec—Brambilla 1 min 13.4 sec—Regazzoni 1 min 13.5 sec—Hoshino 1 min 13.5 sec—Jones 1 min 13.6 sec—Patrese 1 min 13.6 sec—Nilsson 1 min 13.7 sec—Depailler 1 min 14.2 sec—Tambay 1 min 14.2 sec—Jarier 1 min 14.2 sec—Peterson 1 min 14.3 sec—Takahara 1 min 14.4 sec—Villeneuve 1 min 14.5 sec—Binder 1 min 14.7 sec—Takahashi 1 min 14.9 sec—Ribeiro 1 min 15.0 sec—non starter I. Scheckter (March).

1977 WORLD CHAMPIONSHIP

1 N. Lauda 72—2 J. Scheckter 55—3 M. Andretti 47—4 C. Reutemann 42—5 J. Hunt 40—6 J. Mass 25—7 A. Jones 22—8 G. Nilsson 20—8= P. Depailler 20—10 J. Laffite 18—11 H-J Stuck 12—12 E. Fittipaldi 11—13 J. Watson 9—14 R. Peterson 7—15 C. Pace 6—15= V. Brambilla 6—17 C. Regazzoni 5—17= P. Tambay 5—19 J-P Jarier 1—19= R. Zorzi 1—19= R. Patrese 1.

1978

ARGENTINE GRAND PRIX

Buenos Aires; 15 January; 52 laps 310 km/193 miles
1 M. Andretti (Lotus) 1 hr 37 min 04.5 sec 191.82 kph/119.19 mph—2 N. Lauda (Brabham) 1 hr 37 min 17.7 sec—3 P. Depailler (Tyrrell) 1 hr 37 min 18.1 sec—4 J. Hunt (McLaren) 1 hr 37 min 20.5 sec—5 R. Peterson (Lotus) 1 hr 38 min 19.3 sec—6 P. Tambay (McLaren) 1 hr 38 min 24.4 sec—7 C. Reutemann (Ferrari) 1 hr 38 min 27.1 sec—8 G. Villeneuve (Ferrari) 1 hr 38 min 43.3 sec—9 E. Fittipaldi (Fittipaldi) 1 hr 38 min 45.1 sec—10 J. Scheckter (Wolf) 1 hr 38 min 48.0 sec—11 J. Mass (ATS) 1 hr 38 min 53.5 sec—12 J-P Jarier (ATS) 51 laps—13 B. Lunger (McLaren) 51 laps—14 D. Pironi (Tyrrell) 51 laps—15 C. Regazzoni (Shadow) 51 laps—16 J. Laffite (Ligier) 50 laps—17 H-J Stuck (Shadow) 50 laps—18 V. Brambilla (Surtees) 50 laps—fastest lap, Hunt 1 min 50.6 sec 194.3 kph/120.73 mph—retired R. Keegan (Surtees) overheating lap 4—A. Merzario (Merzario) differential lap 9—L. Leoni (Ensign) engine lap 28—D. Ongais (Ensign) ignition lap 35—A. Jones (Williams) fuel vapour lock lap 36—J. Watson (Brabham) engine lap 41.

Starting grid 2-2-2

Andretti 1 min 47.7 sec—Reutemann 1 min 47.8 sec—Peterson 1 min 48.4 sec—Watson 1 min 48.4 sec—Lauda 1 min 48.7 sec—Hunt 1 min 48.7 sec—Villeneuve 1 min 49.0 sec—Laffite 1 min 49.1 sec—Tambay 1 min 49.5 sec—Depailler 1 min 49.7 sec—Jarier 1 min 49.8 sec—Brambilla 1 min 49.9 sec—Mass 1 min 50.1 sec—Jones 1 min 50.1 sec—Scheckter 1 min 50.3 sec—Regazzoni 1 min 50.4 sec—Fittipaldi 1 min 50.8 sec—Stuck 1 min 51.2 sec—Keegan 1 min 51.4 sec—Merzario 1 min 51.7 sec—Ongais 1 min 51.7 sec—Leoni 1 min 51.9 sec—Pironiö 1 min 52.0 sec—Lunger 1 min 52.3 sec—non starters Rebaque (Lotus)—Cheever (Theodore)—Galica (Hesketh).

BRAZIL GRAND PRIX

Rio de Janeiro; 29 January; 63 laps 317 km/197 miles 1 C. Reutemann (Ferrari) 1 hr 49 min 59.9 sec 172.89 kph/107.43 mph—2 E. Fittipaldi (Fittipaldi) 1 hr 50 min 49.0 sec—3 N. Lauda (Brabham) 1 hr 50 min 56.9 sec—4 M. Andretti (Lotus) 1 hr 51 min 33.0 sec—5 C. Regazzoni (Shadow) 62 laps—6 D. Pironi (Tyrrell) 62 laps—7 J. Mass (ATS) 62 laps—8 J. Watson (Brabham) 61 laps—9 J. Laffite (Ligier) 61 laps—10 R. Patrese (Arrows) 59 laps—11 A. Jones (Williams) 58 laps—fastest lap, Reutemann 1 min 43.1 sec 175.72 kph/109.19 mph—retired L. Leoni (Ensign) drive shaft 0 laps—R. Keegan (Surtees) accident lap 5—P. Depailler (Tyrrell) accident lap 8—B. Lunger (McLaren) overheating lap 11—D. Ongais (Ensign) brakes lap 13—R. Peterson (Lotus) accident lap 15—J. Scheckter (Wolf) accident lap 16—J. Hunt (McLaren) accident lap 25—H-J Stuck (Shadow) fuel pump lap 25—P. Tambay (McLaren) accident lap 34—G. Villeneuve (Ferrari) accident lap 35—H. Rebaque (Lotus) fatigue lap 40.

Starting grid 2-2-2

Peterson 1 min 40.4 sec—Hunt 1 min 40.5 sec—Andretti 1 min 40.6 sec—Reutemann 1 min 40.7 sec—Tambay 1 min 40.9 sec—Villeneuve 1 min 41.0 sec—Fittipaldi 1 min 41.5 sec—Jones 1 min 41.9 sec—Stuck 1 min 42.1 sec—Lauda 1 min 42.1 sec—Depailler 1 min 42.1 sec—Scheckter 1 min 42.1 sec—Lunger 1 min 42.6 sec—Laffite 1 min 42.7 sec—Regazzoni 1 min 42.8 sec—Patrese 1 min 43.2 sec—Pironi 1 min 43.5 sec—Mass 1 min 43.7 sec—Watson 1 min 43.7 sec—Rebaque 1 min 43.9 sec—Ongais 1 min 43.9 sec—Keegan 1 min 44.2 sec—non starters Leoni (Ensign) 1 min 43.2 sec—car failed on warming-up lap—Merzario (Merzario) Cheever (Theodore)—Brambilla (Surtees)—Galica (Hesketh).

SOUTH AFRICAN GRAND PRIX

Kyalami; 4 March; 78 laps 199 miles/320 km 1 R. Peterson (Lotus) 1 hr 42 min 15.8 sec 116.7 mph/187.81 kph—2 P. Depailler (Tyrrell) 1 hr 42 min 16.2 sec—3 J. Watson (Brabham) 1 hr 42 min 20.2 sec—4 A. Jones (Williams) 1 hr 42 min 54.7 sec—5 J. Laffite (Ligier) 1 hr 43 min 25.0 sec—6 D. Pironi (Tyrrell) 77 laps—7 M. Andretti (Lotus) 77 laps—8 J-P Jarier (ATS) 77 laps—9 R. Stommelen (Arrows) 77 laps—10 H. Rebaque (Lotus) 77 laps—11 B. Lunger (McLaren) 76 laps—12 V. Brambilla (Surtees) 76 laps—fastest lap, Andretti 1 min 17.1 sec 119.08 mph/191.65 kph—retired J. Hunt (McLaren) engine lap 5—E. Cheever (Hesketh) engine lap 8—E. Fittipaldi (Fittipaldi) drive shaft lap 8—K. Rosberg (Theodore) engine lap 14—J-P Jabouille (Renault) engine lap 38—A. Merzario (Merzario) suspension lap 39—J. Mass (ATS) engine lap 43—N. Lauda (Brabham) engine lap 52—R. Keegan (Surtees) broken oil line lap 52—G. Villeneuve (Ferrari) oil leak lap 55—C. Reutemann (Ferrari) accident lap 55—P. Tambay (McLaren) accident lap 56—J. Scheckter (Wolf) accident lap 59—R. Patrese (Arrows) engine lap 63.

Starting grid 2-2-2

Lauda 1 min 14.6 sec—Andretti 1 min 14.9 sec—Hunt 1 min 15.1 sec—Tambay 1 min 15.3 sec—Scheckter 1 min 15.3 sec—Jabouille 1 min 15.4 sec—Patrese 1 min 15.5 sec—Villeneuve 1 min 15.5 sec—Reutemann 1 min 15.5 sec—Watson 1 min 15.6 sec—Peterson 1 min 15.9 sec—Depailler 1 min 16.0 sec—Pironi 1 min 16.4 sec—Laffite 1 min 16.4 sec—Fittipaldi 1 min 16.5 sec—Mass 1 min 16.6 sec—Jarier 1 min 17.1 sec—Jones 1 min 17.2 sec—Lunger 1 min 17.3 sec—Brambilla 1 min 17.3 sec—Stommelen 1 min 17.5 sec—Rebaque 1 min 17.5 sec—Keegan 1 min 17.6 sec—Rosberg 1 min 17.6 sec—Cheever 1 min 17.8 sec—Merzario 1 min 18.1 sec—non starters Stuck (Shadow)—Regazzoni (Shadow)—Leoni (Ensign)—Arnoux (Martini).

UNITED STATES GRAND PRIX WEST

Long Beach; 2 April; 80½ laps 163 miles/262 km 1 C. Reutemann (Ferrari) 1 hr 52 min 01.3 sec 87.1 mph/140.17 kph—2 M. Andretti (Lotus) 1 hr 52 min 12.4 sec—3 P. Depailler (Tyrrell) 1 hr 52 min 30.2 sec—4 R. Peterson (Lotus) 1 hr 52 min 46.9 sec—5 J. Laffite (Ligier) 1 hr 53 min 24.2 sec—6 R. Patrese (Arrows) 79 laps—7 A. Jones (Williams) 79 laps—8 E. Fittipaldi (Fittipaldi) 79 laps—9 R. Stommelen (Arrows) 79 laps—10 C. Regazzoni (Shadow) 79 laps—11 J-P Jarier (ATS) 75 laps—12 P. Tambay (McLaren) 74 laps—fastest lap, Jones 1 min 22.2 sec 88.41 mph/142.35 kph—retired J. Hunt (McLaren) accident lap 5—J. Watson (Brabham) oil tank lap 9—J. Mass (ATS) brakes lap 11—A. Merzario (Merzario) gearbox lap 17—D. Pironi (Tyrrell) gearbox lap 25—N. Lauda (Brabham) ignition lap 27—G. Villeneuve (Ferrari) accident lap 38—J-P Jabouille (Renault) turbocharger lap 43—V. Brambilla (Surtees) final drive lap 50—J. Scheckter (Wolf) accident lap 59.

Starting grid 2-2-2

Reutemann 1 min 20.6 sec—Villeneuve 1 min 20.8 sec—Lauda 1 min 20.9 sec—Andretti 1 min 21.2 sec—Watson 1 min 21.2 sec—Peterson 1 min 21.5 sec—Hunt 1 min 21.7 sec—Jones 1 min 21.9 sec—Patrese 1 min 22.0 sec—Scheckter 1 min 22.2 sec—Tambay 1 min 22.2 sec—Depailler 1 min 22.4 sec—Jabouille 1 min 22.5 sec—Laffite 1 min 22.6 sec—Fittipaldi 1 min 22.8 sec—Mass 1 min 23.1 sec—Brambilla 1 min 23.2 sec—Stommelen 1 min 23.3 sec—Jarier 1 min 23.4 sec—Regazzoni 1 min 23.4 sec—Merzario 1 min 23.6 sec—Pironi 1 min 23.8 sec—non starters Keegan (Surtees)—Stuck (Shadow)—Lunger (McLaren)—Leoni (Ensign).

MONACO GRAND PRIX

Monte Carlo; 7 May; 75 laps 248 km/154 miles 1 P. Depailler (Tyrrell) 1 hr 55 min 14.7 sec 129.32 kph/80.36 mph—2 N. Lauda (Brabham) 1 hr 55 min 37.1 sec—3 J. Scheckter (Wolf) 1 hr 55 min 46.9 sec—4 J. Watson (Brabham) 1 hr 55 min 48.2 sec—5 D. Pironi (Tyrrell) 1 hr 56 min 22.7 sec—6 R. Patrese (Arrows) 1 hr 56 min 23.4 sec—4 P. Tambay (McLaren) 74 laps—8 C. Reutemann (Ferrari) 74 laps—9 E. Fittipaldi (Fittipaldi) 74 laps—10 J-P Jabouille (Renault) 71 laps—11 M. Andretti (Lotus) 69 laps—fastest lap, Lauda 1 min 28.6 sec 134.5 kph/83.57 mph—retired R. Keegan (Surtees) final drive lap 8—J. Laffite (Ligier) gearbox lap 13—H-J Stuck (Shadow) accident lap 24—J. Ickx (Ensign) brakes lap 27—A. Jones (Williams) oil leak lap 29—R. Stommelen (Arrows) ill lap 38—J. Hunt (McLaren) suspension lap 43—R. Peterson (Lotus) gearbox lap 56—G. Villeneuve (Ferrari) lap 62.

Starting grid 1-1-1

Reutemann 1 min 28.3 sec—Watson 1 min 28.8 sec—Lauda 1 min 28.8 sec—Andretti 1 min 29.1 sec—Depailler 1 min 29.1 sec—Hunt 1 min 29.2 sec—Peterson 1 min 29.2 sec—Villeneuve 1 min 29.4 sec—Scheckter 1 min 29.5 sec—Jones 1 min 29.5 sec—Tambay 1 min 30.1 sec—Jabouille 1 min 30.2 sec—Pironi 1 min 30.5 sec—Patrese 1 min 30.6 sec—Laffite 1 min 30.6 sec—Ickx 1 min 30.7 sec—Stuck 1 min 31.3 sec—Keegan 1 min 31.3 sec—Stommelen 1 min 31.3 sec—Fittipaldi 1 min 31.4 sec—non starters Mass (ATS)—Jarier (ATS)—Regazzoni (Shadow)—Brambilla (Surtees).

BELGIAN GRAND PRIX

Zolder; 21 May; 70 laps 298 km/185 miles
1 M. Andretti (Lotus) 1 hr 39 min 52.0 sec 179.24 kph/111.38 mph—2 R. Peterson (Lotus) 1 hr 40 min 01.9 sec—3 C. Reutemann (Ferrari) 1 hr 40 min 16.4 sec—4 G. Villeneuve (Ferrari) 1 hr 40 min 39.1 sec—5 J. Laffite (Ligier) 69 laps—6 D. Pironi (Tyrrell) 69 laps—7 B. Lunger (McLaren) 69 laps—8 B. Giacomelli (McLaren) 69 laps—9 R. Arnoux (Martini) 68 laps—10 A. Jones (Williams) 68 laps—11 J. Mass (ATS) 68 laps—12 J. Ickx (Ensign) 64 laps—13 V. Brambilla (Surtees) 63 laps—not classified J-P Jabouille (Renault) 56 laps—fastest lap, Peterson 1 min 23.1 sec 184.57 kph/114.68 mph—retired N. Lauda (Brabham) accident 0 laps—J. Hunt (McLaren) accident 0 laps—E. Fittipaldi (Fittipaldi) 0 laps—J. Watson (Brabham) accident lap 18—R. Stommelen (Arrows) accident lap 26—R. Patrese (Arrows) suspension lap 31—C. Regazzoni (Shadow) final drive lap 40—P. Depailler (Tyrrell) gearbox lap 51—J. Scheckter (Wolf) accident lap 53—H-J Stuck (Shadow) accident lap 56.

Starting grid 2-2-2

Andretti 1 min 20.9 sec—Reutemann 1 min 21.7 sec—Lauda 1 min 21.7 sec—Villeneuve 1 min 21.8 sec—Scheckter 1 min 22.1 sec—Hunt 1 min 22.5 sec—Peterson 1 min 22.6 sec—Patrese 1 min 23.2 sec—Watson 1 min 23.3 sec—Jabouille 1 min 23.6 sec—Jones 1 min 23.7 sec—Brambilla 1 min 23.8 sec—Depailler 1 min 23.8 sec—Laffite 1 min 23.9 sec—Fittipaldi 1 min 24.1 sec—Mass 1 min 24.1 sec—Stommelen 1 min 24.1 sec—Regazzoni 1 min 24.2 sec—Arnoux 1 min 24.2 sec—Stuck 1 min 24.5 sec—Giacomelli 1 min 24.8 sec—Ickx 1 min 24.8 sec—Pironi 1 min 24.8 sec—Lunger 1 min 25.0 sec—non starters Keegan (Surtees)—Daly (Hesketh)—Rosberg (Ralt)—Colombo (ATS).

SPANISH GRAND PRIX

Jarama; 4 June; 75 laps 255 km/159 miles
1 M. Andretti (Lotus) 1 hr 41 min 47.1 sec 150.51 kph/93.52 mph—2 R. Peterson (Lotus) 1 hr 42 min 06.6 sec—3 J. Laffite (Ligier) 1 hr 42 min 24.3 sec—4 J. Scheckter (Wolf) 1 hr 42 min 47.1 sec—5 J. Watson (Brabham) 1 hr 42 min 53.0 sec—6 J. Hunt (McLaren) 74 laps—7 V. Brambilla (Surtees) 74 laps—8 A. Jones (Williams) 74 laps—9 J. Mass (ATS) 74 laps—10 G. Villeneuve (Ferrari) 74 laps—11 R. Keegan (Surtees) 73 laps—12 D. Pironi (Tyrrell) 71 laps—13 J-P Jabouille (Renault) 71 laps—14 R. Stommelen (Arrows) 71 laps—15 C. Regazzoni (Shadow) 67 laps—not classified E. Fittipaldi (Fittipaldi) 62 laps—fastest lap, Andretti 1 min 20.1 sec 153.08 kph/95.12 mph—retired P. Tambay (McLaren) accident lap 16—R. Patrese (Arrows) engine lap 21—H. Rebaque (Lotus) broken exhaust lap 21—H-J Stuck (Shadow) suspension lap 45—P. Depailler (Tyrrell) engine lap 51—N. Lauda (Brabham) engine lap 56—C. Reutemann (Ferrari) accident lap 57—J. Ickx (Ensign) engine lap 64.

Starting grid 2-2-2

Andretti 1 min 16.4 sec—Peterson 1 min 16.7 sec—Reutemann 1 min 17.4 sec—Hunt 1 min 17.7 sec—Villeneuve 1 min 17.8 sec—Lauda 1 min 17.9 sec—Watson 1 min 18.0 sec—Patrese 1 min 18.1 sec—Scheckter 1 min 18.2 sec—Laffite 1 min 18.4 sec—Jabouille 1 min 19.0 sec—Depailler 1 min 19.1 sec—Pironi 1 min 19.1 sec—Tambay 1 min 19.3 sec—Fittipaldi 1 min 19.3 sec—Brambilla 1 min 19.7 sec—Mass 1 min 20.0 sec—Jones 1 min 20.0 sec—Stommelen 1 min 20.0 sec—Rebaque 1 min 20.2 sec—Ickx 1 min 20.4 sec—Regazzoni 1 min 20.7 sec—Keegan 1 min 20.8 sec—Stuck 1 min 20.9 sec—non starters Merzario (Merzario)—Lunger (McLaren)—Villota (McLaren)—Colombo (ATS).

SWEDISH GRAND PRIX

Anderstorp; 17 June; 70 laps 282 km/175 miles
1 N. Lauda (Brabham) 1 hr 41 min 00.6 sec 167.61 kph/104.15 mph—2 R. Patrese (Arrows) 1 hr 41 min 34.6 sec—3 R. Peterson (Lotus) 1 hr 41 min 34.7 sec—4 P. Tambay (McLaren) 69 laps—5 C. Regazzoni (Shadow) 69 laps—6 E. Fittipaldi (Fittipaldi) 69 laps—7 J. Laffite (Ligier) 69 laps—8 J. Hunt (McLaren) 69 laps—9 G. Villeneuve (Ferrari) 69 laps—10 C. Reutemann (Ferrari) 69 laps—11 H-J Stuck (Shadow) 68 laps—12 H. Rebaque (Lotus) 68 laps—13 J. Mass (ATS) 68 laps—14 R. Stommelen (Arrows) 67 laps—15 K. Rosberg (ATS) 63 laps—not classified A. Merzario (Merzario) 62 laps—fastest lap, Lauda 1 min 24.8 sec 171.05 kph/106.29 mph—retired V. Brambilla (Surtees) accident lap 7—D. Pironi (Tyrrell) accident lap 8—J. Scheckter (Wolf) overheating lap 16—J. Watson (Brabham) accident lap 19—J-P Jabouille (Renault) piston lap 28—P. Depailler (Tyrrell) suspension lap 42—A. Jones (Williams) wheel bearing lap 46—M. Andretti (Lotus) engine lap 46.

Starting grid 2-2-2

Andretti 1 min 22.1 sec—Watson 1 min 22.7 sec—Lauda 1 min 22.8 sec—Peterson 1 min 23.1 sec—Patrese 1 min 23.4 sec—Scheckter 1 min 23.6 sec—Villeneuve 1 min 23.7 sec—Reutemann 1 min 23.7 sec—Jones 1 min 23.9 sec—Jabouille 1 min 24.0 sec—Laffite 1 min 24.0 sec—Depailler 1 min 24.2 sec—Fittipaldi 1 min 24.3 sec—Hunt 1 min 24.8 sec—Tambay 1 min 25.0 sec—Regazzoni 1 min 25.0 sec—Pironi 1 min 25.8 sec—Brambilla 1 min 26.6 sec—Mass 1 min 26.8 sec—Stuck 1 min 27.0 sec—Rebaque 1 min 27.1 sec—Merzario 1 min 27.5 sec—Rosberg 1 min 27.6 sec—Stommelen 1 min 27.8 sec—non starters Keegan (Surtees)—Ickx (Ensign)—Lunger (McLaren).

FRENCH GRAND PRIX

Paul Ricard; 2 July; 54 laps 314 km/195 miles
1 M. Andretti (Lotus) 1 hr 38 min 51.9 sec 190.4 kph/118.31 mph—2 R. Peterson (Lotus) 1 hr 38 min 54.8 sec—3 J. Hunt (McLaren) 1 hr 39 min 11.7 sec—4 J. Watson (Brabham) 1 hr 39 min 28.8 sec—5 A. Jones (Williams) 1 hr 39 min 33.7 sec—6 J. Scheckter (Wolf) 1 hr 39 min 46.4 sec—7 J. Laffite (Ligier) 1 hr 39 min 46.7 sec—8 R. Patrese (Arrows) 1 hr 40 min 16.8 sec—9 P. Tambay (McLaren) 1 hr 40 min 19.0 sec—10 D. Pironi (Tyrrell) 1 hr 40 min 21.9 sec—11 H-J Stuck (Shadow) 53 laps—12 G. Villeneuve (Ferrari) 53 laps—13 J. Mass (ATS) 53 laps—14 R. Arnoux (Martini) 53 laps—15 R. Stommelen (Arrows) 53 laps—16 K. Rosberg (ATS) 52 laps—17 V. Brambilla (Surtees) 52 laps—18 C. Reutemann (Ferrari) 49 laps—fastest lap, Reutemann 1 min 48.6 sec 192.67 kph/119.72 mph—retired J-P Jabouille (Renault) engine lap 1—C. Regazzoni (Shadow) electrics lap 4—N. Lauda (Brabham) engine lap 10—P. Depailler (Tyrrell) engine lap 10—B. Giacomelli (McLaren) engine lap 28—R. Keegan (Surtees) engine lap 40—E. Fittipaldi (Fittipaldi) suspension lap 43—B. Lunger (McLaren) engine lap 45.

Starting grid 2-2-2

Watson 1 min 44.4 sec—Andretti 1 min 44.5 sec—Lauda 1 min 44.7 sec—Hunt 1 min 44.9 sec—Peterson 1 min 45.0 sec—Tambay 1 min 45.1 sec—Scheckter 1 min 45.2 sec—Reutemann 1 min 45.3 sec—Villeneuve 1 min 45.5 sec—Laffite 1 min 45.7 sec—Jabouille 1 min 45.7 sec—Patrese 1 min 46.3 sec—Depailler 1 min 46.4 sec—Jones 1 min 46.4 sec—Fittipaldi 1 min 46.7 sec—Pironi 1 min 47.1 sec—Regazzoni 1 min 48.5 sec—Arnoux 1 min 48.7 sec—Brambilla 1 min 48.7 sec—Stuck 1 min 48.9 sec—Stommelen 1 min 49.1 sec—Giacomelli 1 min 49.5 sec—Keegan 1 min 49.5 sec—Lunger 1 min 49.5 sec—Mass 1 min 49.9 sec—Rosberg 1 min 50.1 sec—non starters Daly (Ensign)—Rebaque (Lotus)—Merzario (Merzario).

BRITISH GRAND PRIX

Brands Hatch; 16 July; 76 laps 199 miles/320 km
1 C. Reutemann (Ferrari) 1 hr 42 min 12.4 sec 116.61 mph/187.66 kph—2 N. Lauda (Brabham) 1 hr 42 min 13.6 sec—3 J. Watson (Brabham) 1 hr 42 min 49.6 sec—4 P. Depailler (Tyrrell) 1 hr 43 min 25.7 sec—5 H-J Stuck (Shadow) 75 laps—6 P. Tambay (McLaren) 75 laps—7 B. Giacomelli (McLaren) 75 laps—8 B. Lunger (McLaren) 75 laps—9 V. Brambilla (Surtees) 75 laps—10 J. Laffite (Ligier) 73 laps—not classified J. Mass (ATS) 66 laps—fastest lap. Lauda 1 min 18.6 sec 119.71 mph/192.65 kph—retired R.

Peterson (Lotus) fuel leak lap 6—J. Hunt (McLaren) accident lap 7—H. Rebaque (Lotus) gearbox lap 15—G. Villeneuve (Ferrari) drive shaft lap 19—A. Jones (Williams) drive shaft lap 26—M. Andretti (Lotus) engine lap 28—D. Daly (Ensign) lost wheel lap 30—A. Merzario (Merzario) fuel pump lap 32—E. Fittipaldi (Fittipaldi) engine lap 32—J. Scheckter (Wolf) gearbox lap 36—D. Pironi (Tyrrell) gearbox lap 40—R. Patrese (Arrows) puncture lap 40—J-P Jabouille (Renault) engine lap 46—C. Regazzoni (Shadow) gearbox lap 49—K. Rosberg (ATS) suspension lap 59.

Starting grid 2-2-2

Peterson 1 min 16.8 sec—Andretti 1 min 17.1 sec—Scheckter 1 min 17.4 sec—Lauda 1 min 17.5 sec—Patrese 1 min 18.3 sec—Jones 1 min 18.4 sec—Laffite 1 min 18.4 sec—Reutemann 1 min 18.4 sec—Watson 1 min 18.6 sec—Depailler 1 min 18.7 sec—Fittipaldi 1 min 18.8 sec—Jabouille 1 min 18.9 sec—Villeneuve 1 min 19.0 sec—Hunt 1 min 19.0 sec—Daly 1 min 19.1 sec—Giacomelli 1 min 19.8 sec—Regazzoni 1 min 19.8 sec—Stuck 1 min 20.0 sec—Pironi 1 min 20.0 sec—Tambay 1 min 20.1 sec—Rebaque 1 min 20.2 sec—Rosberg 1 min 20.3 sec—Merzario 1 min 20.3 sec—Lunger 1 min 20.4 sec—Brambilla 1 min 20.7 sec—Mass 1 min 20.7 sec—non starters Keegan (Surtees)—Lees (Ensign)—Stommelen (Arrows)—Trimmer (McLaren).

GERMAN GRAND PRIX

Hockenheim; 30 July; 45 laps 305 km/190 miles
1 M. Andretti (Lotus) 1 hr 28 min 00.9 sec 208.26 kph/129.41 mph—2 J. Scheckter (Wolf) 1 hr 28 min 16.2 sec—3 J. Laffite (Ligier) 1 hr 28 min 28.9 sec—4 E. Fittipaldi (Fittipaldi) 1 hr 28 min 37.8 sec—5 D. Pironi (Tyrrell) 1 hr 28 min 58.2 sec—6 H. Rebaque (Lotus) 1 hr 29 min 38.8 sec—7 J. Watson (Brabham) 1 hr 29 min 40.4 sec—8 G. Villeneuve (Ferrari) 1 hr 29 min 57.8 sec—9 R. Patrese (Arrows) 44 laps—10 K. Rosberg (Wolf) 42 laps—11 H. Ertl (Ensign) 41 laps—fastest lap, Peterson 1 min 55.6 sec 211.39 kph/131.35 mph—retired P. Depailler (Tyrrell) accident 0 laps—J. Mass (ATS) accident lap 1—H-J Stuck (Shadow) accident lap 1—J-P Jabouille (Renault) engine lap 5—N. Lauda (Brabham) engine lap 11—C. Reutemann (Ferrari) fuel vaporisation lap 14—P. Tambay (McLaren) accident lap 16—V. Brambilla (Surtees) fuel vaporisation lap 24—N. Piquet (Ensign) engine lap 31—A. Jones (Williams) fuel vaporisation lap 31—J. Hunt (McLaren) disqualified lap 34—R. Peterson (Lotus) gearbox lap 36—R. Stommelen (Arrows) disqualified lap 42.

Starting grid 2-2-2

Andretti 1 min 51.9 sec—Peterson 1 min 52.0 sec—Lauda 1 min 52.3 sec—Scheckter 1 min 52.7 sec—Watson 1 min 52.8 sec—Jones 1 min 53.5 sec—Hunt 1 min 53.5 sec—Laffite 1 min 53.5 sec—Jabouille 1 min 53.6 sec—Fittipaldi 1 min 54.0 sec—Tambay 1 min 54.0 sec—Reutemann 1 min 54.2 sec—Depailler 1 min 54.3 sec—Patrese 1 min 54.3 sec—Villeneuve 1 min 54.4 sec—Pironi 1 min 54.6 sec—Stommelen 1 min 55.2 sec—Rebaque 1 min 55.6 sec—Rosberg 1 min 55.6 sec—Brambilla 1 min 55.9 sec—Piquet 1 min 56.1 sec—Mass 1 min 56.2 sec—Ertl 1 min 56.2 sec—Stuck 1 min 56.4 sec—non starters Jarier (ATS)—Regazzoni (Shadow)—Keegan (Surtees)—Merzario (Merzario).

AUSTRIAN GRAND PRIX

Österreichring; 13 August; 54 laps 321 km/199 miles (race interrupted by rain after 7 laps)
1 R. Peterson (Lotus) 1 hr 41 min 21.6 sec 189.95 kph/118.03 mph—2 P. Depailler (Tyrrell) 1 hr 42 min 09.0 sec—3 G. Villeneuve (Ferrari) 1 hr 43 min 01.3 sec—4 E. Fittipaldi (Fittipaldi) 53 laps—5 J. Laffite (Ligier) 53 laps—6 V. Brambilla (Surtees) 53 laps—7 J. Watson (Brabham) 53 laps—8 B. Lunger (McLaren) 52 laps—9 R. Arnoux (Martini) 52 laps—not classified C. Regazzoni (Shadow) 50 laps—K. Rosberg (Wolf) 49 laps—fastest lap, Peterson 1 min 43.1 sec 207.45 kph/128.91 mph—retired M. Andretti (Lotus) accident 0 laps—H. Rebaque (Lotus) clutch lap 1—N. Piquet (McLaren) accident lap 2—J. Scheckter (Wolf) accident lap 3—R. Patrese (Arrows) accident lap 8—H. Ertl (Ensign) accident lap 8—A. Jones (Williams) accident lap 8—J. Hunt (McLaren) accident lap 8—D. Pironi (Tyrrell) accident lap 20—C. Reutemann (Ferrari) disqualified lap 27—N. Lauda (Brabham) accident lap 28—J-P Jabouille (Renault) gearbox lap 31—H-J Stuck (Shadow) accident lap 33—P. Tambay (McLaren) accident lap 40—D. Daly (Ensign) disqualified lap 43.

Starting grid 2-2-2

Peterson 1 min 37.7 sec—Andretti 1 min 37.8 sec—Jabouille 1 min 38.3 sec—Reutemann 1 min 38.5 sec—Laffite 1 min 38.7 sec—Fittipaldi 1 min 38.8 sec—Scheckter 1 min 38.8 sec—Hunt 1 min 39.1 sec—Pironi 1 min 39.2 sec—Watson 1 min 39.3 sec—Villeneuve 1 min 39.4 sec—Lauda 1 min 39.5 sec—Depailler 1 min 39.5 sec—Tambay 1 min 39.6 sec—Jones 1 min 39.8 sec—Patrese 1 min 40.1 sec—Lunger 1 min 40.8 sec—Rebaque 1 min 40.8 sec—Daly 1 min 41.0 sec—Piquet 1 min 41.1 sec—Brambilla 1 min 41.2 sec—Regazzoni 1 min 41.4 sec—Stuck 1 min 41.6 sec—Ertle 1 min 41.6 sec—Rosberg 1 min 41.7 sec—Arnoux 1 min 41.8 sec—non starters Mass (ATS)—Binder (ATS)—Keegan (Surtees)—Merzario (Merzario).

DUTCH GRAND PRIX

Zandvoort; 27 August; 75 laps 317 km/197 miles
1 M. Andretti (Lotus) 1 hr 41 min 04.2 sec 188.16 kph/116.91 mph—2 R. Peterson (Lotus) 1 hr 41 min 04.5 sec—3 N. Lauda (Brabham) 1 hr 41 min 16.4 sec—4 J. Watson (Brabham) 1 hr 41 min 25.1 sec—5 E. Fittipaldi (Fittipaldi) 1 hr 41 min 25.7 sec—6 G. Villeneuve (Ferrari) 1 hr 41 min 50.2 sec—7 C. Reutemann (Ferrari) 1 hr 42 min 04.7 sec—8 J. Laffite (Ligier) 74 laps—9 P. Tambay (McLaren) 74 laps—10 J. Hunt (McLaren) 74 laps—11 H. Rebaque (Lotus) 74 laps—12 J. Scheckter (Wolf) 73 laps—fastest lap, Lauda 1 min 19.6 sec 191.2 kph/118.8 mph—retired D. Pironi (Tyrrell) accident 0 laps—R. Patrese (Arrows) accident 0 laps—D. Daly (Ensign) drive shaft lap 10—P. Depailler (Tyrrell) engine lap 13—N. Piquet (McLaren) drive shaft lap 16—A. Jones (Williams) throttle cable lap 17—K. Rosberg (Wolf) accident lap 21—B. Lunger (McLaren) engine lap 35—J-P Jabouille (Renault) engine lap 35—V. Brambilla (Surtees) disqualified lap 37—A. Merzario (Merzario) engine lap 40—R. Arnoux (Martini) rear wing lap 40—H-J Stuck (Shadow) final drive lap 56—B. Giacomelli (McLaren) accident lap 60.

Starting grid 2-2-2

Andretti 1 min 16.4 sec—Peterson 1 min 17.0 sec—Lauda 1 min 17.3 sec—Reutemann 1 min 17.3 sec—Villeneuve 1 min 17.5 sec—Laffite 1 min 17.5 sec—Hunt 1 min 17.7 sec—Watson 1 min 17.7 sec—Jabouille 1 min 18.3 sec—Fittipaldi 1 min 18.3 sec—Jones 1 min 18.4 sec—Depailler 1 min 18.4 sec—Patrese 1 min 18.5 sec—Tambay 1 min 18.5 sec—Scheckter 1 min 18.6 sec—Daly 1 min 19.4 sec—Pironi 1 min 19.6 sec—Stuck 1 min 19.6 sec—Giacomelli 1 min 19.8 sec—Rebaque 1 min 20.0 sec—Lunger 1 min 20.0 sec—Brambilla 1 min 20.3 sec—Arnoux 1 min 20.3 sec—Rosberg 1 min 20.5 sec—Piquet 1 min 20.6 sec—Merzario 1 min 20.6 sec—non starters R. Keegan (Surtees) 1 min 20.5 sec accident on warming-up lap—Mass (ATS)—Bleekemolen (ATS)—Regazzoni (Shadow).

ITALIAN GRAND PRIX

Monza; 10 September; 40 laps 232 km/144 miles
1 N. Lauda (Brabham) 1 hr 7 min 04.5 sec 207.53 kph/128.95 mph—2 J. Watson (Brabham) 1 hr 7 min 06.0 sec—3 C. Reutemann (Ferrari) 1 hr 7 min 25.0 sec—4 J. Laffite (Ligier) 1 hr 7 min 42.1 sec—5 P. Tambay (McLaren) 1 hr 7 min 44.9 sec—6 M. Andretti (Lotus) 1 hr 7 min 50.9 sec (including penalty)—7 G. Villeneuve (Ferrari) 1 hr 7 min 53.0 sec (including penalty)—8 E. Fittipaldi (Fittipaldi) 1 hr 7 min 59.8 sec—9 N. Piquet (McLaren) 1 hr 8 min 11.4 sec—10 D. Daly (Ensign) 1 hr 8 min 13.6 sec—11 P. Depailler (Tyrrell) 1 hr 8 min 21.1 sec—12 J. Scheckter (Wolf) 39 laps—13 A. Jones (Williams) 39 laps—14 B. Giacomelli (McLaren) 39 laps—not classified C. Regazzoni (Shadow) 33 laps—fastest

ITALIAN GRAND PRIX—*continued*

lap, Andretti 1 min 38.2 sec 212.56 kph/132.08 mph. The race was stopped following the accident which resulted in the death of R. Peterson (Lotus). The following also did not restart. D. Pironi (Tyrrell)—H-J Stuck (Shadow)—V. Brambilla (Surtees)—B. Lunger (McLaren). Retired following restart J-P Jabouille (Renault) engine lap 6—A. Merzario (Merzario) engine lap 14—J. Hunt (McLaren) distributor lap 19—R. Patrese (Arrows) engine lap 29.

Starting grid 2-2-2

Andretti 1 min 37.5 sec—Villeneuve 1 min 37.9 sec—Jabouille 1 min 37.9 sec—Lauda 1 min 38.2 sec—Peterson 1 min 38.3 sec—Jones 1 min 38.3 sec—Watson 1 min 38.6 sec—Laffite 1 min 38.9 sec—Scheckter 1 min 38.9 sec—Hunt 1 min 38.9 sec—Reutemann 1 min 39.0 sec—Patrese 1 min 39.2 sec—Fittipaldi 1 min 39.4 sec—Pironi 1 min 39.6 sec—Regazzoni 1 min 39.6 sec—Depailler 1 min 39.6 sec—Stuck 1 min 39.7 sec—Daly 1 min 40.1 sec—Tambay 1 min 40.2 sec—Giacomelli 1 min 40.2 sec—Lunger 1 min 40.3 sec—Merzario 1 min 40.7 sec—Brambilla 1 min 40.8 sec—Piquet 1 min 40.8 sec—non starters Bleekemolen (ATS)—Ertl (ATS)—Rebaque (Lotus)—'Gimax' (Surtees).

UNITED STATES GRAND PRIX

Watkins Glen; 1 October; 59 laps 199 miles/320 km
1 C. Reutemann (Ferrari) 1 hr 40 min 48.8 sec 118.58 mph/190.84 kph—2 A. Jones (Williams) 1 hr 41 min 08.5 sec—3 J. Scheckter (Wolf) 1 hr 41 min 34.5 sec—4 J-P Jabouille (Renault) 1 hr 42 min 13.8 sec—5 E. Fittipaldi (Fittipaldi) 1 hr 42 min 16.9 sec—6 P. Tambay (McLaren) 1 hr 42 min 30.0 sec—7 J. Hunt (McLaren) 58 laps—8 D. Daly (Ensign) 58 laps—9 R. Arnoux (Surtees) 58 laps—10 D. Pironi (Tyrrell)—11 J. Laffite (Ligier) 58 laps—12 B. Rahal (Wolf) 58 laps—13 B. Lunger (Ensign) 58 laps—14 C. Regazzoni (Shadow) 56 laps—15 J-P Jarier (Lotus) 55 laps—16 R. Stommelen (Arrows) 54 laps—fastest lap, Jarier 1 min 39.6 sec 122.11 mph/196.52 kph—retired H. Rebaque (Lotus) clutch 0 laps—H-J Stuck (Shadow) fuel pump lap 1—K. Rosberg (ATS) gear linkage lap 21—G. Villeneuve (Ferrari) engine lap 22—P. Depailler (Tyrrell) hub assembly lap 23—J. Watson (Brabham) engine lap 25—M. Andretti (Lotus) engine lap 27—N. Lauda (Brabham) engine lap 28—M. Bleekemolen (ATS) oil pump lap 43—A. Merzario (Merzario) gearbox lap 46.

Starting grid 2-2-2

Andretti 1 min 38.1 sec—Reutemann 1 min 39.2 sec—Jones 1 min 39.7 sec—Villeneuve 1 min 39.8 sec—Lauda 1 min 39.9 sec—Hunt 1 min 40.0 sec—Watson 1 min 40.0 sec—Jarier 1 min 40.0 sec—Jabouille 1 min 40.1 sec—Laffite 1 min 40.2 sec—Scheckter 1 min 40.8 sec—Depailler 1 min 40.8 sec—Fittipaldi 1 min 41.0 sec—Stuck 1 min 41.7 sec—Rosberg 1 min 41.8 sec—Pironi 1 min 41.8 sec—Regazzoni 1 min 41.8 sec—Tambay 1 min 42.0 sec—Daly 1 min 42.2 sec—Rahal 1 min 42.4 sec—Arnoux 1 min 42.5 sec—Stommelen 1 min 42.7 sec—Rebaque 1 min 43.0 sec—Lunger 1 min 43.1 sec—Bleekemolen 1 min 43.6 sec—Merzario 1 min 44.3 sec—non starter Gabbiani (Surtees).

CANADIAN GRAND PRIX

Montreal; 8 October; 70 laps 196 miles/315 km
1 G. Villeneuve (Ferrari) 1 hr 57 min 49.2 sec 99.67 mph/160.4 kph—2 J. Scheckter (Wolf) 1 hr 58 min 02.6 sec—3 C. Reutemann (Ferrari) 1 hr 58 min 08.6 sec—4 R. Patrese (Arrows) 1 hr 58 min 13.9 sec—5 P. Depailler (Tyrrell) 1 hr 58 min 17.7 sec—6 D. Daly (Ensign) 1 hr 58 min 43.7 sec—7 D. Pironi (Tyrrell) 1 hr 59 min 10.4 sec—8 P. Tambay (McLaren) 1 hr 59 min 15.8 sec—9 A. Jones (Williams) 1 hr 59 min 18.1 sec—10 M. Andretti (Lotus) 69 laps—11 N. Piquet (Brabham) 69 laps—12 J-P Jabouille (Renault) 65 laps—not classified K. Rosberg (ATS) 58 laps—fastest lap, Jones 1 min 38.1 sec 102.63 mph/165.17 kph—retired E. Fittipaldi (Fittipaldi) accident 0 laps—H-J Stuck (Shadow) accident lap 1—N. Lauda (Brabham) accident lap 5—J. Watson (Brabham) accident lap 8—B. Rahal (Wolf) fuel system lap 16—R. Arnoux (Surtees) oil pressure lap 37—J-P Jarier (Lotus) oil cooler lap 49—J. Hunt (McLaren) accident lap 51—J. Laffite (Ligier) transmission lap 52.

Starting grid 2-2-2

Jarier 1 min 38.0 sec—Scheckter 1 min 38.0 sec—Villeneuve 1 min 38.2 sec—Watson 1 min 38.4 sec—Jones 1 min 38.9 sec—Fittipaldi 1 min 38.9 sec—Lauda 1 min 39.0 sec—Stuck 1 min 39.1 sec—Andretti 1 min 39.2 sec—Laffite 1 min 39.4 sec—Reutemann 1 min 39.4 sec—Patrese 1 min 39.5 sec—Depailler 1 min 39.6 sec—Piquet 1 min 39.6 sec—Daly 1 min 40.0 sec—Arnoux 1 min 40.5 sec—Tambay 1 min 40.7 sec—Pironi 1 min 41.0 sec—Hunt 1 min 41.0 sec—Rahal 1 min 41.0 sec—Rosberg 1 min 41.6 sec—Jabouille 1 min 41.7 sec—non starters Bleekemolen (ATS)—Regazzoni (Shadow)—Gabbiani (Surtees)—Rebaque (Lotus)—Stommelen (Arrows)—Merzario (Merzario).

1978 WORLD CHAMPIONSHIP

1 M. Andretti 64—2 R. Peterson 51—3 C. Reutemann 48—4 N. Lauda 44—5 P. Depailler 34—6 J. Watson 25—7 J. Scheckter 24—8 J. Laffite 19—9 G. Villeneuve 17—9= E. Fittipaldi 17—11 A. Jones 11—11= R. Patrese 11—13 J. Hunt 8—13= P. Tambay 8—15 D. Pironi 7—16 C. Regazzoni 4—17 J-P Jabouille 3—18 H-J Stuck 2—19 H. Rebaque 1—19= V.Brambilla 1—19= D. Daly 1.

1979

ARGENTINE GRAND PRIX

Buenos Aires; 21 January; 53 laps 316 km/197 miles
1 J. Laffite (Ligier) 1 hr 36 min 3.2 sec 197.53 kph/122.77 mph—2 C. Reutemann (Lotus) 1 hr 36 min 18.1 sec—3 J. Watson (McLaren) 1 hr 37 min 32.0 sec—4 P. Depailler (Ligier) 1 hr 37 min 44.9 sec—5 M. Andretti (Lotus) 52 laps—6 E. Fittipaldi (Fittipaldi) 52 laps—7 E. de Angelis (Shadow) 52 laps—8 J. Mass (Arrows) 51 laps—9 A. Jones (Williams) 51 laps—10 C. Regazzoni (Williams) 51 laps—11 D. Daly (Ensign) 51 laps—fastest lap, Laffite 1 min 16.9 sec 200.92 kph/124.87 mph—retired R. Arnoux (Renault) engine lap 6—N. Lauda (Brabham) fuel pressure lap 8—J-P Jabouille (Renault) engine lap 15—J-P Jarier (Tyrrell) engine lap 15—J. Hunt (Wolf) electrics lap 41—J. Lammers (Shadow) transmission lap 42—H. Rebaque (Lotus) suspension lap 46—G. Villeneuve (Ferrari) engine lap 48.

Starting grid (Following a first lap accident involving Pironi, Watson, Scheckter, Andretti, Tambay, Piquet, and Merzario, the race was stopped. Only Watson and Andretti were able to restart.) **2-2-2**

Laffite 1 min 44.2 sec—Depailler 1 min 45.2 sec—Reutemann 1 min 45.3 sec—Jarier 1 min 45.3 sec—Scheckter 1 min 45.6 sec—Watson 1 min 45.8 sec—Andretti 1 min 45.9 sec—Pironi 1 min 46.4 sec—Tambay 1 min 46.6 sec—Villeneuve 1 min 46.9 sec—Fittipaldi 1 min 47.1 sec—Jabouille 1 min 47.5 sec—Mass 1 min 48.3 sec—Jones 1 min 48.4 sec—de Angelis 1 min 48.5 sec—Regazzoni 1 min 48.6 sec—Hunt 1 min 48.8 sec—Rebaque 1 min 49.4 sec—Piquet 1 min 49.5 sec—Lammers 1 min 49.5 sec—Merzario 1 min 50.2 sec—Lauda 1 min 50.3 sec—Daly 1 min 50.1 sec—Arnoux 1 min 51.5 sec—non starters D. Pironi (Tyrrell) J. Scheckter (Ferrari)—P. Tambay (McLaren)—N. Piquet (Brabham)—A. Merzario (Merzario).

BRAZIL GRAND PRIX

Interlagos; 4 February; 40 laps 318 km/198 miles
1 J. Laffite (Ligier) 1 hr 40 min 09.6 sec 188.63 kph/117.23 mph—2 P. Depailler (Ligier) 1 hr 40 min 14.9 sec—3 C.

Reutemann (Lotus) 1 hr 40 min 53.8 sec—4 D. Pironi (Tyrrell) 1 hr 41 min 35.5 sec—5 G. Villeneuve (Ferrari) 39 laps—6 J. Scheckter (Ferrari) 39 laps—7 J. Mass (Arrows) 39 laps—8 J. Watson (McLaren) 39 laps—9 R. Patrese (Arrows) 39 laps—10 J-P Jabouille (Renault) 39 laps—11 E. Fittipaldi (Fittipaldi) 39 laps—12 E. de Angelis (Shadow) 39 laps—13 D. Daly (Ensign) 39 laps—14 J. Lammers (Shadow) 39 laps—15 C. Regazzoni (Williams) 38 laps—fastest lap, Laffite 1 min 28.8 sec—190.51 kph/118.40 mph—retired J-P Jarier (Tyrrell) electrics, warm-up lap—non starter M. Andretti (Lotus) fuel leak, lap 2—N. Lauda (Brabham) gearbox lap 5—N. Piquet (Brabham) ill lap 5—J. Hunt (Wolf) steering lap 7—P. Tambay (McLaren) accident lap 7—R. Arnoux (Renault) accident lap 28—H-J Stuck (ATS) broke steering wheel lap 31—A. Jones (Williams) fuel pressure lap 33.

Starting grid 2-2-2

Laffite 2 min 23.0 sec—Depailler 2 min 24.0 sec—Reutemann 2 min 24.1 sec—Andretti 2 min 24.3 sec—Villeneuve 2 min 24.3 sec—Scheckter 2 min 24.5 sec—Jabouille 2 min 24.8 sec—Pironi 2 min 25.1 sec—Fittipaldi 2 min 26.3 sec—Hunt 2 min 26.4 sec—Arnoux 2 min 26.4 sec—Lauda 2 min 27.6 sec—Jones 2 min 27.7 sec—Watson 2 min 27.8 sec—Jarier 2 min 27.9 sec—Patrese 2 min 28.1 sec—Regazzoni 2 min 28.9 sec—Tambay 2 min 29.4 sec—Mass 2 min 29.4 sec—de Angelis 2 min 30.3 sec—Lammers 2 min 31.6 sec—Piquet 2 min 31.6 sec—Daly 2 min 31.8 sec—Stuck 2 min 32.3 sec.

SOUTH AFRICAN GRAND PRIX

Kyalami; 3 March; 78 laps 199 miles/320 km
1 G. Villeneuve (Ferrari) 1 hr 41 min 49.9 sec 117.19 mph/188.56 kph—2 J. Scheckter (Ferrari) 1 hr 41 min 53.4 sec—3 J-P Jarier (Tyrrell) 1 hr 42 min 12.1 sec—4 M. Andretti (Lotus) 1 hr 42 min 17.8 sec—5 C. Reutemann (Lotus) 1 hr 42 min 56.9 sec—6 N. Lauda (Brabham) 77 laps—7 N. Piquet (Brabham) 77 laps—8 J. Hunt (Wolf) 77 laps—9 C. Regazzoni (Williams) 76 laps—10 P. Tambay (McLaren) 75 laps—11 R. Patrese (Arrows) 75 laps—12 J. Mass (Arrows) 74 laps—13 E. Fittipaldi (Fittipaldi) 74 laps—fastest lap, Villeneuve 1 min 14.41 sec 123.37 mph/198.5 kph—retired J. Lammers (Shadow) accident lap 2—P. Depailler (Ligier) accident lap 4—E. de Angelis (Shadow) accident lap 16—D. Pironi (Tyrrell) throttle lap 25—J. Laffite (Ligier) accident lap 45—J-P Jabouille (Renault) engine lap 47—H-J Stuck (ATS) accident lap 57—J. Watson (McLaren) ignition lap 61—A. Jones (Williams) accident lap 63—R. Arnoux (Renault) accident lap 67—H. Rebaque (Lotus) engine lap 71.

Starting grid 2-2-2

Jabouille 1 min 11.8 sec—Scheckter 1 min 12.0 sec—Villeneuve 1 min 12.1 sec—Lauda 1 min 12.1 sec—Depailler 1 min 12.1 sec—Laffite 1 min 12.3 sec—Pironi 1 min 12.3 sec—Andretti 1 min 12.4 sec—Jarier 1 min 12.6 sec—Arnoux 1 min 12.7 sec—Reutemann 1 min 12.7 sec—Piquet 1 min 13.1 sec—Hunt 1 min 14.2 sec—Watson 1 min 14.4 sec—de Angelis 1 min 14.4 sec—Patrese 1 min 14.5 sec—Tambay 1 min 14.6 sec—Fittipaldi 1 min 14.6 sec—Jones 1 min 14.6 sec—Mass 1 min 15.0 sec—Lammers 1 min 15.3 sec—Regazzoni 1 min 15.7 sec—Rebaque 1 min 16.1 sec—Stuck 1 min 16.3 sec.

UNITED STATES GRAND PRIX WEST

Long Beach; 8 April; 80 laps 162 miles/260 km
1 G. Villeneuve (Ferrari) 1 hr 50 min 25.4 sec 87.81 mph/141.29 kph—2 J. Scheckter (Ferrari) 1 hr 50 min 54.8 sec—3 A. Jones (Williams) 1 hr 51 min 25.1 sec—4 M. Andretti (Lotus) 1 hr 51 min 29.7 sec—5 P. Depailler (Ligier) 1 hr 51 min 48.9 sec—6 J-P Jarier (Tyrrell) 79 laps—7 E. de Angelis (Shadow) 78 laps—8 N. Piquet (Brabham) 78 laps—9 J. Mass (Arrows) 78 laps—fastest lap, Villeneuve 1 min 21.2 sec—retired J. Hunt (Wolf) transmission lap 1—P. Tambay (McLaren) accident lap 8—N. Lauda (Brabham) accident lap 8—J. Laffite (Ligier) brakes lap 8—A. Merzario (Merzario) engine lap 13—E. Fittipaldi (Fittipaldi) drive shaft lap 19—C. Reutemann (Lotus) drive shaft lap 21—R. Patrese (Arrows) brakes lap 40—J. Lammers (Shadow) accident lap 47—C. Regazzoni (Williams) engine lap 48—H. Stuck (ATS) disqualified lap 49—J. Watson (McLaren) engine lap 62—D. Daly (Ensign) accident lap 68—H. Rebaque (Lotus) accident lap 71—D. Pironi (Tyrrell) accident lap 73.

Starting grid 1-1-1

Villeneuve 1 min 18.8 sec—Reutemann 1 min 18.9 sec—Scheckter 1 min 18.9 sec—Depailler 1 min 19.0 sec—Laffite 1 min 19.0 sec—Andretti 1 min 19.4 sec—Jarier 1 min 19.6 sec—Hunt 1 min 19.6 sec—Patrese 1 min 19.7 sec—Jones 1 min 19.9 sec—Lauda 1 min 20.0 sec—Piquet 1 min 20.5 sec—Mass 1 min 20.6 sec—Lammers 1 min 20.7 sec—Regazzoni 1 min 20.8 sec—Fittipaldi 1 min 21.0 sec—Pironi 1 min 21.2 sec—Watson 1 min 21.3 sec—Tambay 1 min 21.4 sec—de Angelis 1 min 22.0 sec—Stuck 1 min 22.8 sec—Merzario 1 min 22.9 sec—Rebaque 1 min 23.0 sec—Daly 1 min 23.9 sec—non starters Arnoux (Renault)—Jabouille (Renault).

SPANISH GRAND PRIX

Jarama; 29 April; 75 laps 255 km/159 miles
1 P. Depailler (Ligier) 1 hr 39 min 11.8 sec 154.37 kph/95.94 mph—2 C. Reutemann (Lotus) 1 hr 39 min 32.8 sec—3 M. Andretti (Lotus) 1 hr 39 min 39.1 sec—4 J. Scheckter (Ferrari) 1 hr 39 min 40.5 sec—5 J-P Jarier (Tyrrell) 1 hr 39 min 42.2 sec—6 D. Pironi (Tyrrell) 1 hr 40 min 00.3 sec—7 G. Villeneuve (Ferrari) 1 hr 40 min 04.1 sec—8 J. Mass (Arrows) 1 hr 40 min 26.7 sec—9 R. Arnoux (Renault) 74 laps—10 R. Patrese (Arrows) 74 laps—11 E. Fittipaldi (Fittipaldi) 74 laps—12 J. Lammers (Shadow) 73 laps—13 P. Tambay (McLaren) 72 laps—14 H-J Stuck (ATS) 69 laps—fastest lap, Villeneuve 1 min 16.4 sec 160.42 kph/99.7 mph—retired N. Piquet (Brabham) fuel metering unit lap 15—J. Laffite (Ligier) engine lap 15—J-P Jabouille (Renault) turbo lap 21—J. Watson (McLaren) engine lap 21—J. Hunt (Wolf) brakes lap 26—C. Regazzoni (Williams) engine lap 32—E. de Angelis (Shadow) lap 52—A. Jones (Williams) gear linkage lap 54—H. Rebaque (Lotus) engine lap 58—N. Lauda (Brabham) water leak lap 63.

Starting grid 2-2-2

Laffite 1 min 14.5 sec—Depailler 1 min 14.8 sec—Villeneuve 1 min 14.8 sec—Andretti 1 min 15.1 sec—Scheckter 1 min 15.1 sec—Lauda 1 min 15.4 sec—Piquet 1 min 15.6 sec—Reutemann 1 min 15.7 sec—Jabouille 1 min 15.8 sec—Pironi 1 min 16.0 sec—Arnoux 1 min 16.1 sec—Jarier 1 min 16.1 sec—Jones 1 min 16.2 sec—Regazzoni 1 min 16.6 sec—Hunt 1 min 16.9 sec—Patrese 1 min 16.9 sec—Mass 1 min 17.0 sec—Watson 1 min 17.1 sec—Fittipaldi 1 min 17.3 sec—Tambay 1 min 17.4 sec—Stuck 1 min 17.6 sec—de Angelis 1 min 17.8 sec—Rebaque 1 min 18.4 sec—Lammers 1 min 18.8 sec—non starters Daly (Ensign)—Merzario (Merzario)—Brancatelli (Kauhsen).

BELGIAN GRAND PRIX

Zolder; 13 May; 70 laps 298 km/185 miles
1 J. Scheckter (Ferrari) 1 hr 39 min 59.5 sec 178.98 kph/111.24 mph—2 J. Laffite (Ligier) 1 hr 40 min 14.9 sec—3 D. Pironi (Tyrrell) 1 hr 40 min 34.7 sec—4 C. Reutemann (Lotus) 1 hr 40 min 46.0 sec—5 R. Patrese (Arrows) 1 hr 41 min 03.8 sec—6 J. Watson (McLaren) 1 hr 41 min 05.4 sec—7 G. Villeneuve (Ferrari) 69 laps—8 H-J Stuck (ATS) 69 laps—9 E. Fittipaldi (Fittipaldi) 68 laps—10 J. Lammers (Shadow) 68 laps—11 J-P Jarier (Tyrrell) 67 laps—fastest lap, Scheckter 1 min 22.4 sec 186.19 kph/115.72 mph—retired C. Regazzoni (Williams) accident lap 2—J-P Jabouille (Renault) engine lap 13—H. Rebaque (Lotus) drive shaft lap 17—J. Mass (Arrows) accident lap 17—B. Giacomelli (Alfa Romeo) accident lap 21—E. de Angelis (Shadow) accident lap 21—R. Arnoux (Renault) engine lap 22—N. Lauda (Brabham) engine lap 23—N. Piquet (Brabham) engine lap 23—M. Andretti (Lotus) brakes lap 27—A. Jones (Williams) electrics lap 39—J. Hunt (Wolf) accident lap 40—P. Depailler (Ligier) accident lap 46.

BELGIAN GRAND PRIX—*continued*

Starting grid 2-2-2

Laffite 1 min 21.1 sec—Depailler 1 min 21.2 sec—Piquet 1 min 21.3 sec—Jones 1 min 21.6 sec—Andretti 1 min 21.8 sec—Villeneuve 1 min 22.1 sec—Scheckter 1 min 22.1 sec—Regazzoni 1 min 22.4 sec—Hunt 1 min 22.5 sec—Reutemann 1 min 22.6 sec—Jarier 1 min 22.7 sec—Pironi 1 min 22.8 sec—Lauda 1 min 22.9 sec—Giaxomelli 1 min 23.1 sec—Rebaque 1 min 23.6 sec—Patrese 1 min 23.9 sec—Jabouille 1 min 24.0 sec—Arnoux 1 min 24.3 sec—Watson 1 min 24.4 sec—Stuck 1 min 24.6 sec—Lammers 1 min 24.8 sec—Mass 1 min 25.1 sec—Fittipaldi 1 min 25.2 sec—de Angelis 1 min 25.5 sec—non starters Tambay (McLaren)—Merzario (Merzario)—Daly (Ensign).

MONACO GRAND PRIX

Monte Carlo; 27 May; 75 laps 249 km/154 miles
1 J. Scheckter (Ferrari) 1 hr 55 min 22.5 sec 130.88 kph/81.34 mph—2 C. Regazzoni (Williams) 1 hr 55 min 22.9 sec—3 C. Reutemann (Lotus) 1 hr 55 min 31.0 sec—4 J. Watson (McLaren) 1 hr 56 min 03.8 sec—5 P. Depailler (Ligier) 73 laps—6 J. Mass (Arrows) 68 laps—fastest lap, Depailler 1 min 28.8 sec 132.21 kph/82.17 mph—retired R. Patrese (Arrows) suspension lap 3—J. Hunt (Wolf) transmission lap 4—R. Arnoux (Renault) steering lap 7—E. Fittipaldi (Fittipaldi) engine lap 16—M. Andretti (Lotus) suspension lap 21—D. Pironi (Tyrrell) accident lap 21—N. Lauda (Brabham) accident lap 21—H-J Stuck (ATS) wheel lap 30—J-P Jarier (Tyrrell) suspension lap 34—A. Jones (Williams) steering lap 42—G. Villeneuve (Ferrari) gearbox lap 53—J. Laffite (Ligier) transmission lap 55—J-P Jabouille (Renault) engine lap 68—N. Piquet (Brabham) transmission lap 68.

Starting grid 1-1-1

Scheckter 1 min 26.4 sec—Villeneuve 1 min 26.5 sec—Depailler 1 min 27.1 sec—Lauda 1 min 27.2 sec—Laffite 1 min 27.3 sec—Jarier 1 min 27.4 sec—Pironi 1 min 27.4 sec—Mass 1 min 27.5 sec—Jones 1 min 27.7 sec—Hunt 1 min 28.0 sec—Reutemann 1 min 28.0 sec—Stuck 1 min 28.2 sec—Andretti 1 min 28.2 sec—Watson 1 min 28.2 sec—Patrese 1 min 28.3 sec—Regazzoni 1 min 28.5 sec—Fittipaldi 1 min 28.5 sec—Piquet 1 min 28.5 sec—Arnoux 1 min 28.6 sec—Jabouille 1 min 28.7 sec—non starters de Angelis (Shadow)—Tambay (McLaren)—Lammers (Shadow)—Daly (Ensign)—Brancatelli (Merzario).

FRENCH GRAND PRIX

Dijon-Prenois; 1 July; 80 laps 304 km/189 miles
1 J-P Jabouille (Renault) 1 hr 35 min 20.4 sec 191.23 kph/118.85 mph—2 G. Villeneuve (Ferrari) 1 hr 35 min 35.0 sec—3 R. Arnoux (Renault) 1 hr 35 min 42.2 sec—4 A. Jones (Williams) 1 hr 35 min 57.0 sec—5 J-P Jarier (Tyrrell) 1 hr 36 min 24.9 sec—6 C. Regazzoni (Williams) 1 hr 36 min 24.9 sec—7 J. Scheckter (Ferrari) 79 laps—8 J. Laffite (Ligier) 79 laps—9 K. Rosberg (Wolf) 79 laps—10 P. Tambay (McLaren) 78 laps—11 J. Watson (McLaren) 78 laps—12 H. Rebaque (Lotus) 78 laps—13 C. Reutemann (Lotus) 77 laps—14 R. Patrese (Arrows) 77 laps—15 J. Mass (Arrows) 75 laps—18 E. de Angelis (Shadow) 75 laps—17 B. Giacomelli (Alfa Romeo) 75 laps—18 J. Lammers (Shadow) 73 laps—fastest lap, Arnoux 1 min 9.16 sec 197.58 kph/122.88 mph—retired N. Lauda (Brabham) engine lap 16—J. Ickx (Ligier) engine lap 17—M. Andretti (Lotus) suspension lap 51—N. Piquet (Brabham) accident lap 53—E. Fittipaldi (Fittipaldi) engine lap 53—D. Pironi (Tyrrell) suspension lap 71—non starter H-J Stuck (ATS).

Starting grid 2-2-2

Jabouille 1 min 1.2 sec—Arnoux 1 min 7.4 sec—Villeneuve 1 min 7.6 sec—Piquet 1 min 8.1 sec—Scheckter 1 min 8.1 sec—Lauda 1 min 8.2 sec—Jones 1 min 8.2 sec—Laffite 1 min 8.6 sec—Regazzoni 1 min 8.6 sec—Jarier 1 min 8.9 sec—Pironi 1 min 8.9 sec—Andretti 1 min 9.3 sec—Reutemann 1 min 9.4 sec—Ickx 1 min 9.7 sec—Watson 1 min 10.0 sec—Rosberg 1 min 10.1 sec—Giacomelli 1 min 10.6 sec—Fittipaldi 1 min 10.6 sec—Patrese 1 min 10.7 sec—Tambay 1 min 10.9 sec—Lammers 1 min 11.1 sec—Mass 1 min 11.1 sec—de Angelis 1 min 12.2 sec—Rebaque 1 min 12.0 sec.

BRITISH GRAND PRIX

Silverstone; 14 July; 68 laps 199 miles/321 km
1 C. Regazzoni (Williams) 1 hr 26 min 11.2 sec 138.8 mph/223.33 kph—2 R. Arnoux (Renault) 1 hr 26 min 35.4 sec—3 J-P Jarier (Tyrrell) 67 laps—4 J. Watson (McLaren) 67 laps—5 J. Scheckter (Ferrari) 67 laps—6 J. Ickx (Ligier) 67 laps—7 P. Tambay (McLaren) 66 laps—8 C. Reutemann (Lotus) 66 laps—9 H. Rebaque (Lotus) 66 laps—10 D. Pironi (Tyrrell) 66 laps—11 J. Lammers (Shadow) 65 laps—12 E. de Angelis (Shadow) 65 laps (including penalty)—13 P. Gaillard (Ensign) 63 laps—fastest lap, Regazzoni 1 min 14.4 sec 141.87 mph/228.27 kph—retired N. Piquet (Brabham) accident lap 2—M. Andretti (Lotus) wheel bearing lap 3—N. Lauda (Brabham) brakes lap 12—J-P Jabouille (Renault) engine lap 21—E. Fittipaldi (Fittipaldi) overheating lap 25—A. Jones (Williams) engine lap 39—J. Laffite (Ligier) engine lap 44—K. Rosberg (Wolf) metering unit lap 44—R. Patrese (Arrows) fuel vaporisation lap 45—J. Mass (Arrows) gearbox lap 56—G. Villeneuve (Ferrari) fuel vaporisation lap 63.

Starting grid 2-2-2

Jones 1 min 11.9 sec—Jabouille 1 min 12.5 sec—Piquet 1 min 12.6 sec—Regazzoni 1 min 13.1 sec—Arnoux 1 min 13.3 sec—Lauda 1 min 13.4 sec—Watson 1 min 13.6 sec—Reutemann 1 min 13.9 sec—Andretti 1 min 14.2 sec—Laffite 1 min 14.4 sec—Scheckter 1 min 14.6 sec—de Angelis—1 min 14.9 sec—Villeneuve 1 min 14.9 sec—Rosberg 1 min 15.0 sec—Pironi 1 min 15.3 sec—Jarier 1 min 15.6 sec—Ickx 1 min 15.6 sec—Tambay 1 min 15.7 sec—Patrese 1 min 15.8 sec—Mass 1 min 16.2 sec—Lammers 1 min 16.7 sec—Fittipaldi 1 min 16.7 sec—Gaillard 1 min 17.1 sec—Rebaque 1 min 17.3 sec—non starters H-J Stuck (ATS)—A. Merzario (Merzario).

GERMAN GRAND PRIX

Hockenheim; 29 July; 45 laps 305 km/189.91 miles
1 A. Jones (Williams) 1 hr 24 min 48.8 sec 215.99 kph/134.24 mph—2 C. Regazzoni (Williams) 1 hr 24 min 51.7 sec—3 J. Laffite (Ligier) 1 hr 25 min 7.2 sec—4 J. Scheckter (Ferrari) 1 hr 25 min 20.1 sec—5 J. Watson (McLaren) 1 hr 26 min 26.6 sec—6 J. Mass (Arrows) 44 laps—7 G. Lees (Tyrrell) 44 laps—8 G. Villeneuve (Ferrari) 44 laps—9 D. Pironi (Tyrrell) 44 laps—10 J. Lammers (Shadow) 44 laps—11 E. de Angelis (Shadow) 43 laps—12 N. Piquet (Brabham) 42 laps—fastest lap, Villeneuve 1 min 51.9 sec 218.31 kph/135.68 mph—retired H-J Stuck (ATS) suspension lap 1—C. Reutemann (Lotus) accident lap 2—E. Fittipaldi (Fittipaldi) electrics lap 5—J-P Jabouille (Renault) accident lap 8—R. Arnoux (Renault) puncture lap 10—M. Andretti (Lotus) transmission lap 17—H. Rebaque (Lotus) handling lap 23—J. Ickx (Ligier) puncture lap 25—N. Lauda (Brabham) engine lap 25—K. Rosberg (Wolf) engine lap 30—P. Tambay (McLaren) suspension lap 31—R. Petrese (Arrows) puncture lap 35.

Starting grid 2-2-2

Jabouille 1 min 48.5 sec—Jones 1 min 48.7 sec—Laffite 1 min 49.4 sec—Piquet 1 min 49.5 sec—Scheckter 1 min 50.0 sec—Regazzoni 1 min 50.1 sec—Lauda 1 min 50.4 sec—Pironi 1 min 50.4 sec—Villeneuve 1 min 50.4 sec—Arnoux 1 min 50.5 sec—Andretti 1 min 50.7 sec—Watson 1 min 50.9 sec—Reutemann 1 min 50.9 sec—Ickx 1 min 51.1 sec—Tambay 1 min 51.5 sec—Lees 1 min 51.5 sec—Rosberg 1 min 52.0 sec—Mass 1 min 52.7 sec—Patrese 1 min 52.9 sec—Lammers 1 min 53.6 sec—de Angelis 1 min 53.7 sec—Fittipaldi 1 min 54.0 sec—Stuck 1 min 54.5 sec—Rebaque 1 min 55.9 sec.

AUSTRIAN GRAND PRIX

Österreichring; 12 August; 54 laps 321 km/199 miles
1 A. Jones (Williams) 1 hr 27 min 38.0 sec 219.61 kph/136.49 mph—2 G. Villeneuve (Ferrari) 1 hr 28 min 14.1 sec—3 J. Laffite (Ligier) 1 hr 28 min 24.8 sec—4 J. Scheckter (Ferrari) 1 hr 28 min 25.2 sec—5 C. Regazzoni (Williams) 1 hr 28 min 26.9 sec—6 R. Arnoux (Renault) 53 laps—7 D. Pironi (Tyrrell) 53 laps—8 D. Daly (Tyrrell) 53 laps—9 J. Watson (McLaren) 53 laps—10 P. Tambay (McLaren) 53 laps—fastest lap, Arnoux 1 min 35.8 sec 223.78 kph/139.08 mph—retired M. Andretti (Lotus) clutch lap 1—J. Mass (Arrows) engine lap 2—J. Lammers (Shadow) accident lap 4—E. Fittipaldi (Fittipaldi) engine lap 15—K. Rosberg (Wolf) electrics lap 15—J-P Jabouille (Renault) transmission lap 16—C. Reutemann (Lotus) handling lap 22—J. Ickx (Ligier) engine lap 26—H-J Stuck (ATS) engine lap 28—N. Piquet (Brabham) engine lap 32—E. de Angelis (Shadow) engine lap 34—R. Patrese (Arrows) suspension lap 34—P. Gaillard (Ensign) suspension lap 42—N. Lauda (Brabham) engine lap 45.

Starting grid 2-2-2

Arnoux 1 min 34.1 sec—Jones 1 min 34.3 sec—Jabouille 1 min 34.4 sec—Lauda 1 min 35.5 sec—Villeneuve 1 min 35.7 sec—Regazzoni 1 min 35.8 sec—Piquet 1 min 35.8 sec—Laffite 1 min 35.9 sec—Scheckter 1 min 36.1 sec—Pironi 1 min 36.3 sec—Daly 1 min 36.4 sec—Rosberg 1 min 36.7 sec—Patrese 1 min 36.7 sec—Tambay 1 min 36.7 sec—Andretti 1 min 37.1 sec—Watson 1 min 37.2 sec—Reutemann 1 min 37.3 sec—Stuck 1 min 37.9 sec—Fittipaldi 1 min 38.4 sec—Mass 1 min 38.8 sec—Ickx 1 min 39.3 sec—de Angelis 1 min 39.4 sec—Lammers 1 min 39.4 sec—Gaillard 1 min 41.1 sec.

DUTCH GRAND PRIX

Zandvoort; 26 August; 75 laps 317 km/197 miles
1 A. Jones (Williams) 1 hr 41 min 19.8 sec 187.59 kph/116.59 mph—2 J. Scheckter (Ferrari) 1 hr 41 min 41.6 sec—3 J. Laffite (Ligier) 1 hr 42 min 23.0 sec—4 N. Piquet (Brabham) 74 laps—5 J. Ickx (Ligier) 74 laps—6 J. Mass (Arrows) 73 laps—7 H. Rebaque (Lotus) 73 laps—fastest lap, Villeneuve 1 min 19.4 sec 191.44 kph/118.98 mph—retired R. Arnoux (Renault) accident lap 1—C. Regazzoni (Williams) accident lap 1—C. Reutemann (Lotus) accident lap 1—E. Fittipaldi (Fittipaldi) engine lap 2—N. Lauda (Brabham) injury lap 4—P. Tambay (McLaren) engine lap 6—R. Patrese (Arrows) accident lap 7—M. Andretti (Lotus) suspension lap 9—J. Lammers (Shadow) gearbox lap 12—H-J Stuck (ATS) transmission lap 19—J-P Jarier (Tyrrell) throttle lap 20—J. Watson (McLaren) misfire lap 22—J-P Jabouille (Renault) clutch lap 26—K. Rosberg (Wolf) engine lap 33—A. de Angelis (Shadow) drive shaft lap 40—G. Villeneuve (Ferrari) puncture lap 49—D. Pironi (Tyrrell) suspension lap 51.

Starting grid 2-2-2

Arnoux 1 min 15.5 sec—Jones 1 min 15.6 sec—Regazzoni 1 min 16.2 sec—Jabouille 1 min 16.3 sec—Scheckter 1 min 16.4 sec—Villeneuve 1 min 16.9 sec—Laffite 1 min 17.1 sec—Rosberg 1 min 17.3 sec—Lauda 1 min 17.5 sec—Pironi 1 min 17.6 sec—Piquet 1 min 17.7 sec—Watson 1 min 17.7 sec—Reutemann 1 min 18.0 sec—Tambay 1 min 18.1 sec—Stuck 1 min 18.3 sec—Jarier 1 min 18.4 sec—Andretti 1 min 18.4 sec—Mass 1 min 18.6 sec—Patrese 1 min 18.6 sec—Ickx 1 min 18.7 sec—Fittipaldi 1 min 19.4 sec—de Angelis 1 min 20.7 sec—Lammers 1 min 21.1 sec—Rebaque 1 min 21.3 sec.

ITALIAN GRAND PRIX

Monza; 9 September; 50 laps 232 km/144 miles
1 J. Scheckter (Ferrari) 1 hr 22 min 0.2 sec 212.1 kph/131.82 mph—2 G. Villeneuve (Ferrari) 1 hr 22 min 0.7 sec—3 C. Regazzoni (Williams) 1 hr 22 min 5.0 sec—4 N. Lauda (Brabham) 1 hr 22 min 54.6 sec—5 M. Andretti (Lotus) 1 hr 22 min 54.6 sec—6 J. Laffite (Ligier) 1 hr 23 min 1.8 sec—7 C. Reutemann (Lotus) 1 hr 23 min 24.4 sec—8 E. Fittipaldi (Fittipaldi) 49 laps—9 A. Jones (Williams) 49 laps—10 D. Pironi (Tyrrell) 49 laps—11 H-J Stuck (ATS) 49 laps—12 V. Brambilla (Alfa Romeo) 49 laps—13 R. Patrese (Arrows) 47 laps—14 J-P Jabouille (Renault) 45 laps—fastest lap, Regazzoni 1 min 35.6 sec 210.3 kph/135.68 mph—retired N. Piquet (Brabham) accident lap 2—J. Mass (Arrows) suspension lap 3—P. Tambay (McLaren) engine lap 4—R. Arnoux (Renault) engine lap 14—J. Watson (McLaren) accident lap 14—B. Giacomelli (Alfa Romeo) accident lap 29—E. de Angelis (Shadow) gearbox lap 34—J. Ickx (Ligier) engine lap 41—K. Rosberg (Wolf) engine lap 42—J. Laffite (Ligier) engine lap 42.

Starting grid 2-2-2

Jabouille 1 min 34.6 sec—Arnoux 1 min 34.7 sec—Scheckter 1 min 34.8 sec—Jones 1 min 34.9 sec—Villeneuve 1 min 35.0 sec—Regazzoni 1 min 35.3 sec—Laffite 1 min 35.4 sec—Piquet 1 min 35.6 sec—Lauda 1 min 36.2 sec—Andretti 1 min 36.6 sec—Ickx 1 min 37.1 sec—Pironi 1 min 37.2 sec—Reutemann 1 min 37.2 sec—Tambay 1 min 37.2 sec—Stuck 1 min 37.3 sec—Jarier 1 min 37.6 sec—Patrese 1 min 37.7 sec—Giacomelli 1 min 38.0 sec—Watson 1 min 38.1 sec—Fittipaldi 1 min 38.1 sec—Mass 1 min 38.2 sec—Brambilla 1 min 38.6 sec—Rosberg 1 min 38.8 sec—de Angelis 1 min 39.1 sec.

CANADIAN GRAND PRIX

Montreal; 30 September; 72 laps 198 miles/319 km
1 A. Jones (Williams) 1 hr 52 min 6.9 sec 105.96 mph/170.49 kph—2 G. Villeneuve (Ferrari) 1 hr 52 min 7.9 sec—3 C. Regazzoni (Williams) 1 hr 53 min 20.5 sec—4 J. Scheckter (Ferrari) 71 laps—5 D. Pironi (Tyrrell) 71 laps—6 J. Watson (McLaren) 70 laps—7 R. Zunino (Brabham) 70 laps—8 E. Fittipaldi (Fittipaldi) 67 laps—9 J. Lammers (Shadow) 67 laps—fastest lap, Jones 1 min 31.3 sec 105.96 mph/170.49 kph—retired J. Laffite (Ligier) engine lap 10—H-J Stuck (ATS) accident lap 14—P. Tambay (McLaren) accident lap 19—R. Patrese (Arrows) accident lap 20—C. Reutemann (Lotus) suspension lap 23—J-P Jabouille (Renault) throttle lap 24—E. de Angelis (Shadow) engine lap 24—H. Rebaque (Lotus) engine mounting lap 26—D. Daly (Tyrrell) engine lap 28—J-P Jarier (Tyrrell) brakes lap 33—J. Ickx (Ligier) transmission lap 47—V. Brambilla (Alfa Romeo) ignition lap 52—N. Piquet (Brabham) gearbox lap 61.

Starting grid 2-2-2

Jones 1 min 29.9 sec—Villeneuve 1 min 30.5 sec—Regazzoni 1 min 30.8 sec—Piquet 1 min 30.8 sec—Laffite 1 min 30.8 sec—Pironi 1 min 31.9 sec—Jabouille 1 min 32.1 sec—Arnoux 1 min 32.1 sec—Scheckter 1 min 32.3 sec—Andretti 1 min 32.6 sec—Reutemann 1 min 32.7 sec—Stuck 1 min 32.8 sec—Jarier 1 min 33.1 sec—Patrese 1 min 33.1 sec—Fittipaldi 1 min 33.3 sec—Ickx 1 min 33.3 sec—Watson 1 min 33.4 sec—Brambilla 1 min 33.4 sec—Zunino 1 min 33.5 sec—Tambay 1 min 33.6 sec—Lammers 1 min 34.1 sec—Rebaque 1 min 34.1 sec—de Angelis 1 min 34.2 sec—Daly 1 min 34.3 sec.

UNITED STATES GRAND PRIX

Watkins Glen; 7 October; 59 laps 199 miles/321 km
1 G. Villeneuve (Ferrari) 1 hr 52 min 17.7 sec 106.46 mph/171.29 kph—2 R. Arnoux (Renault) 1 hr 53 min 6.5 sec—3 D. Pironi (Tyrrell) 1 hr 53 min 10.9 sec—4 E. de Angelis (Shadow) 1 hr 53 min 48.2 sec—5 H-J Stuck (ATS) 1 hr 53 min 49.0 sec—6 J. Watson (McLaren) 58 laps—7 E. Fittipaldi (Fittipaldi) 55 laps—fastest lap, Piquet 1 min 40.0 sec 121.5 mph/195.49 kph—retired B. Giacomelli (Alfa Romeo) accident lap 1—J. Ickx (Ligier) accident lap 2—J. Laffite (Ligier) accident lap 3—C. Reutemann (Lotus) accident lap 6—M. Andretti (Lotus) gearbox lap 16—J-P Jarier (Tyrrell) accident lap 18—K. Rosberg (Wolf) oil leak lap 20—P. Tambay (McLaren) accident lap 20—J-P Jabouille (Renault) engine lap 24—R. Zunino (Brabham) accident lap 25—C. Regazzoni (Williams) accident lap 29—M. Surer (Ensign) engine lap 32—A. Jones (Williams) wheel lap 36—R. Patrese (Arrows) suspension lap 44—J. Scheckter (Ferrari) puncture lap 48—D. Daly (Tyrrell) accident lap 52—N. Piquet (Brabham) engine lap 53.

UNITED STATES GRAND PRIX—*continued*

Starting grid 2-2-2

Jones 1 min 35.6 sec—Piquet 1 min 36.9 sec—Villeneuve 1 min 36.9 sec—Laffite 1 min 37.1 sec—Regazzoni 1 min 37.1 sec—Reutemann 1 min 37.9 sec—Arnoux 1 min 38.2 sec—Jabouille 1 min 38.2 sec—Zunino 1 min 38.5 sec—Pironi 1 min 38.8 sec—Jarier 1 min 38.9 sec—Rosberg 1 min 39.0 sec—Watson 1 min 39.2 sec—Stuck 1 min 39.3 sec—Daly 1 min 39.5 sec—Scheckter 1 min 39.6 sec—Andretti 1 min 40.1 sec—Giacomelli 1 min 40.3 sec—Patrese 1 min 40.3 sec—de Angelis 1 min 40.6 sec—Surer 1 min 40.6 sec—Tambay 1 min 40.7 sec—Fittipaldi 1 min 40.7 sec—Ickx 1 min 40.7 sec.

1979 WORLD CHAMPIONSHIP

1 J. Scheckter 51—2 G. Villeneuve 47—3 A. Jones 40—4 J. Laffite 36—5 C. Regazzoni 29—6 P. Depailler 20—6= C. Reutemann 20—8 R. Arnoux 17—9 J. Watson 15—10 M. Andretti 14—10= J-P Jarier 14—10= D. Pironi 14—13 J-P Jabouille 9—14 N. Lauda 4—15 A. de Angelis 3—15= J. Mass 3—15= J. Ickx 3—15= N. Piquet 3—19 R. Patrese 2—19= H-J Stuck 2—21 E. Fittipaldi 1.

RACING WITH GUINNESS

Derek Daly would probably have won the European Formula 2 Championship in 1979 had he not been taking the opportunities presented to him in the world of Formula 1. His efforts gained the recognition of a drive with the Tyrrell team in 1980. *Photo by David Phipps; permission by Arthur Guinness Son and Company (Park Royal) Limited.*

Index

Thirty years of Grand Prix Motor Racing

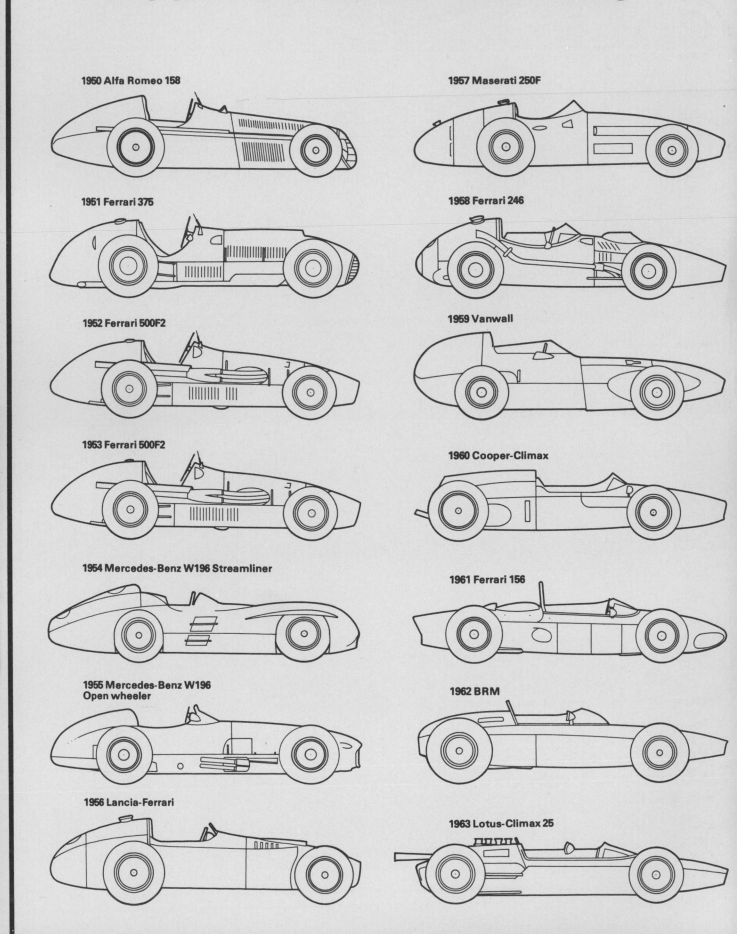

1950 Alfa Romeo 158

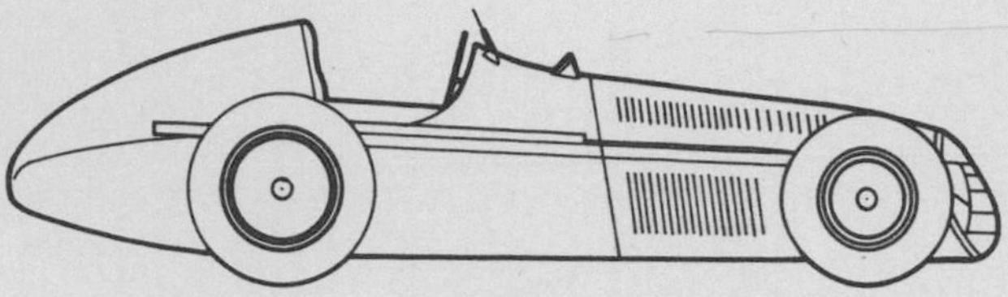

1951 Ferrari 375

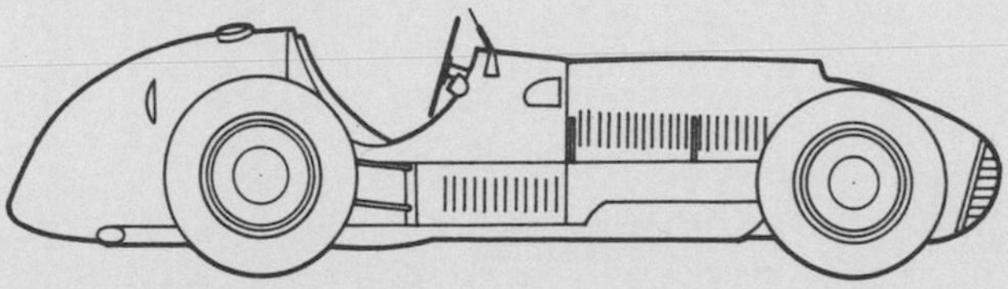

1952 Ferrari 500F2

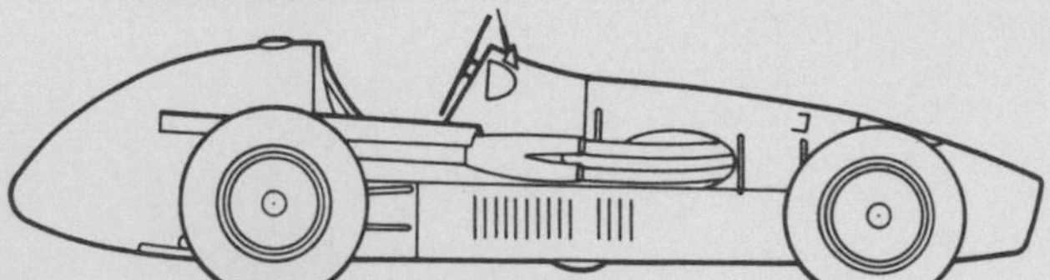

1953 Ferrari 500F2

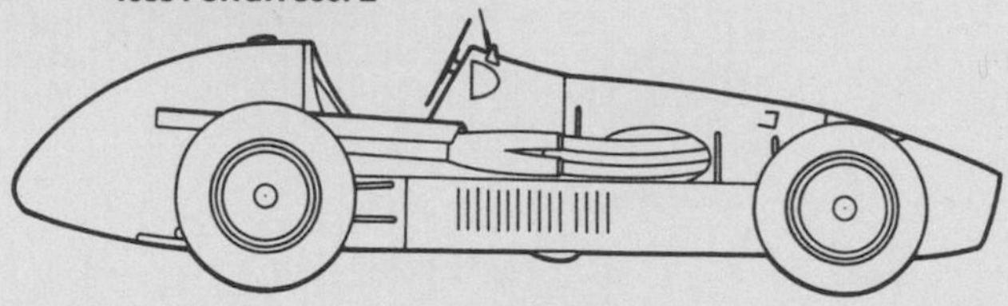

1954 Mercedes-Benz W196 Streamliner

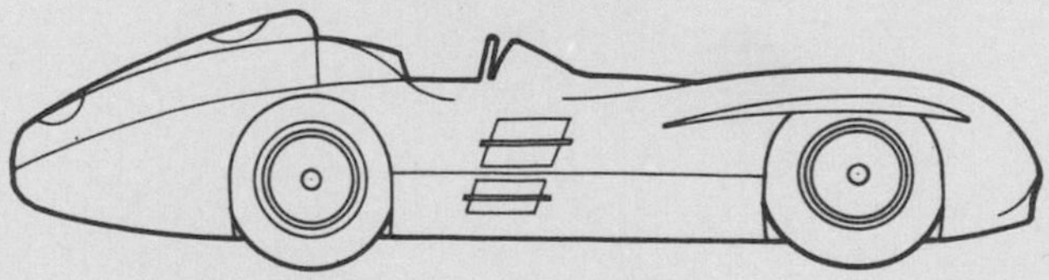

1955 Mercedes-Benz W196
Open wheeler

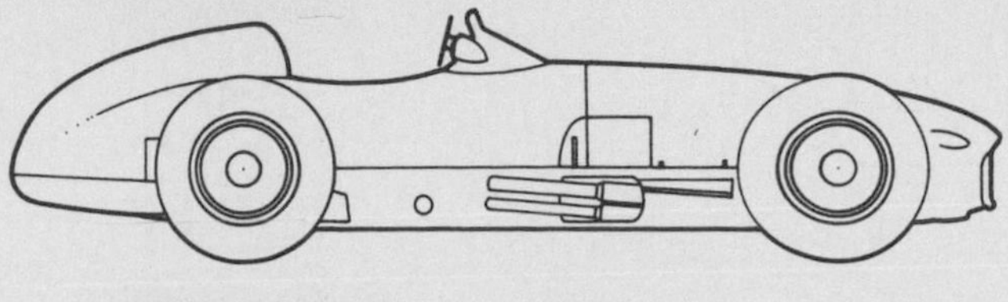

1956 Lancia-Ferrari

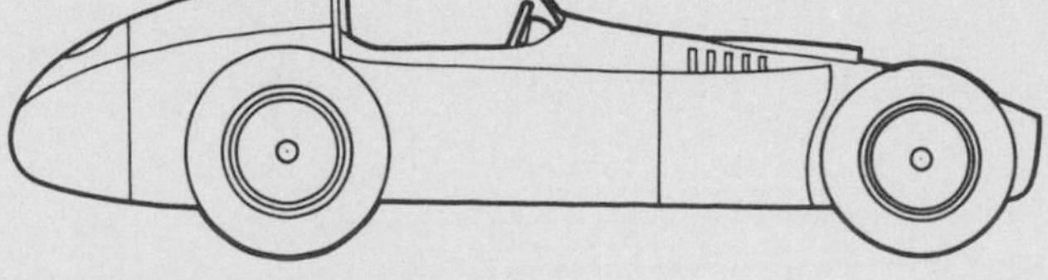

1957 Maserati 250F

1958 Ferrari 246

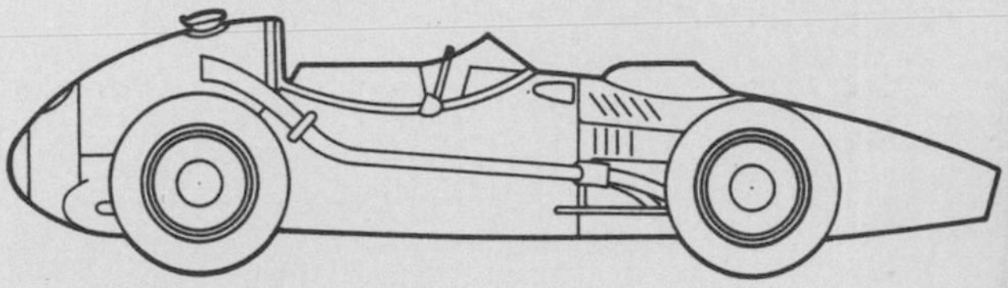

1959 Vanwall

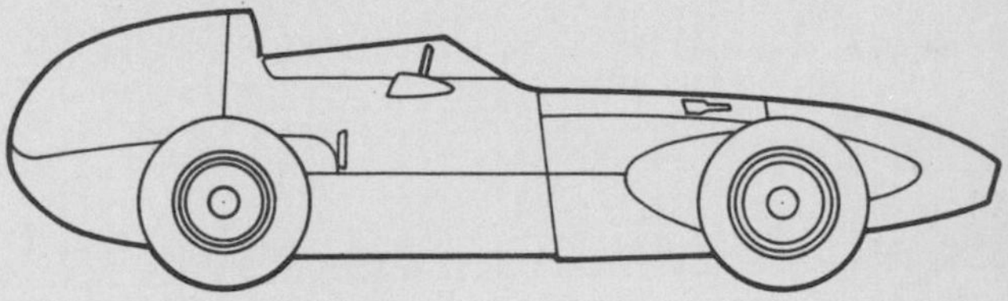

1960 Cooper-Climax

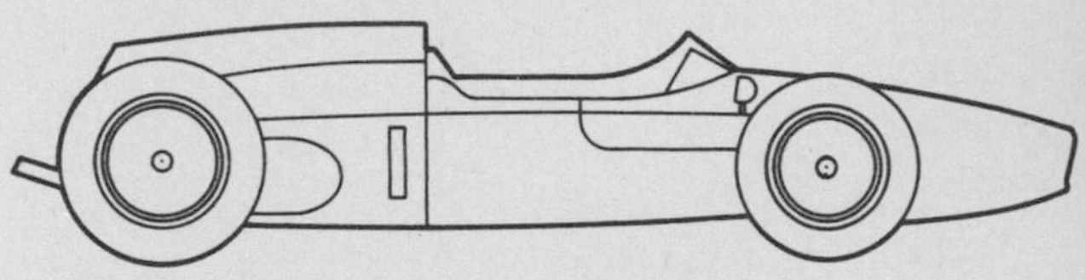

1961 Ferrari 156

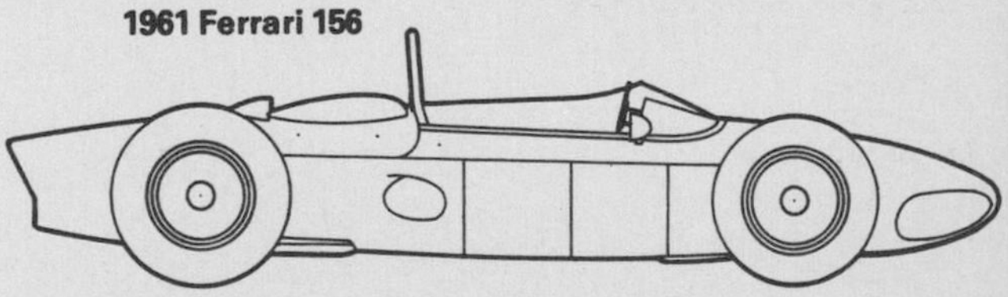

1962 BRM

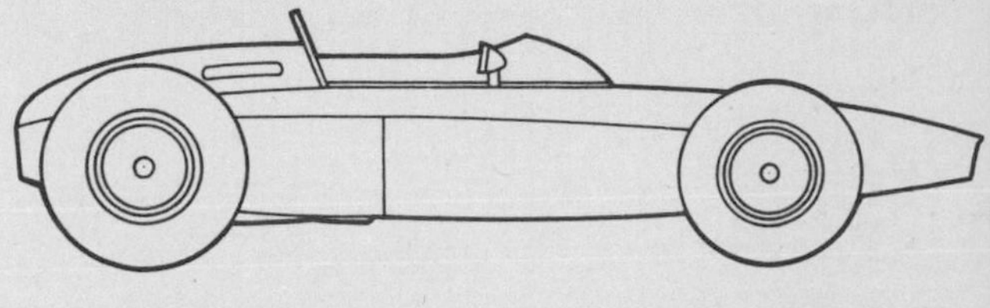

1963 Lotus-Climax 25

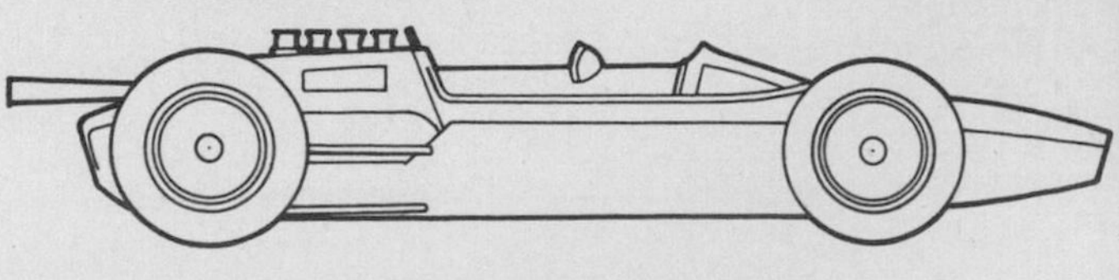